STONE SCULPTURE IN THE ALLAHABAD MUSEUM

Volume II

STONE SCULPTURE IN THE ALLAHABAD MUSEUM

Volume II

KRISHNA DEVA
S.D. TRIVEDI

MANOHAR
AMERICAN INSTITUTE OF INDIAN STUDIES
NEW DELHI
1996

ISBN 81-7304-140-7

First Published 1996

Published by
Ajay Kumar Jain
Manohar Publishers & Distributors
2/6, Ansari Road, Daryaganj
New Delhi - 110002

Lasertypeset by
A J Software Publishing Co. Pvt. Ltd.
305, Durga Chambers,
1333, D.B. Gupta Road,
Karol Bagh, New Delhi - 110005

Printed at
Rajkamal Electric Press
G.T. Karnal Road
Delhi

CONTENTS

PREFACE

Pramod Chandra's *Stone Sculpture in the Allahabad Museum* (1970) was the first model catalogue of an archaeological museum specialising in sculpture in India with a thorough documentation of each piece, lavish illustration and a brief but perceptive review of ancient Indian art in general and of the art styles involved in particular. Since the Allahabad Museum has been singularly fortunate in possessing a large collection of Śuṅga sculptures from Bharhut, Gupta art pieces from Bhumara, late Gupta and early medieval art specimens from places around Allahabad and medieval sculptures from Jamsot, the sculptures called for a chronological classification with an emphasis on the sites of their provenance which aptly suited the collection.

Since the publication of Pramod Chandra's book a sizable number of sculptures have been added, most of which pertain to the early medieval and medieval art styles that flourished with the numerous centers in Madhyadeśa such as Garhwa, Gurgi, Kauśāmbī, Bhita, etc. The medieval period is well known for an increasing proliferation in the iconic forms pertaining to all the three principal Indian religions, viz. Brahmanism, Jainism and Buddhism, though the last was on a decline. The present catalogue documents nearly 400 sculptures which have been broadly classified sect-wise starting with various categories of Brahmanical gods and goddesses, followed by deities of the Buddhist and Jaina pantheons and terminating with secular and miscellaneous themes including architectural members. With few exceptions all the documented specimens have also been illustrated by photographic reproductions.

The catalogue is preceded by Introduction which deals with the history of the collection, iconographical peculiarities of some images, chronological range and special traits of the various art centres and concerned art styles, followed by a review of the aesthetics of the art specimens discussed.

Though this book is a result of the collaborative effort of the two authors, the Introduction is mainly written by S.D.Trivedi and the Catalogue by Krishna Deva. The authors claim no originality for the Glossary which has been largely copied from Pramod Chandra's work. The authors gratefully acknowledge the scholarly help of Sri Shriranjan Shukla, Curatorial Associate of the Allahabad Museum, who has an intimate knowledge of the collection. The photographs have been prepared by Sri D.P. Nanda, the talented photographer of the Varanasi Centre of the American Institute of Indian Studies and the layout designed by Sri S. Dorai, the gifted Artist-Draftsman of the Institute. Thanks are also due to Sri P.K. Ramachandran of the Institute for the care and diligence with which he has typed the manuscript and prepared the press-copy. The main credit, however, for conceiving the entire project and seeing it through is indeed due to the inspiring leadership and enlightened patronage of Dr. P.R. Mehendiratta, Director of the Institute.

23 September 1992 AUTHORS
American Institute of Indian Studies,
Ramnagar,
Varanasi-221 008

ABBREVIATIONS

Accn. No.	Accession Number of the Museum
ASI	Archaeological Survey of India
BMA	*Bulletin of Museums and Archaeology in U.P.*, Lucknow
EHI	*Elements of Hindu Iconography* by T.A.G. Rao
SML	State Museum, Lucknow
SSAM	*Stone Sculpture in the Allahabad Museum* by Pramod Chandra, AIIS Publication No.2 (1970)

LIST OF ILLUSTRATIONS

Figure

45. Umā-Maheśvara, Gaya, Gaya District, Bihar, 11th century A.D., ht. .480 m.
46. Rāvaṇānugrahamūrti, Soraon, Allahabad District, UP, 10th century A.D., .440 X .375 m.
47. Rāvaṇānugrahamūrti, Lacchagir, Allahabad District, UP, 10th century A.D., .787 X .406 m.
48. Gajāntaka Śiva, site not known, 11th century A.D., .685 X .595 m.
49. Śukanāsa with Śiva's head, site not known, 9th century A.D., .385 X .555 m.
50. Head of God, site not known, 10th century A.D., .170 X .082 m.
51. Head of Śiva, Soraon, Allahabad District, UP, 10th century A.D., ht. .285 m.
52. Śiva Head, Jhusi, Allahabad District, UP, 11th century A.D., ht. .285 m.
53. Head of Śiva, Provenance unknown, 11th century A.D., .330 X .135 m.
54. Bhairava, site not known, 10th century A.D., .770 X .490 m.
55. Bust of Bhairava, Kauśāmbī, Allahabad District, UP, 8th century A.D., .470 X .360 m.
56. Bust of God, UP, 8th century A.D., .400 X .270 m.
57. Head of Bhairava, Kauśāmbī, Allahabad District, UP, 9th century A.D., ht. .220 m.
58. Head of Bhairava (?), site not known, 10th century A.D., .175 X .195 m.
59. Head of Bhairava, Lacchagir, Allahabad District, UP, 11th century A.D., ht. .220 m.
60. Head of Bhairava, Jhusi, Allahabad District, UP, 11th century A.D., ht. .160 m.
61. Dancing Gaṇeśa, site not known, 10th century A.D., .410 X .295 m.
62. Dancing Gaṇeśa, Gurgi, Rewa District, MP, 10th century A.D., .630 X .400 m.
63. Gaṇeśa seated, UP, 10th century A.D., 570 X .430 m.
64. Gaṇeśa, site not known, 10th century A.D., .495 X .300 m.
65. Dancing Gaṇeśa, site not known, 10th century A.D., .485 X .340 m.
66. Kārttikeya, site not known, 6th century A.D., .355 X .230 m.
67. Kārttikeya, Kauśāmbī, Allahabad District, UP, 7th century A.D., ht. .240 m.
68. Head of Brahmā (?), Bhita, Allahabad District, UP, 9th century A.D., ht. .240 m.
69. Brahmā, Bara, Allahabad District, UP, 11th century A.D., .660 X .597 m.
70. Brahmā, Kauśāmbī, Allahabad District, UP, 11th century A.D., .380 X .430 m.
71. Brahmā, Rajasthan (?), 11th century A.D., .490 X .440 m.
72. Three-headed Brahmā (?), site not known, 11th century A.D., .595 X .340 m.
73. Three-faced Agni, UP, 8th century A.D., ht. 430 m.
74. Agni surrounded by sages, Gurgi, Rewa District, MP, 10th century A.D., .890 X .760 m.
75. Seated Agni, 10th century A.D., .350 X .170 m.
76. Seated Agni, site not known, 10th century A.D., .400 X .270 m.
77. Dikpāla Indra, MP, 11th century A.D., .730 X .470 m.
78. Dikpāla Agni, MP, 11th century A.D., .730 X .470 m.
79. Dikpāla Agni, site not known, 11th century A.D., .785 X .300 m.
80. Dikpāla Agni, site not known, 11th century A.D., .690 X .525 m.
81. Dikpāla Agni, site not known, 12th century A.D., .535 X .230 m.
82. Dikpāla Nirṛti, site not known, 10th century A.D., .785 X .520 m.
83. Dikpāla Nirṛti (?), Chilla near Bhita, Allahabad District, UP, 10th century A.D., .405 X .380 m.
84. Standing Varuṇa, UP, 10th century A.D., .640 X .490 m.
85. Kubera, site not known, 6th century A.D., 1.355 X .738 m.
86. Kubera, site not known, 6th-7th century A.D., .290 X .240 m.
87. Architectural fragment with Kubera, Lacchagir, Allahabad District, UP, 10th century A.D., .210 X .495 m.
88. Dikpāla Īśāna, Baghaura, Allahabad District, UP, 10th century A.D.
89. Sūrya, site not known, 10th century A.D., .435 X .340 m.
90. Sūrya, Kauśāmbī, Allahabad District, UP, 10th century A.D., .305 X .350 m.
91. Sūrya in Rathikā, site not known, 10th century A.D., 1 m X .760 m.
92. Sūrya, site not known, 12th century A.D., .530 X .460 m.
93. Solar deity (?), site not known, 11th century A.D., .395 X .318 m.
94. Revanta, Durgaganj (Soraon), Allahabad District, UP, 10th century A.D., .270 X .510 m.
95. Navagraha panel, site not known, 9th century A.D., .85 X .26 m.
96. Navagraha panel, site not known, 10th century A.D., .275 X .550 m.
97. Navagraha panel, Kauśāmbī, Allahabad District, UP, 10th century A.D., .275 X .477 m.
98. Deity, headless, Mathura, Mathura District, UP, 2nd century A.D., .160 X .110 m.
99. Head of deity, Mathura, Mathura District, UP, 2nd century A.D., .102 X .065 m.
100. Head of deity, site not known, 3rd century A.D., .165 X .09 m.
101. Fragment of deity, Mathura, Mathura District, UP, 3rd century A.D., .150 X .170 m.

158. Naigameṣa, Mathura, Mathura District, UP, 2nd century A.D., .165 X .115 m.
159. Vidyādhara, site not known, 10th century A.D., .375 X .205 m.
160. Vidyādhara Mithuna, site not known, 11th century A.D., .395 X .395 m.
161. Vidyādhara, site not known, 12th century A.D., .220 X .130 m.
162. Apsarā and Vyāla, Khajuraho, Chhatarpur District, MP, 11th century A.D., .420 X .260 m.
163. Apsarā, Gurgi, Rewa District, MP, 10th century A.D., 635 X .355 m.
164. Apsaras, Jamsot, Allahabad District, UP, 11th century A.D., .585 X .405 m.
165. Apsarā Karpūramañjarī, site not known, 11th century A.D., .470 X .300 m.
166. Māyādevī in Lumbinī Forest, Gandhara (Pakistan), 2nd century A.D., .345 X .127 m.
167. Buddha Head, Gandhara (Pakistan), 2nd-3rd centuries A.D., .105 X .075 m.
168. Male Head, Gandhara (Pakistan), 2nd-3rd centuries A.D., .098 X .065 m.
169. Male Head, Gandhara (Pakistan), 2nd-3rd centuries A.D., .120 X .087 m.
170. Bust of Bodhisattva (?), Kauśāmbī, Allahabad District, UP, 1st century A.D., .165 X .128 m.
171. Buddha (Headless), Mathura, Mathura District, UP, 3rd century A.D., .320 X .230 m.
172. A-D Life Scenes of Buddha, site not known, c.4th century A.D., .200 X .570 m.
173. Standing Buddha, UP, 5th century A.D., ht. .280 m.
174. Preaching Buddha, UP, 5th century A.D., .320 X .230 m.
175. Buddha Head, Mathura, Mathura District, UP, 5th century A.D., ht. .220 m.
176. Head of Buddha, Sarnath, Varanasi District, UP, 6th century A.D., .190 X .120 m.
177. Head of Buddha, Sarnath, Varanasi District, UP, 7th century A.D., ht. .275 m.
178. Bust of Buddha, site not known, 7th century A.D., .115 X .082 m.
179. Bust of Tārā, Gaya, Gaya District, Bihar, 9th century A.D., ht. .220 m.
180. Tārā, site not known, 11th century A.D., .120 X .160 m.
181. Ṣaḍakṣarī Lokeśvara, Gurgi, Rewa District, MP, 10th century A.D. .410 X .480 m.
182. Ṣaḍakṣarī Lokeśvara, site not known, 11th century A.D., .152 X .094 m.
183. Ṣaḍakśarī Lokeśvara Group, Gurgi, Rewa District, MP, 12th century A.D., .470 X .335 m.
184. Seated Buddha, Gaya, Gaya District, Bihar, 10th century A.D., ht. .310 m.
185. Buddhist Image Pedestal, Kauśāmbī, Allahabad District, UP, 10th century A.D., .230 X .470 m.
186. Ornate Stūpa base, Gaya, Gaya District, Bihar, 10th century A.D., .390 X .360 m.
187. A-B Buddhist Goddess, Kauśāmbī, Allahabad District, UP, 10th century A.D., ht. .430 m.
188. Buddhist Goddess, Gurgi, Rewa District, MP, 11th century A.D., .530 X .370 m.
189. Miniature stūpa, Kauśāmbī, Allahabad District, UP, 11th century A.D., .185 X .160 m.
190. A-D. Miniature stūpa, Sarnath, Varanasi District, UP, 12th century A.D., .685 X .395 m.
191. Jina Head, Mathura, Mathura District, UP, 2nd century A.D., ht. .260 m.
192. Jina Head, Mathura, Mathura District, UP, 2nd century A.D., .120 X .107 m.
193. Jina Head, Sarnath, Varanasi District, UP, 3rd century A.D., ht. .260 m.
194. Ādinātha, Bharwari, Allahabad District, UP, 5th century A.D., .292 X .343 m.
195. Bust of Ādinātha, UP, 6th century A.D., .400 X .270 m.
196. Head of Pārśvanātha, Kauśāmbī, Allahabad District, UP, c.6th century A.D., ht. .410 m.
197. Jina Head, Bhita, Allahabad District, UP, 8th century A.D., ht. .160 m.
198. Head of Jina, Bhita, Allahabad District, UP, 8th century A.D., ht. .180 m.
199. Jina Head, site not known, 8th century A.D., .250 X .185 m.
200. Jina Head, Kauśāmbī, Allahabad District, UP, 9th century A.D., .305 X .430 m.
201. Caturviṁśati-paṭṭa, Gurgi, Rewa District, MP, 9th century A.D., 530 X .370 m.
202. Jaina Tutelary couple, UP, 10th century A.D., .620 X .530 m.
203. Seated Ambikā, Kauśāmbī, Allahabad District, UP, 7th century A.D., .390 X .250 m.
204. A-B. Gomukha Yakṣa, site not known, 10th century A.D., .375 X .250 m.
205. Jaina Lintel, site not known, 10th century A.D., .590 X 1.51 m.
206. Jaina Lintel, site not known, 10th century A.D., .450 X 1.05 m.
207. Jaina Lintel, site not known, 10th century A.D., 330 X .810 m.
208. Jaina Śilāpaṭṭa, site not known, 10th century A.D., .230 X .440 m.
209. Jina-Paṭṭa, site not known, 10th century A.D., .285 X .370 m.
210. Seated Ādinātha, site not known, 10th century A.D., .740 X .450 m.
211. Jina Head, Agra, Agra District, UP, 10th century A.D., ht. .210 m.
212. Jina Head, Agra, Agra District, UP, 10th century A.D., ht. .220 m.

.293 X .203 m.

269. Female Bust, site not known, 10th century A.D., .165 X .122 m.
270. Railing Post, Bhita, Allahabad District, UP, 1st century B.C., .490 X .170 m.
271. Lotus on Sūcī, Mathura, Mathura District, UP, 2nd century A.D., .255 X .370 m.
272. Pillar Fragment, Bhumara, Satna District, MP, 5th century A.D., .410 X .230 m.
273. Pillar Base, Bhumara, Satna District, MP, 5th century A.D., .450 X .210 m.
274. Architectural fragment, Bhumara, Satna District, MP, 5th century A.D., .355 X .318 m.
275. Candraśālā with Head, Bhumara, Satna District, MP, 5th century A.D., .340 X .280 m.
276. Siṁhamukha-praṇāla, Bhita, Allahabad District, UP, 6th century A.D., .258 X .185 m.
277. Yakṣī on Praṇāla, site not known, 7th century A.D., .350 X .200 m.
278. A-B. Siṁha-mukha Praṇala, site not known, 8th century A.D., .215 X .195 (Lion face only)
279. Pillar Capital, site not known, 7th century A.D., .325 X .175 m.
280. Śukanāsa with head, Rewa, Rewa District, MP, 8th century A.D., .450 X .650 m.
281. Base of Door-jamb, UP, 9th century A.D., .430 X .190 m.
282. Gaṅgā on Doorjamb, UP, 9th century A.D., .555 X .320 m.
283. Yamunā and Mahākāla, site not known, 10th century A.D. .490 X .255 m.
284. River-Goddess on Jamb, Manikpur, Allahabad District, UP, 10th century A.D., .925 X .235 m.
285. Door-sill fragment, site not known, 9th century A.D., .220 X .770 m.
286. Door-sill, site not known, 9th century A.D., .110 X .730 m.
287. Door-sill, site not known, 10th century A.D., .280 X 1.270 m.
288. Door-sill, site not known, 12th century A.D., .395 X 1.725 m.
289. Door-lintel with Mātṛkās, site not known, 9th century A.D., .280 X .530 m.
290. Lintel of Viṣṇu Shrine, UP, 10th century A.D., .320 X 1.06 m.
291. Lintel Fragment, site not known, 10th century A.D., .520 X .910 m.
292. Vaiṣṇava Lintel, site not known, 11th century A.D., .285 X .1.02 m.
293. Lintel showing Pārśvanātha, Gurgi, Rewa District, MP, 10th century A.D., .250 X 1.650 m.
294. Miniature shrine, Hissar, Hissar District, Haryana, 10th century A.D., .380 X .390 m.
295. Gandharva Musicians, site not known, 10th century A.D., ht. .225 to .235 m.
296. Pillar fragment, site not known, 10th century A.D., .800 X .240 m.
297. Nāgī on pillar, site not known, 10th century A.D., .385 X .205 m.
298. Pillar fragment, site not known, 11th century A.D. .945 X .413 m.
299. Erotic Panel, site not known, 11th century A.D. .240 X .80 m.
300. Teacher and Disciple, site not known, 11th century A.D., .280 X .380 m.
301. Makara and Gladiator, Khajuraho, Chhatarpur District, MP, 11th century A.D., .375 X .280 m.
302. Makara and Gladiator, Khajuraho, Chhatarpur District, MP 11th century A.D., .380 X .310 m.
303. Kumāra-bracket, site not known, 10th century A.D., .330 X .310 m.
304. Kumāra-bracket, site not known, 10th century A.D., .315 X .635 m.
305. A-C. Bracket with Animal-headed gods, site not known, 12th century A.D., .410 X 1.05 m.
306. Grotesque bracket-figure, Bhita, Allahabad district, UP, 12th century A.D., length .350 m.
307. Ornate Āmalasāraka, site not known, 12th century A.D., .30 X Dia.1.05 m.
308. A-D. Memorial Pillar with Kṛṣṇalīlā scenes, site not known, 13th century A.D., .870 X .225 m.
309. A-D. Memorial pillar with Kṛṣṇalīlā scenes, site not known, 13th century A.D., .970 X .270 m.
310. A-D. Memorial Pillar Fragment, site not known, 13th century A.D., .410 X .170 m.
311. Horse's Head, Bharhut, Satna District, MP, 2nd century B.C., .190 X .153 m.
312. Fish-tailed Makara, site not known, 1st century B.C., .140 X .255 m.
313. Cow with calf, Mathura, Mathura District, UP, 2nd century A.D., .130 X .08 m.
314. Owl Family, site not known, 8th century A.D., .350 X .170 m.
315. Nandī, Garhwa, Allahabad District, UP, 9th century A.D., .342 X .431 m.
316. Elephant, site not known, 10th century A.D., .280 X .480 m.
317. Lion's Head, site not known, 10th century A.D., ht. 280 m.
318. Siṁha-vyāla, Khajuraho, Chhatarpur District, MP, 10th century A.D., .380 X .180 m.
319. Siṁha-vyāla, UP, 10th century A.D., ht. .200 m.
320. Gaja-vyāla, Khajuraho, Chhatarpur District, MP, 11th century A.D., .470 X .150 m.
321. Aśva-vyāla, Khajuraho, Chhatarpur District, MP, 11th century A.D., .405 X .165 m.
322. Gajākrānta-siṁha, provenance unknown, 11th century A.D., .345 X .470 m.
323. Miniature shrine, UP, 10th century A.D., .910 X .360 m.

INTRODUCTION

The Collection

Find Places

The Art

Iconography

Present Study

References

INTRODUCTION

The Collection

The Allahabad Museum has a good representation of stone sculptures in its wide range of collection. These were acquired through exploration, purchase, gift, etc. Most of quality art pieces were received from the sites in the course of expeditions involving personal effort of curatorial staff. The late Pandit Brij Mohan Vyas, the then Executive Officer of Allahabad Municipality, is credited with bringing Bharhut and Bhumara sculptures, exerting his personal influence and a strong dedicated will. The remains of Jamsot were shifted *en bloc* to the Museum through the untiring efforts of Dr. S.C. Kala, the then Director of the Museum. During his tenure, several sculptres from various other sites were collected from time to time. With the meagre funds at the disposal of the Museum under Municipal Corporation, much could not be spent for the purchase of antiquities. The collection was largely augmented until 1980s through exploration and purchase, paying nominal prices even for very valuable pieces.

After the take-over by the Government of India as an autonomous body,[1] some sculptures have been purchased from private collectors and antique dealers.

The first lot of acquired antiquities through purchase includes an image of Umā-Maheśvara, a couple in *āliṅgana* pose, Nirṛiti and some heads, all belonging to the Mediaeval period. The Nṛvarāha image was a good selection of the second lot. Three mutilated sculptures depicting an identical theme were acquired from different owners which throw welcome light on the prevalence of Yoginī cult around Kauśāmbī. Out of these one (Cat.No.168, Fig.138) is inscribed and provides a clue for identification of the other fragmentary pieces.

Find Places

A knowledge of the findspot of a particular sculpture has multi-fold importance. This helps to reconstruct the religious, political and cultural history of the region. The development of artistic and architectural activities of the place is also revealed by the context of the find. Sometimes sculptures of other art schools are found at distant places which throw light on the inter-state cultural contact at that time. Often the exact find place of the antiquities is not known because of their acquisition through purchase, gift, etc. Occasionally on the basis of regional characteristics or traits of the particular school of art, original provenance could be determined.

The sculptures of the Allahabad Museum have been acquired from different sites. Their brief review in relation to the collection of the Museum may be worth considering.

Bharhut

The village Bharhut is situated 15 km. south of District Satna in Madhya Pradesh. It is nearly half-way between Allahabad and Jabalpur. As many as 54 pieces of Bharhut Stupa railings were gifted to the Allahabad Museum by Maharaja of Nagod State.[2] This is the second largest collection of Bharhut sculptures, the first being at the Indian Museum, Calcutta. The Bharhut pieces have already been catalogued in Pramod Chandra's *Stone Sculptures in the Allahabad Museum.* Only one was left which has been taken into account in this monograph.

Kauśāmbī

The ruins of ancient Kauśāmbī lie near the village Kosam on the left bank of the Yamuna, about 51 km. west of Allahabad. It was the capital of Vatsa *Mahājanapada* and regarded as one of the six principal cities of north India. The site yielded a phenomenal number of antiquities including coins, beads, terracottas, sculptures and other archaeological material. The excavations, were conducted there by Department of Ancient Indian History and Archaeology, University of Allahabad[3] and the exposed finds deposited in the departmental Museum. The Allahabad Museum also possesses a big chunk of repositories from this site. The sculptures found from this place reveal that the art flourished right from the 2nd century B.C. to the late Mediaeval period. This was an important centre for all the three principal faiths as reflected by numerous images and carvings relating to Brahmanical, Buddhist and Jaina religions found from Kauśāmbī and its neighborhood. Many Yakṣa figures throw light on the popularity of Folk Cult in olden days.

Bhita

The mounds at the site of Bhita were excavated in 1909-10 and 1911-12 which reveal cultural sequence of at least five periods.[4] The unearthed material includes pottery, terracottas, seals and sealings, inscriptions, coins and sculptures, etc. The earliest *Pañcamukhī* Śivalinga belongs to Bhita. Early images of Yakṣas found from this site are noteworthy specimens of the sculptural art of India. Fortunately the Allahabad Museum has acquired one massive image of Yakṣa recently. Finding of mediaeval sculptures from the site is a testimony of continuous artistic activities in the region.

Mathura

The city is situated on the right bank of the Yamuna about 145 km. to the south-east of Delhi. In ancient times it was well-connected with all important towns. Mathura *maṇḍala* has a unique place in the cultural history of India. A large number of stone sculptures have been found from this region. They represent Brahmanical, Buddhist and Jaina pantheons apart from secular themes and constitute a distinct school of art because of their special characteristics. It seems that there was a well-established industry of stone carving which catered to the needs of places, far and near. The finding of Mathura sculptures at different archaeological sites clearly proves this.

The Allahabad Museum also has some icons of the Mathura school. A few of them may be categorised remarkable on various counts. The Buddha image belonging to the second regnal year of Kaniṣka is also in the possession of the Allahabad Museum.[5] A small *mātṛkā* icon (Cat.No.134, Fig.112) is a solitary example of a rare iconographic type.

Jhusi

Jhusi (ancient Pratiṣṭhāna) is an adjoining locality of Allahabad city just across the Ganga. The high mounds are scattered around the village and often disturbed by the recent activities of construction here and there. Numerous archaeological objects have been found from these mounds. Some good sculptures of the Gupta period were acquired from this site by the Allahabad Museum.[6] Jhusi is indeed a rich mine of antiquarian wealth and small ancient relics including stone beads, picked up from the surface.

Bhumara

There was a temple dedicated to Śiva at Bhumara, a village in the old state of Nagod and now in the Satna District of Madhya Pradesh.[7] The loose remains from this Gupta temple are housed in the Allahabad Museum and the Indian Museum, Calcutta. This museum has numerous fragments of slabs pertaining to the upper parts of the Gupta temple depicting *gaṇas* in different poses. The major part of the remains have been described in the earlier Catalogue of Dr.Pramod Chandra. Only a few, which were left inadvertently, have been included in this monograph.

Garhwa

Garhwa lies 40 km. south-west of Allahabad. This place was known as Bhaṭṭagrāma in the Gupta period.[8] Some architectural members of the Gupta temple, found from this place, are now preserved in the State Museum Lucknow.[9] Garhwa means a fort and inside the ruined fortification there are a few temples of the mediaeval period. An image of Śeṣaśāyī Viṣṇu from this site (Cat.18, Fig.14) belonging to the 10th century A.D. has been discussed here in detail.

Sarnath

Sarnath is a famous archaeological site situated 9 km. from Varanasi. The Buddha preached his first sermon here in the Deer park (*mṛgadāva*). Ruins of stūpas, temples and monasteries are scattered here over an extensive area.[10] The stone sculptures from the site are divided in several museums, the major chunk being in the local museum. The Director-General of Archaeological Survey of India has loaned some pieces discovered from Sarnath to this Museum. They represent deities of the Buddhist and Brahmanical pantheons.

Khajuraho

Khajuraho situated 46 km. from Chhatarpur in Madhya Pradesh is famous for its magnificent temples built by Candellas.[11] The loose remains from Khajuraho are divided at different places. Some of the antiquities from this place were loaned to some established museums. The Khajuraho sculptures of this Museum were presented by the Maharaja of Chhatarpur. Apart from Brahmanical and Jaina images, a good number of secular sculptures from Khajuraho are also well-represented in the Museum. These include *Apsarās, Vyālas,* and some architectural members.

Gurgi

The ruins of monuments of Gurgi are situated 20 km. to the east of Rewa.[12] Numerous statues and fragments, collected from the mounds, passed through several hands. The sculptures mostly belong to the mediaeval period. The place was sacred to all the three important faiths—

Brahmanical, Jaina and Buddhist, which is testified by the findings. With the efforts of Pt. Brij Mohan Vyas, a number of sculptures were collected from Gurgi which have been dealt with in this Catalogue.

Gaya

Gaya is situated 9 km. from Bodh Gaya, an important ancient site of Bihar. Though the place has no extant monument, yet most of the present temples have been built on original sites with old materials.[13] A number of antiquities have been found from this place and now distributed in different collections. They are mostly Buddhist and belong to the mediaeval period. Plenty of miniature stūpas were modelled to satisfy the demand of the followers. The State Museum, Lucknow has a representative collection of sculptures of the Eastern School of Art, particularly from Gaya.[14] The Allahabad Museum has also collected such pieces including some good examples of miniature votive stūpas from various sources.

Jamsot

The village of Jamsot is situated in Meja Tahsil of the Allahabad District. The debris of a ruined Candella temple was lying buried here near a tank. It was removed *en bloc* to the Allahabad Museum during 1962-63. The old relics constituting parts of a Śiva temple are important from iconographic point of view. The Apsarā figures are remarkable for their postures (*bhaṅgimās*) combining sensuous beauty. More than one hundred pieces from this place are now the property of this Museum.

Other Sites

Temples were erected at many sites of the Allahabad District during early mediaeval period. With the passage of time they were dilapidated and remains were scattered here and there. The Allahabad Museum possesses such statues from Kara, Karchhana, Unchadih, Lachhagir, Soraon and Bara.[15]

Dr. Panna Lall also lent some Gāndhāra and Mediaeval sculptures, the latter collected from the hill districts of Kumaon.[16] A number of sculptures were also acquired through purchase but their exact find-spots often are unknown.

The Art

The stone sculptures of the Allahabad Museum belong to a long time span ranging from 3rd century B.C. to the Modern period. Each distinct period had its own special features. The artistic characteristics of some select statues are discussed here.

Among Śuṅga sculptures, the figure of Yakṣa (Cat.No.179, Fig.148) is noteworthy. The delineation is flat. The dwarfish figure has colossal muscular body bedecked with long heavy earrings. The rope entwined round the belly of the Yakṣa is an interesting feature. He shares the thick lower garment with some coeval Yakṣa images.[17] This double-faced Yakṣa appears to be engaged in bearing some load, other *bhāravāhaka* Yakṣas are also known from this period. Bhita has yielded an almost contemporary Yakṣa figure with four faces.[18]

Spotted red sandstone was the medium of Mathura school of sculpture. Though Mathura sculptures are easily identifiable by special type of sandstone yet their distinctive characteristics constitute a style popularly known as the Mathura Art. A sculpture representing Naigmeṣa (Cat.No.189, Fig.158) may be taken as an early example of this art. The figure stands straight without any bend in the body. The heavy garment is worn in a peculiar manner as found in the early Kuṣāṇa images of Yakṣas, Bodhisattvas and Nāga deities.[19] The pose of *abhaya* is not frontal. A crowned figure of Kubera (Cat. No.182, Fig.151) has a robust body, a typical sitting posture and protruding belly, peculiar to such images. A headless image (Cat. No. 116. Fig. 28) has all the Kuṣāṇa features of the Mathura art. Several heads mostly detached from Jina figures have been found from Mathura, with variant types of modelling. The early heads are shaven and have almond-shaped eyes (Cat. No. 234, Fig. 192). The elaborate head-gear of a head (Cat. No. 117, Fig. 99) is typical of some Bodhisattva images of the Kuṣāṇa period.[21] A smiling expression (Cat. No. 281, Fig. 232) is beautifully portrayed on another head. Its cap-like turban is quite different from bicornate turban of the Śuṅga period. The eyes, half open and half closed (*ardhonmīlita*), are indicative of its transitional phase before the advent of the Gupta features.

Sculptural art was vigorously pursued in the Vatsa Mahājanapada right from the 2nd century B.C. to the Gupta period. Among several pieces, the fragmentary bust of Bodhisattva (Cat. No. 210, Fig. 170) seems to be a product of the Kauśāmbī workshop, though it bears partial resemblance to the Kuṣāṇa art of Mathura.

Examples of the classical Gupta art command heightened aesthetic consciousness and mark definite change in the plastic idiom and expressive quality. The square pedestal showing important events of Buddha's life (Cat. No. 213, Fig. 172 A-D) is a fine example of the Sarnath school. It bears resemblance to the Mathura School of Art in the delineation of drapery. The serenity and poise of the figures constitute a great achievement of this period.

The *Gaṇas* from Bhumara are depicted in playful action.[22] Their hair-styles have beautiful variations. The wig-type coiffure of a *Gaṇa* (Cat.No.185, Fig.154) is remarkable. The preaching Buddha (Cat. No. 215, Fig.

174) is another notable example of the Sarnath school. The *ubhayāṁsika saṁghāṭī* has been shown as transparent without any parallel folds, its presence indicated by few incised lines.

In the 6th-7th century A.D. the classical traditions of Indian sculpture continued on a lower scale. Two Kubera images have identical sitting posture typical of this god. The figure within *candraśālā* (Cat. No. 101, Fig. 85) seems to be earlier than the other (Cat. No. 102, Fig. 86) which may belong to the 7th century A.D. He has a plain halo behind the head and twisted locks of hair dangle on his shoulders. These characteristics occasionally continued in the later period. The modelling of the *Ekamukhaliṅga* (Cat. No. 41, Fig. 34) is also reminiscent of the Gupta idiom. The eyes resembling lotus petal, sharp eye-brows, moist lips, full cheeks, serenity on the face - all classical features are present in this sculpture. The Kārttikeya image (Cat. No. 80, Fig. 67) belongs to the transitional phase of the Gupta and early mediaeval art. It has a slim and balanced body but reveals the beginning of conventionalization which dominates in later centuries.

The Allahabad Museum has a good collection of heads, fragmented from stone sculptures. These have artistic variations. Some heads (Cat. No. 288, Fig. 238) are adorned with wig-type hair arrangement with roundish face and smiling look, partly resembling the specimen (Cat. No. 282, Fig. 232). Another head (Cat. No. 7, Fig.6) wears an intricately ornamented cylindrical crown. The arch-like eyebrows are peculiar to this piece. A face (Cat. No. 243, Fig. 200) has almost closed elongated eyes, with the eye-brows spaced apart. The halo is made of beautiful lotus petals.

The Pāla head of Viṣṇu (Cat. No. 15, Fig. 11) is adorned with *mukuṭa* carved with typical *kīrttimukha* which looks like a close- fitting cap. The lines of eyebrows are thick and joined together. The face is oval. Some heads are depicted wearing *kulah* cap, alien feature, illustrated in Fig. Nos. 234 and 241 (Cat. Nos. 284 and 291).

After the death of Harṣavardhana, the country could not remain under one umbrella for long. Several small and big kingdoms emerged with a new political scenario. Consequently, different regional styles were developed.[23]

In general the sculptural art of the post-Gupta period received setback so far as aesthetics and elegance are concerned.[24] The grace and serenity of the Gupta idiom gradually faded in the following centuries. The slim and balanced body was now replaced by heavy and podgy anatomy. In many cases limbs were disproportionate and lifeless. Stylization of certain postures and motifs dominated. Emphasis was shifted from artistic achievement to the iconographic delineation of the image. The treatment of drapery is now generally coarse and ornamentation becomes conventionalised. In spite of these deteriorating trends of mediaeval art, some sculptures are quite beautiful.[25]

The Allahabad Museum has a rich collection of mediaeval sculptures, representing the regional art styles that flourished in different parts under Pratīhāra, Candella, Kalacūri and Pāla royal dynasties.

Some small icons made of slate coloured stone have been found from different parts of North India. These are in low relief and the treatment is usually linear. As a systematic study of this art form has not been done so far,[26] the dating of icons of this class is problematical.[27] Such an image of Pārvatī (Cat. No. 146, Fig. 119) appears to be a work of the 8th century A.D. The hairdo, drapery and other decorations have been suggested by incised lines. A number of similar icons are preserved in the State Museum, Lucknow.[28]

Amongst the art-styles of the mediaeval period, the early creations of the Gurjara-Pratīhāras are more akin to the classical traditions.[29] But gradually ornamentation and conventional elaboration dominated over the figural form. A standing image of Viṣṇu (Cat. No. 4, Fig. 4) is a fine example of Pratīhāra art which flourished in the Kauśāmbī *maṇḍala*.[30] The oval-shaped nimbus carved out of foliage, high crown, *muktāyajñopavīta*, incised lower garment - these traits are peculiar to this art. The serenity of expression could not be achieved but the proportion of the physique is maintained to a large extent.

Another sculpture representing Hanumān from the same place is a testimony of continued artistic creativity. This (Cat. No. 39, Fig. 32) is a stylised figure with increased and differently delineated ornaments. An image of goddess (Cat. No. 168, Fig. 138) bears similar anatomy and embellishment, belonging to the same period and site.

An icon of Nṛvarāha (Cat. No. 21, Fig. 17) pertains to the late Pratīhāra period. The modelling is dull and stale. Another image of this god (Cat. No. 20, Fig. 16) provides different features. He is surrounded by several small figures and art motifs. The ornamentation is sumptuous, and exaggerated by decorating even the club and the wheel, the *āyudhas* of the god. This is a specimen of the early Candella art, which is represented in this Museum by numerous late Candella sculptures from Jamsot. A typical figure of Śiva (Cat.No. 46, Fig.38) from Jamsot has elliptical face, fleshy lips, curved eye-brows, exaggerated treatment of jewellery and drapery, all traits of the Candella art. Many types of female damsels (*nāyikās*), dancers and celestial figures from this site share these features.

An independent art style was developed in Bengal and Bihar and the adjoining areas under the sway of the Pāla and Sena rulers.[31] The early Pāla sculpture is much influenced by classical idiom but the images of later phase reveal mediaeval traits. The Allahabad Museum possesses only a few sculptures of the Pāla school, belonging to the later phase (10th-11th century A.D.). An image of Śiva-Pārvatī (Cat. No. 55, Fig. 45) is a good example of this art. The treatment here has a metallic look and the lotus dominates the whole composition as evidenced also in other images (Cat. No. 14, Fig. 10 and Cat. No. 222, Fig. 180). A fragmentary piece (Cat. No. 33, Fig. 27) represents the Sena art of the 12th century A.D. The delineation of the figures is crude and the decoration conventional. There are a few images from Gaya which represent the Eastern School of Art (also known as the Magadha School). The medium of these sculptures is black schist. An image of Pārvatī (Cat. No. 15, Fig. 124) is a fine example of the Katyūri Art which flourished in the Garhwal and Kumaon region.[32] This is influenced by the Pāla art and has a pronounced metallic appearance. Her close-fitting lower garment (*sāṛī*) is tastefully treated with folds. She stands on lotus petals, has a stalked lotus in her hand and the halo is also decorated with lotus petals. Thus the domination of lotus motif is clearly evident.

The mediaeval sculptures from Ḍāhala *maṇḍala* represent the Kalacuri art.[33] An image of Agni (Cat. No. 88, Fig. 74) is a representative example of this style. The legs are elongated and decorated with typical stringed ornaments. A Viṣṇu icon (Cat. No. 16, Fig. 12) is the only specimen of the mediaeval Karṇāṭa style which is quite different from the art styles of North India.

After the twelfth century A.D. sculptural art showed further decline. The figures are lifeless with disproportionate limbs. The facial expression is crude. An image of Rāma (Cat. No. 34, Fig. 28) appears to be a product of the last phase of mediaeval sculpture. The artistic decadence is quite evident from the rough and listless modelling of the image.

Iconography

The iconography of Kuṣāṇa deities is simple. There is not much variety of postures, attributes and other details. The number of sculptures is also meagre as compared with later times. In some cases, particularly Jina images, the monotonous presentation dominates the iconic forms. As time rolled on, new forms were conceived and representations of some more deities added. The process of replacing the alien features with new indigenous elements was started and received significant patronage under the Gupta rule. Apart from the images of gods and goddesses narrative scenes were also given a prominent place in stone carvings.

In the mediaeval period iconography becomes progressively more complex. Several Pauranic deities got representation in sculptural art. With multiplicity of hands, the number of attributes and *āyudhas* also proliferated. Their postures became more varied. Different iconographic texts and literary descriptions helped to shape new forms and compositions. Sometimes the sculptors or the commissioning authority also used their discretion in shaping an image. Due to assimilation of all these features of varied nature, it is very difficult to understand some images of mediaeval period. An attempt has been made to highlight only new features and rare characteristics of the images covered in this monograph.

Brahmanical Trinity (Brahmatrayī)

The depiction of gods and goddesses in a row with equal status started from the Kuṣāṇa period.[34] The Brahmanical Trinity (Brahmā, Viṣṇu, Maheśa) became popular in the mediaeval period. They are generally shown on the top of sculpture representing Brahmanical gods. Their independent images are also known. The Allahabad Museum also houses one (Cat. No. 1, Fig. 1) wherein the gods are depicted in *samapāda* standing pose with their associated attendants.[35] It seems that the image was evolved to accommodate the feelings of the followes of diverse sects.[36]

Viṣṇu and His Incarnations

Early images of Viṣṇu are simple in execution. The four-armed god is invariably shown with *śaṅkha, cakra* and *gadā*, the fourth hand being usually in the *abhaya* pose. There is no attendant or subsidiary deity around the god. The modelling of Viṣṇu icons continued to be simple with select ornaments like *kirīṭamukuṭa, ekāvalī* and *vanamālā*. Dangling of matted hair locks on the shoulders was a special trait of the Gupta Art (Cat. No. 2, Fig. 2). Apart from the usual *lāñchanas* Viṣṇu sometimes holds a fruit (*śrīphala*).[39] A revolutionary change is effected by the introduction of *āyudhapuruṣas* (personification of *āyudhas*). A few representative Viṣṇu images of the Gupta period are preserved in the Allahabad Museum.[40]

Generally the composition of Viṣṇu images of the early mediaeval period appears to be complex. Now he is surrounded by a number of *parivāradevatās*. The fourth *lāñchana padma* was associated with him. Generally the right hand of the god is shown in *varadamudrā* with lotus mark. He is flanked by *āyudhapuruṣas*, along with his consort Lakṣmī and mount Garuda in human form. In some images the figures of Sarasvatī, Bhūdevī, Trinity (Brahmā, Viṣṇu and Maheśa), Vidyādharas and donors are also depicted. The *parikara* is usually adorned with miniature figures of incarnations of Viṣṇu whose number varies from two to ten. A fragment of Viṣṇu image (Cat. No. 14, Fig. 10) shows the tortoise and fish incarnations in their therianthropomorphic forms in place of their usual representation in zoomorphic form.[41] This sculpture belongs to the Pāla school of art and interestingly enough this rare feature can be seen in another Pāla sculpture of the State Museum, Lucknow where these two incarnations were treated in the same manner.[42]

Independent images of some incarnations of Viṣṇu are also in the collection. The zoomorphic form of boar incarnation known as *Yajña-Varāha* or *Mahāvarāha* was very popular in Central India during the early mediaeval period. A couple of such figures have been acquired from Khajuraho in the Allahabad Museum. A standing image of Vāmana (Cat. No. 32, Fig. 26) is identifiable by his short stature and peculiar hair treatment. Similar images of Vāmana in *vaṭuka* form are known from Bundelkhand.[43] Many of these icons are carved almost in three dimensions.

A powerful depiction of Nṛvarāha (Cat.No.20, Fig.16) represents two preceding incarnations of Matsya and Kūrma on the *parikara* (frame).[44] A broad lotus leaf (*kamala-dala*), treated as a canopy over the head, is surmounted by a miniature figure of Viṣṇu in meditation. This is rarely found in Varāha images.

A small fragment from Viṣṇu image (Cat. No. 26, Fig. 21) shows the fish incarnation along with Liṅga within *arghya*. Sometimes worship of Liṅga[45] is depicted but here a male figure is standing in *tribhaṅga* with the right hand raised in *abhaya*. Only the bust of the second figure is visible. A plausible explanation or literary corroboration has not been found so far.[46]

Some columns have been found on which some incarnations of Viṣṇu have been depicted. Sometimes importance is given to one incarnation making the figure bigger so as to enshrine it within the temple edifice.[47] Usually the accepted sequence was not adopted. The sculpture (Cat. No. 27, Fig. 22) gives prominence to Nṛsiṁha *avatāra*. A frieze (Cat. NO. 35, Fig. 29) depicts a scene of Kṛṣṇalīlā where a small child is shown being offered butter instead of being caught stealing for which Kṛṣṇa became famous (*mākhanacora*).

The figure (Cat. No. 39, Fig. 32) of Hanumān, the staunch devotee of Rāma, is fashioned in a uniform style, at several places in the early mediaeval period. An early Pratīhāra period image in the Allahabad Museum also belongs to the same class. His pose is typical and probably based on some literary narration. The right hand of the god is raised above the head and the other one is in the *vitarka-mudrā*. His face is open as if he is saying something. Significantly enough this beautiful icon comes from Kauśāmbī. The image resembles one from Siron Khurd (Distt. Latitpur).[48]

Śiva in Liṅga and Vigraha Forms

Śiva has been represented in many forms in the plastic art from very early times. His symbolic form in the shape of Liṅga (*Liṅga-vigraha*) and human form (*mānasa-vigraha*) have a wide variety of manifestations. The Allahabad Museum possesses a good number of *mukhaliṅgas* in its collection. One Ekamukhaliṅga (Cat. No. 41, Fig. 34) has a striking feature on the face shown attached with the shaft (*liṅga* part). Several beautiful Ekamukhaliṅgas of the Gupta period have been found from different parts of northern India.[49] Though the number of Ekamukhaliṅgas decreased in the mediaeval period yet this exhibit belongs to the post-Gupta period and, as such, provides testimony of continuity of the art tradition and popularity of the Liṅga worship. Evidently the idea behind the representation was to combine the symbolic and anthromorphic forms in one.

The *Caturmukhaliṅgas* were also popular in mediaeval art. The four faces shown around the *liṅga* denote four aspects of Śiva, viz., Sadyojāta, Aghora, Umā and Tatpuruṣa. The fifth face Īśāna is invisible.[50] A beautiful *Caturmukhaliṅga* of the Gupta period was found from Kauśāmbī.[51] In these *liṅgas*, one face is shown in the fierce (*Aghora*) aspect depicting bare teeth, beard and moustaches while the other face just opposite is always in beatific form denoting Umā aspect. Exceptionally the crescent is depicted adorning Umā face in one *Caturmukhaliṅga*.

The theme of Umā-Maheśvara was very popular in the mediaeval art. Several images have been found from different parts of India with varying treatment. The artists took special fancy to endow new postures to Śiva and Pārvatī. Geographical factor and regional art idioms also contributed to provide novelty. A variety is observed in some such images in the Allahabad Museum. A Pāla sculpture (Cat. No. 55, Fig. 45) seems to be a copy of the one preserved in the State Museum, Lucknow.[52]

A mutilated image (Cat. No. 53, Fig. 43) of this class is peculiar in composition. Three miniature Śivaliṅgas in a row on running pedestal are shown in the extreme right corner instead of in the middle. A small figure of Brahmā is shown standing irrespective of his usual seated position. Between the feet of the divine parents is depicted a standing figure of Gaṇeśa. Usually dancing figure of Bhṛṅgī is carved in this place. Umā is holding a child in her lap, probably her son Kārttikeya.[53] The concept of Skandamātā is highlighted and the *āliṅgana* pose was avoided in this case. An image (Cat. No. 51, Fig. 41) of mediaeval period is important because of its unique depiction. Though a definite cognizance is not traceable, yet the very posture, the *jaṭājūṭa*, and the trident-like arrow suggest it to be a representation of Umā-Maheśvara. A bow is held in the left hand of the god which is a rare feature with Umā-Maheśamūrti.

In many places the icons of Rāvaṇānugraha have been simply labelled as Umā-Maheśvara because of their prominent position. But on account of the depiction below the pedestal of Rāvaṇa in the act of lifting Kailāśa, these images should be categorised under *Rāvaṇānugrahamūrti*.[54] In some sculptures the folded hillscape denotes the Kailāśa mountain.[55] To assure Pārvatī that there was no cause for fear or nervousness, the right hand of Śiva is shown facing towards his consort in *abhaya*. The frontal look of this posture is not altogether unknown in such images.

The representations of Gaja-saṁhāramūrti are meagre

in northern India. Usually they are combined with other aspects of Śiva like Bhairava or Andhākasuravadha.[56] A good example of multi-armed Gajāsuravadhamūrti (Cat. No. 58, Fig. 48) is preserved in the Allahabad Museum. The *gajacarma* is beautifully portrayed, though the image is not in a good state of preservation. The presence of female deities on either side of the top of the stele is also an interesting feature. The face of Śiva is composed in placid attitude.

The architectural member *śukanāsa* (Cat. No. 59, Fig. 49), once adorning a mediaeval Śiva temple, shows a beautiful head. This can be identified as Śiva because of the third eye and matted locks of hair on the head. This beautiful sculpture hails from Kara, a site in the Allahabad District.

Gaṇeśa and Kārttikeya

The images of Gaṇapati were quite popular in the mediaeval period. He was represented in various forms. The dancing posture of the multi-armed deity was a special craze for sculptors. In a niche (*rathikā*) four-headed Gaṇeśa (Cat. No. 74, Fig. 62) is shown as if he is in a dancing mood. One is so convinced from the way Ganesa has placed his foot on his *vāhana* rat even in the absence of the rhythm of the dance or any accomplice. His lower right hand is placed on *kaṭi* as usually found in a dance pose. Another icon (Cat. No. 77, Fig. 65) presents him performing dance in full swing.

Gaṇeśa is *Ekadanta* (having only one tusk) and the sculptors took liberty to show either the right (Cat. No. 74, Fig. 62) or the left tusk (Cat. No. 77, Fig. 65). His trunk is either turned to the right or left but in some cases it has got a frontal position falling on his belly (Cat. Nos. 75-76, Figs. 63-64). The serpent is, in some cases, shown hanging from the shoulder in the *upavīta* fashion (Cat. Nos. 76-77, Figs. 64-65).

A two-armed standing figure of Kārttikeya (Cat. No. 80, Fig. 67), though in a highly mutilated condition, commands unique gesture. The feeding of the peacock bears affinity to the early Gupta images of Kārttikeya.[57]

Brahmā

Caturmukha Brahmā is normally depicted with faces attached to each other in a row' the fourth face at the back being invisible. Usually the central face is bearded (*lambakūrca*) (Cat. Nos. 83-84, Figs. 69, 70). But exceptions are there as seen in a fragmentary piece of the Allahabad Museum (Cat. No. 82, Fig. 68). He is also shown a little pot-bellied. Probably the sculpture (Cat. No. 84, Fig. 70) was chiselled in the manner of Viṣṇu image wherein he is shown flanked by female figure in a separate niche.[58] The right part of the image is wanting.

Dikpālas

The images of Agni may be classified in two groups. One belongs to the independent cult icon and the other represents his position as guardian of the south-east direction. The Dikpāla form is depicted on one of the faces of an upright pilaster once adorning the outer wall of a temple. In one sculpture (Cat. No. 88, Fig. 74) of the category of independent cult images Agni is represented in *Brahmacārin* form. He wears a broad *Yajñopavīta* and wooden sandals (*pādukas*) and is surrounded by several bearded figures, probably sages, holding sacrificial tools in their hands. At least in one example the tenon is attached below the sculpture (Cat. No. 87, Fig. 73). This might be for insertion on a high pillar with groove, meant for prominent display at a religious place. The flames are shown around the body of the god. This feature continued from the Kuṣāṇa to the mediaeval period.[59] The naked figure (Cat. No. 98, Fig. 82) of Nirṛti holding a sword is flanked by *apsarās* on recesses, a unique composition of cruelty and beauty at one place. He wears a long garland composed of human skulls. The *vāhana*, probably bull, is also unusual to Dikpāla Nirṛti. Some of the feaures of Bhairava, a ferocious form of Śiva are also assimilated with this image. The other image (Cat . No. 99, Fig. 83) of this god is quite different in treatment.

The Allahabad Museum houses a beautiful sculpture (Cat. No. 100, Fig. 84) representing *Varuṇa*, the lord of the west direction. Interestingly he has deer as his mount, usually associated with Vāyu.[60] But he can be easily identified as Varuṇa because of his attribute noose. Kubera has a typical pose of sitting known in texts as *mahārājalīlāsana*, and his figure can be recognised by this posture alone (Cat. 101, Fig. 85). Mongoose-shaped purse (*nakulaka*) and *caṣaka* (wine-cup) are his *lāñchanas* as seen in a sculpture of the Museum (Cat. No. 102, Fig. 86).

Sūrya and Revanta

The mutilated image (Cat. No. 107, Fig. 89) of Sūrya with Daṇḍa and Piṅgala shows two Pratihāras on pilasters on each side. The protective dress worn on the arms is also a rare feature in this example (Cat. No. 108, Fig. 90). The sitting posture of a Sūrya image (Cat. No. 110, Fig. 92) reminds of Kuṣāṇa icons of the Mathura school.[61]

A stele (Cat. No. 112, Fig. 94) showing Revanta accompanying Daṇḍa and Piṅgala, all riding on horse-back, depicts a vivid scene of hunting (*mṛgayā*) as prescribed in iconographic texts.[62] The figures are shown in action. Such images are known from other parts of India[63] and the Allahabad Museum also has almost a similar image[64] with some unique features.

Brahmanical Goddesses

A small fragment (Cat. No. 134, Fig.112) of Mathura red sandstone depicts a hitherto unknown feature of bird-faced baby of a bird- headed mother-goddess, a biological phenomenon. The piece belongs to the 2nd century A.D. Different forms of Durgā have been found in the sculptural art of India. The Museum collection has a good example (Cat. No. 138, Fig. 114) of four-armed standing figure of Durgā carrying wine flask, sword (now wanting), shield and long trident. The surviving upper part of Mahiṣāsuramardinī shows her upper raised hands holding a garland with which she adorned herself after victory. It has resemblance with one in the Mathura Museum.[65] The icons of Lajjāgaurī are rare. In such representations the face of the goddess is not shown and her private part is exposed. The Museum has one piece (Cat. No. 139 Fig. 51) though not in a good state of preservation. Independant images of Lakṣmī are not many in the early mediaeval period. The two-armed image (Cat. No. 140, Fig. No. 115) of Lakṣmī is depicted in modest way carrying a long-stalked lotus in her left hand.

There are two beautiful examples of Tapasvinī Pārvatī in the Museum. The first (Cat. No. 148, Fig. 120) is flanked by animals probably deer and lion and without any attendant. The other (Cat. No. 153, Fig. 124) is surrounded by several female attendants. Such images have been found from the Uttarākhaṇḍa region and Central India.[66]

The *saptamātṛkā* panels are found all over India. On some panels, the goddesses are depicted in dancing posture. A fragmentary piece (Cat. No. 158, Fig. 129) consists of three surviving *mātṛkās* in the attitude of dancing. Kaumārī and Indrānī have children in their laps highlighting their motherly aspect (*mātṛtva*). Vārāhī, holding a wine-pot (*caṣaka*) and fish (*matsya*) in her hands, has no inclination to play a mother. The independent four-armed image of Vārāhī (Cat. No. 161, Fig. 132) is also in a dancing pose. Thunderbolt and dagger (*churikā*) as attributes are associated with the goddess, a noteworthy feature.

There are a number of Cāmuṇḍā images. The sculpture (Cat. No. 162, Fig. 133) depicting *Ulūkavāhinī* Devi is rare. It is in good state of preservation. A skeletal figure of Cāmuṇḍā (Cat. No. 163, Fig. 134) shows exposed details of bones both in the front and back. Sculptures of Cāmuṇḍā carved in the round are rare. The goddess Cāmuṇḍā has human mount as seen in many images.

Three sculptures (AM 92.130, 92.146, 91.1914), almost identical in treatment, have been found from Kauśāmbī. Fortunately one (Cat. No. 168, Fig. 138) has got a two-line mutilated inscription which gives clue that the sculpture belongs to some Pāla king. Yaśaḥpāla was the last ruler of Gurjara Pratihāra dynasty in the Kauśāmbī *maṇḍala* in the early eleventh century A.D.[67] This sculpture seems to belong to the same period. Its identification is a matter of further research but, anyway, this represents a Yoginī. Another interesting image (Cat. No. 172, Fig. 142) of *Aśvarohinī* Devī defies attempts at correct identification. A mutilated image depicting the same subject was recently unearthed from the premises of the Jarai Temple, Barwasagar which belongs to the late ninth century A.D. A human figure in adoration is obstructing the advancement of the horse. This gives an impression that the representation has some narrative intent. The Tantric character of the goddess is evident from associated attributes like sword, shield, *kapāla*, etc. A lady holding a conch with both hands along the chest is a novel experiment of the sculptor. She has no other attribute or mark for proper identification. For the sake of convenience, we may designate her as *Śaṅkhadhāriṇī Devī*. Female figures holding a deep bowl have been named as *Dīpālakṣmī*. The figure (Cat. No. 176, Fig. 145) resembles bronze-images of the goddess preserved in the Lucknow Museum Collection. Bronze *Dīpālakṣmī* is a familiar theme in South India.

Minor Deities Common to all Sects

Yakṣa cult has been popular right from the 3rd century B.C. Even today local folk-deities are worshipped under various names. Several Yakṣa-images have been found from important archaeological sites. Generally they are disproportionate, dwarfish and pot-bellied. A double-sided Yakṣa figure of the 2nd century B.C. (Cat. No. 179, Fig. 148) was recently acquired and was reported to have been found from Bhita. A four-faced image of Yakṣa from the same site and belonging to the same period is housed in the State Museum, Lucknow.[68] The Yakṣas engaged in wilfully stretching their mouth are also known from well-known sites.[69] From Mathura comes another image almost in similar posture. Probably these were meant for amusement of children.

The panels in stone as well as in terracotta representing Kubera and Hārītī have been found from Mathura and its vicinity. Kubera and Kārttikeya both were associated with mothers.[70] The Allahabad Museum has two such images (Cat. Nos. 182-183, Figs. 151-152) of the Kuṣāṇa period. The sitting posture of deities is standardised. A crossed line on the pedestal might be the indication of a couch.

The figures holding a staff with both hands and sitting in squatting pose are a problem for identification. These are found on *śukanāsas*, chaitya-windows and facades of miniature shrines. Independent images of this theme are also known.[71] The staff is associated with several gods like Yama, Indra, Śiva, etc. Several suggestions have been offered but the exact meaning of these images remains a puzzle. Naigameṣa is a presiding deity of child birth.[72] He is shown goat-headed and in most cases associated with children. He is also mentioned in Jaina literature. His female counterpart, Naigameṣī, is also known to early Mathura art.[73] The sculpture (Cat. No. 189, Fig. 158) described in the monograph belongs to the Kuṣāṇa art of Mathura. The style of his drapery resembles that of early Kuṣāṇa images of Yakṣas, Bodhisattvas and Nāgas. In the *Mahābhārata* and *Purāṇas* Naigmeya was enumerated as one of the names of Skanda. Interestingly, the hairdo of the figure is divided in three parts which became a cognizable mark of the god in later times. He is accompanied by four children, two on the shoulders and two on each side of the god. In a similar image deposited in the Mathura Museum four children are seen seated on the shoulders of Naigameśa.

The most striking character of mediaeval Indian sculptural art lies in various renderings of feminine beauty, particularly as *Apsarās* and *Nāyikās*. These damsels are generally engaged in one or the other playful act. Some of the beautiful *Apsarā* figures were already included in the catalogue by Dr. Pramod Chandra.[74] A few are described here, exhibiting different *mudrās* and *bhaṅgimās*.

Buddhist Deities

Buddhist icons included here may be classified under three heads, viz. (1) Bodhisattva and Buddha images, (2) depiction of life stories, and (3) other minor deities. The number of Buddhist images less in comparison to other pantheons in the Museum collection. The head (Cat. No. 211) seems to belong to an image of Bodhisattva. It could be identified as such on the basis of the typical crown worn by most of the Kuṣāṇa Bodhisattva figures. But some early figures having features of Buddha are designated as Boddhisattva on their pedestal inscriptions.[75] A small bust (Cat. No. 210, Fig. 170) wearing ornaments and in *abhaya* pose may also be representation of Bodhisattva.

Generally seated images of Buddha in the Mathura art are portrayed in two ways. Buddha is seated either in meditation placing his palms on each other or in a cross-legged position of *yogāsana* with the right hand in *abhaya*. A very mutilated image (Cat. No. 21, Fig. 171) of the Mathura art belongs to this latter group.

The *mudrās* have significant role in Buddhist iconography. Standing Buddhas are rarely shown in *varada-mudrā* in the Mathura school of art. But it was popular in the Sarnath school of the Gupta period. The Buddha image (Cat. No. 214, Fig. 173) of this art must have been in the *varada* pose.

Several heads of Buddha have been found from different places. These might be detached from full-size images. But it seems that this is not the case with the stucco heads which might have been prepared for independent use. Three stucco heads (Cat. Nos. 207-209, Figs.167-168), though mutilated, are distinguished by their expression and other details.

The scenes of Buddha's life have also got a special place in Indian art. Apart from four most important events, namely, Nativity, Temptation, First Sermon and *Mahāparinirvāṇa*, some other life-scenes have also been portrayed on stone slabs and friezes. A fragmentary piece of blue schist stone (Cat. No. 206, Fig. 166) shows the nativity scene. A better preserved piece of Gāndhāra art is also kept in the Allahabad Museum.[76] A square stone slab fashioned as *chowki* (Cat. No. 213, Figs. 172 A-D) depicts principal incidents of Buddha's life. It has carvings on four sides. Three side niches accommodate three scenes, each on one side, which may be identified as *Māradharṣaṇa*, *Dharmacakrapravartana*, and *Mahāparinirvāṇa*. The fourth niche has at least three scenes. Though these are very badly defaced yet the identification is possible on the basis of mere traces of figures. The scenes are Birth of Buddha, first bath by two *nāgas* Nanda-Upananda, and Indra's visit to Buddha. It is interesting to note that two less important events were also presented along with a principal one.

Some Buddhist icons of the Eastern school of art are inscribed. The Museum has also inscribed images out of which three are described here. One represents a group of Ṣaḍakṣarī Lokeśvara (Cat.No. 224, Fig. 182) and the other shows Buddhist goddess Tārā.

There was a tradition of making miniature stūpas probably for convenience of worship. This might have been inspired from the figural representation of stūpas on the early stone sculpture. This new trend received tremendous popularity in Bihar resulting in several small stūpa shrines in the Pāla and Magadha Schools of Art. A beautiful base of stūpa (Cat. No. 228, Fig. 186) depicts niched Buddha and Bodhisattva along with outlines of several stūpas. Another miniature stūpa showing Buddha on the sides hails from Sarnath, an important Buddhist site.

In the mediaeval period, Buddhism was strongly influenced by the Tantric wave. Several sculptures were produced which have Tantric traits. An image of goddess (Cat. No. 229, Fig. 187 A-B) seems to be an outcome of such influence.

Jaina Deities

In the pre-Christian era Jainism was accepted as one of the important religious faiths of India. It continued to flourish with same fervour from early times to the present-day. This is also evident from the find of numerous images, temples, inscriptions, etc. relating to the Jaina religion.

The Allahabad Museum has a representative collection of Jaina images. Barring a few, the majority of them belong to the Mediaeval period. There are some heads detached from the Tīrthaṅkara images which could be recognized on the basis of their typical modelling. In the mediaeval Jina heads the upraised part in the form of *uṣṇīṣa* is also found (Cat. Nos. 255-256, Figs. 211-212) and often confusion prevails whether a particular head belongs to a Jina or the Buddha.

The Tīrthaṅkaras have the highest position in the Jaina religion. Their number is twenty-four among whom Ādinātha or Ṛṣabhanātha is regarded as the earliest. The last Tīrthaṅkara Mahāvīra is a historical figure, contemporary with the Buddha. The iconography of Jinas is very simple. They are depicted only in two postures, viz., seated in *dhyānamudrā* or standing straight without any bend in the body (*kāyotsargamudrā*). Their main characteristics are well-contained in the popular verse of *Bṛhatsaṁhitā* of *Varāhamihira*. According to this, the Arhats should be depicted nude, young and beautiful. The image should have placid expression, long arms and *śrīvatsa* mark on the chest.[77]

The early Jina images had no distinguishing marks for identification.[78] Only three Tīrthaṅkaras - Ādinātha, Neminātha and Pārśvanātha - can be recognized because of their special features. The assimilation of their distinctive marks (*lāñchanas*), *Śasanadevatās* and attendants (*Gaṇadharas*) in the image of Jinas was a development during the early medieval period.

Even the fragmentary upper part of the image (Cat. No. 237-238, Figs. 194-195) of Ādinātha can be easily identified because of hair-locks falling on the shoulders. Likewise the Pārśvanātha image (Cat. No. 239, Fig. 196) has always a snake canopy around the head. The other Jina figures have their respective marks of cognizance usually carved on the pedestals.[79] Some sculptures, made of black marble or granite, have mirror-like polish and some Jina images bear a short inscription on the pedestal normally giving the date of installation of the image.[80] The obelisk carved with a Tīrthaṅkara on each side is technically known as *sarvatobhadrapratimā*. Such images started taking shape right from the Kuṣāṇa period and generally represented Ṛṣabhanātha, Neminātha, Pārśvanātha and Mahāvīra. In the mediaeval period too these four-fold images continued to be in great demand. A *sarvatobhadra pratimā*[81] of the Allahabad Museum (Cat No. 268, Fig. 222 A-B) is simple in composition. But the figures have a short stature. Two-corner stone-slabs (Cat. No. 269-270, Figs. 223 A-B) carved with Supārśvanātha and Pārśvanātha are almost identical.

A fragmentary stone-slab (Cat. No. 274, AM 542) seems to be a part of an auspicious column (*Mānastambha*). This shows some Tīrthaṅkara figures. In the mediaeval period several stone tablets (*śilāpaṭṭa*) were prepared bearing a number of Jina figures carved in a row. All three such tablets of the Museum collection are interesting. One (Cat. No. 252, Fig. 208) has sixty-four Jina figures seated in *dhyānamudrā*. The other (Cat. No. 245, Fig. 201) has twenty-four Tīrthaṅkaras shown in four horizontal rows but only Ādinātha is seated in *yogāsana*. A female devotee is seen on the extreme right in the *namaskāra-mudrā*. The third *paṭṭa* (Cat. No. 253, Fig. 209) has only sixteen Tīrthaṅkaras among whom the central figure in the lower row may be identified as Pārśvanātha with snake hoods shown in the shape of a halo.

Some lintels of Jaina temples are also profusely carved with Tīrthaṅkaras, decorative motifs and *śāsanadevatās*. A lintel (Cat. No. 249, Fig. 205) depicting 24 Tīrthaṅkaras in different positions gives an idea of the elevation of a Jaina temple. The central part of the other slab (Cat. No. 250, Fig. 206) is occupied by Ambikā flanked by the figures of Pārśvanātha and Ādinātha.

Secular Subjects

The presence of figures in highly amorous poses and engaged in sexual acts on the temples is still a mystery. Several explanations were offered by scholars but an authentic objective could not be determined for erotism on the religious edifices.

The Allahabad Museum has one erotic couple (Cat. No. 292, Fig. 241) from the famous site of temples - Khajuraho. On a horizontal slab (Cat. No. 295, Fig. 245) loving couples are shown in different poses within pillared niches. This piece also belongs to the Candella Art. A unique sculpture (Cat. No. 293, Fig. 243) depicting bestiality scene bears a long inscription. A donkey-like animal is engaged in sexual intercourse with a woman who is bent low from her waist. Almost identical representations have been found from Roda and in the temples at Khajuraho and Ambarnath.[82] Several other depictions highlighting animal-woman coitus are known from various sites but their exact meaning has not been ascertained. It might have some symbolic or perhaps imprecatory significance.

There are several male and female heads which could not be identified with a particular religion. A few of them (Cat. Nos. 284, 291, 299, Figs. 234, 241, 248) have some alien features particularly in their head-dresses. An unidentified scene carved on a stone-slab (Cat. No. 289, Fig. 239) arouses an interest because of peculiar gesture of figures. A male holding a sword stands unperturbed and a female figure is kneeling towards him. A lady standing nearby seems to be busy in persuasion while a couple is proceeding towards the opposite direction. This might be some sort of story. A portrait of some royal dignitary (Cat. No. 297, Fig. 246) is also noteworthy for its majestic look and rich decoration.

Architectural Members

There are a number of architectural members in the Museum. These are fragmented parts of temples and other monuments in the shape of pillars, door-sills, lintels, gargoyles, doorjambs, brackets, panels, *śukanāsas*, *āmalakas*, etc. They are carved with art motifs, geometrical designs, creeper pattern, divine and secualr figures. A part of pillar capital (Cat. No. 341, Fig. 279) shows a beautiful example of *kīrttimukha* resembling a human face instead of the usual lion face.[83]

There are some Kumāra brackets showing Atlantean figures bearing load with their hands. A bracket (Cat. No. 373, Fig. 305 A-C) with animal-headed gods is most interesting. On the four sides of the piece, elephant-headed Gaṇeśa, monkey-faced Hanumān, lion- faced Narasiṁha and boar-faced Nṛvarāha, the last two incarnations of Viṣṇu, have been shown. The very purpose of this arrangement and presentation is not known. Only those gods were selected for the purpose of load-bearing who have animal faces.

Memorial Pillars

Some obelisks depicting various scenes including *Kṛṣṇalīlā* have been found from different sites.[84] The sites of these memorial pillars prserved in the Allahabad Museum are not known. But they seem to belong to the same place or region and the arrangement of scenes in separate compartments is quite similar to those found from Central India.

Animals

Animals were closely associated with the sculptural art of India. The Aśokan pillars are crowned with animal figures. Sanchi and Bharhut reliefs represented a variety of animals and birds. They are depicted not only in association with gods and goddesses or in narrative scenes but their independent figures were also frequently sculptured. A small architectural fragment (Cat.No. 382, Fig. 314) shows an owl family, a rare subject for the sculptor. A hybrid animal motif, popularly known as *Śārdūla* or *Vyāla*, has an enormous variety.[85] The Allahabad Museum has a few which have been illustrated in the monograph.

The foregoing account of iconographic details reveals that deities were represented in varied forms, some of which were quite rare and unique.

Present Study

The exposition of material through descriptive catalogues is of prime importance for advanced study and research. This catalogue covers about 400 stone sculptures of the Allahabad Museum. Their details are highlighted and most of them are also illustrated with photographs. Similarities and other related useful information are given for making the documentation comprehensive.

The arrangement of the catalogued pieces is based on iconography. First of all Brahmanical gods and goddesses are classified under different heads, followed by Buddhist and Jaina icons, after which the secular subjects are dealt with. The architectural members have been discussed in relation to their original placement in structure.

The precise information consisting of a short caption, name of the site, if known, approximate date, the variety of material used, measurements in metric system and the Accession number of the Allahabad Museum is given at the outset. It is followed by a brief description of the piece. Only a few are not described but their illustrations are given. Obviously they are self- explanatory.

Thus the present study provides useful data for further indepth study of the sculptural art and iconography of North India.

References

1. The Allahabad Museum was taken over as an autonomous body by the Government of India on 29th April 1986.
2. For detailed study, please see *Bharhut Bedika* by Dr. S.C. Kala, Allahabad, 1951.
3. For details please see *The Excavation at Kausambi* by G.R. Sharma, 1957-59.
4. *Archaeological Survey of India - Annual Report*, 1911-12, pp. 29-94.
5. Sharma, R.C., *Buddhist Art of Mathura*, Delhi, 1984, p. 183, fig. 93.
6. *SSAM*, plate LXI, fig. 196.
7. For detailed study, please refer to *Memoir* No. 16 of ASI entitled *The Temple of Siva at Bhumara* by R.D. Banerji, 1924.
8. *Gazetteer of India. Uttar Pradesh, Allahabad*, 1968 (Allahabad), p.32.
9. Joshi, N.P., *Catalogue of Brahmanical Sculptures in the State Museum, Lucknow*, Part I, Lucknow, 1972, pp. 82, 85-89.
10. Hargreaves, H., *Excavation at Sarnath, A.S.I.*, 1914-15.
11. For detailed study, please see *Temples of Khajuraho*, Vols. I-II, by Krishna Deva, New Delhi (1990).
12. Cunningham, A., *Archaeological Survey Report*, XXI, p. 151.
13. *Ibid.*, pp. 5-6.
14. *SML* Nos. B.260-B.288.
15. *Uttar Pradesh District Gazetteers, Allahabad*, pp. 371-396.
16. Kala, S.C., *Sculptures in the Allahabad Municipal Museum*, Allahabad, 1946, p. 19.
17. Misra, Ram Nath, *Yaksha Cult and Iconography*, New Delhi, 1981, Figs. 23-26.
18. *SML* No. 56. 394; *Ibid.*, figs. 35-37.
19. Agrawala, V.S., *Indian Art*, Varanasi 1966, Figs. 325, 380, 382, etc.
20. Joshi, N. P., *Catalogue*, Part I, p. 115, Figs. 45-48.
21. Joshi, N. P., *Mathura Sculptures*, Mathura, 1966, Figs. 42, 71.
22. *SSAM*, pp. 79-86, Pl.LVIII & LIX.
23. Ray, Nihar Ranjan, "Sculpture (Ch.)" *The Struggle for Empire*, The History and Culture of the Indian People, Vol.V (1957), p. 641.
24. Saraswati, S.K., *A Survey of Indian Sculpture*, p. 151.
25. Śivaramamurti, C., *Indian Sculpture*, New Delhi, 1961, Figs. 21, 23, 33, 34, 35, etc.
26. Such images are housed in the State Museum, Lucknow, Allahabad Museum, and Government Museums at Jhansi and Almora.
27. Dr. N.P. Joshi published an article in *BMA* No. 40 dealing

with allied problems.
28. Joshi N.P., *Catalogue*, Part 2, Vol. II, Figs. 33, 37, 60.
29. Brijesh Krishna, *The Art under the Gurjara-Pratiharas*, New Delhi, 1989, p. 121.
30. *District Gazetteer, Allahabad*, pp. 30-31.
31. For detailed study, please refer to : Kramrisch Stella, "Pāla and Sena Sculpture," *Rupam* No. 40, Calcutta, 1929. And also *The Art of the Pāla Empire of Bengal*, Oxford, 1928.
32. Joshi, Maheshwar P., Katyuri Art: *Introduction*: *BMA* Nos. 43- 44 (1989), pp. 17-28.
33. For detailed account, please see *Sculpture of Dahala and Dakshina Kosals and their Background; Kalachuri Phase* by Dr. R.N. Misra, Delhi, 1987.
34. Misra, Ram Nath, *Yaksha Cult and Iconography*, New Delhi, 1981, Figs., 8, 9 & 22.
35. A similar image found from Etah is preserved in the State Museum, Lucknow, Joshi N.P., *Catalogue*, Part 2, Vol. I, p. 234, Fig. 56, Accn. No. 57.
36. Some scholars classified such images under "Syncretic icon" Singh, Sheo Bahadur, *Brahmanical Icons in Northern India*, New Delhi, 1977, p. 189, Fig. 72.
37. Joshi, N.P., 'Early Viṣṇu Images', *BMA* No. 2 (1968), pp. 6- 28.
38. *Ibid.*, p.12; Mathura Museum Accn. Nos. 34.2520, 34.2487. 15.956, 15.1168, 57.4267 etc.
39. Joshi, N.P., *Catalogue of the Brahmanical Sculptures in the State Museum, Lucknow*, p.19.
40. Tripathi, Rishi Raj, *Masterpieces in the Allahabad Museum*, Allahabad (1984), pp. 12-13, Fig. Nos. 18 & 19.
41. *'Matsyāvatāriṇaṁ devaṁ Matsyākāraṁ prakalpayet'*, *Śilparatna* as quoted in *EHI*, Vol. I, Part II.
42. Joshi, N.P., *Brahmanical Sculptures in the State Museum, Lucknow*, Part II, Vol. I, p. 107.
43. Trivedi, S.D., *Archaeology of Bundelkhand* (in Hindi), Jhansi, 1984, 47-48.
44. Generally the incarnations are depicted in the '*Prabhavali*' of Viṣṇu icons but their number is not always ten. It varies from two to ten.
45. Trivedi, S.D., *Sculptures in the Jhansi Museum*, Jhansi, 1983, p.45, Fig.10
46. Joshi, N.P., *Cataloque*, Part 2, Vol.I, p. 140.
47. Trivedi. *op.cit.*, pp. 51-52, Fig. 25.
48. Government Museum, Jhansi Accn. No. 81.175.
49. Joshi, N.P., *Catalogue*, Part I, p. 32 D 29-31.
50. *Pañcamañca tathaiśānaṁ Yogināmapyagocaraṁ* = *Rūpamaṇḍana* 4.94.
51. Joshi, N.P., *Catalogue*, Part I, pp. 103-104, Plates 5, 6, Fig. 31.
52. *Ibid.*, Part 2, Vol. I, Figs. 32 & 33.
53. Kārttikeya is regarded as elder brother of Gaṇeśa but in this case the former is shown in the lap while the Younger brother is standing. This is somewhat unusual.
54. In several museums the position is the same. Dr. Pramod Chandra has also overlooked the presence of Ravaṇa, *SSAM*, Plate No. CXLII, Fig.426 and Plate No. CXLVIII, Fig.44.
55. *...daśamukhabhujocchvāsitaprasthasandheḥ/Kailāsasya...*, *Meghadūta I, 62.*
56. Sivaramamurti, C., "Geographical and Chronological Factors in Indian Iconography", *Ancient India* (Bulletin of the Archaeological Survey of India) No. 6 (Jan. 1950), p. 59.
57. Banerjea, J.N., *Development of Hindu Iconography* (2nd Edn.) p. 366, PI.XVI, Fig.2
58. Trivedi, *op.cit.*, p. 42, Fig. 3.
59. Sahai, Bhagwant, *Iconography of Minor Hindu and Buddhist Deities*, New Delhi (1975), pp. 28-34.
60. *Agni Purāṇa*, 52.14.
61. Srivastava, V.C., *Sun-Worship in Ancient India*, Allahabad (1972), pp. 297-298, Pl.12a, b, 13a.
62. *Bṛhatsaṁhitā* 58.56.
63. Sharma, B.N., *Iconography of Revanta*, New Delhi (1975), p. 56, Fig. 13.
64. *SSAM*, p. 113, Plate XCVIII, Fig. 278.
65. Sharma, R.C., *Mathura Museum Introduction*, p. 49, Fig. XLIII.
66. Trivedi, R.D., *Iconography of Parvati*, pp.31-72.
67. *District Gazetteer Allahabad*, p. 31; J.R.A.S. 1927, p. 694.
68. Joshi, N.P., Some unpublished images (in Hindi), *BMA* No. 4 (Dec. 1969), pp. 9-10, Figs. 1-4.
69. Misra, Rama Nath, *op.cit*, Fig.66.
70. Agrawala, Prithvi Kumar, *Skanda-Karttikeya*, Varanasi (1967), pp. 48-52.
71. Trivedi, *op. cit.* p. 75, Fig. 76.
72. Agrawala, V.S., "The Presiding Deity of Child-Birth", *Jaina Antiquity*, Vol. II, no.4, pp. 75-79.
73. Agrawala, Prithvi Kumar, *op. cit.*, Plate XII, Fig.d.
74. *SSAM*, pp. 126-130, Figs. 333-347.
75. Sharma, R.C., *Buddhist Art of Mathura*, Delhi (1984), p. 178.
76. *SSAM*, Fig.110.
77. *Ājānulambabāhuḥ śrīvatsāṅkaḥ praśāntamūrtiśca digvāsastaruṇo rūpavāṅsca kāryo arhatāmdevaḥ*, *Bṛhatsaṁhitā*, 58.45.
78. Bhattacharya, B.C., *The Jaina Iconography*, 1974 (Revised Edn.) p. 28 and p. 34.
79. *Ibid., Foreword*, p. XXIII.
80. Trivedi, *op. cit.*, pp. 87-89.
81. Also known as '*Caumukhi*'; Bhattacharya, *op. cit.*, p. 34.
82. Desai, Devangana, *Erotic Sculpture in India*, Bombay, (1985) p. 93, Figs. 129, 130.
83. On the pillars of the Gupta period we find the *Kīrttimukha* decoration in which the lion face has been accepted as a natural member of the pattern. Agrawala, V.S., *Studies in Indian Art*, Varanasi, 1965, p. 244.
84. Joshi, N.P., *Catalogue*, Part II, Vol.I, pp. 228-232, Figs. 49-54.
85. M.A.Dhaky discussed in detail in his book *The Vyala Figures on the Medieval Temples of India*, Varanasi, 1965.

CATALOGUE

BRAHMANICAL TRINITY

1. BRAHMANICAL TRINITY
   Sudrupur, Allahabad District, UP
   12th century A.D.
   Grey Sandstone, .330 x .495 m.
   AM 706 Fig. 1

Standing Brahmanical Trinity, each four-armed with characteristic attributes and a pair of attendants. Viṣṇu occupies the center while Brahmā and Śiva are on the right and left. Brahmā is three-headed and carries *varadākṣa*, *sruk*, book and *kamaṇḍalu*. Viṣṇu's lower right and upper left hands are chipped off while his remaining hands bear *gadā* and *śaṅkha*. Śiva holds in his four hands *varadākṣa, triśūla*, serpents and water-pot (mutilated).

VIṢṆU AND HIS INCARNATIONS

2. BUST OF VIṢṆU
   Bhita, Allahabad District, UP
   6th century A.D.
   Buff Sandstone, ht. .275 m.
   AM 274 Fig. 2

Bust of Viṣṇu with cascading locks of curls falling on both shoulders. The figure has a handsome face and wears a *kirīṭamukuṭa* and torque, both luxuriously ornamented, besides *kuṇḍalas, keyūras* and *yajñopavīta*. Traces of *vanamālā* wind round the left arm. The figure bears affinity to the Gupta Viṣṇu image from Kankali Tila, Mathura, now in the State Museum, Lucknow (H.111).

3. STANDING VIṢṆU
   Lacchagir, Allahabad District, UP
   9th century A.D.
   Buff Sandstone, .430 x .215 m.
   AM 401 Fig. 3

Viṣṇu standing in *samabhaṅga*, hands and feet broken off. The god has a well-built physique and a handsome oval face. He wears a short *kirīṭamukuṭa, kundalas*, torque and necklace and is draped in a *dhotī* secured by a *mekhalā* with pendant jewelled loops and tassels.

4. STANDING VIṢṆU
   Kauśāmbī, Allahabad District, UP
   9th century A.D.
   Buff Sandstone, .760 x .430 m.
   AM 1093 Fig. 4

Sensitively modelled four-armed Viṣṇu standing in *samabhaṅga*. The god stretches his lower right hand in *varada* and holds *gadā* in the upper right and *cakra* and *śaṅkha* in the left hands. He is flanked by Lakṣmī on the right and Garuḍa on the left besides the donor couple. He has a handsome oval face crowned by a highly ornamented *kirīṭamukuṭa* set against an oval lotus nimbus and also wears *ratnakuṇḍalas*, torque, *yajñopavīta, vanamālā, keyūras*, and wristlets, He is draped in a *dhotī* secured by a *kaṭisūtra* and a scarf.

5. HEAD OF VIṢṆU
   site not known
   9th century A.D.
   Greyish buff sandstone, .235 x .115 m.
   AM 803

Head of Viṣṇu or Sūrya wearing jewelled *kirīṭamukuṭa*.

6. VIṢṆU HEAD
   Unchdih, Allahabad District, UP
   7th century A.D.
   Buff sandstone, .235 x .178 m.
   AM 831 Fig. 5

Oval head of Viṣṇu, figured against lotus halo, has a conspicuously tall *kirīṭamukuṭa* with jewelled ornament on the lower part.

7. VIṢṆU HEAD
   Site not known
   9th century A.D.
   Grey sandstone, .235 x .170 m.
   AM 1107 Fig. 6

Viṣṇu's head sporting profusely bejewelled tall *kirīṭamukuṭa*.

8. BUST OF VIṢṆU
Kauśāmbī, Allahabad District, UP
10th century A.D.
Buff sandstone, .270 x .200 m.
AM 356 Fig. 7

Of this Viṣṇu stele only the right upper portion showing a nimbate bust of the god flanked by a garland-bearing *vidyādhara* has survived together with the cakra *āyudha* borne in his upper left hand. Viṣṇu wears *kirīṭamukuṭa, kuṇḍalas,* torque, pearl necklace, *yajñopavīia* and *keyūra.* All four hands broken. A large *kaustubha-maṇi* is depicted on the chest.

9. VIṢṆU
Site not known
10th century A.D.
Buff sandstone, .445 x .280 m.
AM 953 Fig. 8

Upper part of stele showing upper half of Viṣṇu holding *cakra* in the only surviving upper left hand. Śiva is represented above the *cakra.* In addition to the usual motifs, the *parikara* also shows figures of *avatāras* including Nṛsiṁha. Viṣṇu wears *kirīṭamukuṭa, kuṇḍalas,* torque, *kaustubha-maṇi, yajñopavīta, keyūras* and wristlets.

10. HEAD OF VIṢṆU
Site not known
10th century A.D.
Buff sandstone, .270 x.410 m.
AM 1413

Upper part of Viṣṇu image stele showing nimbate head of Viṣṇu flanked by seated Brahmā and Śiva.

11. BUST OF VIṢṆU
Site not known
10th century A.D.
Buff sandstone, .205 x .195 m.
AM 466

Upper part of Viṣṇu image stele showing the god's bust wearing *kirīṭamukuṭa* and holding *cakra* in the only surviving upper left hand. The lotus nimbus is flanked by a garland-bearing *vidyādhara.*

12. BUST OF VIṢṆU
Kauśāmbī, Allahabad District, UP
11th century A.D.
Grey sandstone, ht. .400 m.
AM 270

Upper part of image stele showing bust of Viṣṇu, hands broken. The god wears *kirīṭamukuṭa, kuṇḍalas,* torque, necklace and the distinguishing *kaustubha-maṇi.*

13. STANDING VIṢṆU
Kalyanpur, Allahabad District, UP
12th century A.D.
Pink sandstone, .720 x .600 m.
AM 713 Fig. 9

Image of Viṣṇu standing in *samabhaṅga* holding *varada, gadā, cakra* and *śaṅkha.* Lower part of image stele with the god's feet broken. Viṣṇu wears *kirīṭamukuṭa* which projects against a perforated lotus-shaped nimbus and other usual ornaments. The nimbus is flanked by two seated gods of whom Brahmā appears on the left. The *parikara* also shows the incarnations of Matsya, Varāha and Vāmana on the right and the Tortoise, Narasiṁha and another seated incarnation on the left above the usual motifs of rearing *vyāla* and elephant.

14. VIṢṆU IMAGE FRAGMENT
Site not known
12th century A.D.
Black schist, .690 x .395 m.
AM 1328 Fig. 10

Upper right fragment of Viṣṇu image of the Pāla style displaying crowning umbrella at the pointed top and *gadā* in the upper right hand of the god. Among relief figures carved on the right margin are incarnations including Nṛvarāha. Below Nṛvarāha are figured Kacchapa nd Matsya in therianthropomorphic forms with distinctive Vaiṣṇava attributes.

15. VIṢṆU HEAD
Site not known
12th century A.D.
Black schist, .265 x .255 m.
AM 615 Fig. 11

Head of Viṣṇu wearing elaborate *kirīṭamukuṭa* adorned centrally with a *kīrttimukha.* A typical specimen of late Pāla sculpture from Eastern India.

16. VIṢṆU
Site not known
12th century A.D.
Greenish soapstone, .760 x .355 m.
AM 235 Fig. 12

Four-armed Viṣṇu standing carrying *gadā* and *cakra* in the upper pair of hands, the lower pair being mutilated. The figure is a typical specimen of the medieval Karṇāta style, revealed by the scrolls encircling the *gadā* and *cakra* and characteristic jewellery and dress worn by the god.

17. NIMBUS OF VIṢṆU-VIŚVARŪPA
UP
7th century A.D.
Red Sandstone, ht. .460 m.
AM 939 Fig. 13

Fragment of oval nimbus of Viṣṇu-Viśvarūpa, full of miniature reliefs, depicting four heads of the Ekādaśa-Rudra group along the edges and numerous gods on the remaining portion. Among carved gods, eight of the Twelve Ādityas can be made out. Figures of Viṣṇu-Viśvarūpa with similar carved nimbus are known from sites of Deogarh, Kannauj and Bhuili in U.P. Ref. T.S.Maxwell, *Visvarupa* (Oxford University Press, 1988), figs 63-69.

18. ŚEṢAŚĀYĪ VIṢṆU
Garhwa, Allahabad District, UP
10th century A.D.
Sandstone, .290 x .600 m.
AM 546 Fig. 14

Four-armed Viṣṇu reclining on the coils of Ādiśeṣa. Viṣṇu supports his head, canopied by serpent-hoods, with the upper right hand and holds *gadā* in the lower right and *cakra* and *śaṅkha* in the left hands. His feet are being massaged by Lakṣmī (head missing) while from his navel rises a lotus stalk supporting Brahmā. The upper field is adorned by seated Navagrahas.

The god's couch is flanked on the proper right by a devotee while below the couch are carved objects including a pot and a horse. The pot and horse may respectively represent the pot of ambrosia and the horse Uccaiḥśravā recovered from the Churning of the Ocean.

19. ŚEṢAŚĀYĪ VIṢṆU
Site not known
10th century A.D.
Pink sandstone, .395 x .495 m.
AM 919 Fig. 15

Four-armed Viṣṇu reclining on the coils of Ādiśeṣa with the upper right hand supporting his head and the lower holding *gadā* and the left hands bearing *cakra* and *śaṅkha*. From his navel issues a lotus stalk but the emerging figure (of Brahmā) is fully defaced. Viṣṇu's figure is broken below thighs and only the proper right corner of the upper part showing a pair of devotees is preserved.

20. NṚ-VARĀHA
Phaphamau, Allahabad District, UP
10th century A.D.
Buff sandstone, .700 x .395 m.
AM 432 Fig. 16

Nṛ-varāha (four-armed) standing in the characteristic *pratyālīḍha* pose with the flexed left foot, placed on a lotus, being adored by Śeṣa and his consorts. The god lifts up Pṛthvī on his left arm and sniffs at her face. His right hands hold *kaṭi* and *gadā* while his upper left hand bears *cakra*. His lower left hand and the face of Pṛthvī are mutilated. Lakṣmī and Garuḍa together with a donor couple are figured on the flanks of the god and Yogāsana Viṣṇu on the crest.

21. NṚ-VARĀHA
Site not known
10th century A.D.
Buff sandstone, .515 x .700 m
AM 91-1913 Fig. 17

Nṛ-Varāha standing in *ālīḍhāsana* rescuing Pṛthvī seated on the god's upraised left arm. The god stands under a canopy of lotus leaf and holds *gadā, kaṭi, cakra* and *śaṅkha* in the four hands. He is flanked by Surasundarīs carrying lotus stalks. A dagger is suspended from his waist-band.

22. YAJÑA-VARĀHA
Khajuraho, Chhatarpur District, MP
11th century A.D.
Greyish buff sandstone, .545 x 1.245 m.
AM 664 Fig. 18

Boar incarnation of Viṣṇu in zoomorphic form. Three legs together with a part of the back mutilated. The tail is beautifully braided and has complicated knots. The entire massive body is carved with circular clusters of miniature divinities seated either in *padmāsana* or *mahārājalīlāsana*. The ribbon round the neck is also adorned with miniature deities. Most of the figures are defaced and their features obliterated. Yet groups of Viṣṇu and Gaṇeśa are identifiable, the latter on the right flank of the back. On the snout is seen a figure of Sarasvatī with *vīṇā* while Bhūdevī appears close to the boar's tusk with her mutilated hand clutching the left side of the snout.

23. YAJÑA-VARĀHA
Khajuraho, Chhatarpur District, MP
12th century A.D.
Greyish buff sandstone, .610 x 1.170 m.
AM 665 Fig. 19

Yajña-Varāha carved all over with figures of divinities. All four legs broken.

24. NṚ-VARĀHA HEAD
Bhita, Allahabad District, UP
10th century A.D.
Grey sandstone, .127 x .210 m.
AM 324 Fig. 20

Beautifully executed and well finished head of Nṛ-Varāha. The flowing hair on the head is secured by double pearl string. Care has been taken to delineate also the protruding fang and the folds of skin on the neck.

25. KACCHAPĀVATĀRA
Site not known
10th century A.D.
Red sandstone, .230 x .400 m.
AM 1438

Mutilated top of Viṣṇu image stele showing Kacchapāvatāra supporting the hill Mandara as a churning stick for the cosmic event of the Churning of Ocean by the gods and the demons. Figure of Lakṣmī (one of the 14 jewels recovered) or Pṛthvī is addorsed to the defaced hill. This is comparable to a much better preserved specimen in the State Museum, Lucknow (No. 42. 189), from Kalakankar (UP) (N.P. Joshi, *Catalogue of Brahmanical Sculptures in State Museum, Lucknow,* Part 2, Vol. 1, pp. 186-187 and Plate.)

26. VIṢṆU IMAGE FRAGMENT
Site not known.
10th century A.D.
Red sandstone, .250 x .275 m.
AM 1189 Fig. 21

Upper right corner of Viṣṇu image stele showing the Matsya crowned by Śivaliṅga in *arghya* flanked by devotees. A Vidyādhara carrying lotus stalk (hovering on the right side of Viṣṇu's head) is also seen alongwith a well-preserved Nṛvarāha and the top end of Viṣṇu's *gadā.* The Matsya has conspicuous scales.

27. PARAŚURĀMA AND NṚSIṀHA
Mt. Abu, Sirohi District, Rajasthan
12th century A.D.
Marble, .440 x .210 m.
AM 793 Fig. 22

Fragment of pilaster carved with of Nṛsiṁha eviscerating Hiraṇyakaśipu in a niche crowned by a *toraṇa*-arch. Paraśurāma flanked by attendants, is depicted above Nṛshiṁha and a miniature figure of Kūrma below Nṛsiṁha.

28. NṚ-SIṀHA CRUSHING DEMONS
Site not known.
10th century A.D.
Buff sandstone, .270 x .445 m.
AM 1358 Fig. 23

Feet of Nṛ-siṁha crushing three associates of the demon Hiraṇyakaśipu. Two associates are slain and lie pellmell, while a third one is still struggling to fight with a sword.

29. SEATED NṚSIṀHA
UP
11th century A.D.
Greyish buff sandstone, .710 x .660 m.
AM 1348 Fig. 24

Four-armed Nṛsiṁha (head missing) seated in *lalitāsana,* eviscerating the demon Hiranyakaśipu who is placed on the god's flexed left knee with pendant right foot supported on lotus, flanked by devotees. Two aides of the demon (one fighting) shown below the god's seat on the left. *Vidyādharas* carrying garland flank the god's missing head.

30. STANDING VĀMANA
UP
10th century A.D.
Grey sandstone, .590 x .460 m.
AM 428 Fig. 25

Vāmana incarnation of Viṣṇu standing in *samabhaṅga.* All four hands broken but the lotus stalk originally held in the upper right hand is intact. Only the upper part of the image stele is preserved showing, besides the usual motifs of *makara* transom and *vyāla, Varāhāvatāra* on the right side and *Narasiṁhāvatāra* on the left. Vāmana is depicted as *vaṭuka* with small curls and a pot belly.

31. TORSO OF VĀMANA
Site not known.
10th century A.D.
Buff sandstone, ht. .440 m.
AM 612

Torso of Vāmanāvatāra of Viṣṇu adorned with torque, necklace, *kaustubha maṇi, urabandha, vastropavīta, ratnopavīta* and *vanamālā* (abraded). He wears *dhotī* secured by *kaṭisūtra* with jewelled pendant loops and tassels. The figure represents a *vaṭuka* with a pot belly.

32. VĀMANA
Site not known
8th century A.D.
Buff sandstone, .247 x .108 m.
AM 590 Fig. 26

Vāmana as *vaṭuka,* hands and feet broken.

33. FRAGMENT OF VIṢṆU IMAGE
Site not known

12th century A.D.
Black schist, .520 x .255 m.
AM 1434 Fig. 27

Fragment of Viṣṇu image of Sena style showing figures of Paraśurāma and Rāma in niches and Matsya and Kūrma in the margin.

34. RĀMA
Site not known.
12th century A.D.
Red sandstone, .635 x .520 m.
AM 1359 Fig. 28

Two-armed Rāma standing, wearing *kirīṭamukuṭa* and other ornaments and carrying bow and arrow.

35. KṚṢṆALĪLĀ-SLAB
Site not known
9th century A.D.
Greyish red sandstone, .285 x .855 m.
AM 1363 Fig. 29

Slab bearing in a niche child Kṛṣṇa being offered butter while it is being churned by two Gopīs. A pair of *gaṇa*-like Gopas and a Gopī depicted in adjoining niches.

36. VIṢṆU IMAGE FRAGMENT
Site not known
9th century A.D.
Buff sandstone, .480 x .145 m.
AM 1391 Fig. 30

Parikara of Viṣṇu image showing figures of Varāha and Buddha incarnations, besides a *vyāla* on the edge of the frame.

37. FRAGMENT OF VIṢṆU IMAGE
Site not known
10th century A.D.
Greyish buff sandstone, .255 x .180 m.
AM 1334

Fragment of Viṣṇu image stele showing some *parikara* figures of Viṣṇu, viz.incarnations of Rāma and Buddha on the proper right edge of of the frame together with parts of Garuḍa and an *āyudha- puruṣa.*

38. FRAGMENT OF VAIṢṆAVA IMAGE
Site not known.
10th century A.D.
Buff sandstone, .520 x .370 m.
AM 1119 Fig. 31

Lower part of image stele showing Lakṣmī holding lotus stalk, accompanied by a female attendant and a Vaiṣṇava guardian. A donor's figure is also partly preserved.

39. HANUMĀN
Kauśāmbī, Allahabad District, UP
10th century A.D.
Grey sandstone, .600 x .310 m.
AM 1075 Fig. 32

Hanumān standing in the characteristic *pratyālīḍha* pose with the right hand raised up and the left held in *tarjanīmudrā.* The god wears *karaṇḍamukuṭa* and other ornaments and carries a *kṛpāṇa* suspended from the waistband. Lower part of the figure is broken.

ŚIVA IN LIṄGA AND VIGRAHA FORMS

40. EKAMUKHALIṄGA
Bhita, Allahabad District, UP
6th century A.D.
Greyish sandstone, ht. .780 m.
AM 701 Fig. 33

The Śivaliṅga has preserved the plain octagonal section (Viṣṇu- bhāga) surmounted by the circular Rudrabhāga from which projects Śiva's head, wearing an elaborate *jaṭājūṭa* tied in the middle, *karṇakuṇḍalas* and *ekāvalī.* The third eye is marked vertically on the forehead.

41. EKAMUKHALIṄGA
Site not known
7th century A.D.
Purple red sandstone, .215 x .110 m
AM 911 Fig. 34

Ekamukhaliṅga with the third eye shown prominently. Even with wide open eyes the face exudes inner concentration.

42. EKAMUKHALIṄGA
Sarnath, Varanasi District, UP
8th century A.D.
Greyish buff sandstone, ht. 610 m.
AM 784 Fig. 35

Śiva's head projecting from the *liṅga* has an unusually oblong shape with an elaborate *jaṭājūṭa,* a horizontal third eye on the forehead and a smiling face.

43. CATURMUKHALIṄGA
Site not known
9th century A.D.
Grey sandstone, ht. .570 m.
AM. 947 Fig. 36 A-B

Śivaliṅga showing four faces viz. Tatpuruṣa, Aghora, Vāmadeva and Sadyojāta. But for the Aghora face which is terrific with pair of fangs and moustaches, goggle eyes and raised curls adorned with a pair of human skulls, the three other faces are identical and pleasant showing a two-tiered *jaṭaāūṭa* and third eye on the forehead.

44. CATURMUKHALIṄGA
Site not known
9th century A.D.
Grey sandstone, .600 x .340 m.
AM 1397 Fig. 37 A-B

Caturmukhaliṅga with Tatpuruṣa, Aghora, Umā and Sadyojāta faces of Śiva. While its Tatpuruṣa and Sadyojāta faces are quite alike and identical with those of the previous Caturmukhaliṅga (No.43) with finely delineated hair-lines on the *jaṭājūṭa* and the third eye marked on the forehead, the Umā face has simpler *jaṭājūṭa* adorned with crescent. The Aghora face, though abraded, shows goggle eyes and gaping mouth with moustaches.

45. CATURMUKHALIṄGA
Site not known
11th century A.D.
Greyish sandstone, .650 x .210 m.
AM 215

Caturmukha Siva-liṅga with four faces representing four aspects of Siva, viz. Tatpuruṣa, Aghora, Vāmadeva and Sadyojāṭa.

46. SEATED ŚIVA
Jamsot, Allahabad District, UP
12th century A.D.
Buff sandstone, .610 x .430 m
AM 1007 Fig. 38

Śiva seated in *ardhaparyaṅkāsana* holding *varada, triśūla,* lotus stalk with spiral end and *kamaṇḍalu* in the four hands. The god wears *jaṭājūṭa* and *karṇakuṇḍalas,* normal *kuṇḍala* in one ear and *sarpa-kuṇḍala* in the other, torque, *hāra, yajñopavīta,* armlets and wristlets and is draped in *adhovastra.* He also has a *kaustubha-maṇi* on his chest.

47. ŚIVA BUST
Site not known
11th century A.D.
Grey sandstone, .380 x .190 m.
AM 956

Bust of Śiva wearing *jaṭājūṭa* and ornaments which include normal *kuṇḍala* in the left ear and *sarpa-kuṇḍala* in the right ear. The third eye is incised on the forehead.

48. SEATED ŚIVA
Site not known
10th century A.D.
Buff sandstone, .250 x .130 m.
AM 1311 Fig. 39

Part of an image showing four-armed Śiva seated in *lalitāsana,* carrying serpent and water-vessel in left hands, right hands broken.

49. STANDING ŚIVA
10th century A.D.
Greyish sandstone, .410 x .320 m.
AM 1325

Headless Śiva standing in *tribhaṅga,* flanked by two attendants. Nandī is depicted behind the god.

50. UMĀ-MAHEŚVARA
Gaya, Gaya District, Bihar
9th century A.D.
Grey schist, ht. 400 m.
AM 240 Fig. 40

Sensitively modelled figure of Umā-Maheśvara in *ālingaṅa-mudrā.* Maheśvara's head with a lotus halo is flanked on the proper left side by seated Viṣṇu. The image stele is only partially preserved. Śiva's right hand holds mutilated *vījapūraka,* while his upper left hand carries a serpent and the lower left embraces Pārvatī. Pārvatī is seated in *sukhāsana* on the lap of her lord embracing him with the right hand and holding mirror (defaced) in the left hand. Śiva is *ūrdhvameḍhra* and wears a *jaṭāmukuṭa* while Pārvatī dons a *dhammilla.* Adorned with appropriate ornaments, both have a tall proportionate physique with attenuated waist.

The image is remarkable for its high aesthetic quality.

51. UMĀ-MAHEŚVARA
Site not known
10th century A.D.
Pink sandstone, .900 x .560
AM 1389 Fig. 41

Umā-Maheśvara seated in *āliṅgana.* Maheśvara holds trident and bow in the upper pair of hands and has placed the lower left hand below Umā's breast. The image is much mutilated, particularly in the lower part. The presence of the weapon bow in the hands of Śiva's *āliṅgana-mūrti* is unusual.

52. UMĀ-MAHEŚVARA
Site not known
10th century A.D.

Greyish red sandstone, .660 x .455 m.
AM 464 Fig. 42

Āliṅgna-mūrti of seated Umā-Maheśvara. Śiva has a smiling face and wears a tall *jaṭājūṭa* and cups Umā's breast with his lower left hand.

53. UMĀ-MAHEŚVARA
Bharwari, Allahabad District, UP
11th century A.D.
Grey sandstone, .560 x .370 m.
AM 993 Fig. 43

Seated Umā-Maheśvara on the upper right corner of a damaged large image. Śiva is four-armed and carries *triśūla* in the upper left hand. Pārvatī carries infant Skanda in her lap. Gaṇeśa stands between the feet of the divine parents. Traces of *liṅgas* are seen above Śiva's head.

54. UMĀ-MAHEŚVARA
Site not known
11th century A.D.
Buff sandstone. .275 x .280 m.
AM 1111 Fig. 44

Bust of Umā-Maheśvara in *āliṅgana-mudrā.* Upper left hand of Maheśvara carries serpent while the god caresses Umā's breast with his lower left hand, right hands broken. Gaṇeśa is seated on the top left of the stele and probably Kubera on the top right.

55. UMĀ-MAHEŚVARA
Gaya, Gaya District, Bihar
11th century A.D.
Black schist, ht. .480 m.
AM 237 Fig. 45

Umā-Maheśvara seated in *āliṅgana-mudrā* with their feet respectively on the back of the Lion and Nandī. Umā seated in the lap of her lord embraces him with the right hand and holds mirror in the left. Maheśvara has placed his lower right hand on the chin of Umā and carries *nīlotpala* and trident in the upper right and left hands while he caresses the breast of Umā with his lower left hand.

56. RĀVAṆĀNUGRAHAMŪRTI
Soraon, Allahabad District, UP
10th century A.D.
Buff sandstone, .440 x .375 m.
AM 711 Fig. 46

Śiva-Pārvatī seated in *āliṅgana-mudrā* on the Kailāsa mountain which is being shaken by Rāvaṇa. Śiva's lower right hand is held in *vitarkamudrā* while he carries serpent in the upper right hand. His upper left hand is broken while he caresses Pārvatī's breast with the lower left hand. Pārvatī embraces Śiva with her right hand and holds mirror in her left hand. Side figures on the pedestal represent *gaṇas.*
The pedestal centrally bears four-armed Rāvaṇa trying to dislodge Kailāsa flanked by Śiva-*gaṇas* who are making a fun of Rāvaṇa by showing their anus. Below the couch supporting the divine couple are shown their mounts viz. bull and lion intervened by skeletal Bhṛṅgī. The couch is flanked on the right by Gaṇeśa and on the left by Kārttikeya.

57. RAVAṆĀNUGRAHAMŪRTI
Lacchagir, Allahabad District, UP
10th century A.D.
Buff sandstone, .787 x .406 m.
AM 657 Fig. 47

Śiva-Pārvatī seated in *āliṅgana* on Mount Kailāsa which is being vainly shaken by Rāvaṇa. Śiva's head is flanked by seated Brahmā and Garuḍāsana Viṣṇu while a crown held by a pair of *vidyādharas* acts as a canopy above Śiva's head. Śiva's lower right hand is held in *abhaya* while his upper right carries a lotus flower canopied by serpent hood. His upper left hand bears trident while he caresses Pārvatī's breast with his lower left hand. Kārttikeya and Gaṇeśa are seated beside Śiva's seat and the bull and lion mounts are shown below the seat. Śiva's *pratihāras* stand above Gaṇeśa and Kārttikeya. Rāvaṇa is shown on the pedestal flanked by Śivagaṇas who are represented with their upraised hands supporting Kailāsa.

58. GAJĀNTAKA ŚIVA
Site not known
11th century A.D.
Grey sandstone, .685 x .595 m.
AM 297 Fig. 48

Multi-armed Śiva dancing, carrying *gajacarma* in the upper pair of hands after slaying Gajāsura and Andhakāsura. Two seated Mātṛkās are represented flanking Śiva's head. The figure is much damaged.

59. ŚUKANĀSA WITH ŚIVA'S HEAD
Site not known
9th century A.D.
Greyish white sandstone .385 x .555 m.
AM 1172 Fig. 49

Well-preserved *śukanāsa* containing in its medallion handsome head of Śiva adorned with *jaṭājūṭa.* The forehead is marked by the third eye.

60. HEAD OF GOD
Site not known
10th century A.D.
Greyish red sandstone, .170 x .082 m.
AM 484 Fig. 50

Head of god wearing *jaṭāmukuṭa*.

61. HEAD OF ŚIVA
Soraon, Allahabad District, UP
10th century A.D.
Pink sandstone, ht. .285 m.
AM 369 Fig. 51

Śiva's head has an elaborate *jaṭāmukuṭa* and the third eye marked horizontally on the forehead.

62. ŚIVA HEAD
Jhusi, Allahabad District, UP
11th century A.D.
Greyish sandstone, ht. .180 m.
AM 1074 Fig. 52

Head of Śiva with tall *jaṭāmukuṭa* and the third eye.

63. HEAD OF ŚIVA
Provenance unknown
11th century A.D.
Light red sandstone, .330 x .135 m.
AM 384 Fig. 53

Beautifully chiselled head of Śiva with long eye-brows, large half-closed eyes, thick lower lips and projecting chin. The head sports a tall *jaṭāmukuṭa*.

64. BHAIRAVA
Site not known
10th century A.D.
Greyish sandstone, .770 x .490 m.
AM 1393 Fig. 54

Four-armed Bhairava standing in elegant *tribhaṅga* flanked by supple figures of male and female attendants also standing in *tribhaṅga*. The god wears a heavy *jaṭāmukuṭa* and other ornaments including long *vanamālā* and carries *varada, khaṭvāṅga*, serpent and *kapāla* in the four hands. The male attendant also carries *kapāla* in one of his hands. The female attendant dons a beautiful *dhammilla*.

65. BUST OF BHAIRAVA (?)
Kauśāmbī, Allahabad District, UP
8th century A.D.
Greyish white sandstone, .470 x .360 m.
AM 268 Fig. 55

Pot-bellied bust of Bhairava (?) having *ūrdhvapiṅgalakeśa* with few curly strands falling on both shoulders. The figure has extended ear-lobes adorned with heavy *ratnakuṇḍalas*. The god also wears *keyūras, vakṣabandha*, and broad *graiveyaka* and *hāra* of an unusual type. The nimbus is very large and adorned with a lotus design of enormous size.

66. BUST OF GOD
UP
8th century A.D.
sandstone, .400 x .270 m.
AM 974 Fig. 56

Bust of god (Bhairava ?) with a plain halo behind *jaṭājūṭa* and an unusually broad scarf worn as *upavīta*. The figure has *ūrdhvapiṅgalakeśa* and goggle eyes, which are attributes of Bhairava.

67. HEAD OF BHAIRAVA
Kauśāmbī, Allahabad District, UP
9th century A.D.
Sandstone, ht. 220 m.
AM 847 Fig. 57

Fierce head of Bhairava with *ūrdhvapiṅgalakeśa*, third eye on the forehead and bared teeth.

68. HEAD OF BHAIRAVA (?)
Site not known
10th century A.D.
Greyish red sandstone, .175 x .195 m.
AM 1102 Fig. 58

Beautiful oval head of Bhairava (?) with *ūrdhvapiṅgalakeśa*.

69. HEAD OF BHAIRAVA
Lacchagir, Allahabad District, UP
11th century A.D.
Buff sandstone, ht. .220 m.
AM 475 Fig. 59

Terrific head of Bhairava, moustached and bearded, with human skulls projecting from *jaṭāmukuṭa*, third eye on the forehead, bulging eyes and knit eye-brows.

70. HEAD OF BHAIRAVA
Jhusi, Allahabad District, UP
11th century A.D.
Pink sandstone, ht. .160 m.
AM 483 Fig. 60

Moustached and bearded head of Bhairava wearing *jaṭāmukuṭa*.

71. MINIATURE HARIHARA (?)
Site not known
9th century A.D.
Greyish sandstone, .178 x .120 m.
AM 872

Four-armed Harihara (?), much worn-out with details damaged. Traces of *triśūla* in upper right hand and of *cakra* in lower left hand. Flanking attendants figured in *atibhaṅga*.

GAṆEŚA AND KĀRTTIKEYA

72. DANCING GAṆEŚA
Site not known
10th century A.D.
Buff sandstone, .410 x .295 m.
AM 1357 Fig. 61

Twelve-armed dancing Gaṇeśa. Uppermost right hand holds spiral lotus stalk, uppermost left hand carries radish and lowermost holds serpent. All other hands broken. Right leg missing, left leg broken below the knee. The god is shown as *ekadanta* and wears a low crown, *hāra, armlets, wristlets, urumālā* and a *vakṣabandha* of snake. Every limb of the corpulent god including his trunk turned to the proper right and his pot belly are moving to the rhythm of the dance.

73. TORSO OF GAṆEŚA
Bhita, Allahabad District, UP
10th century A.D.
Buff sandstone, .390 x .410 m.
AM 447

Torso of corpulent seated Gaṇeśa holding *abhayākṣa* in the only surviving right hand. The god uses snake (seen on the belly) as an ornament and also wears torque, necklace, *pādāṅgada* and anklet.

74. DANCING GAṆEŚA
Gurgi, Rewa District, MP
10th century A.D.
Plum coloured sandstone, .630 x .400 m.
AM 449 Fig. 62

Niched figure of dancing four-armed Gaṇeśa with his left foot gently placed on the rat mount. His trunk is turned to the bowl of sweets placed in the lower left hand, while his upper right hand is held in *abhaya*. The niche is crowned by a *candraśālikā*.

75. SEATED GAṆEŚA
UP
10th century A.D.
Buff sandstone, .570 x .430 m.
AM 1267 Fig. 63

Four-armed seated Gaṇeśa, with the rat mount beneath his left knee. The trunk drops centrally with a supple spiral twist.

76. GAṆEŚA
Site not known
10th century A.D.
Buff sandstone, .495 x .300 m.
AM 1375 Fig. 64

Four-armed corpulent Gaṇeśa seated, holding mutilated *akshamālā*, and *paraśu* in right hands, attributes of left hands abraded. He wears a distinctive tiara and wristlets and *nāga* as an adornment. His trunk is pendant centrally. A tiny rat mount is depicted below his left knee.

77. DANCING GAṆEŚA
Site not known
10th century A.D.
Greyish black sandstone, .485 x .340 m.
AM 1130 Fig. 65

Four-armed Gaṇeśa dancing, holding tall *paraśu* in lower right hand, sweets in lower left hand, the other pair of hands in dance poses.

78. SEATED GAṆEŚA
Jamsot, Allahabad District, UP
12th century A.D.
Buff sandstone, .510 x .380 m.
AM 1320

Four-armed Gaṇeśa seated with trunk turned to his left. A devotee is carved on the pedestal. The *ekadanta* feature of the god has been brought out prominently.

79. KĀRTTIKEYA
Site not known
6th century A.D.
Grey sandstone, .355 x .230 m.
AM 994 Fig. 66

Kārttikeya seated on peacock, *śakti* (spear) in the left hand. The peacock is pecking at the mutilated fruit held in the god's right hand. It has strong affinity to the Kārttikeya figure from Bharat Kala Bhawan of the Gupta period.

80. KĀRTTIKEYA
Kauśāmbī, Allahabad District, UP
7th century A.D.
Grey sandstone, .390 x .280 m.
AM 1097 Fig. 67

Kārttikeya standing, feeding peacock. Kārttikeya wears *śikhaṇḍaka* hairdo and *ekāvalī*.

81. STANDING KĀRTTIKEYA
Site not known
7th century A.D.
Greyish sandstone, .270 x .210 m.
AM 1304

Kārttikeya standing in *ābhaṅga* holding defaced *śakti* in his right hand, left hand placed on his left thigh.

BRAHMĀ

82. HEAD OF BRAHMA (?)
Bhita, Allahabad District, UP
9th century A.D.
Pink sandstone, ht. .240 m.
AM 648 Fig. 68

Of the three heads of the deity (probably Brahmā) a complete one and part of another have survived. They wear *jaṭājūṭa*.

83. BRAHMĀ
Bara, Allahabad District, UP
11th century A.D.
Red sandstone, .660 x.597 m.
AM 459 Fig. 69

Three-headed and four-armed corpulent Brahmā standing in *samabhaṅga*, carrying *varadākṣa* and *sruk* in the right hands, left hands broken. The central head of the god is bearded. Brahmā wears *jaṭāmukuṭa, yajñopavīta* and the usual dress and jewellery and is flanked on the right by a female attendant, the left side being chipped off.

84. BRAHMĀ
Kauśāmbī, Allahabad District, UP
11th century A.D.
Greyish sandstone, .380 x .430 m.
AM 399 Fig. 70

Damaged figure of corpulent four-armed Brahmā seated in *lalitāsana*, right hands broken, objects in left hands mutilated. A female attendant stands in an adjacent niche on his left.

85. BRAHMĀ
Rajasthan ?
11th century A.D.
Buff sandstone, .490 x .440 m.
AM 715 Fig. 71

Part of a large figural composition showing four-armed corpulent Brahmā wearing *vastropavīta* and armlet and a peculiar head dress. The figure is much mutilated and has lost all hands and the entire portion below the pot belly.

86. THREE-HEADED BRAHMĀ ?
Site not known
11th century A.D.
Buff sandstone, .595 x .340 m.
AM 1319 Fig. 72

Three-headed and six-armed god standing in *tribhaṅga*. All hands with attributes broken. The heads wear *jaṭāmukuṭa* and the typical dress and ornaments of the deities from Khajuraho.

AGNI

87. THREE-FACED AGNI
UP
8th century A.D.
Red sandstone, ht. .430 m.
AM 275 Fig. 73

Three-faced and two-armed Agni stands in *samabhaṅga* against an oval *prabhāmaṇḍala* which together with the entire backslab is covered with flames. The god wears diaphanous drapery and elegant *jaṭājūṭa* (on all heads) and prominent *yajñopavīta*. His right hand which was held akimbo is mutilated and the left hand carries *kamaṇḍalu*. The stele has tenon meant for insertion.

88. AGNI SURROUNDED BY SAGES
Gurgi, Rewa District, MP
10th century A.D.
Buff sandstone, .890 x .760 m.
AM 461 Fig. 74

Standing figure of four-armed Agni (head missing) wearing *pādukās*; surrounded by numerous bearded sages, standing as well as seated, most of them carrying *sruk* and *sruvā*. The ram mount is depicted on the lower right corner of the stele. The figure may represent worship of Agni as a prelude to the performance of a sacrifice.

89. SEATED AGNI
10th century A.D.
Greyish sandstone, .350 x .170 m.
AM 1439 Fig. 75

Two-armed Agni seated with *yogapaṭṭa* tied around the knees. Traces of flames visible around the oval nimbus.

Agni wears *jaṭāmukuṭa* and beard and holds *kamaṇḍalu* in the left hand while the right hand is mutilated. A tenon projects from the base of the image.

90. SEATED AGNI
Site not known
10th century A.D.
Light red sandstone, .400 x .270 m.
AM 1238 Fig. 76

Damaged figure of four-armed corpulent Agni seated in *padmāsana* holding book (mutilated) and *kamaṇḍalu* in left hands, right hands broken. The god is bearded and wears a heavy *jaṭājūṭa* and *yajñopavīta* and is distinguished (from Brahmā) by partially surviving nimbus bearing marks of flames.

DIKPĀLAS

91. DIKPĀLA INDRA
MP
11th century A.D.
Red sandstone, .730 x .470 m.
AM 1341 Fig. 77

Corner block showing Indra and Agni on adjacent faces, each in a niche adorned with scrolls crowned by a *kīrttimukha.* Dikpāla Indra stands in *tribhaṅga* with all hands broken. The god wears the typical dress and ornaments including *kaustubha-maṇi* and *vanamālā* of the Candella style. Airāvata mount is carved to the right of the god's feet.

The lower part of the niche is carved with miniature atlantid figures, as though supporting the weight of the stele. The adjacent face represents Dikpāla Agni.

92. DIKPĀLA AGNI
MP
11th century A.D.
Red sandstone, .730 x .470 m.
AM 1341 Fig. 78

Dikpāla Agni, bearded and wearing *jaṭāmukuṭa,* stands in *tribhaṅga.* All hands except the lower right holding *varadākṣa* broken. Ram mount carved near the god's feet below. Load-bearing atlantid figures carved beneath the pedestal.

93. DIKPĀLA AGNI
Site not known
11th century A.D.
Buff sandstone, .785 x .300 m.
AM 1395 Fig. 79

Dikpāla Agni, wearing beard and *jaṭāmukuṭa,* stands in *tribhaṅga.* All hands broken.

94. DIKPĀLA AGNI
Site not known
11th century A.D.
Dark grey sandstone, .690 x .525 m.
AM 1365 Fig. 80

Four-armed Agni standing with a *prabhāmaṇḍala* around bearded head, donning *jaṭājūṭa* and other ornaments including long *vanamālā.* All hands broken. Damaged ram mount depicted below.

95. DIKPĀLA AGNI
Site not known
11th century A.D.
Red sandstone, 1.00 x .430 m.
AM 1367

Four-armed figure of standing Agni/Brahmā with bearded head wearing *jaṭāmukuṭa.* All hands with attributes broken. The feet and pedestal also lost.

96. DIKPĀLA AGNI
Site not known
12th century A.D.
Grey sandstone, .535 x .230 m.
AM 1164 Fig. 81

Corpulent and bearded figure of two-armed Dikpāla Agni. The adjacent face of the corner piece shows two-armed Indra.

97. DIKPĀLA AGNI
Jamsot, Allahabad District, UP
12th century A.D.
Greyish red sandstone, .745 x .500 m.
AM 1394

Corner piece showing four-armed figures of Indra and Agni. Indra is mutilated but his elephant mount is intact. Agni is pot-bellied with a bearded head with *jaṭājūṭa* and holds book in the only preserved upper left hand. Ram mount depicted below.

98. DIKPĀLA NIRṚTI
Site not known
10th century A.D.
Red spotted coarse-grained sandstone, .785 x .520 m.
AM 1122 Fig. 82

Dikpāla Nirṛti, four-armed, nude standing in *tribhaṅga,* flanked by *apsaras.* The god has an animal mount and carries sword (mutilated) in the right hand, left hand broken.

99. DIKPĀLA NIRṚTI (?)
Chilla near Bhita, Allahabad District, UP
10th century A.D.
Buff sandstone, .405 x .380 m.
AM 1429 Fig. 83

God (Nirṛti ?) wearing *karaṇḍamukuṭa* and holding sword and kaṭi. Traces of animal mount behind.

100. STANDING VARUṆA
UP
10th century A.D.
Greyish sandstone, .640 x .490 m.
AM 1385 Fig. 84

Dikpāla Varuṇa standing in *ābhaṅga* with the right hand held in *vitarkamudrā* and left carrying *pāśa*. Deer mount below, which is unusual since deer is recognized as *vāhana* of Dikpāla Vāyu.

101. KUBERA
Site not known
6th century A.D.
Grey sandstone, 1.355 x .738 m.
AM 206 Fig. 85

Corpulent Kubera in *candraśālā* medallion seated in *mahārājalīlāsana* against a bolster, holding circular object in right hand.

102. KUBERA
Site not known
6th-7th century A.D.
Buff sandstone, .290 x .240 m.
AM 1216 Fig. 86

Corpulent Kubera seated at ease against an invisible bolster, holding wine-cup in the right hand and a well-carved *nakulaka* in the left. He wears a cap from which emerge cascading ringlets of curls falling on his shoulders. His dress and ornaments and the ovate nimbus are very sketchily incised.

103. ARCHITECTURAL FRAGMENT WITH KUBERA
Lacchagir, Allahabad District, UP
10th century A.D.
Sandstone, .210 x .495 m.
AM 626 Fig. 87

Architectural fragment with three compartments showing Kubera seated in *mahārājalīlāsana* flanked by female attendants in the middle panel, a pair of apsarases in the right panel and a pair of musicians in the left panel.

104. DIKPĀLA ĪŚĀNA
Jamsot, Allahabad District, UP
12th century A.D.
Buff sandstone, .560 x .345 m.
AM 1179

Dikpāla Īśāna standing in *tribhaṅga* carrying serpent and *kamaṇḍalu* in the left hands, right hands broken.

105. DIKPĀLA ĪŚĀNA
Baghaura, Allahabad District, UP
10th century A.D.
Red sandstone,
AM 780 Fig. 88

Dikpāla Īśāna standing in *tribhaṅga* carrying sword, serpent and *kaṭi* in three hands, the attribute of the fourth hand mutilated.

106. DIKPĀLA
Site not known
10th century A.D.
Red sandstone, .575 x .280 m.
AM 1321

Four-armed Dikpāla standing in *tribhaṅga* with all hands broken.

SŪRYA AND REVANTA

107. SŪRYA
Site not known
10th century A.D.
Grey sandstone, .435 x .340 m.
AM 1437 Fig. 89

Standing Sūrya flanked by Daṇḍa and Piṅgala in a miniature niche. Pratihāras of the god are carved on the pilasters framing the niche.

108. SŪRYA
Kauśāmbī, Allahabad District, UP
10th century A.D.
Grey sandstone, .305 x .350 m.
AM 863 Fig. 90

Upper part of stele showing bust of Sūrya holding full blown lotus stalk in the two hands. Sūrya dons a *kirīṭamukuṭa* figured against an oval lotus halo, which is flanked by figures of Uṣā and Pratyūṣā shooting arrows. Sūrya also wears *kuṇḍalas,* torque, *kavaca, yajñopavīta* and wristlets.

109. SŪRYA IN RATHIKĀ
Site not known
10th century A.D.
Redish sandstone, 1 m. x .760 m.
AM 1156 Fig. 91

Wall fragment showing standing Sūrya in *rathikā* and figures of Dikpāla Indra and Agni on adjacent faces.

110. SŪRYA
Site not known
12th century A.D.
Light red sandstone, .530 x .460 m.
AM 1440 Fig. 92

Sūrya seated in *utkuṭikāsana*, hands broken. Defaced figure of Mahāśvetā represented between the feet, damaged *vidyādharas* carved on the flanks of the head of Sūrya. Donors/devotees carved on either side of Sūrya.

111. SOLAR DEITY (?)
Site not known
11th century A.D.
Greyish sandstone, .395 x .318 m.
AM 820 Fig. 93

Four-armed god seated in *lalitāsana* carrying lotus-buds in the upper pair of hands. But for *jaṭājūṭa* he could be identified with one of the Ādityas.

112. REVANTA
Durgaganj (Soraon), Allahabad District, UP
10th century A.D.
Grey sandstone, .270 x .510 m.
AM 298 Fig. 94

Panel showing Revanta as horse-rider out hunting, preceded and followed respectively by Daṇḍa and Piṅgala, also figured as riding horses and marching in the same direction. Two attendants of Revanta are shown in the background, one behind, holding a parasol and the other facing and approaching the god with a wine-jar in hand. Hunting hounds are represented beneath all the three horses mauling and, in two cases almost devouring the hunted animals which resemble deer. In two cases the hunted games are being trampled upon by the horses, that beneath the leading horse being a wild boar. An attendant behind the last horse-rider carries on his shoulders the complete carcass of a hunted stag. This is a most lively representation of the divine hunter Revanta, son of Sūrya, whose iconographic traits fully accord with the description given in the ancient Silpa texts including Varāhamihira's *Bṛahatsaṁhitā* (c. 6th century A.D.).

This sculpture bears close affinity to a figure from Mathura (Mathura Museum No. 68. 2-4) : Ref. B.N. Sharma, *Revanta* (Delhi, 1975), Fig. 24.

NAVAGRAHAS

113. NAVAGRAHA PANEL
Site not known
9th century A.D.
Buff sandstone, .85 x .26 m.
AM 1302 Fig. 95

Panel with seated figures of Navagrahas, damaged at both ends. Rāhu is represented by a head and it is not certain whether or how Ketu was represented.

114. NAVAGRAHA PANEL
Site not known
10th century A.D.
Buff sandstone, .275 x .550 m.
AM 396 Fig. 96

The right end of the panel bearing figure of Ketu is broken and Sūrya is partly mutilated. But for Sūrya and Rāhu, other Grahas stand in exaggerated *tribhaṅga*. Rāhu is elegantly depicted as a bust with hands in *tarpaṇa-mudrā*.

115. NAVAGRAHA PANEL
Kauśāmbī, Allahabad District, UP
10th century A.D.
Greyish sandstone, .275 x .477 m.
AM 834 Fig. 97

Damaged Navagraha panel showing only four standing Grahas beginning with the Sun. The moon has a crescent incised at the crest.

MISCELLANEOUS GODS

116. DEITY, HEADLESS
Mathura, Mathura District, UP
2nd century A.D.
Spotted red sandstone, .160 x .110 m.
AM 894 Fig. 98

Deity (headless) seated in *pralambapādāsana*, with right hand held in *abhayamudrā*.

117. HEAD OF DEITY
Mathura, Mathura District, UP
2nd century A.D.
Spotted red sandstone, .102 x .065 m.
AM 111 Fig. 99

Head of deity wearing fan-shaped headdress typical of the Kuṣāṇa period.

118. HEAD OF DEITY
Site not known
3rd century A.D.
Buff sandstone, .165 x .09 m.
AM 474 Fig. 100

Head of deity wearing headdress typical of the Kuṣāṇa period.

119. FRAGMENT OF DEITY
Mathura, Mathura District, UP
3rd century A.D.
Spotted red sandstone, .150 x .170 m.
AM 899 Fig. 101

Fragmentary torso of a deity wearing a girdle of three pearl strands and a *vanamālā*. The nudity of the figure is concealed by a small strip of cloth hanging centrally from the girdle in flaring pleats.

120. CROWNED HEAD
Site not known
8th century A.D.
Greyish sandstone, .242 x .223 m.
AM 804 Fig. 102

Head of god wearing short jewelled *kirīṭamukuṭa*.

121. CROWNED HEAD
Kauśāmbi, Allahabad District, UP
8th century A.D.
Sandstone, ht. .200 m.
AM 906

Head of either Sūrya or Viṣṇu wearing *kirīṭamukuṭa*.

122. BUST OF GOD
MP
9th century A.D.
Sandstone, ht. .230 m.
AM 972 Fig. 103

Bust of god wearing jewelled *kirīṭamukuṭa,* heavy *ratnakuṇḍalas,* torques and *keyūra.* The ornate headdress and the cascading curls are notable.

123. HEAD OF DIVINITY
Jhusi, Allahabad District, UP
9th century A.D.
Pink sandstone, ht. .125 m.
AM 1073

Crowned head of god with a dignified oval face.

124. HEAD OF DEITY
Soraon, Allahabad District, UP
9th century A.D.
Greyish sandstone, .260 x .190 m.
AM 369

Head of deity, probably Śiva, wearing *jaṭāmukuṭa* with a mutilated lotus halo.

125. CROWNED HEAD
Site not known
9th century A.D.
Pink sandstone, ht. .390 m.
AM 964 Fig. 104

Head of deity wearing jewelled *karaṇḍamukuṭa.*

126. CROWNED HEAD
Site not known
9th century A.D.
Buff sandstone, .135 x .082 m.
AM 482

Head wearing short mutilated crown.

127. STANDING DEITY
10th century A.D.
Buff sandstone, .407 x .120 m.
AM 745 Fig. 105

Male deity standing in *samabhaṅga,* wearing profuse jewellery including *kaustubha-maṇi.* Hands and feet broken.

128. HEAD OF DEITY
Site not known
10th century A.D.
Grey sandstone, .280 x .150 m.
AM 1109 Fig. 106

Head of deity donning *karaṇḍamukuṭa* adorned centrally with jewelled ornament.

129. HEAD OF ĪŚĀNA (?)
Site not known
10th century A.D.
Buff sandstone, ht. .200 m.
AM 1072 Fig. 107

Head of Īśāna (?) with handsome oval face, ornate *karaṇḍamukuṭa* and third eye on the forehead.

130. CROWNED HEAD
Agroha, Hissar District, Haryana
11th century A.D.
Sandstone, ht. .140 m.
AM 874 Fig. 108

Head of either Viṣṇu or Sūrya wearing ornate *kirīṭamukuṭa* and *kuṇḍalas*.

131. HEAD OF DIVINITY
Site not known
11th century A.D.
Buff sandstone, ht. .250 m.
AM 849 Fig. 109

Head of divinity wearing crown adorned with pearl festoons. It is notable for dignified facial expression with sharp eyebrows and forehead adorned with *tilaka*.

132. MALE HEAD
Site not known
12th century A.D.
Greyish sandstone, .180 x .127 m.
AM 373 Fig. 110

Male head wearing damaged crown, a peculiar *tilaka* and whiskers.

133. CROWNED HEAD
Bhita, Allahabad District, UP
13th century A.D.
Sandstone, .190 x .100 m.
AM 310 Fig. 111

Head of deity wearing *karaṇḍamukuṭa*.

BRAHMANICAL GODDESSES

134. BIRD-HEADED MOTHER-GODDESS
Mathura, Mathura District, UP
2nd century A.D.
Spotted red sandstone .128 x .108 m.
AM 109 Fig. 112

Bird-headed Mother-goddess with bird-headed child in her lap. The presence of bird-headed child is a rare and interesting feature. Bird-headed Mātṛkās of the Kuṣāṇa period are known in several combinations from Mathura. Ref: N.P. Joshi, *Matrkas - Mothers in Kuṣāṇa Art* (Delhi, 1986).

135. BUST OF MOTHER-GODDESS
Mathura, Mathura District, UP
2nd century A.D.
Spotted Red Sandstone, .202 x .150 m.
AM 92

Bust of Mother-goddess under an arched canopy. The goddess has close-set breasts and wears heavy ear-ornaments and a torque. AM 116 is a better preserved specimen of a similar figure from Mathura.

136. STANDING DURGĀ
Mathura, Mathura District, UP
6th century A.D.
Red spotted sandstone, .180 x .145 m.
AM 82 Fig. 113

Standing four-armed Durgā, carrying a long trident in the lower left hand, a wine-pot in the upraised lower right and a circular rayed shield in the upper left hand. Upper right corner of the stele broken with the upper right hand which might have held a sword.

137. FEMALE HEAD
UP
6th century A.D.
Greyish sandstone, ht. .290 m.
AM 1212

Head of female deity (Durgā?) with a *dhammilla* hair-do.

138. MAHIṢĀSURAMARDINĪ
Site not known
8th century A.D.
Red sandstone, .95 x .102 m.
AM 983 Fig. 114

Miniature four-armed Mahiṣāsuramardinī slaying the buffalo demon whose muzzle with protruding tongue is preserved together with the upper part of the goddess. She holds a garland in her uplifted pair of hands to celebrate her victory.

139. LAJJĀGAURĪ
Bhita, Allahabad District, UP
7th century A.D.
Buff sandstone, .145 x .140 m.
AM 299

Defaced figure of headless nude Lajjāgaurī. Better preserved specimens of comparable (as well as earlier) dates are known from Bhita, Alampur, Nāgārjunakondā, Ter, etc.

Ref. J.N. Tiwari, *Goddess Cults in Ancient India*, (Delhi, 1985), pp. 182-219.

140. LAKṢMĪ
Kauśāmbī, Allahabad District, UP
7th century A.D.
Buff sandstone, Ht. .370 m.
AM 853 Fig. 115

Lakśmī standing in *samabhaṅga* with right hand held up in *abhaya* and left carrying lotus stalk. She has a large circular lotus shaped nimbus and wears *dhammilla* coiffure, *kuṇḍalas,* torque, necklace with *lalantikā* and wristlets.

141. LAKṢMĪ
Sarnath, Varanasi District, UP
7th century A.D.
Buff sandstone, .370 x .170 m.
AM 489

Lakṣmī standing in *samabhaṅga* with the right hand stretched in *varada* and left carrying lotus stalk, feet broken. The *adhovastra* is prominently shown with multiple incised lines.

142. BUST OF DEVĪ
Kauśāmbī, Allahabad District, UP
7th century A.D.
Buff sandstone, ht. .360 m.
AM 273 Fig. 116

Bust of Devī wearing crown and *ekāvalī.* The figure is beautifully modelled.

143. BUST OF GODDESS
Lacchagir, Allahabad District, UP
8th century A.D.
Buff sandstone, ht. .190 m.
AM 359

Mutilated bust of goddess. Her upraised right hand holds a snake.

144. FEMALE HEAD
8th century A.D.
Grey sandstone, .230 x .160 m.
AM 913 Fig. 117

Female head with elaborate coiffure, resembling *ūrdhvapiṅgalakeśa* with a central jewel.

145. BUST OF DEITY
UP
9th century A.D.
Pale sandstone, ht. .340 m.
AM 681 Fig. 118

The deity (probably goddess) has an oval face, wearing a highly ornate *mukuṭa* against an oval nimbus formed by double lotus, *kuṇḍalas* and torque. The sculpture probably comes from a Himalayan site.

146. MINIATURE PĀRVATĪ
Site not known
8th century A.D.
Slate stone, .172 x .120 m.
AM 930 Fig. 119

Two-armed miniature Pārvatī standing with right hand in *abhaya,* attribute of the left hand abraded. *Pancaliṅgas* depicted above. The figure sports a circular headdress and large leaf-like ears, which together with the fanlike objects on the sides of her head, her hands and drapery are all embellished with hatched incisions.

147. PĀRVATĪ IN PAÑCĀGNITAPA
Site not known
9th century A.D.
Red sandstone, .710 x .620 m.
AM 1344

Niche displaying standing four-armed Pārvatī engaged in *pañcāgnitapa.* The figure is much mutilated but fires are seen held in her two upper hands and a *kamaṇḍalu* in lower left hand. The niche is framed by *ghaṭapallava* pilasters also embellished with *kīrttimukha* pattern.

148. ARCHITECTURAL MEMBER WITH PĀRVATĪ
Kauśāmbī, Allahabad District, UP
9th century A.D.
Buff sandstone, .680 x .460 m.
AM 1271 Fig. 120

Architectural member showing niched Pārvatī doing penance. The piece is carved with typical Pratīhāra motifs of *ghaṭapallava* pillaret and festoon of *ardhapadmas.*

Four-armed Pārvati stands in *samabhaṅga* holding probably lotus stalks in upper pair of hands, the objects in her lower pair of hands are unclear. She is flanked by frisking animals on both sides, that on the right being deer.

149. PĀRVATĪ
Site not known
10th century A.D.
Greyish sandstone, .340 x .340 m.
AM 92.148 Fig. 121

Image stele showing bust of Pārvatī. She has a lotus halo crowned by Pañcaliṅgas and flanked by Mālādhara Vidyādharas and wears a *jaṭāmukuṭa* and other usual ornaments.

150. PĀRVATĪ HEAD
Bhita, Allahabad District, UP
10th century A.D.
Grey sandstone, .215 x .102 m.
AM 338 Fig. 122

Beautifully chiselled head of Pārvatī, donning *jaṭājūṭa* (abraded), with the third eye and sharp eye-brows marked on the forehead.

151. PĀRVATĪ IMAGE FRAGMENT
Site not known
10th century A.D.
Buff sandstone, .760 x .330 m.
AM 167

Parikara of Pārvatī image fragment showing attendants and the lion mount.

152. SKANDA-MĀTĀ
Kara, Allahabad District, UP
10th century A.D.
Grey sandstone, .335 x .293 m.
AM 260 Fig. 123

Skandamātā (headless) seated in *lalitāsana* on lion mount, holding infant Skanda in her lap.

153. STANDING PĀRVATĪ
10th century A.D.
Grenish schist, .420 x .240 m.
AM 1076 Fig. 124

Four-armed Pārvatī, standing in *samabhaṅga,* stretches the lower right hand in *varada* and holds lotus flower in the upper right and *triśūla* and *ghaṇṭā* in the left hands. She is flanked by female *cauri*-bearers as well as Jayā and Vijayā carrying *daṇḍa* or sword on the sides. Lion is represented on the proper right and mutilated deer (?) on the left of her feet placed on a lotus. Her head is flanked by a *mālāvidyādhara* on each side, that on the left being defaced. She wears a *jaṭāmukuṭa, kuṇḍalas,* torque, *hāra,* wristlets and anklets and is draped in a *sārī* and scarf which winds round both her arms. This is a typical early medieval art-specimen from the Himālayan hills, characterised by metallic finish, elongation of the figures and an ornamental arched canopy crowning the image.

154. STANDING PĀRVATĪ
Site not known
11th century A.D.
Sandstone, .540 x .320 m.
AM 846 Fig. 125

Image stele showing four-armed Pārvatī standing in *samabhaṅga* with the right hands broken and left hands carrying spiral lotus stalk and *kamaṇḍalu. Pañcaliṅgas* flanked by *vidyādharas* are carved at the top while on either side of her head are depicted Gaṇeśa and Śiva. She is flanked in the lower field by female *chauri*-bearers, each with two other attendants. Seated donor couple are also depicted.

155. MĀTṚKĀS
Site not known
7th century A.D.
Buff sandstone, .330 x .450 m.
AM 1266 Fig. 126

Two seated Mātṛkās partly surviving out of a badly damaged early Saptamātṛkā group. The less damaged one wears a *dhammilla* headdress, *kuṇḍalas,* torque and wristlets and shows elegant modelling with close-set globular breasts. She is two-armed, holding a *ratna* in the right hand and some mutilated *āyudha* in the left hand.

156. BUST OF KAUMĀRĪ
UP
7th century A.D.
Buff sandstone, ht. .360 m.
Am 974 Fig. 127

Kaumārī wears *śikhaṇḍaka* coiffure, *ekāvalī* and a broad scarf as *kucabandha.*

157. SAPTAMĀTṚKĀ PANEL
UP
9th century A.D.
Buff sandstone, .390 x .385 m.
AM 1201 Fig. 128

Right extremity of mutilated Saptamātṛkā panel showing seated Vīṇādhara Vīrabhadra (head missing) and Brahmāṇī. Vīrabhadra is seated in *lalitāsana,* holding *vīṇā* in the main pair of hands and trident in the upper left hand. Brahmāṇī is three-headed and seated in *utkuṭikāsana* on a lotus seat with *yogapaṭṭa* tied round her knees.

158. SAPTAMĀTṚKĀ PANEL
Shivadvara, Mirzapur District, UP
9th century A.D.
Grey sandstone, .380 x .355 m.
AM 904 Fig. 129

Kaumārī, Vārāhī and Indrāṇī survive out of the panel of dancing Saptamātṛkās. Kaumārī (face abraded) and Indrāṇī hold child in their lap besides their special cognizances, viz *śakti* and *vajra.* Vārāhi is corpulent and sow-faced and holds fish in her left hand.

159. HEADLESS VAIṢṆAVĪ
Jhusi, Allahabad District, UP
10th century A.D.
Buff sandstone, .370 x .240 m.
AM 251 Fig. 130

Vaiṣṇavī (head lost) seated on her mount Garuḍa, depicted as winged and wearing *ūrdhvapiṅgalakeśa.* All four hands of the goddess are broken.

160. BUST OF VAIṢṆAVĪ (?)
UP
10th century A.D.
Buff sandstone, .240 x .190 m.
AM 984 Fig. 131

The goddess with a handsome oval face is probably Vaiṣṇavī wearing a tall *kirīṭamukuṭa* against a lotus shaped *nimbus, kuṇḍalas,* torque, pearl necklace and *keyūras.* All four hands are broken.

161. VĀRĀHĪ
Gadhaiya, Allahabad District, UP
Late 9th century A.D.
Greyish red sandstone, .600 x .450 m.
AM 1094 Fig. 132

Four-armed Vārāhī dancing, holding *vajra* and dagger in the right hands, licking blood from the skull-cup held in the upper left- hand and carrying fish in the lower left hand. She wears torque, necklace, armlet, wristlets and is draped in a lower garment and scarf.

162. CĀMUṆḌĀ ON OWL
UP
8th century A.D.
Sandstone, .700 x .430 m.
AM 948 Fig. 133

Four-armed Cāmuṇḍā seated on owl. She has stretched her mouth with the upper pair of hands and holds *kartari* and *kapāla* (?) in the lower pair of hands.

163. BUST OF CĀMUṆḌĀ
Bhita, Allahabad District, UP
9th century A.D.
Buff sandstone, .350 x .220 m.
AM 971 Fig. 134

Skeletal bust of fierce Cāmuṇḍā with third eye marked on the forehead, goggle eyes, gaping mouth, pendant breasts and sunken belly. She wears *kuṇḍalas* and a long pearl necklace. The back of the stele is also carefully modelled.

164. STANDING CĀMUṆḌĀ
Site not known,
10th century A.D.
Sandstone, .320 x .250 m.
AM 1323 Fig. 135

Multi-armed figure of standing Cāmuṇḍā with the main right hand holding *kapāla* and the main left touching with its index finger her chin. Her left arm also supports the *khaṭvāṅga.* Other details defaced.

165. DANCING CĀMUṆḌĀ
Provenance unknown.
11th century A.D.
Greyish red sandstone. .620 x .450 m.
AM 1406 Fig. 136

Eight-armed dancing skeletal figure of Cāmuṇḍā with *ūrdhvakeśa,* sagging breasts, and sunken belly, wearing *muṇḍamālā.* She stands on a disintegrated corpse. All hands mutilated except two left ones, one held on the chin and the other carrying shield. A sword was obviously held in one of the mutilated right hands.

166. DANCING CĀMUṆḌĀ
Jamsot, Allahabad District, UP
12th century A.D.
Greyish red sandstone, .610 x .445 m.
AM 1054 Fig. 137

Ten-armed dancing Cāmuṇḍā with a skeletal figure, all hands broken. She stands on *nara-vāhana* and wears *muṇḍamālā.*

167. NARA-VĀHANĀ DEVĪ
Site not known
10th century A.D.
Red sandstone, .560 x .410 m.
AM 949

Four-armed Tantric goddess seated on reclining human mount, carrying serpents in the two right hands and a pot in the surviving left hand.

168. NARA-VĀHANĀ YOGINĪ
Kauśāmbī, Allahabad District, UP
10th century A.D.
Greyish red sandstone, .770 x .470 m.
AM 92.130 Fig. 138

Inscribed four-armed Yoginī, much damaged and broken in two parts, seated in *lalitāsana* on a *nara-vāhana.* She is seated under a canopy of mango fruits and wears *jaṭājūṭa, asthi-kuṇḍalas, asthi-mālā* and armlets studded with minute human skulls, besides normal torque and *ratnopavīta* and a peculiar *mekhalā* of jingle-bells. All her hands are mutilated but the upper left one is seen to carry a long staff (*dhvajadaṇḍa*) with its upper part chipped off. Her head is flanked on each side by a dancing female attendant carrying *kapāla* and mutilated *daṇḍa.* The *naravāhana* is also flanked on each side by a defaced attendant standing in *tribhaṅga.*

A two-line damaged inscription appears on the right margin engraved in 10th century proto-Nāgarī characters reading:

1. (ī) mahahara......sa Śrī...
2. (de) hapāla Mahā (r) ....

169. LOTUS PEDESTAL OF NARAVĀHANĀ YOGINĪ
Kauśāmbī, Allahabad District, UP
10th century A.D.
Buff sandstone .410 x .445 m.
AM 92.146 Fig. 139

Large lotus (*mahāmbuja*) pedestal issuing from the navel of a nude reclining *nara-vāhana*. The *nara-vāhana* is flanked on both sides by figures, those on the right are chipped off, while those on the left represent two cavorting figures, one a skeletal *gaṇa* and the other a headless female.

The deity is missing from the lotus pedestal.

170. LOTUS PEDESTAL OF NARAVĀHANĀ YOGINĪ
Kauśambī, Allahabad District, UP
10th century A.D.
Buff sandstone, .380 x .760 m.
AM 91.1914 Fig. 140

Large lotus (*mahāmbuja*) pedestal issuing from the navel of a reclining *nara-vāhana*. The lotus is flanked on each side by a standing attendant, that on the left is a male carrying *daṇḍa* and an object with a curved top while the figure on the right looks like a female carrying a *kapāla*. The lotus is mutilated together with whatever was left of the surmounting deity.

171. COW-FACED GODDESS
Gurgi, Rewa District, MP
10th century A.D.
Plum coloured sandstone, ht. .460 m.
AM 500 Fig. 141

Tantric cow-faced goddess standing in *ābhaṅga* holding *kapāla* in the lower right hand and bell and *khaṭvāṅga* in the left hands.

172. GODDESS RIDING A HORSE
Provenance unknown
10th century A.D.
Greyish sandstone, .545 x .370 m.
AM 554 Fig. 142

Multi-armed goddess riding a striding horse. A seated devotee is shown in front obstructing the stride of the horse. The goddess holds a skull-cup and the rein in the normal pair of hands and defaced dagger and *khaṭvāṅga* in the other left hands. The remaining hands and their attributes are mutilated. The female figures flanking her head seem to carry sword of staff. Ref: Padma Upadhyaya, *Female Images in Museums of U.P* (Varanasi, 1978) p. 67.

173. HEAD OF GODDESS
Site not known
9th century A.D.
Buff sandstone, .152 x .162 m.
AM 476 Fig. 143

Head of goddess wearing tall *jaṭāmukuṭa*.

174. BUST OF GODDESS
Site not known
10th century A.D.
Greyish red sandstone, .250 x .127 m.
AM 390

Damaged bust of goddess wearing *jaṭāmukuṭa*.

175. ŚAṄKHADEVĪ IN RATHIKĀ
Site not known
9th century A.D.
Greyish sandstone, .515 x .380 m.
AM 545 Fig. 144

Śaṅkhadevī standing in *samabhaṅga* in a *rathikā*, flanked by vertical bands of chequer design.

176. DĪPALAKṢMĪ
UP
9th century A.D.
Sandstone, ht. .820 m.
AM 995 Fig. 145

Unfinished sculpture of standing Dīpalakṣmī.

177. BHAIRAVĪ
Gaya, Gaya District, Bihar
11th century A.D.
Black schist, ht. .530 m.
AM 239 Fig. 146

Bhairavī standing in *tribaṅga* with a fierce face marked by *ūrdhvapiṅgalakeśa* tied with a serpent (hood visible), third eye, and gaping mouth, holding *kapāla* in the left hand, right hand broken. She has a bulky body with a pot belly and stands amidst luxuriant lotus stalks.

178. MAHIṢĀSURAMARDINĪ
Site not known
16th century A.D.
Slate, 530 x 300 m.
AM 1326 Fig. 147

Eight-armed Mahiṣāsuramardinī killing the demon with

triśūla, held in the main pair of hands. Other hands carry attributes such as sword and shield, bow and arrow, etc. A specimen of late medieval degenerate style, probably from the hills.

MINOR DEITIES COMMON TO ALL SECTS

179. YAKṢA
Bhita, Allahabad District, UP
2nd century B.C.
Grey sandstone, .980 x .520 m.
AM 92.12 Fig. 148

Massive figure of crude dwarfish Yakṣa with hands upraised and knees bent under the sheer weight of unshapely plump body. The squat face wearing the typical Śuṅga turban and heavy ear-ornaments sits directly over the shoulders. The figure wears a *dhoti* secured by a two-strand *kaṭisūtra* with a central knot, while the upper body is draped by a peculiar scarf with a serpentine knot. Face and hands damaged. Feet broken off. This figure is comparable to the coeval and equally massive and ugly three-faced Yakṣa from Rajghat (Varanasi): Ref. R.N. Misra, *Yaksa Cult and Iconography* (Delhi, 1981), Plates 39-41.

Yakṣa with upraised hands are also known from sites such as Sanchi and Pitalkhora.

180. HEAD OF YAKṢA
Kauśāmbī, Allahabad District, UP
1st century B.C.-A.D.
Greyish sandstone, ht. .250 m.
AM 860 Fig. 149

Dignified head of Yakṣa wearing a heavy turban and *vapra-kuṇḍalas.*

181. HEAD OF YAKṢA
Bhita, Allahabad District, UP
2nd century A.D.
Spotted red sandstone, .127 x .165 m.
AM 830 Fig. 150

Yakṣa head with puffed cheeks, bulging eye and mouth stretched with the fingers of hands as in a comic play. An identical head also from Bhita is published in Pramod Chandra's *Stone Sculpture in the Allahabad Museum,* PL. XXXIII No.83. A similar head (part of a quern) bearing Kuṣāna inscription is also known from Ahicchatra.

182. KUBERA
Mathura, Mathura District, UP
2nd century A.D.
Spotted red sandstone, .210 x .180 m.
AM 296 Fig. 151

Pot-bellied Kubera squatting, holding wine-cup in the left hand, right hand in *abhaya* (defaced).

183. KUBERA AND HĀRĪTĪ
Mathura, Mathura District, UP
2nd century A.D.
Spotted red sandstone, .197 x .260 m.
AM 118 Fig. 152

Squatting Kubera (headless) and Hārītī. The pedestal is flanked by devotees, that on the right wearing the Scythian dress.

184. TORSO OF YAKṢA
Mathura, Mathura District, UP
4th century A.D.
Red spotted sandstone, .340 x .260 m.
AM 93 Figs. 153 A-B

Heavily built torso of a Yakṣa (?) carrying mutilated *musala* in left hand, right hand broken. The god is draped in a *dhoti* and a scarf which passes over the left shoulder and going cross-wise at the back flutters down the left arm after loosely winding round the waist. *Ekāvalī* is the only ornament worn by the god. The broad scarf worn cross-wise at the back is an unusual feature. Is he Mudgarapāṇi Yakṣa?

185. GAṆA
Bhumara, Satna District, MP
5th century A.D.
Red sandstone, .315 x .690 m.
AM 1442 Fig. 154

Dwarf *gaṇa* with long torso and short legs gesticulating. The *gaṇa* is framed in a niche, flanked by lotus design on both sides. Bhumara is known for a large variety of cavorting and gesticulating *gaṇas* which are published in *Pramod Chandra's Cat.*, Pls. LVIII-LIX.

186. GAṆA
Jhusi, Allahabad District, UP
5th century A.D.
Reddish sandstone, .155 x .09 m.
AM 977 Fig. 155

Pot-bellied dwarf *gaṇa* with a distinctive headdress, wearing earrings and *ekāvalī.*

187. DAṆḌAPĀṆI YAKṢA(?)
Mau (near Robertsganj), Mirzapur District, UP
5th century A.D.
Sandstone, . 230 x .290 m.
AM 905 Fig. 156

Architectural fragment showing a deity seated in

utkuṭikāsana, holding a *daṇḍa* or sceptre. The figure is two-armed and wears an *ekāvalī*.

A similar coeval deity appears within a *candraśālā* at Bhumara and subsequently on the seventh century Muṇḍeśvarī temple at Ramgarh and Paraśurāmeśvara temple at Bhubaneswar. For comparable figures also see:

1. S.D. Trivedi, *Sculptures in the Jhansi Museum*, (Jhansi, 1983) Fig. 76]

2. F.M. Asher, *The Art of Eastern India, 300-800*, (Minneapolis, 1980), Pl.103.

188. DAṆḌAPĀNI YAKṢA IN MINIATURE SHRINE
Allahabad, Allahabad District, UP
10th century A.D.
Pink sandstone, .875 x .330 m.
AM 663 Fig. 157

Front view of a miniature shrine showing Śiva-liṅga enshrined in the sanctum and squatting figure of Daṇḍapāṇi Yakṣa in the *śukanāsa* medallion. This shrine was published earlier in *P. Chandra's Cat.*, p. 171 item 502 but not illustrated. Figures of Daṇḍapāṇi Yakṣa in the *śukanāsa* medallion also appear in the Miniature Shrines, bearing accession Nos. AM 674, 675, 678 and 1077 published earlier in *P. Chandra's Catalogue.*

The *Matsya-purāṇa* (chapters 180 and 183) refer to Yakṣa Harikeśa, son of Yakṣa Pūrṇabhadra and grandson of Yakṣa Maṇibhadra, settling down at Varanasi as an ardent devotee of Śiva, who appointed Harikeśa as his Daṇḍadhara, charged with the responsibility of awarding liberation or punishment to men according to their merits or demerits. Ref. R.N. Mishra, *Yakṣa Cult and Iconography* (Delhi, 1981), p. 34.

Harikeśa is also called Daṇḍapāṇi Yakṣa and is frequently represented on the *śukanāsa* of the Miniature Shrines, generally enshrining Śivaliṅga, which seem to be memorial monuments of funerary character.

189. NAIGAMEṢA
Mathura, Mathura District, UP
2nd century A.D.
Spotted red sandstone, .165 x .115 m.
AM 462 Fig. 158

Goat-headed Yakṣa Naigameṣa carrying a child on the left shoulder. He is flanked by two attendants whose mutilated busts are shown below. Naigameṣa seems to be originally a folk deity who was subsequently appropriated by the Jainas and charged with the task of transferring the foetus of Jina Mahāvīra from the womb of Devānandā to that of Triśalā.

190. VIDYĀDHARA
Site not known
9th century A.D.
Buff sandstone, ht . 310 m.
AM 989

Vidyādhara in flight, holding full blown lotus flower by stalk in the right hand, left hand broken.

191. Vidyādhara
Site not known
10th century A.D.
Greyish red sandstone, .375 x .205 m.
AM 1215 Fig. 159

Vidyādhara wielding dagger.

192. VIDYĀDHARA COUPLE
Site not known
10th century A.D.
Buff sandstone, .230 x .155 m.
AM 1287

193. VIDYĀDHARA MITHUNA
Site not known
11th century A.D.
Buff sandstone, .395 x .395 m.
AM 1431 Fig. 160

The figure resembles types represented at Jamsot.

194. VIDYĀDHARĪ
Site not known
11th century A.D.
Red sandstone, .178 x .152 m.
AM 963

Bust of *vidyādharī* with hands in *añjalimudrā.*

195. VIDYĀDHARĪ
Jamsot, Allahabad District, UP
12th century A.D.
Buff sandstone, ht. .370 m.
AM 1061

Flying *vidyādharī.*

196. VIDYĀDHARA
Site not known
12th century A.D.
Grey sandstone, .220 x .130 m.
AM 1192 Fig. 161

Sword-wielding *vidyādhara* bust. The figure has bearded and moustached round face and wears *karṇa-kuṇḍalas*, torque and wristlets.

197. APSARĀ AND VYĀLA
Site not known.
10th century A.D.
Pink sandstone, .785 x .230 m.
AM 443

Ghaṭapallava pilaster carved with a standing Apsarā depicted in *añjalimudrā.* A vyāla is represented on the adjoining recessed facet. Apsarā and *vyāla* are used as favorite architectural motifs on early medieval and medieval art of North India.

198. APSARĀ AND VYĀLA
Khajuraho, Chhatarpur District, MP
11th century A.D.
Buff sandstone , .420 x .260 m.
AM 248 Fig. 162

Apsarā standing, viewed from behind, with her head in profile, holding bunch of flowers in her right hand. Rearing *siṁha-vyāla* with a boar below is depicted on the adjacent recessed facet.

199. APSARĀ
Gurgi, Rewa District, MP
10th century A.D.
Light red sandstone, .635 x .355 m.
AM 517 Fig. 163

Apsarā standing in a charming *tribhaṅga* posture with feet in *svastikapāda,* adjusting her braids in the mirror held in her left hand.

200. APSARASES
Jamsot, Allahabad District, UP
11th century A.D.
Buff sandstone, .585 x .405 m.
AM 1053 Fig. 164

Apsarases on a corner piece, one of them holding mirror in the left hand.

201. APSARĀ KARPŪRAMAÑJARĪ
Site not known
11th century A.D.
Buff sandstone, .470 x .300 m.
AM 1360 Fig. 165

Apsarā (*Karpūramañjarī*) in three-quarters back view, rinsing water from wet plaits of hair. Portion below thighs broken. The figure is in the typical Khajuraho style.

202. APSARĀ
Jamsot, Allahabad District, UP
12th century A.D.
Buff sandstone, ht. 1.790 m.
AM 1130

Architectural fragment with dancing Apsarā at the base. The Apsarā wears the typical dress and ornaments of the art of Jamsot.

203. APSARĀ
Jamsot, Allahabad District, UP
12th century A.D.
Buff sandstone, 1.740 x .450 m.
AM 1138

Architectural fragment depicting Apsarā with all characteristics of the art of Jamsot.

204. ARCHITECTURAL FRAGMENT WITH ATTENDANT
Bhita, Allahabad District, UP
10th century A.D.
Buff sandstone, ht. .560 m.
AM 453

Male attendant, probably subsidiary to a missing central deity. The attendant with hands and feet broken stands in *tribhaṅga* and wears dress and ornaments (notice double *urumālā*) typical of late 11th century art.

205. VIDYĀDHARA AND PRATIHĀRA
Site not known
12th century A.D.
Buff sandstone, 1.09 x 255 m.
AM 557

Architectural fragment with two plain niches showing a *mālā-vidyādhara* and a *gadādhārī pratihāra.*

BUDDHIST DEITIES

Gandhara Art

206. MĀYĀDEVĪ IN LUMBINĪ FOREST
Gandhara (Pakistan)
2nd century A.D.
Blue schist, .345 x .127 m.
AM 372 Fig. 166

Māyādevī standing in the typical posture of the Nativity Scene in the Lumbinī Forest beneath a *śāla* tree. She stands in the *śālabhañjikā* pose and is figured in the typical Greco-Roman style. Hands and feet mutilated.

207. BUDDHA HEAD
Gandhara (Pakistan)
2nd-3rd centuries A.D.
Stucco, .105 x .075 m.
AM 1445 Fig. 167

Buddha head with prominent *uṣṇīṣa.* Nose chipped.

208. MALE HEAD
Gandhara (Pakistan)
2nd-3rd centuries A.D.
Stucco, .098 x .065 m.
AM 1443 Fig. 168

Turbaned head of probably Bodhisattva. Curls fall on the proper right side covering the ear, corresponding left side damaged.

209. MALE HEAD
Gandhara (pakistan)
2nd-3rd centuries A.D.
Stucco, .120 x .087 m.
AM 1444 Fig. 169

Portrait head of male figure with damaged ornate headdress.

Art of Indian Mainland

210. BUST OF BODHISATTVA(?)
Kauśāmbī, Allahabad District, UP
1st century A.D.
Pale buff sandstone, .165 x .128 m.
AM 149 Fig. 170

The god has turbaned head and holds the right hand in *abhaya.*

211. BODHISATTVA
Mathura, Mathura District, UP
2nd century A.D.
Spotted red sandstone, .110 x .065 m.
AM 86

Head of deity, probably Bodhisattva, wearing typical fan-shaped Kuṣāṇa crown and heavy *kuṇḍalas.*

212. BUDDHA (HEADLESS)
Mathura, Mathura District, UP
3rd century A.D.
Spotted red sandstone, .320 x .230 m.
AM 1337 Fig. 171

Seated Buddha with head and hands broken. This is a typical seated Kuṣāṇa image of Buddha wearing *ubhayāṁsika saṅghāṭī.*

213. LIFE SCENES OF BUDDHA
Site not known
c. 4th century A.D.
Buff sandstone, .200 x .570 m.
AM 92.13 Fig. 172 A-D

Square pedestal of a Buddhist image, carved with scenes of Buddha's Nativity, Temptation, First Preaching, and Parinirvāṇa on the four faces.

214. STANDING BUDDHA
UP
5th century A.D.
Red sandstone, ht. .280 m.
AM 278 Fig. 173

Standing Buddha figure, broken below waist. The pendant right hand, probably held in *varada,* is broken while the upraised left hand carries the end of *saṅghāṭī.* The figure is a specimen of Sarnath Gupta Buddha type, with sensitive modelling, diaphanous drapery, luminous face with half-closed meditative eyes and snail shell curls with *uṣṇīṣa.*

215. PREACHING BUDDHA
UP
5th century A.D.
Buff sandstone, .320 x .230 m.
AM 600 Fig. 174

Buddha (head broken) seated turning the wheel of Law (*Dharma-cakra*) at Sarnath, indicated by a depiction of the Five Chosen Monks (*Pañca-Vargīya Bhikkhus*) with a wheel between carved on the pedestal. The scene represents the first preaching by Buddha, forming the most important event in the history of Buddhism. This figure is essentially a miniature version of the celebrated image of the Preaching Buddha of the Gupta period from Sarnath, with minor difference of details.

216. Buddha Head
Mathura, Mathura District, UP
5th century A.D.
Spotted red sandstone, ht. .220 m.
AM 980 A Fig. 175

Buddha head of typical Mathura Gupta type with *uṣṇīṣa* damaged.

217. HEAD OF BUDDHA
Sarnath, Varanasi District, UP
6th century A.D.
Buff sandstone, .190 x .120 m.
AM 611 Fig. 176

218. BUDDHA HEAD
Sarnath, Varanasi District, UP
7th century A.D.
Buff sandstone, .205 x .115 m.
AM 352

219. HEAD OF BUDDHA
Sarnath, Varanasi District, UP
7th century A.D.
Grey sandstone, ht. .275 m.
AM 743 Fig. 177

The face is oval with chiselled features and snail shell curls with a prominent *uṣṇīṣa.*

220. BUST OF BUDDHA
Site not known
7th century A.D.
Buff sandstone, .115 .082 m.
AM 491 Fig. 178

Nimbate bust of Buddha

221. BUST OF TĀRĀ
Gaya, Gaya District, Bihar
9th century A.D.
Grey schist, ht. .220 m.
AM 735 Fig. 179

Upper part of inscribed image stele showing bust of Tārā holding lotus stalk in the left hand, right hand broken. A stūpa is carved on the proper right side. The Buddhist formula is inscribed in the 9th century script along the upper edge of the circular *prabhāvalī.*

222. TĀRĀ
Site not known
11th century A.D.
Black schist, .120 x .160 m.
AM 592 Fig. 180

Lower part (feet only) of an inscribed image of Tārā of the Pāla style. The goddess is seated in *lalitāsana* on a lotus seat, her pendant right foot also rests on a lotus, flanked by a female donor, also seated in a supplicant pose on a smaller lotus.

One line inscription on the lowest fringe of the pedestal in 11th century script, saying that this is pious gift of a lady who is called *dānapati.*

223. ṢAḌAKṢARĪ LOKEŚVARA
Gurgi, Rewa District, MP
10th century A.D.
Red sandstone, .410 x .480 m.
AM 656 Fig. 181

Upper half of stele showing a handsome figure of Ṣaḍakṣarī Lokeśvara with the folded hands (defaced), flanked by Maṇidhara and Ṣaḍakṣarī Mahāvidyā also with hands folded. Lokeśvara is flanked by a pair of stūpas while his head is canopied by trefoil arch flanked by garland-bearing *vidyādharas.*

224. ṢAḌAKṢARĪ LOKEŚVARA
Site not Known
11th century A.D.
Greenish schist .152 x .094 m.
AM 584 Fig. 182

Part of Ṣaḍakṣarī Lokeśvara image of the Pāla School showing Maṇidhara (four-armed) seated, with main pair of hands folded on lotus, springing from a winding stalk. The central figure of Lokeśvara and the left figure of Ṣaḍakṣarī Mahāvidyā are lost.

225. ṢAḌAKṢARĪ LOKEŚVARA GROUP
Gurgi, Rewa District, MP
12th century A.D.
Greyish green sandstone, .470 x .335 m.
AM 531 Fig. 183

Lokeśvara flanked by Maṇidhara and Ṣaḍakṣarī Mahāvidyā, all four- armed and seated with the main pair of hands in the *añjalimudrā* under arched canopy, crowned by distinctive type of stūpa-like spires. The figure of Lokeśvara is larger and the arched canopy is correspondingly higher and flanked by *Vidyādharas.* The pedestal is ornamented with bold scrolls, flanked by a seated figure of devotee on either side.

226. SEATED BUDDHA
Gaya, Gaya District, Bihar.
10th century A.D.
Black schist, ht. .310 m.
AM 225 Fig. 184

Figure of Buddha (head broken) seated in *bhūmisparśamudrā* on a double lotus resting on a *pañcaratha* pedestal. The figure is surrounded by seven principal scenes from Tathāgata's life starting with Nativity shown on the lower right and ending with *parinirvāṇa* depicted at top.

227. BUDDHIST IMAGE PEDESTAL
Kauśāmbī, Allahabad District, UP
10th century A.D.
Sandstone, .230 x .470 m.
AM 525 Fig. 185

Image pedestal of *triratha* design, showing five miniature niched figures of seated Buddha in the corner *ratha* and a standing Buddha in the fragmentary recessed middle *ratha.*

228. ORNATE STŪPA BASE
Gaya, Gaya District, Bihar
10th century A.D.
Black schist, .390 x .360 m.
AM 242 Fig. 186

Stūpa base simulating *vedibandha* mouldings ornamented with figures of Buddha and Bodhisattva and a row of miniature *stūpas.*

229. BUDDHIST GODDESS
Kauśāmbī, Allahabad District, UP
10th century A.D.
Buff sandstone, ht. .430 m.
AM 272 Fig. 187 A-B

Bust of Tantric Buddhist goddess with four hands (three front heads female and back head male) and eight hands, all broken. The crown is carved with five Dhyānī Buddhas.

230. BUDDHIST GODDESS
Gurgi, Rewa District, MP
11th century A.D.
Red sandstone, .530 x .370 m.
AM 503 Fig. 188

Buddhist goddess seated in *bhūmisparśamudrā* on a double lotus under an arched canopy flanked by devotees. A pair of devotees also flank the lotus pedestal. The goddess is profusely decked with ornaments.

231. MINIATURE STŪPA
Kauśāmbī, Allahabad District, UP
11th century A.D.
Greyish sandstone, .185 x.160 m.
AM 741 Fig. 189

Miniature *stūpa* uniformly adorned with niched Buddha figures on four sides, three sides in *dhyāna* and one in *bhūmisparśamudrā*

232. MINIATURE STŪPA
Sarnath, Varanasi District, UP
12th century A.D.
Grey sandstone, .685 x .395 m.
AM 687 Fig. 190 A-D

Miniature *stūpa* with niched figures of Buddha, Maitreya, Tārā and Padmapāṇi Avalokiteśvara.

JAINA DEITIES

233. JINA HEAD
Mathura, Mathura District, UP
2nd century A.D.
Spotted red sandstone, ht. .260 m.
AM 120 Fig. 191

Head of Jina with shaven crown, a typical specimen of Kuṣāṇa Jina figure from Mathura.

234. Jina Head
Mathura, Mathura District, UP
2nd century A.D.
Spotted red sandstone, .120 x .107 m.
AM 73 Fig. 192

Shaven head of Jina with staring eyes, of typical Kuṣāṇa style from Mathura, defaced and damaged.

235. JINA HEAD
Sarnath, Varanasi District, UP
3rd century A.D.
Red sandstone, ht. .260 m.
AM 386 Fig. 193

Jina head with curly hair and damaged *uṣṇīṣa.*

236. JINA HEAD
Mathura, Mathura District, UP
4th century A.D.
Spotted red sandstone,
AM 980

Abraded head of Jina with snail curls and damaged *uṣṇīṣa.*

237. ĀDINĀTHA
Bharwari, Allahabad District, UP
5th century A.D.
Greyish black stone, .292 x .343 m.
AM 996 Fig. 194

Bust of Jina Ādinātha with shaven head, wide open eyes and curls falling on shoulders.

238. BUST OF ĀDINĀTHA
UP
6th century A.D.
Buff sandstone, .400 x .270 m.
AM 929 Fig. 195

Bust of Ādinātha with a plain circular halo, half-closed meditative eyes and curls falling on shoulders, the last being a cognizance of Ādinātha, The image also bears *Śrīvatsa* sign on the chest. The plain circular halo combined with attenuated and elongated torso indicate late Gupta art conventions.

239. HEAD OF PĀRŚVANĀTHA
Kauśāmbī, Allahabad District, UP
c.6th century A.D.
Buff sandstone, ht. .410 m.
AM 523 Fig. 196

Head of Pārśvanātha with a circular canopy of serpent hoods, resembling peacock's plumes, which represents a rare artistic feature.

240. JINA HEAD
Bhita, Allahabad District, UP
8th century A.D.
Buff sandstone, ht. .160 m.
AM 486 Fig. 197

241. HEAD OF JINA
Bhita, Allahabad District, UP
8th century A.D.
Buff sandstone, ht. .180 m.
AM 825 Fig. 198

242. JINA HEAD
Site not known
8th century A.D.
Greyish sandstone, .250 x .185 m.
AM 1312 Fig. 199

243. JINA HEAD
Kauśāmbī, Allahabad District, UP
9th century A.D.
Grey sandstone, .305 x .430 m.
AM 528 Fig. 200

Jina image of which only the head with chiselled oval features and snail shell curls with *uṣṇīṣa* is preserved. A *mālā-vidyādhara* is depicted on the right of the lotus halo.

244. HEADLESS JINA
Agra, Agra District, UP
9th century A.D.
Red sandstone, ht. .470 m.
AM 645

Headless Jina seated in *dhyānāsana*. The figure has a well-modelled youthful build with *Śrīvatsa* mark on the chest.

245. CATURVIMŚATI-PAṬṬA
Gurgi, Rewa District, MP
9th century A.D.
Red sandstone, .530 x .370 m.
AM 496 Fig. 201

A rare early Caturviṁśati-Jina-Paṭṭa with all Jinas standing except one probably representing Ṛṣabhanātha who is shown seated in *dhyānāsana*. A kneeling devotee is depicted in the right corner of the lowest row.

246. JAINA TUTELARY COUPLE
UP
10th century A.D.
Grey sandstone, .620 x .530 m.
AM 619 Fig. 202

The tutelary couple seated on elevated couches has each a child in the lap. The middle upper part of the stele with the presiding Jina figure is broken. The upper right corner bears a *vidyādhara* figure. The pedestal is carved with a group of seven similar male figures seated in *lalitāsana*.

247. SEATED AMBIKĀ
Kauśāmbī, Allahabad District, UP
7th century A.D.
Red sandstone, .390 x .250 m.
AM 861 Fig. 203

Ambikā seated on lion mount, hands and legs defaced. A dwarf male devotee stands on proper right. Of the seated presiding Jina only the locked feet are extant on the pedestal at the top centre.

248. GOMUKHA YAKṢA
Site not known
10th century A.D.
Buff sandstone, .375 x .250 m.
AM 1424 Fig. 204 A-B

Four-armed Gomukha Yakṣa (*śāsanadevatā* of Ādinātha) seated in *ardhaparyaṅkāsana*, holding lotus stalks in the upper pair of hands, while the lower right hand is held in *abhaya* and the lower left hand carries an abraded *kamaṇḍalu*. An identical figure of Gomukha Yakṣa is represented on the adjacent face. The god is shown as corpulent wearing a low crown, necklace, *yajñopavīta*, armlets and wristlets.

249. JAINA LINTEL
Site not known
10th century A.D.
Brownish sandstone, .590 x 1.51 m.
AM 1282 Fig. 205

Exquisitely finished lintel of a Jaina shrine showing three projecting niches roofed by Latina *śikharas*. The central niche has a seated figure of Ādinātha and the side niches bear figures of Pārśvanātha and Supārśvanātha. The intervening recess on the proper right shows seated Ambikā and that on the left shows Padmāvatī Yakṣī. The seated figures of Jinas and Yakṣīs are all flanked by a pair of standing Jinas. The upper space between the *śikharas* was also filled with two rows of seated Jinas of which only the lower row is preserved. The number of Jinas thus totalled twenty-four.

250. JAINA LINTEL
Site not known
10th century A.D.
Buff sandstone, .450 x 1.05 m.
AM 1380 Fig. 206

Ornate Jaina lintel with niches crowned by *Phāṁsanā* roof. Central niche has seated figure of Ādinātha, right niche has Pārśvanātha, left end broken. Ambikā Yakṣī is figured in the recess between the two preserved niches. The seated Jinas and Ambikā are flanked each by a pair of standing Jinas. The arched space between the two *Phāṁsanā* roofs is ornamented with seated Jinas, *vidyādharas* and floral motifs. The carvings are of a high quality. This lintel generally resembles the preceding one (AM 1282) in overall design.

251. JAINA LINTEL
Site not known
10th century A.D.
Greyish sandstone, .330 x .810 m.
AM 1181 Fig. 207

Lintel of a Jaina shrine showing two of the three niches containing seated Jina figures with an intervening recess occupied by a seated Jaina Yakṣī. All the seated figure are flanked on both sides by standing Jinas. On the upper part of the lintel occur four seated Jinas, two in niches.

252. JAINA ŚILĀPAṬṬA
Site not known
10th century A.D.
Red sandstone, .230 x .440 m.
AM 524 Fig. 208

Śilāpaṭṭa carved with 64 figures of seated Jinas in four rows. A *paṭṭa* with 64 Jinas is rare.

253. JINA-PAṬṬA
Site not known
10th century A.D.
Red sandstone, .285 x .370 m.
AM 618 Fig. 209

Jina-*paṭṭa* with 16 standing Jinas in two rows. The central figure in the lower row is Pārśvanātha. It is likely that the central figure in the upper row was Ādinātha, though details are obliterated.

254. SEATED ĀDINĀTHA
Site not known
10th century A.D.
Sandstone, .740 x .450 m.
AM 620 Fig. 210

Ādinātha, seated in meditation, recognized by the *lānchana* bull carved below seat and by his curls falling on both shoulders. The Jina is seated on lion pedestal which is flanked by tiny figures of Gomukha Yakṣa and Cakreśvari Yakṣī carved on recessed facets. The Jina is also attended by Indra and Upendra as *Caurī*-bearers, while the upper part of the stele bears the usual designs of pair of elephants and parasols flanked by *vidyādharas*,

255. JINA HEAD
Agra, Agra District, UP
10th century A.D.
Buff sandstone, ht. .210 m.
AM 744 Fig. 211

The curly hair with conspicuous *uṣṇīṣa* is modelled after the Buddha image.

256. JINA HEAD
Agra, Agra District, UP
10th century A.D.
Sandstone, ht. .220 m.
AM 354 Fig. 212

The head has a round face with half-closed meditative eyes and curly hair with *uṣṇīṣa.*

257. STANDING JINA
Bhita, Allahabad District, UP
10th century A.D.
Buff sandstone, .580 x .360 m.
AM 501

Part of a stele showing nude Jina standing in *kāyotsarga,* flanked on the left by either Indra or Upendra, wearing *kirīṭamukuṭa* and carrying *caurī.*

258. ĀDINĀTHA
Site not known
10th century A.D.
Grey sandstone, .415 x .580 m.
AM 1354 Fig. 213

Lower part (below navel) of inscribed image of Ādinātha seated on *triratha* pedestal. Bull cognizance and inscription on the lappet. Gomukha Yakṣa and Cakreśvari Yakṣī together with donor couple and a group of Aṣṭagrahas also carved on the pedestal.

259. SEATED ĀDINĀTHA
Gurgi, Rewa District, MP
11th century A.D.
Plum coloured sandstone, .600 x .390 m.
AM 621 Fig. 214

Seated Ādinātha flanked by Indra and Upendra below which are carved miniature figures of seated Jinas. Design of bull is carved as Jina's cognizance on the lion pedestal.

260. JINA CANDRAPRABHA
UP
11th century A.D.
Greyish sandstone, .603 x .407 m.
AM 92-159 Fig. 215

The seated Jina is flanked by Indra and Upendra. Seated as well as standing figures of Jinas are carved on the *parikara*, besides the usual motifs. The cresent cognizance is marked on the pedestal.

261. SEATED NEMINĀTHA
Site not known
11th century A.D.
Grey Sandstone, .610 x .390 m.
AM 633 Fig. 216

Figure of Neminātha seated in *dhyānāsana*, recognized by *śaṅkha* sign carved on the pedestal. The Jina is flanked by Indra and Upendra. The stele also shows six standing Jinas and two seated Jinas, besides the usual figures and motifs on the *parikara*.

262. PEDESTAL OF ĀDINĀTHA IMAGE
Site not known
11th century A.D.
Buff sandstone, .430 x .780 m.
AM 669 Fig. 217

Lion pedestal of an image of Jina Ādinātha, carved centrally with a *kīrttimukha*. A small figure of seated Gomukha Yakṣa appears on proper left end.

263. ĀDINĀTHA
Kauśāmbī, Allahabad District, UP
11th century A.D.
Greyish sandstone, .675 x .560 m.
AM 561 Fig. 218

Seated Ādinātha flanked on left by standing Pārśvanātha. Yakshī Cakreśvarī is carved below on the left end of the pedestal.

264. SEATED JINA
Site not known
11th century A.D.
Buff sandstone, .335 x .235 m.
AM 370 Fig. 219

A Jina seated in niche flanked by a pair of standing Jinas.

265. JINA MAHĀVĪRA
Gurgi, Rewa District, MP
11th century A.D.
Purple sandstone, 1.31 x .38 m.
AM 495 Fig. 220

Standing Jina Mahāvīra indicated by lion face resembling *kīrttimukha* carved on the pedestal. Five seated Jinas vertically depicted in a line on the right side of the *parikara*.

266. PĀRŚVANĀTHA
Site not known
11th century A.D.
Grey sandstone, .585 x .280 m.
AM 530 Fig. 221

Standing Pārśvanātha flanked by Indra and Upendra. A seated Jina is depicted on the lower right side.

267. PĀRŚVANĀTHA
Kauśāmbī, Allahabad District, UP
12th century A.D.
Purple sandstone, .590 x .317 m.
AM 527

Crude figure of standing Pārśvanātha flanked by Indra and Upendra and donor couple.

268. SARVATOBHADRA IMAGE OF JINA
Kauśāmbī, Allahabad District, UP
11th century A.D.
Greyish buff sandstone, .420 x .240 m.
AM 522 Fig. 222 A-B

A slab with a standing Jina on each of the four faces. Cognizance marks absent.

269. CORNER PIECE WITH TWO JINAS
Gurgi, Rewa District, MP
11th century A.D.
Plum coloured sandstone, .580 x .390 m.
AM 540 Fig. 223 A-B

Corner block with two Jina figures viz. Pārśvanātha and Supārśvanātha, standing in *daṇḍasana*. Elegant serpent coils form immediate background of the Jina figures. Both Jinas are flanked by Indra and Upendra, besides two seated figures of Jinas.

270. CORNER PIECE WITH TWO JINAS
Site not Known
11th century A.D.
Red sandstone, .585 x .480 m.
AM 538

Corner piece of architecture with standing figures of Pārśvanātha and Supārśvanātha on adjacent faces. This corner piece is practically a replica of the preceding one (AM 540).

271. STANDING ĀDINĀTHA
Gurgi, Rewa District, MP
12th century A.D.

Plum coloured sandstone, .129 x .430 m.
AM 504 Fig. 224

Standing Ādinātha (arms broken) recognized by bull cognizance on the pedestal. The Jina is flanked by Indra and Upendra and seated devotees. His head is flanked by *vidyādharas* carrying garland. Triple parasol depicted above the head. The recessed *parikara* on proper left is carved with Jina's devotees and decorative motifs.

272. STANDING JINA
Gurgi, Rewa District, MP
12th century A.D.
Pink sandstone, .110 x .350 m.
AM 502 Fig. 225

Standing Jina figure, portion below thighs missing. The upper part of the stele shows parasol lustrated by elephants. Flying *vidyādharas* flank both sides of Jina's head.

273. STANDING NEMINĀTHA
Gurgi, Rewa District, MP
12th century A.D.
Pink sandstone, .129 x .390 m.
AM 536 Fig. 226

Standing figure of Jina Neminātha indicated by *śaṅkha* cognizance carved on the lion pedestal. Jina's head is disproportionately large and all subsidiary figures are poorly carved.

274. UPPER PART OF JINA IMAGE
Site not known
12th century A.D.
Buff sandstone, .400 x .560 m.
AM 542

Upper part of stele showing Jina's head flanked by *vidyādhara* couple and embellished with motifs of parasol, elephants and heavenly musicians.

275. JINA HEAD
Kara, Allahabad District, UP
13th century A.D.
Sandstone, ht. .310 m.
AM 351 Fig. 227

The head has highly stylized features.

276. JINA HEAD
Site not known
12th century A.D.
Greyish sandstone, .230 x .190 m.
AM 360

Squat head with petrified expression.

277. JINA HEAD
Site not known
12th century A.D.
Greyish sandstone, .268 x .215 m.
AM 601 Fig. 228

Head with highly stylized features.

278. STANDING JINA
Gaya, Gaya District, Bihar,
12th century A.D.
Black schist, .495 x .342 m.
AM 543 Fig. 229

Lower part (knees downwards) of a standing Jina flanked by Indra and Upendra. The pedestal bears an inscription saying that the slab containing a Tritīrthī of Ariṣṭanemi, Pārśvanātha and Vardhamāna was set up in (VS) 1234.

279. MĀNASTAMBHA FRAGMENT
Site not known
11th century A.D.
Light red sandstone, .290 x .245 m.
AM 1170

Upper part of Mānastambha with two worn out rows of Jina figures. The central Jina figure in the top row is seated in *dhyānamudrā*.

MISCELLANEOUS FIGURES INCLUDING SECULAR MALES

280. MALE HEAD
Mathura, Mathura District, UP
2nd century A.D.
Spotted red sandstone, .110 x .065 m.
AM 86 Fig. 230 A-B

Turbaned male head of Mathura Kuṣāṇa style.

281. MALE HEAD
Mathura, Mathura District, UP
3rd century A.D.
Spotted red sandstone .095 x .076 m.
AM 1069 Fig. 231

Male head with tight-fitting cap.

282. MALE HEAD
Kauśāmbī, Allahabad District, UP
4th century A.D.
Pale buff sandstone, .230 x .215 m.
AM 859 Fig. 232

Nose and lips damaged. Curls are disposed in symmetrically wavy lines with a central parting.

283. MALE HEAD
Site not known
6th century A.D.
Greyish sandstone, .190 x .165 m.
AM 389 Fig. 233

Male head wearing tight-fitting headdress.

284. HEAD WITH PEAKED CAP
Site not known
6th century A.D.
Greyish sandstone, .190 x .111 m.
AM 588 Fig. 234

Head of jester (?) wearing peaked cap.

285. MALE HEAD
Site not known
6th century A.D.
Greyish sandstone, .240 x .134 m.
AM 318 Fig. 235

Male bust with round face and wig-shaped curls, torque with a pendant and *urabandha* with a central knot.

286. GROTESQUE HEAD
Kauśāmbī, Allahabad Diṣtt., UP
7th century A.D.
Pale buff sandstone, ht. .215 m.
AM 986 Fig. 236

Grotesque head with grizzly hair, goggle eyes and knit eyebrows, carrying foot of a female figure. This may be either Yakṣa's head or Śiva-gaṇa's head (carrying Pārvatī's foot).

287. BEARDED HEAD
Site not known
9th century A.D.
Buff Sandstone, .205 x .160 m.
AM 346 Fig. 237

Bearded head wearing a close-fitting cap of Iranian type.

288. MALE HEAD
Site not known
10th century A.D.
Greyish sandstone, .165 x .115 m.
AM 1108 Fig. 238

Male head with snail-shell curls, staring eyes and smiling expression.

289. UNIDENTIFIED SCENE
Site not known
9th century A.D.
Greyish sandstone, .485 x .815 m.
AM 1159 Fig. 239

Much worn out scene showing a standing male on proper right and a couple walking away on left with a female figure crouching to a standing female in the middle. This may perhaps depict some story.

290. AMOROUS COUPLE
Site not known
10th century A.D.
Buff sandstone, .500 x .250 m.
AM 1118 Fig. 240

Amorous couple standing in *tribhaṅga* in *āliṅganamudrā*. The male is bearded: the female wears a *dhammilla* coiffure and holds *līlākamala* in typical Khajuraho style.

291. HEAD WITH CONICAL CAP
Kara, Allahabad District, UP
10th century A.D.
Pink sandstone, ht. .375 m.
AM 107 Fig. 241

Bearded head wearing a conical cap, forming part of a large damaged stele. It may represent Piṅgala, Sūrya's attendant.

292. EROTIC COUPLE
Khajuraho, Chhatarpur District, MP
10th century A.D.
Buff sandstone, .570 x .280 m.
AM 92.158 Fig. 242

A Digambara *Kṣapaṇaka* having *paśubandha* intercourse with a female. The *Kṣapaṇaka* holds a *rajoharaṇa* in his armpit.

293. DONKEY COOPULATTING WITH HUMAN FEMALE
Site not known
10th century A.D.
Greyish red sandstone, .420 x .350 m.
AM 1165 Fig. 243

Inscribed slab carved with a donkey coopulating with a human female. The long inscription starts with *Mahārājādhirāja Someśvara* engraved in the 10th century script.

294. AMOROUS COUPLE
Khajuraho, Chhatarpur District, MP
10th century A.D.
Buff sandstone, .490 x .290 m.
AM 4738 Fig. 244

Couple standing in *tribhaṅga*, embracing each other. The right hand of the male is in *kaṭi* while the female holds a lotus bud in her left hand. This figure is a typical specimen of 10th century Khajuraho art.

295. LOVING MITHUNAS
Site not known
11th century A.D.
Grey sandstone, .350 x .700 m.
AM 1404 Fig. 245

Slab showing five loving couples in projecting and recessed niches.

296. BATTLE FRIEZE
Site not known
11th century A.D.
Sandstone, .300 x 1.150 m.
AM 694

Battle scene depicting some foot soldiers, a horse-rider and an elephant.

297. BUST OF MALE DIGNITARY
MP
11th century A.D.
Sandstone, .330 x .190 m.
AM 1209 Fig. 246

This bust from Central India shows a male dignitary or even a prince. The figure with conspicuous beard and moustaches has an impressive bearing with an officious tilt. He wears torque and *hāra,* while *kaustubha-maṇi* among his ornaments is a hallmark of medieval Central Indian art.

298. BUST OF MALE FIGURE
Site not known
12th century A.D.
Buff sandstone, .270 x .190 m.
AM 1210 Fig. 247

Bust of moustached and bearded male figure with smiling expression. The figure wears *karṇakuṇḍalas,* torque and a pearl necklace.

299. BEARDED HEAD
Site not known
12th century A.D.
Buff sandstone, .203 x .180 m.
AM 309 Fig. 248

Bearded head of a Śaiva ascetic wearing *jaṭājūṭa.*

300. BEARDED HEAD
Site not known
13th century A.D.
Sandstone, .300 x .265 m.
AM 1315

Bearded head of probably a dignitary.

SECULAR FEMALES

301. FEMALE HEAD
Mathura, Mathura District, UP
2nd-3rd century A.D.
Red spotted sandstone, ht. .130 m.
AM 76 Fig. 249

Smiling female head with wide open eyes. She wears a close-fitting headdress familiar from the Kushāṇa art of Mathura.

302. FEMALE HEAD
Mathura, Mathura District, UP
2nd centuries A.D.
Spotted red sandstone, ht. .120 m.
AM 78 Fig. 250 A-B

Female head of typical Mathura Kusāṇa style.

303. FEMALE HEAD
Mathura, Mathura District, UP
2nd century A.D.
Spotted red sandstone, .290 x .310 m.
AM 113 Fig. 251

Female head on a railing fragment.

304. FEMALE HEAD
Kauśāmbī, Allahabad District, UP
4th century A.D.
Greyish sandstone, .200 x .250 m.
AM 852 Fig. 252

Female head wearing a circular ornament on the *sīmanta* and heavy ear-ornaments.

305. FEMALE HEAD
Kauśāmbī, Allahabad District, UP
4th century A.D.
Sandstone, ht. .230 m.
AM 480 Fig. 253

Beautifully modelled female head with wide-open eyes and minute snail curls parted in the middle.

306. FEMALE HEAD
Mathura, Mathura District, UP
6th century A.D.
Spotted red sandstone, .120 x .130 m.
AM 87

Female head detached from a large figural stele.

307. FEMALE TORSO
Site not known
6th century A.D.
Buff sandstone, .292 x .165 m.
AM 742 Fig. 254

Sensitively modelled female torso with close-set full breasts, thin waist and broad hips, draped in a lower garment which is notable for its multiple series of delicate folds. She wears armlets and *hāra* with a *lalantikā* which forms a loop at the waist.

308. FEMALE HEAD
Site not known
7th century A.D.
Greyish sandstone, .133 x .133 m.
AM 907 Fig. 255

Female head wearing *dhammilla* coiffure.

309. FEMALE TORSO
Site not known
7th century A.D.
Sandstone, .390 x .250 m.
AM 350 Fig. 256

Female (head lost) standing *en face*, wearing *ekāvalī*, armlets, wristlets and *mekhalā* of two strands which secures her lower garment. She has close-set round breasts and thin waist with *trivalī* marked on her belly. A scarf winds round her arms and she holds in her hands fluttering ends of the scarf.

310. FEMALE HEAD
Jhusi, Allahabad District, UP
8th century A.D.
Buff sandstone, .230 x .165 m.
AM 468 Fig. 257

Beautifully chiselled circular female head with smiling expression, sporting *cakra*-shaped *dhammilla.* curls are delineated by fine lines and their central parting is embellished with a jewelled ornament.

311. FEMALE BUST
Jasra, Allahabad District, UP
8th century A.D.
Sandstone, .200 x .110 m.
AM 472

Smiling head with a floriate ornament centrally adorning her cascading curls. Portion below head mutilated.

312. FEMALE HEAD
UP
6th century A.D.
Buff sandstone, ht. .290 m.
AM 1212 Fig. 258

Female head with damaged oval face and bun-shaped chignon behind, with two tiers of curly locks in front.

313. FEMALE TORSO
Jhusi, Allahabad District, UP
9th century A.D.
Pink sandstone, .280 x .210 m.
AM 882 Fig. 259

Delicately modelled female torso with curls falling on shoulders. She wears torque, necklace and armlet. The necklace is placed between her close-set globular breasts.

314. FEMALE HEAD
Sirsa, Allahabad District, UP
9th century A.D.
Sandstone, ht. .250 m.
AM 379 Fig. 260

Female head with a beautiful oval face, donning a circular *jaṭājūṭa*.

315. FEMALE BUST
Site not known
9th century A.D.
Buff sandstone, ht. .200 m.
AM 985 Fig. 261

She has close-set globular breasts and wears *kuṇḍalas* and torque. Her headdress shows a central circular ornament.

316. FEMALE HEAD
Soraon, Allahabad District, UP
9th century A.D.
Sandstone, ht. .280 m.
AM 821 Fig. 262

Female head wearing a luxuriously ornamented *dhammilla* headdress with triple pearl pendants in the central parting. The arch of the *dhammilla* is formed of spirally twisted strands of pearls.

317. FEMALE BUST
Site not known
9th century A.D.
Sandstone, ht. .100 m.
AM 469 Fig. 263

Female bust wearing *dhammilla* coiffure, *kuṇḍalas* and torque. She holds a mutilated object in her upraised left hand.

318. FEMALE BUST
Bhita, Allahabad District, UP
9th century A.D.
Buff sandstone, .230 x .250 m.
AM 269 Fig. 264

Female bust with background carved with scrolls resembling peacock plumes.

319. FEMALE STANDING
UP
10th century A.D.
Buff sandstone, .730 x .130 m.
AM 817

Apsarā (head missing) standing in elegant *ābhaṅga* holding scarf in the pendant left hand, right hand broken.

320. FEMALE TORSO
UP
10th century A.D.
Buff sandstone, .380 x .170 m.
AM 1283 Fig. 265

Graceful female torso with left hand placed on *kaṭi*.

321. FEMALE BUST
Site not known
10th century A.D.
Sandstone, ht. .360 m.
AM 271

Female bust wearing *dhammilla* coiffure, torques and *hāra*. Badly mutilated.

322. FEMALE TORSO
MP
10th century A.D.
Buff sandstone, .420 x .210 m.
AM 1317

323. FEMALE BUST
MP
10th century A.D.
Sandstone, ht. 480 m.
AM 275 Fig. 266

Bust of female with handsome oval face wearing *dhammilla* coiffure, *kuṇḍalas*, torques with *lalantikā* and necklace winding over her globular breasts. She has a coquetish tilt of head.

324. FEMALE STANDING
Lacchagir, Allahabad District, UP
10th century A.D.
Buff sandstone, ht. .550 m.
AM 400 Fig. 267

Female standing in *tribhaṅga,* hands and feet broken.

325. FEMALE TORSO
Site not known
10th century A.D.
Buff sandstone, .293 x .203 m.
AM 710 Fig. 268

Female torso standing in *tribhaṅga* and wearing profuse jewellery including torque with *lalantikā*, *stanahāra* and *keyūras* and draped in a lower garment, fastened by *ratnamekhalā* with jewelled pendant loops and tassels.

326. FEMALE BUST
Site not known
10th century A.D.
Buff sandstone, .165 x .122 m.
AM 493 Fig. 269

Female bust wearing *dhammilla* coiffure and torque.

ARCHITECTURAL MEMBERS

327. RAILING POST
Bhita, Allahabad District, Up
1st century B.C.
Grey sandstone, .490 x .170 m.
AM 814 Fig. 270

Railing post (*vedikā*) of square design carved with one full and two half lotuses with intervening plain fluted sections. Atop the post is a tenon meant to receive a coping stone.

328. RAILING FRAGMENT
2nd century A.D.
Buff sandstone, .275 x .345 m.
AM 122

Fragment of railing (*vedikā*) complete with heavy base and a pair of pillars and cross-bars. The carvings are confined to the square sections of the pillars, showing lotus and floral designs.

329. LOTUS ON SŪCĪ
Mathura, Mathura District, UP
2nd century A.D.
Cream buff sandstone, .255 x .370 m.
AM 123 Fig. 271

Beautifully carved lotus on a *sūcī* (cross-bar) of a railing.

330. PILLAR FRAGMENT
Sarnath, Varanasi District, UP
5th century A.D.
Buff sandstone, diam. .170 m, ht. .610 m.
AM 217

Circular pillar fragment with an octagonal band carved with scrolls of typical Gupta design. The pillar fragment is crowned by lotus motif.

331. PILLAR BASE
Bhumara, Satna District, MP
5th century A.D.
Red sandstone, .380 x .220 m.
AM 729

Pillar base of square shape with a luxuriously ornamented *ghaṭapallava* design.

332. PILLAR FRAGMENT
Bhumara, Satna District, MP
5th century A.D.
Red sandstone, .410 x .230 m.
AM 813 Fig. 272

Pillar or pilaster fragment with two squarish sections ornamented respectively with a half lotus and a *kīrttimukha* spewing pearl chain (*muktāgrāsà*), intervened by a plain octagonal section.

333. PILLAR BASE
Bhumara, Satna District, MP
5th century A.D.
Red sandstone, .450 x .210 m.
AM 604 Fig. 273

Pillar base with plain square sections below and four ornate circular zones above. From bottom these comprise a globular *āmalaka*-like cushion, a jewelled cable design, a circular abacus carved with paralled wavy design with fan-like attachments and a plain fluted globe, partly preserved.

334. ARCHITECTURAL FRAGMENT
Bhumara, Satna District, MP
5th century A.D.
Red sandstone, .355 x .318 m
AM 776 Fig. 274

Architectural fragment with a *candraśālā* carved with a full blown lotus flower.

335. ARCHITECTURAL FRAGMENT
Bhumara, Satna District, MP
5th century A.D.
Red sandstone, .360 x .333 m.
AM 775

Architectural fragment showing a complete *candraśālā* carved with lotus design.

336. CANDRAŚĀLĀ WITH HEAD
Bhumara, Satna District, MP
5th century A.D.
Red sandstone, .340 x .280 m.
AM 348 Fig. 275

Candraśālā fragment inset with head with snail curls, typical of the Gupta period.

337. DOORWAY FRAGMENT
Bhumara, Satna District, MP
5th century A.D.
Red sandstone, .395 x .460 m.
AM 697

Doorway fragment with four surviving *śākhās* respectively carved with datepalm motif, jewelled garland and two varieties of scrolls.

338. SIṀHAMUKHA-PRAṆĀLA
Bhita, Allahabad District, UP
6th century A.D.
Greyish sandstone, .258 x .185 m.
AM 387

339. YAKṢĪ ON PRAṆĀLA
Site not known
7th century A.D.
Greyish sandstone, .350 x .200 m.
AM 91-1916 Fig. 277

Corpulent Yakṣī with a pot belly associated with *praṇāla* (gargoyle). The Yakṣī has a pensive countenance and wears ear-rings, *ekāvalī* and *stana-hāra*.

340. SIṀHA-MUKHA PRAṆĀLA
Site not known
8th century A.D.
Deep red sandstone, .215 x .195 (Lion face only)
AM 1416 Fig. 278 A-B

Praṇāla with lion-face at the discharge end.

341. PILLAR CAPITAL
Site not known
7th century A.D.
Buff sandstone, .325 x .175 m.
AM 1188 Fig. 279

Fragment of an ornate pillar capital carved with circular zones terminating with *āmalaka*-shaped vase supporting a square block adorned with an exquisitely carved *kīrttimukha*. A similar pillar is known from the late Gupta site of Piparia, District Satna, MP. (J.G. Williams, *The Art of Gupta India*, New Delhi, 1983, fig. 176).

342. PILLAR
UP
7th century A.D.
Sandstone, .960 x .210 m.
AM 1268

Pillar of square section with late Gupta motifs of *kīrttimukha*, *ghaṭapallava* and scrolls on the capital and luxuriant *ghaṭapallava* at the base.

343. ŚUKANĀSA WITH HEAD
Rewa, Rewa District, MP
8th century A.D.
Red sandstone, .450 x .650 m.
AM 553 Fig. 280

Śukanāsa fragment of a shrine with the medallion containing head of a deity, flanked by worshipful *vidyādharas*.

344. ARCHITECTURAL FRAGMENT
Site not known
8th century A.D.
Buff sandstone, .380 x .300 m.
AM 1355

Architectural piece of *Latina śikhara* top carved with a female head.

345. BASE OF DOOR-JAMB
UP
9th century A.D.
Red sandstone, .430 x .190 m.
Am 1327 Fig. 281

Base of door-jamb of a Śaiva shrine showing a river-goddess with attendant, flanked by Mahākāla, a *pratihāra* of Śiva.

346. GAṄGĀ ON DOORJAMB
UP
9th century A.D.
Buff sandstone, .555 x .320 m.
AM 1180 Fig. 282

Base of door-jamb (*pedyā*) carved with a beautiful figure of Gaṅgā standing in elegant *tribhaṅga* followed by an umbrella-bearer and a divine headless *pratihāra*. Gaṅgā's face is chipped off. She is shown standing on a pedestal carved with a beautiful well-preserved *makara* (her *vāhana*) with scroll tails.

347. GAṄGĀ AND ŚAIVA PRATIHĀRA
Site not known
9th century A.D.
Grey sandstone, .500 x .290 m.
AM 1163

Door-jamb showing Gaṅgā and Śaiva pratihāra (Nandī).

348. YAMUNĀ AND MAHĀKĀLA
Site not known
10th century A.D.
Grey sandstone, .490 x .255 m.
AM 914 Fig. 283

Yamunā and Mahākāla carved below the *triśākha* door-jamb of a Śaiva shrine.

349. JAMB WITH GAṄGĀ
Site not known
11th century A.D.
Light red sandstone, .650 x .230 m.
AM 1405

Jamb of a Śaiva shrine showing at the base Gaṅgā flanked by Mahākāla.

350. RIVER-GODDESS ON JAMB
Manikpur, Allahabad District, UP
10th century A.D.
Buff sandstone, .925 x .235 m.
AM 441 Fig. 284

Rūpaśākhā of a fragmentary doorway carved with two standing Śaiva figures. The *pedyā* at the base bears the figures of river-goddess and a flanking Śaiva *pratihāra*.

351. DOOR-SILL FRAGMENT
Site not known
9th century A.D.
Grey sandstone, .220 x .770 m.
AM 1166 Fig. 285

Doorsill, right end, showing a pair of *Udadhi-kumāras* riding *makaras* with luxurious scroll tails, and a niched figure of Kubera flanked by attendants and two pairs of dancers and musicians in niches.

352. DOOR-SILL
Site not known
9th century A.D.
Greyish sandstone, .110 x .730 m.
A 1331 Fig. 286

Door-sill fragment of a temple carved with designs of *kīrttimukha*, elephant and lion, the last at the extremity.

353. DOOR-SILL
Site not known
10th century A.D.
Light red sandstone, .280 x .1.270 m.
AM 748 Fig. 287

Door-sill of shrine carved centrally with scene of dance and music flanked by *Udadhi-kumāra* pairs and terminated by lion pouncing on elephant at the ends.

354. DOOR-SILL
Site not known
12th century A.D.
Greyish black sandstone, .395 x 1.725 m.
AM 1153 Fig. 288

The door-sill is adorned with lotus stalks in the central projection flanked by elephant figures and with recumbent lions at the ends.

355. DOOR-LINTEL WITH MĀTṚKĀS
Site not known
9th century A.D.
Buff sandstone, .280 x .530 m.
AM 258 Fig. 289

Side fragment of the door-lintel of a shrine carved with a beautiful figure of *śālabhañjikā*, flanked by rearing *vyālas*, at the proper left end. The lintel has three horizontal registers, respectively adorned with scrolls, *vyāla* heads and three (of the seven) seated *Mātṛkās* with Gaṇeśa at the terminal end.

356. LINTEL OF VIṢṆU SHRINE
UP
10th century A.D.
Greyish buff sandstone, .320 x 1.06 m.
AM 1273 Fig. 290

Lintel of a Viṣṇu shrine carved with projecting figures of Brahmā, Viṣṇu and Śiva (head missing) and Navagrahas in the recesses.

357. LINTEL FRAGMENT
Site not known
10th century A.D.
Buff sandstone, .520 x .910 m.
AM 1361 Fig. 291

Lintel fragment of a Viṣṇu shrine showing standing Viṣṇu, flanked by female attendants on *lalāṭa* and Navagrahas in recesses.

358. VAIṢṆAVA LINTEL
Site not known
11th century A.D.
Buff sandstone, .285 x 1.02 m.
AM 1175 Fig. 292

Lintel of Vaiṣṇava shrine showing seated Viṣṇu on *lalāṭa* and Brahmā and Śiva at ends. In between are depicted standing Navagrahas in the recesses.

359. LINTEL SHOWING PĀRŚVANĀTHA
Gurgi, Rewa District, MP
10th century A.D.
Red sandstone, .250 x 1.650 m.
AM 288 Fig. 293

Jina Pārśvanātha, seated in *dhyāna*, is shown as the *lalāṭa-bimba* of the lintel carved with stencilled scroll design.

360. MINIATURE SHRINE
Hissar, Hissar District, Haryana
10th century A.D.
Sandstone, .380 x .390 m.
AM 876 Fig. 294

Miniature shrine (probably upper part of an image stele) showing a two-armed seated deity carrying axe in the left-hand in the middle niche, flanked by attendants in side niches. The shrine with a fine model of *Latina śikhara* takes off from a *makara-toraṇa*.

361. GANDHARVA MUSICIANS
site not known
10th century A.D.
Greyish buff sandstone, ht. .225 to .235 m.
AM 1101 Fig. 295

Arched top of the same or two identical image stelae, carved with flying *gandharva* musicians.

362. PILLAR FRAGMENT
Site not known
10th century A.D.
Light red sandstone, .800 x .240 m.
AM 752 Fig. 296

Octagonal pillar fragment carved with *ghaṭapallava*, *kīrttimukha* and scrolls.

363. NĀGĪ ON PILLAR
Site not known
10th century A.D.
Red sandstone, .385 x .205 m.
AM 1398 Fig. 297

Ghaṭapallava pillar fragment carved with figure of Nāgī

(only head intact) on the lower part.

364. PILLAR FRAGMENT
Site not known
11th century A.D.
Greyish sandstone, .945 x .413 m.
AM 781 Fig. 298

Fragment of medieval pillar with three ornate zones carved with a large *ghaṭapallava*, niched deities and foliate diamond design.

365. PILLAR FRAGMENT
Site not known
11th century A.D.
Buff sandstone, .420 x .540 m. (dia.)
AM 1082

Fragment of a circular pillar carved with a row of *kīrttimukhas* spewing chain-and-bell (a typical medieval motif).

366. EROTIC PANEL
Site not known
11th century A.D.
Buff sandstone, .240 x .80 m,.
AM 1353 Fig. 299

Bevelled horizontal architectural piece bearing a group of erotic pairs preparing possibly for *rati-cakra*.

367. TEACHER AND DISCIPLE
Site not known
11th century A.D.
Light red sandstone, .280 x .380 m.
AM 400 Fig. 300

Slab with four-armed god in *yogāsana* in projected niche and a bearded teacher and disciple in recess. The teacher and disciple are seated unusually close to each other.

368. MAKARA AND GLADIATOR
Khajuraho, Chhatarpur District, MP
11th century A.D.
Greyish red sandstone, .375 x .280 m.
AM 357 Fig. 301

Right end of *makara-toraṇa* marked by a gladiator.

369. MAKARA AND GLADIATOR
Khajuraho, Chhatarpur District, MP
11th century A.D.
Greyish Sandstone, .380 x .310 m.
AM 358 Fig. 302

370. KUMĀRA-BRACKET
Site not known
10th century A.D.
Grey sandstone, .330 x .310 m.
A 1377 Fig. 303

371. KUMĀRA-BRACKET
Site not known
10th century A.D.
Red sandstone, .315 x .635
AM 1346 Fig. 304

A complex type of bracket with a two-armed *kumāra* seated between a pair of load-bearing four-armed *kumāras* (Atlantaen figures).

372. KUMĀRA-BRACKET
Provenance unknown
10th century A.D.
Buff sandstone, .240 x .170 m.
AM 1290

373. BRACKET WITH ANIMAL-HEADED GODS
Site not known
12th century A.D.
Greyish black sandstone, .410 x 1.05 m.
AM 1144 Fig. 305 A-C

Bracket with four-armed animal-headed gods (Gaṇeśa, Hanumān, Nṛsiṁha and Nṛvarāha) on the four sides and adoring *nāgas* in the corners. Gaṇeśa appears on the east.

374. GROTESQUE BRACKET-FIGURE
Bhita, Allahabad District, UP
12th century A.D.
Red sandstone, length .350 m.
AM 944 Fig. 306

A rare type of grotesque bracket figure resembling an old man (*Yakṣa ?*) carrying on the back a female figure seated facing the back of the man. Of the female rider only the right foreleg and foot adorned with anklet, tenderly supported on the left palm of the man, has survived.

375. ORNATE ĀMALASĀRAKA
Site not known
12th century A.D.
Grey sandstone, .30 x Dia. 1.05 m.
AM 1152 Fig. 307

Crowning *āmalasāraka* of a Nāgara temple carved with four large faces sporting *jaṭājūṭa* and four smaller seated figures of female devotees, seated in meditation, each holding *akṣamālā* in the left hand.

MEMORIAL PILLARS

376. MEMORIAL PILLAR WITH KṚṢṆALĪLĀ SCENES
Site not known
13th century A.D.
Buff sandstone, .870 x .225 m.
AM 1390 Fig. 308 A-D

Memorial pillar of square section, complete with base and crown, carved with Kṛṣṇalīlā scenes on all the four faces. Of the seven compartments on each face, the lowest bears figure of a cow symbolically representing Gokula and the top one shows three roundels whose significance is not clear. The remaining five compartments bear mostly Kṛṣṇalīla scenes, such as transport of infant Kṛṣṇa across the Yamunā (depicted in two adjacent compartments), theft of butter, Yamalārjuna, Śakaṭabhaṅga, Pūtanā-vadha and killing of bull-demon, horse-demon, storm-demon and the elephant Kuvalayāpīḍa, etc.

377. MEMORIAL PILLAR WITH KṚṢṆALĪLĀ SCENES
Site not known
13th century A.D.
Buff sandstone, .970 x .270 m.
AM 1275. Fig. 309 A-D

Memorial pillar carved on all four faces with scenes mostly pertaining to Kṛṣṇalīlā myths. From the base upwards four compartments are fully preserved together with a portion of the fifth. Upper part is broken. The lowest compartment shows on all faces a cow standing, representing Gokula. Other compartments depict scenes of Yamalārjuna, Govardhana-dhāraṇa, Pūtanā-vadha, Vatsāsura-vadha and Kuvalayāpīḍa-vadha, etc.

378. MEMORIAL PILLAR FRAGMENT
Site not known
13th century A.D.
Buff sandstone, .410 x .170 m.
AM 1233 Fig. 310 A-D

Upper part of a momorial pillar carved on all four faces. Besides the crowning *cūlā* (finial), only two upper compartments are fully preserved and a portion of the third which depicts a river (probably Yamunā). The top compartment invariably shows three globular lumps whose exact significance is not known. The figures in the second compartment are different in the four faces and depict a reclining female, a standing female, a seated male (ascetic ?) and a briskly walking male, all crudely executed.

ANIMALS

379. HORSE'S HEAD
Bharhut, Satna District, MP
2nd century B.C.
Red sandstone, .190 x .153 m.
AM 5 Fig. 311

380. FISH-TAILED MAKARA
Site not known
1st century B.C.
Light red sandstone, .140 x .255 m.
AM 854 Fig. 312

Fish-tailed *makara* carved in a medallion on the cross-bar (*sūcī*) of a railing (*vedikā*). A typical Śuṅga design also known from Kauśāmbī (Ref. Pramod Chandra's *Catalogue*, Pl. XXXI, No. 76).

381. COW WITH CALF
Mathura, Mathura District, UP
2nd century A.D.
Sandstone, .130 x .08 m
AM 81 Fig. 313

Mother cow tenderly licking while suckling her calf. The artist has ably depicted the sentiment of maternal affection in the animal kingdom.

382. OWL FAMILY
Site not known
8th century A.D.
Pink sandstone, .350 x .170 m.
AM 404 Fig. 314

Architectural fragment depicting a family of owls.

383. NANDĪ
Garhwa, Allahabad District, UP
9th century A.D.
Greyish sandstone, .342 x .431 m.
AM 704 Fig. 315

Recumbent Nandī (Śiva's *vāhana*) adorned with chain round the neck. The animal bears an expression of quiet dignity.

384. ELEPHANT
Site not known
10th century A.D.
Light red sandstone, .280 x .480 m.
AM 1418 Fig. 316

385. HORSE'S HEAD
Mathura, Mathura District, UP
10th century A.D.
Red sandstone, ht. .150 m.
AM 609

386. LION'S HEAD

Site not known
10th century A.D.
Red sandstone, ht. .280 m.
AM 4476 Fig. 157

This powerful portrayal represents head of a lion with prominent whiskers and tufts of hair on the crown.

387. SIṀHA-VYĀLA
Khajuraho, Chhatarpur District, MP
10th century A.D.
Greyish red sandstone, .380 x .180 m.
AM 247 Fig. 318

Lion-headed *vyāla* with a warrior counterplayer below.

388. SIṀHA-VYĀLA
Site not known
10th century A.D.
Grey sandstone, .400 x .290 m.
AM 1392

Damaged *Siṁha-vyāla* with a rider.

389. SIṀHA-VYĀLA
UP
10th century A.D.
Red sandstone, ht. .200 m.
AM 868 Fig. 319

390. SIṀHA-VYĀLA
Site not known
11th century A.D.
Red sandstone, ht. .630 m.
AM 629

391. GAJA VYĀLA
Khajuraho, Chhatarpur District, MP
11th century A.D.
Buff sandstone, .470 x .150 m.
AM 249 Fig. 320

A typical rearing *gaja-vyāla* with a warrior counterplayer below.

392. GAJA-VYĀLA
Khajuraho, Chhatarpur District, MP
11th century A.D.
Greyish red sandstone, .548 x .215 m.
AM 408

Gaja-vyāla with rider and warrior counterplayer.

393. AŚVA-VYĀLA
Khajuraho, Chhatarpur District, MP
11th century A.D.
Greyish red sandstone, .405 x .165 m.
AM 246 Fig. 321

Aśva-vyāla (horse headed) *vyāla* (muzzle damaged) with a warrior counterplayer.

394. GAJĀKRĀNTA-SIṀHA
Provenance unknown
11th century A.D.
Red sandstone, .345 x .470 m.
AM 1417 Fig. 322

This is a favourite medieval motif depicted on such architectural members as the *Śukanāsa* and the door-sill.

395. WINGED LION
Provenance unknown
11th century A.D.
Greyish red sandstone, 1.06 x .950 m.
AM. 1149

Crouching winged lion of a large size. Head and forepart damaged. Manes shown over the neck.

396. NANDĪ
Provenance unknown
11th century A.D.
Greyish brown sandstone, .590 x 1.03 m.
AM 1148

Recumbent Nandī bull, adorned with straps lined with jingle-bells around the back. A dwarf *gaṇa* attendant depicted below the muzzle of the bull.

MINIATURE SHRINE

397. MINIATURE SHRINE
UP
10th century A.D.
Buff sandstone, .910 x .360
AM 1077 Fig. 323

Miniature *triratha* shrine with a *Latina śikhara* and a *jaṅghā* niche on three sides containing standing figures of Pārvatī, Sūrya and Gaṇeśa. The sanctum is empty.

Though this shrine is included in Pramod Chandra's *Catalogue* (p. 171, No. 503, Pl.CLXXIII), We illustrate here the front face of the shrine showing figure of Daṇḍapāṇi in the *śukanāsa* medallion. For further details of Daṇḍapāṇi figures see notes under this Catalogue Nos. 187 (AM 905) and 188 (AM 663).

GLOSSARY

abhaya mudrā — A gesture granting freedom from fear, with hand raised, palm forward, fingers pointing upward.

akṣamālā — A rosary.

āliṅganamūrti — An iconographical form in which a god is shown accompanied by his consort, whom he generally embraces.

āmalaka — See *āmalasāraka*.

āmalasāraka — A grooved disc crowning the superstructure of a North Indian temple.

añjali mudrā — A gesture of worship consisting of palms joined to each other near the chest.

apsarā — See *surasundarī*.

ardhaparyaṅkāsana — A seated posture in which one leg is drawn up on the seat, the other, with knee bent, resting on the ground.

Aṣṭagraha — A group of planetary Divinities, similar to the Navagraha, except that Ketu is generally omitted.

āyudha — A weapon, an attribute.

āyudhapuruṣa — A personification of a Deity's weapon or attribute.

bāhyaśākhā — The outermost molding of a doorway surround.

bhadra — The central projection of a temple wall.

bhāravāhaka — An atlantes figure.

bhūmisparśa mudrā — A gesture of the hand touching the earth, by which, generally, the seated Buddha calls the Earth Goddess to witness his triumph over Māra (temptations).

cakra — A wheel, discus.

candraśālā — An arched ornamental motif, with a cavity in the centre, generally filled with figural sculpture or decorative motif.

caturviṁśati paṭṭa — A relief sculpture with the representation of twenty-four divinities, usually the twenty-four Tīrthaṅkaras.

channavīra — An ornament consisting of two strands which cross on the torso and pass one over each shoulder.

chatra — A parasol.

ḍamaru — A small double-headed drum shaped like an hour glass.

dhammilla — A style of coiffure in which the hair is swept into a circular chignon on the top of the head.

dharmacakra mudrā — Abbreviated from *dharmacakra-pravartana mudrā*. A gesture signifying the turning of the wheel of the law, the palms face forward, held close to each other near the chest. In the Buddhist context the gesture is primarily associated with the Buddha preaching the first sermon at Sarnath.

dhotī — A modern apparel consisting of a piece of cloth wrapped around the waist and the legs; the term is also used for designating the lower garment worn in ancient times.

dhyāna mudrā — A gesture of meditation in which the hands are relaxed in the lap, one above the other, with the palms turned upward.

dikpāla — A regent of either one of the four cardinal or four intermediate directions of space.

dvārapāla — A door guardian.

ekāvalī — A necklace consisting of a single strand of pearls or beads often with an oblong spacer in the centre.

gadā — A mace; a weapon commonly carried by Viṣṇu.

gajākrānta-siṁha — An ornamental motif showing an elephant attacked by a lion or a *vyāla*.

gaja-vyāla — A *vyāla* with the head of an elephant.

gaṇa — A grotesque, dwarf goblin; often shown as an attendant and companion of Śiva.

garbhagṛha — literally, womb-house; the dark sanctum of a temple housing the main image of the divinity.

ghaṭa-pallava — An ornamental motif consisting of a pot with overflowing foliage, often used as the capital and /or base of pillars and pilasters.

graha — A planet.

īhāmṛga — A fabulous animal such as a griffin.

jāla — Literally, net; in architecture it denotes the lacelike tracery made up of interwined *candraśālikās* which cover the *śikhara* of North Indian temple.

jaṅghā — Literally, thigh; in architecture the wall proper of the temple, lying between the *varaṇḍikā* and the *vedibandha*.

jaṭājūṭa — A coiffure consisting of long locks of hair piled above the head.

jaṭāmukuṭa — An elaborate *jaṭājūṭa* sometimes adorned with jewels.

kamaṇḍalu — A vase, generally carried by ascetics.

karaṇḍa-mukuṭa — A conical crown with bulging, horizontal sections, resembling piled baskets.

karṇa-kuṇḍala — Ear ornament, usually circular.

kaṭisūtra — Waist-band of textile or thread.

kaṭyavalambita — A gesture of the hand in which it is shown resting on the waist.

kāyotsargva — A standing posture in which the body is held erect, the two hands hanging at the sides; common to images of Jaina Tīrthaṅkaras.

khaḍga — A sword; more specifically a sword with a broad blade.

khaṭvāṅga — A club, the knob of which consists of a human skull.

kinnara — A semi-divine being, half human, half bird.

kirīṭa-mukuta — A type of tall, cylindrical crown worn by Viṣṇu and other gods.

kīrttimukha — A motif consisting of a leonine head with bulging eyes, and flat nose.

kulah — A conical cap, probably of Central Asian origin.

kumbha — Literally, a pot; in architecture, the broad cyma moulding at the base of the *vedibandha*.

lāñchana — A distinctive sign.

latā — In architecture, applied to projections on the superstructure of North Indian temples.

Latina — A type of *śikhara* lacking the subsidiary clusters of *śikharas* surrounding or leaning against the main *śikhara*.

madhyalatā — The central *latā* on the surface of a North Indian *śikhara*.

makara — Ornamental motif, apparently developed from an alligator or crocodile.

mithuna — In art, the representation of an amorous couple,.

nakula — A mongoose.

Navagraha — A group of nine divinities

consisting of the Sun (Ravi); the six planets, Soma (Moon), Mangala (Mars), Budha (Mercury), Bṛhaspati (Jupiter), Śukra (Venus), and Śani (Saturn); to whom are appended Rāhu, the Demon of the Eclipse, and Ketu, a deification of comets or meteors.

padma — A lotus

padmalatā — A creeper mainly yielding lotus flowers.

padmāsana — A seated posture with both legs crossed, feet resting on the thighs.

pañcāgnitapa — A penance done with five fires; it was per-formed by Pārvatī to win the hand of Śiva.

pañcaratha — A surface endowed with five *rathas* or projections, as in a temple wall.

pāśa — A noose, lasso.

patralatā — A lotus rhizome.

pedyā — Base of the vertical jambs of the doorway surround.

phāṁsanā — A type of pyramidal temple superstructure.

pīḍhā — A horizontal slab, which together with others, constitutes the fabric of a North Indian temple *śikhara.*

prabhāvalī — A halo.

pradakṣiṇā — Circumambulation in a clockwise direction.

pralambapādāsana — See *paryaṅkāsana.*

pustaka — A book; in sculpture, generally shown as oblong in shape.

rūpaśākhā — A molding of the doorway surround decorated with figures.

śākhā — A molding of the doorway surround.

śakti — A spear.

samabhaṅga — A posture in which the figure is shown without any flexions of the body.

samapādasthānaka — an erect, standing posture in which the weight of the body is thrown equally on both legs; same as *samabhaṅga.*

saṁghāṭī — A monastic robe, generally worn by the Buddha, that covers one or both shoulders.

śankha — A conch; generally carried by Viṣṇu as one of his attributes.

Sapta mātṛkā — A group of seven Mother Goddesses.

saptaratha — A surface, generally of a temple wall or of a pedestal, with seven projections.

śārdūla — A mythical animal with leonine features.

sarpakuṇḍala — Ear ornament representing or emulating a serpent.

sarvato-bhandrikā — A quadruple image, the representation

pratimā — of a deity or deities being carved on all the four sides.

śikhā — A lock of hair on the cranium; in architecture, the finial of a temple.

śikhara — The superstructure of a temple, rising above the walls.

siṁha-vyāla — A *vyāla* with the head of a lion.

Śrīvatsa — An auspicious sign of varying design, often decorating the chest of Viṣṇu and the Tīrthaṅkaras.

śrīvṛkṣa — In architecture, generally the outermost molding of a doorway surround decorated with a pattern resembling the stem of a palm tree or a design consisting of superimposed palmettes and flowers.

sruk — A type of ladle used for pouring oblations into the sacrificial fire.

stambha — A pillar, column.

stambhaśākhā — A molding of the doorway surround decorated with a pilaster.

śukanāsa	An antefix placed on the *śikhara* of a temple, just above the *antarāla*
śuka-vyāla	A *vyāla* with the head of a parrot.
surasundarī	A heavenly damsel; generally the name for female figures in various attitudes and postures adorning a temple.
toraṇa	An ornate gateway.
tribhaṅga	A posture in which the body is flexed thrice.
tri-ratha	A surface endowed with three *rathas*, or projections, as in a temple wall.
triśūla	A trident.
Udadhikumāra	A divinity, generally carrying a pot and riding a *makara*. Often represented on the sill of a North Indian temple doorframe.
udarabandha	An ornamental belt worn around the stomach.
udgama	A pediment, generally crowning a niche.
udīcyaveśa	A term generally applied to the dress of the Sun god, when it consists of a tunic and boots.
upavīta	A sacred thread worn across the left shoulder and under the right arm.
ūrdhvapiṅgalakeśa	curls rising over the head of a terrific deity like Bhairava or Yama.
ūrṇā	A small, circular protuberance seen on the forehead of the Buddha just above the eyes.
urujāla	An ornament, generally suspended in loops over the thighs.
uṣṇīṣa	Literally, turban; generally applied to the cranial protuberance on the head of the Buddha; also the coping of a *vedikā*.
uttarīya	A shawl-like garment worn over or across the upper part of the body.
vāhana	A vehicle; generally applied to the animal mounts of the various divinities.
vajra	A thunderbolt; a weapon commonly represented with two transverse bolts.
Valabhī	A type of temple superstructure imitating a barrel vaulted roof.
vanamālā	A large garland, reaching almost to the knees.
varada mudrā	A gesture bestowing gift with hand lowered, palm forward, fingers pointing downwards.
vedibandha	The podium; in temple walls, the member intervening between the *pīṭha* (plinth and the *jaṅghā* (wall) and generally consisting of a group of four moldings, viz., *khura, kumbha, kalaśa and kapotapālī.*
vedikā	A railing
Vidyādhara	An angelic being, human in form, and without wings; he is generally shown flying above the principal deity of a sculptural grouping, carrying garlands, casting flowers, etc.
vīṇā	A lute.
vyāla	A mythical composite animal, of leonine form but often endowed with wings and possessing the heads of a large variety of animals and birds.
yajñopavīta	Same as *upavīta*.
yogapaṭṭa	A piece of cloth tied around the legs in order to support the lifted knees.

CONCORDANCE

Catalogue No.	*Figure No.*	*Allahabad Mus. Accn. No.*
1	1	706
2	2	274
3	3	401
4	4	1093
5		803
6	5	831
7	6	1107
8	7	356
9	8	953
10		1413
11		466
12		270
13	9	713
14	10	1328
15	11	615
16	12	235
17	13 A-B	939
18	14	546
19	15	919
20	16	432
21	17	91-1913
22	18 A-B	664
23	19	665
24	20	324
25		1438
26	21	1189
27	22	793
28	23	1358
29	24	1348
30	25	428
31		612
32	26	590
33	27	1434
34	28	1359
35	29	1363
36	30	1391
37		1334
38	31	1119
39	32	1075
40	33	701
41	34	911
42	35 A-B	784
43	36 A-D	947
44	37 A-B	1397
45		215
46	38	1007
47		956
48	39	1311
49		1325
50	40	240
51	41	1389
52	42	464
53	43	993
54	44	1111
55	45	237
56	46	711
57	47	657
58	48	297
59	49	1172
60	50	484
61	51	369
62	52	1074
63	53	384
64	54	1393
65	55	268
66	56	974
67	57	847
68	58	1102
69	59	475
70	60	483
71		872
72	61	1357
73		447
74	62	449
75	63	1267
76	64	1375
77	65	1130
78		1320
79	66	994
80	67	1097
81		1304
82	68	648
83	69	459
84	70	399

Catalogue No.	*Figure No.*	*Allahabad Mus. Accn. No.*
85	71	715
86	72	1319
87	73	275
88	74	461
89	75	1439
90	76	1238
91	77	1314 (Indra)
92	78	1314 (Agni)
93	79	1395
94	80	1365
95		1367
96	81	1164
97		1394
98	82	1122
99	83	1429
100	84	1385
101	85	206
102	86	1216
103	87	626
104		1179
105	88	780
106		1321
107	89	1437
108	90	863
109	91	1156
110	92	1440
111	93	820
112	94	298
113	95	1302
114	96	396
115	97	834
116	98	894
117	99	111
118	100	474
119	101	899
120	102	804
121		906
122	103	972
123		1073
124		369
125	104	964
126		482
127	105	745
128	106	1109
129	107	1072
130	108	874
131	109	849
132	110	373
133	111	310
134	112	109
135		
136	113	82

Catalogue No.	*Figure No.*	*Allahabad Mus. Accn. No.*
137		92
138	114	983
139		299
140	115	853
141		489
142	116	273
143		359
144	117	913
145	118	681
146	119	930
147		1344
148	120	1271
149	121	92.148
150	122	338
151		167
152	123	260
153	124	1076
154	125	846
155	126	1266
156	127	974
157	128	1201
158	129	904
159	130	251
160	131	984
161	132	1094
162	133	948
163	134	971
164	135	1323
165	136	1406
166	137	1054
167		949
168	138	92.130
169	139	92.146
170	140	91.1914
171	141	500
172	142	554
173	143	476
174		390
175	144	545
176	145	995
177	146	239
178	147	1326
179	148	92.12
180	149	860
181	150	830
182	151	296
183	152	118
184	153 A-B	93
185	154	1442
186	155	977
187	156	905
188	157	663

Catalogue No.	*Figure No.*	*Allahabad Mus. Accn. No.*	*Catalogue No.*	*Figure No.*	*Allahabad Mus. Accn. No.*
189	158	462	241	198	825
190		989	242	199	1312
191	159	1215	243	200	528
192		1287	244		645
193	160	1413	245	201	496
194		963	246	202	619
195		1061	247	203	861
196	161	1192	248	204 A-B	1424
197		443	249	205	1282
198	162	248	250	206	1380
199	163	517	251	207	1181
200	164	1053	252	208	524
201	165	1360	253	209	618
202		1130	254	210	620
203		1138	255	211	744
204		453	256	212	454
205		557	257		501
206	166	372	258	213	1354
207	167	1445	259	214	621
208	168	1443	260	215	92-159
209	169	1444	261	216	633
210	170	149	262	217	669
211		86	263	218	561
212	171	1337	264	219	370
213	172	92.13	265	220	495
214	173	278	266	221	530
215	174	600	267		527
216	175	980 A	268	222 A-B	522
217	176	611	269	223 A-B	540
218		352	270		538
219	177	743	271	224	504
220	178	491	272	225	502
221	179	735	273	226	536
222	180	592	274		542
223	181	656	275	227	351
224	182	584	276		360
225	183	531	277	228	601
226	184	225	278	229	543
227	185	525	279		1170
228	186	242	280	230 A-B	86
229	187 A-B	272	281	231	1069
230	188	503	282	232	859
231	189	741	283	233	389
232	190 A-D	687	284	234	588
233	191	120	285	235	318
234	192	73	286	236	986
235	193	386	287	237	346
236		980	288	238	1108
237	194	996	289	239	1159
238	195	924	290	240	1118
239	196	523	291	241	107
240	197	486	292	242	92.158

Catalogue No.	*Figure No.*	*Allahabad Mus. Accn. No.*
293	243 A-B	1165
294	244	4738
295	245	1404
296		694
297	246 A-B	1209
298	247	1210
299	248	309
300		1315
301	249	76
302	250	78
303	251	113
304	252	852
305	253	480
306		87
307	254	742
308	255	907
309	256	350
310	257	468
311		472
312	258	1212
313	259	882
314	260	379
315	261	985
316	262	821
317	263	469
318	264	269
319		817
320	265	1283
321		271
322		1317
323	266	275
324	267	400
325	268	710
326	269	493
327	270	814
328		122
329	271	123
330		217
331		729
332	272	813
333	273	604
334	274	776
335		775
336	275	348
337		697
338	276	387
339	277	91.1916
340	278	1416
341	279	1188
342		1268
343	280	553
344		1355
345	281	1327
346	282	1180
347		1163
348	283	914
349		1405
350	284	441
351	285	1166
352	286	A1331
353	287	748
354	288	1153
355	289	258
356	290	1273
357	291	1361
358	292	1175
359	293	288
360	294	876
361	295	1101
362	296	752
363	297	1398
364	298	781
365		1082
366	299	1353
367	300	1400
368	301	357
369	302	358
370	303	1377
371	304	1346
372		1290
373	305 A-C	1144
374	306	944
375	307 A-B	1152
376	308 A-D	1390
377	309 A-D	1275
378	310 A-D	1233
379	311	5
380	312	854
381	313	81
382	314	404
383	315	704
384	316	1418
385		609
386	317	4476
387	318	247
388		1392
389	319	868
390		629
391	320	249
392	321	246
393		
394	322	1417
395		1149
396		1148
397	323	1077

ILLUSTRATIONS

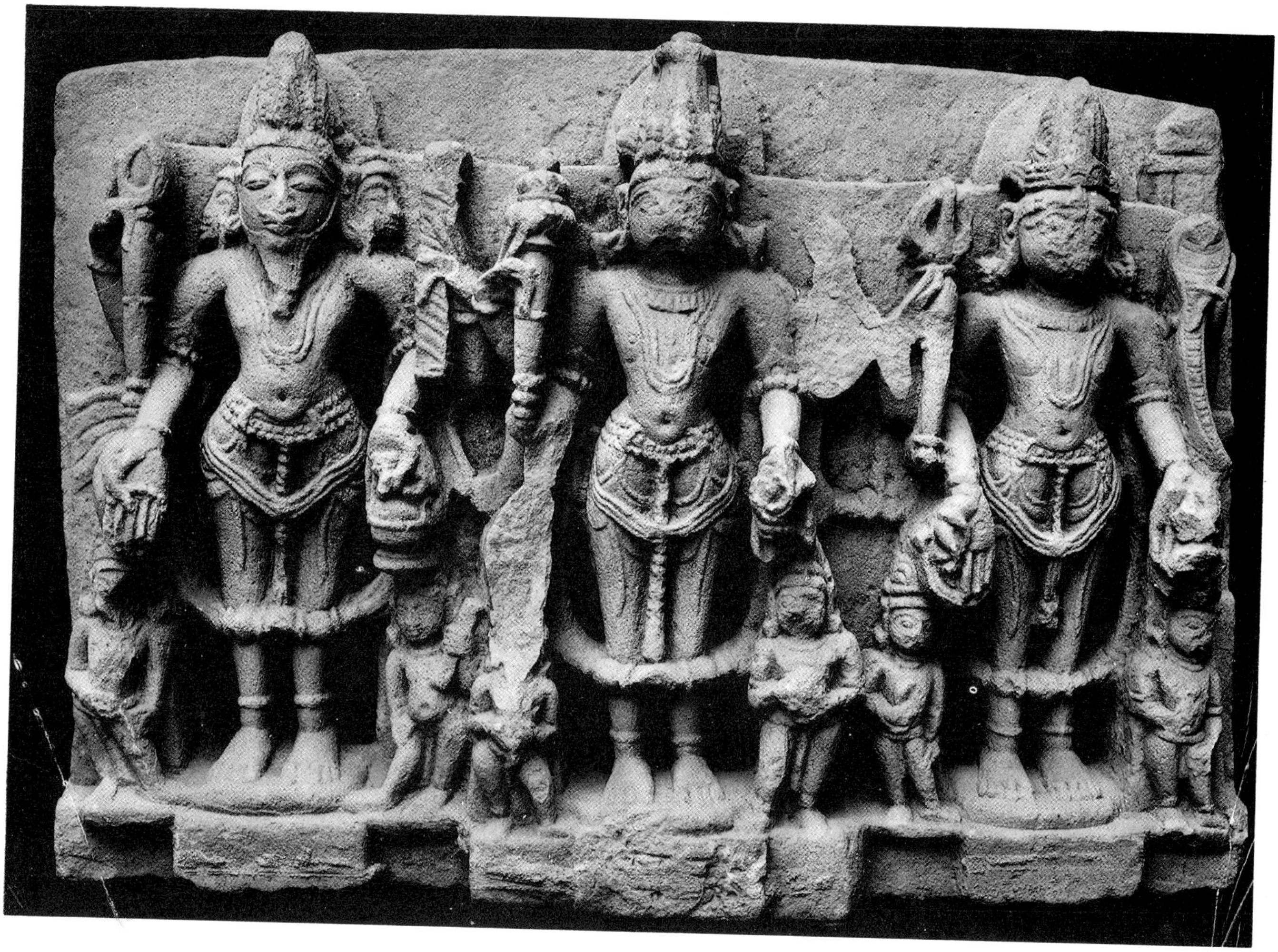

▲ 1

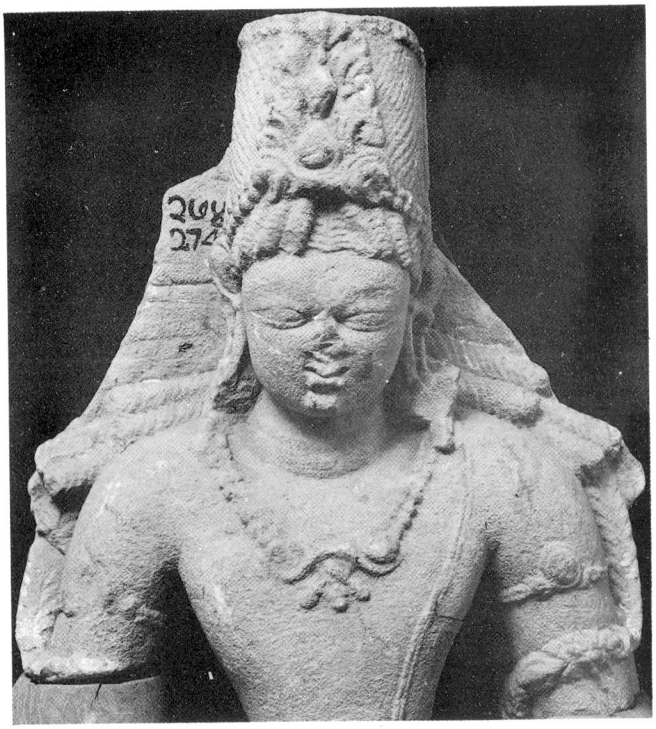

◄ 2

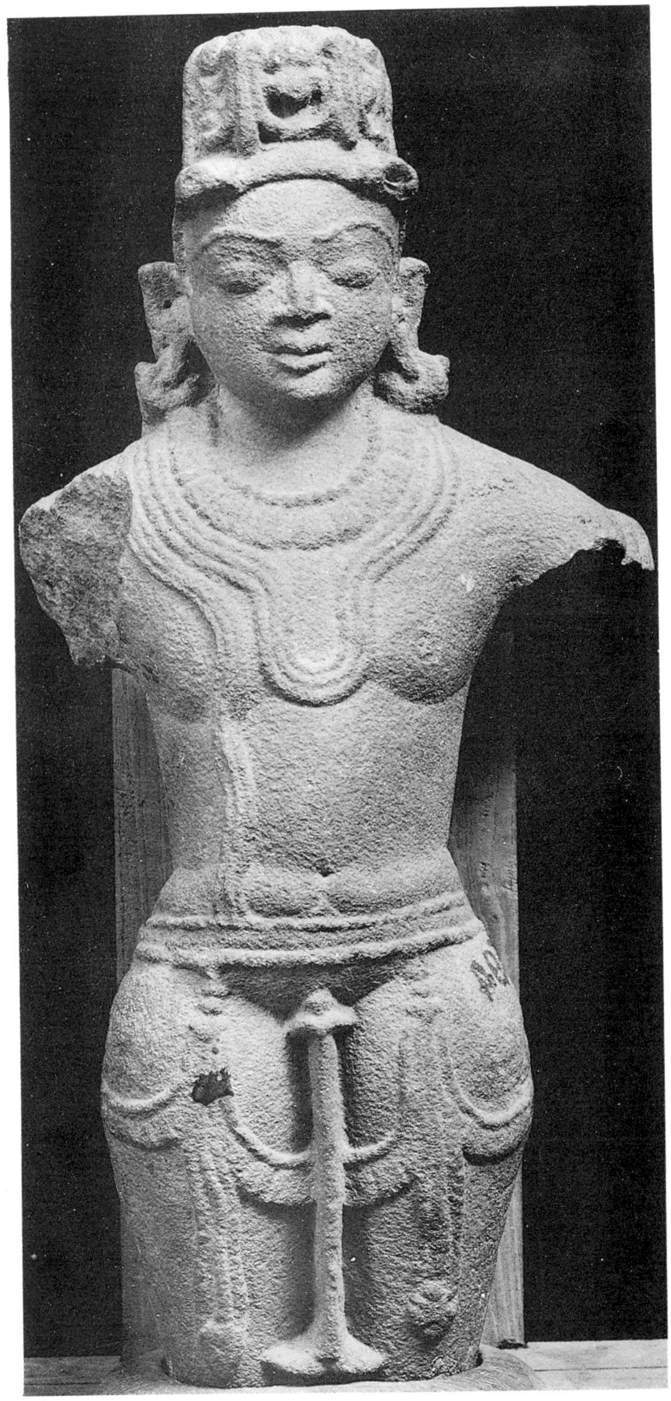

► 3

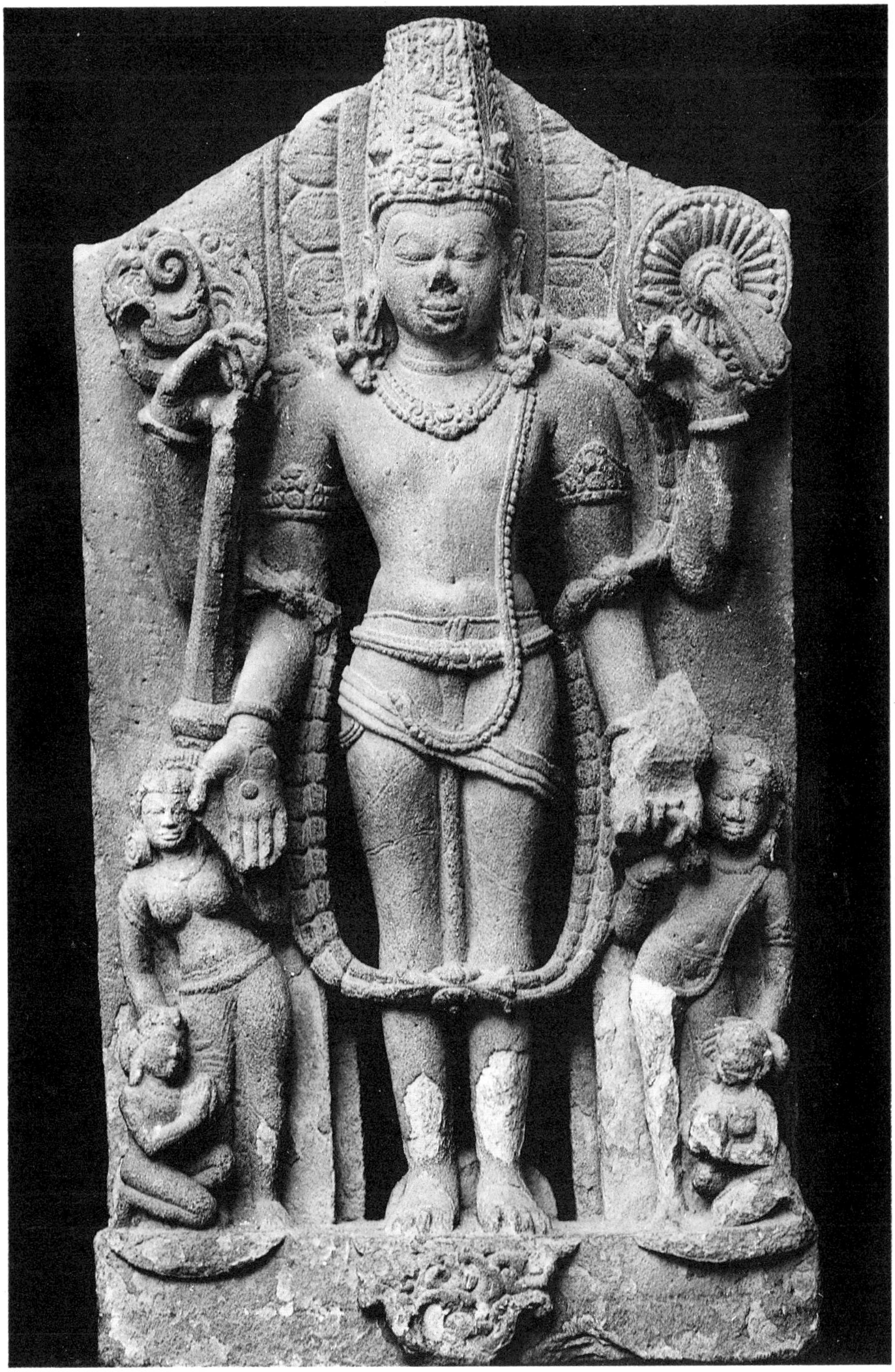

▲4

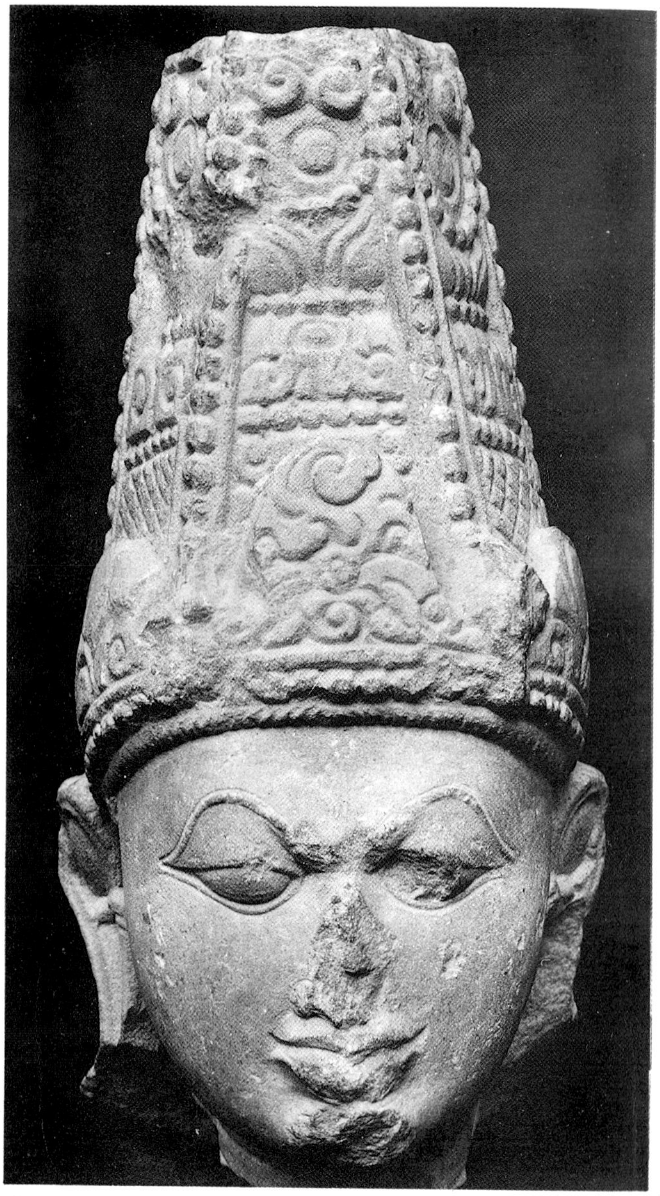

◀
6

▶
5

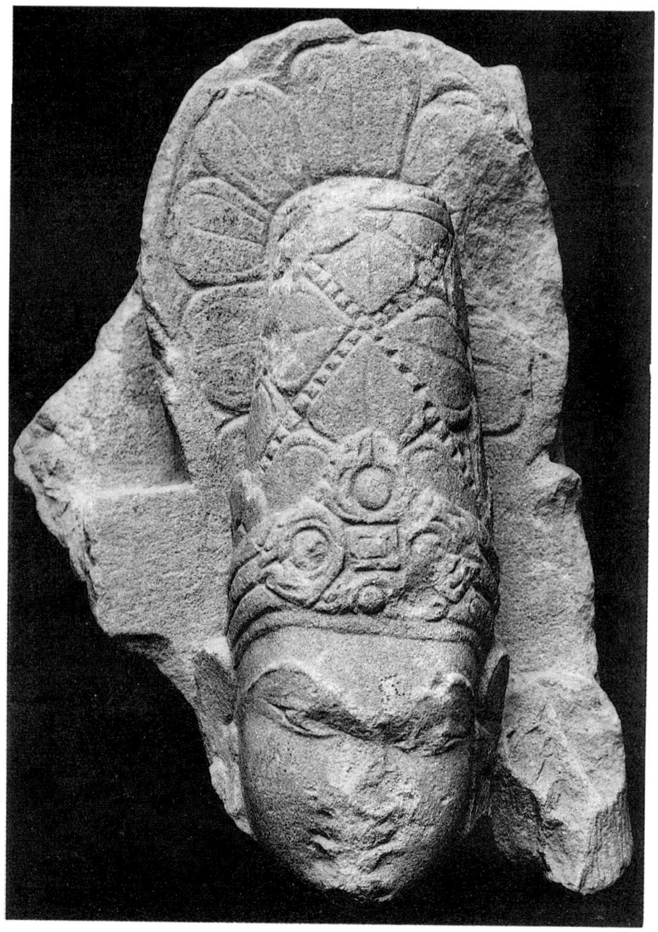

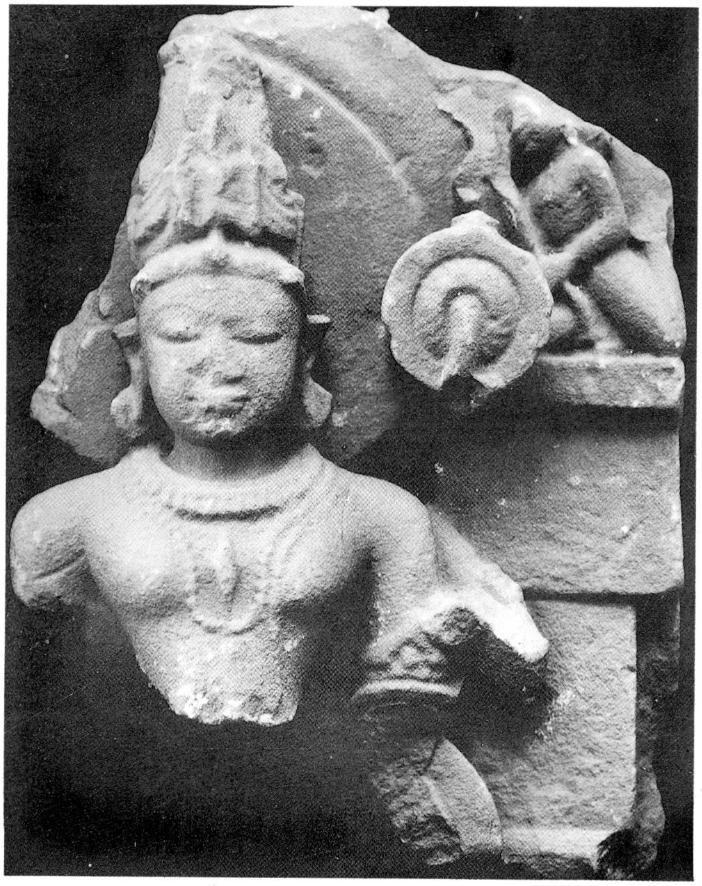

◀
7

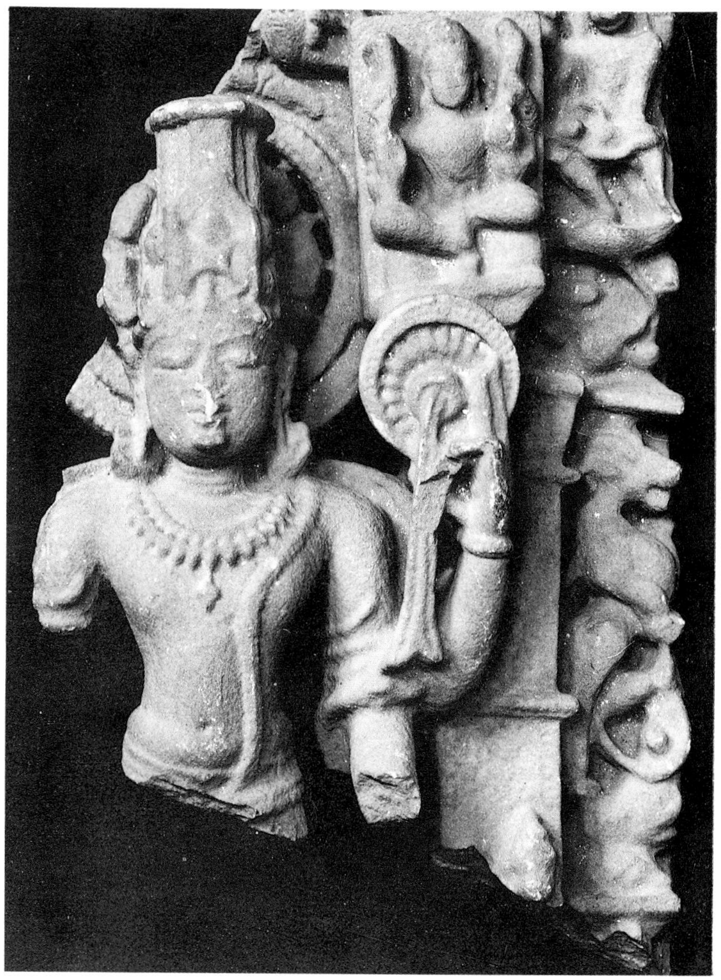

▶
8

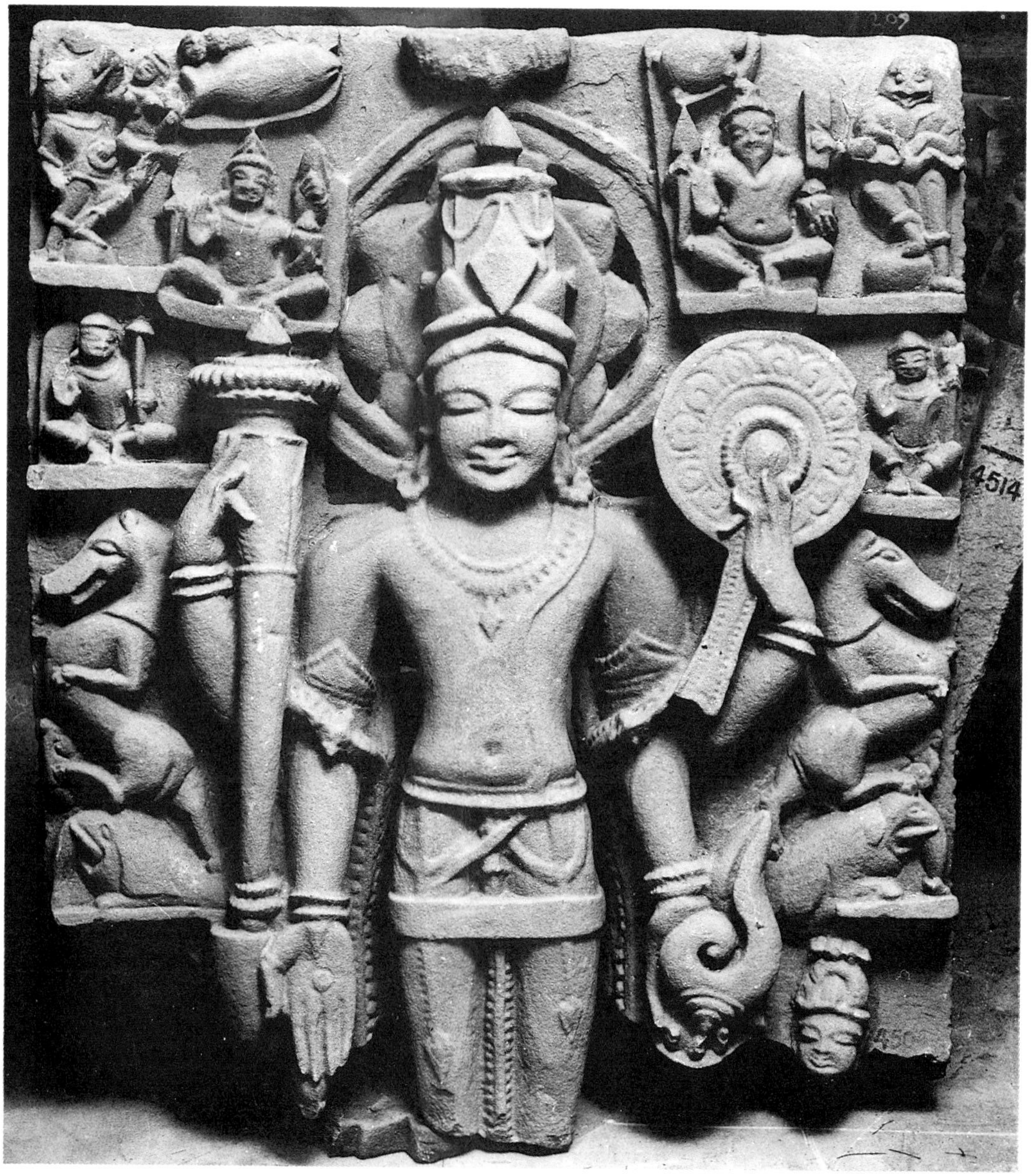

▲9

12

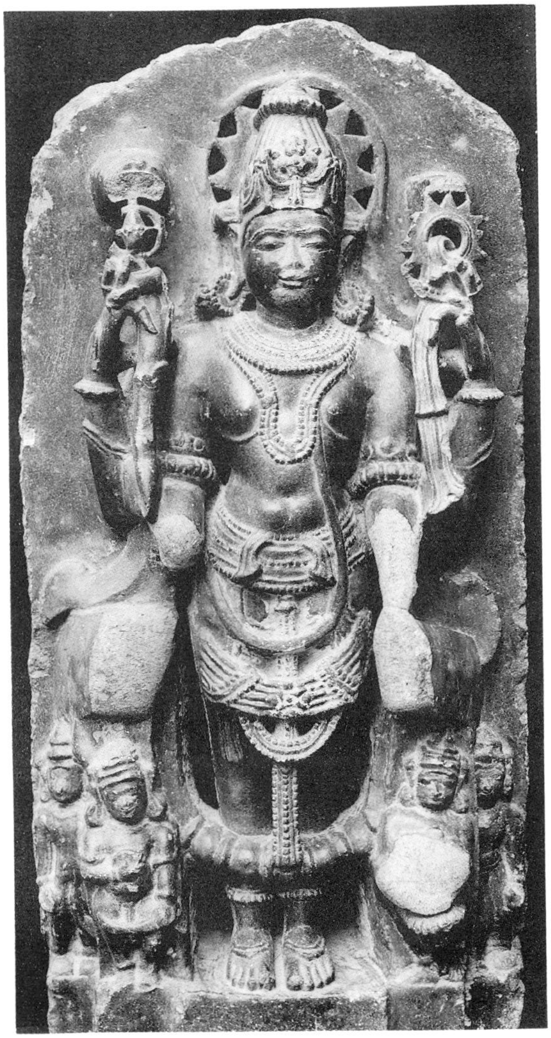

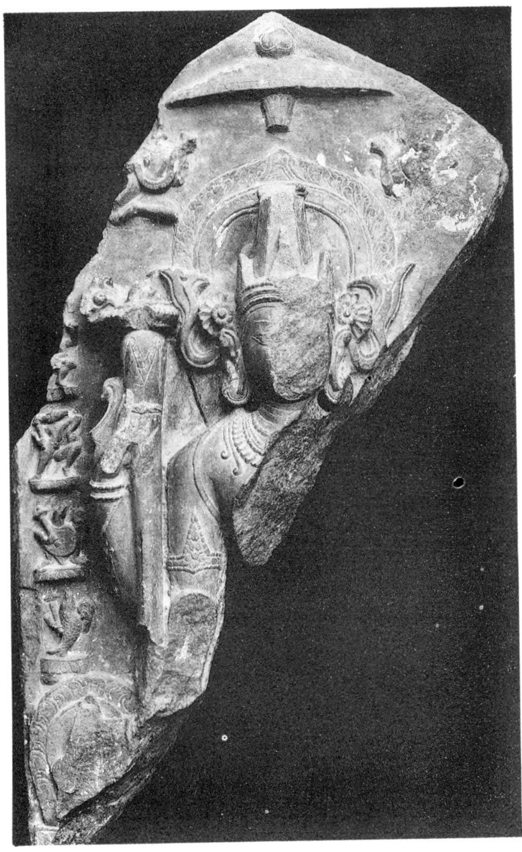

10

11

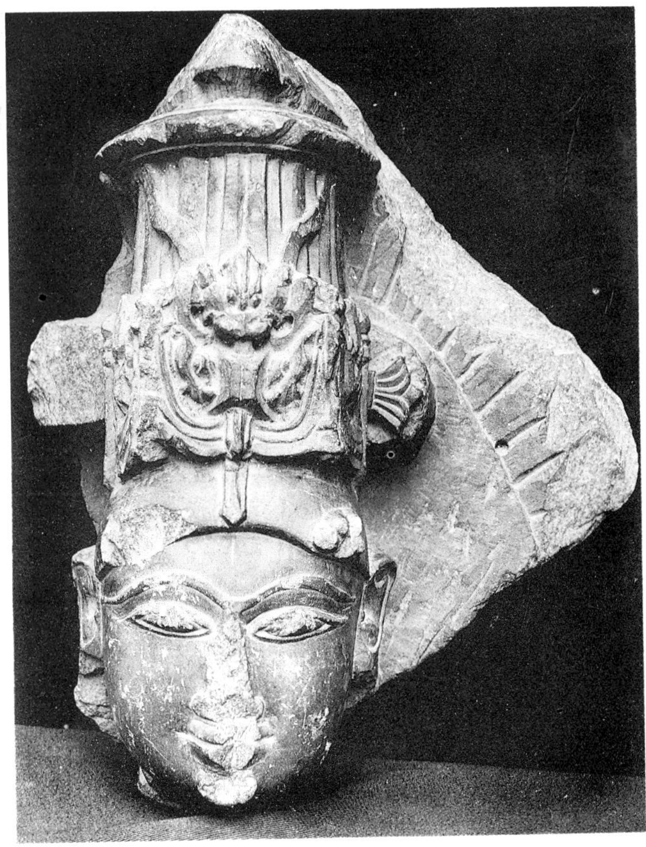

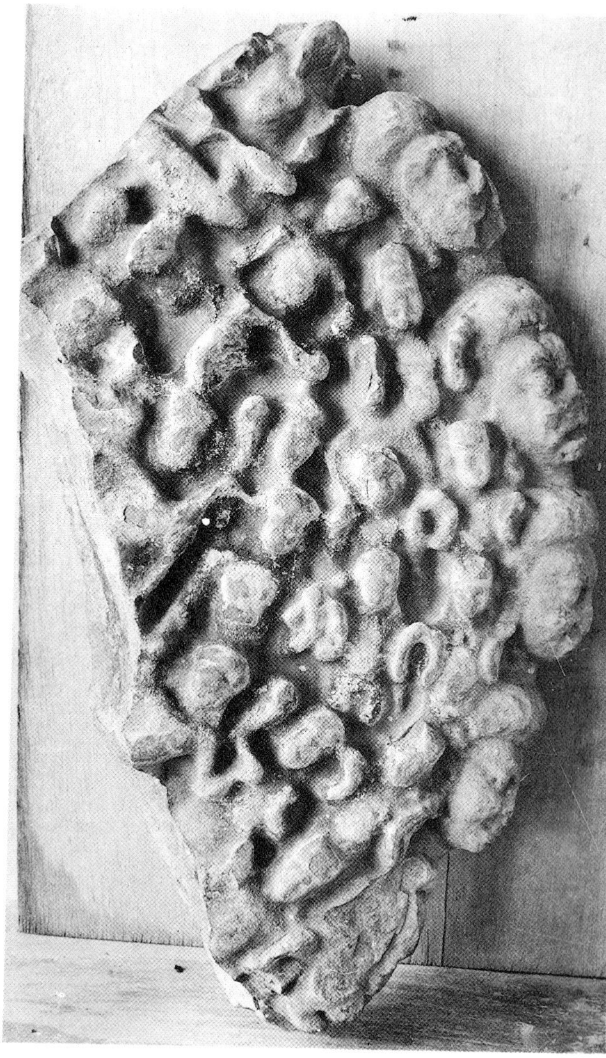

◀
13A

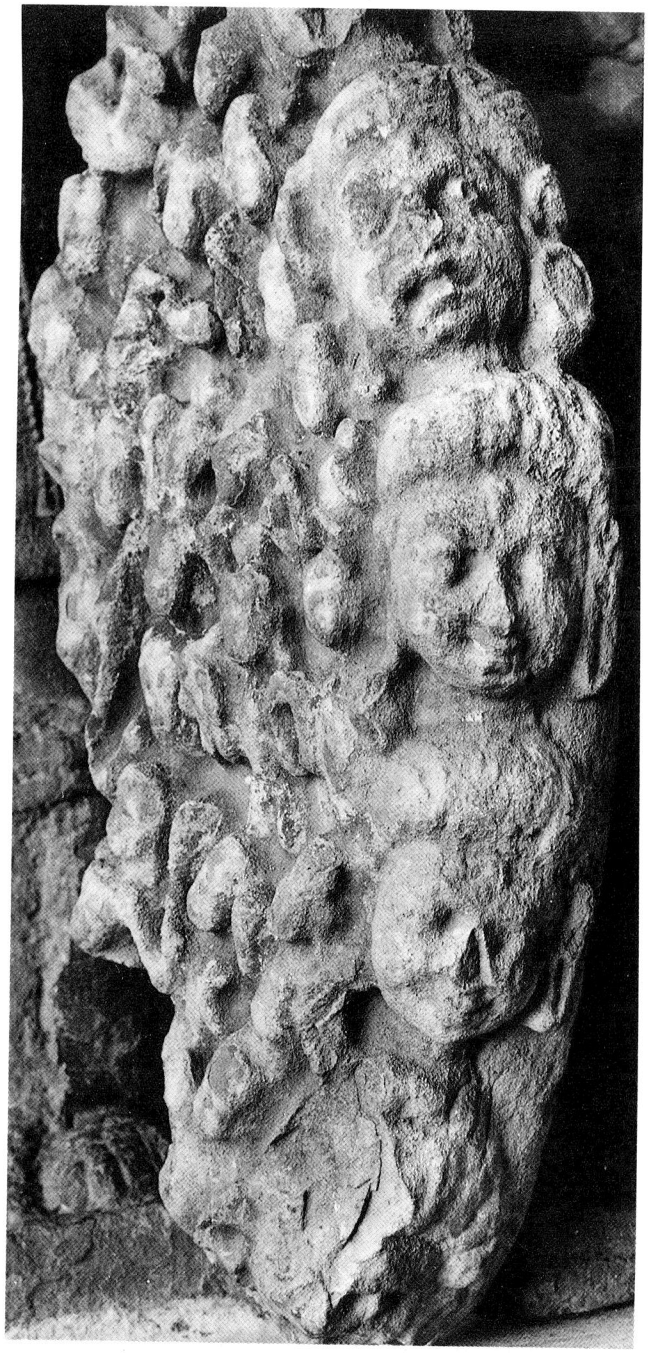

▶
13B

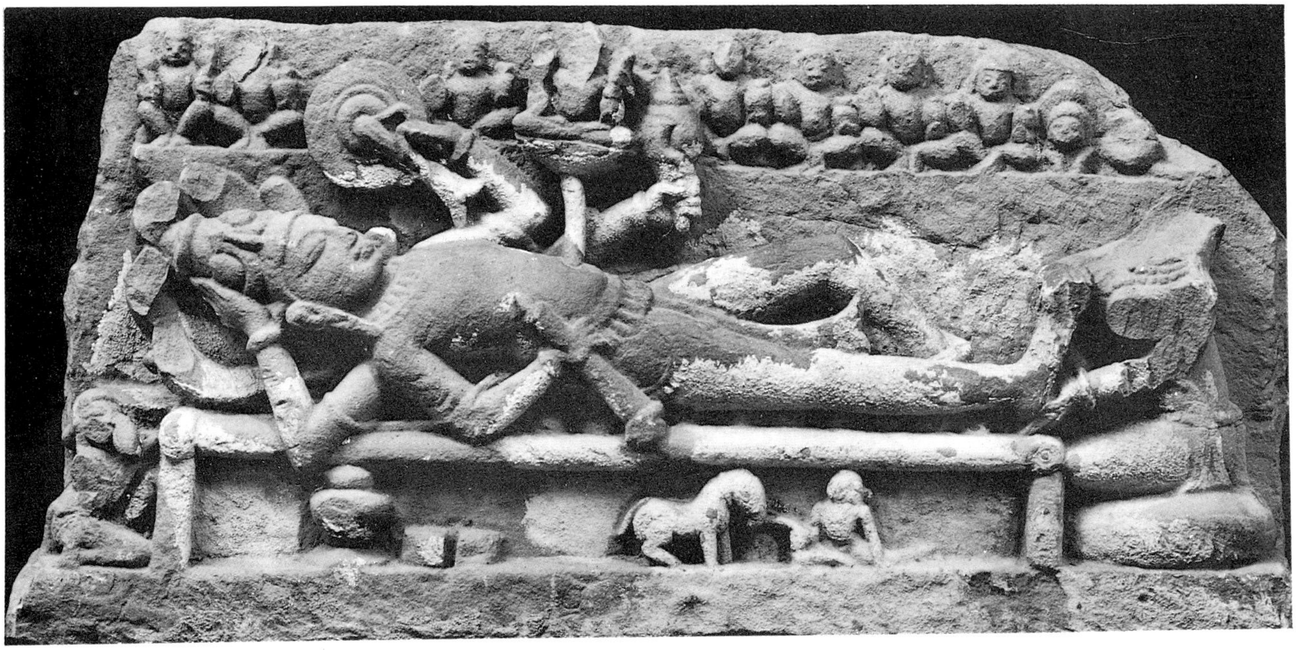

▲ 14

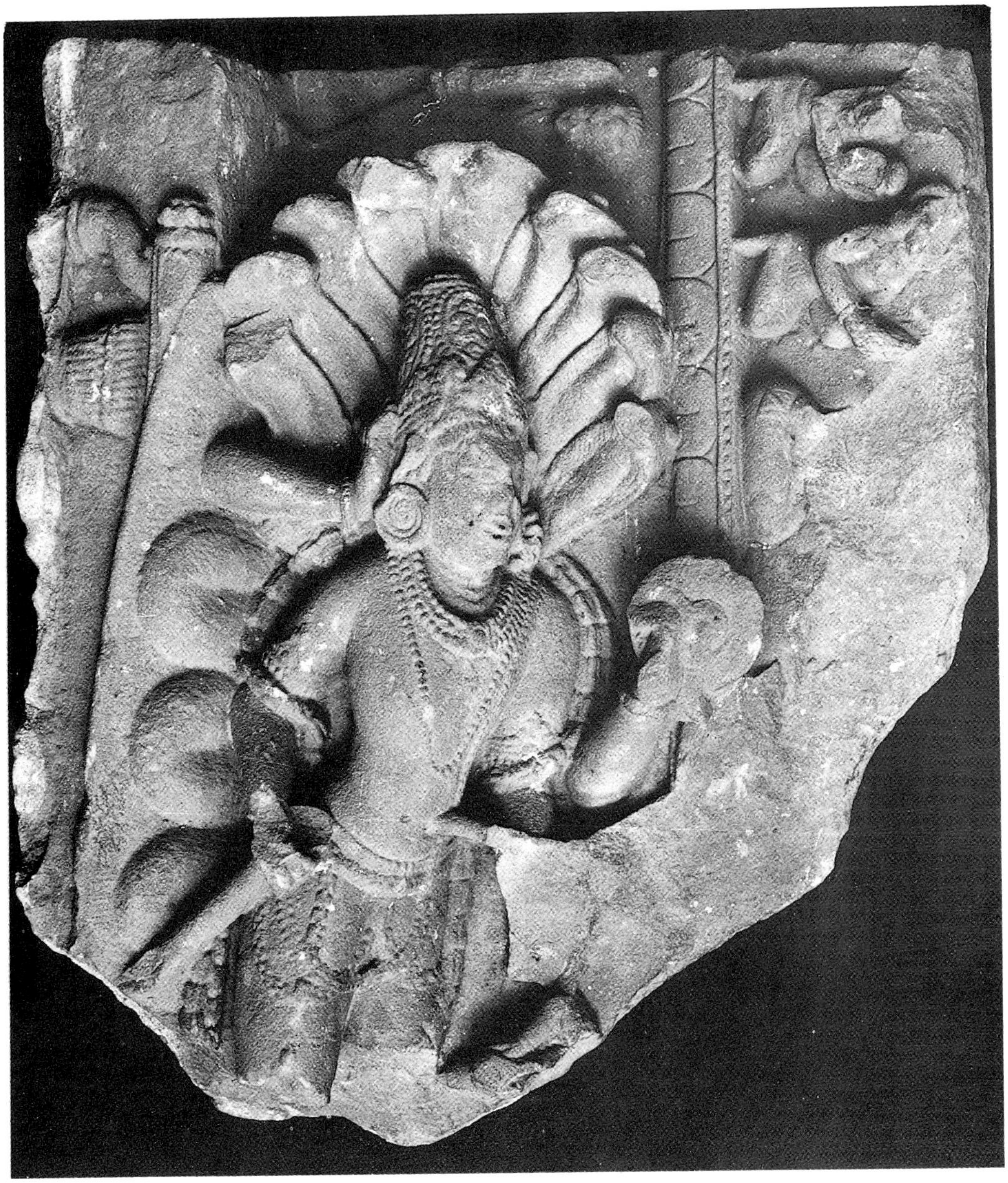

◄ 15

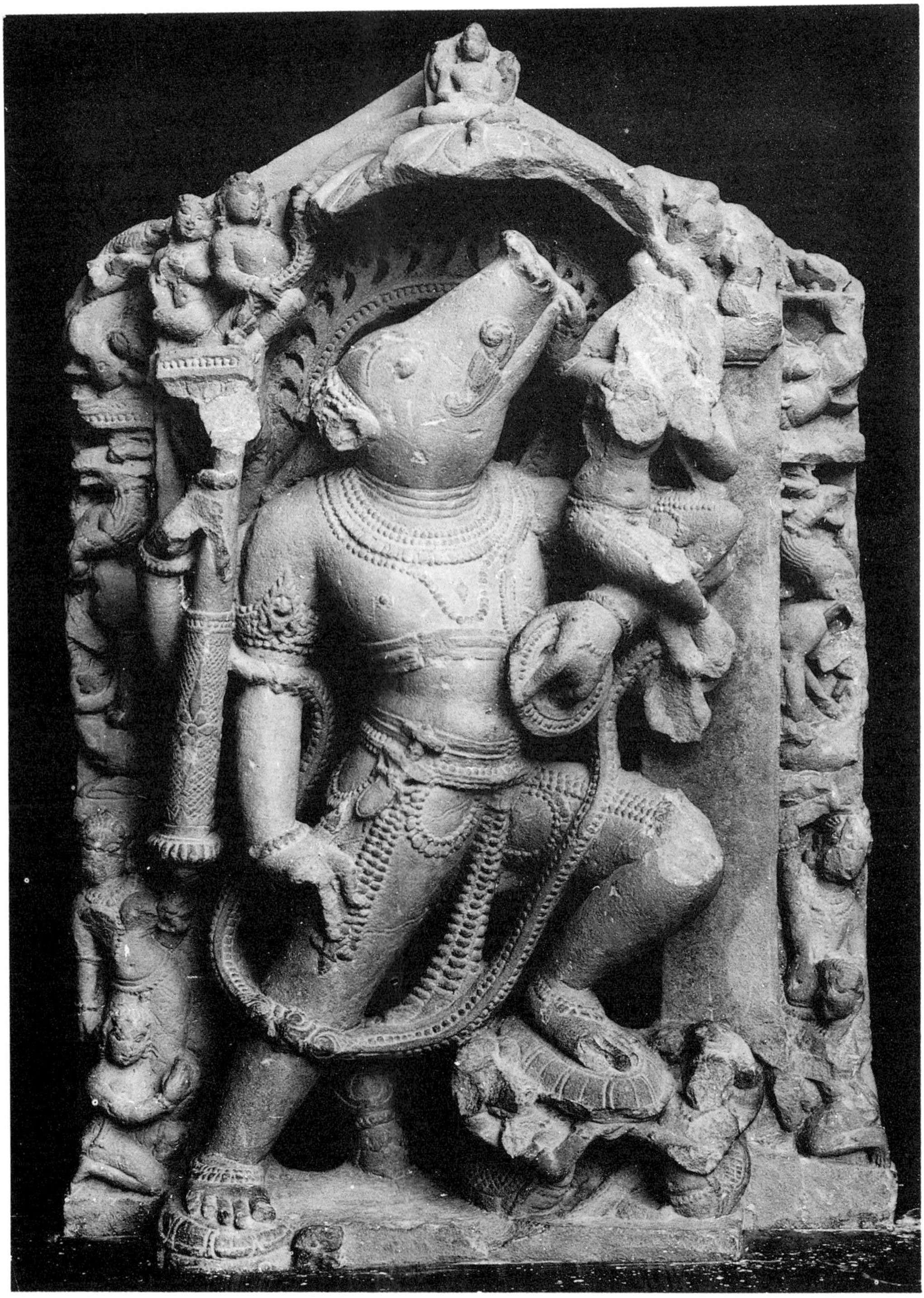

▲ 16

▶
17

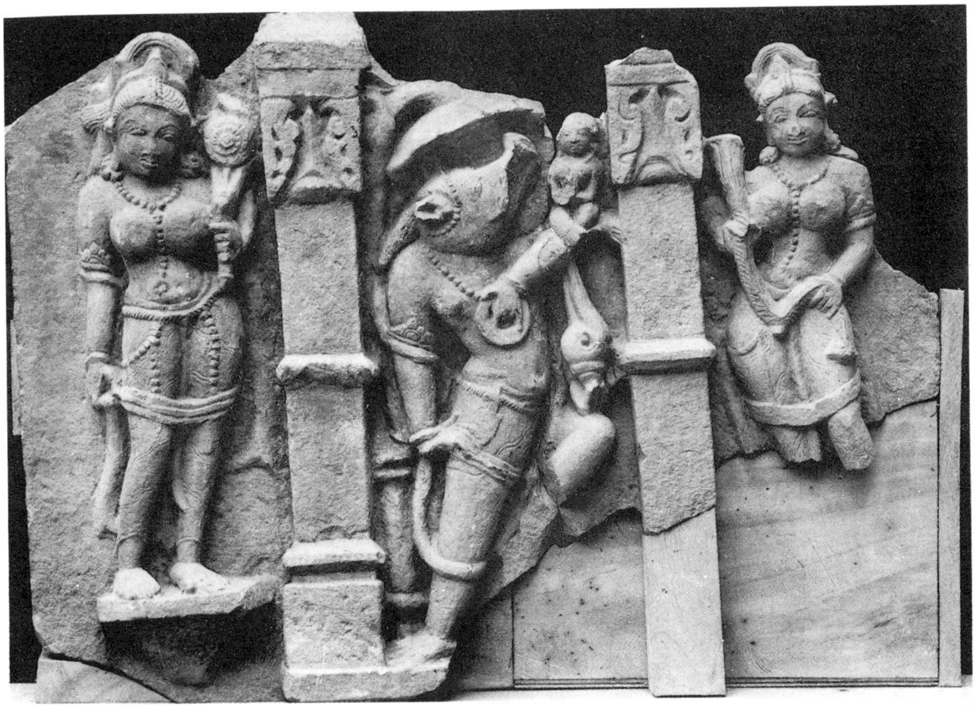

◀
18A

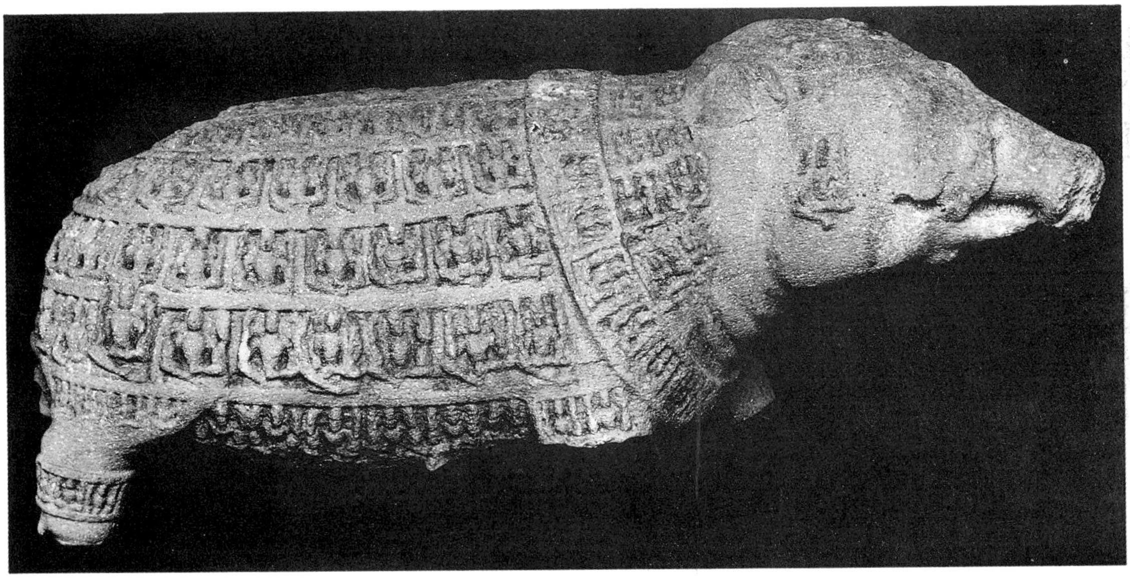

▶
18B

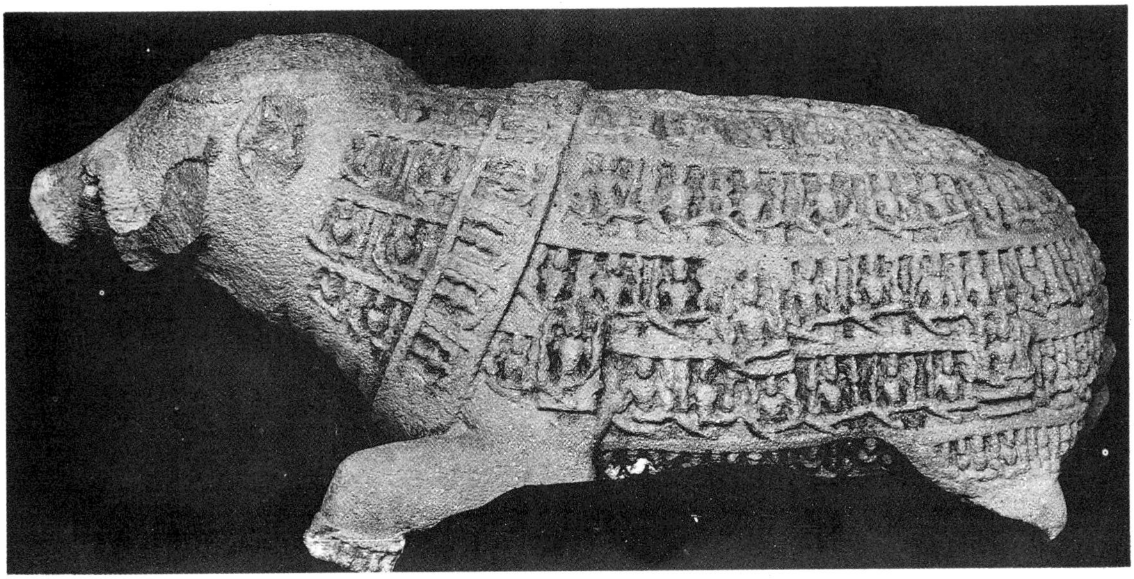

▶
19

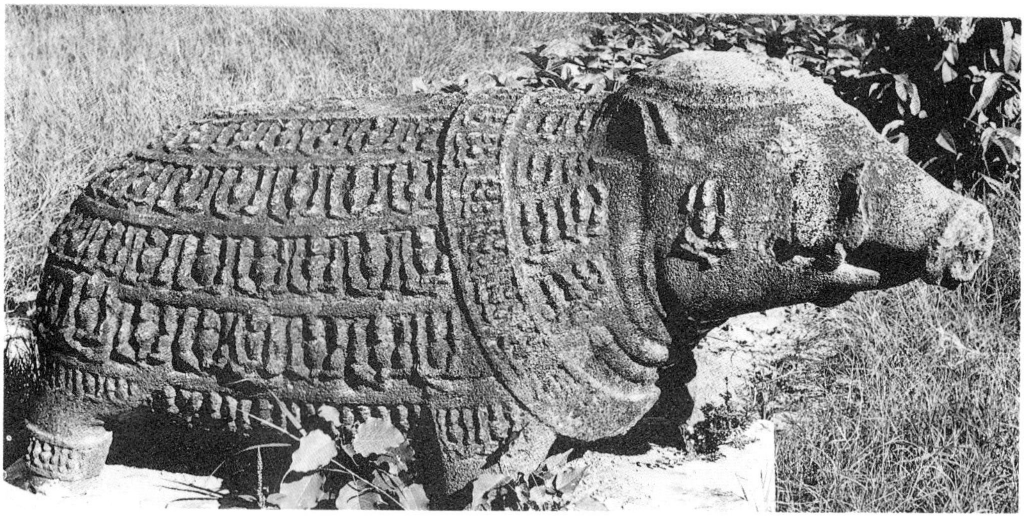

◀
20

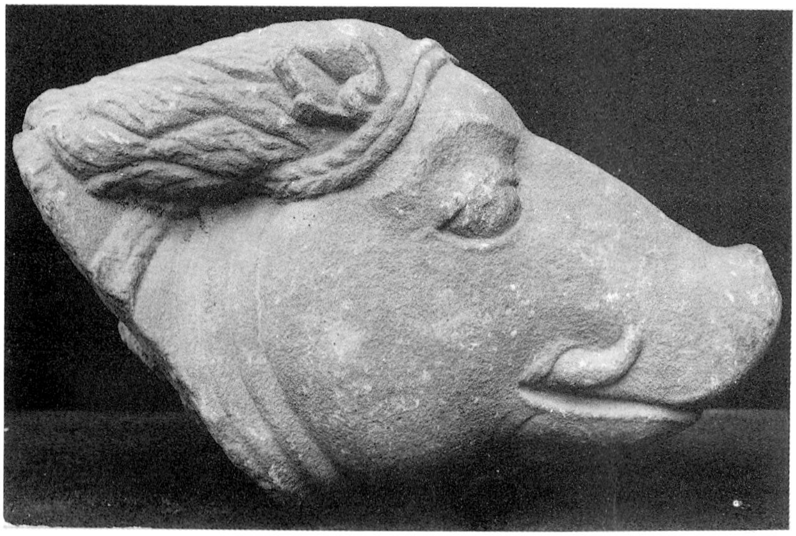

▶
21

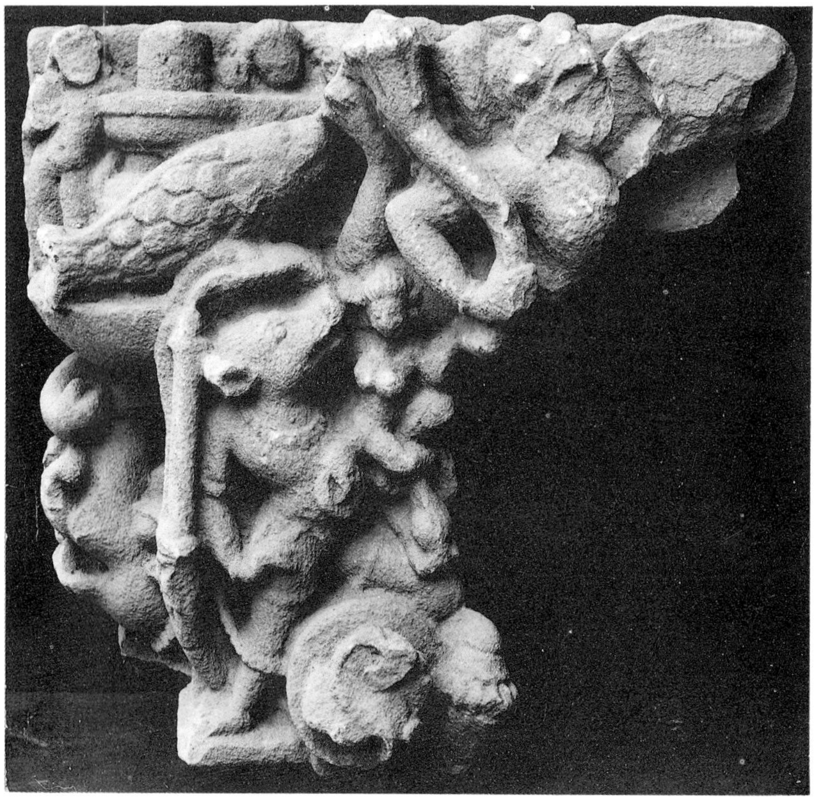

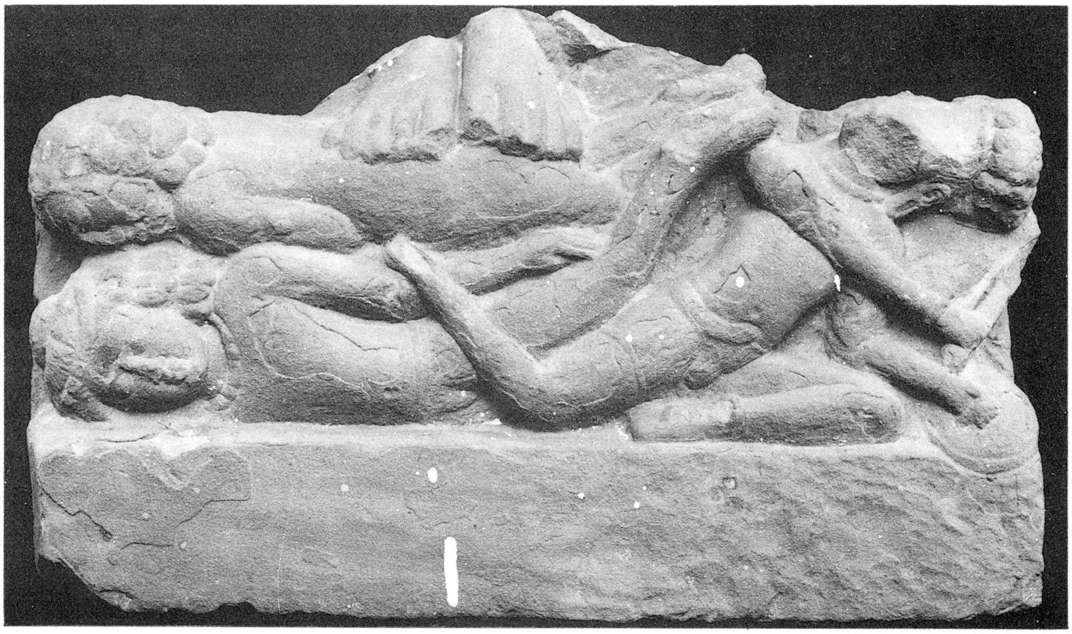

▲ 23

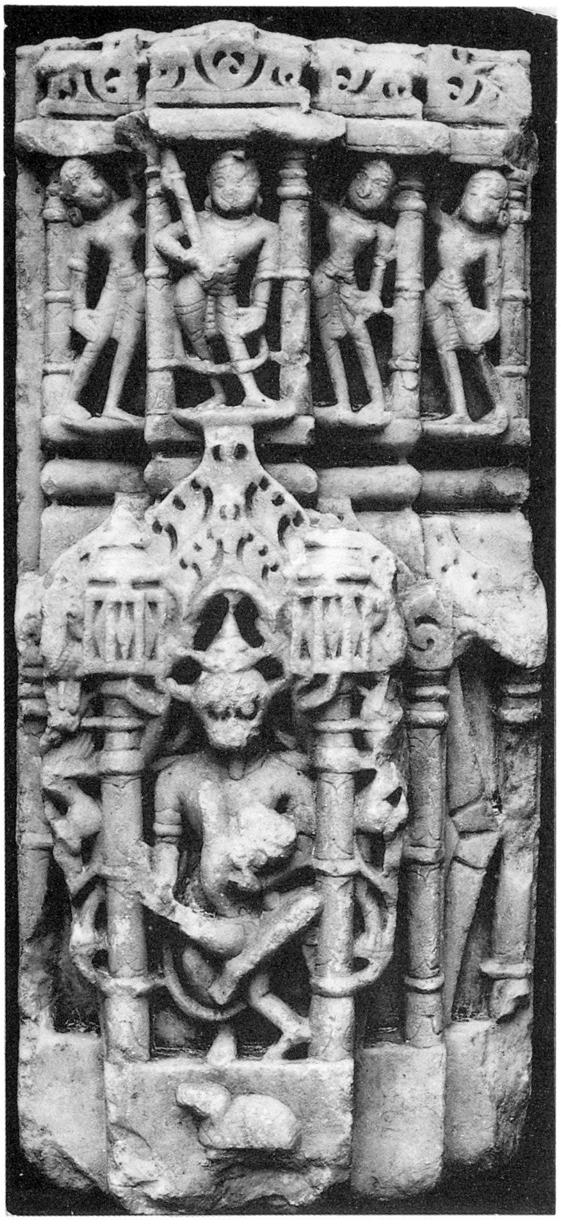

◀ 22

▼ 24

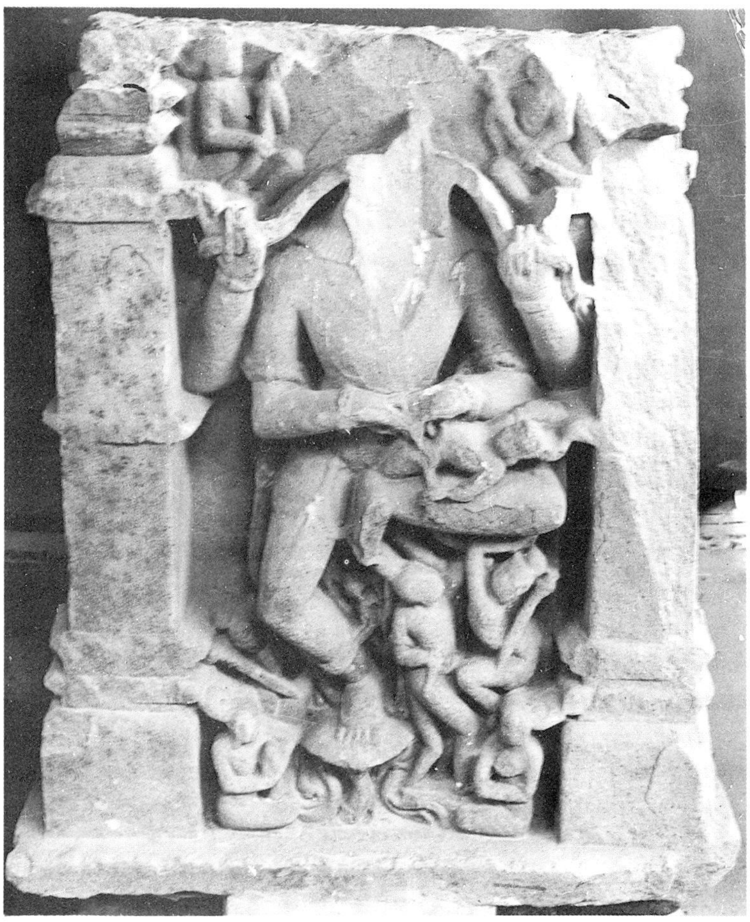

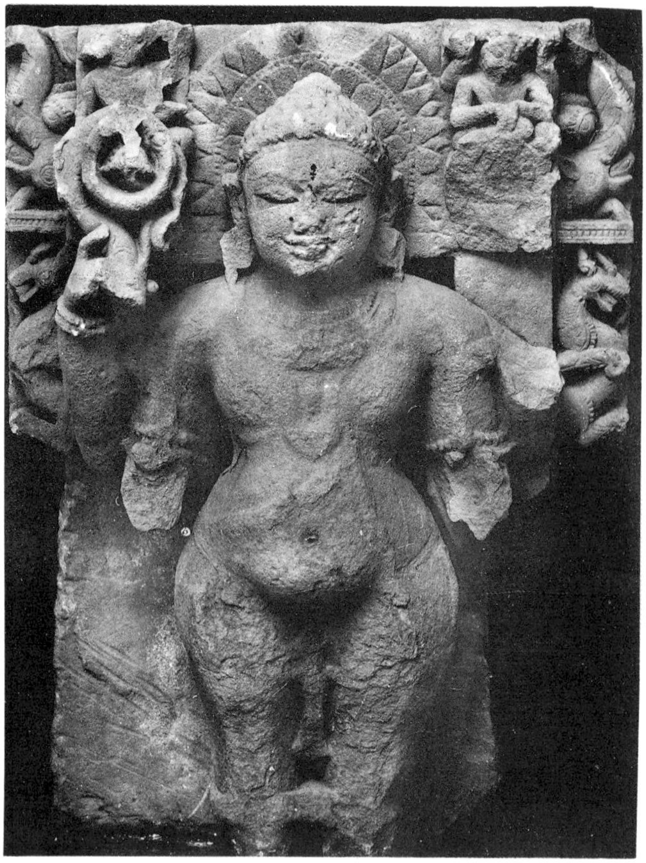

◀
25

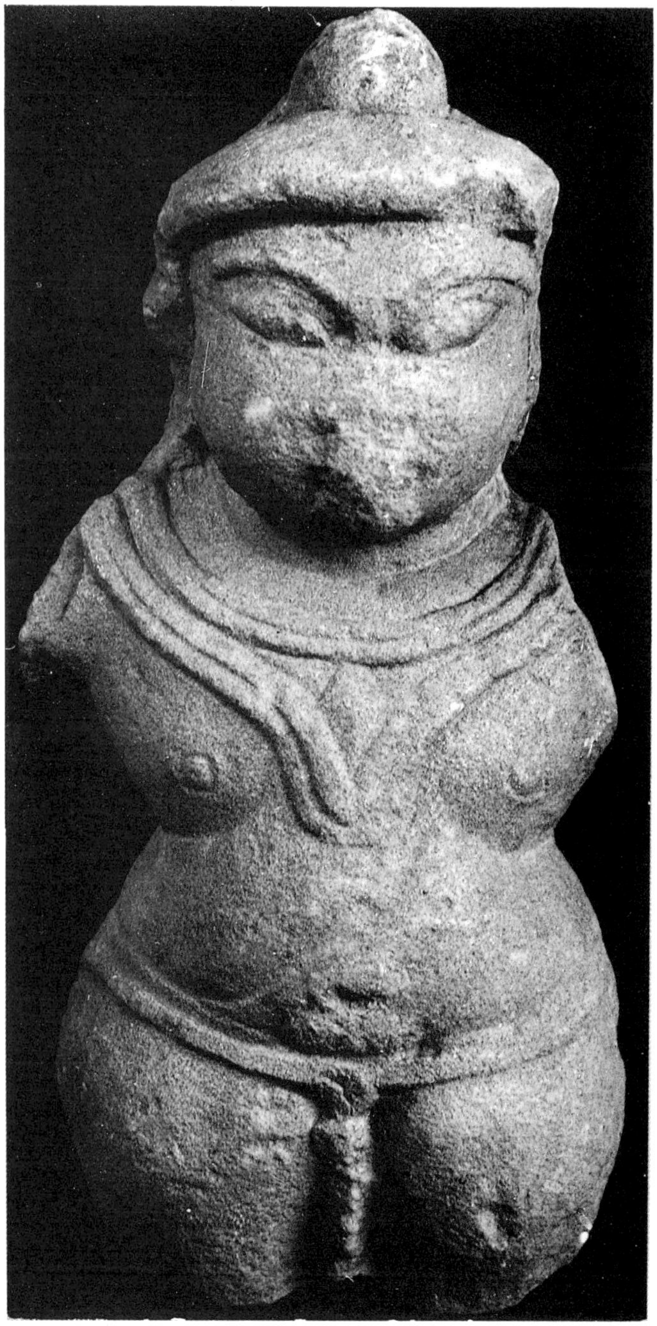

▶
26

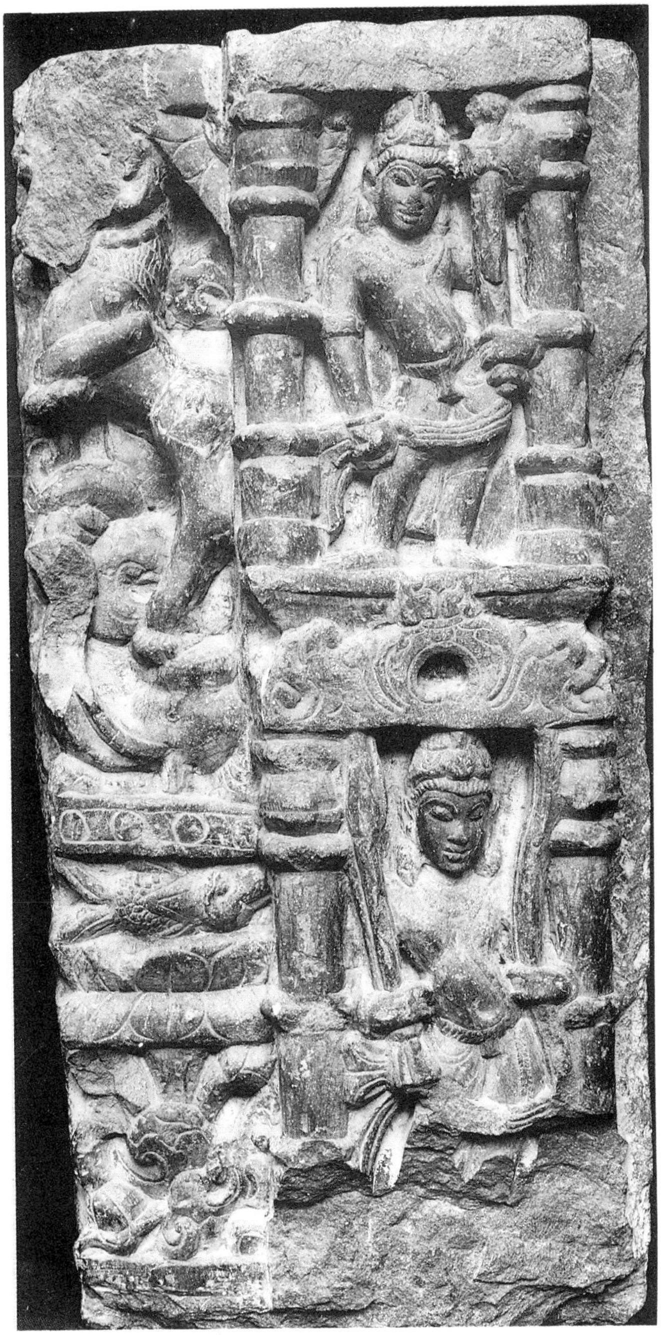

◀ 27

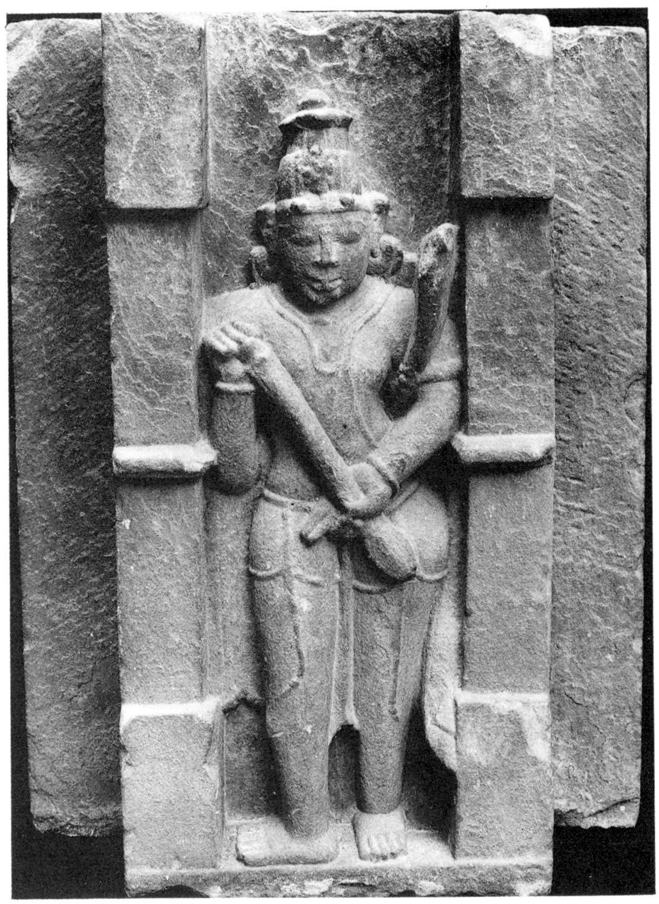

▶ 28

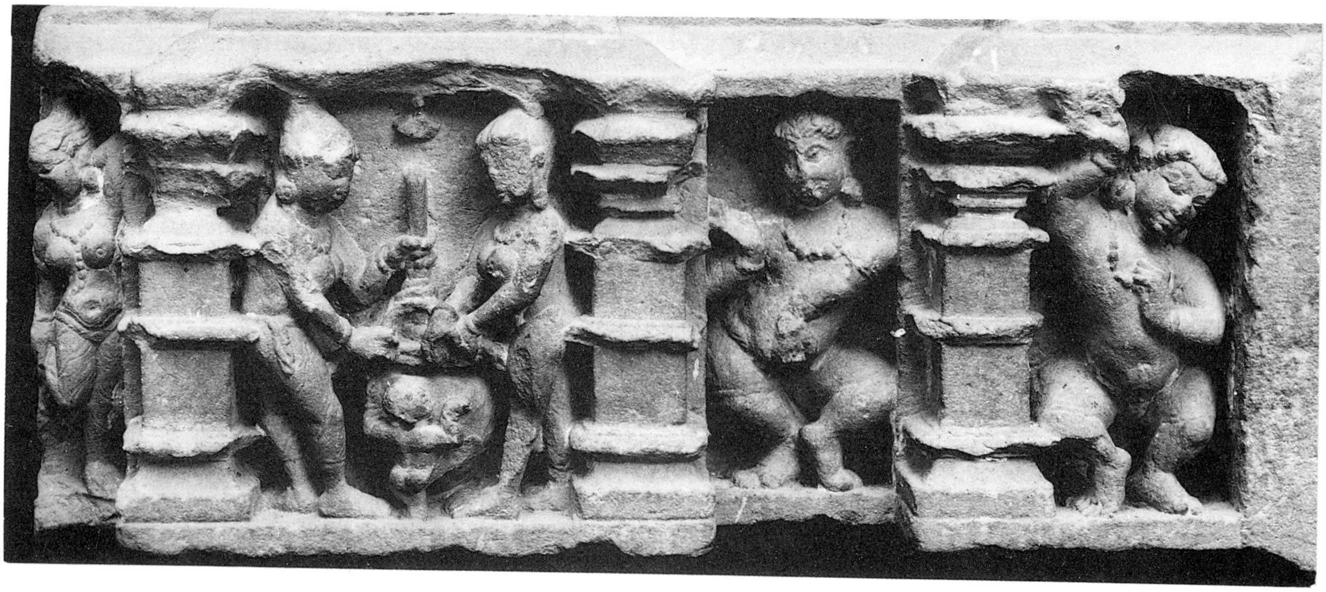

▲ 29

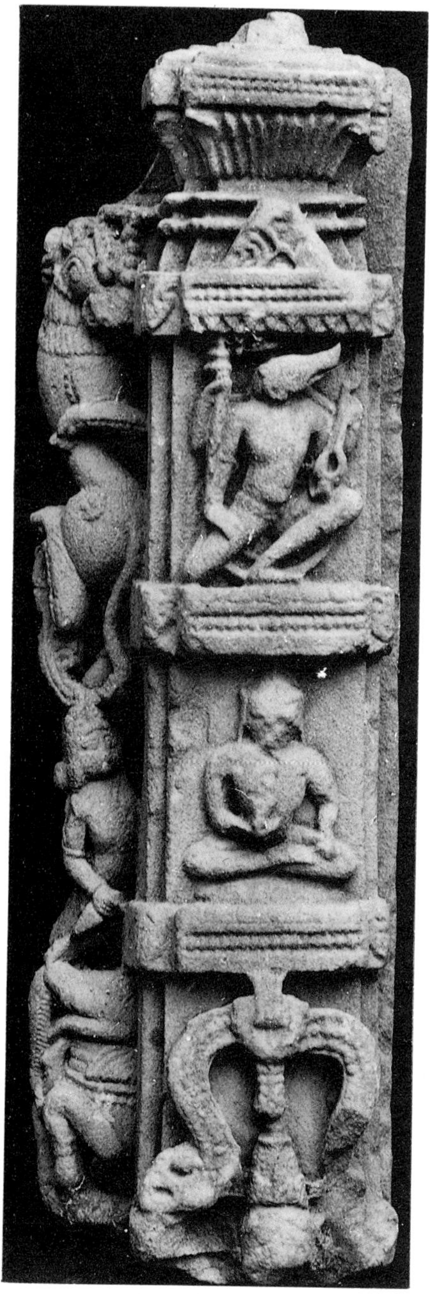

◀ 30

▼ 31

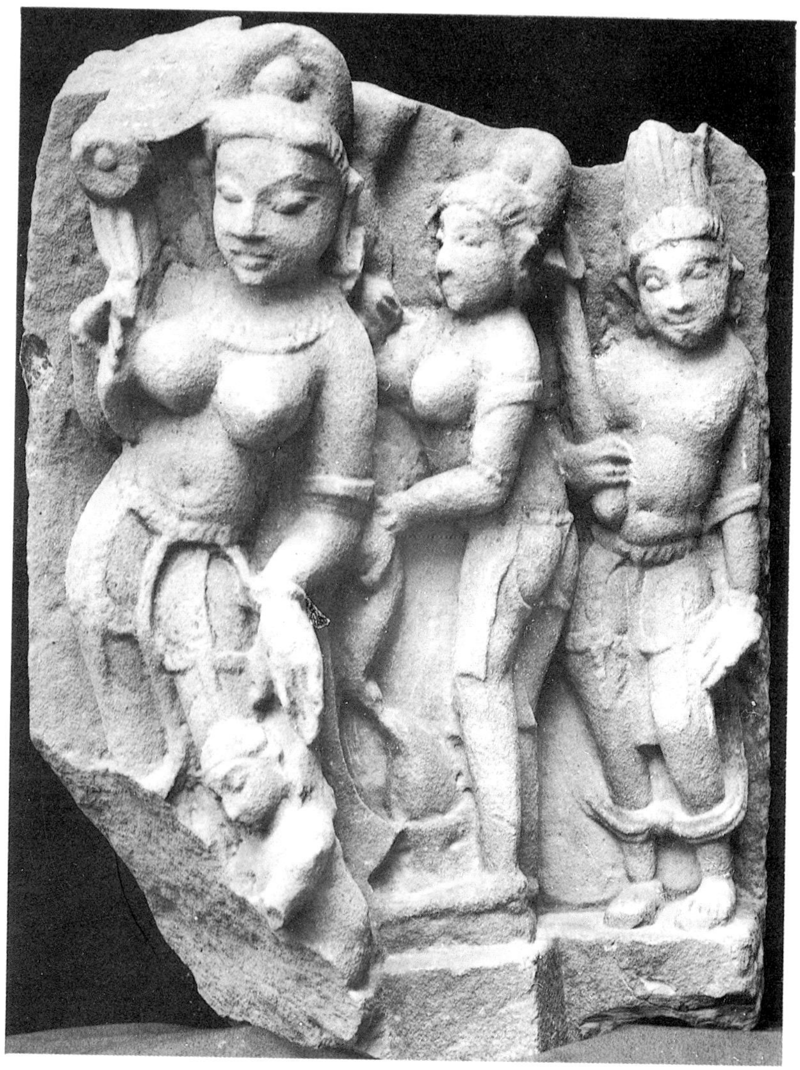

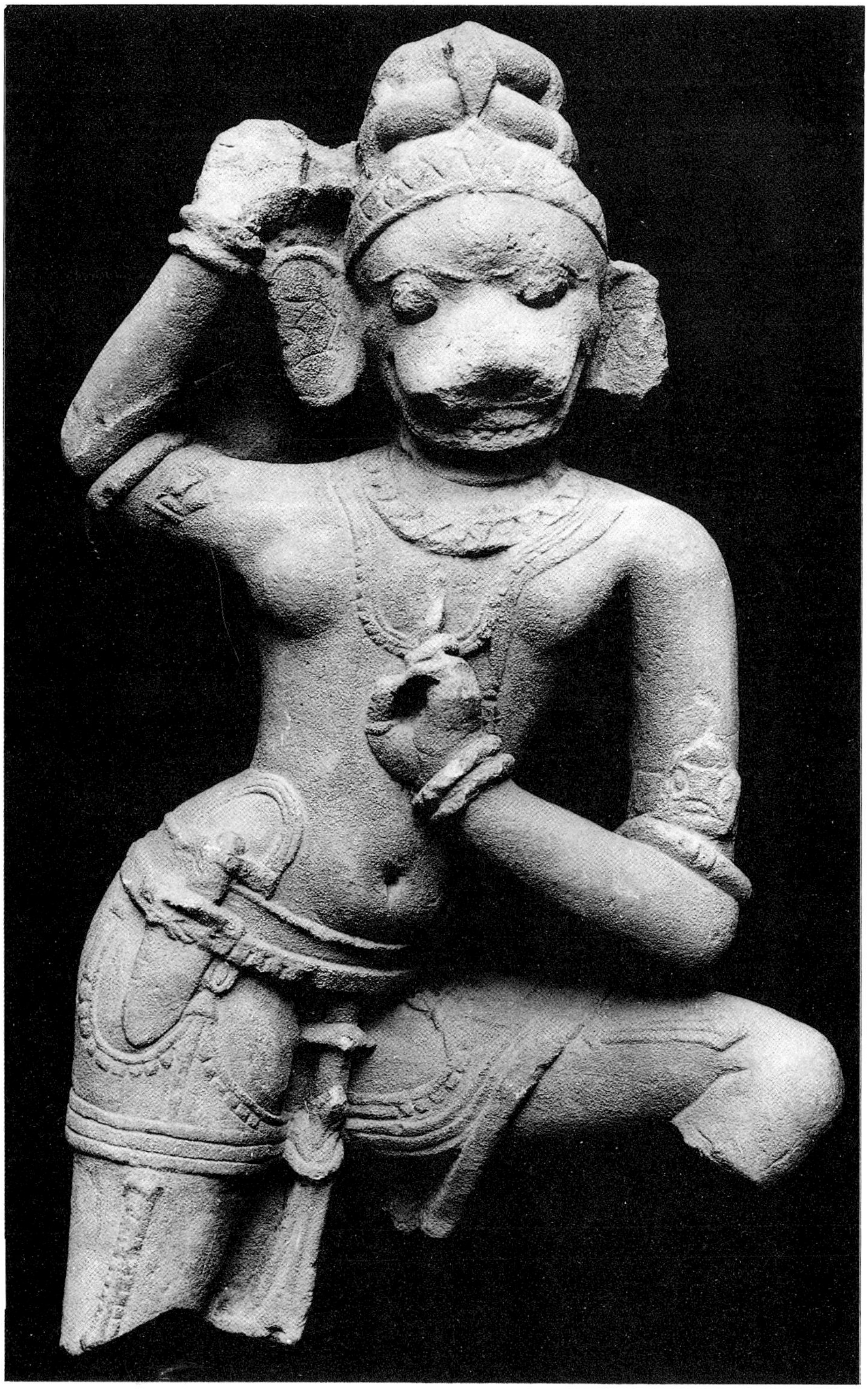

▲ 32

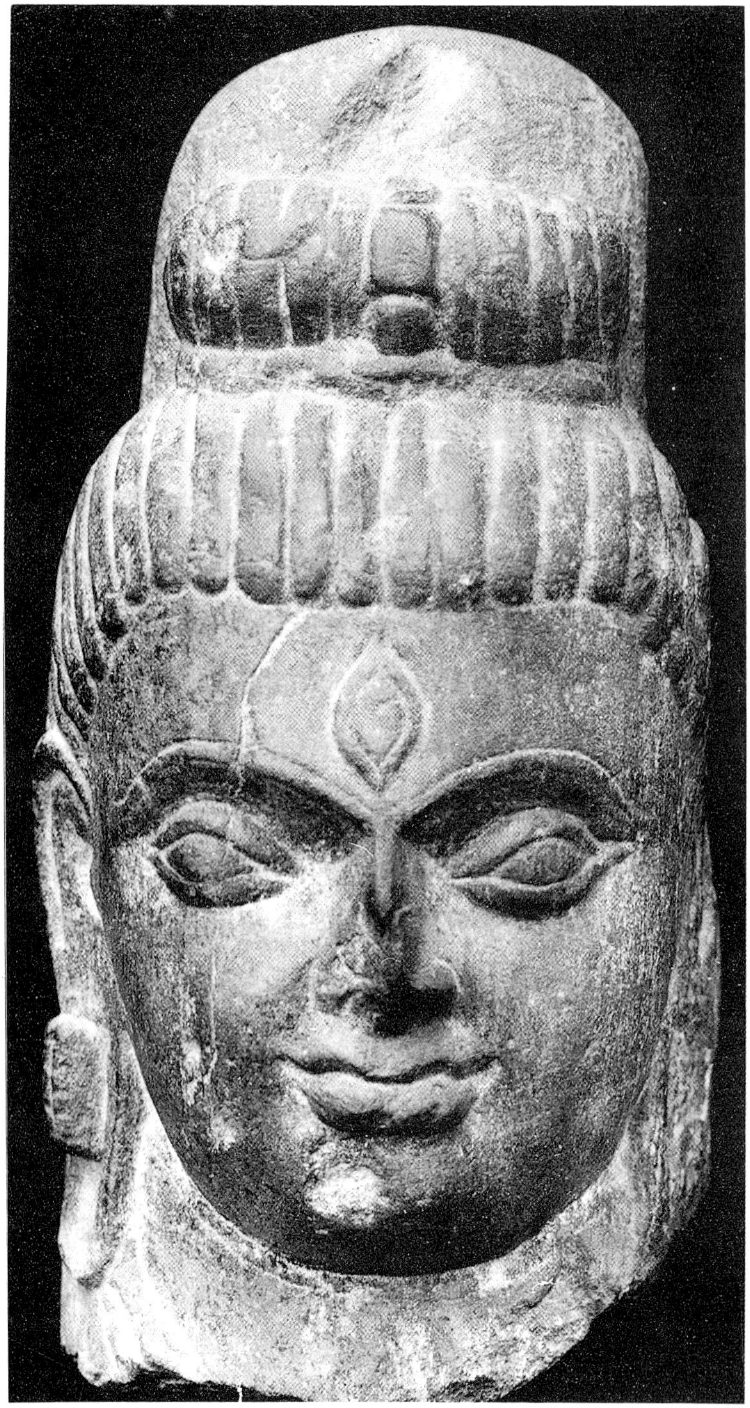

◀
34

▶
33

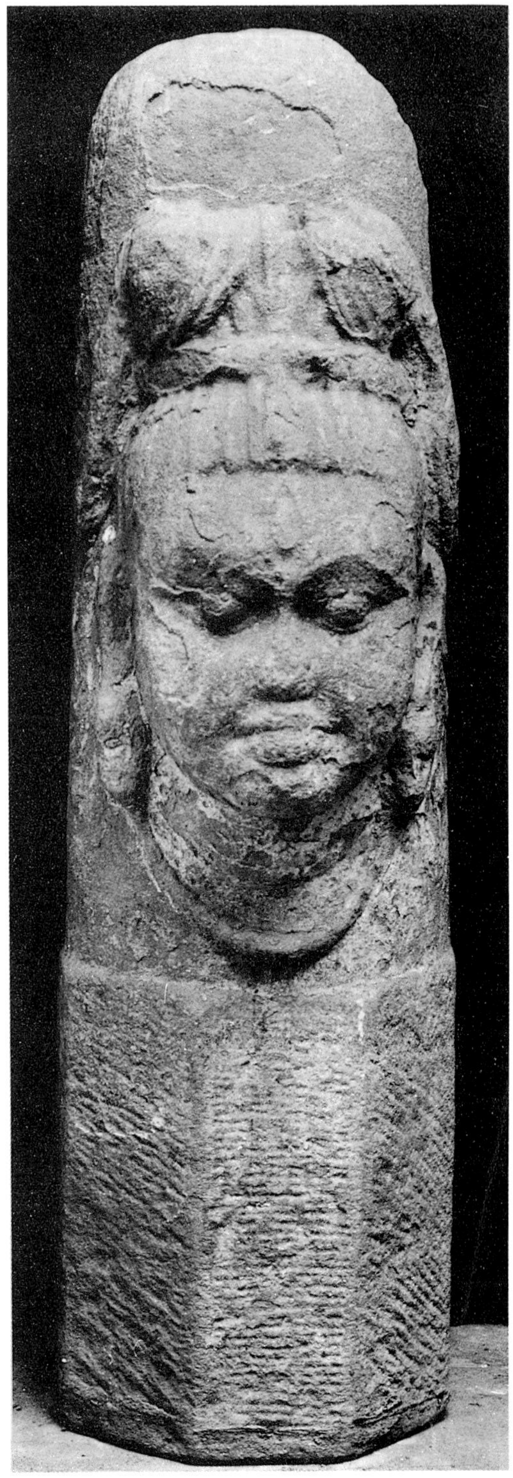

◀
35A

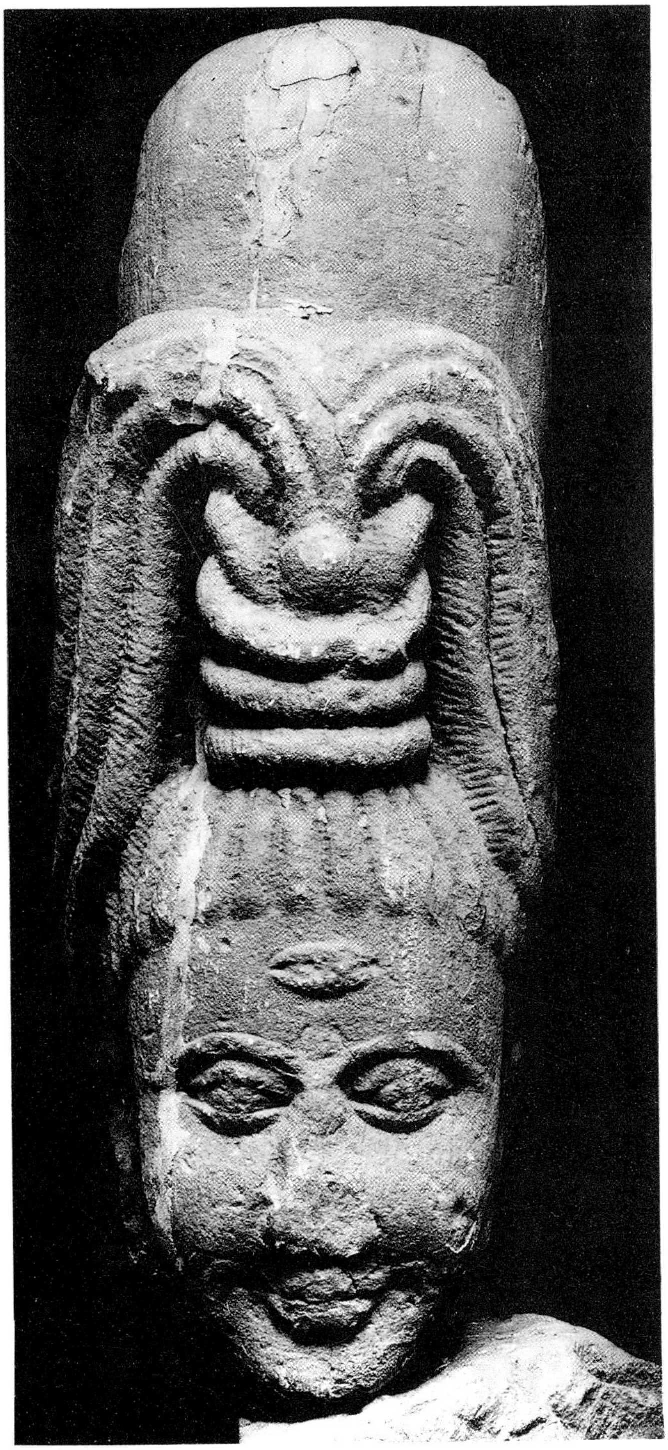

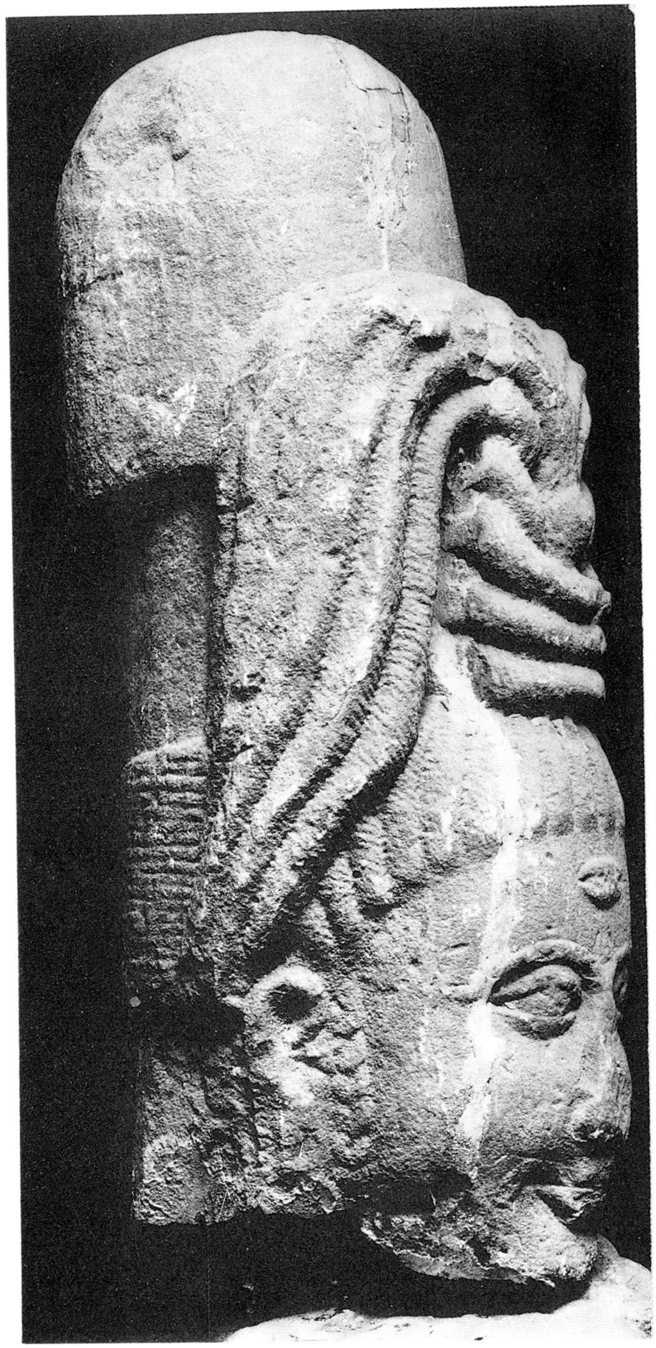

▶
35B

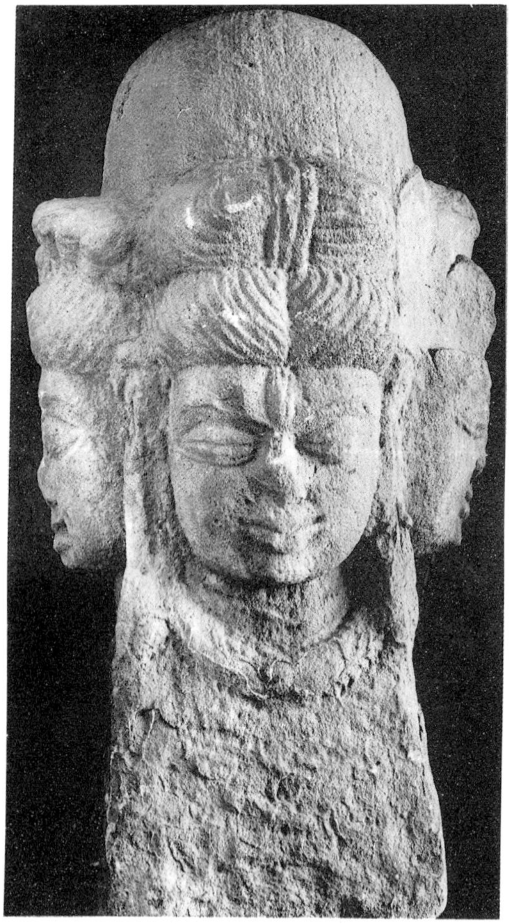

◀ 36A

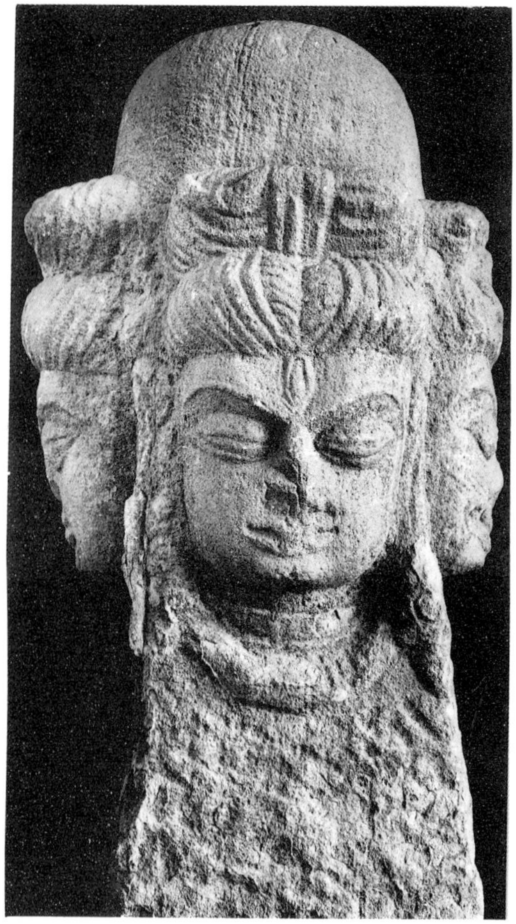

◀ 36B

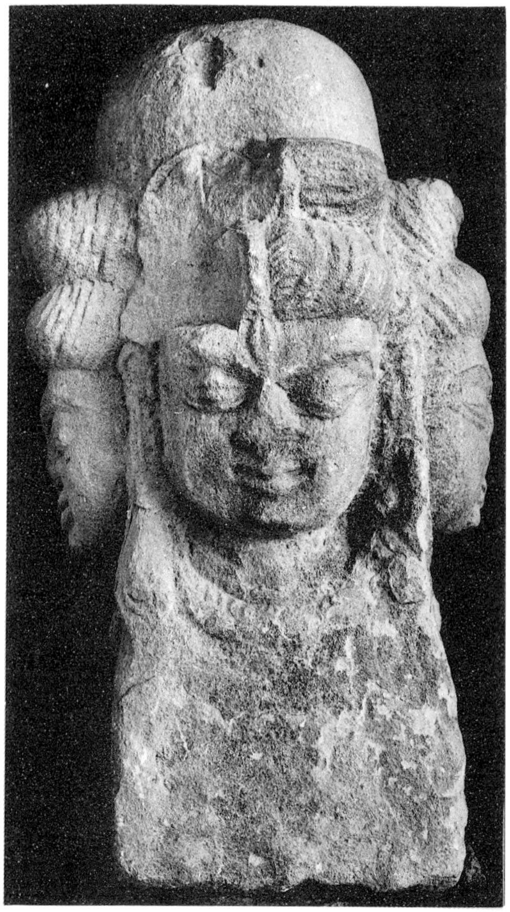

▶ 36C

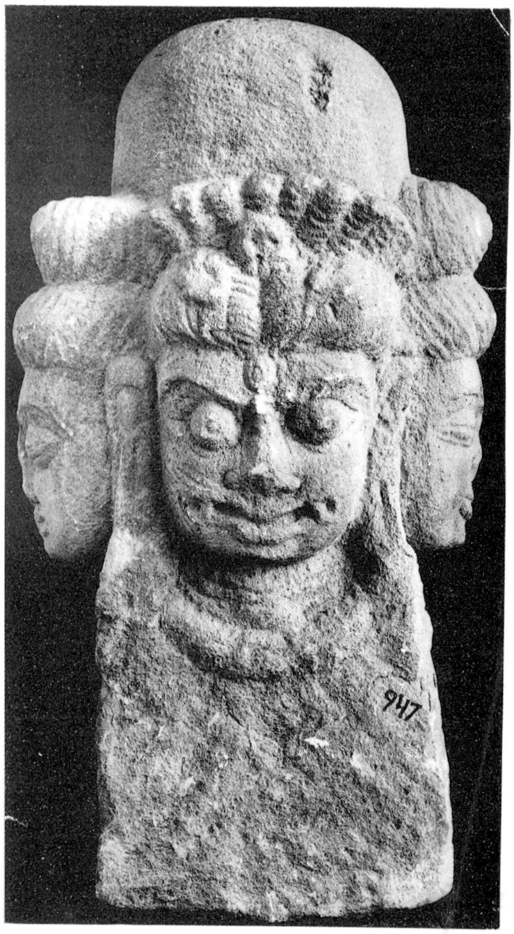

▶ 36D

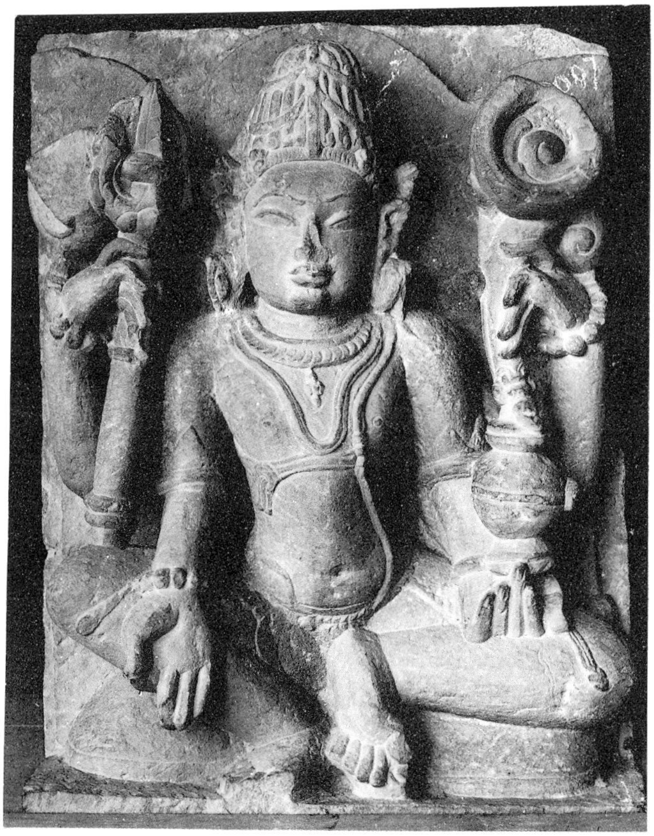

◀
38

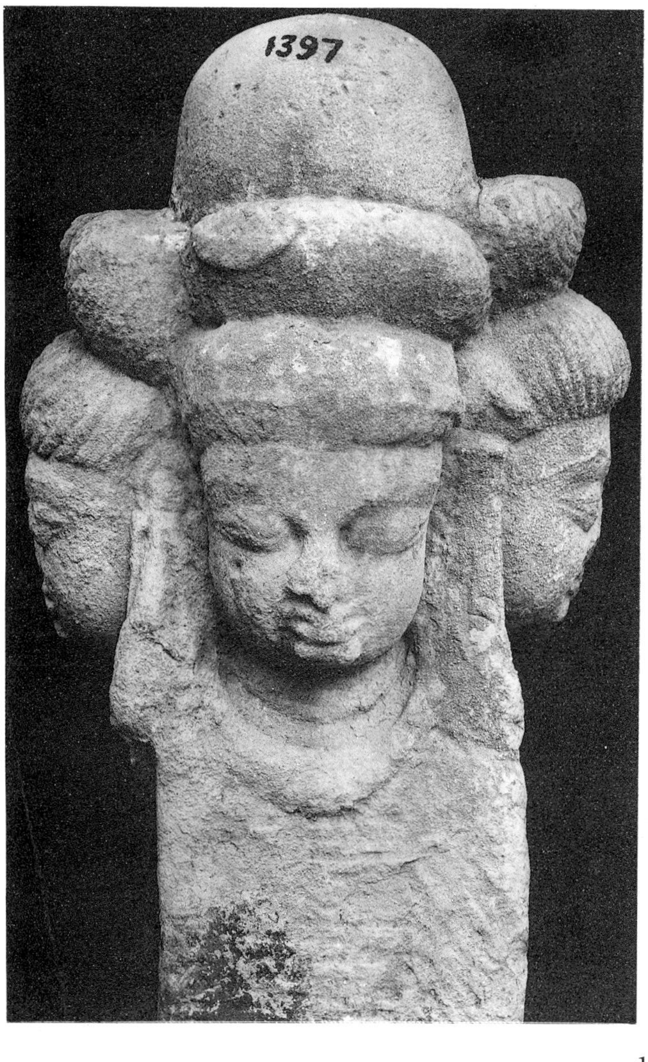

◀
37A

▶
37B

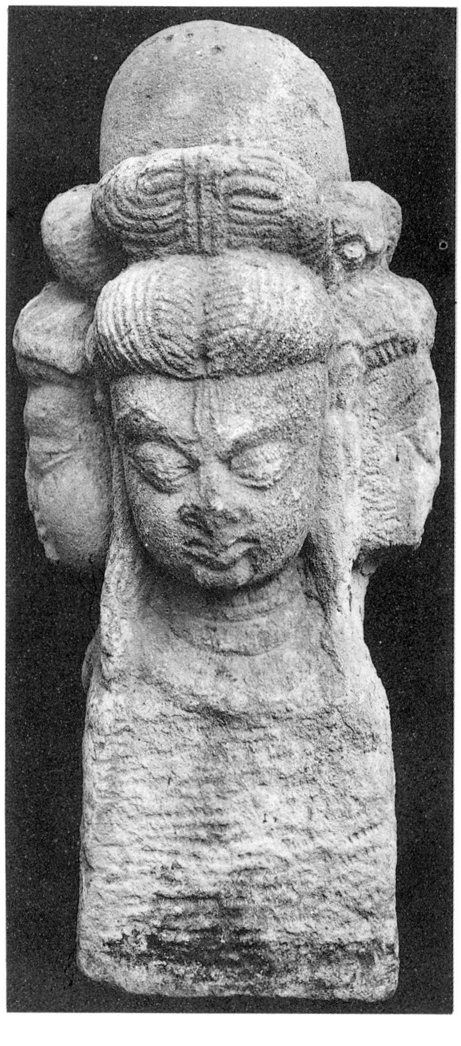

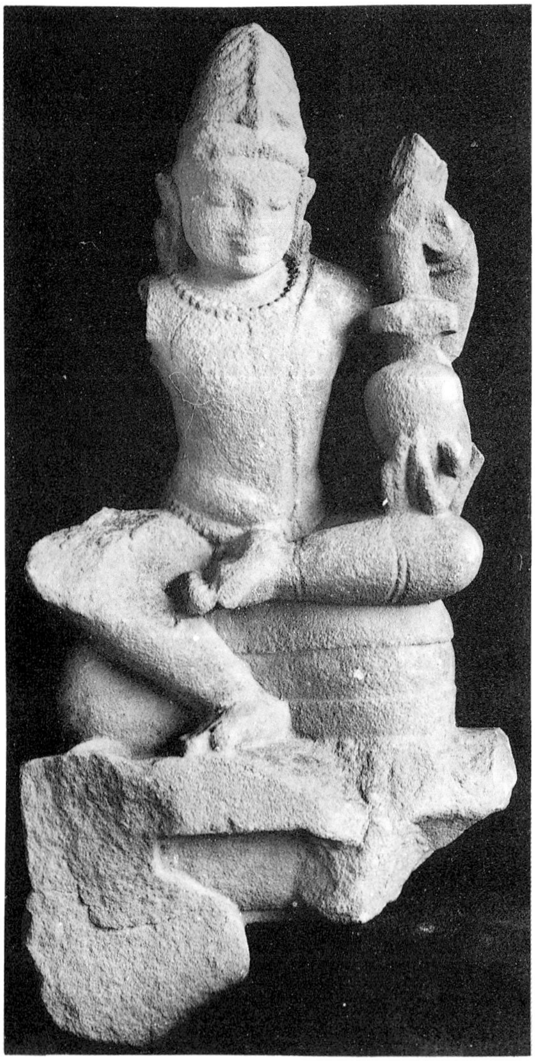

◀ 39

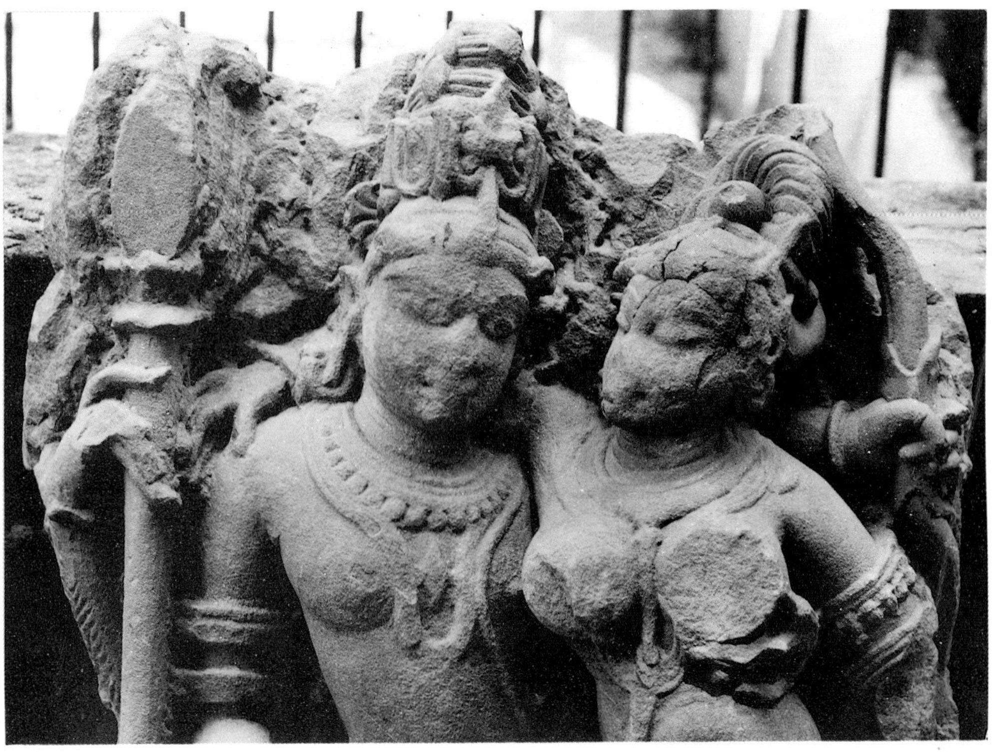

▶ 41

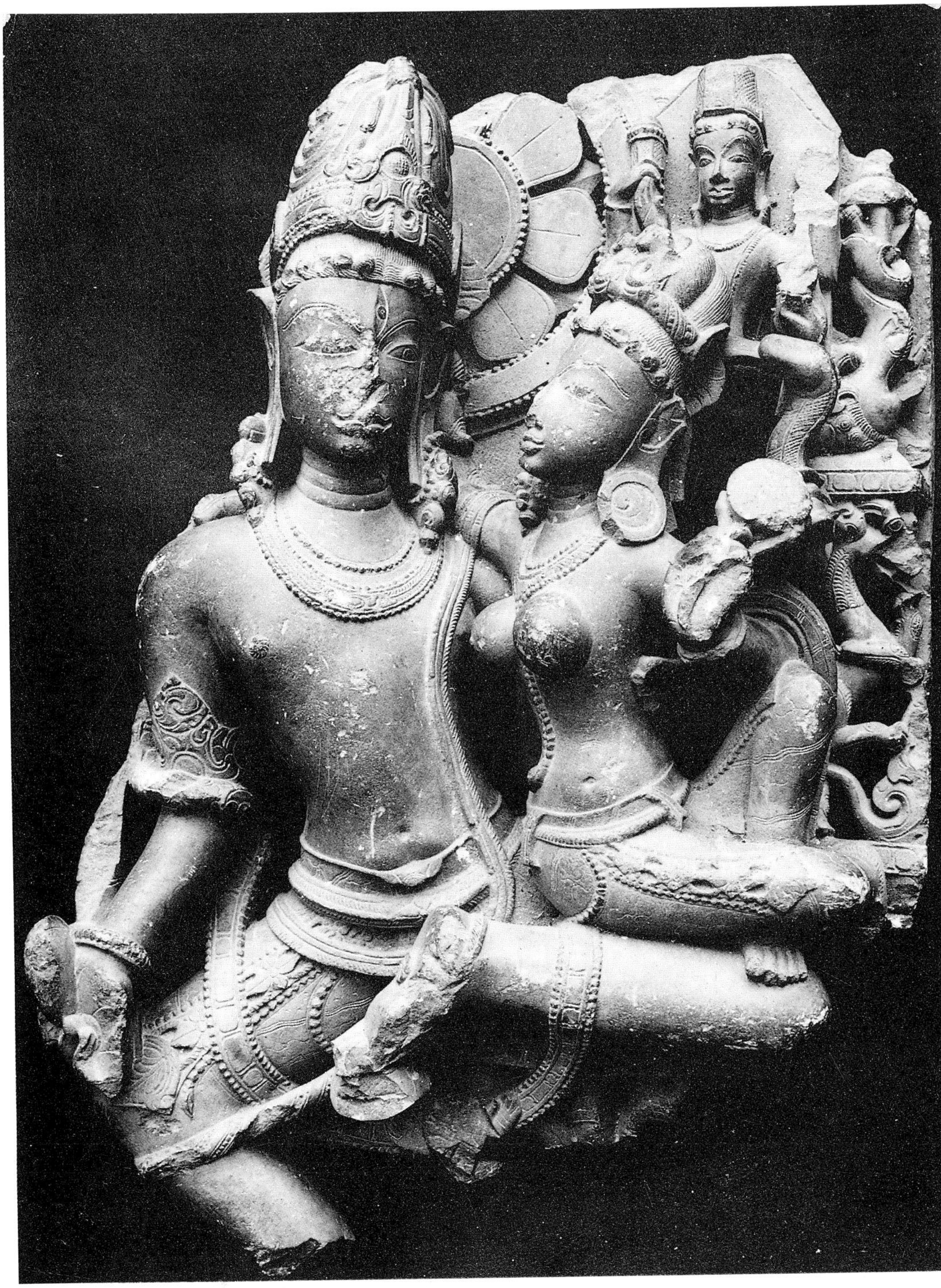

▲40

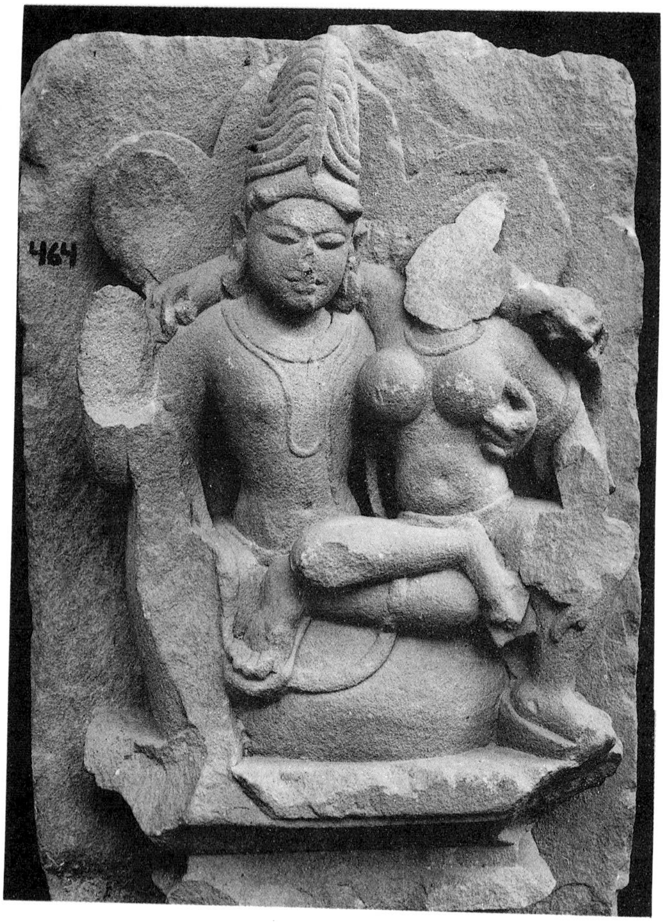

◀
42

◀
43

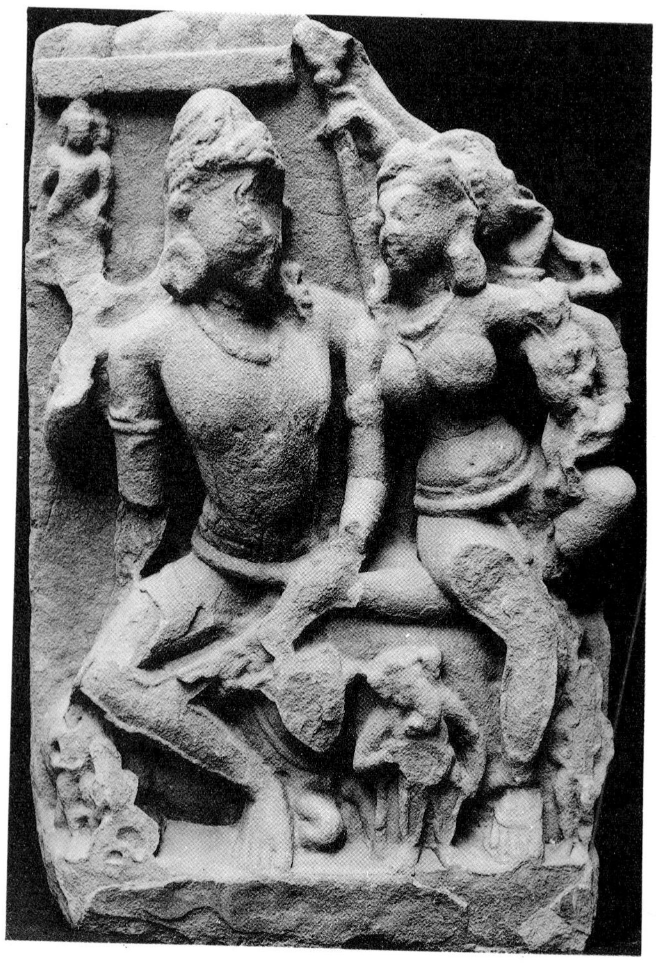

▶
44

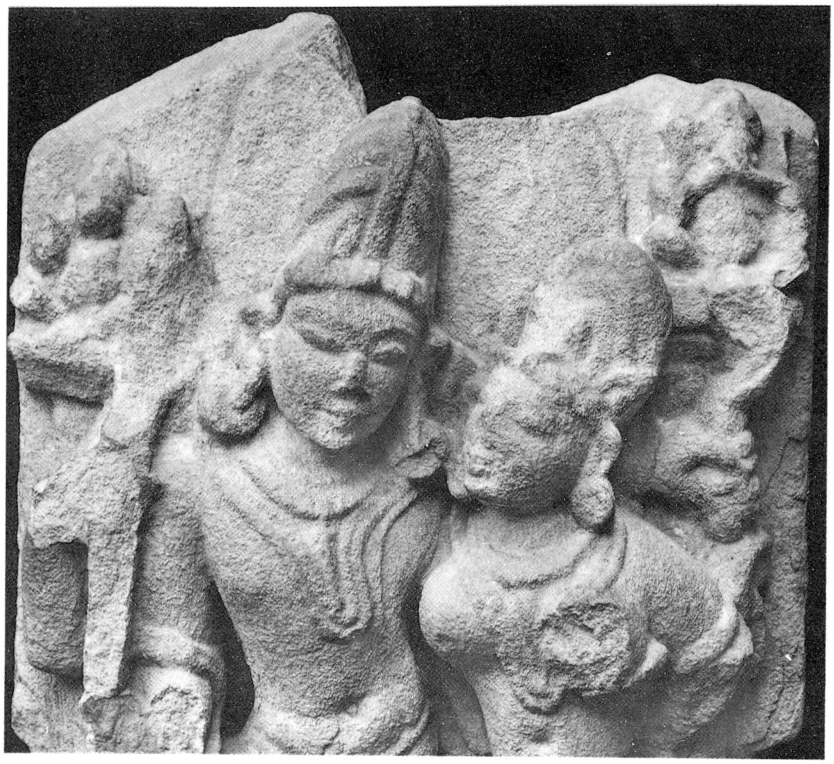

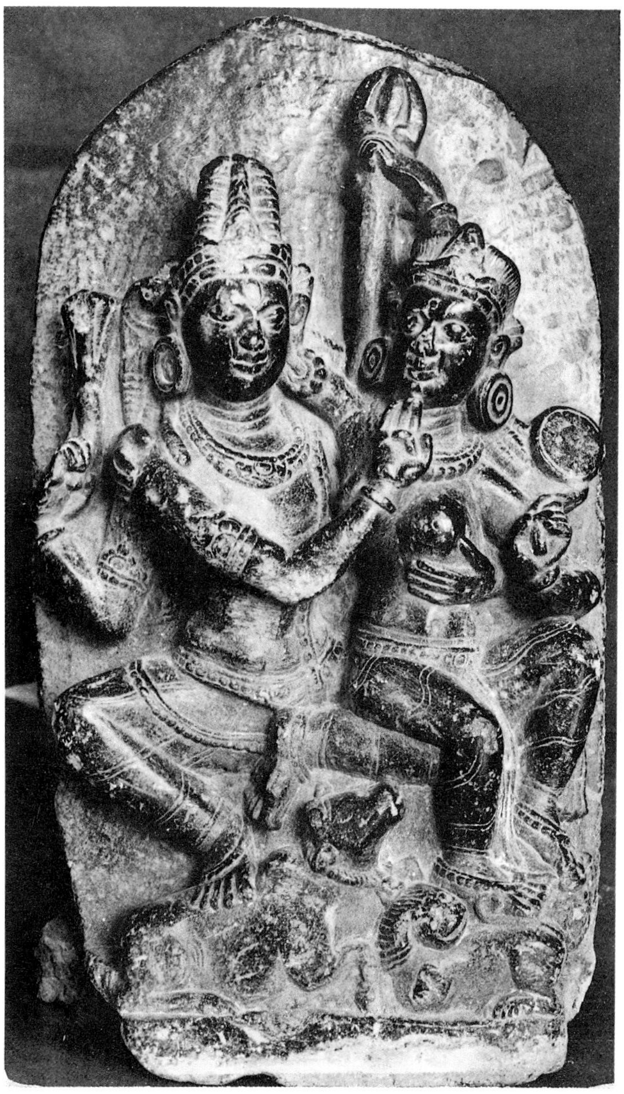

◀
45

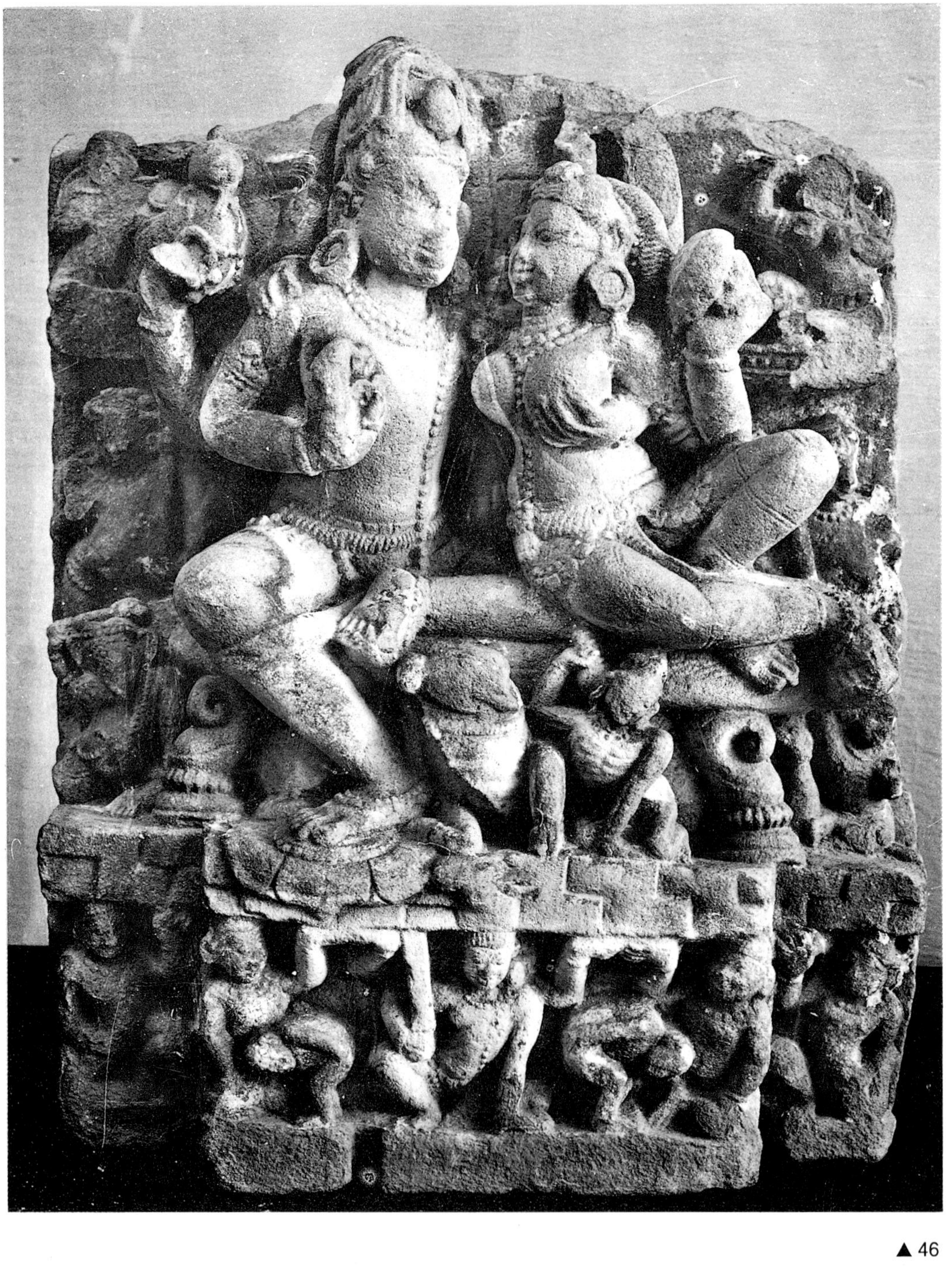

▲46

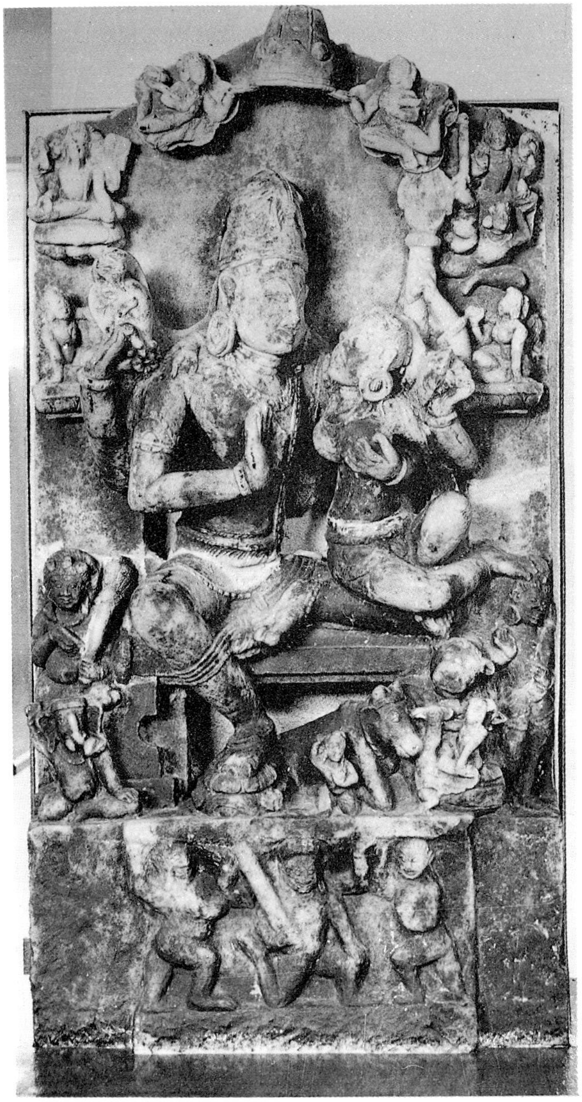

◀ 47

▶ 48

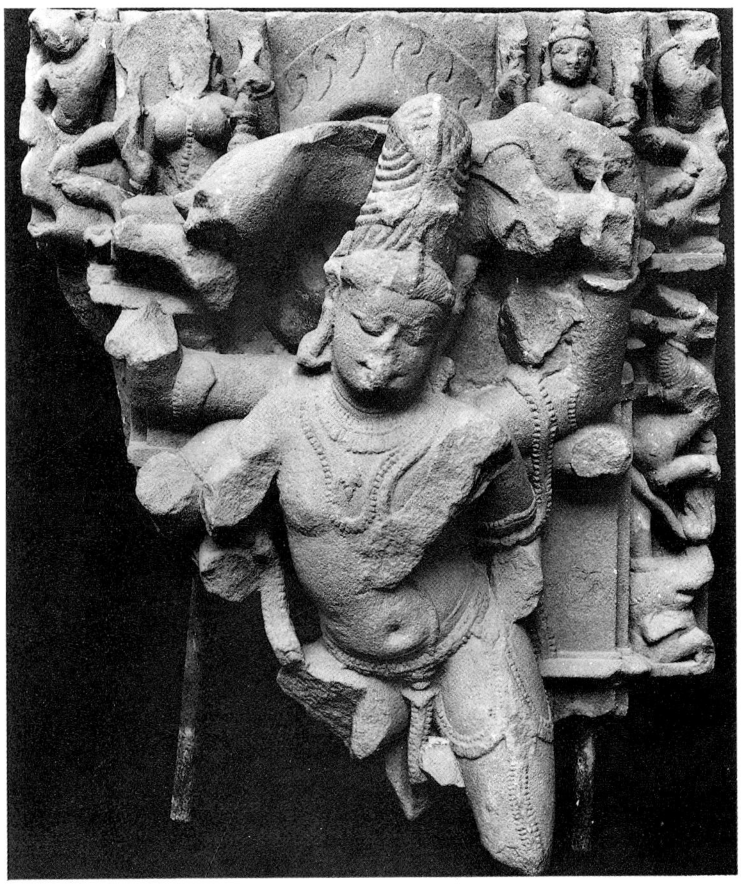

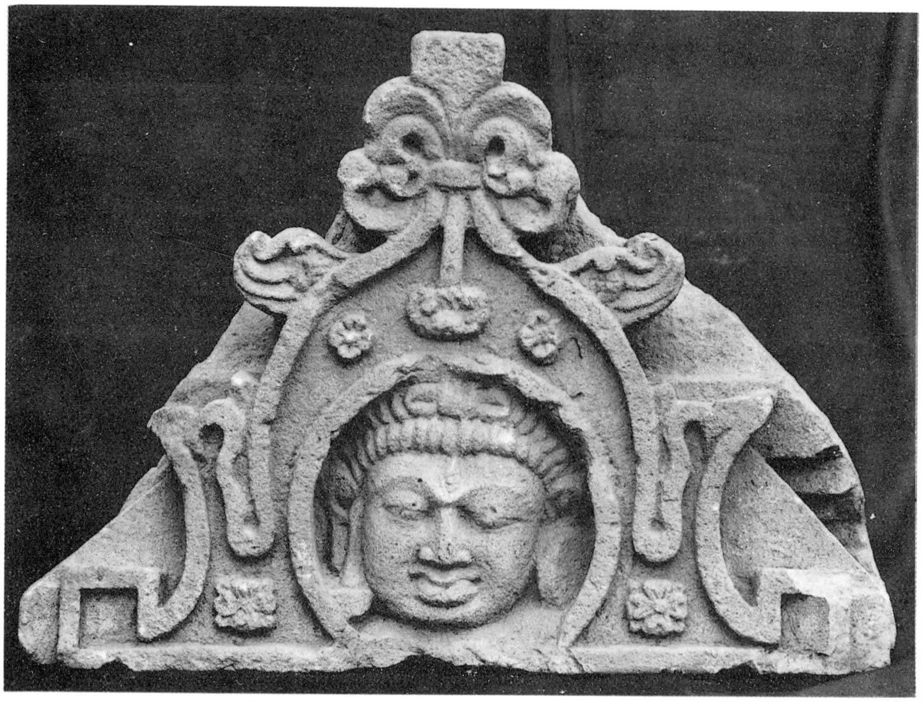

◀
49

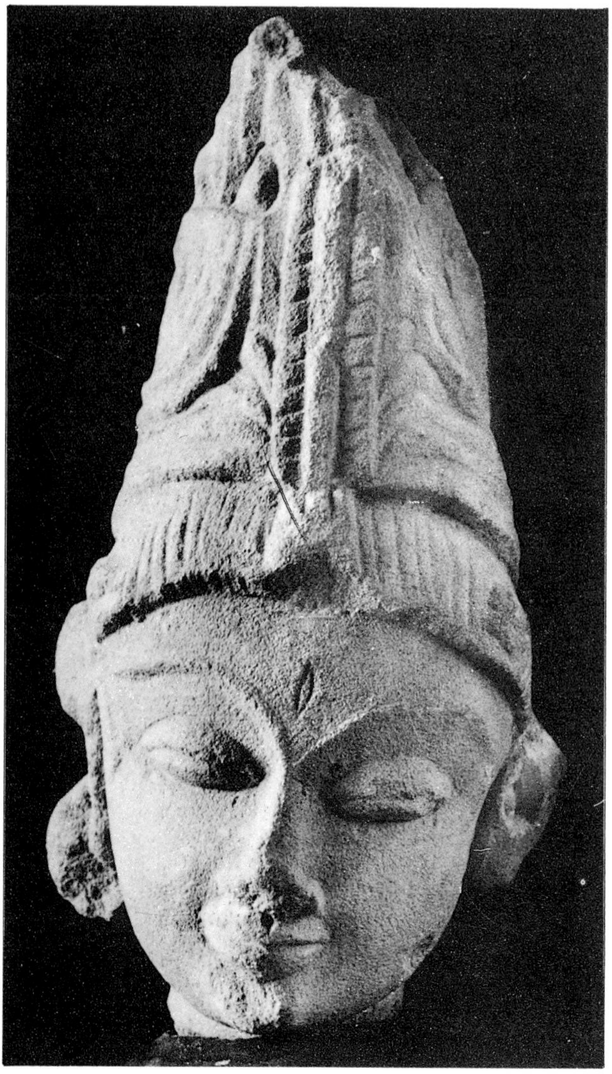

◀
52

▶
53

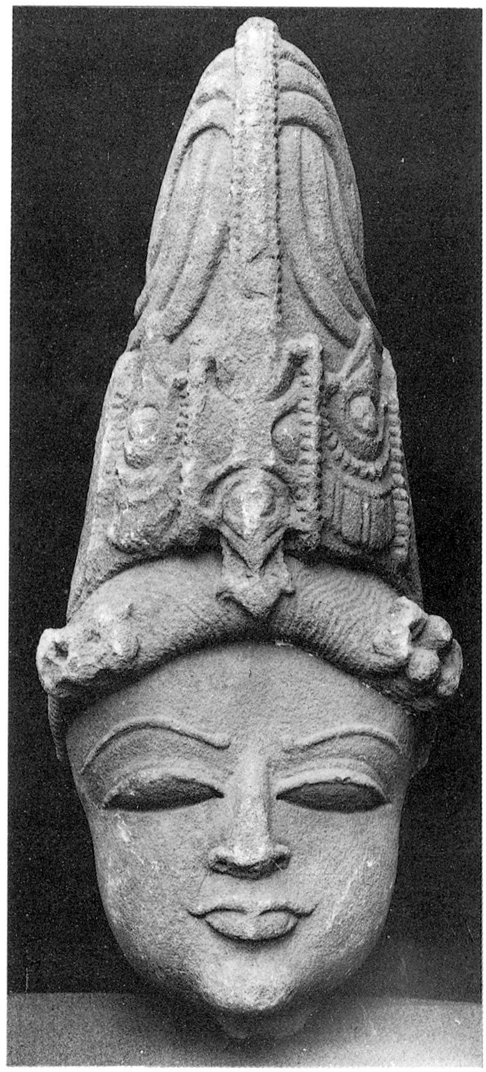

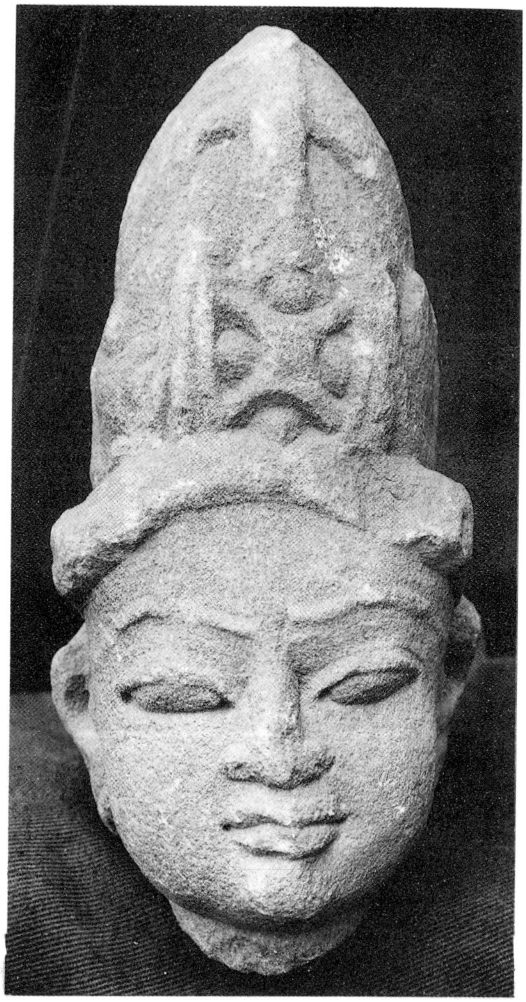

◀ 50

▶ 51

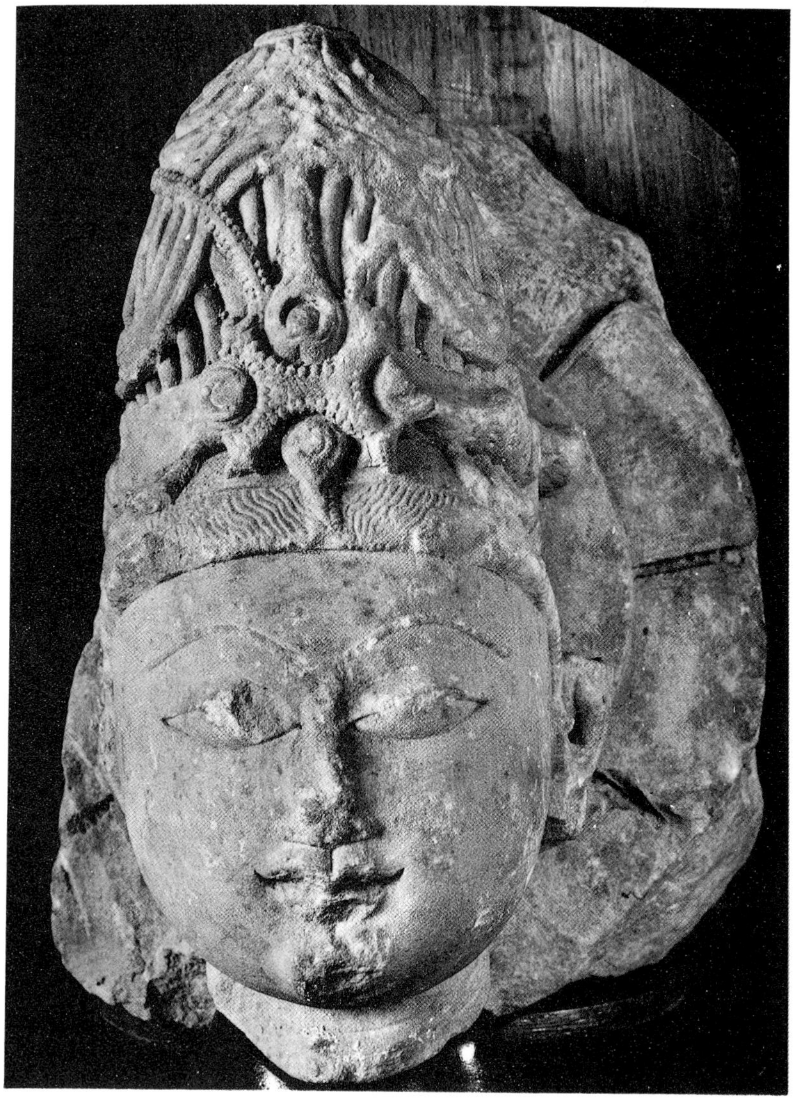

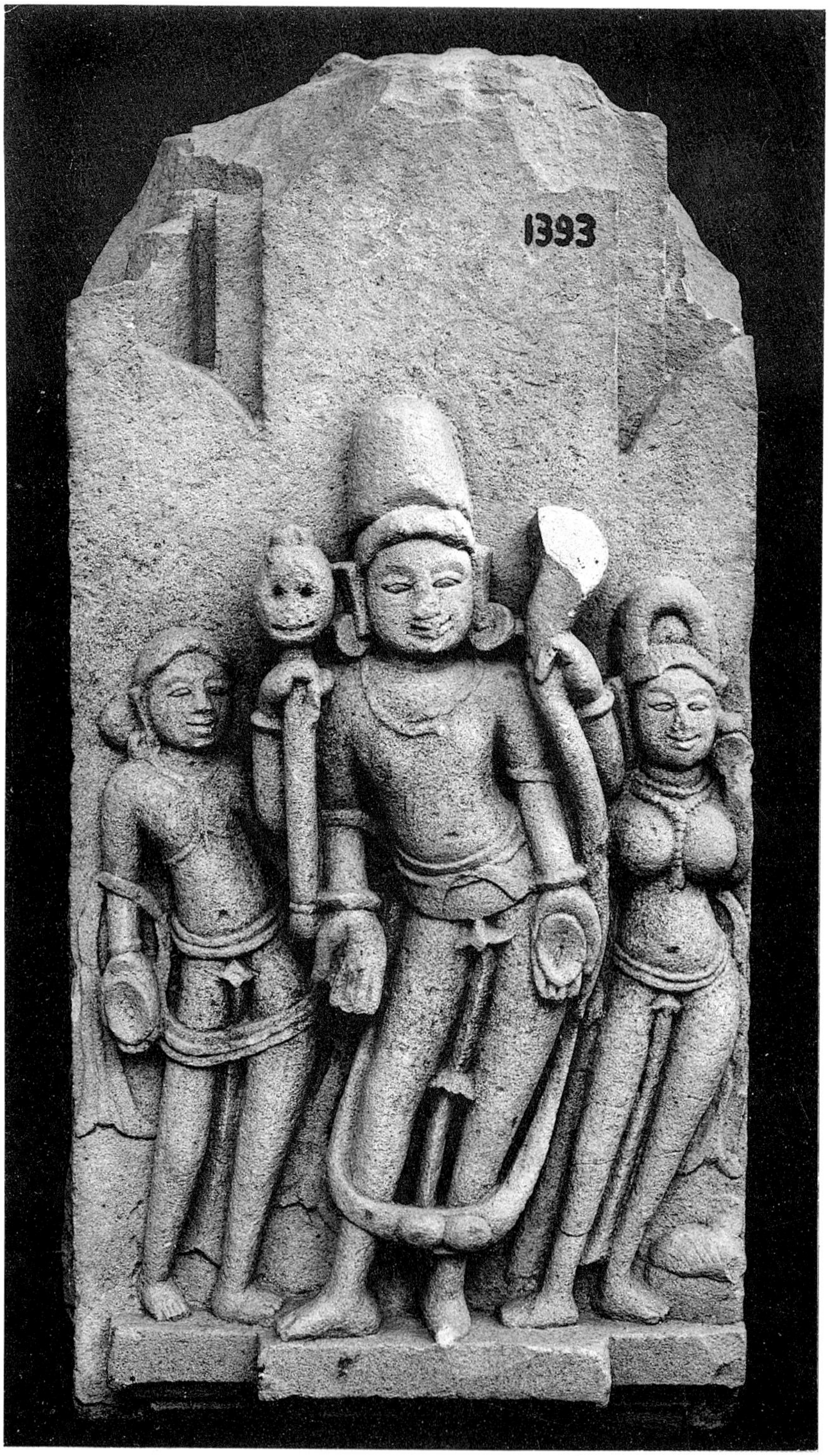

▲54

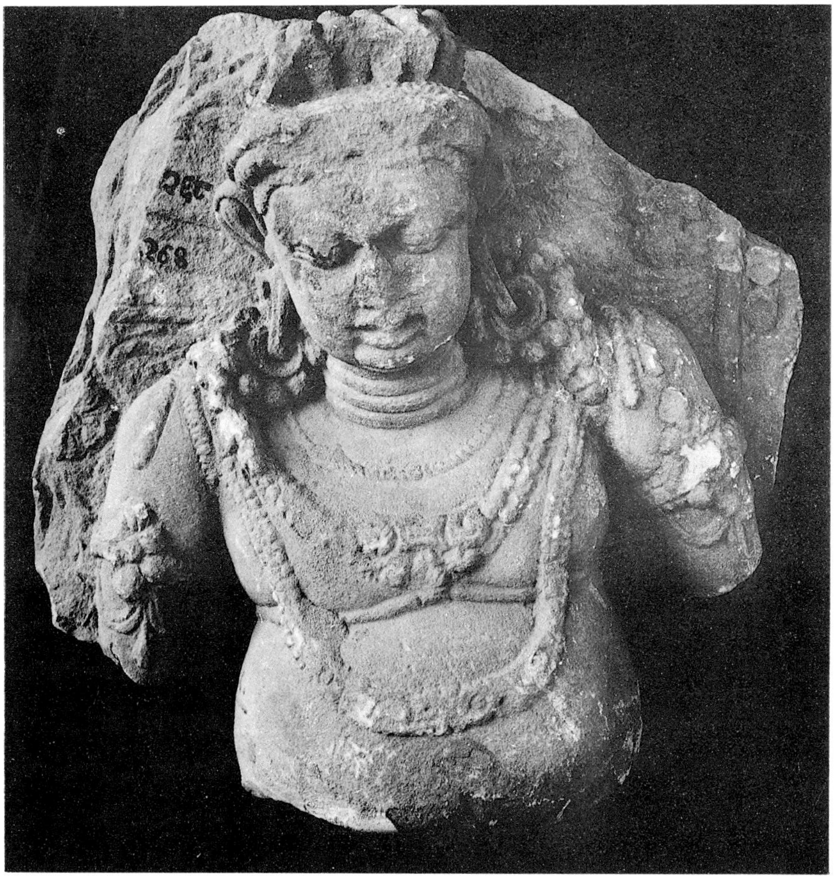

◀ 55

▶ 56

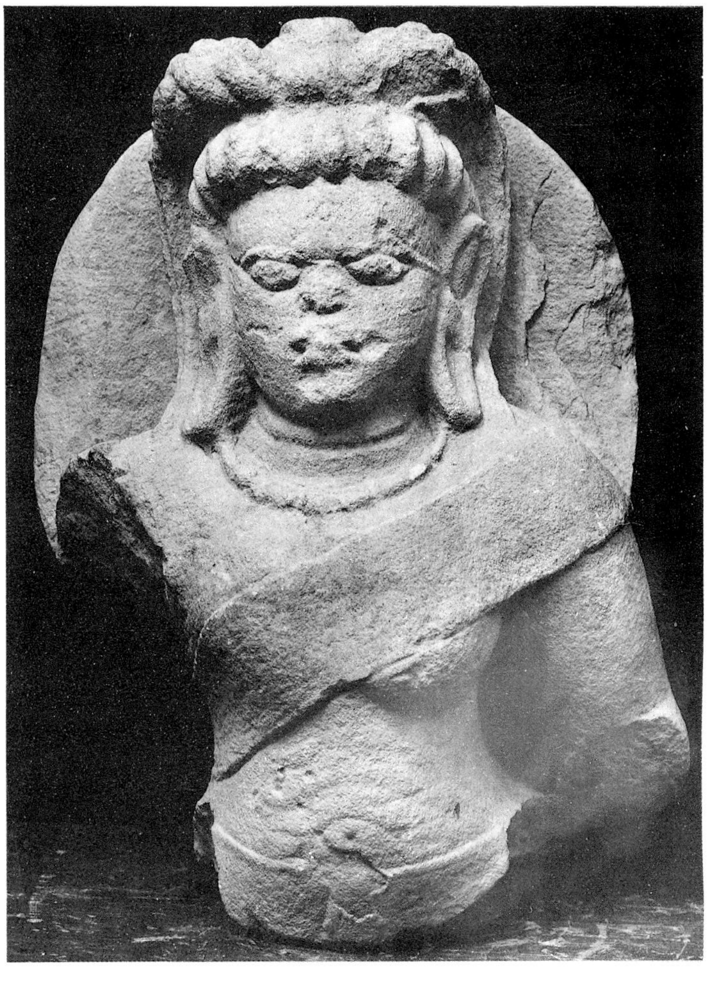

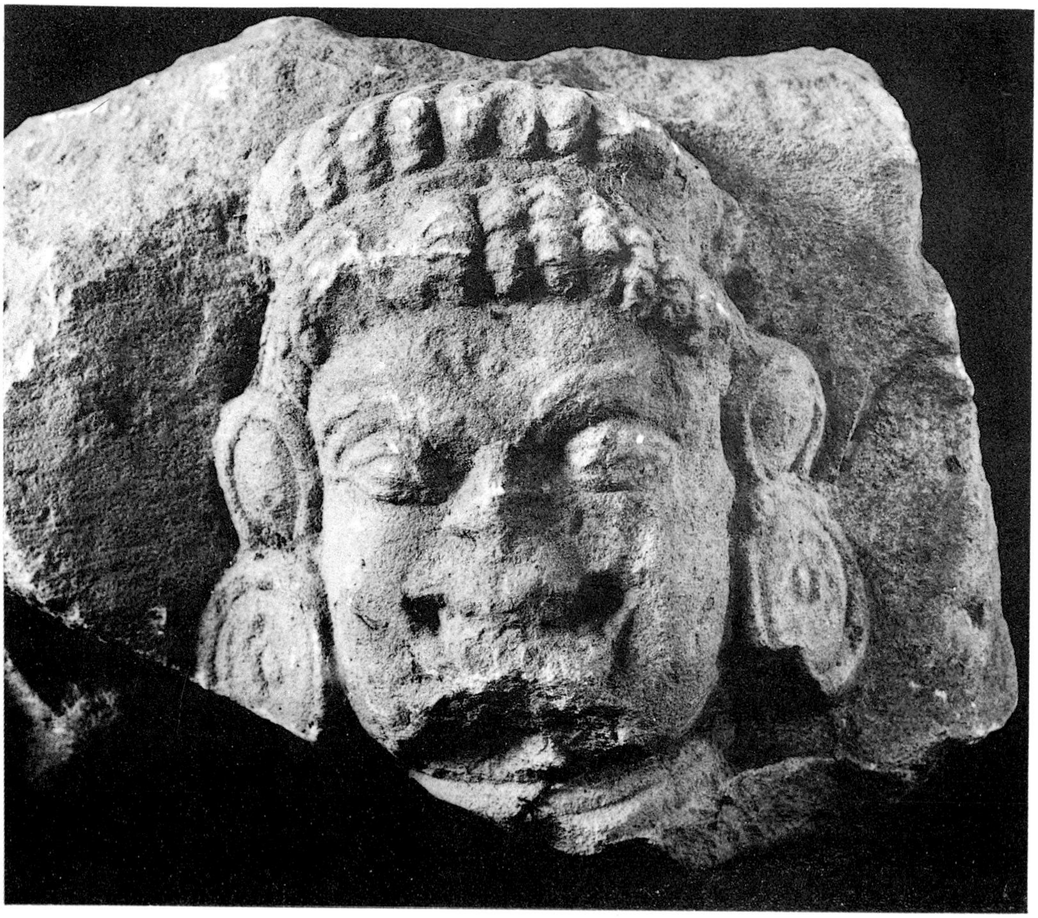

◀ 57

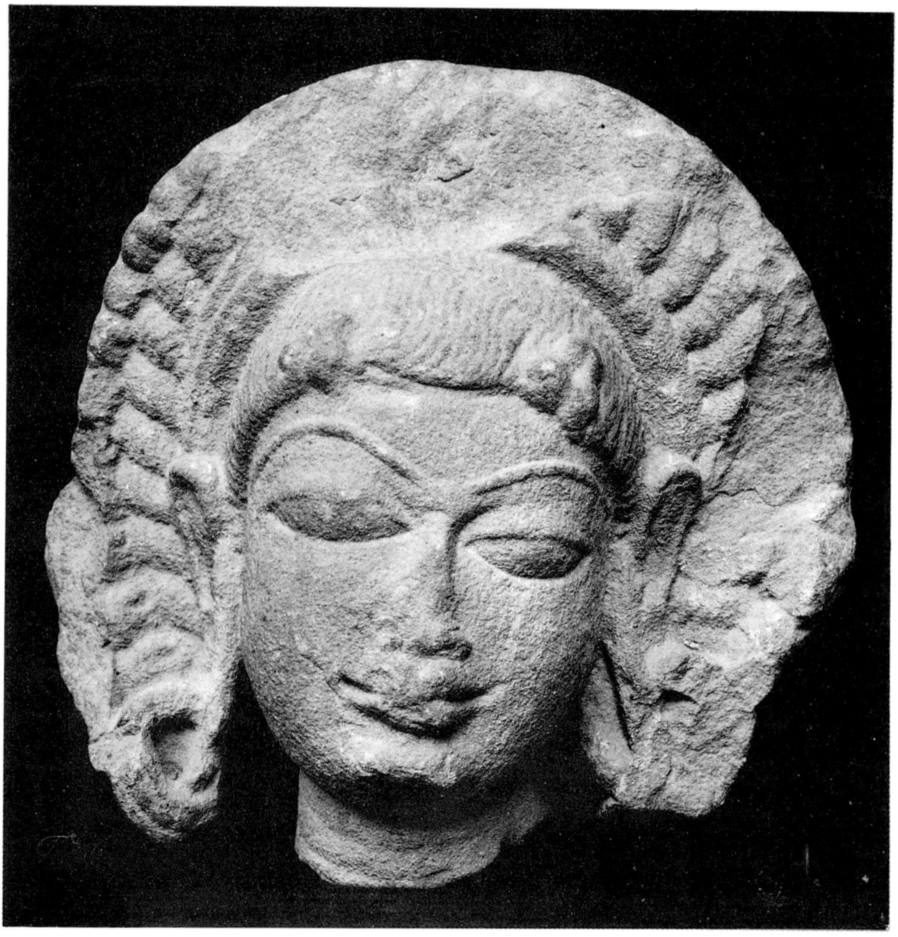

▶ 58

◀ 59

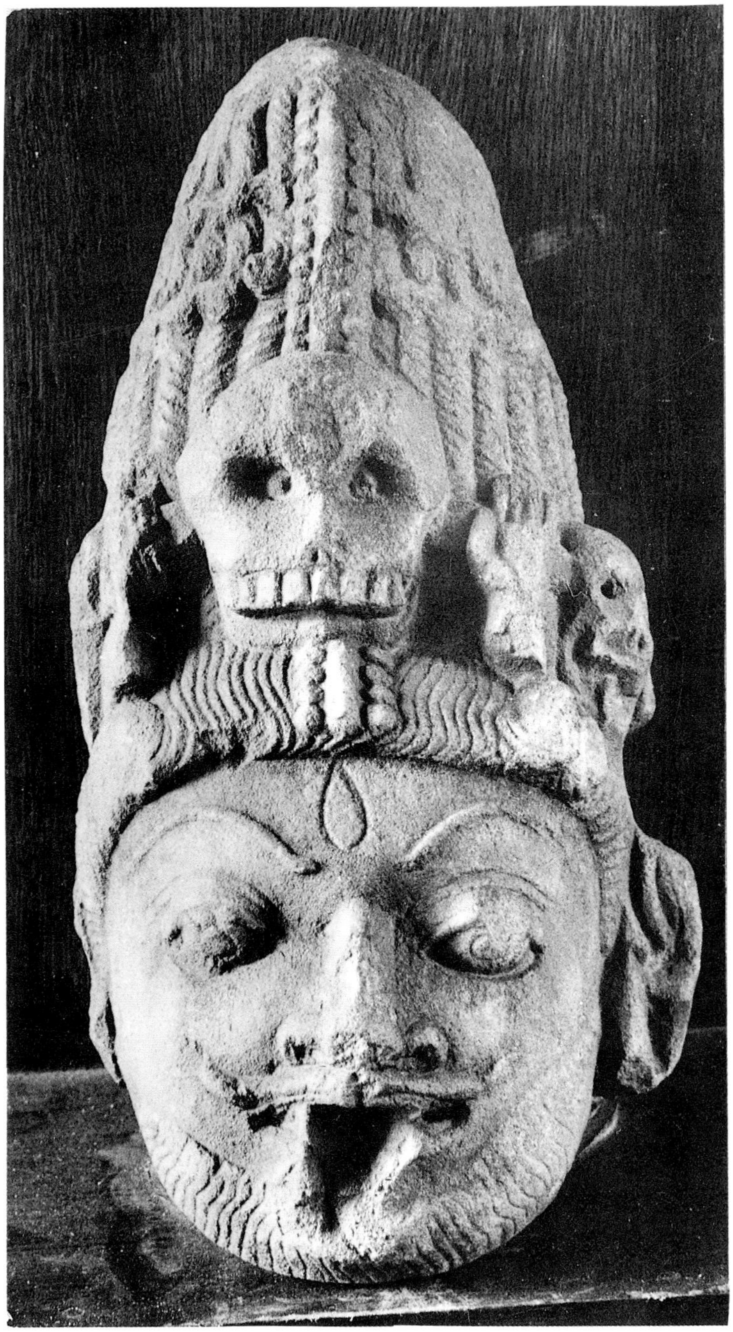

▶ 60

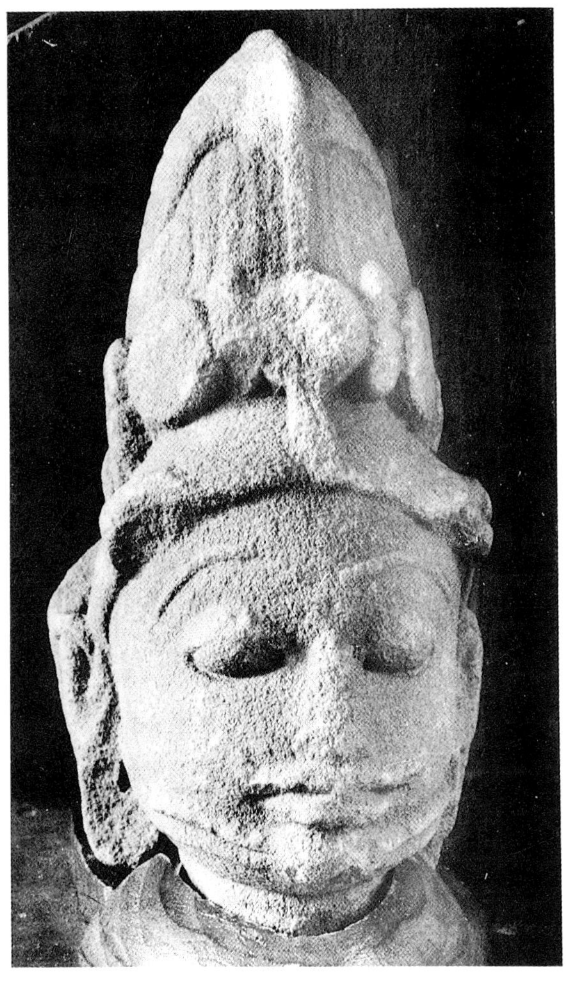

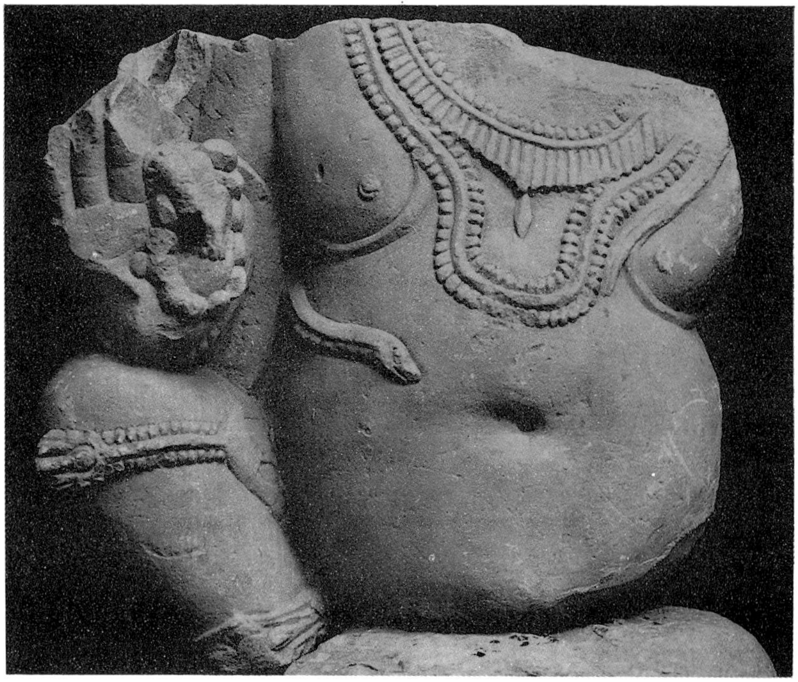

◄ 61

▼ 62

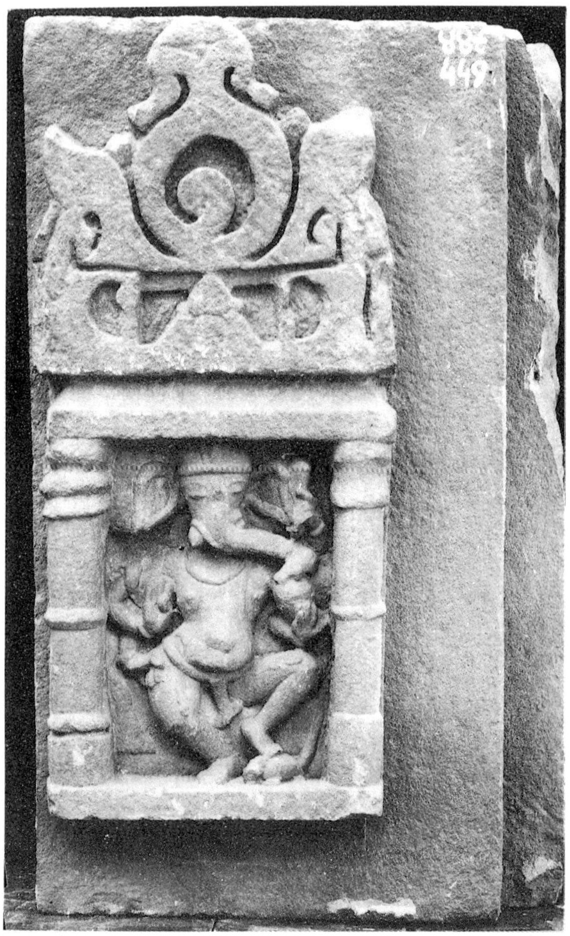

▼ 65

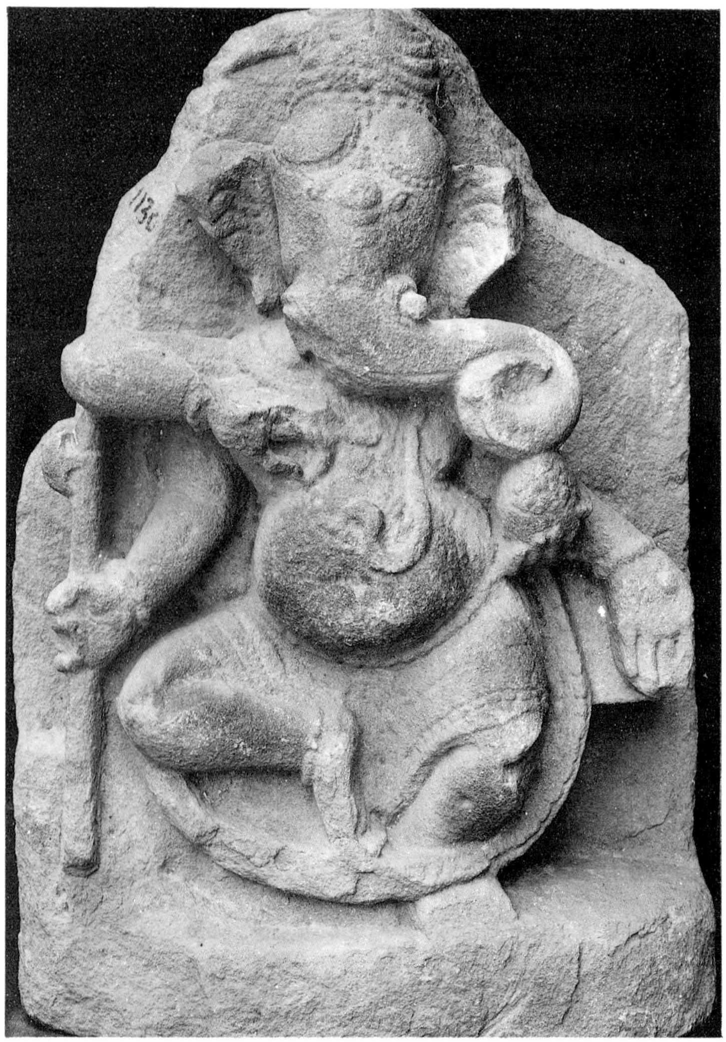

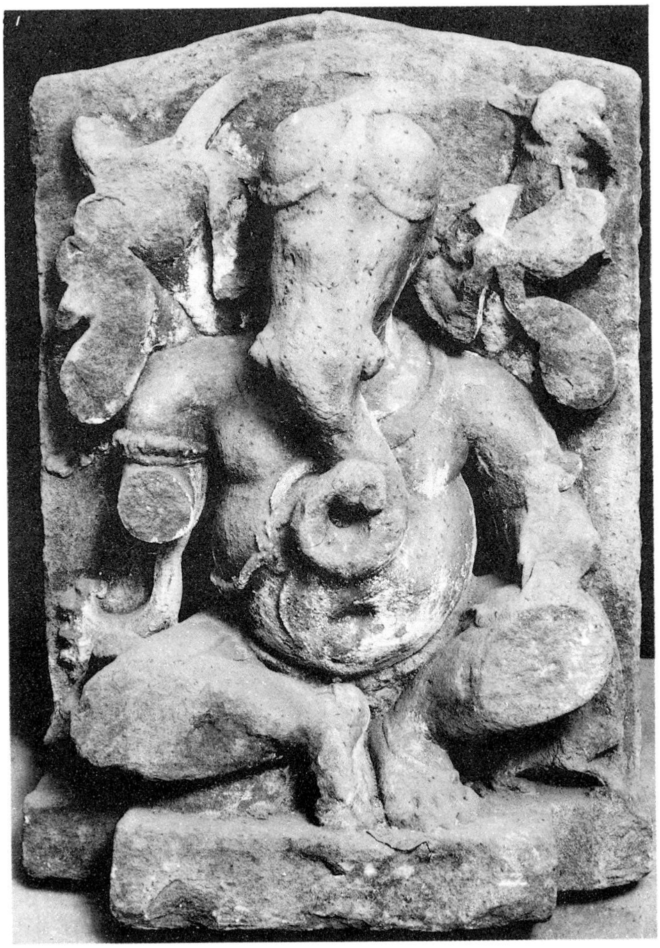

◀
63

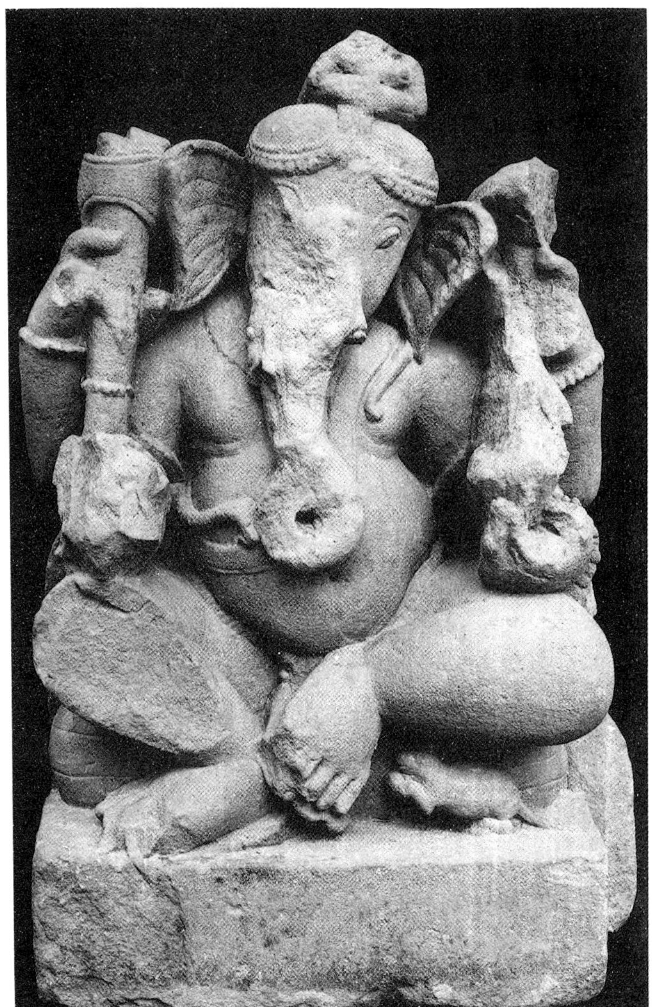

▶
64

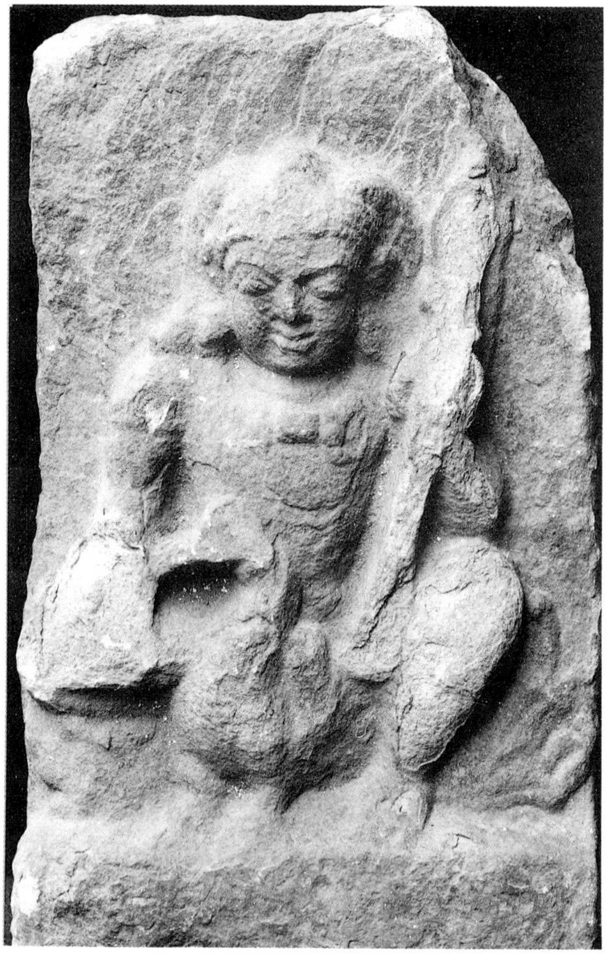

◀
66

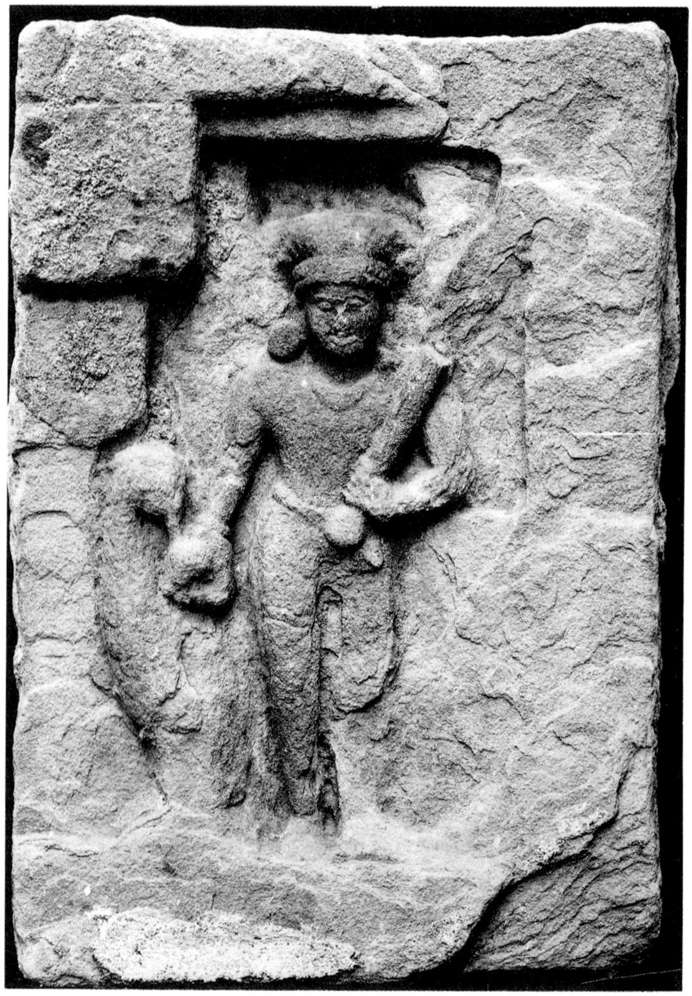

▶
67

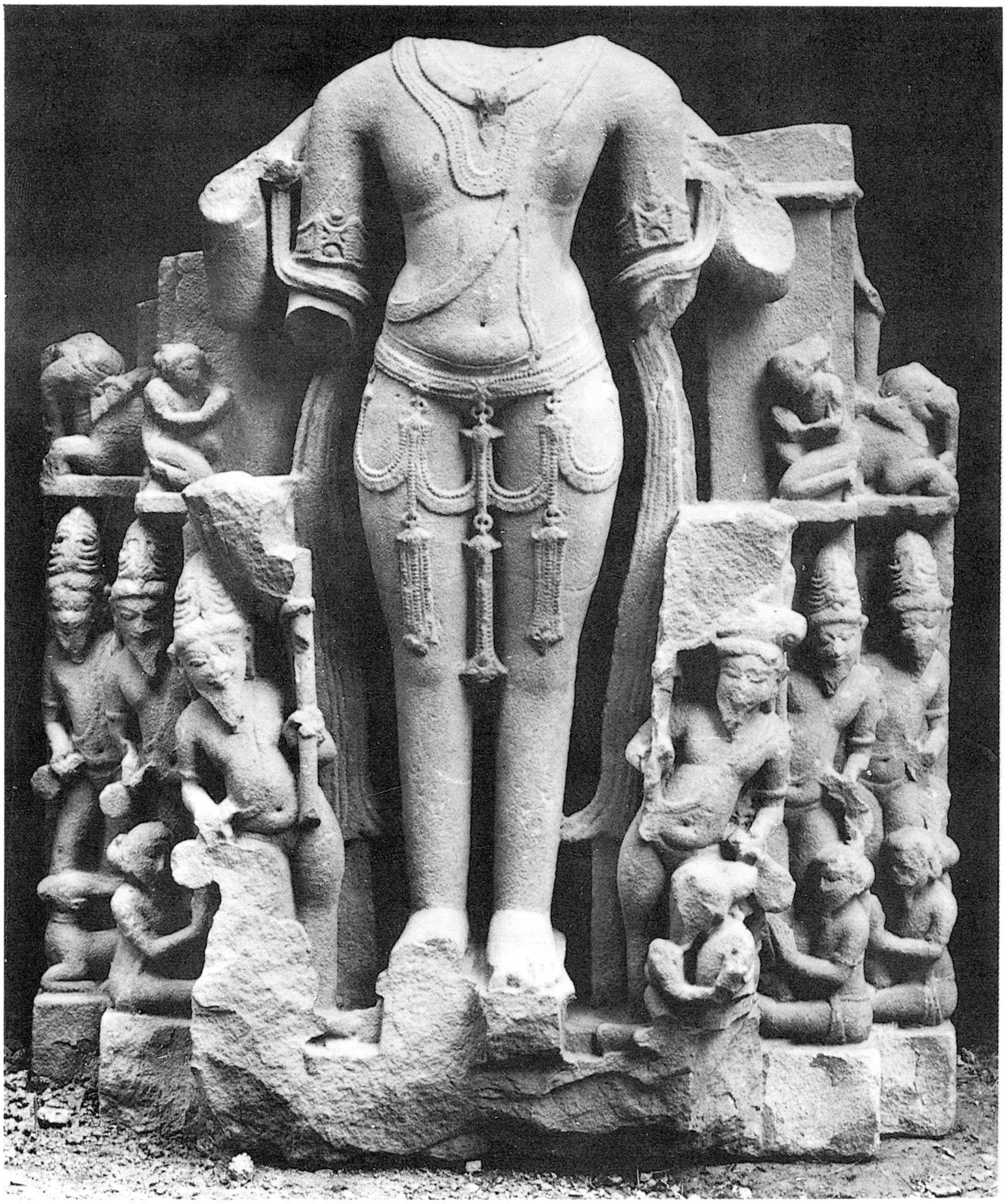

▲74

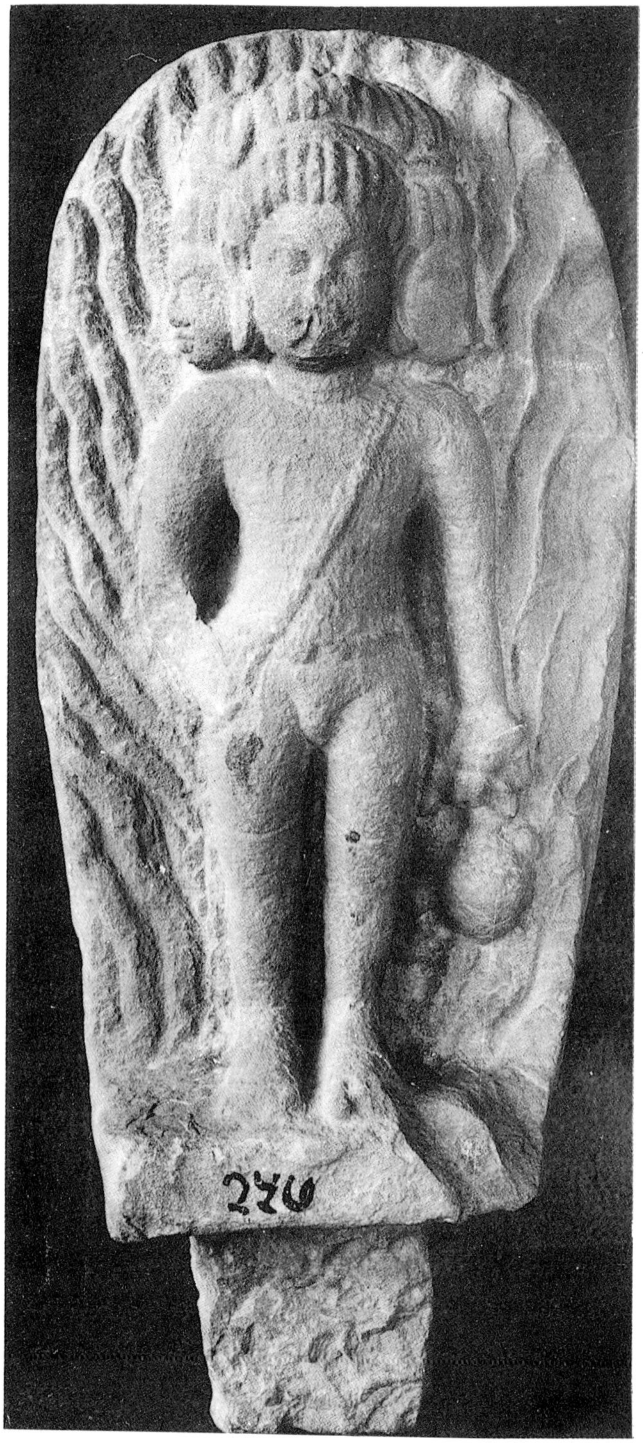

◀
73

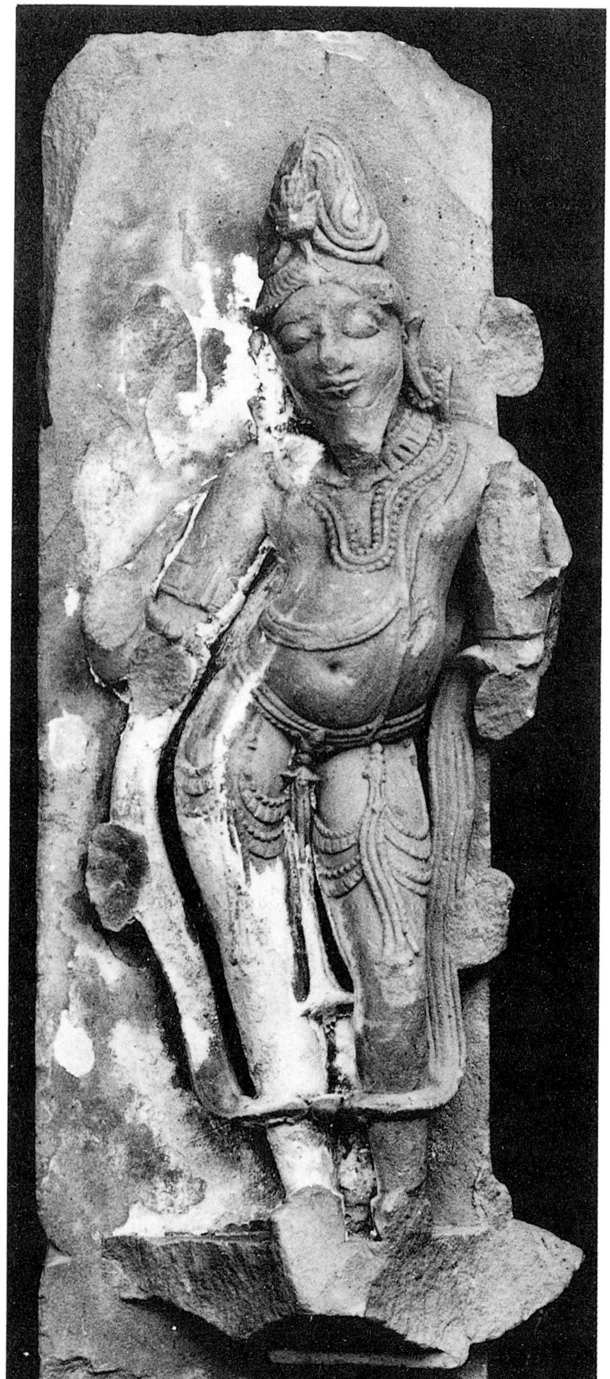

▶
79

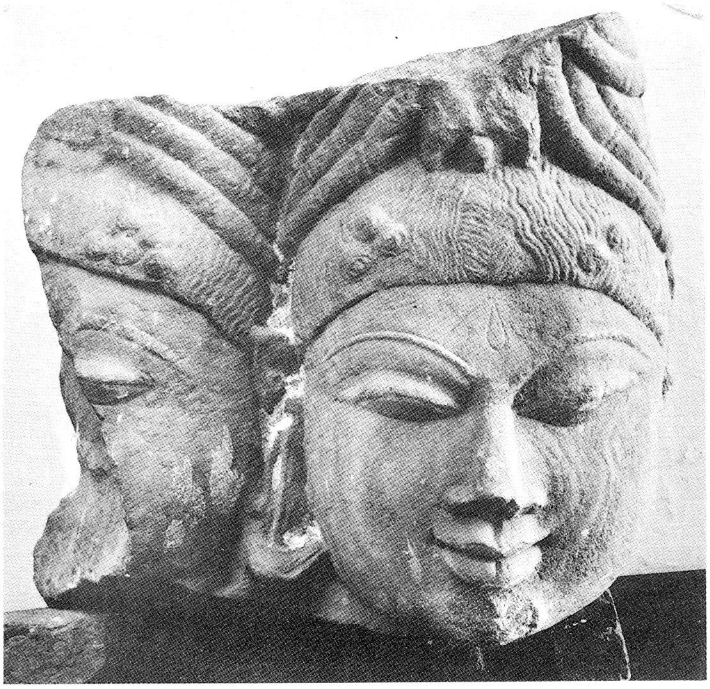

▲ 68

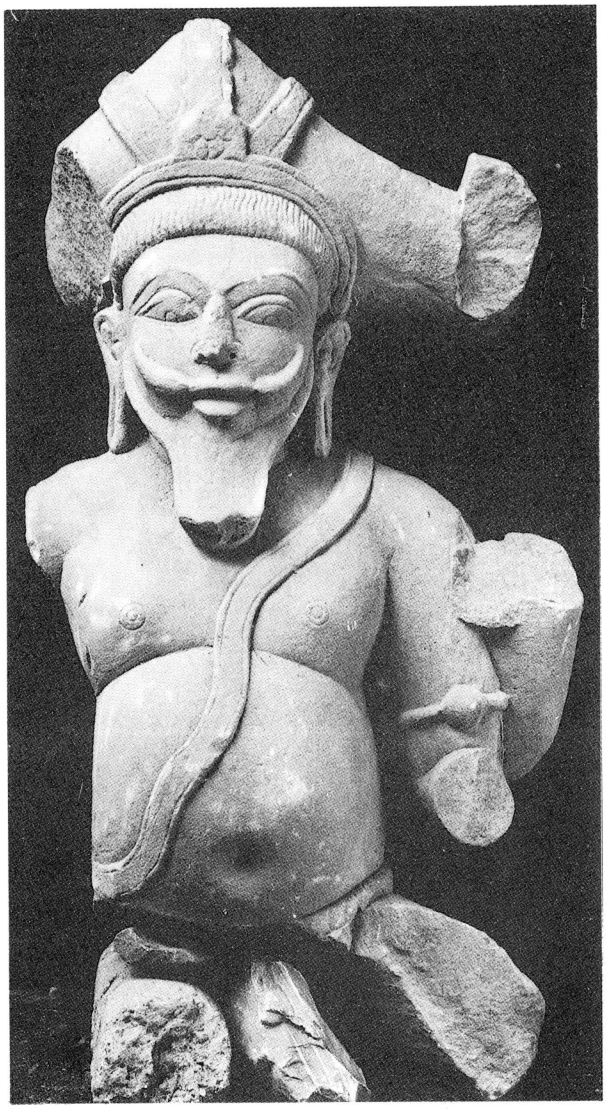

▶
71

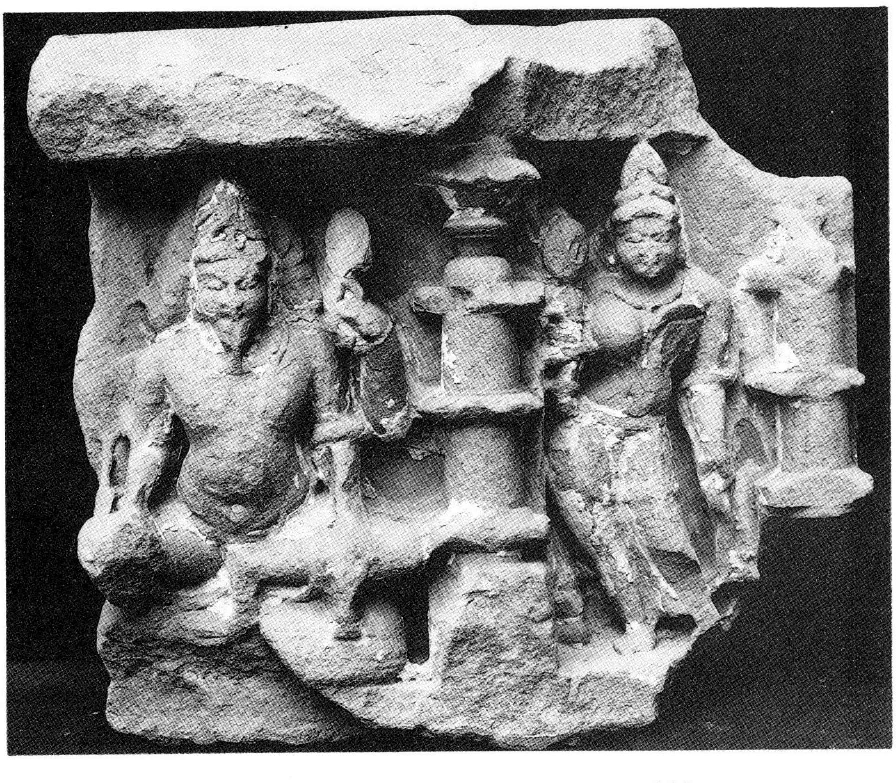

◀
70

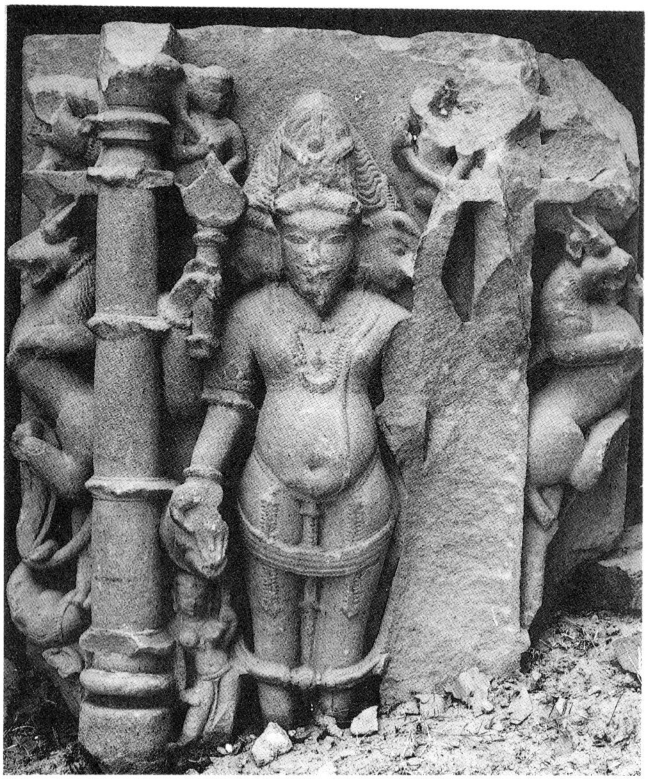

◀
69

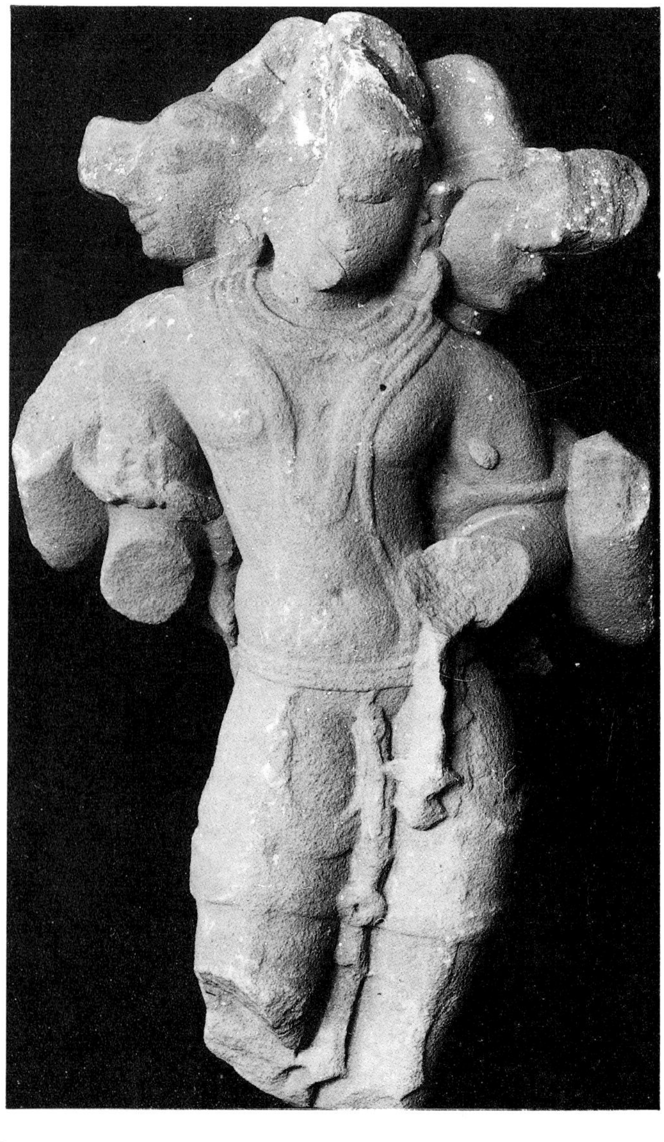

▶
72

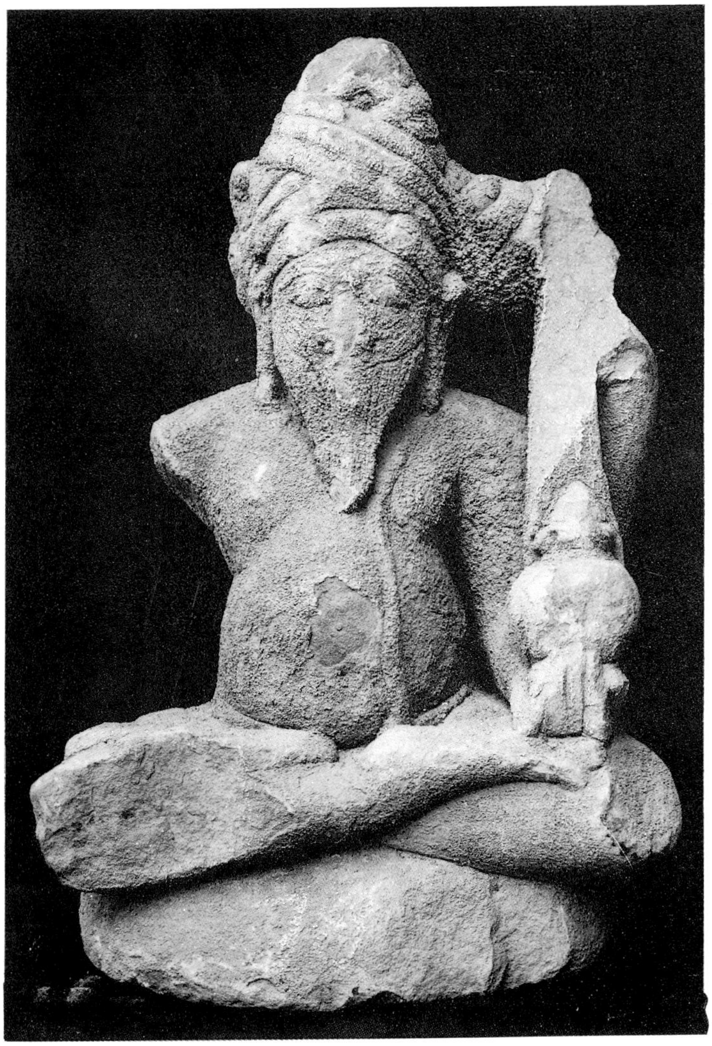

◀
76

▶
75

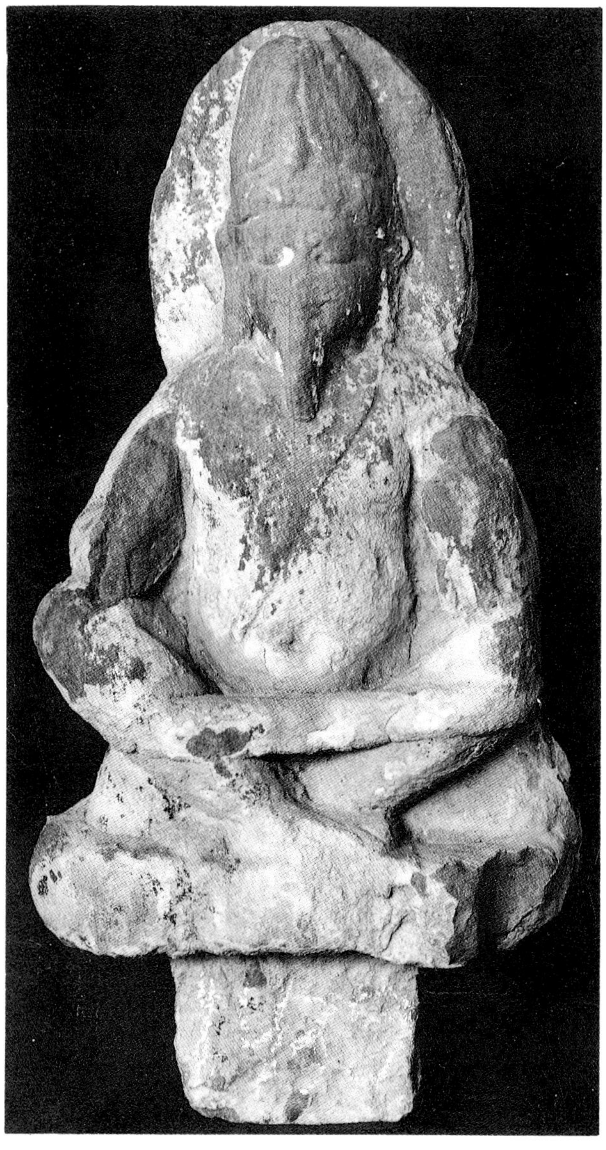

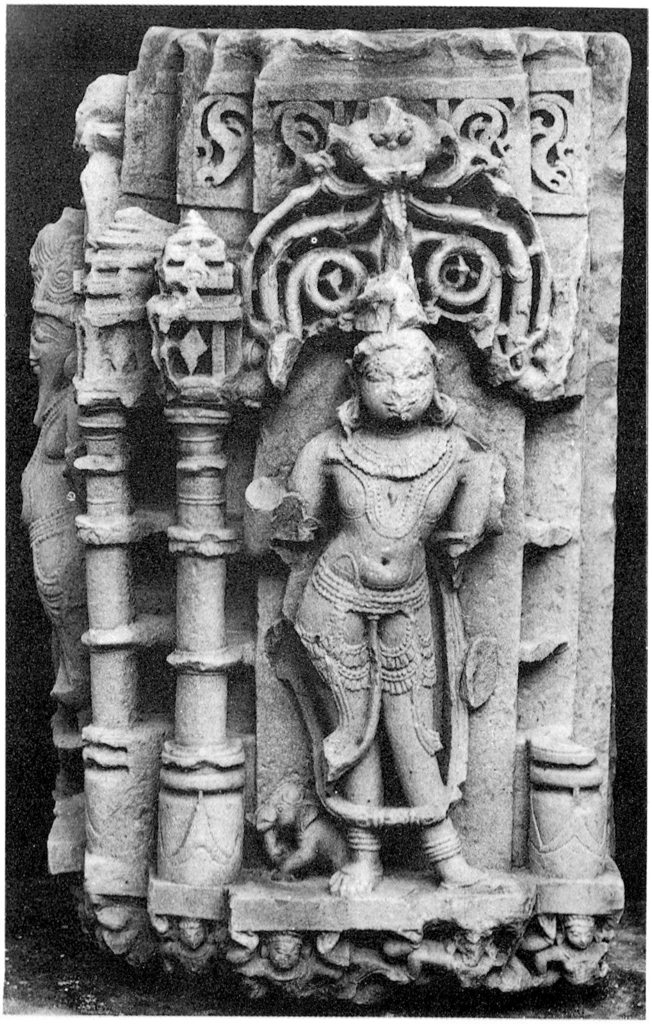

◀
77

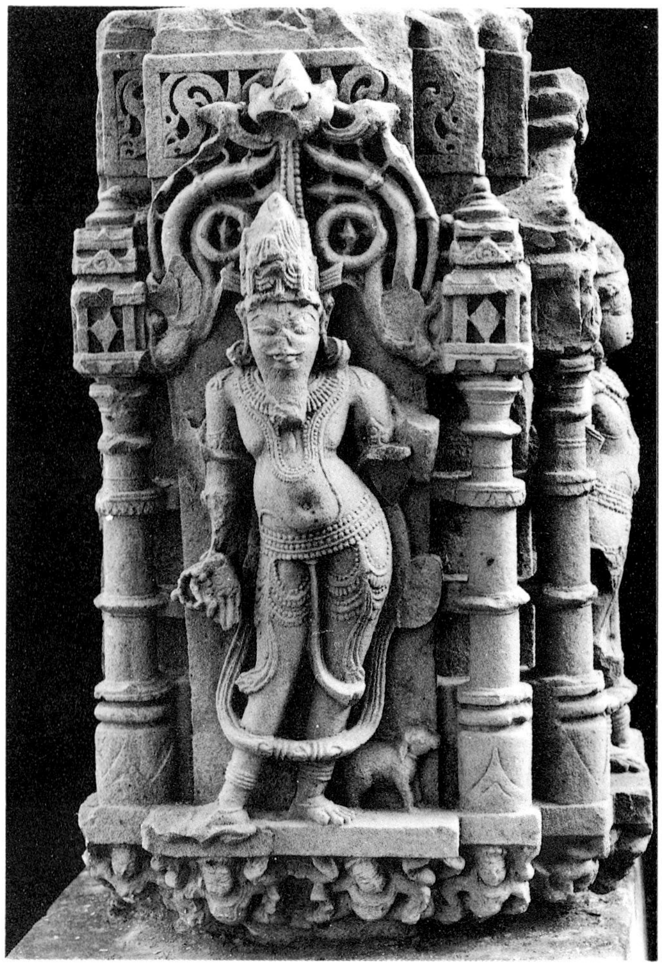

▶
78

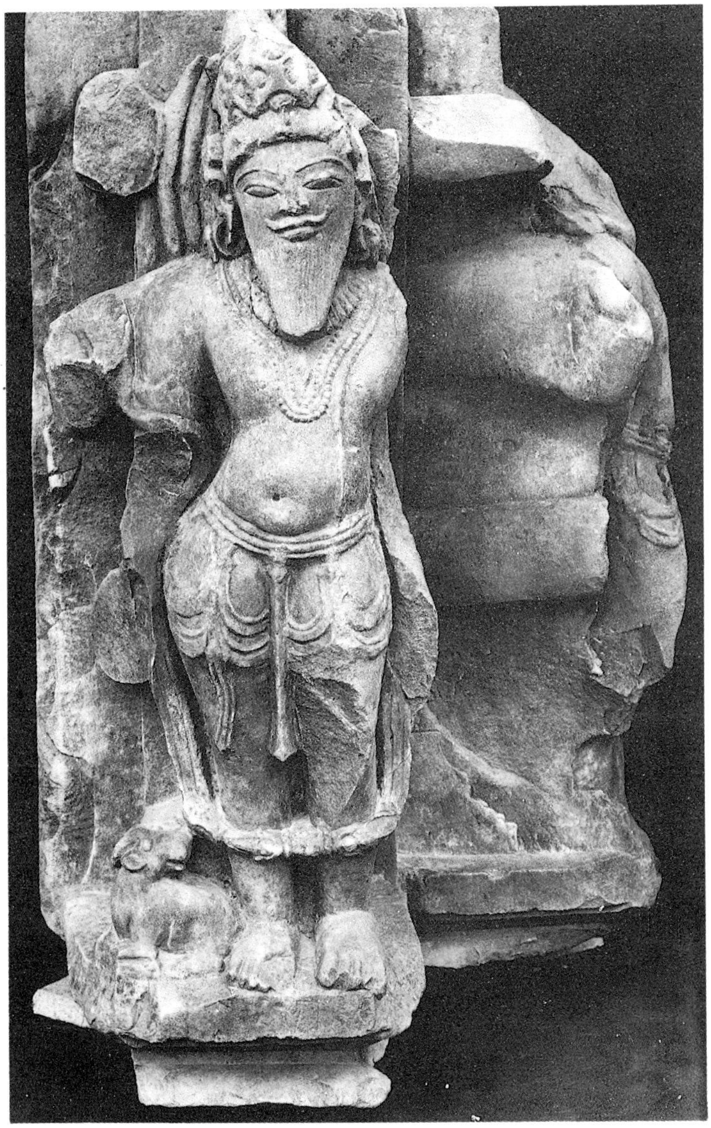

◀
80

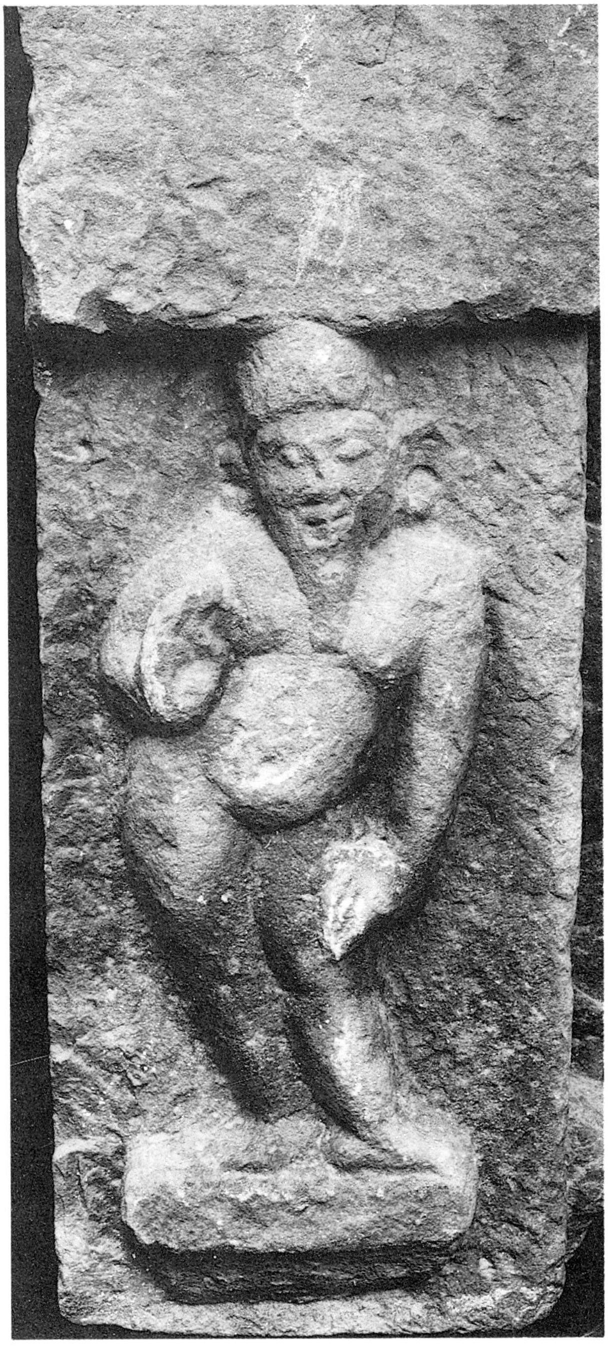

▶
81

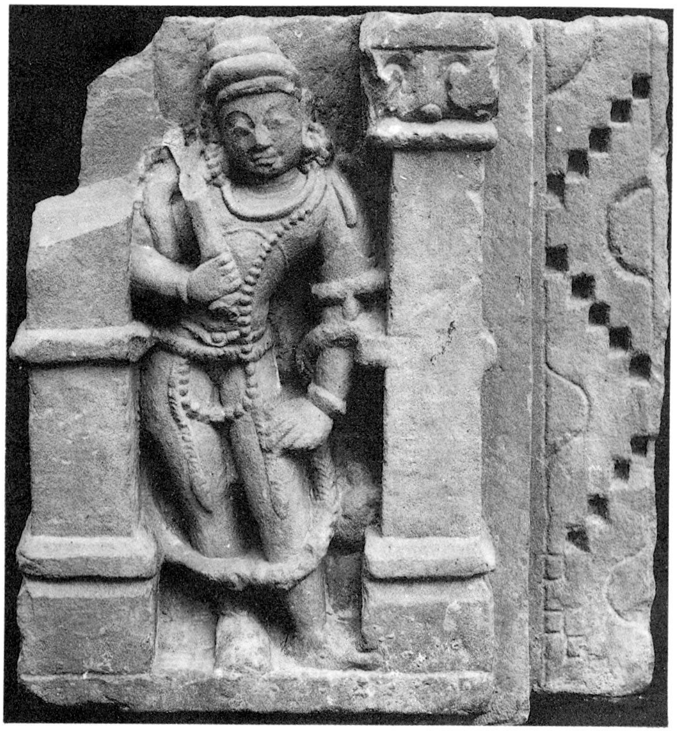

◀ 83

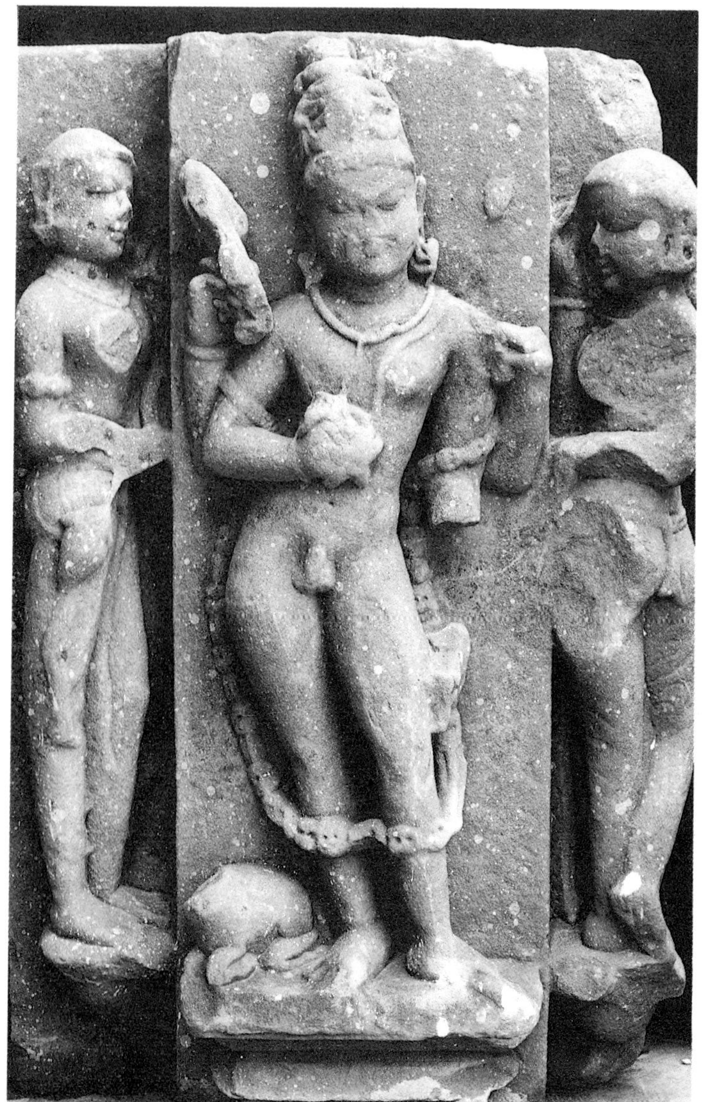

▶ 82

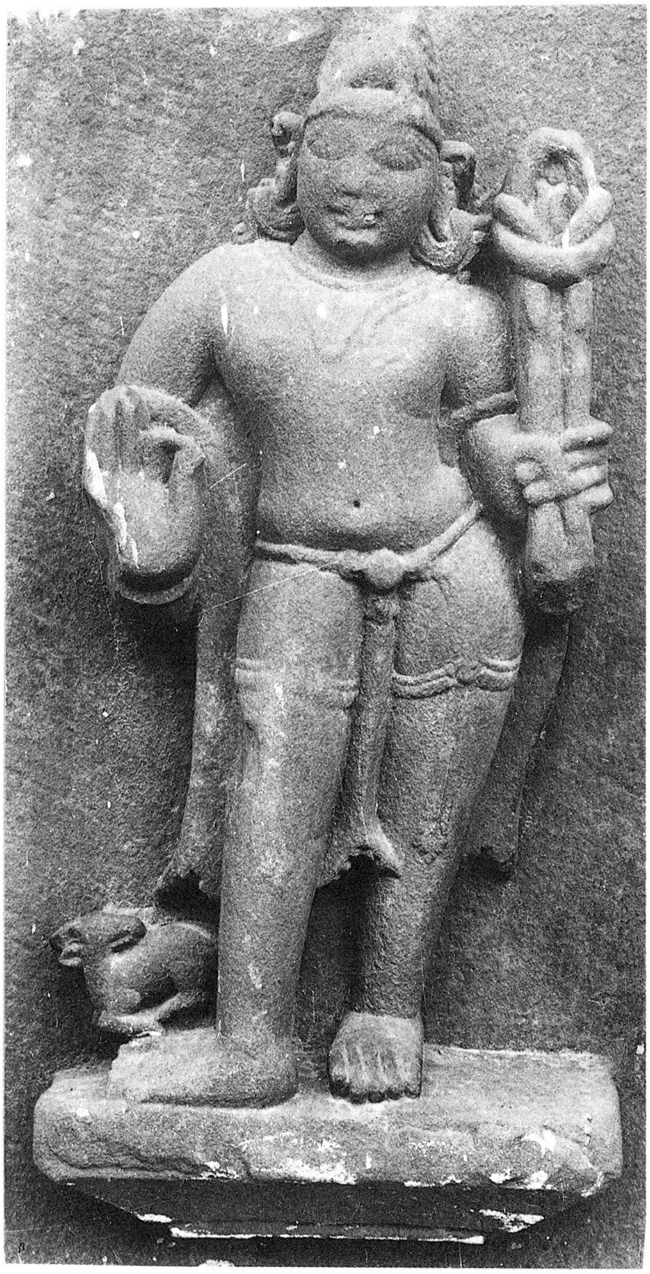

◀ 84

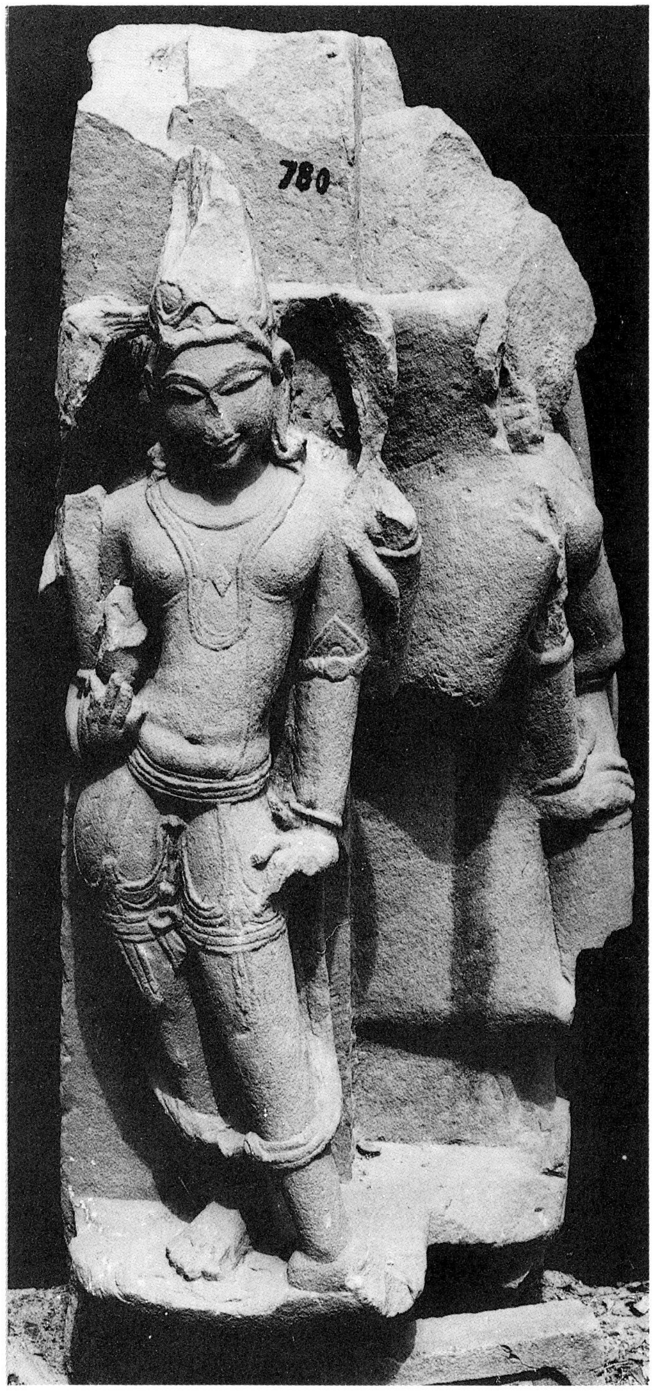

▶ 88

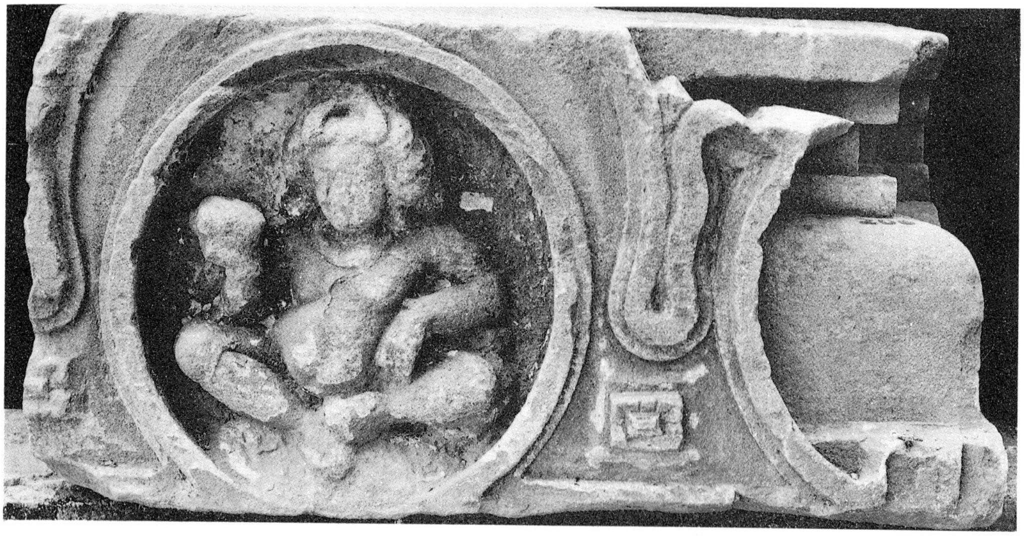

◀ 85

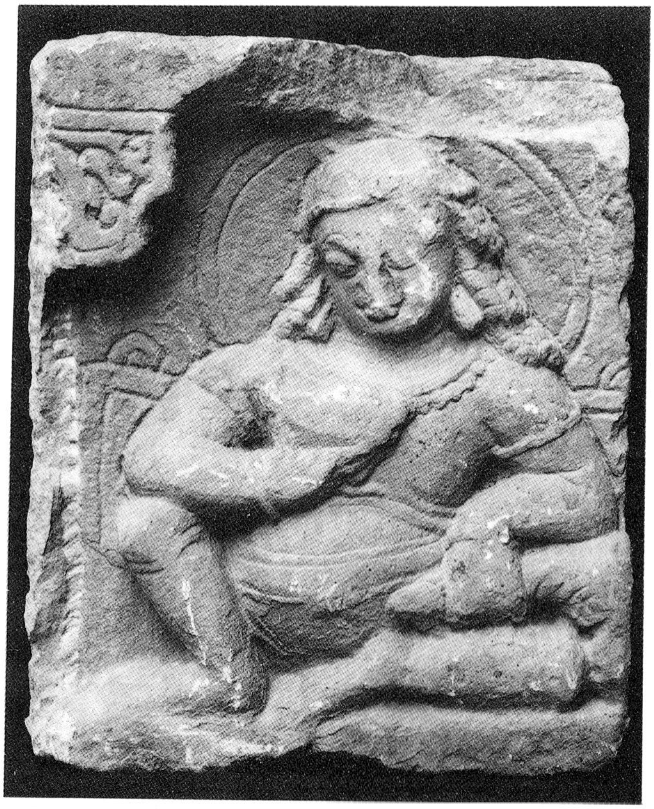

◀ 86

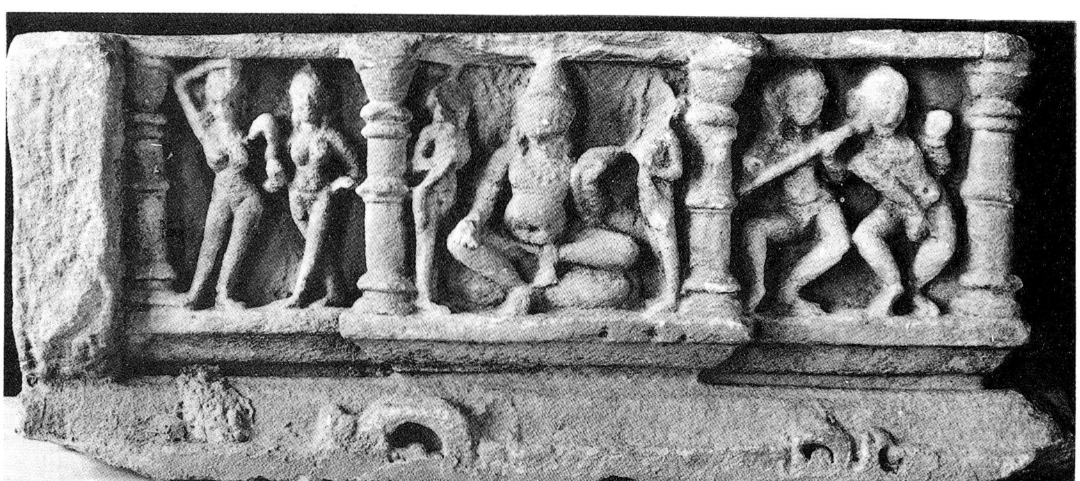

▶ 87

▶ 90

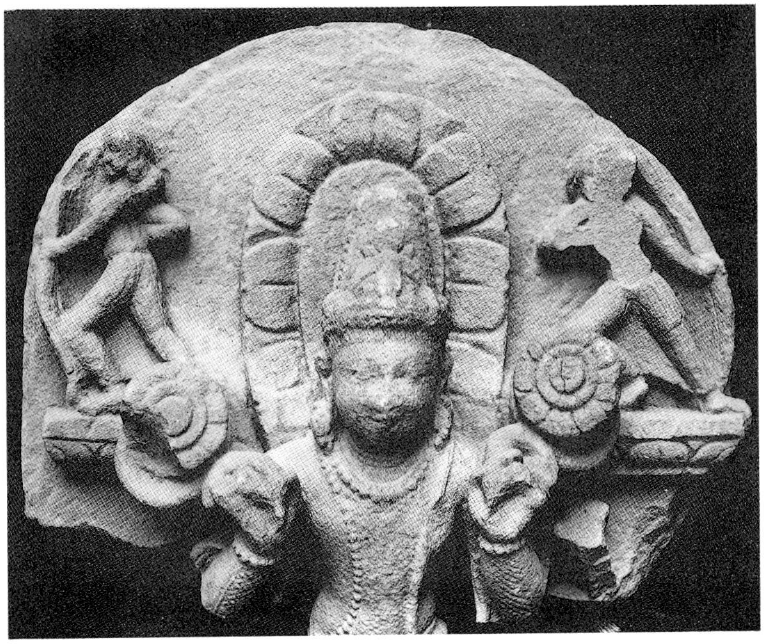

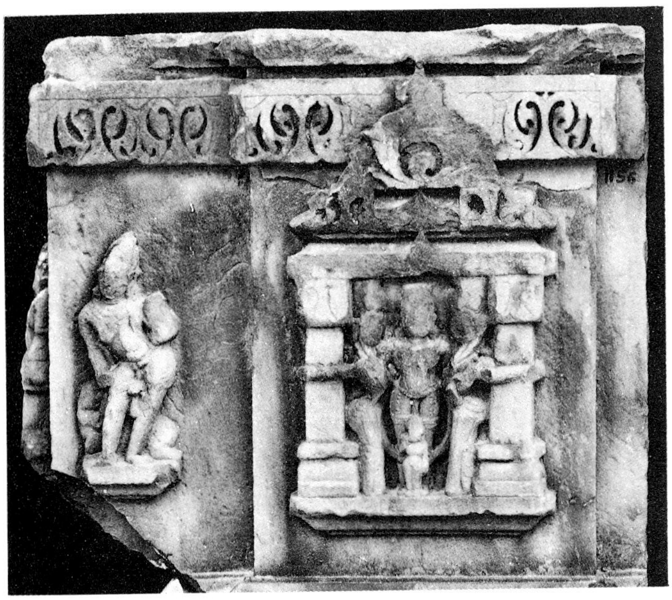

▲ 91

▶ 89

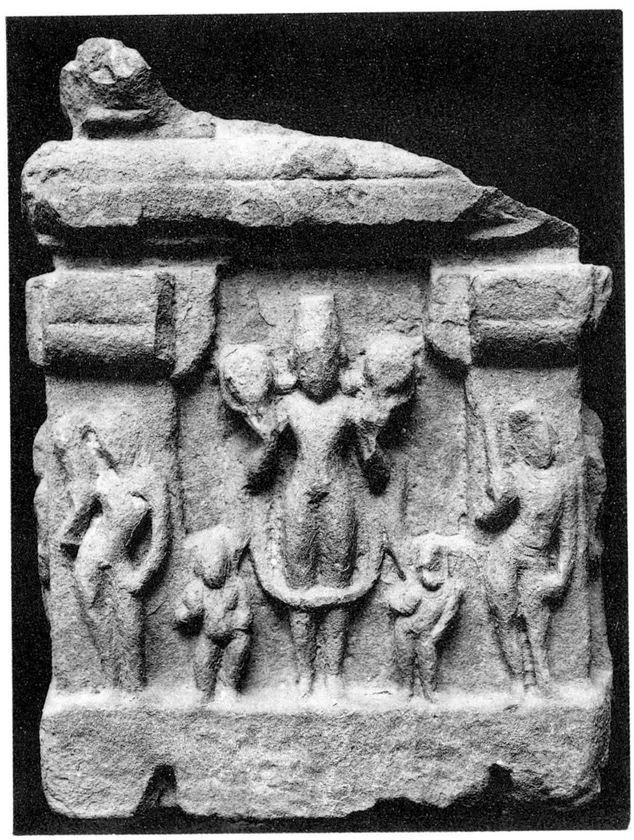

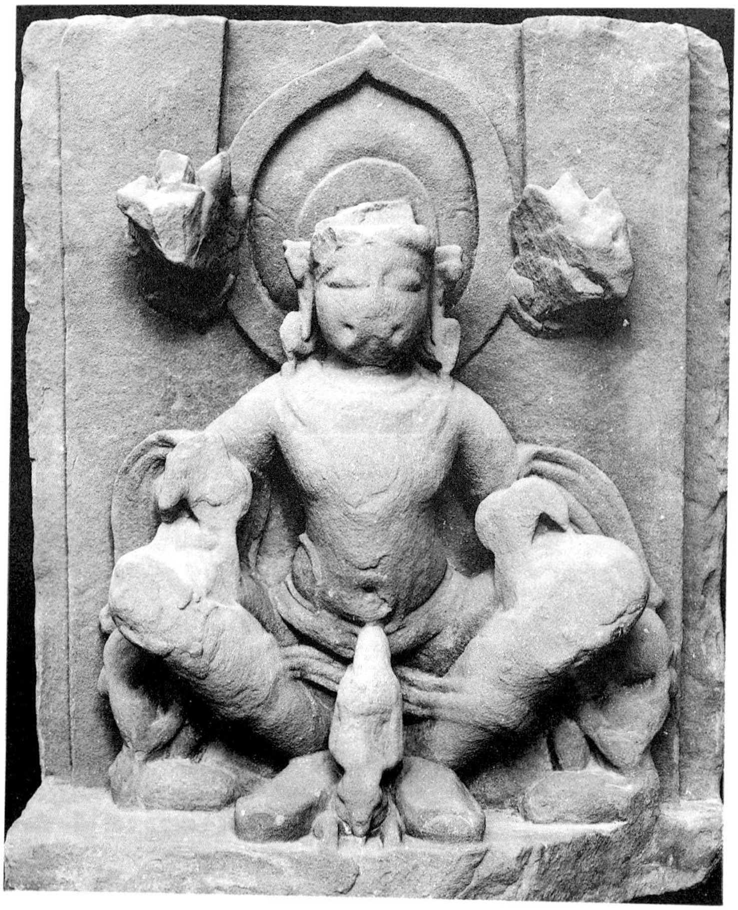

◀
92

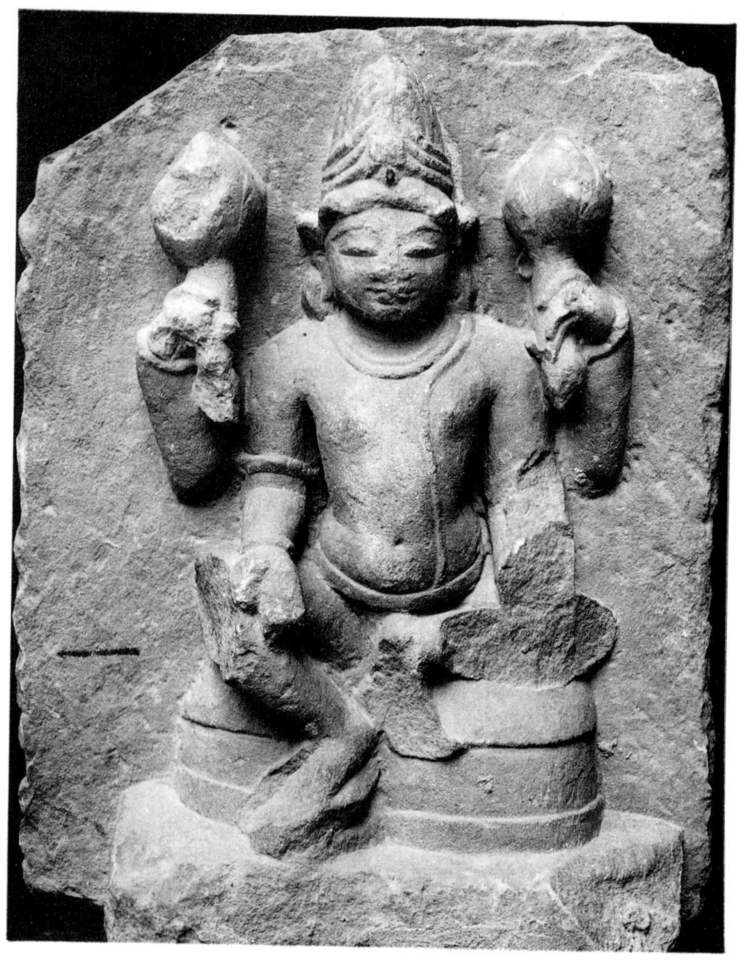

▶
93

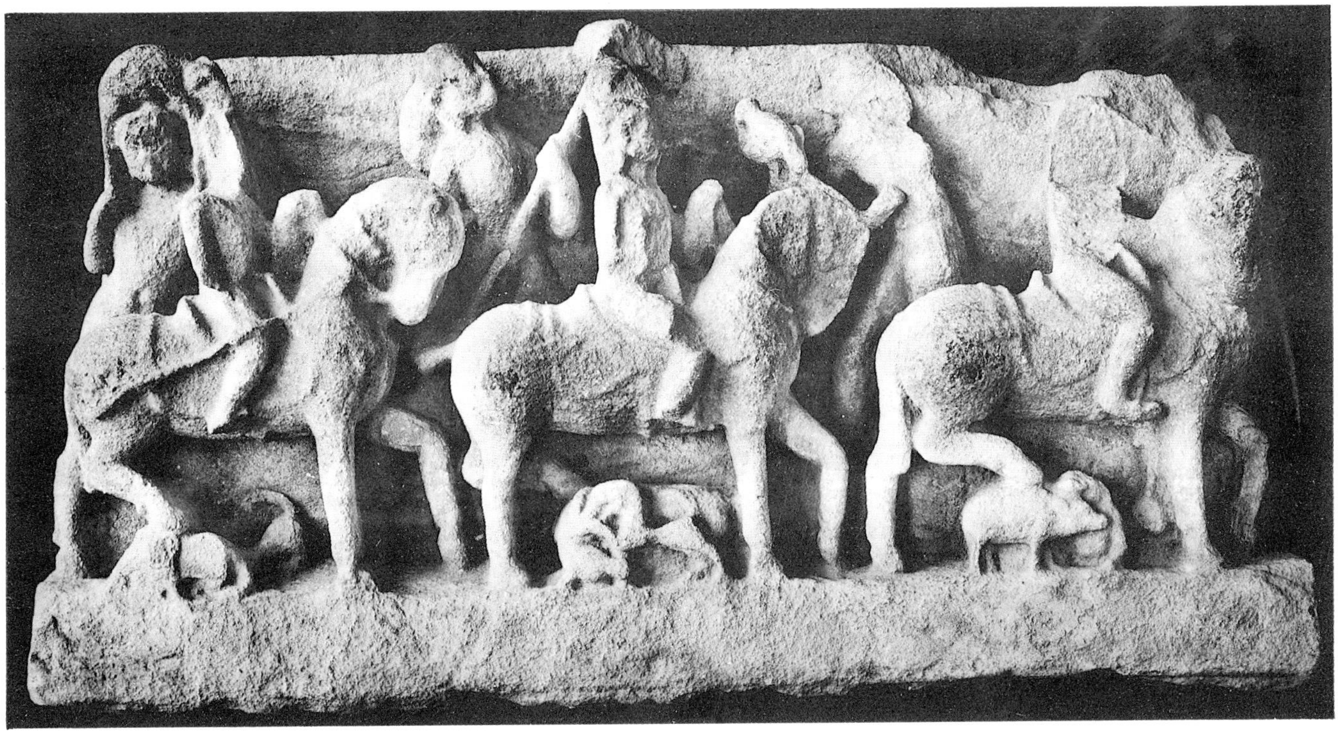

▲ 94

▼ 95

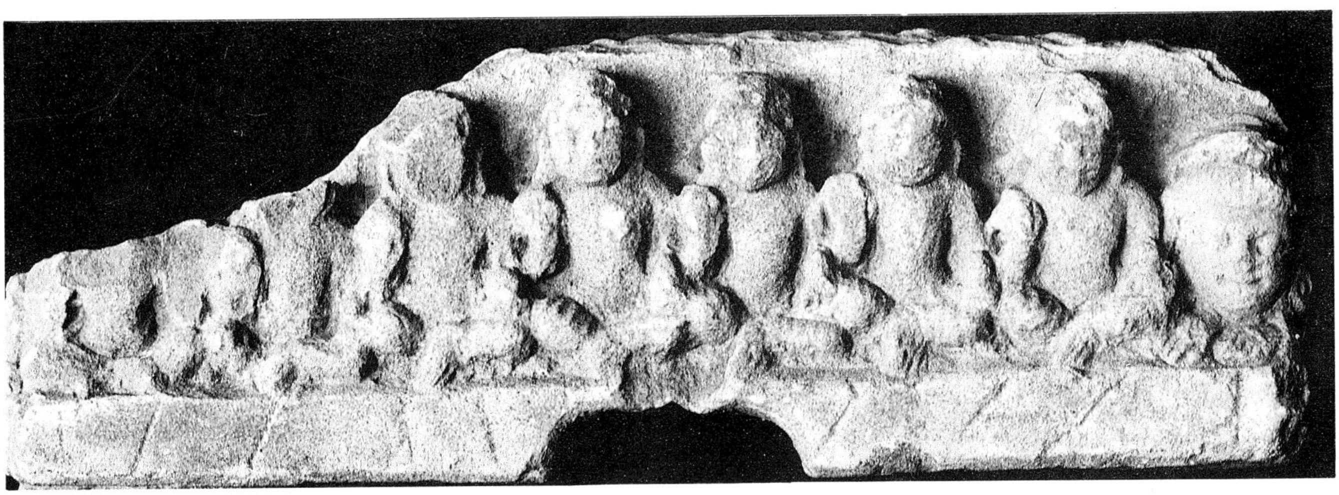

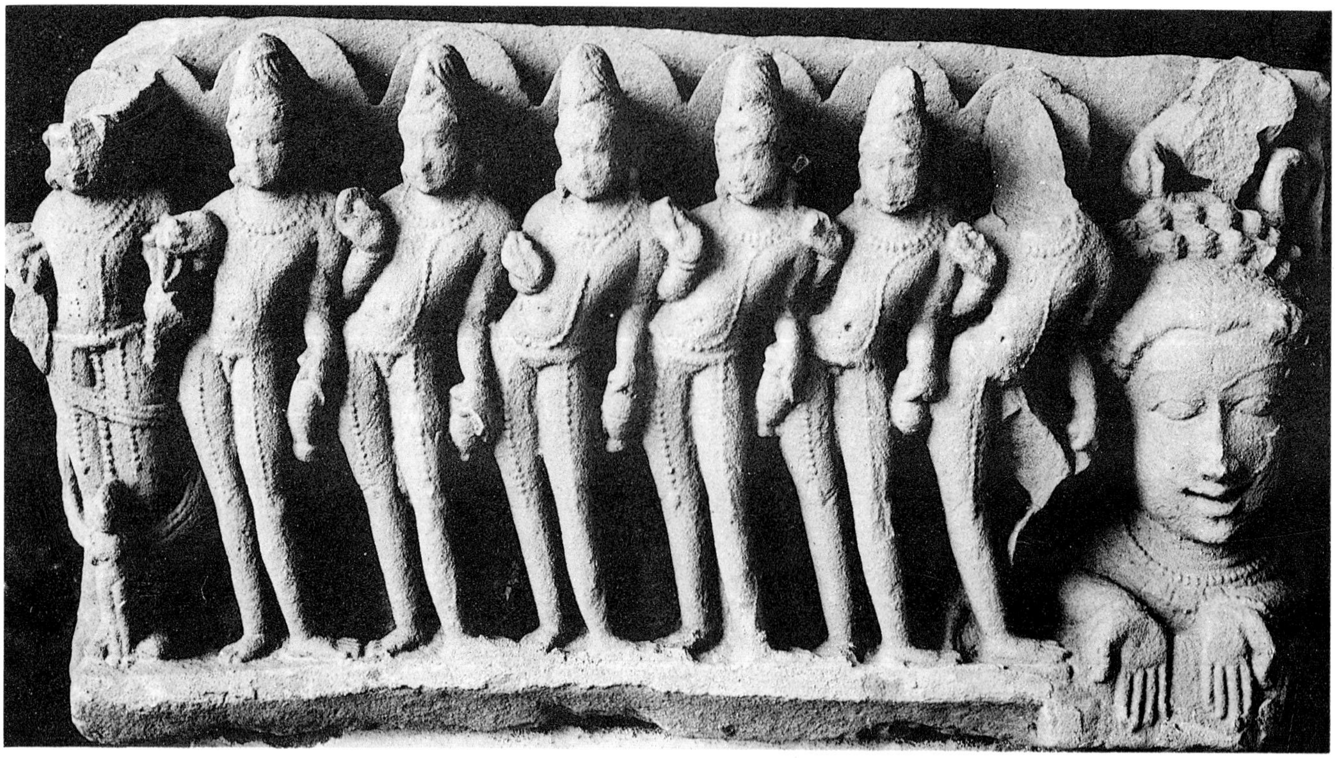

▲96

▼97

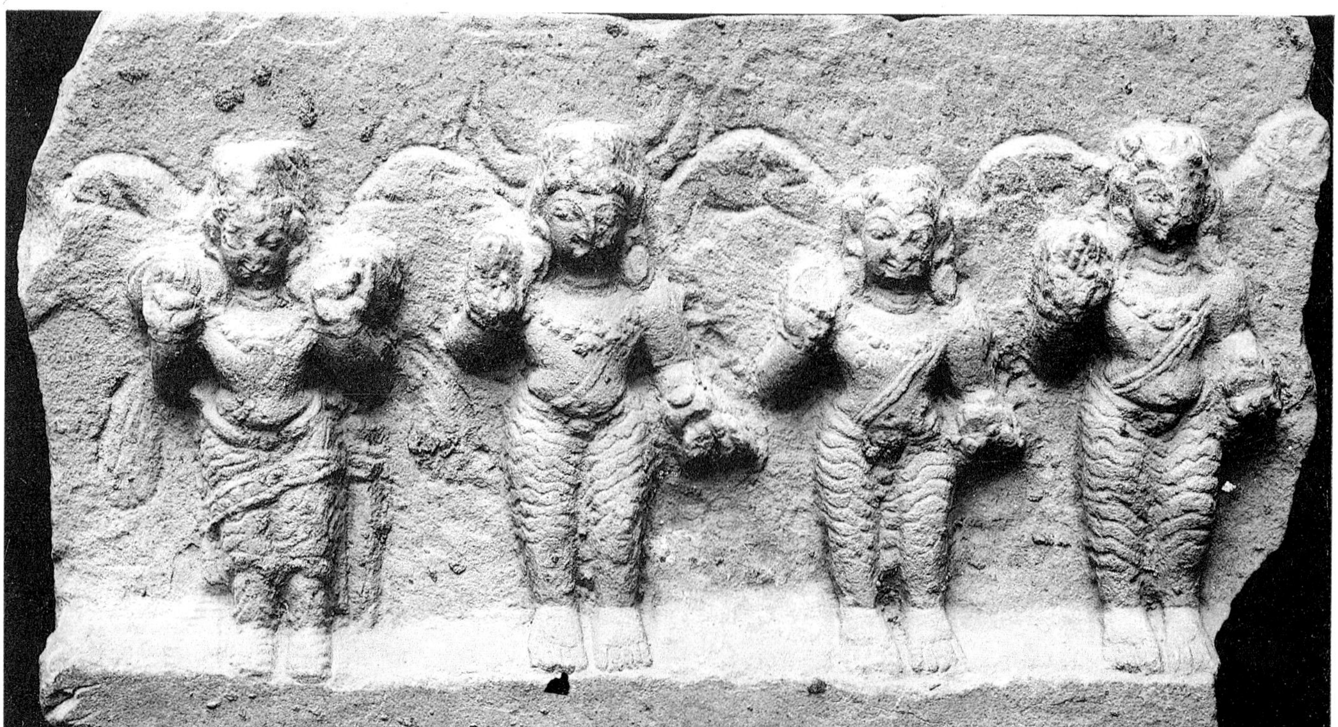

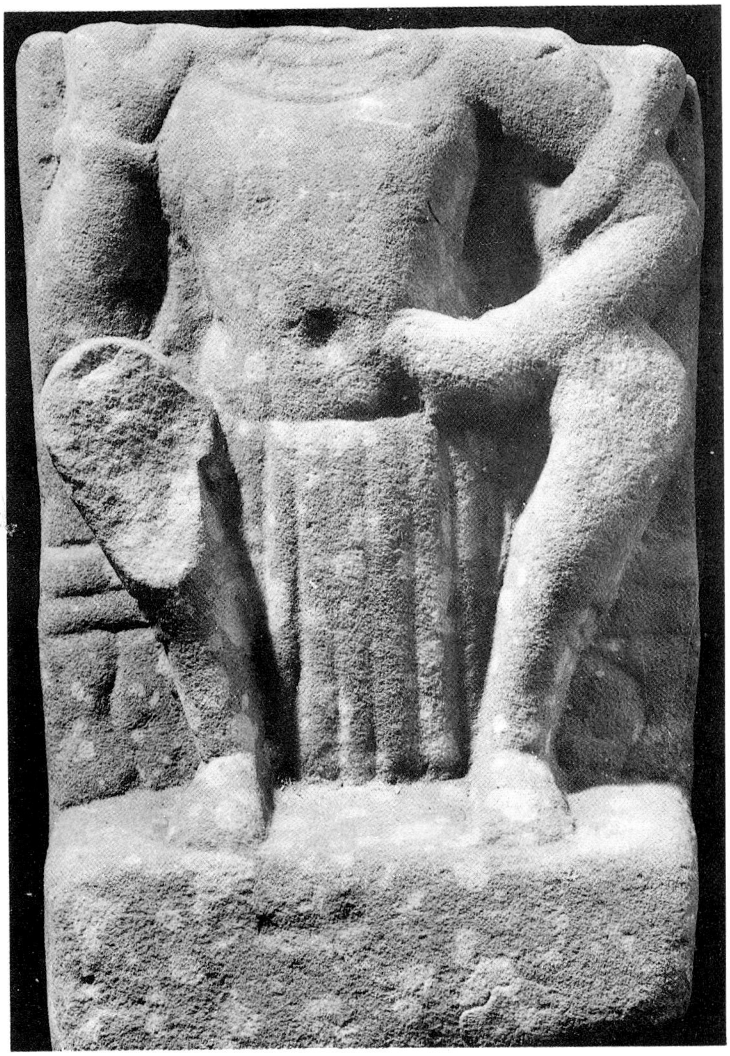

◀
98

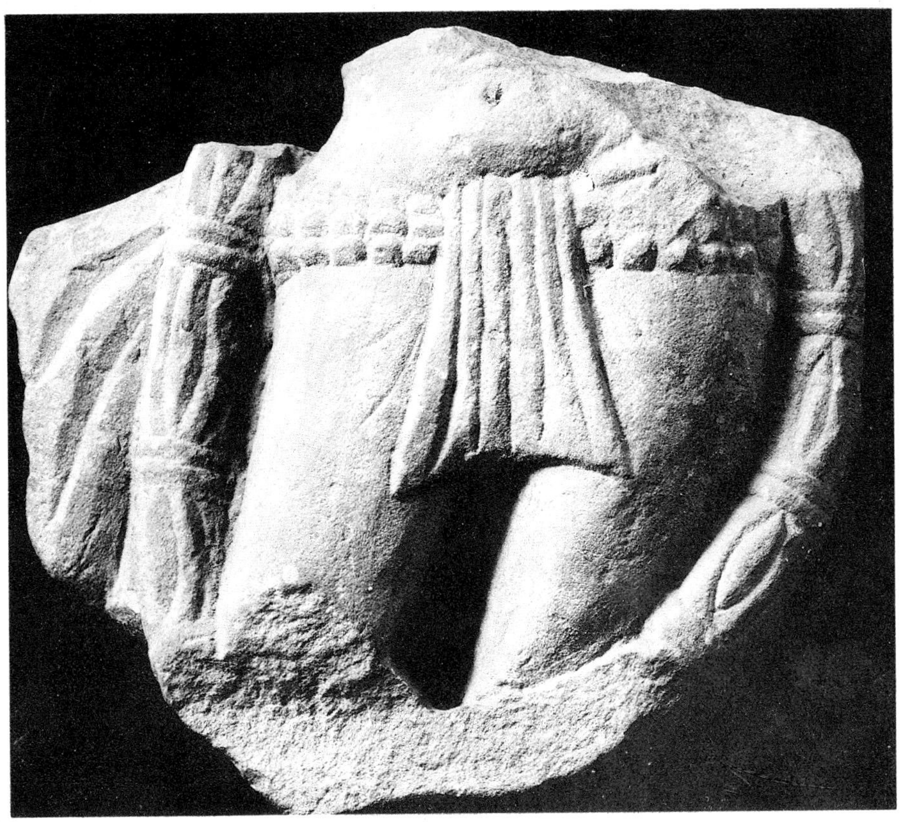

▶
101

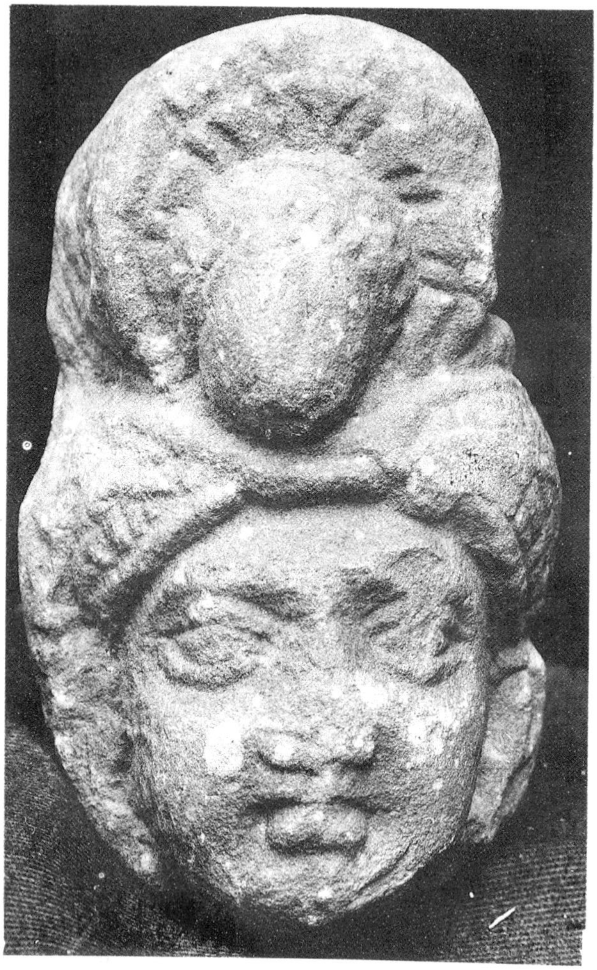

◀ 99

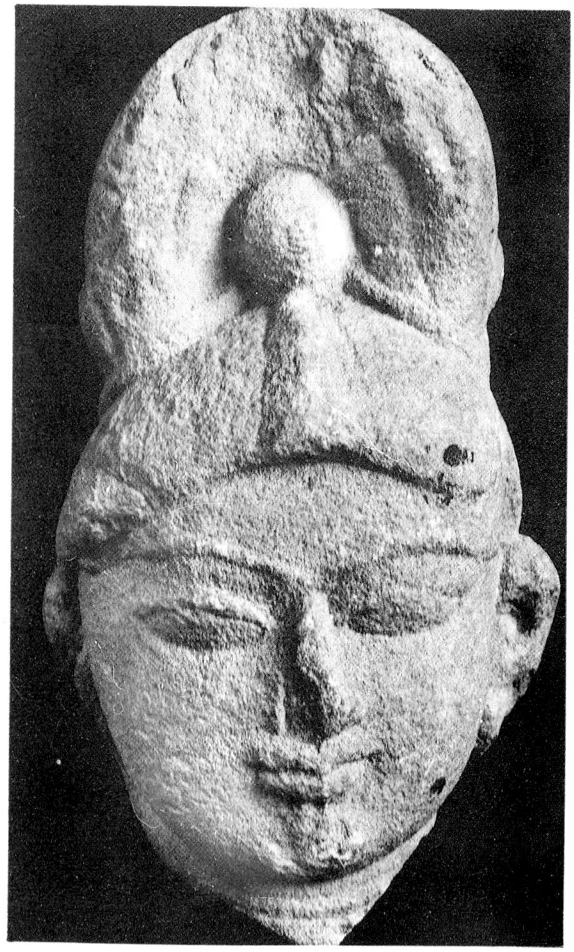

▶ 100

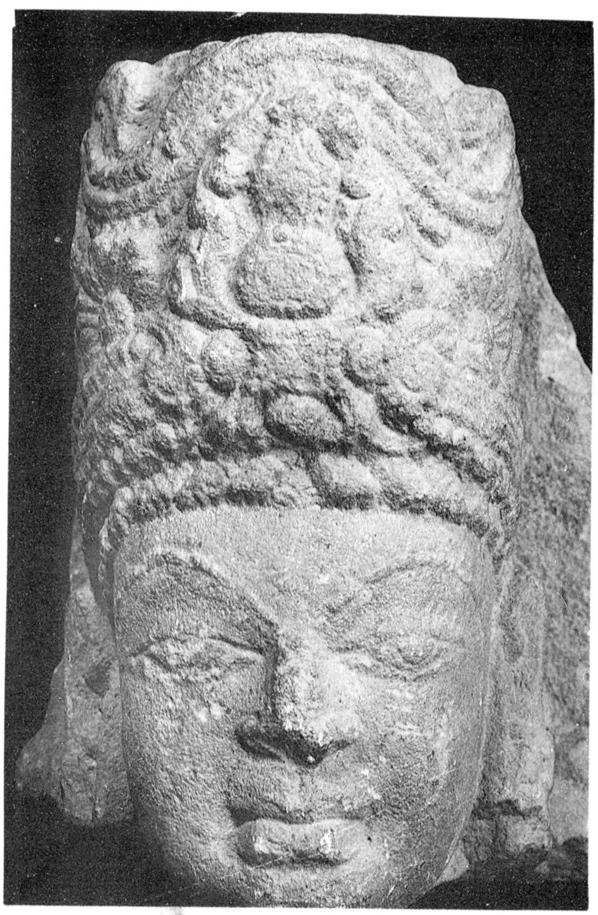

◀ 102

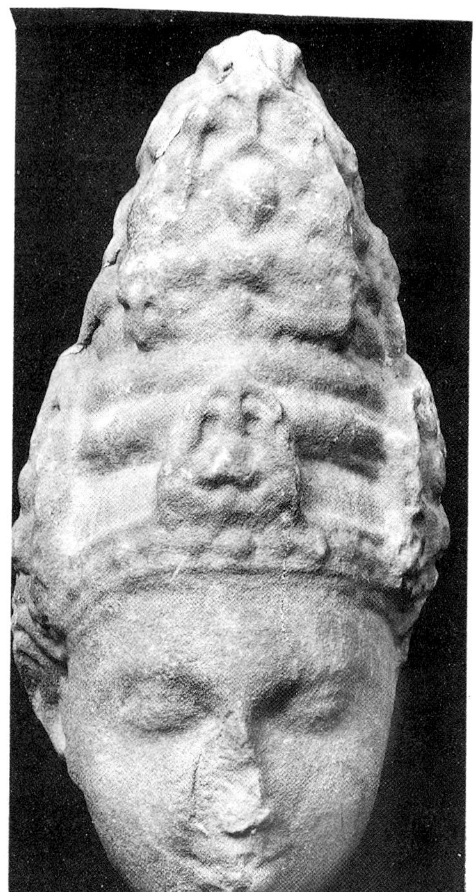

▶ 104

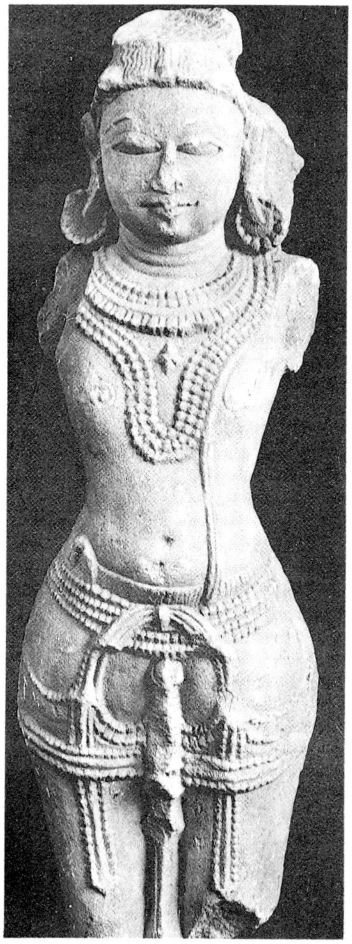

◀
105

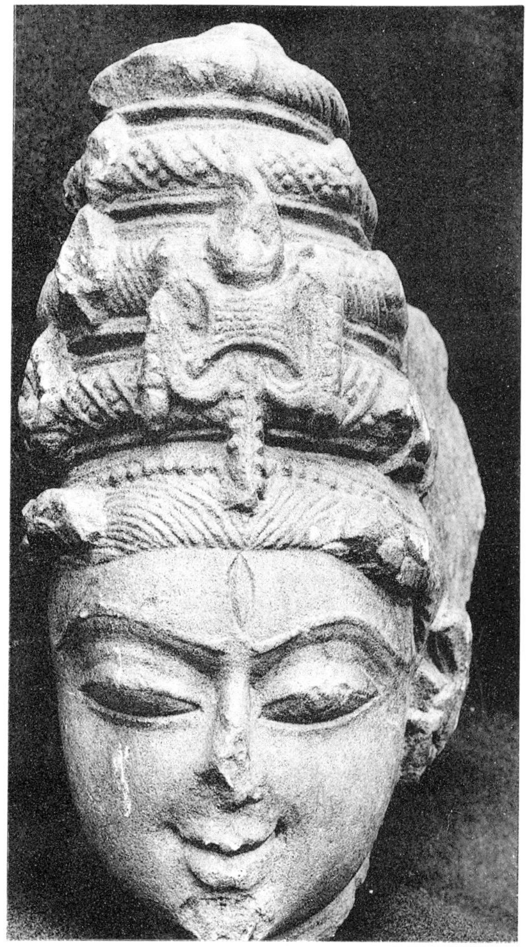

▶
107

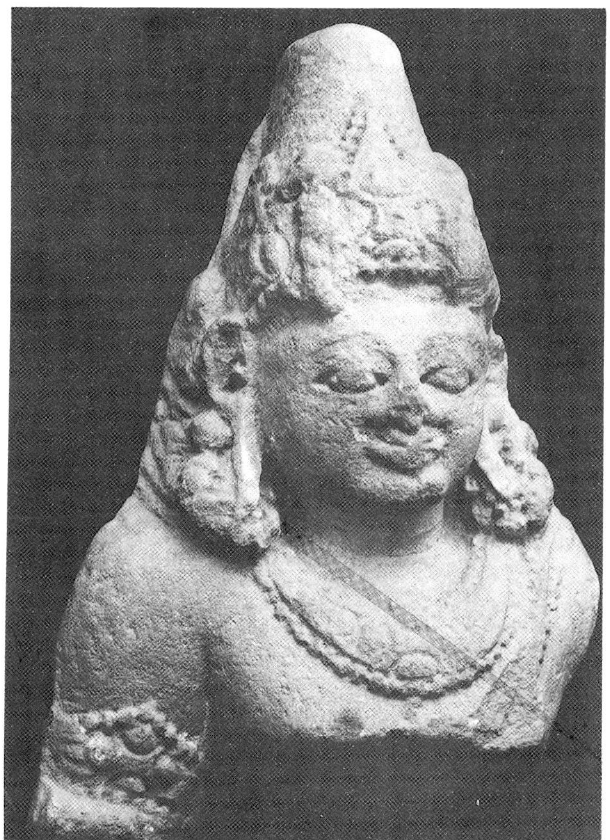

◀
103

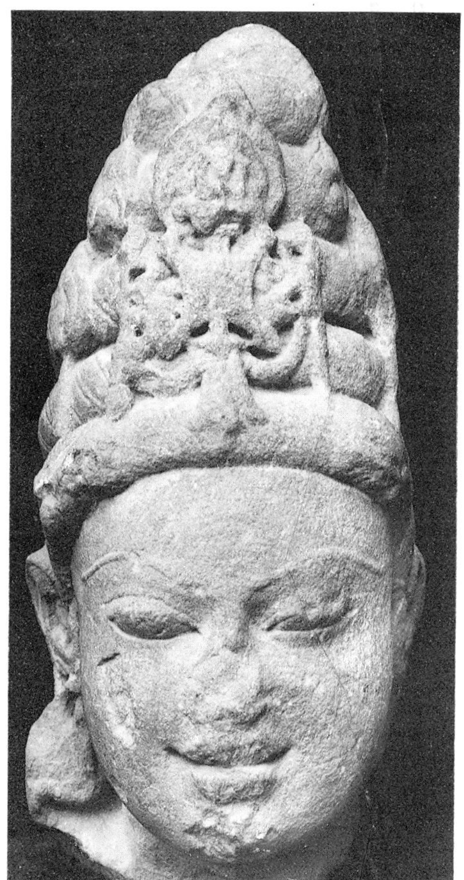

▶
106

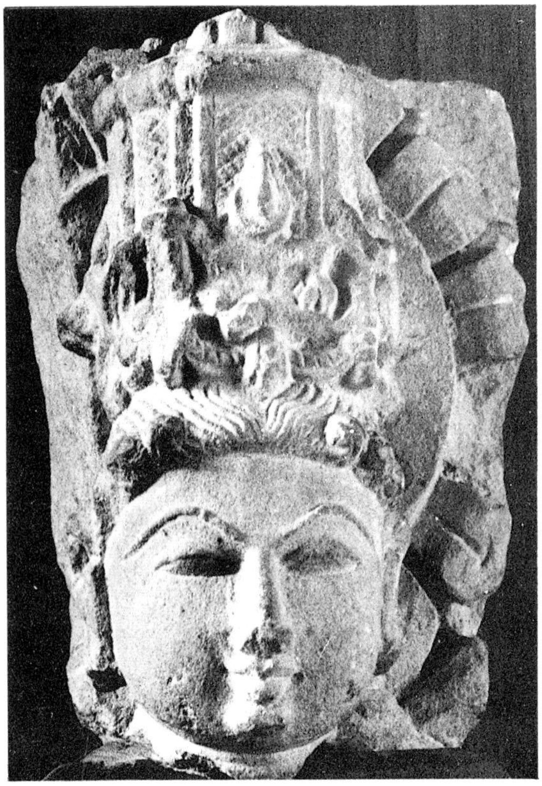

◀ 108

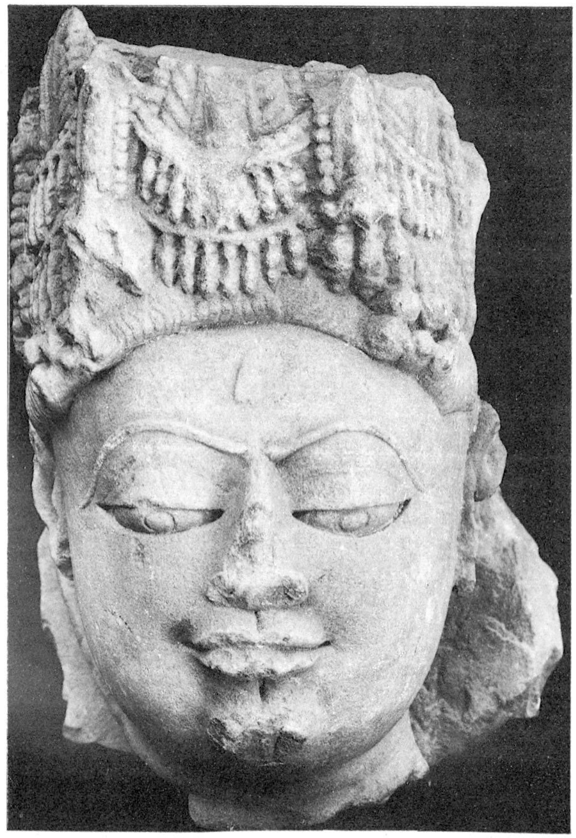

▶ 109

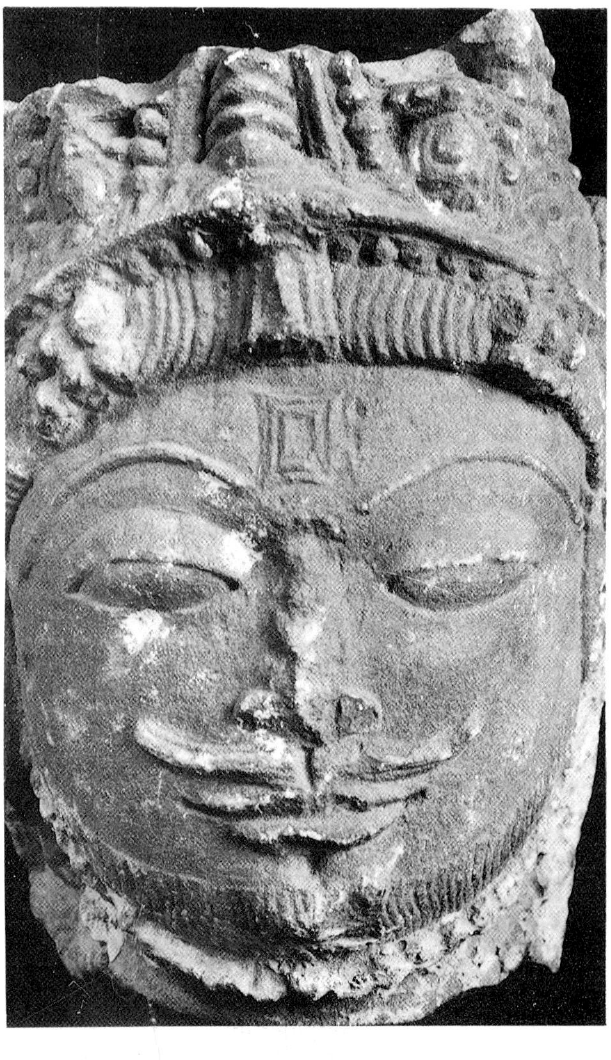

◀ 110

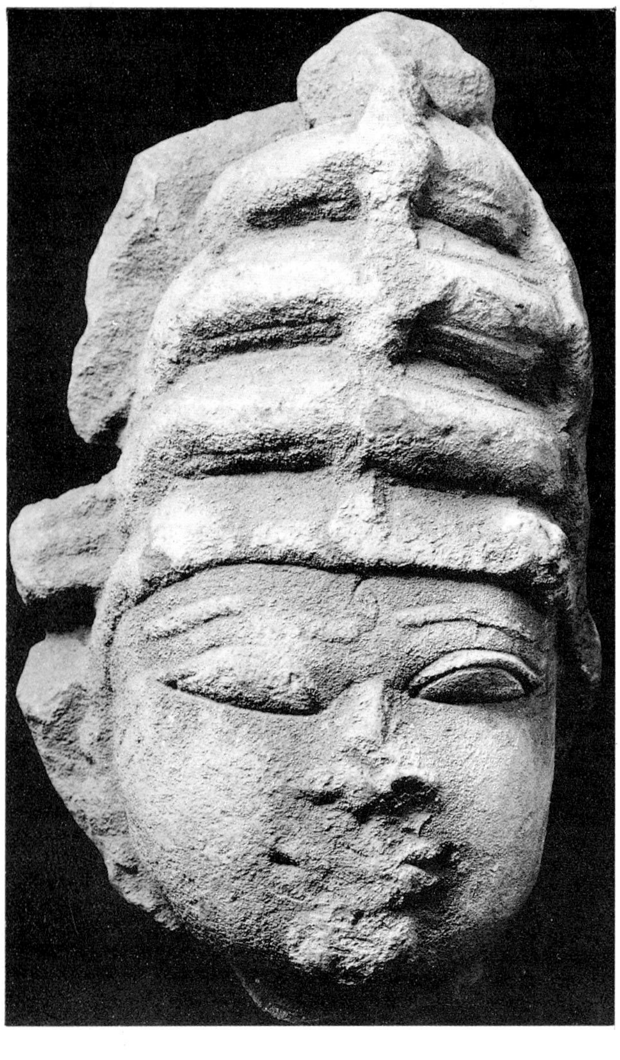

▶ 111

◀
112

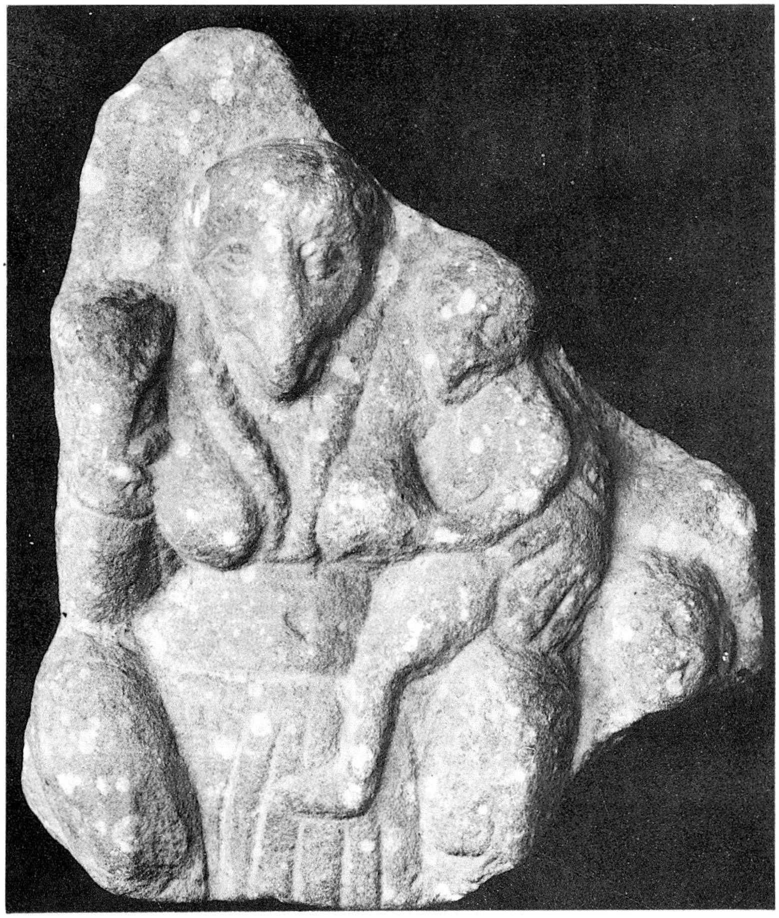

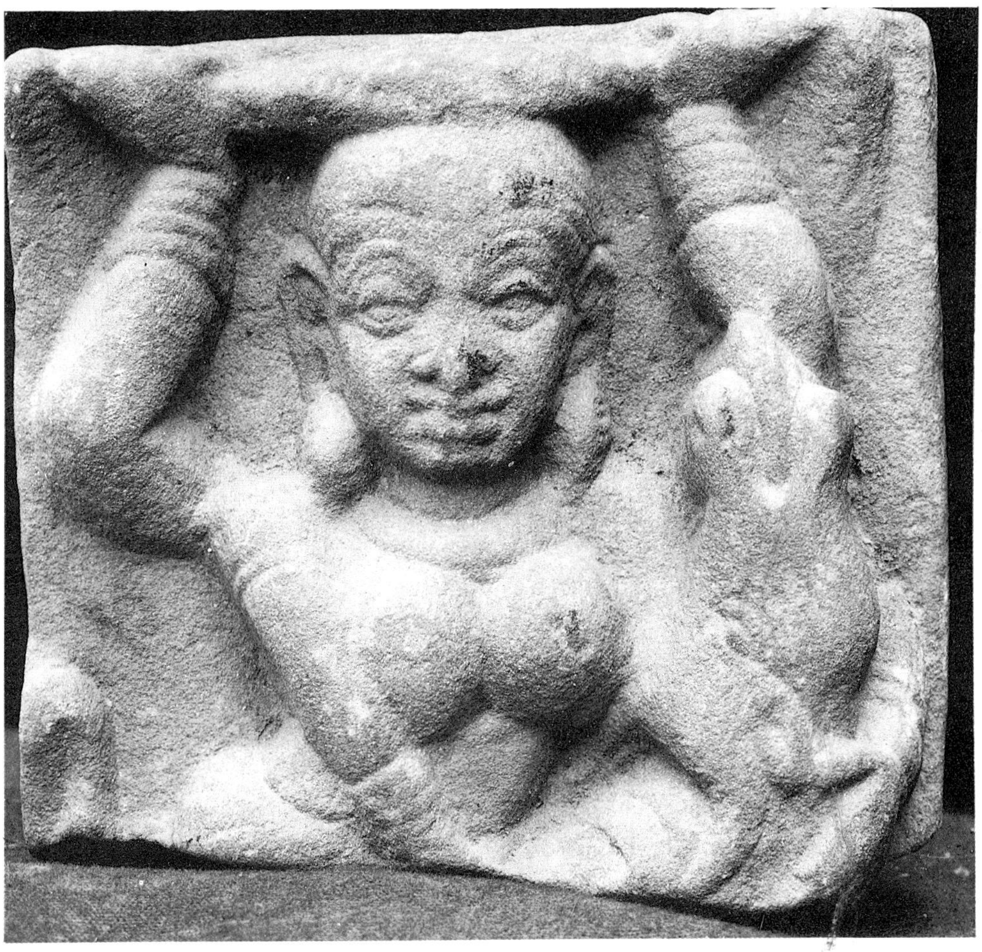

▶
114

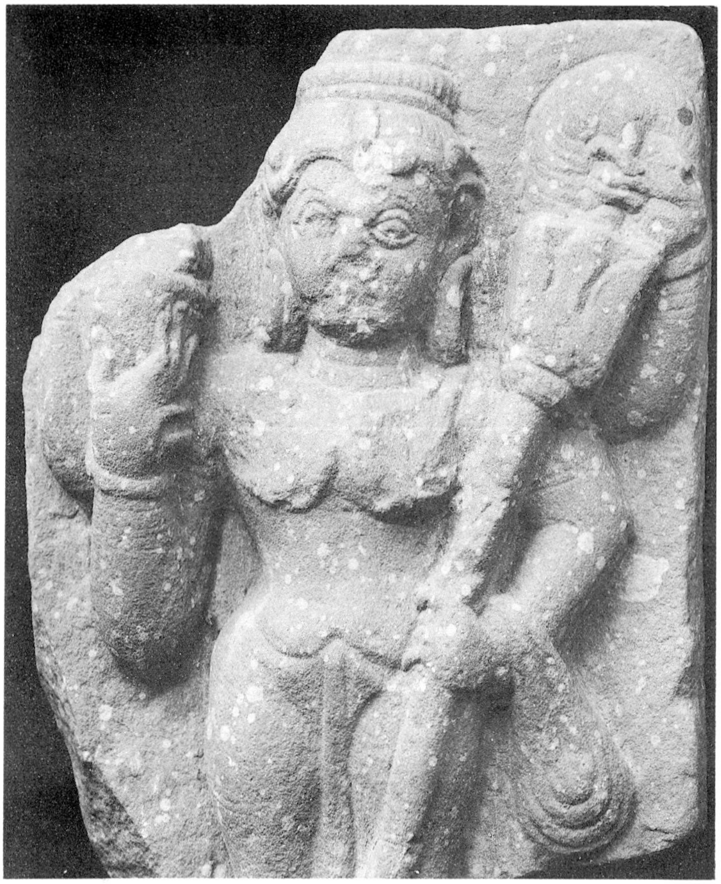

◀
113

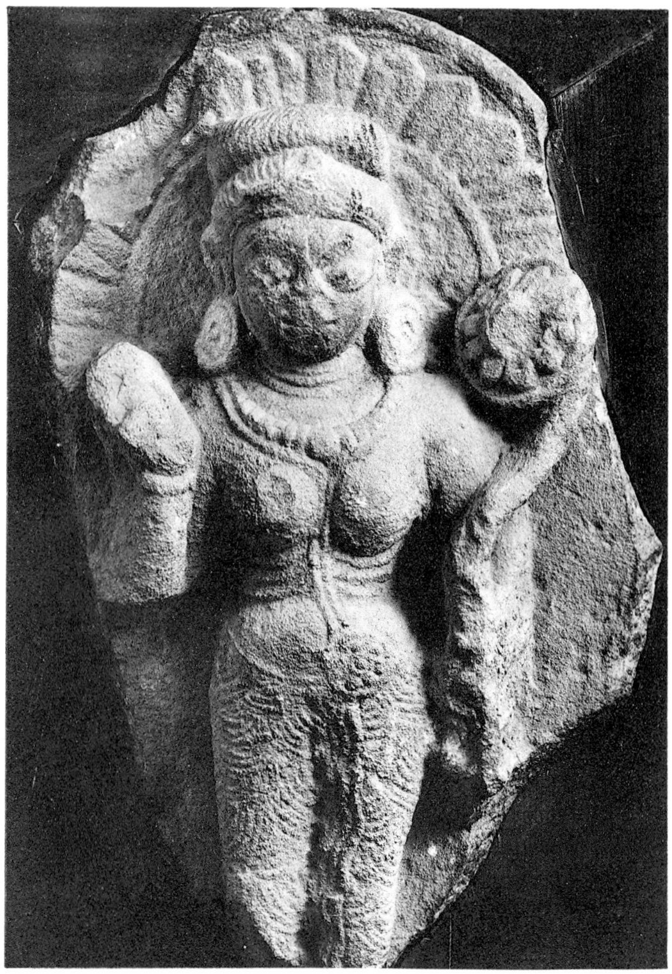

▶
115

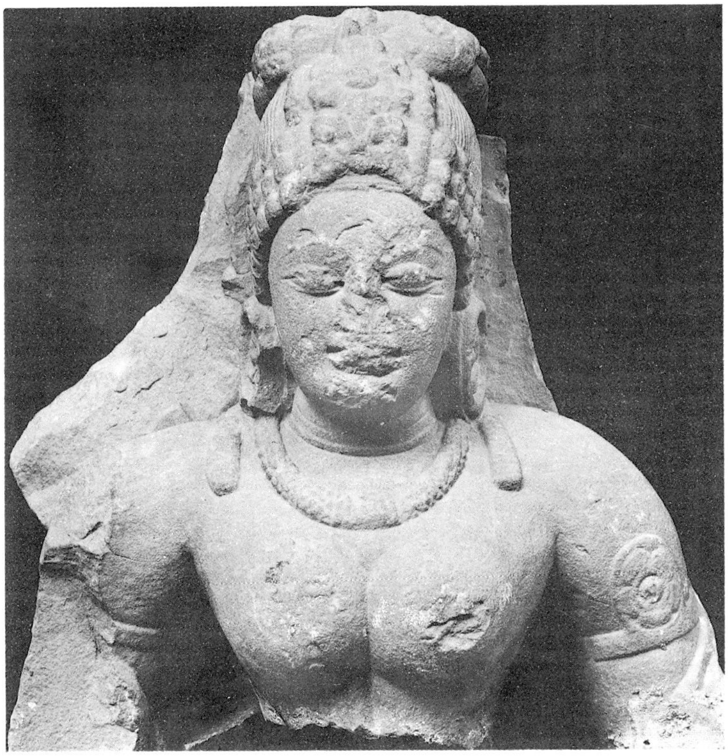

▲ 116

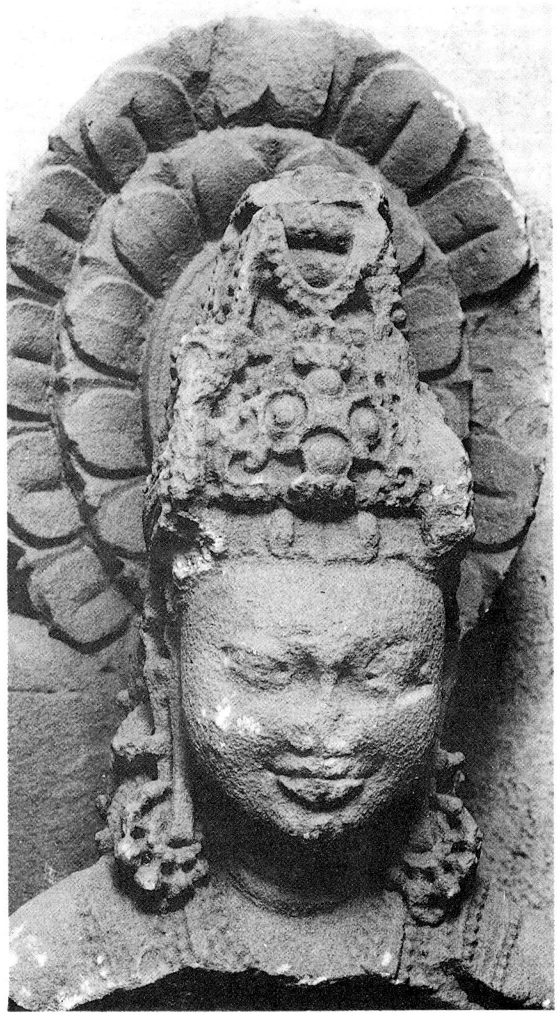

▶
118

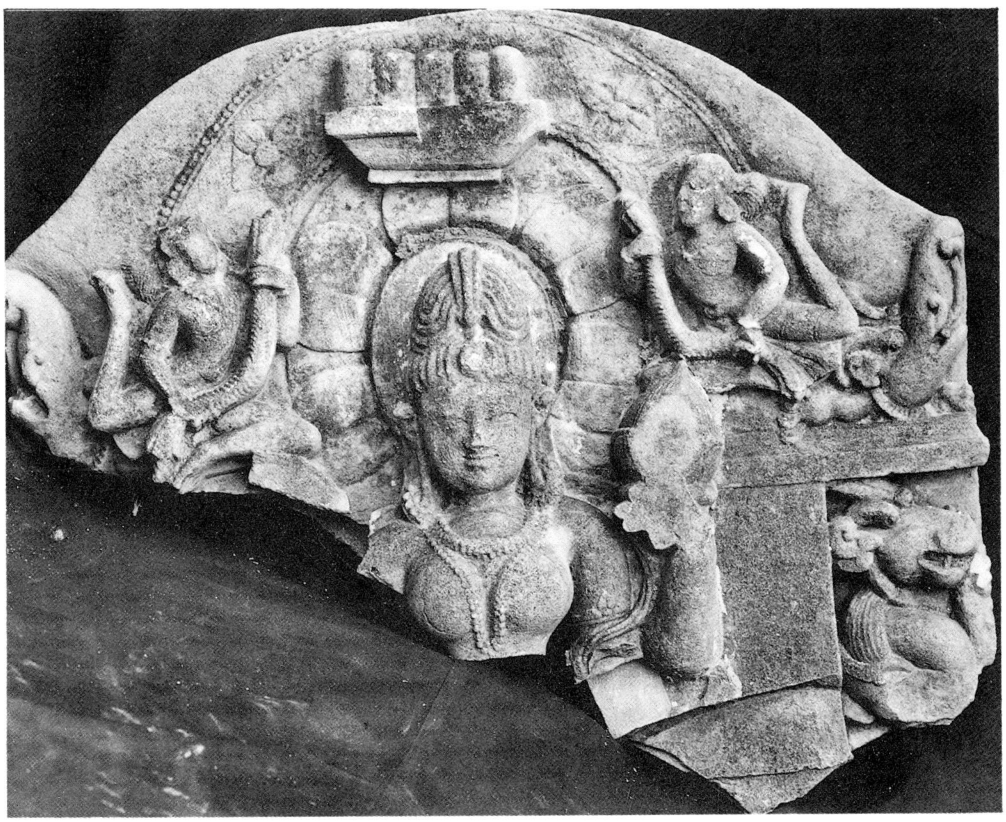

◀
121

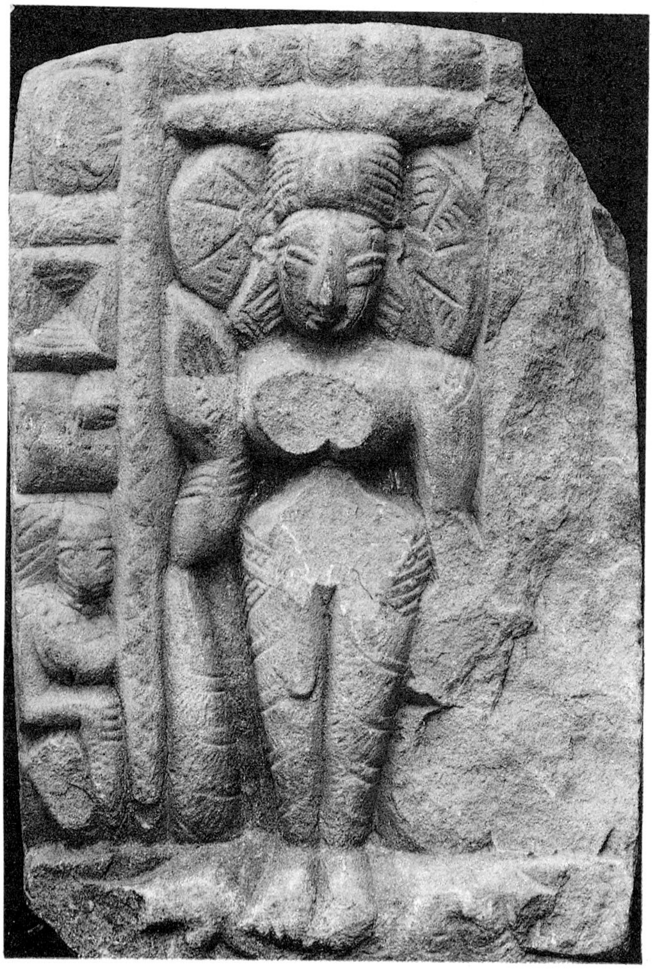

◀ 119

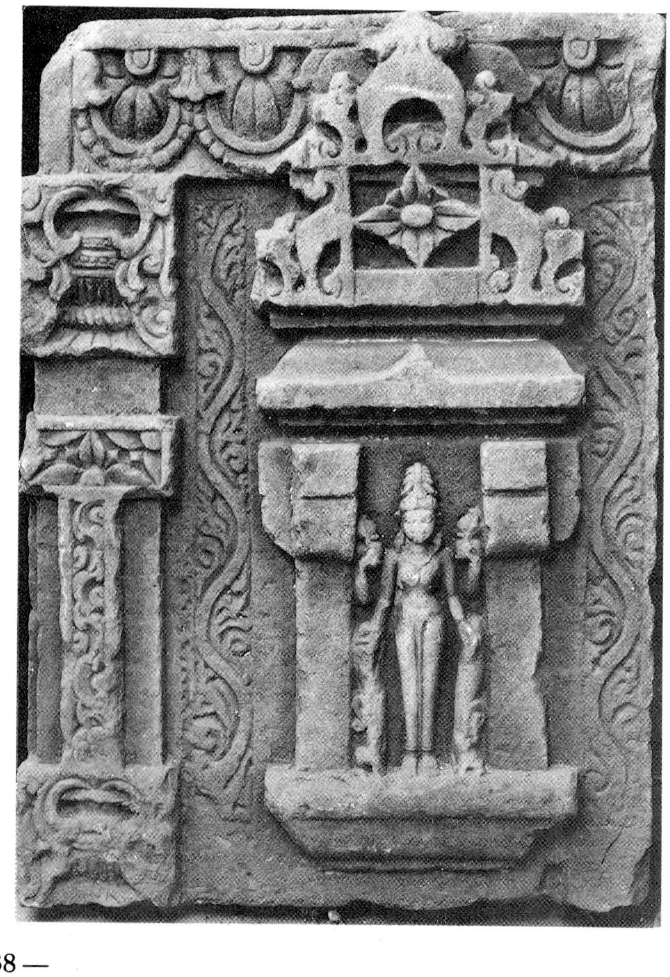

▶ 120

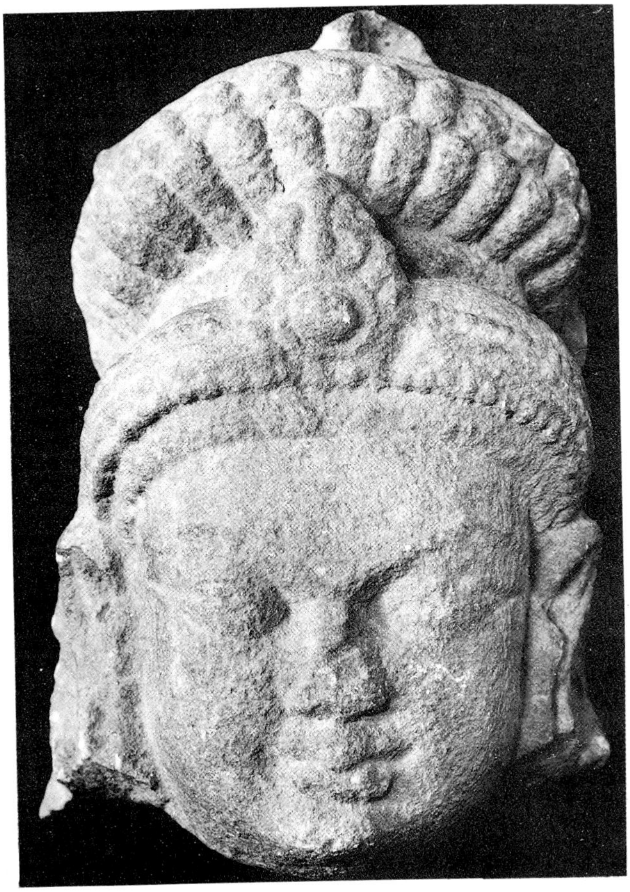

◄
117

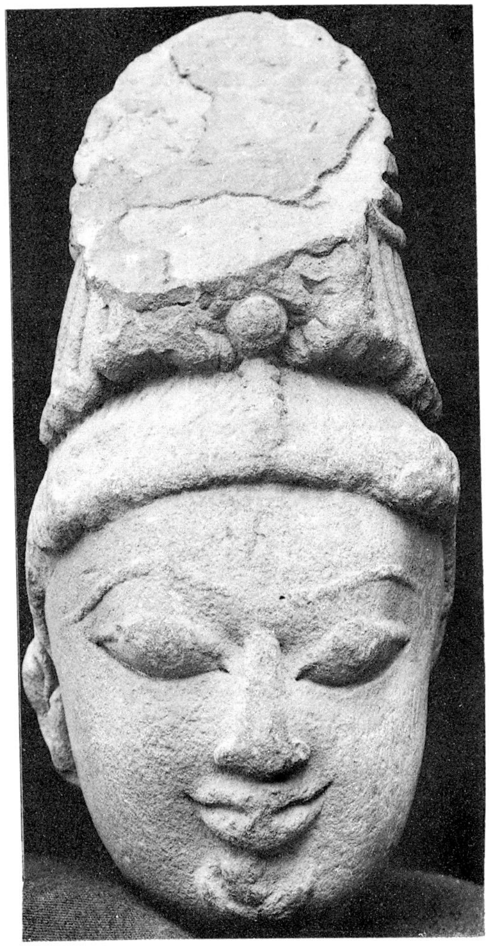

►
122

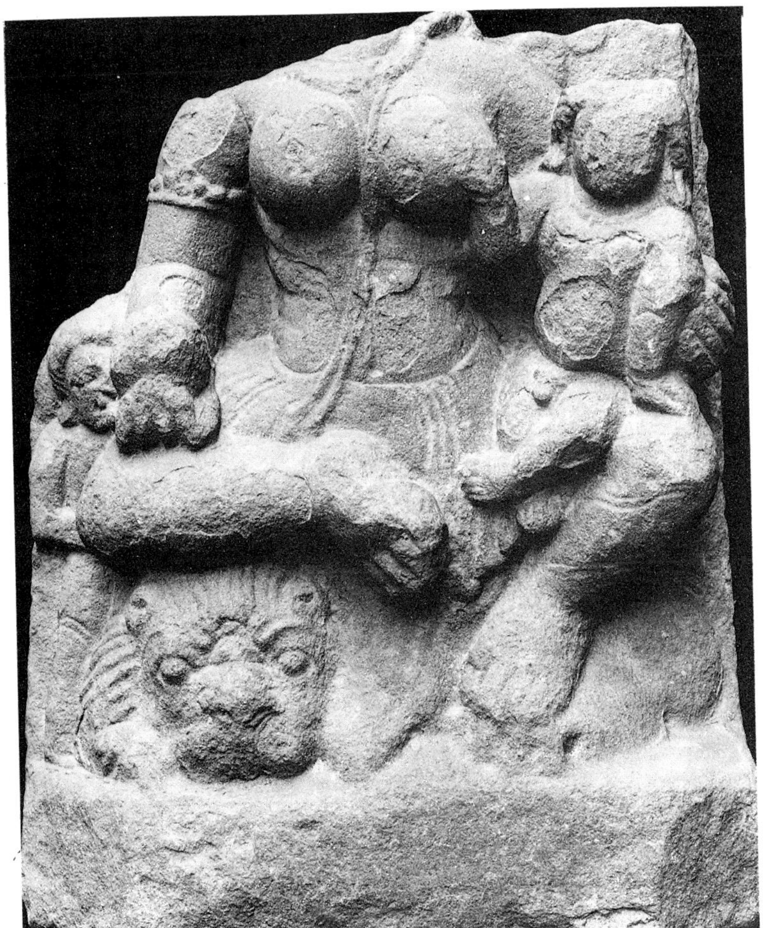

◄
123

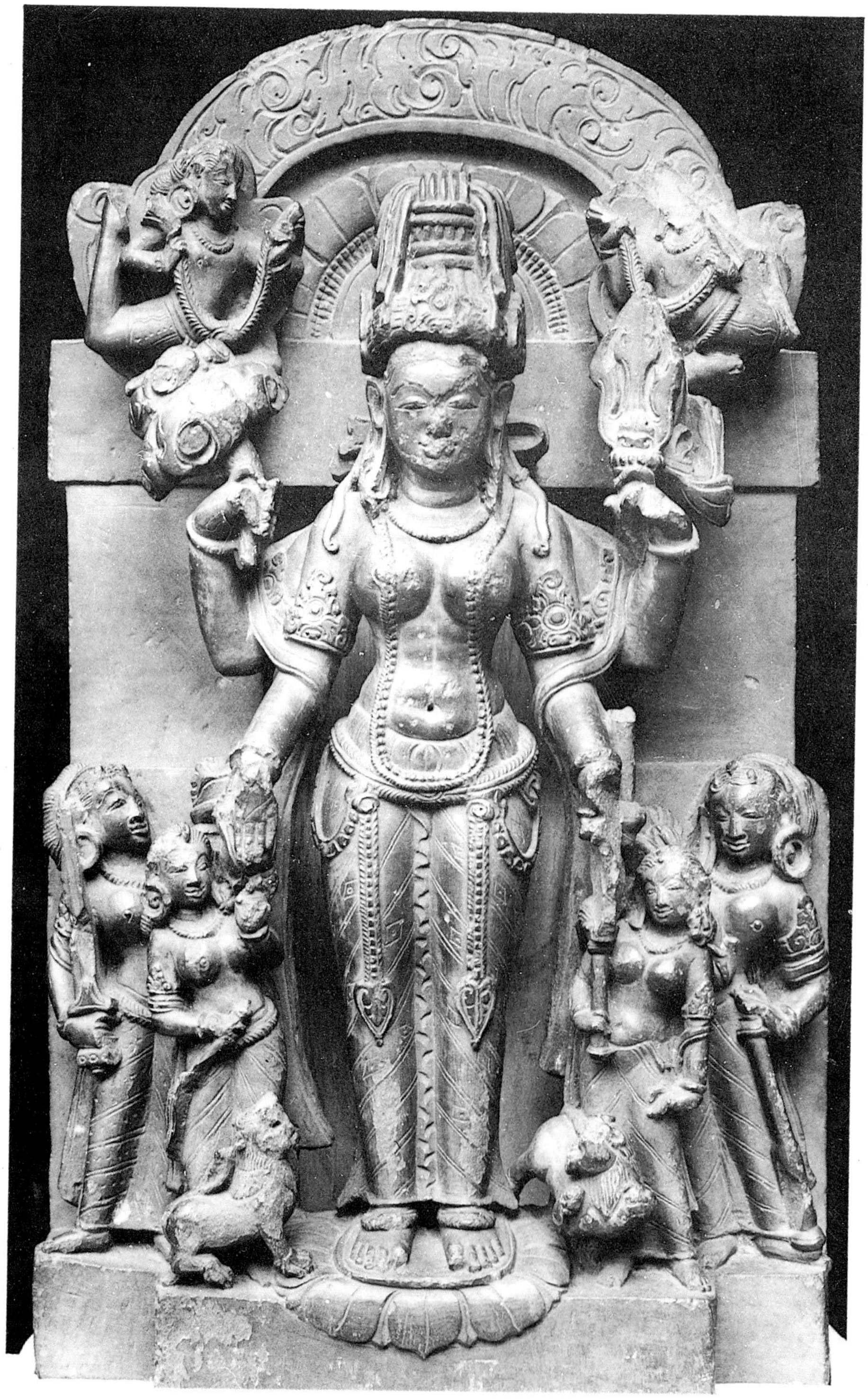

▲ 124

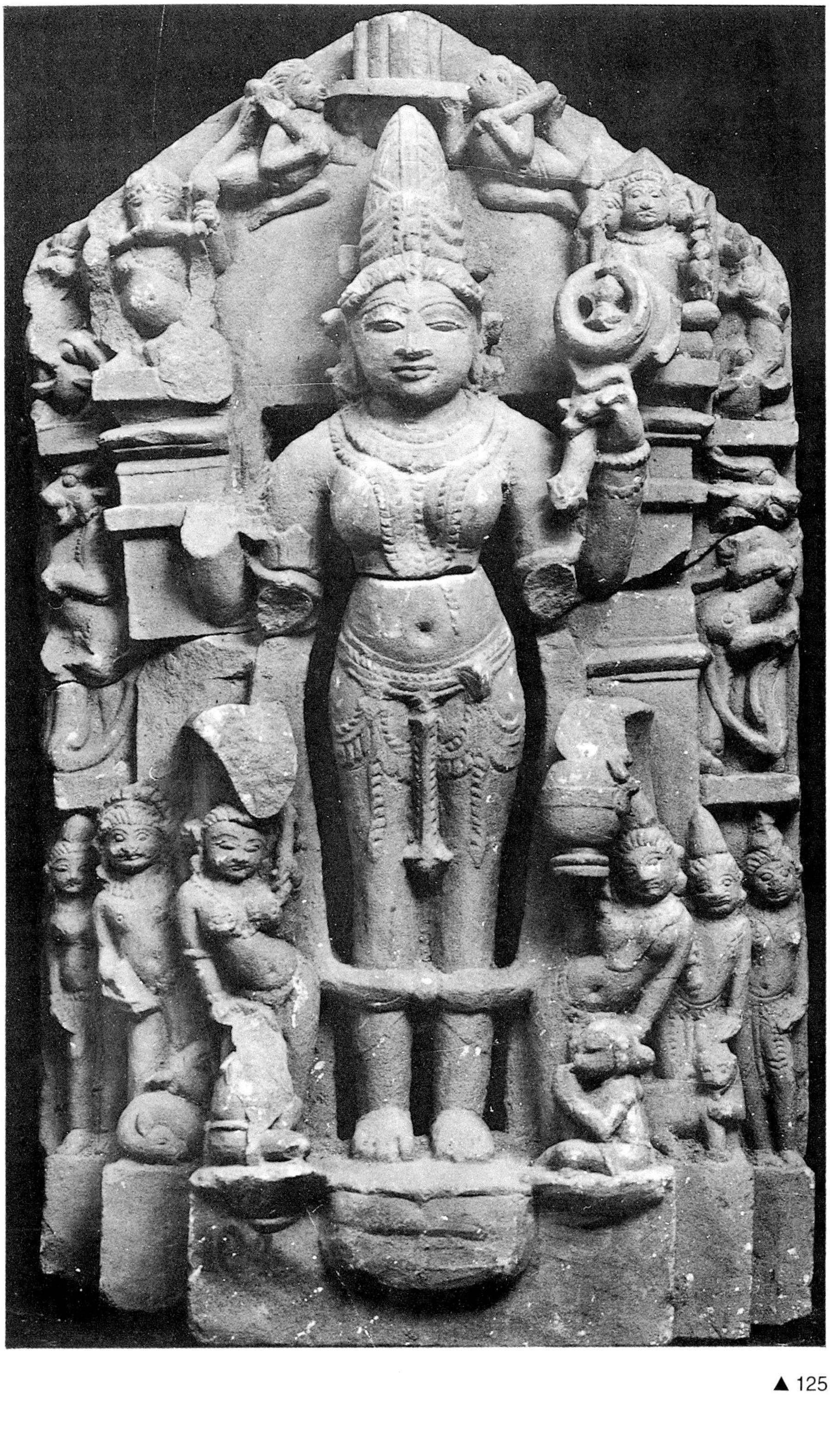

▲ 125

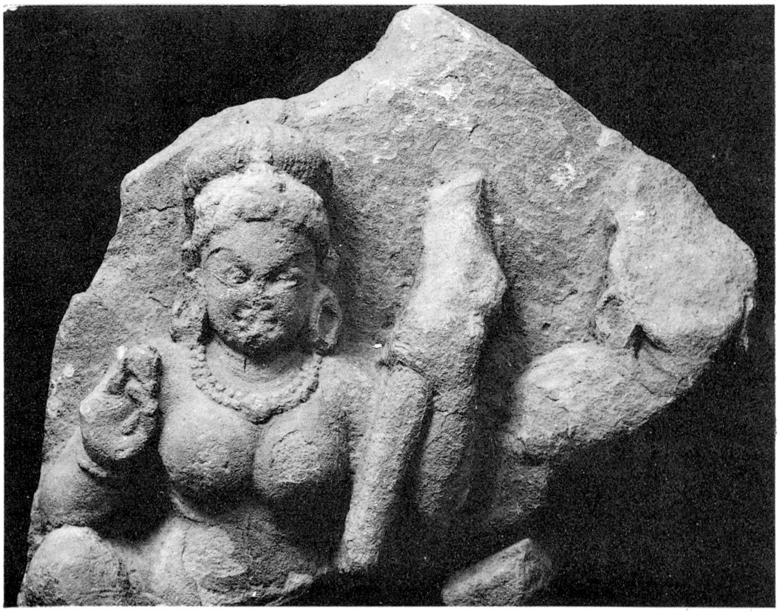

◀ 126

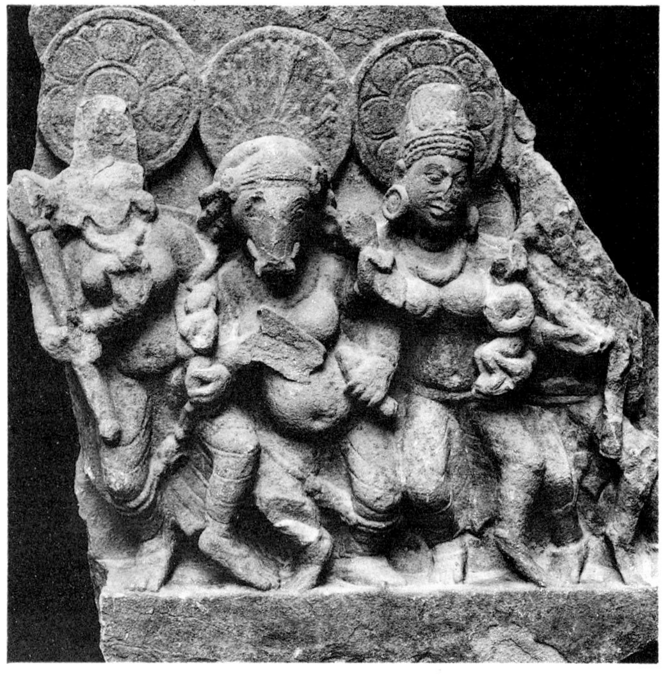

▲ 129

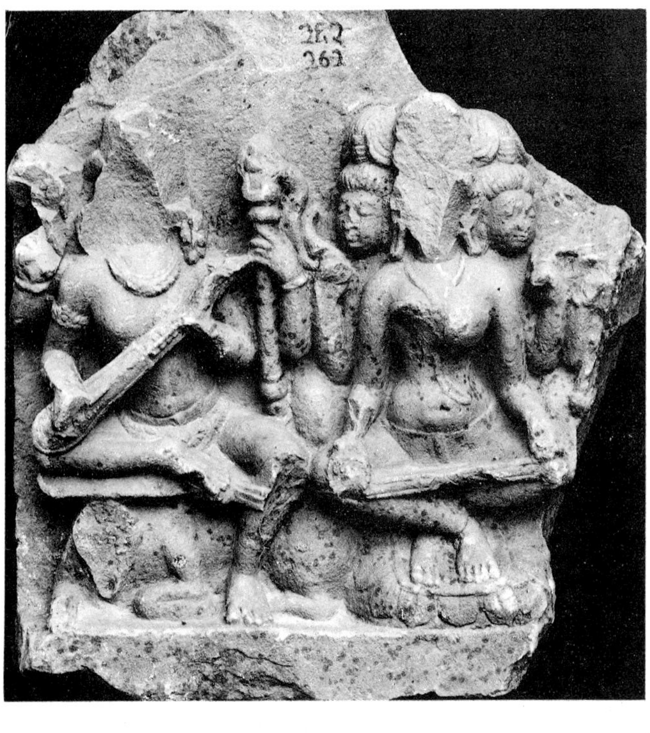

◀ 128

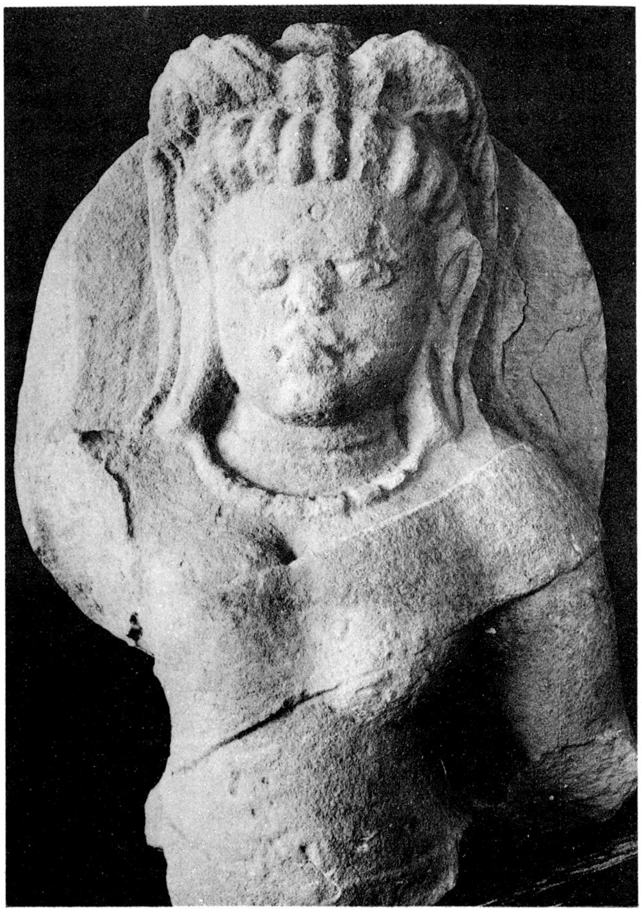

◀ 127

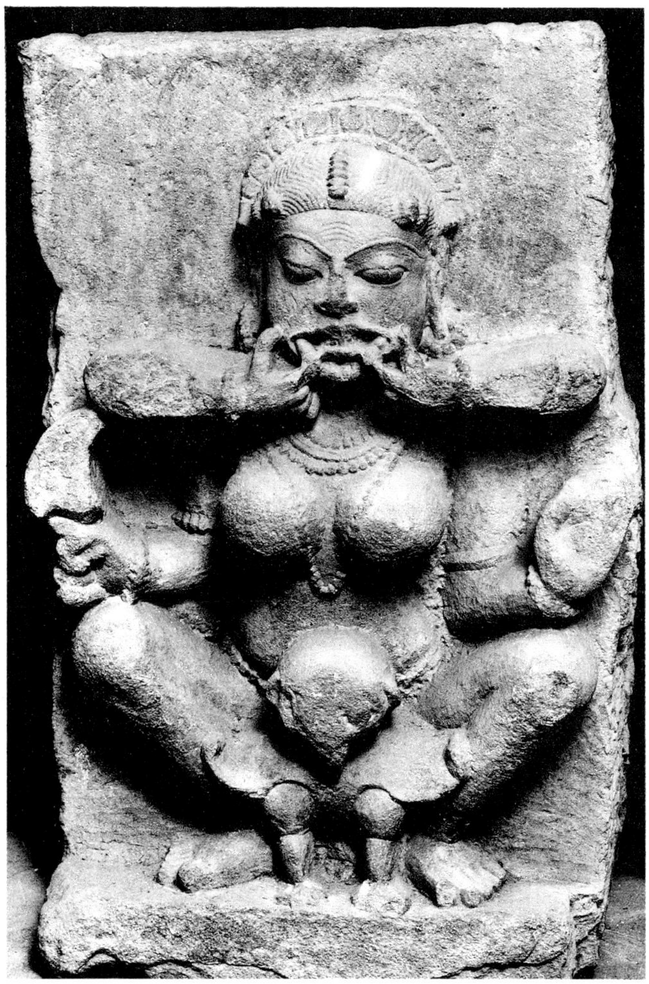

▶ 132

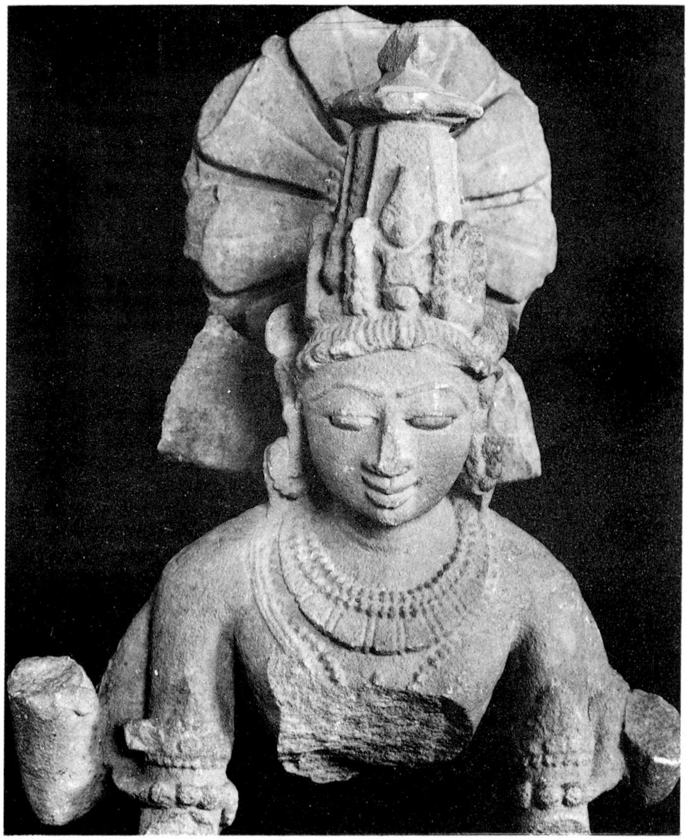

◀
131

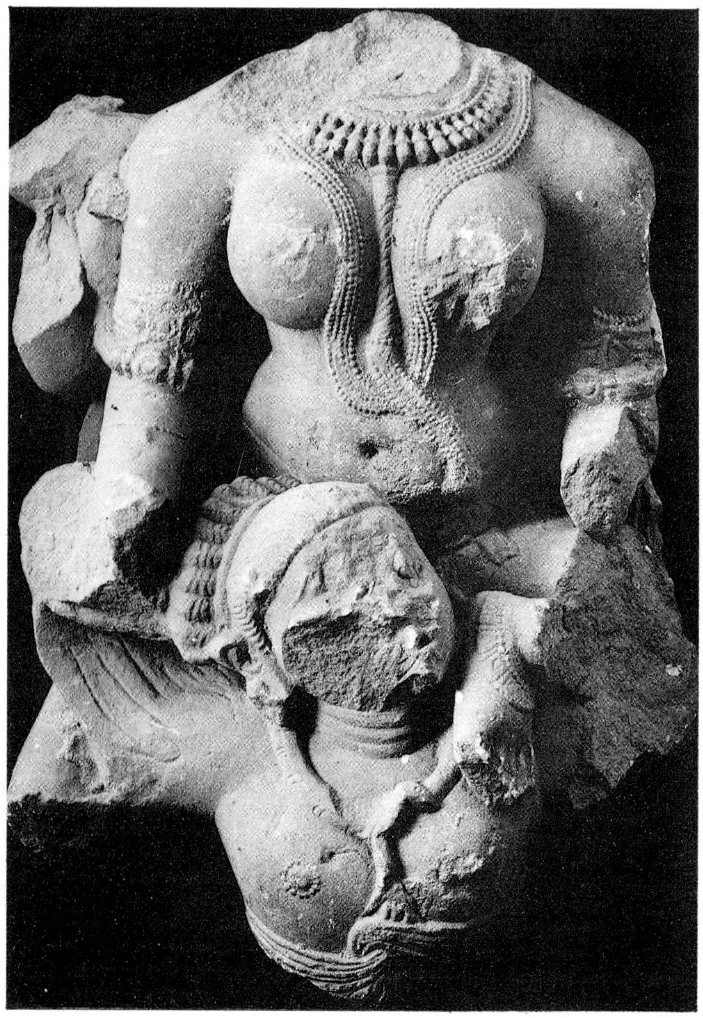

▶
130

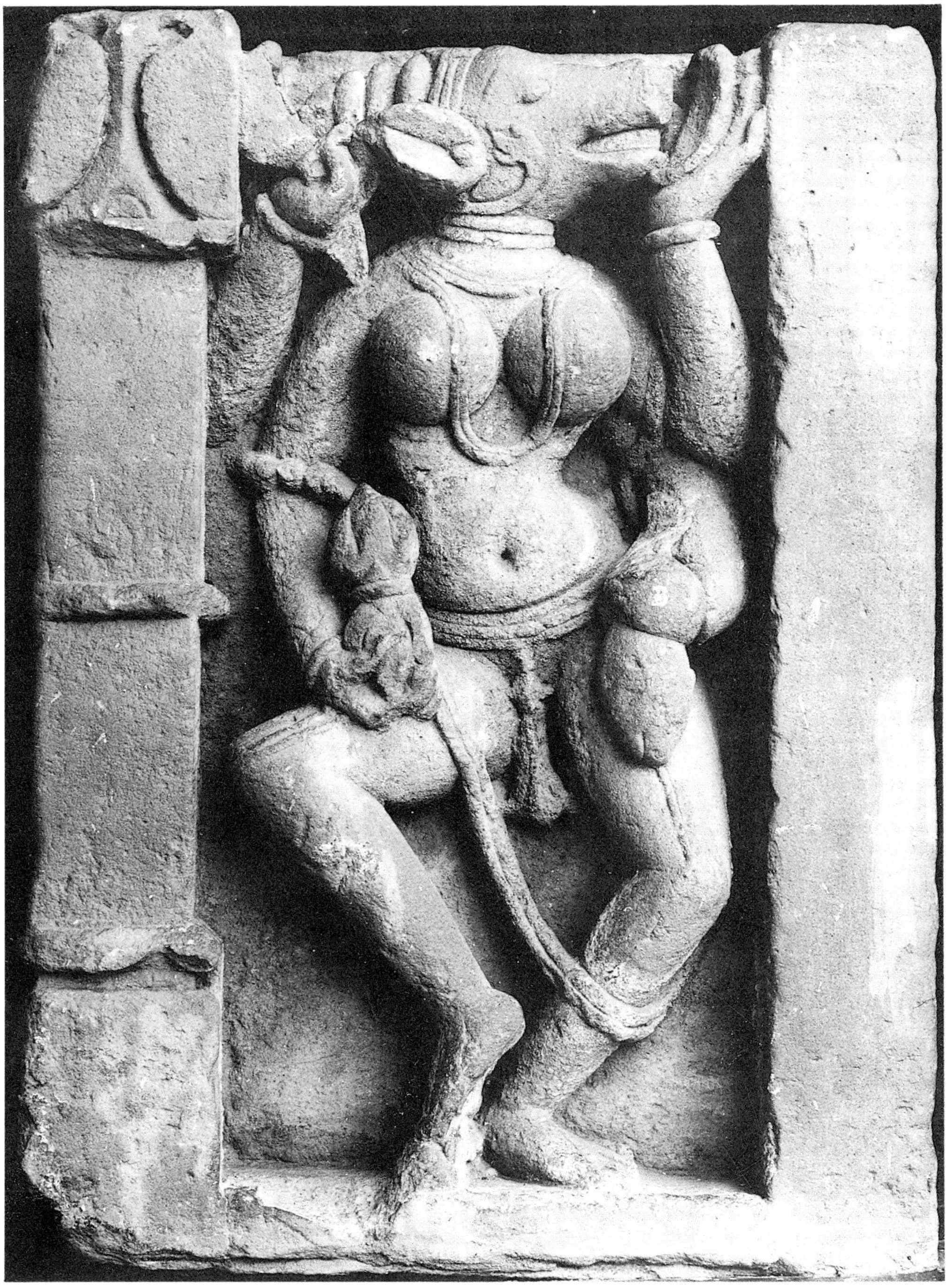

▲133

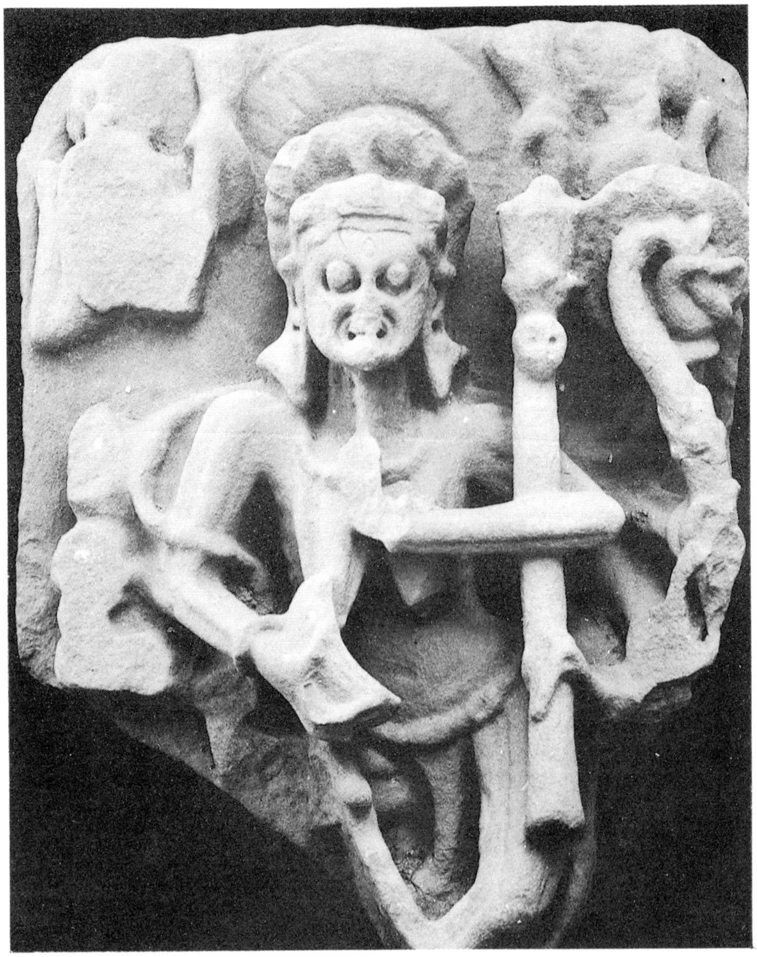

◀ 135

▼ 134A

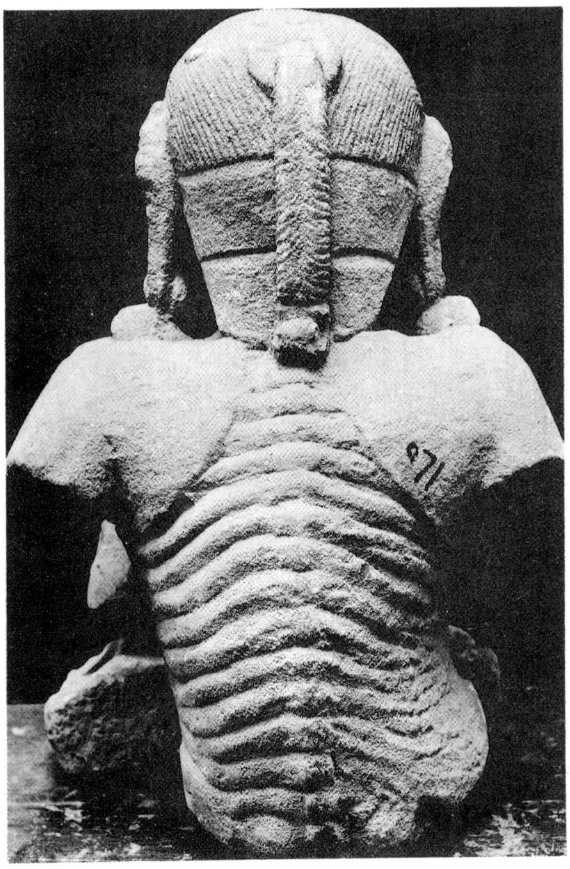

▼ 134B

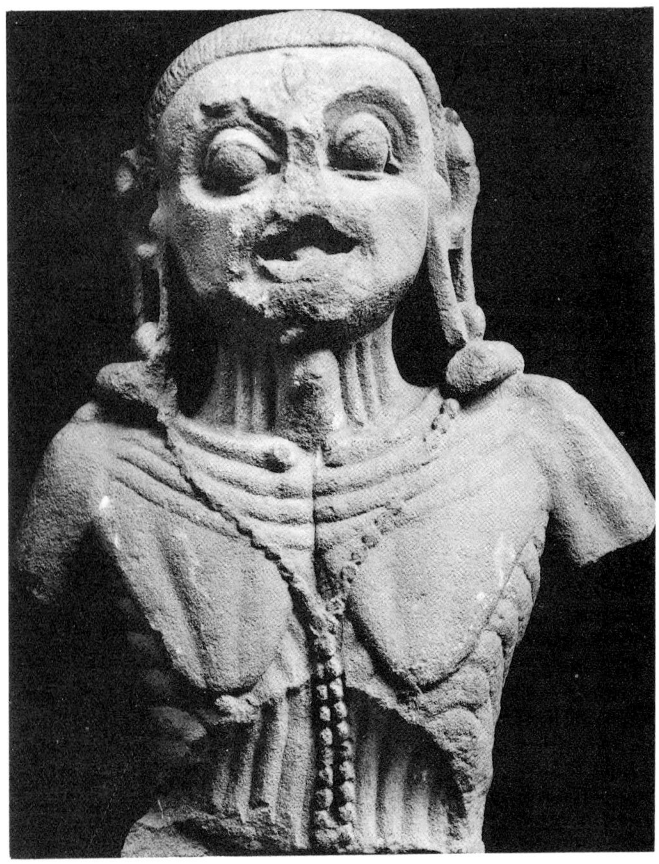

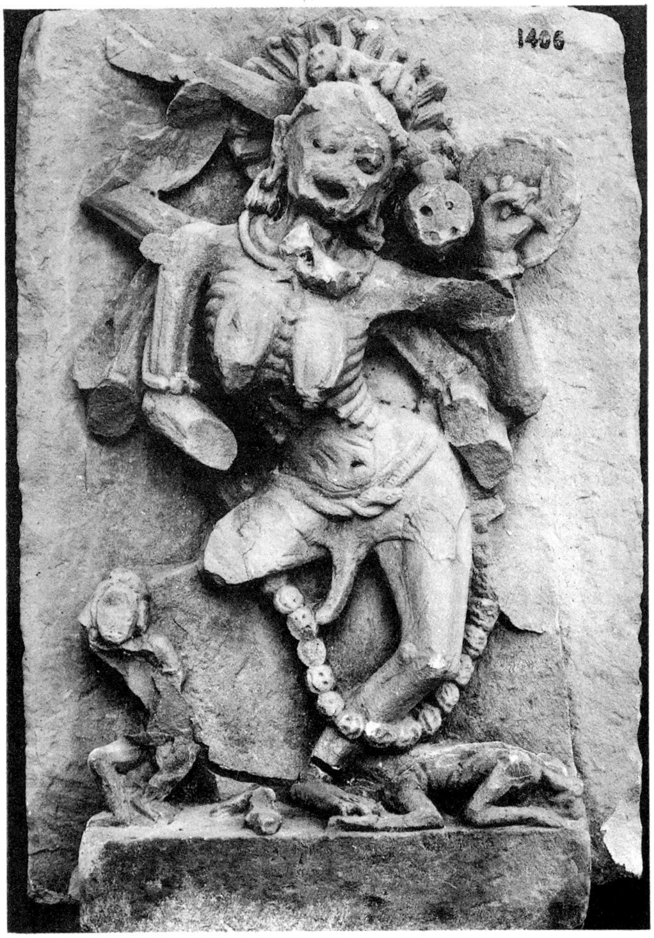

◀ 136

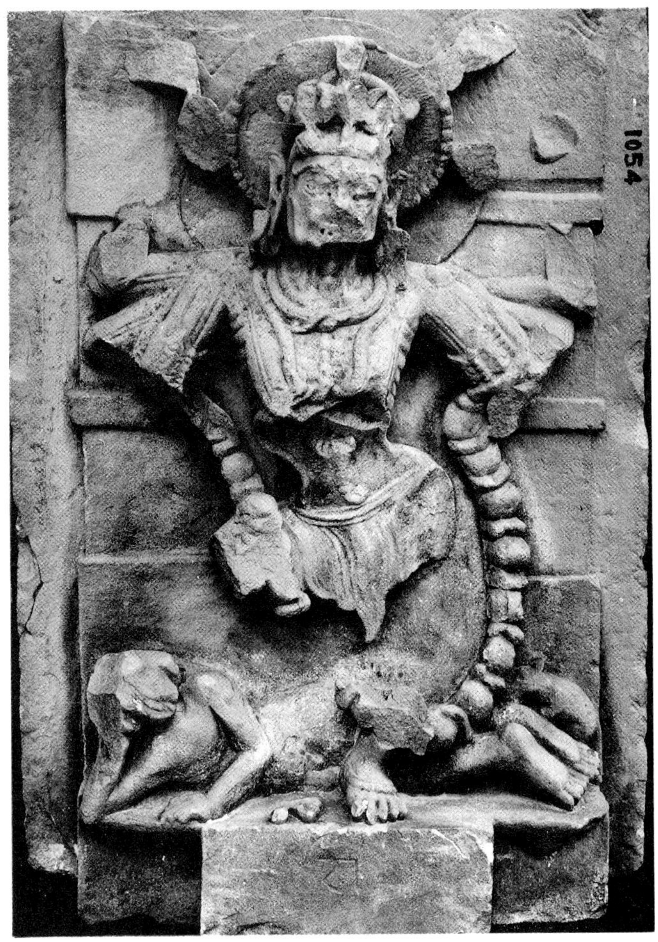

▶ 137

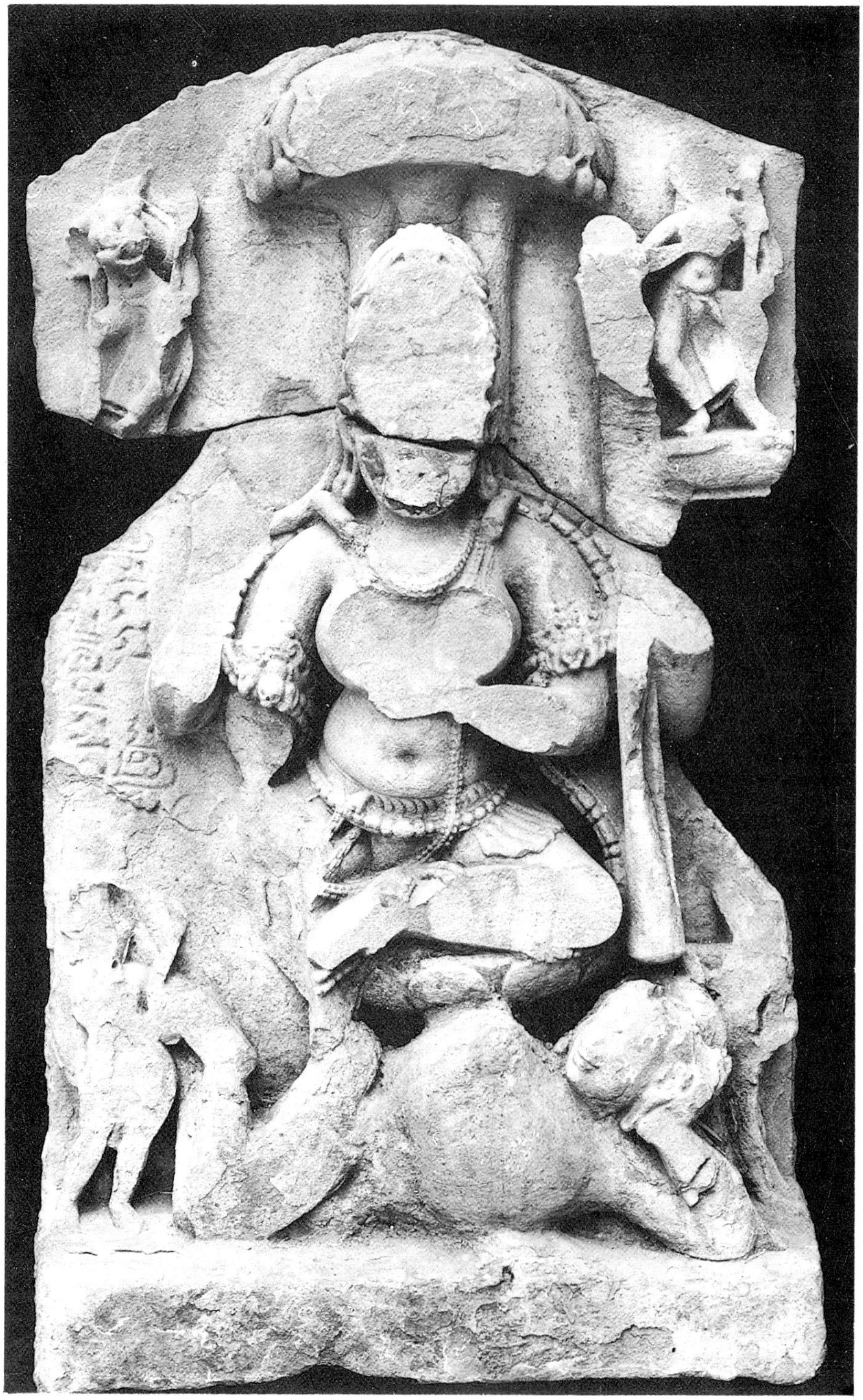

▲ 138

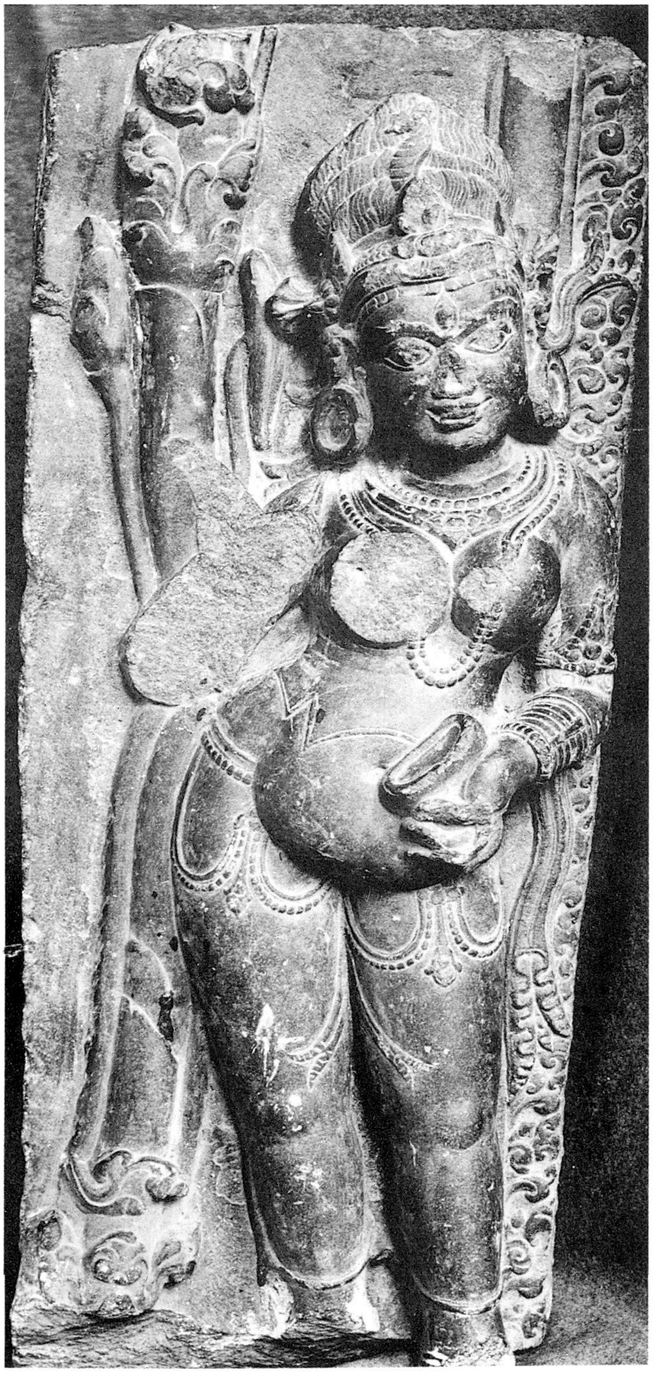

◀
146

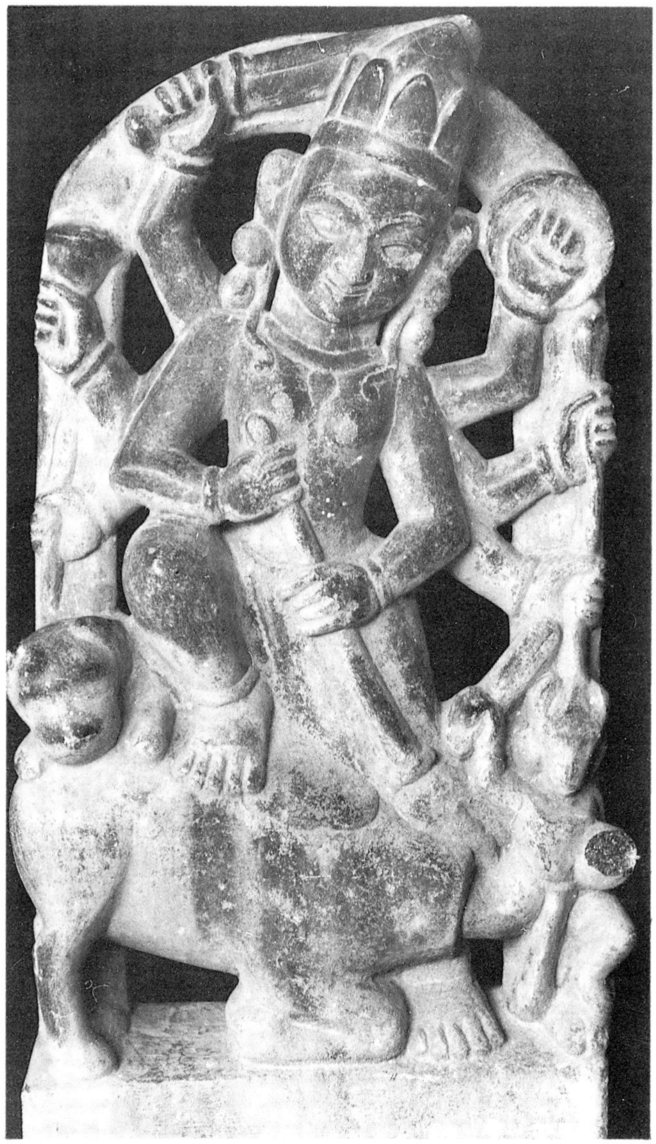

▶
147

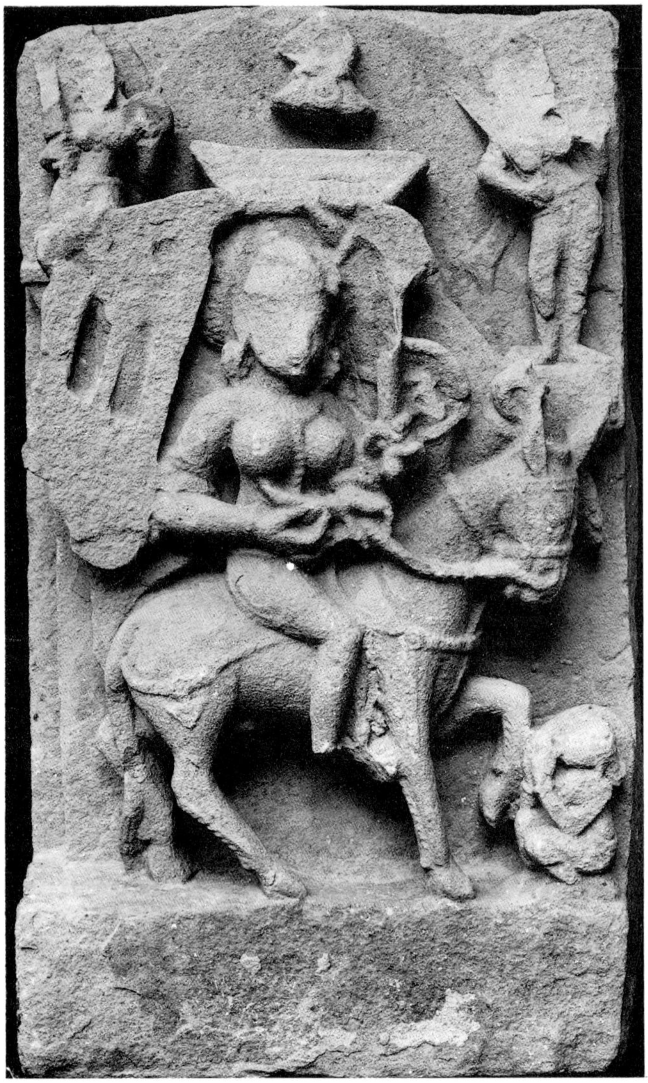

◀
142

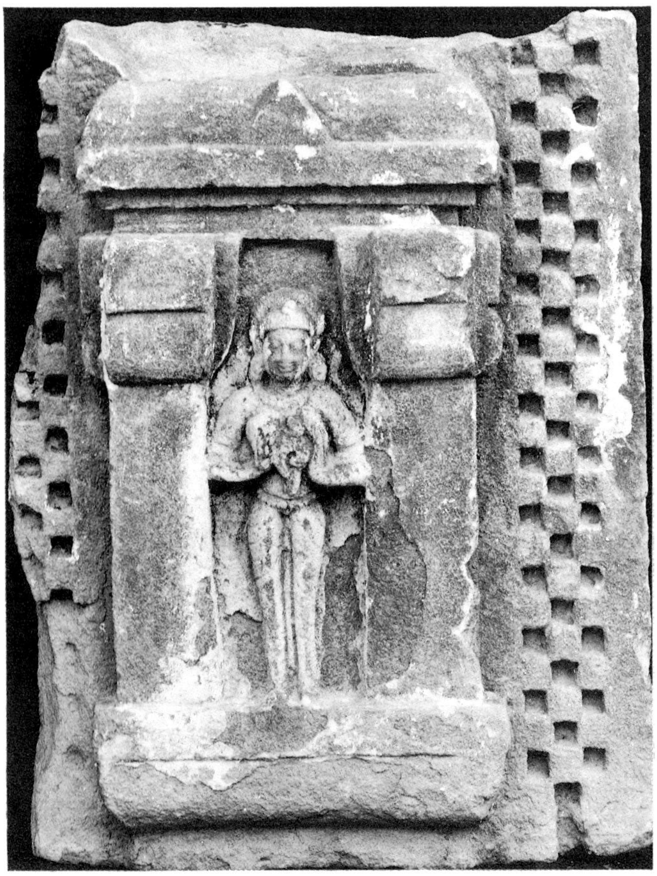

▶
144

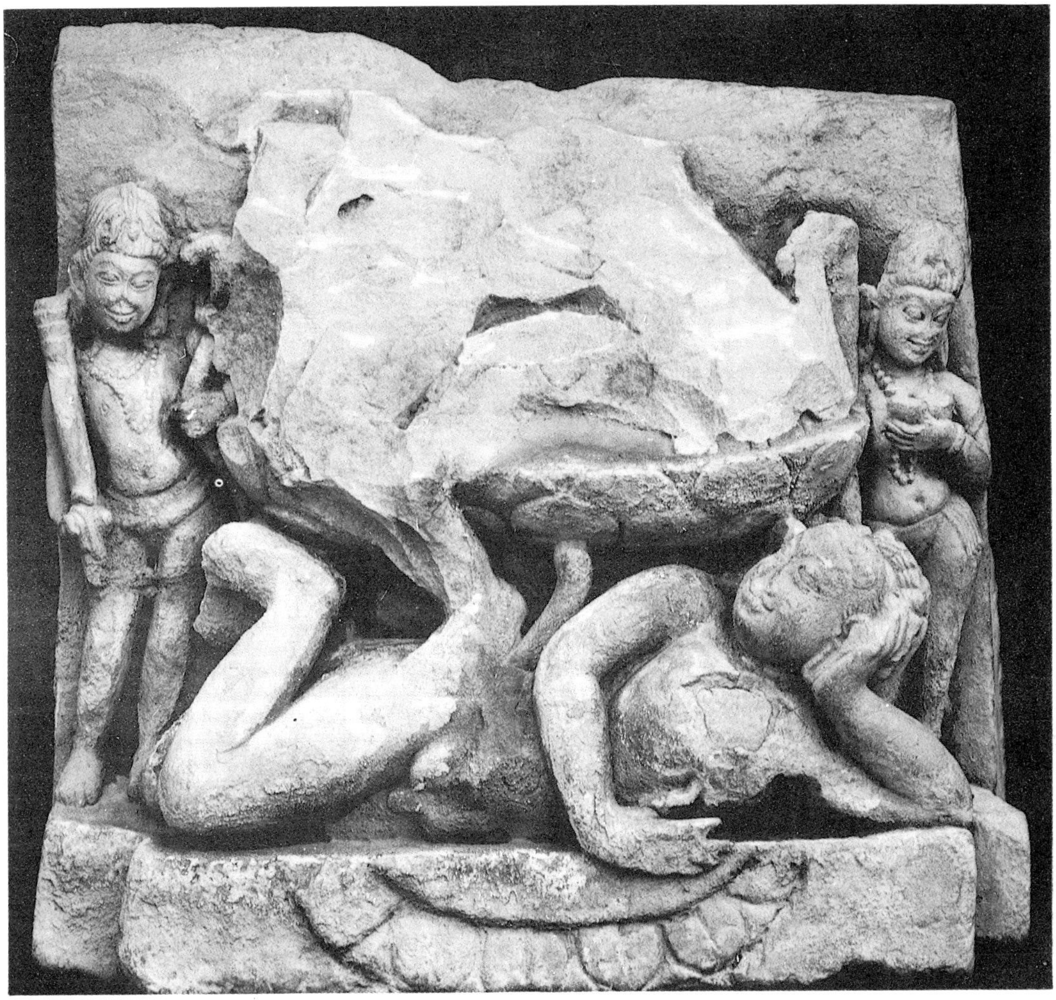

▲ 139

▼ 140

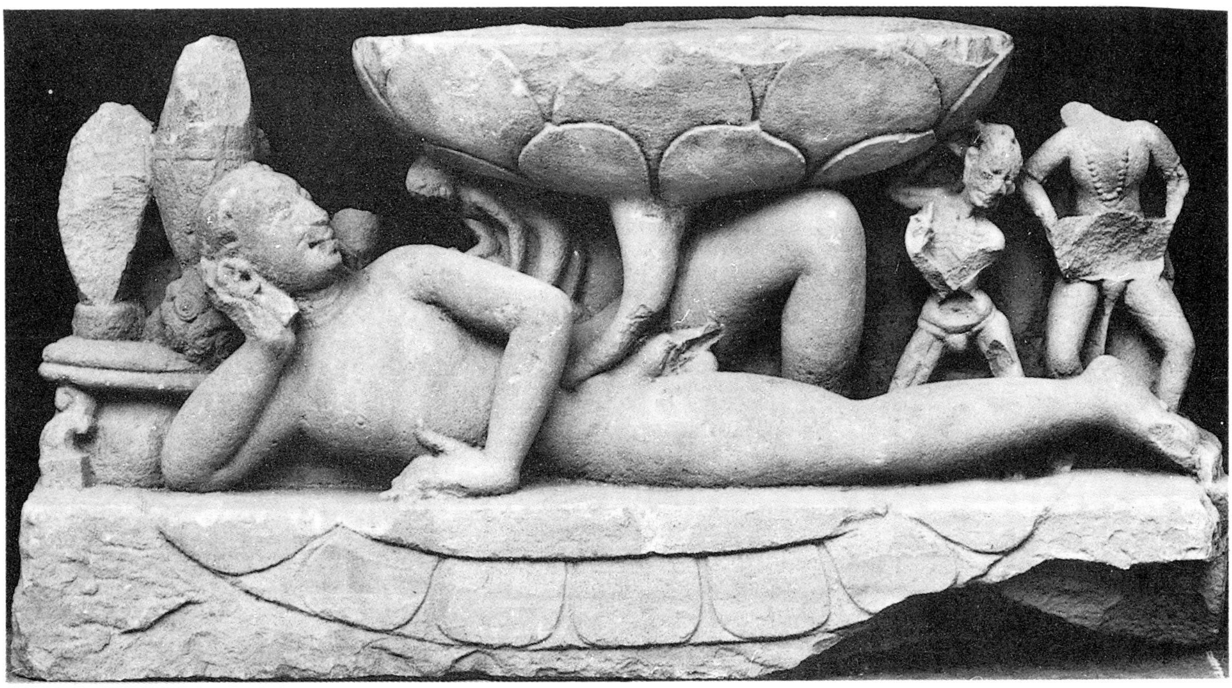

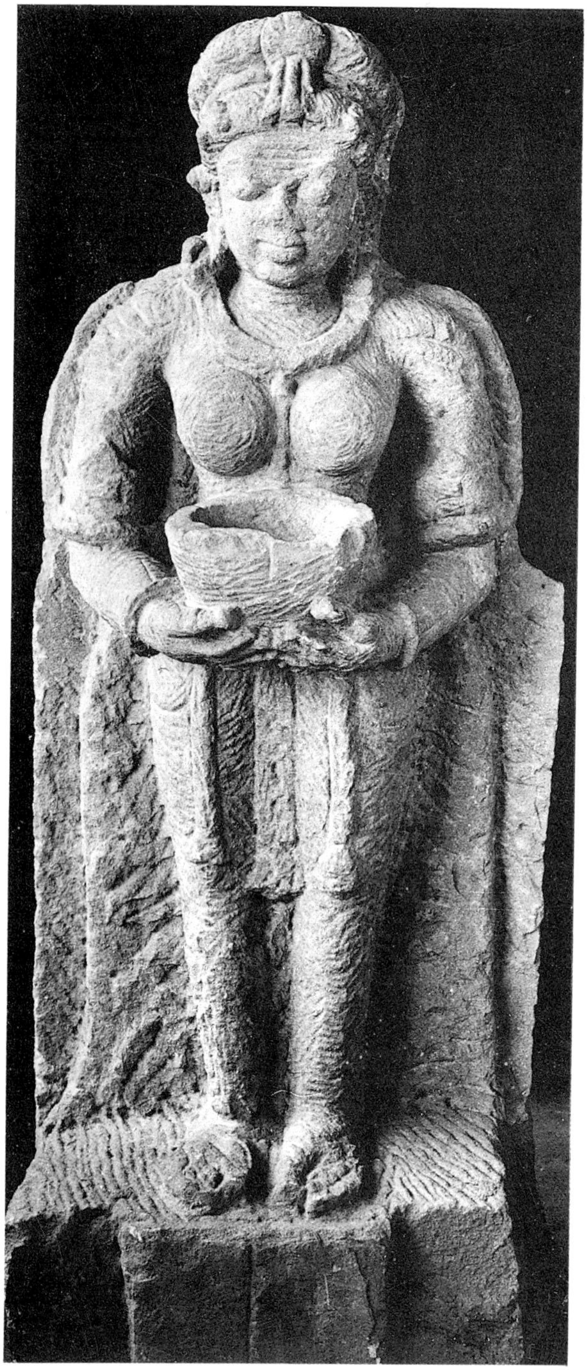

◀
145

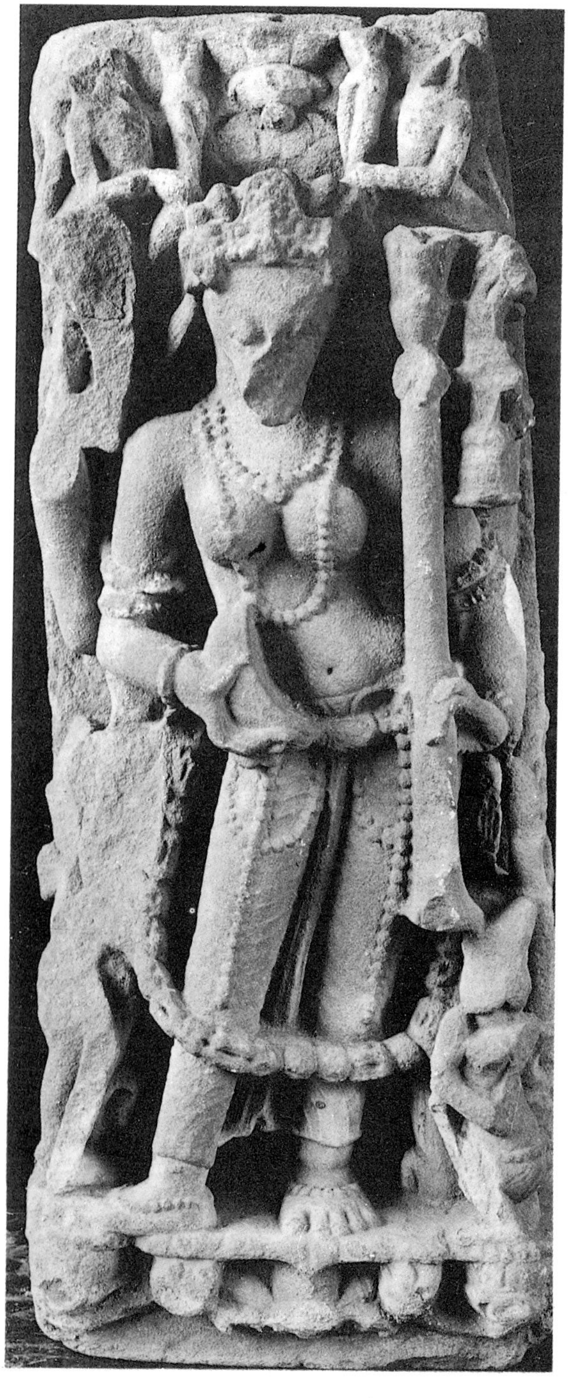

▶
141

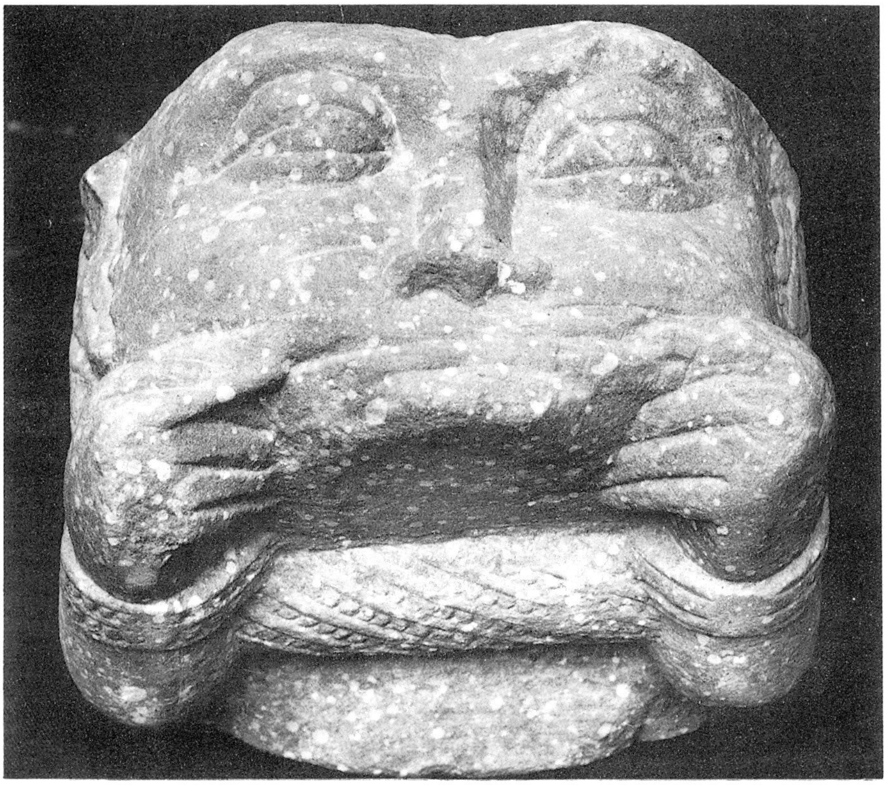

▲ 150

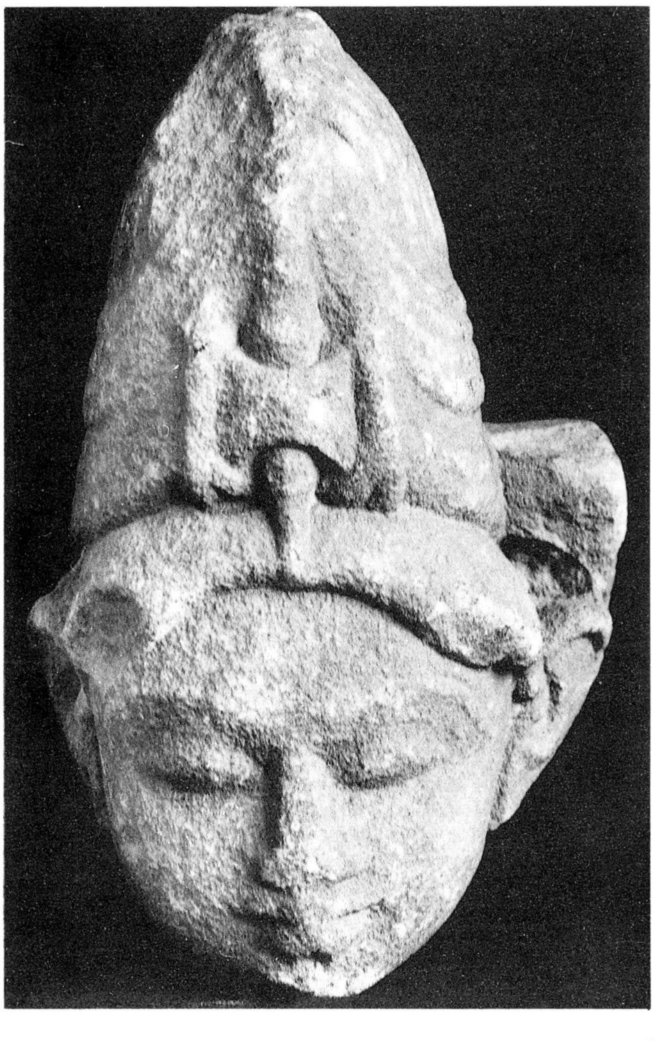

◀ 143

▼ 149

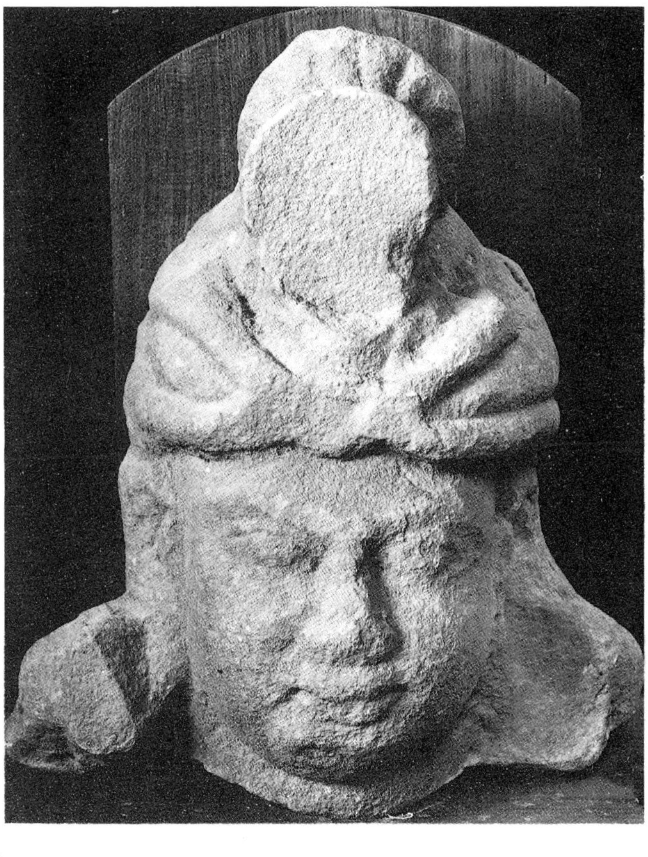

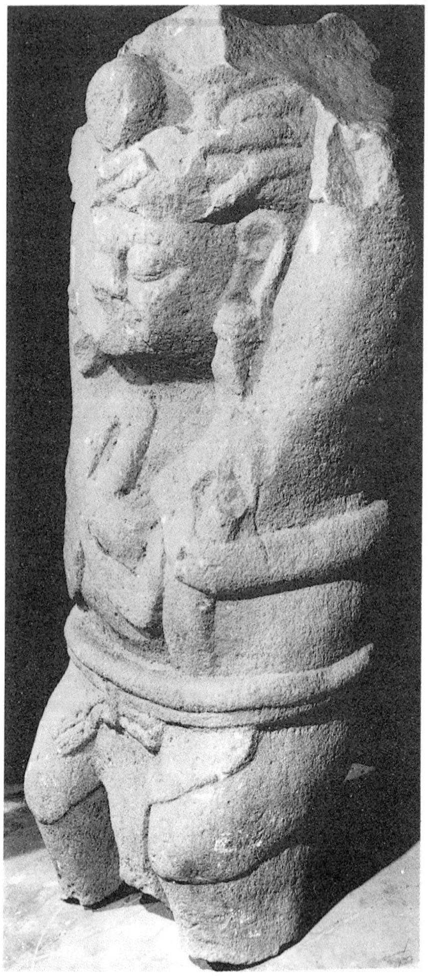

148

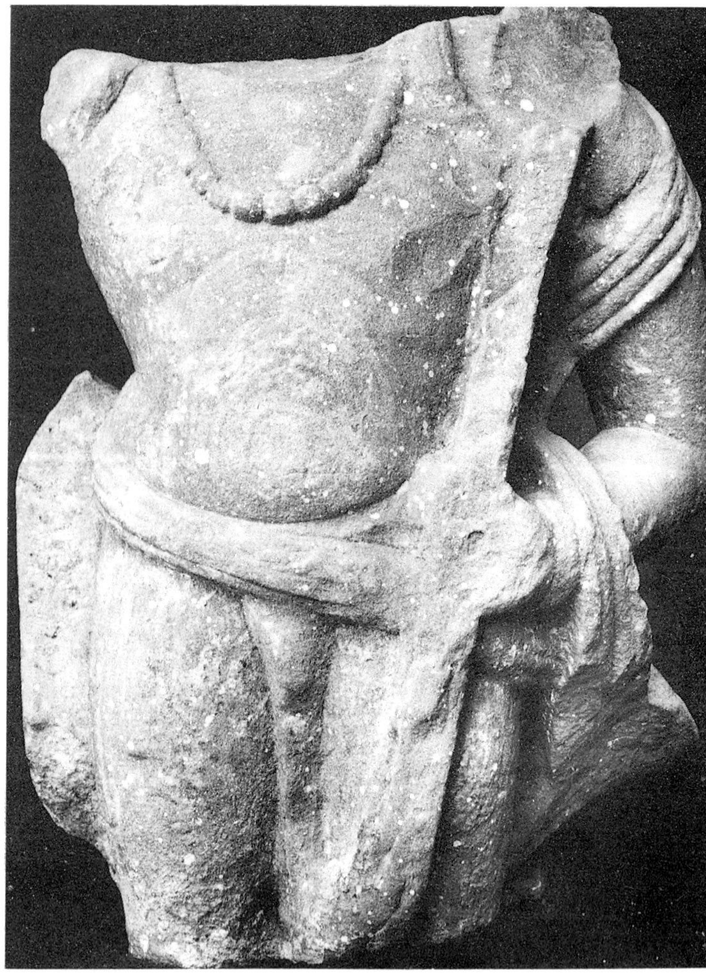

153A

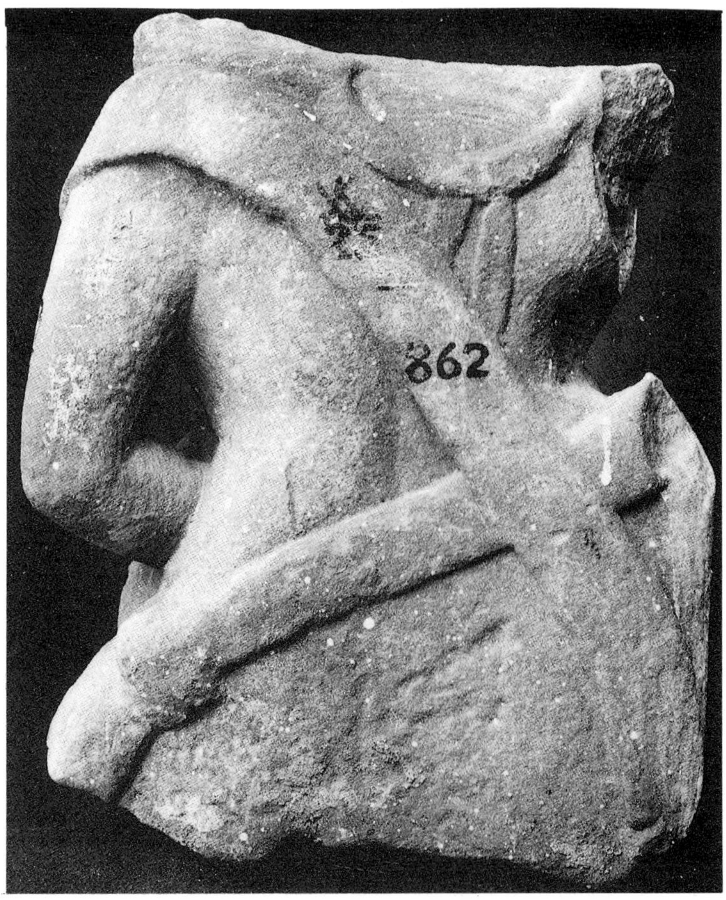

153B

◀
151

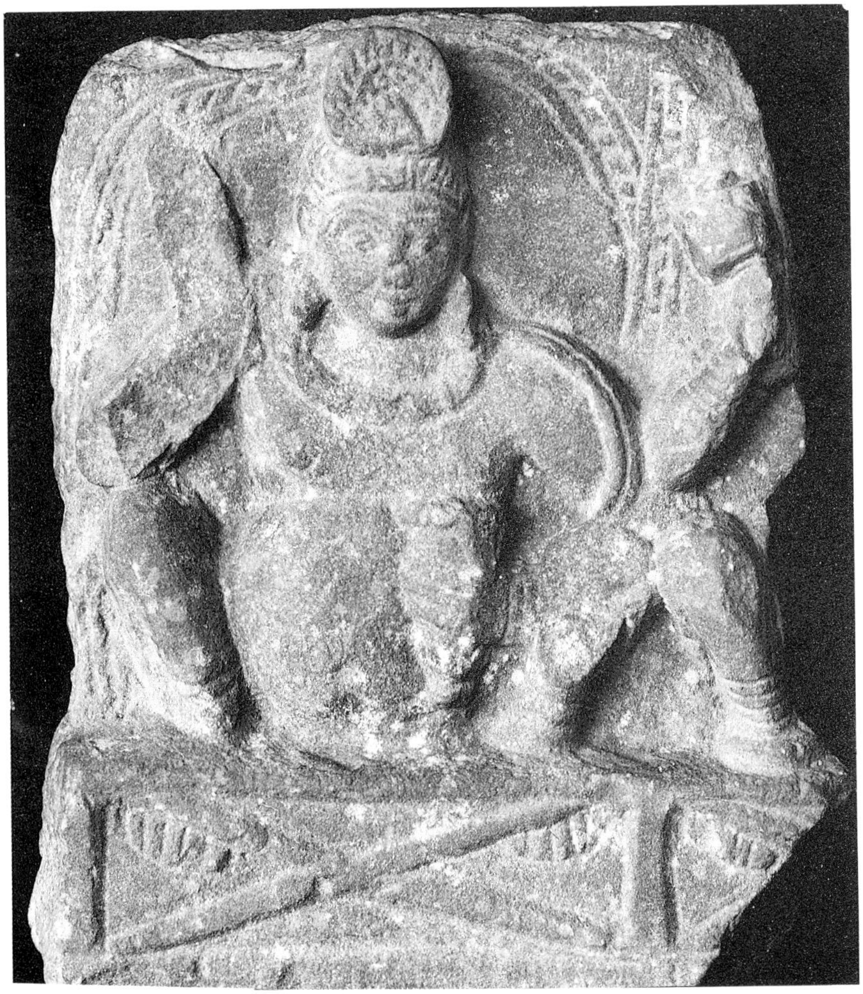

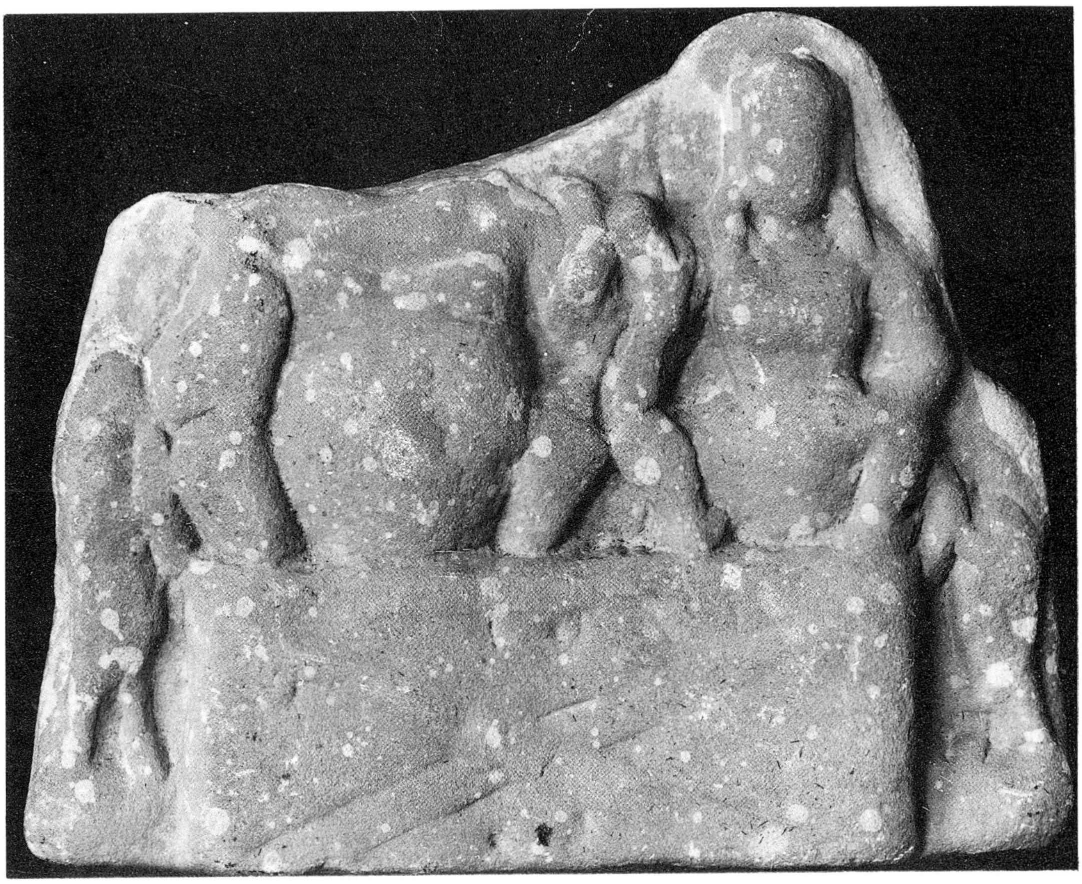

▶
152

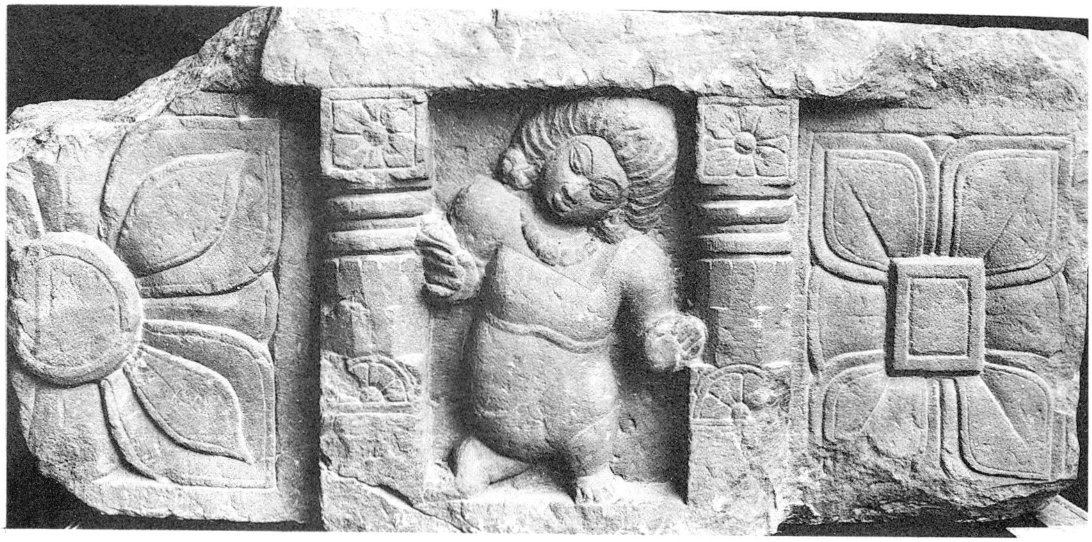

▶ 154

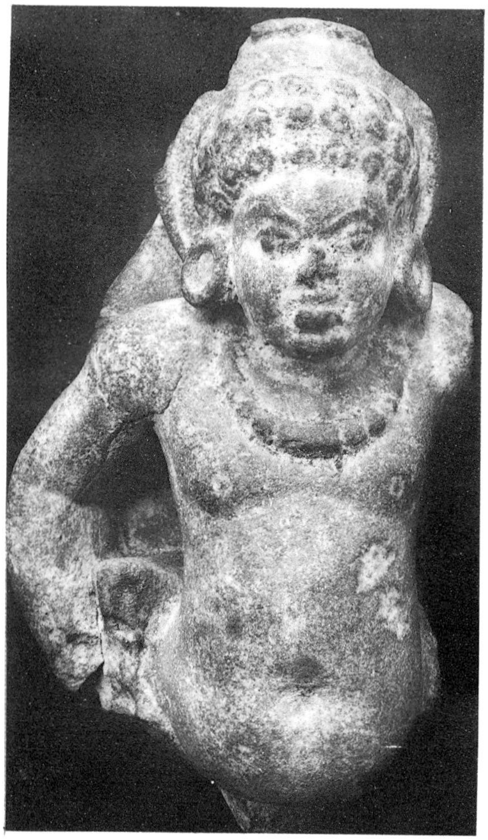

▲ 155

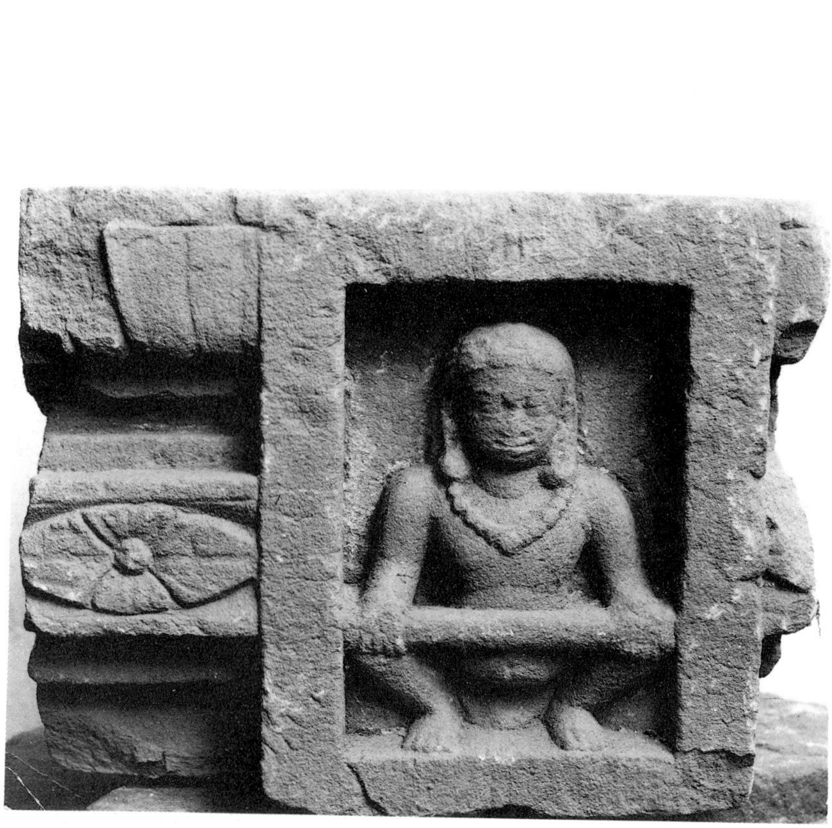

▶ 156

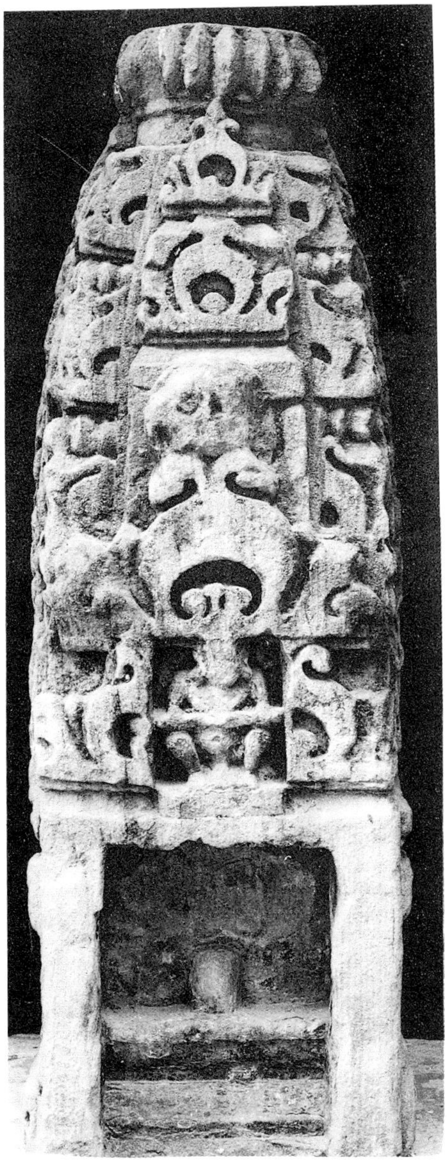

◀
157

▶
158

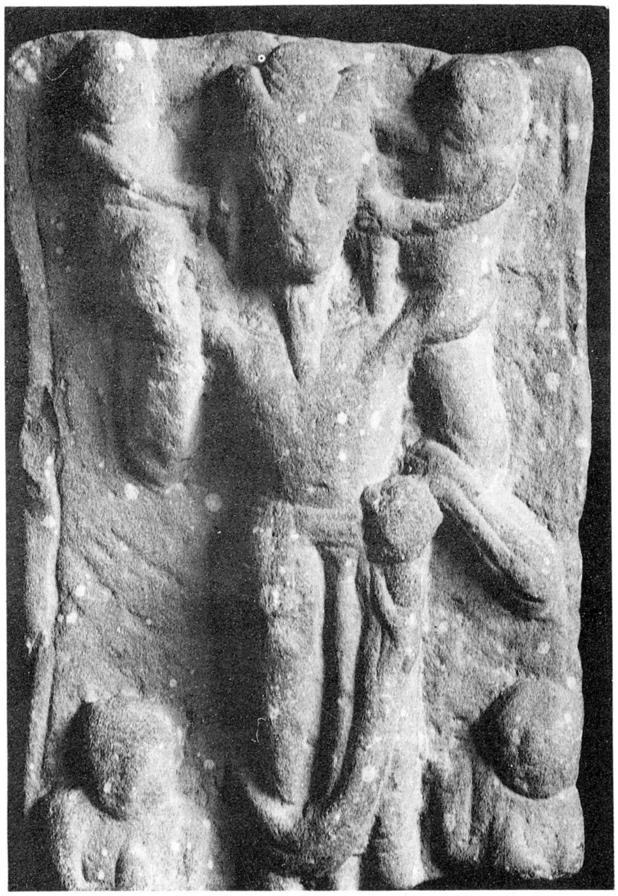

▶
160

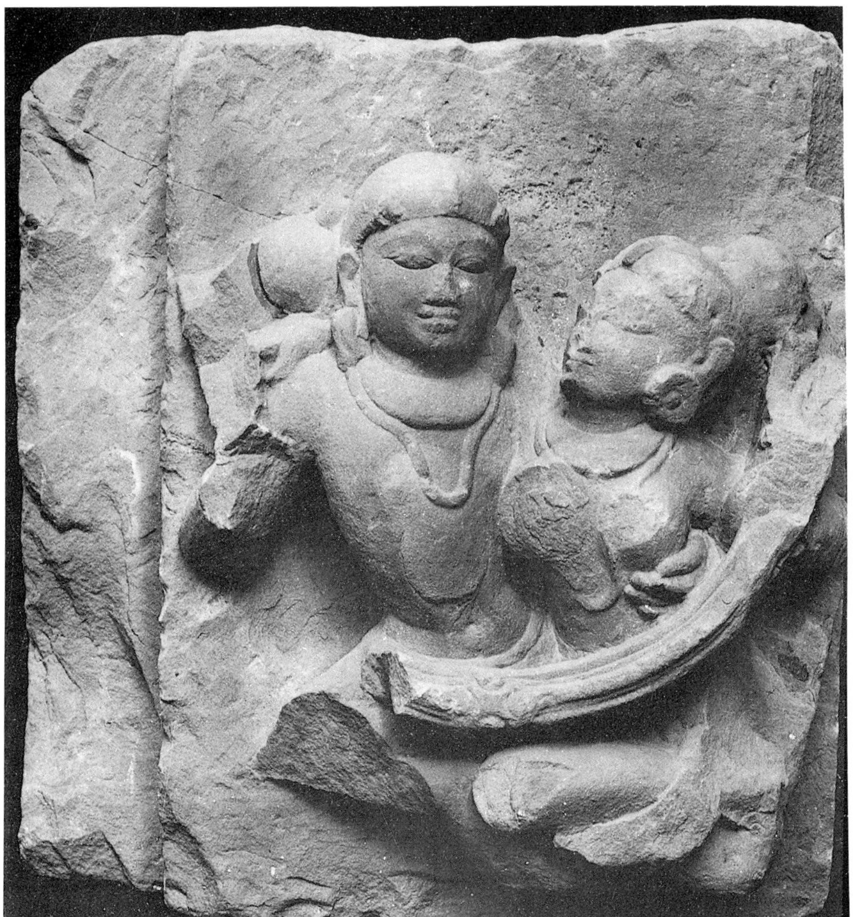

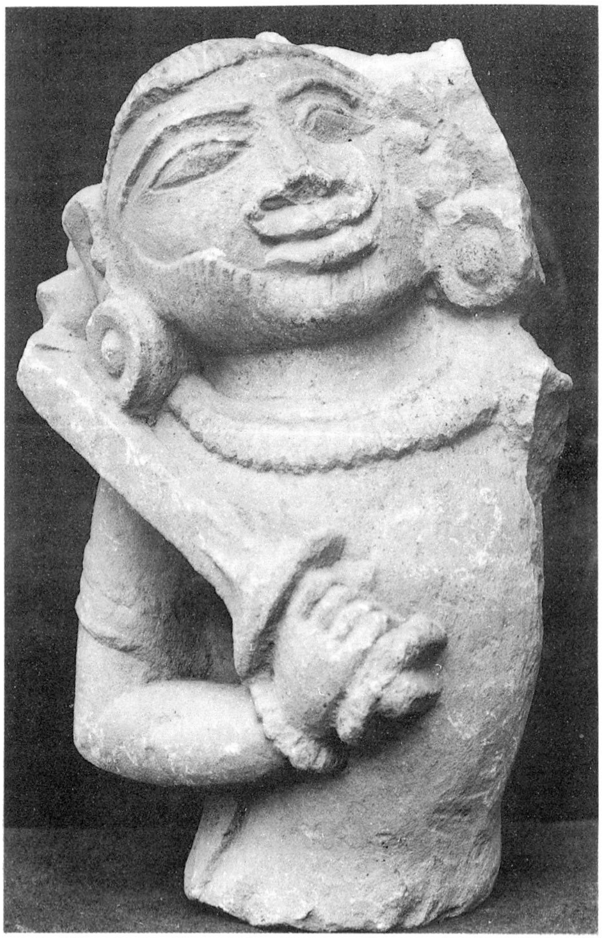

◀
161

▶
159

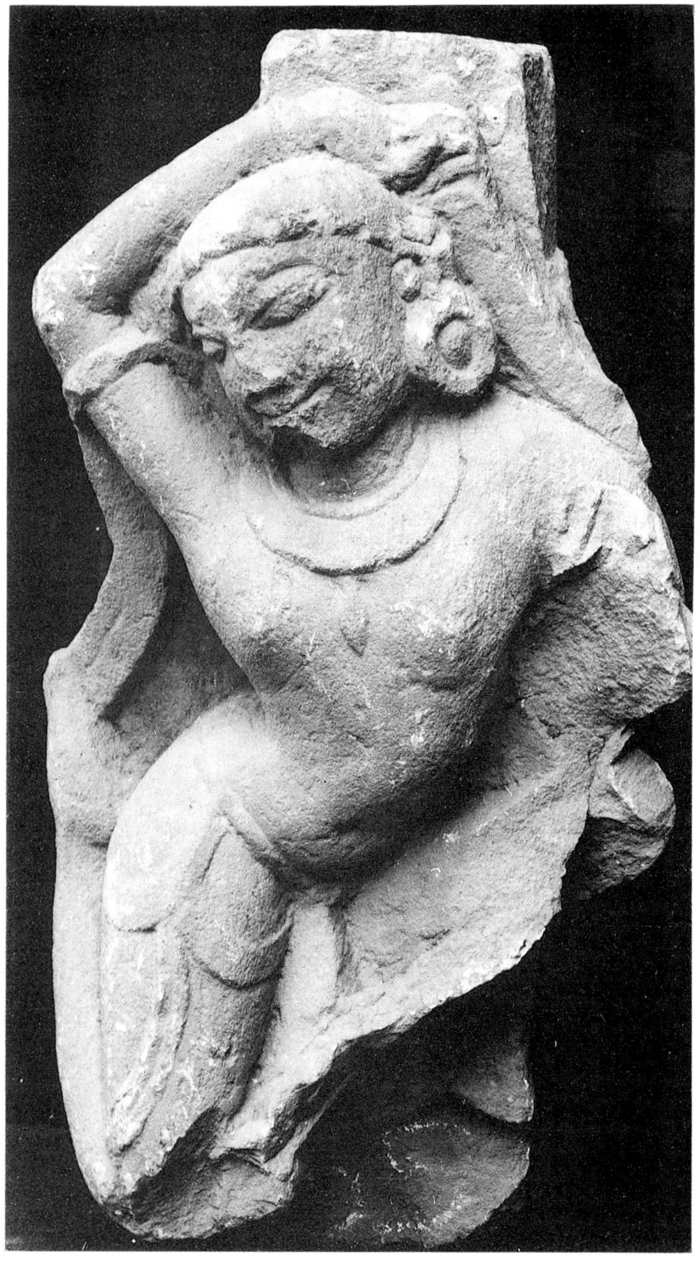

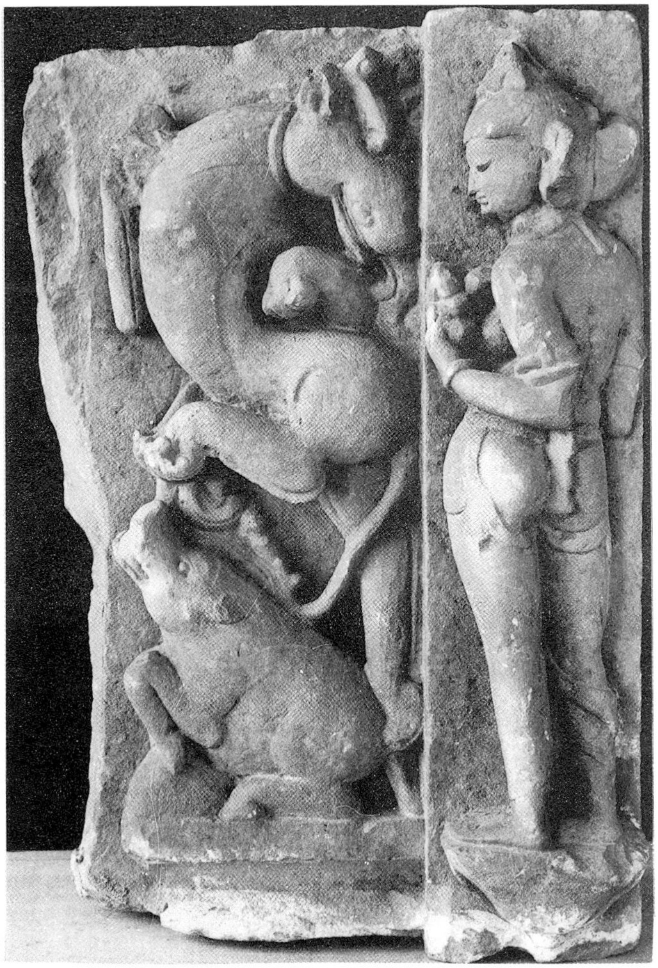

◀
162

▶
164

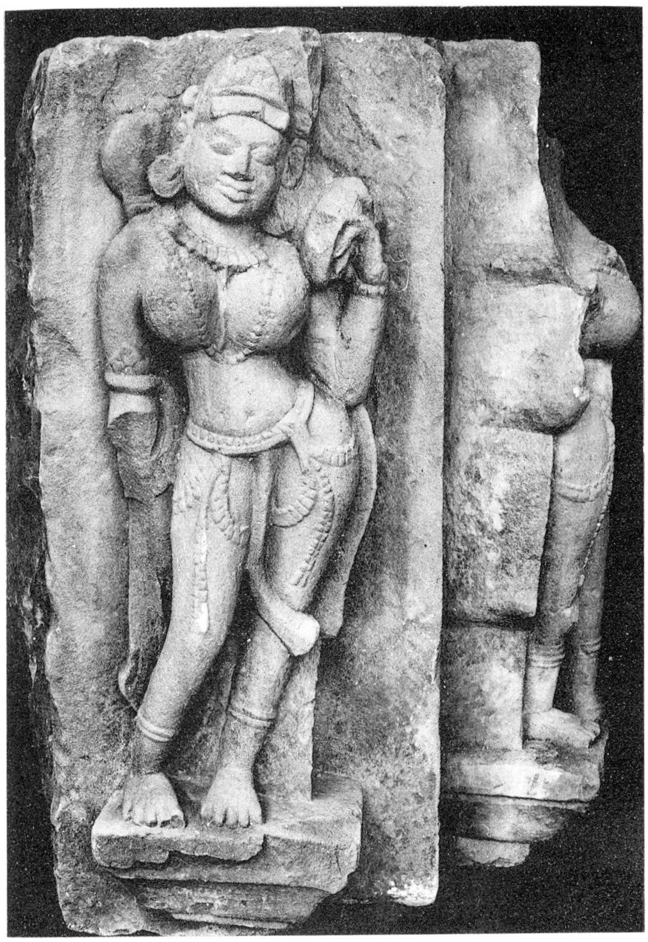

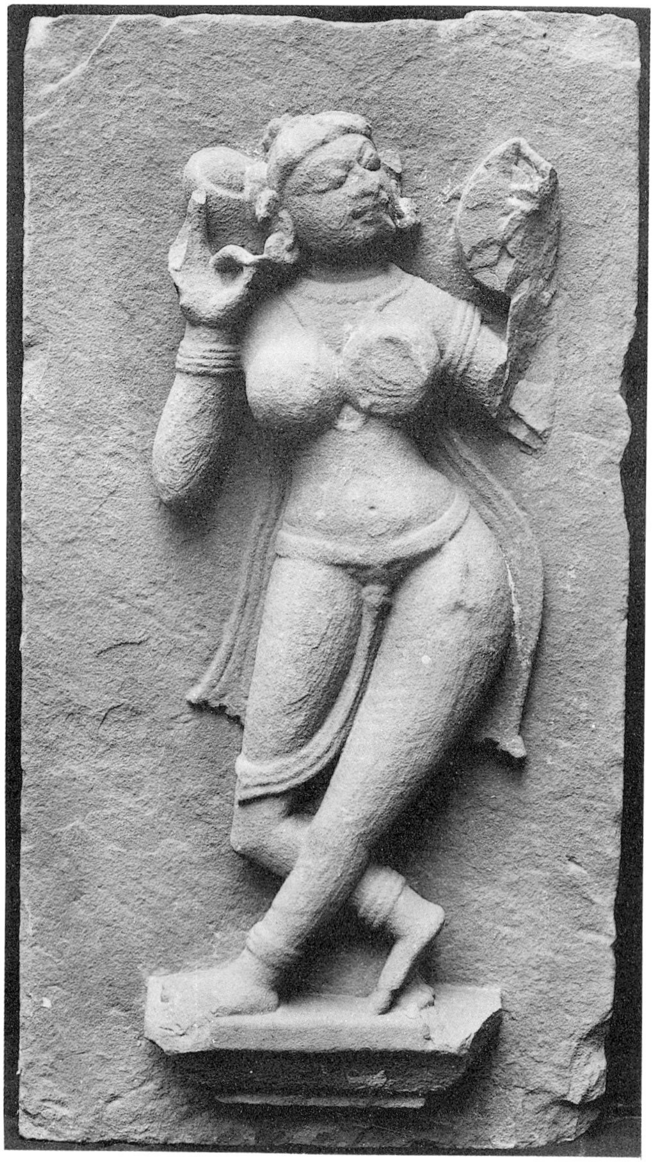

◀
163

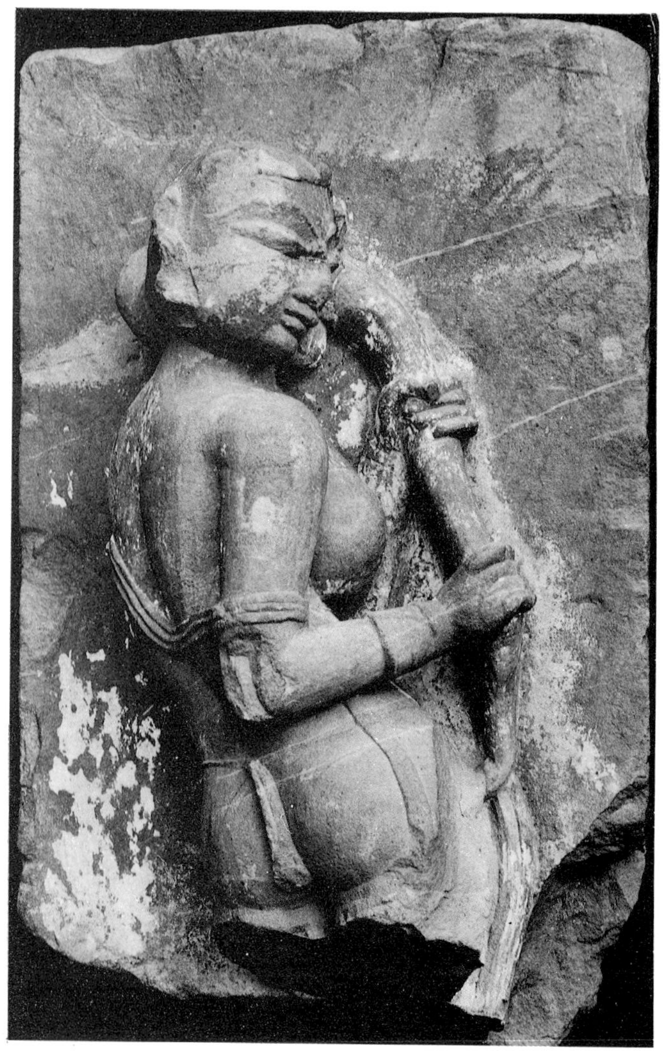

▶
165

◄ 166

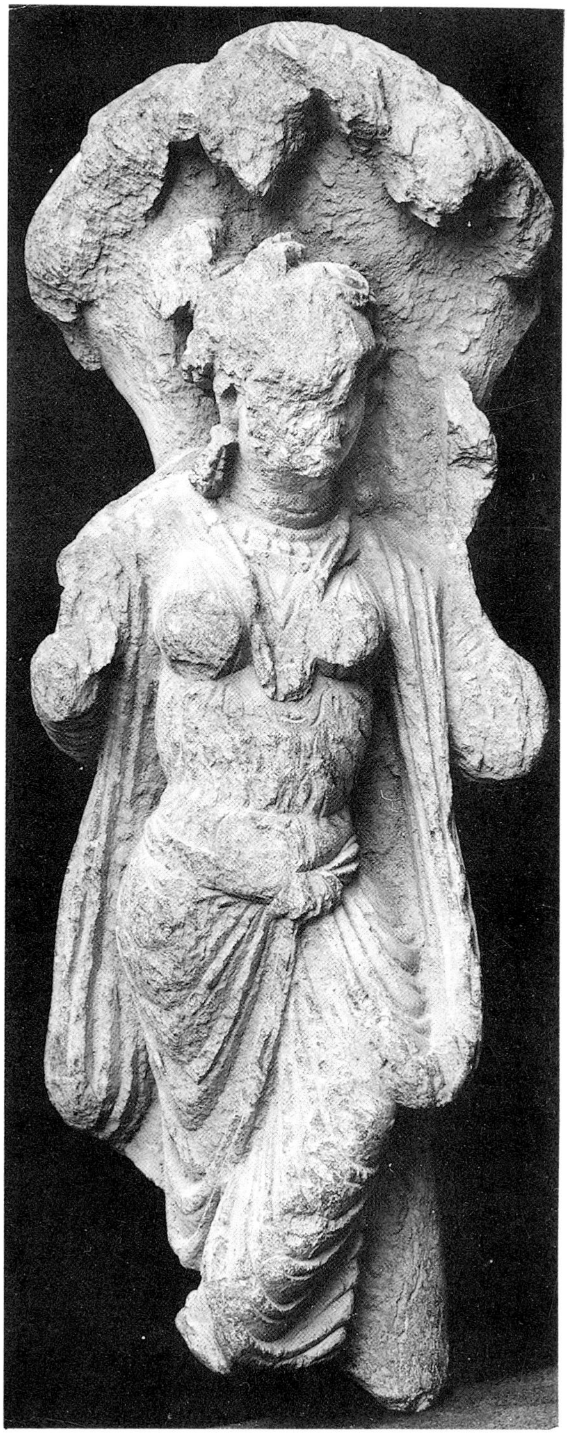

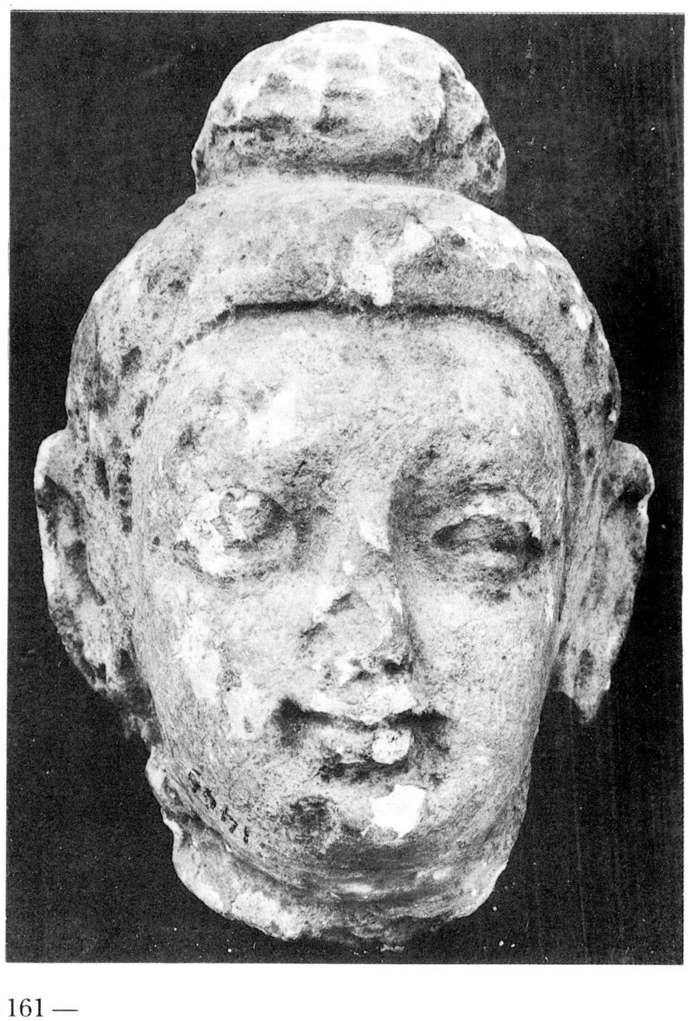

► 167

◀ 170

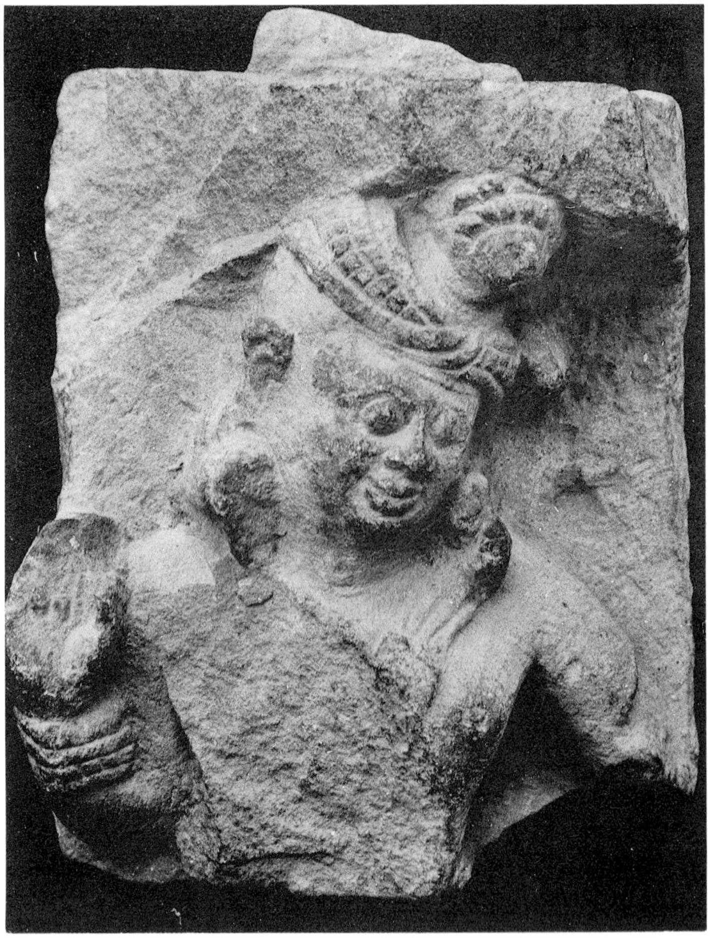

▼ 168

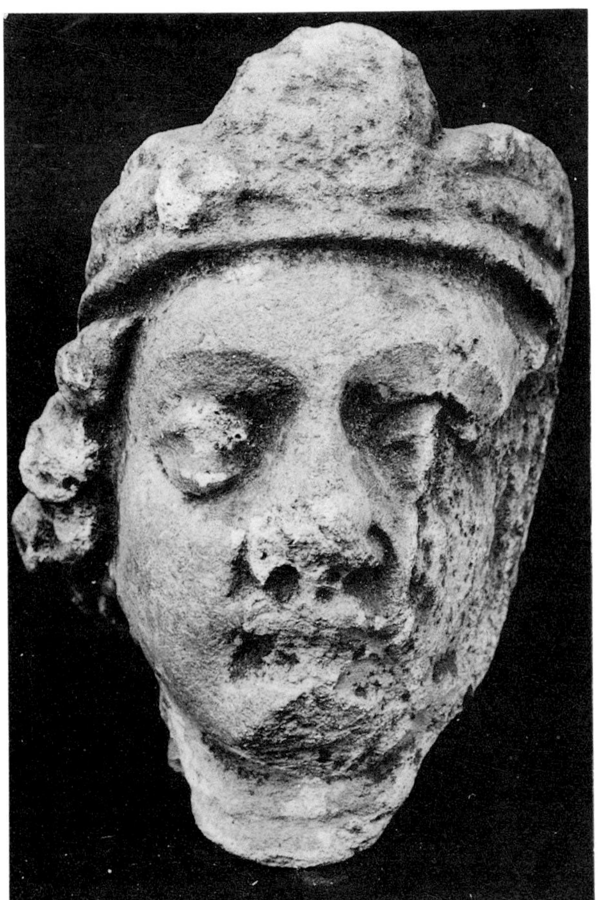

▼ 169

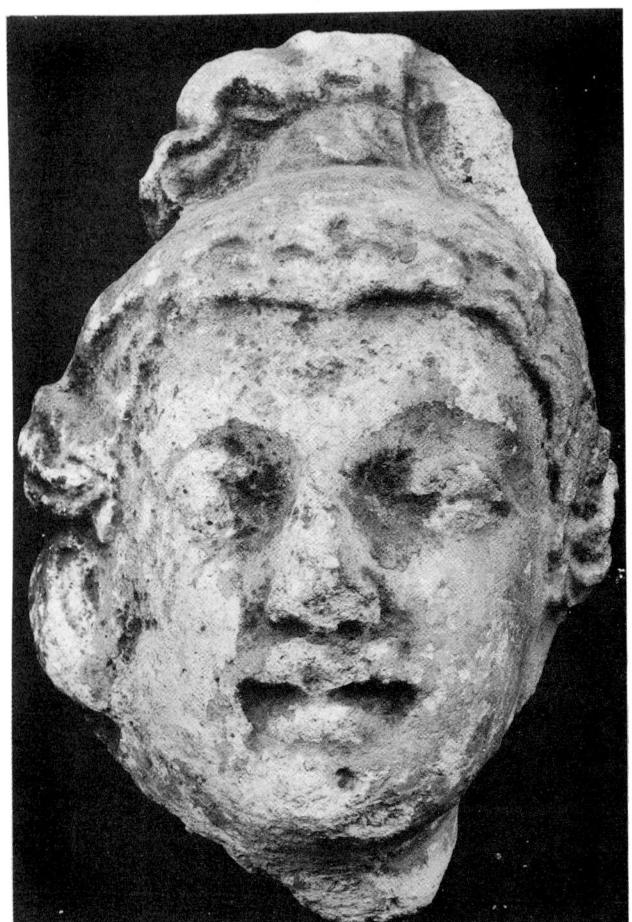

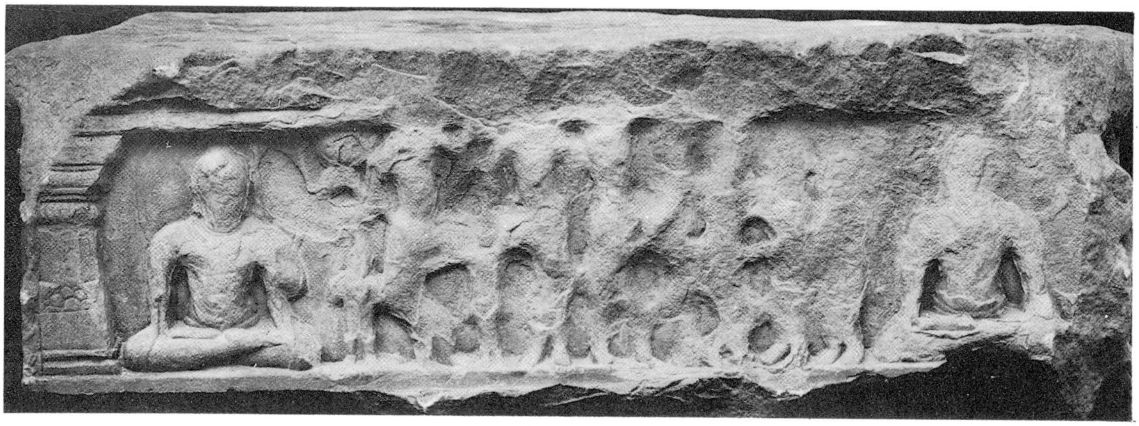

172A

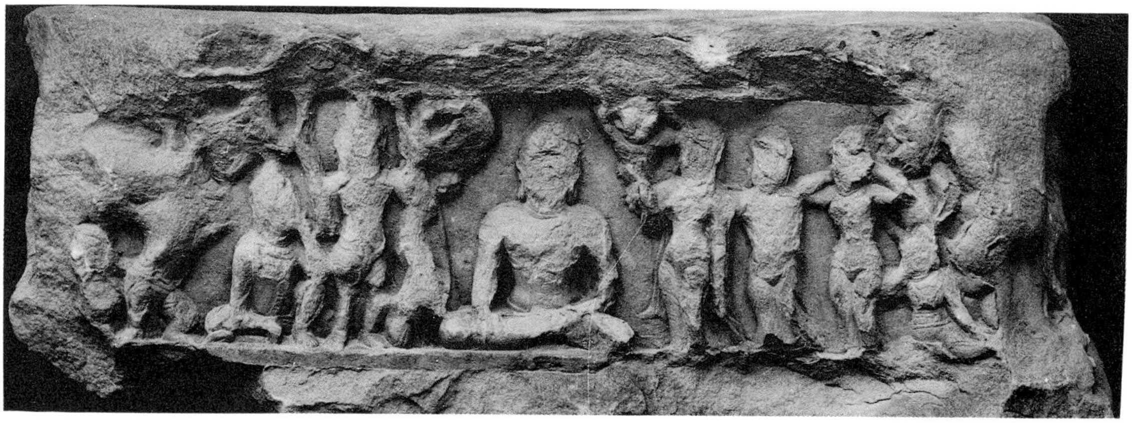

172B

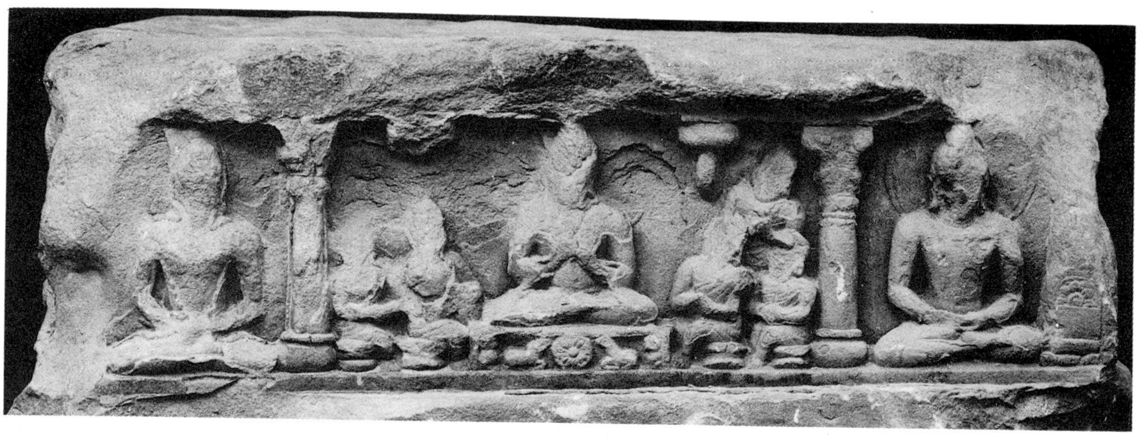

172C

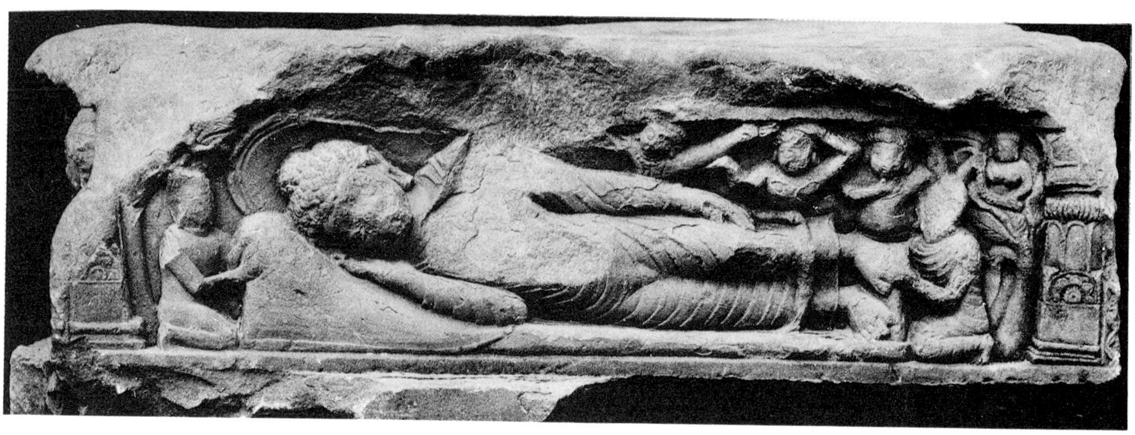

172D

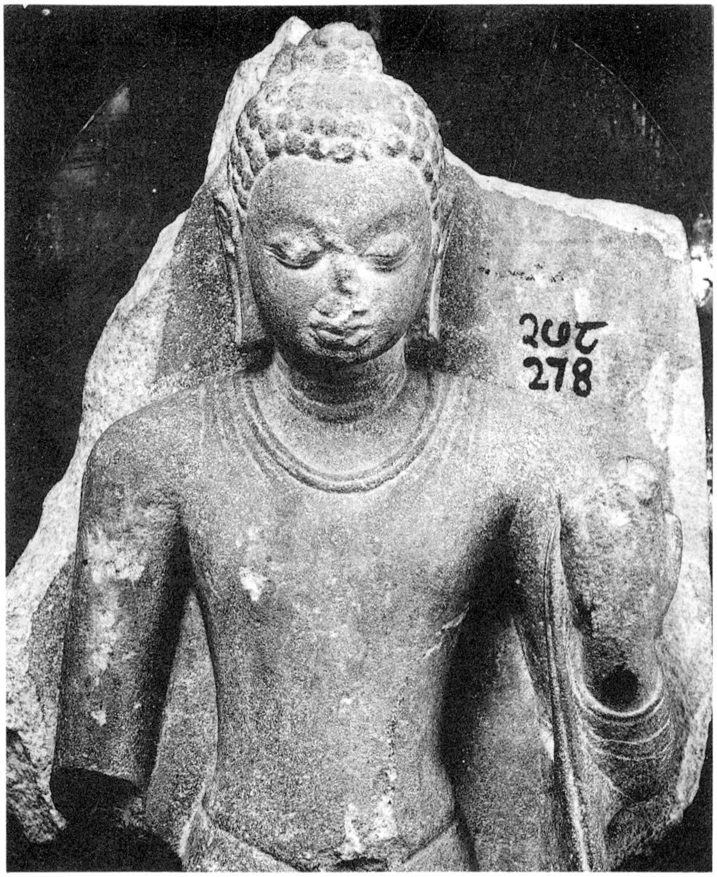

◀ 173

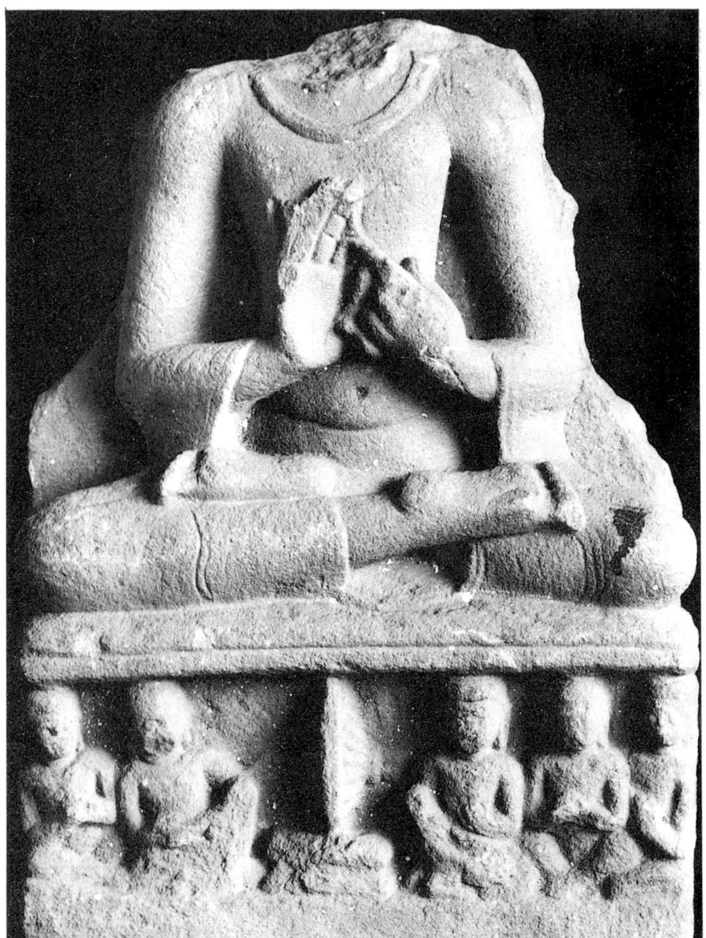

▶ 174

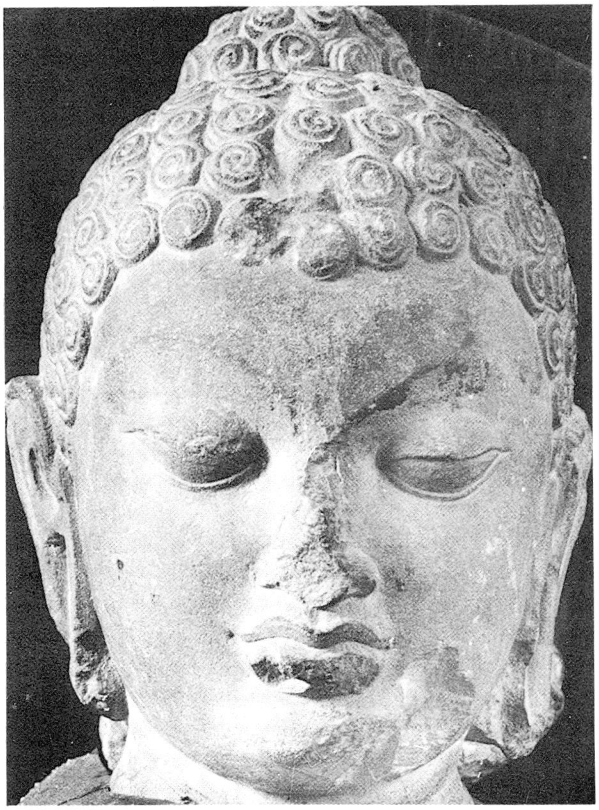

▲ 176

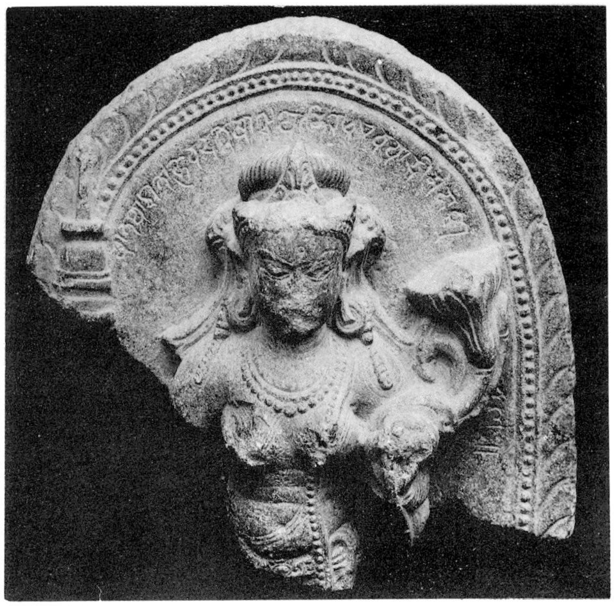

▲ 179

▼ 175

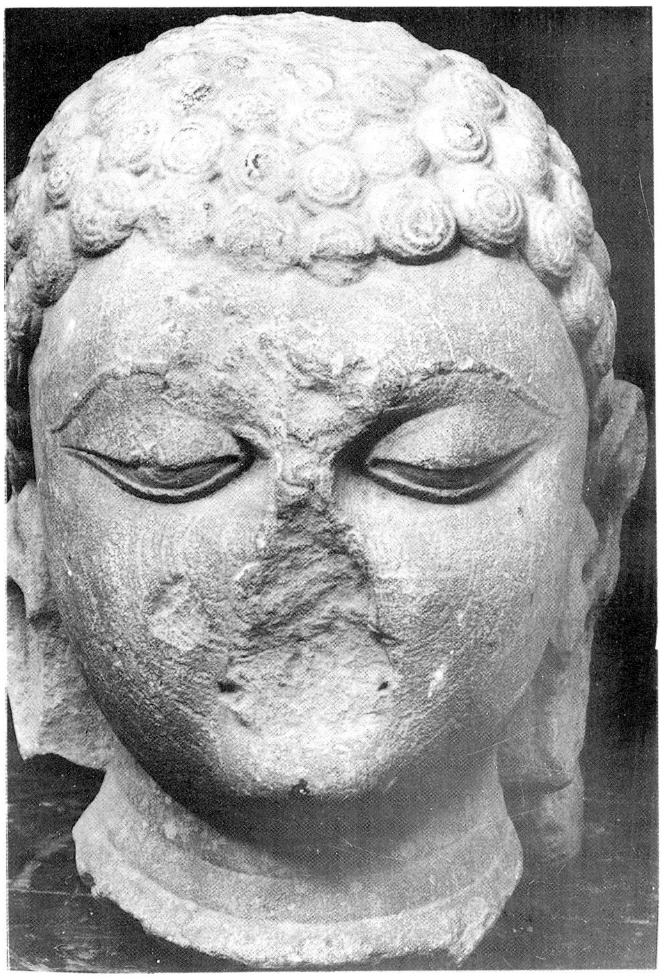

▼ 177

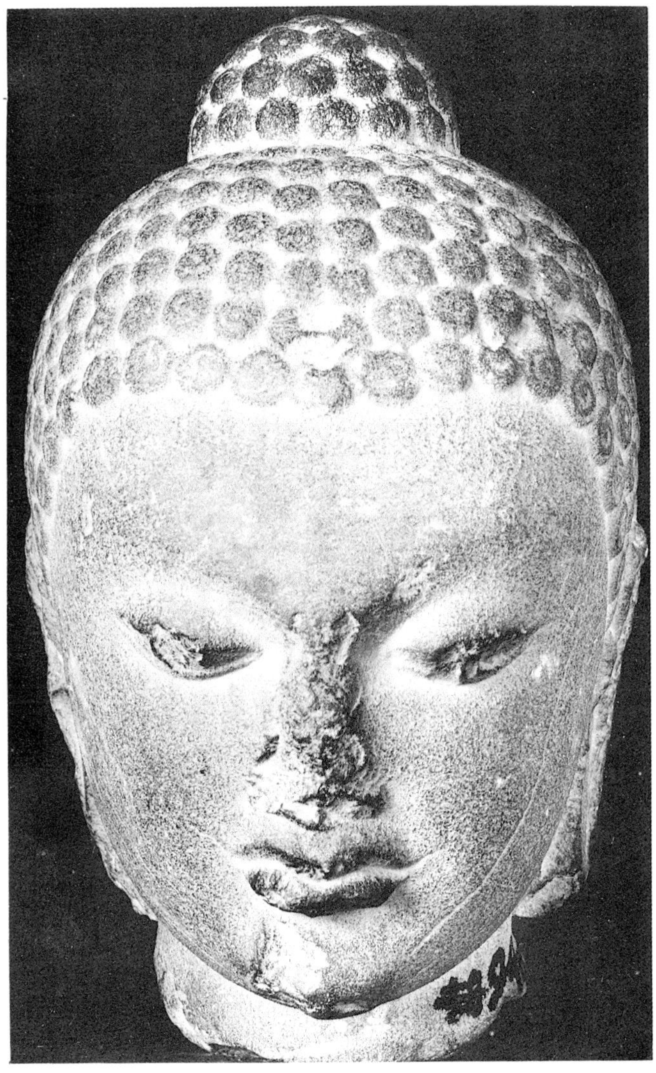

▶ 171

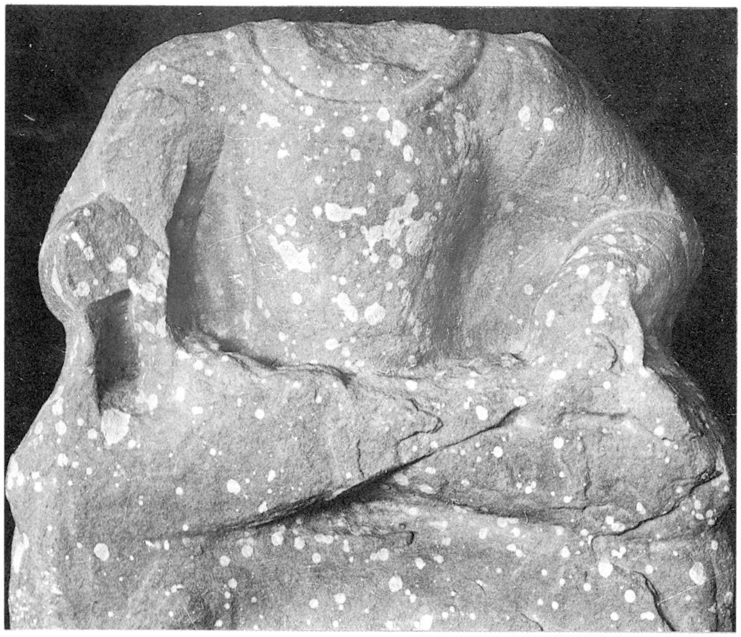

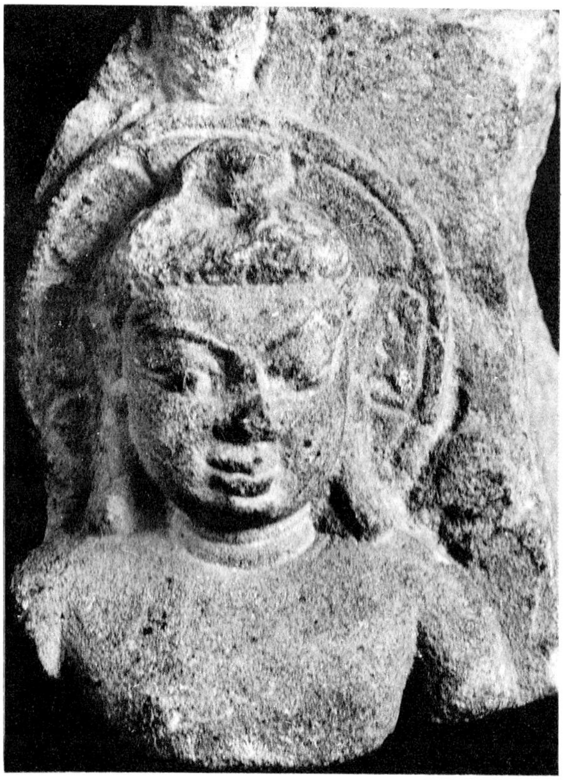

▲ 178

▶ 180

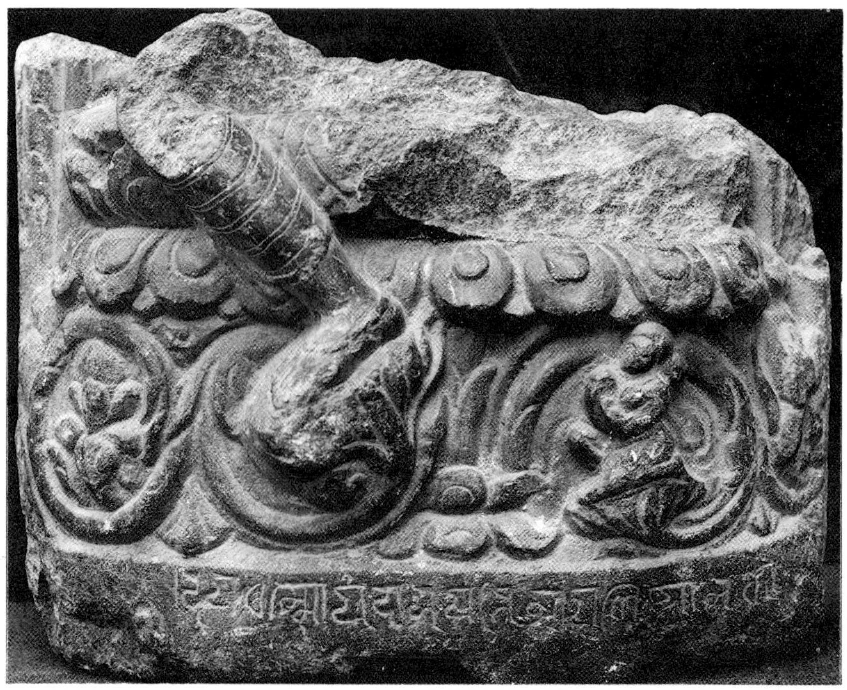

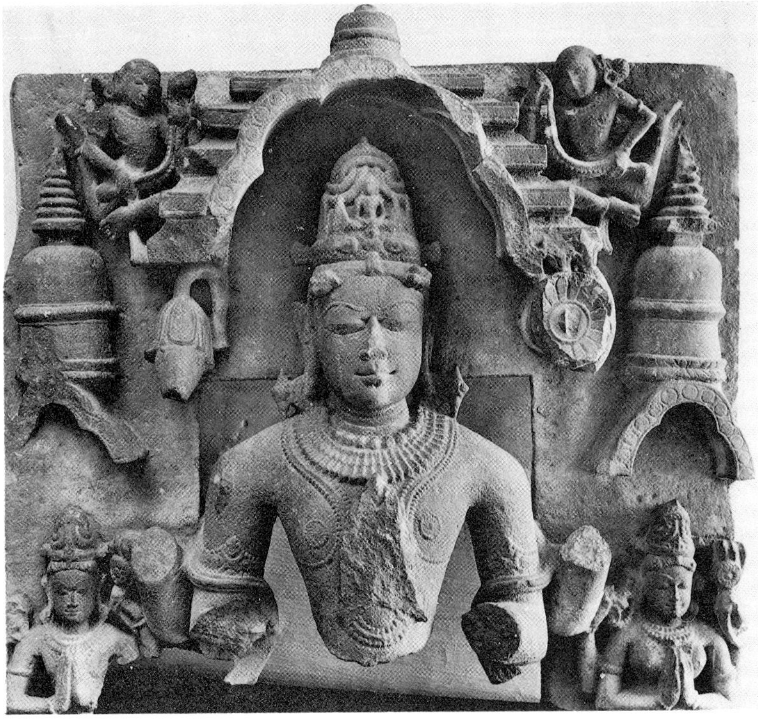

▲ 181

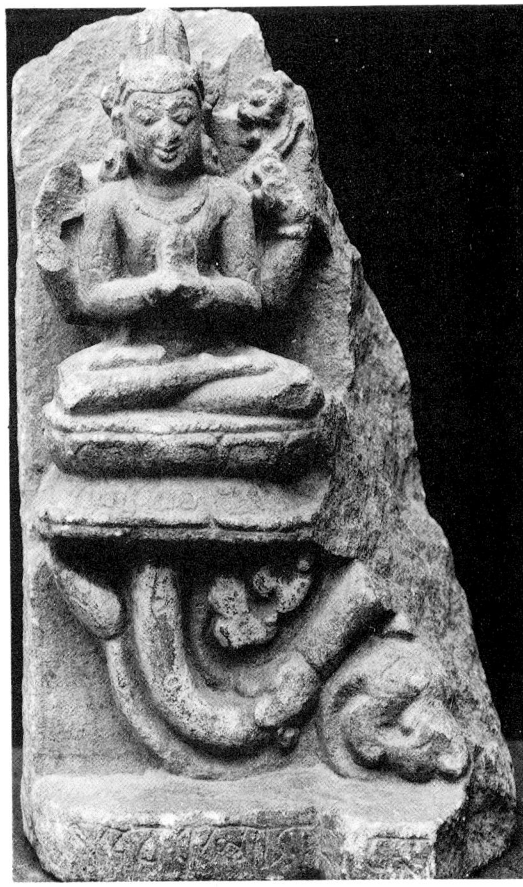

▶
182

▼ 185

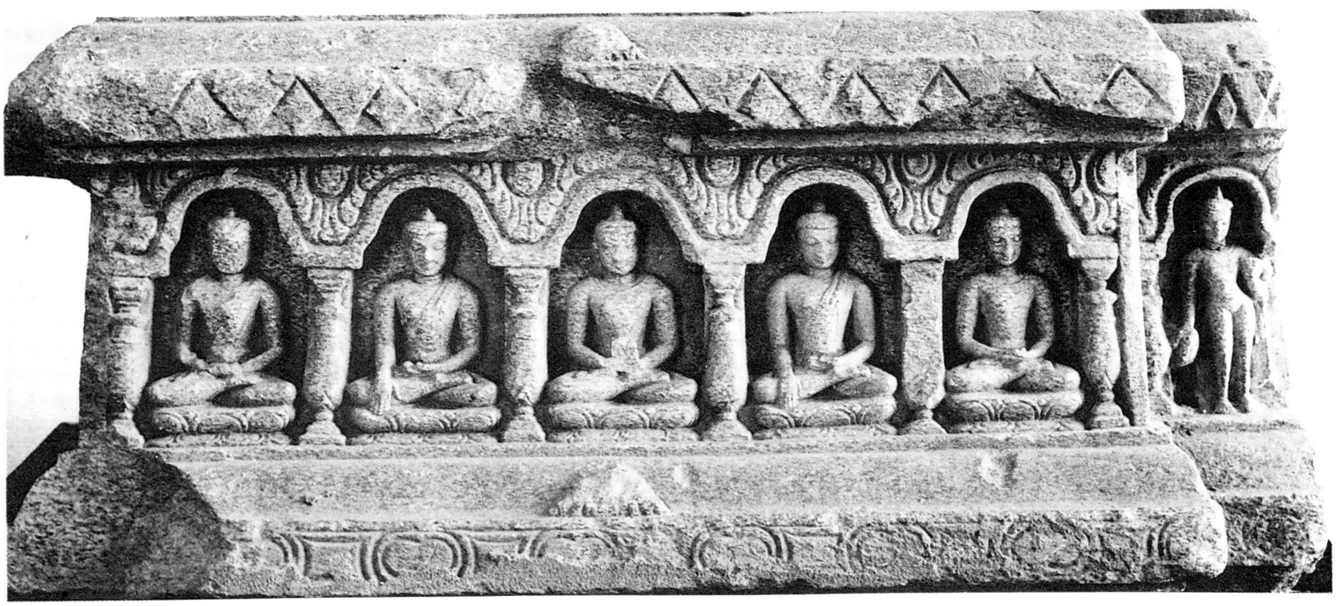

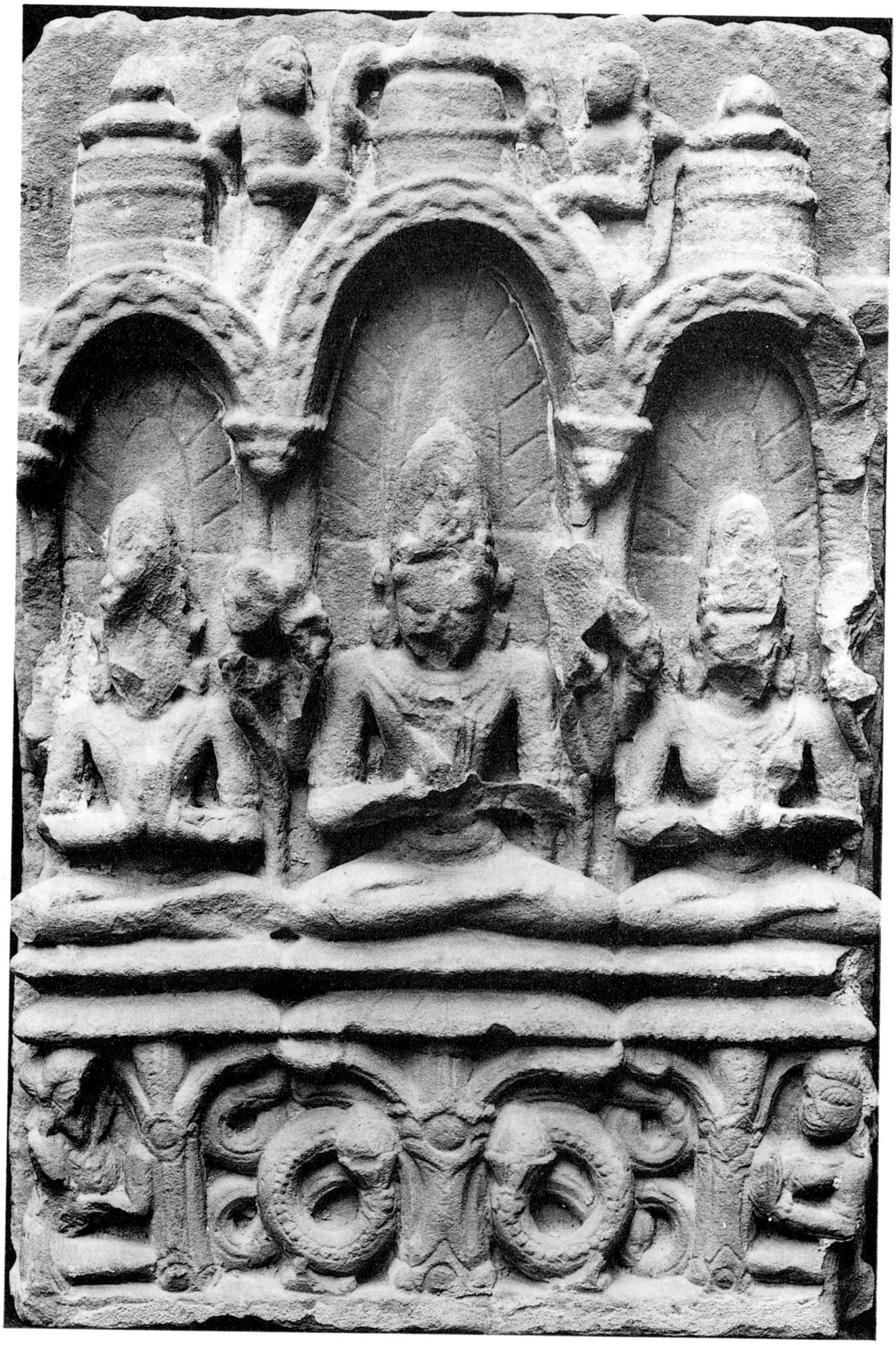

▲ 183

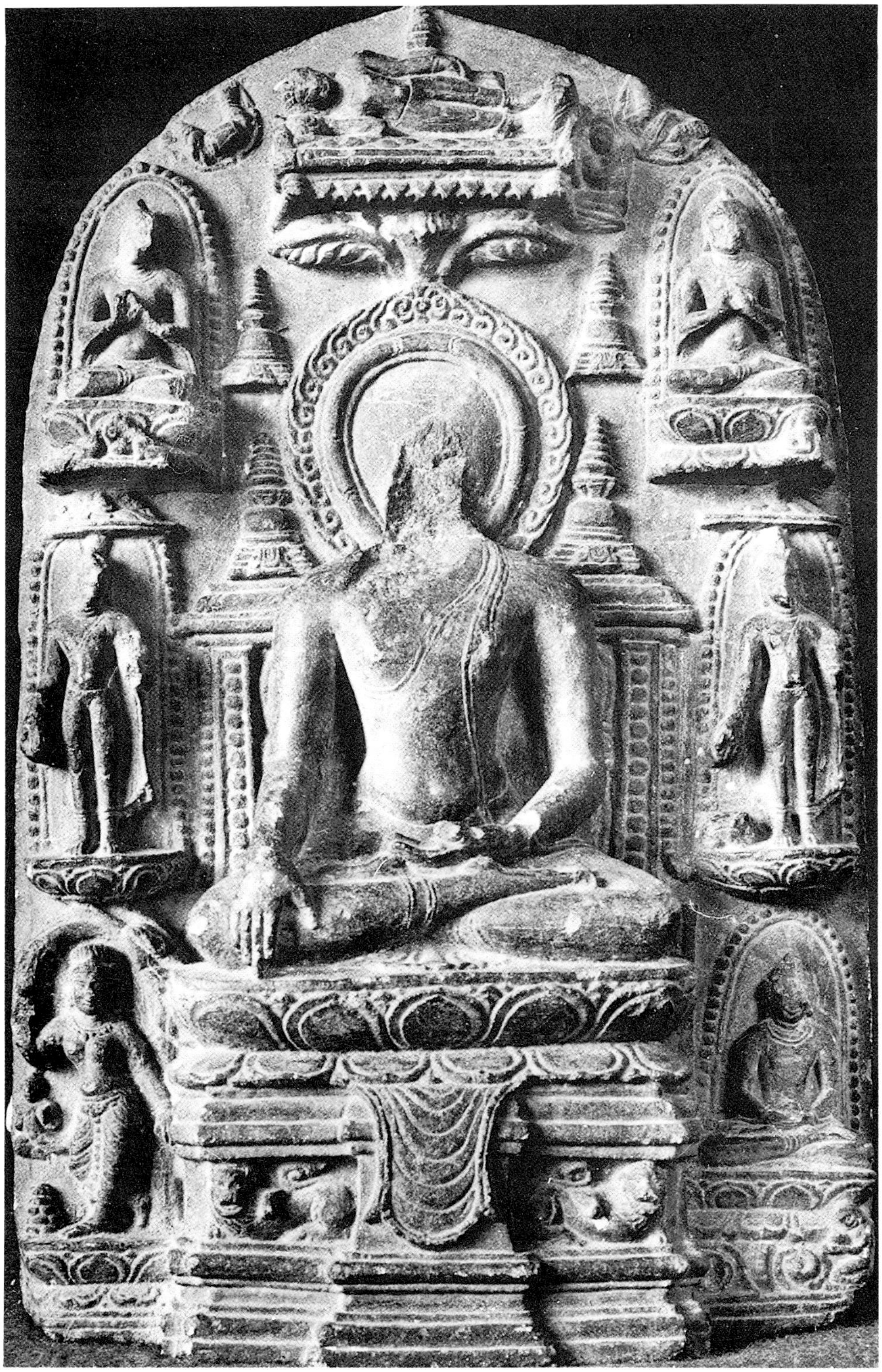

▲ 184

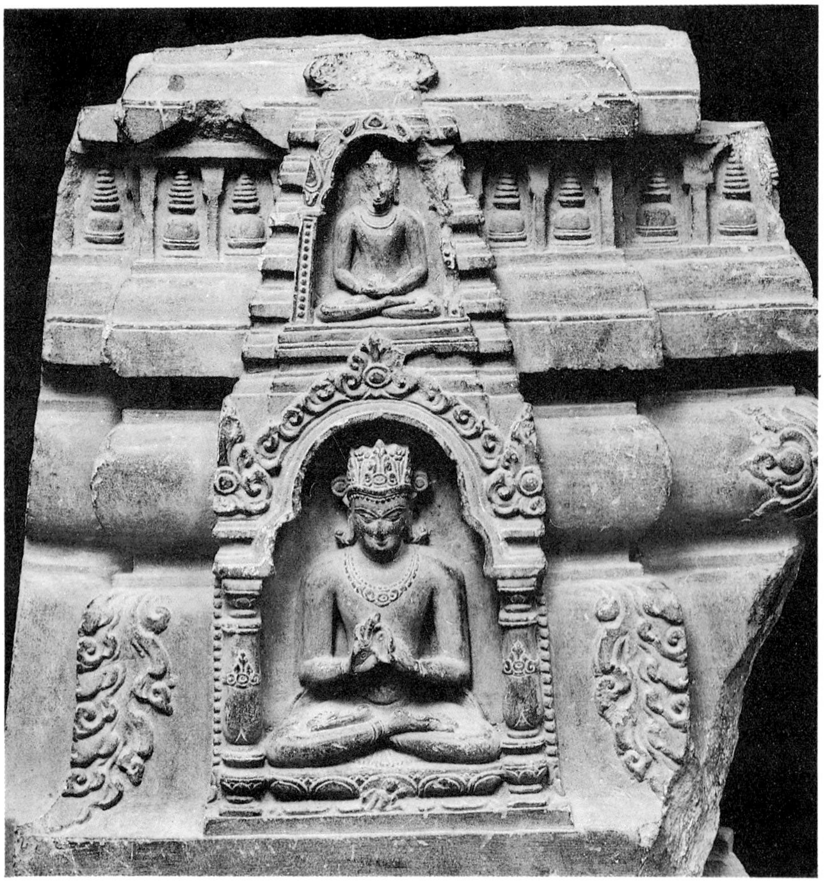

◀ 186

▶ 189

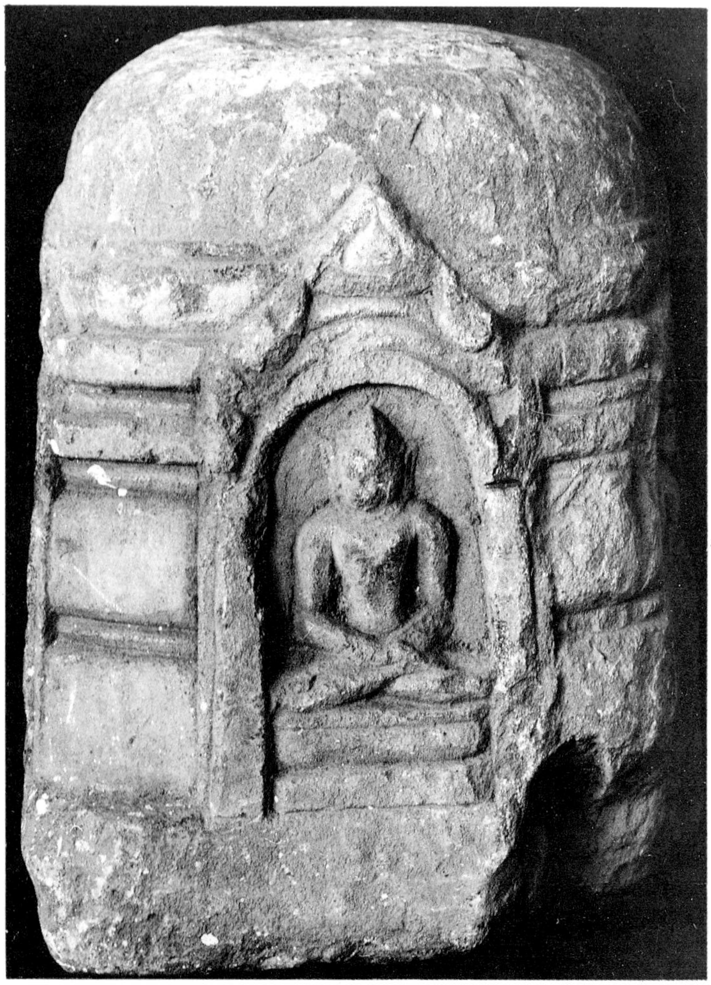

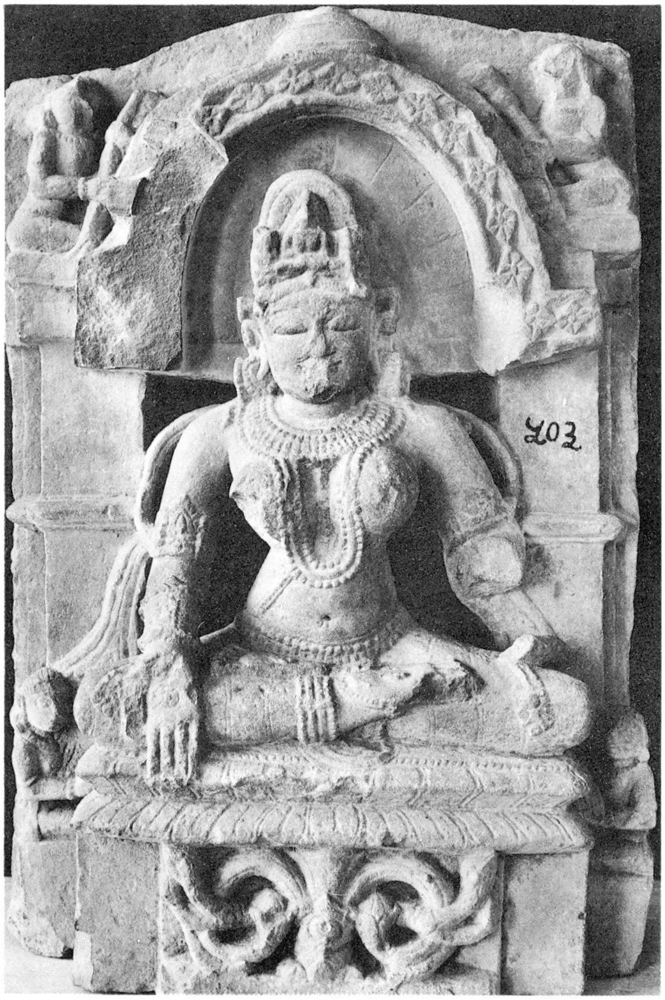

▼ 187A

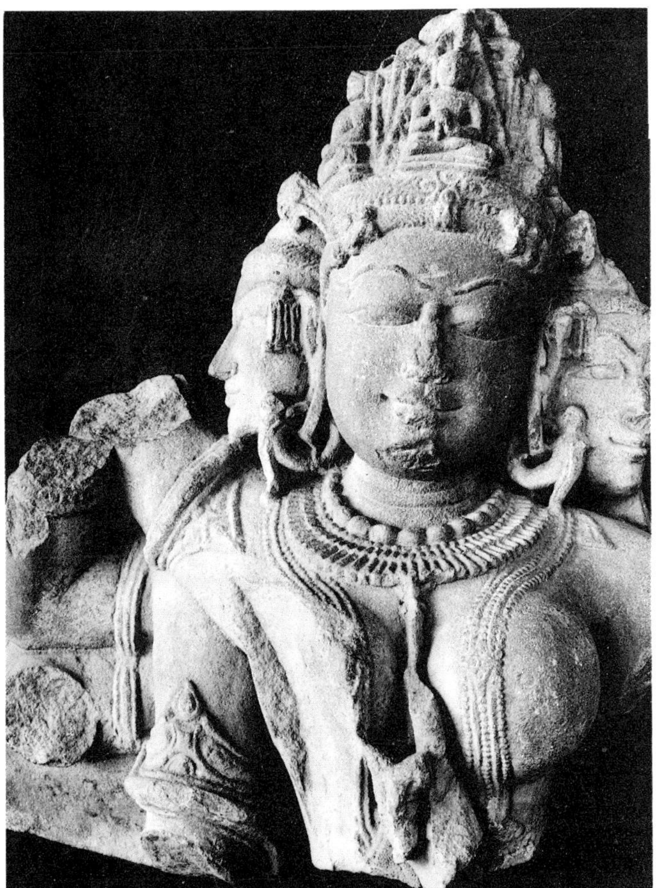

▲ 188

▼ 187B

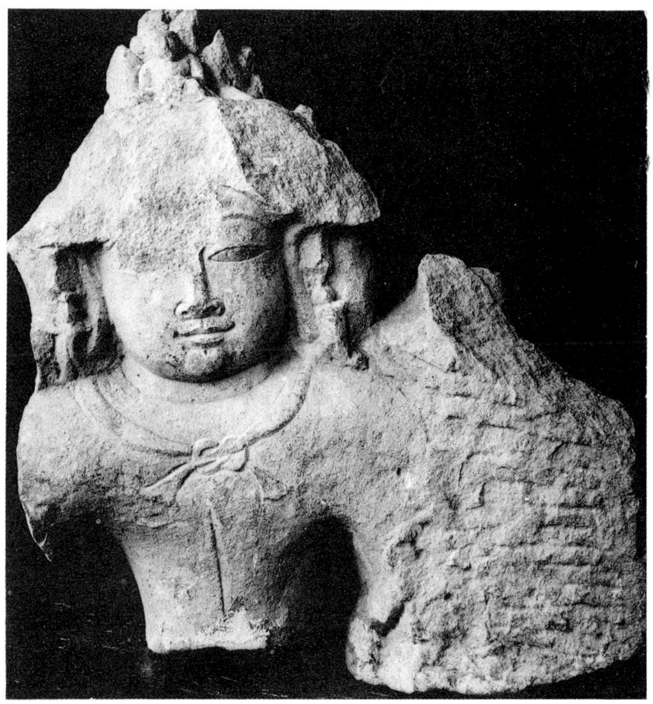

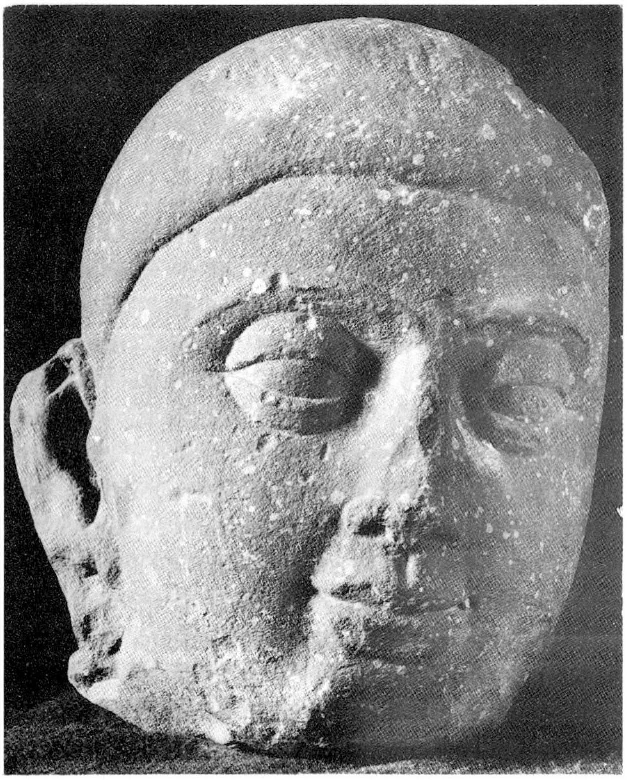

▲ 191

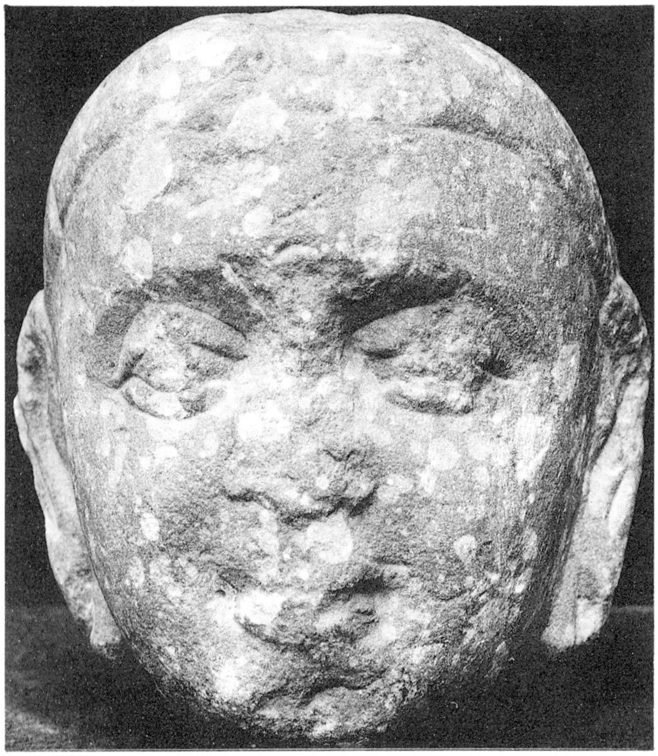

▲ 192

▼ 193

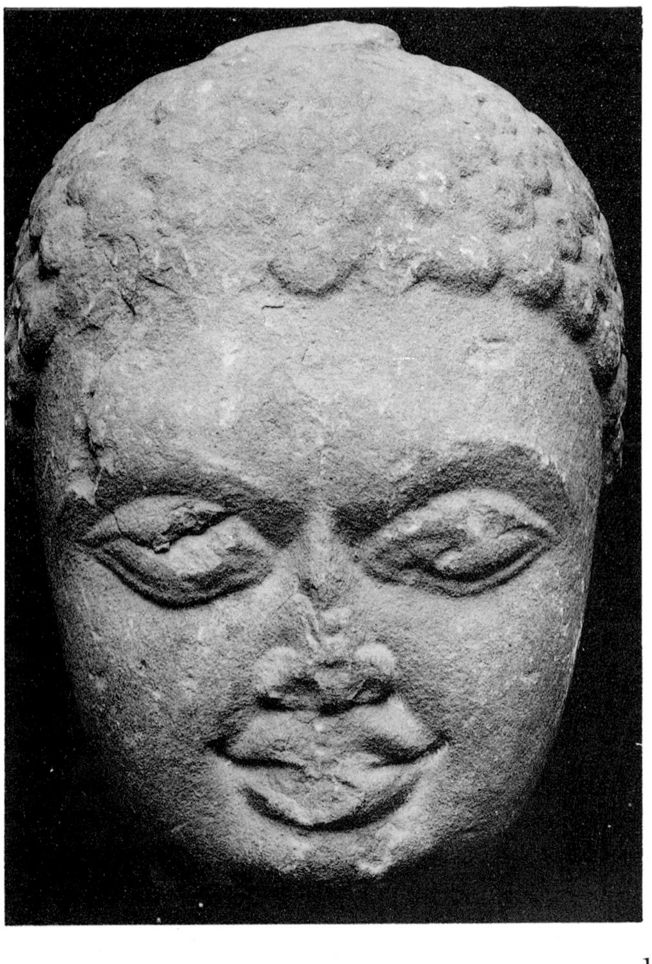

▼ 197

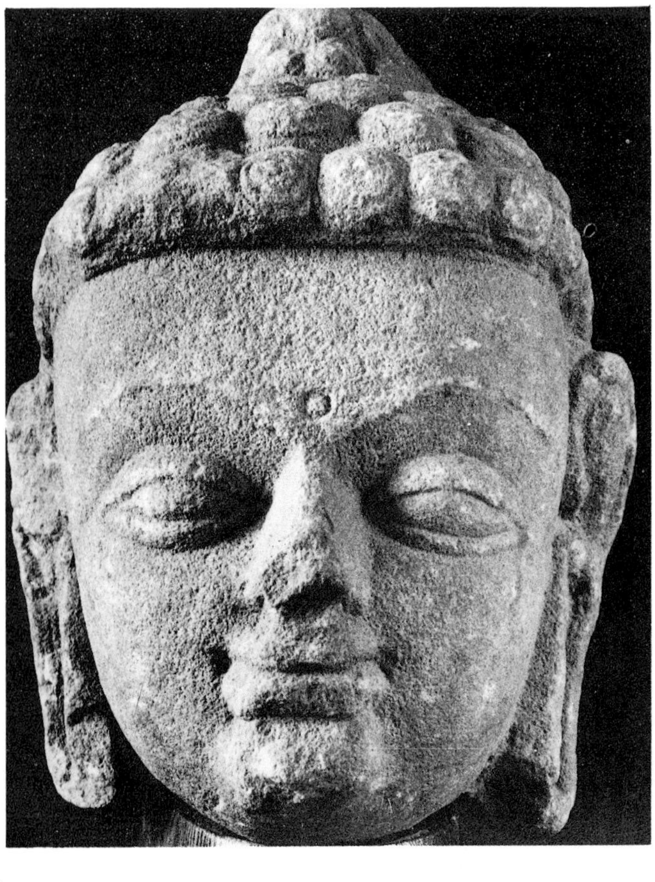

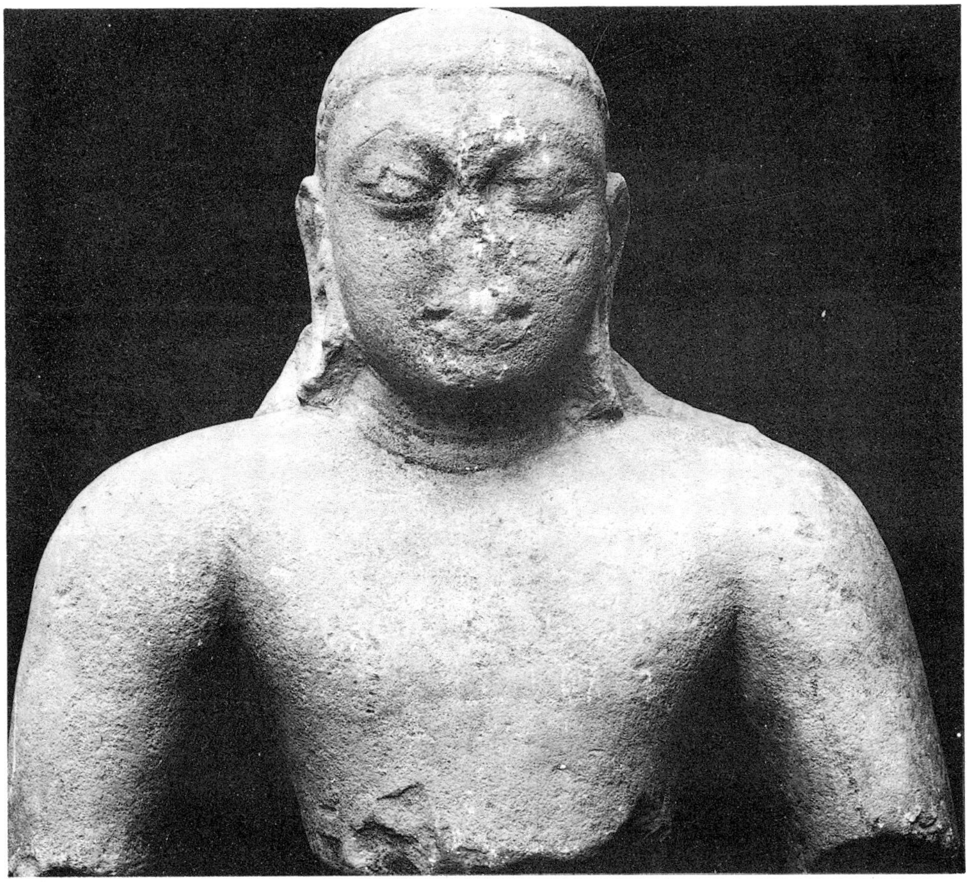

▲ 194

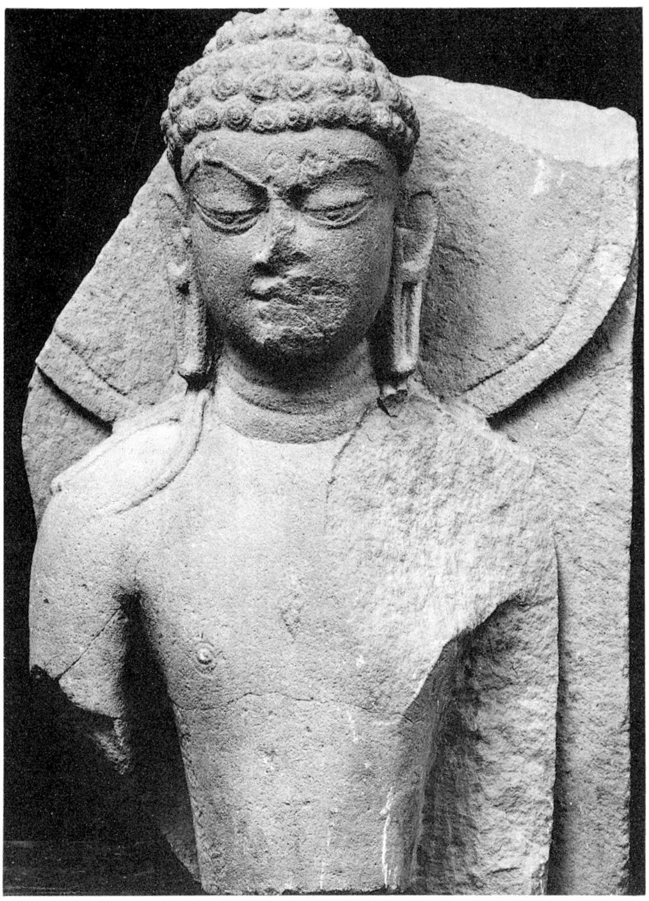

◀ 195

▼ 196

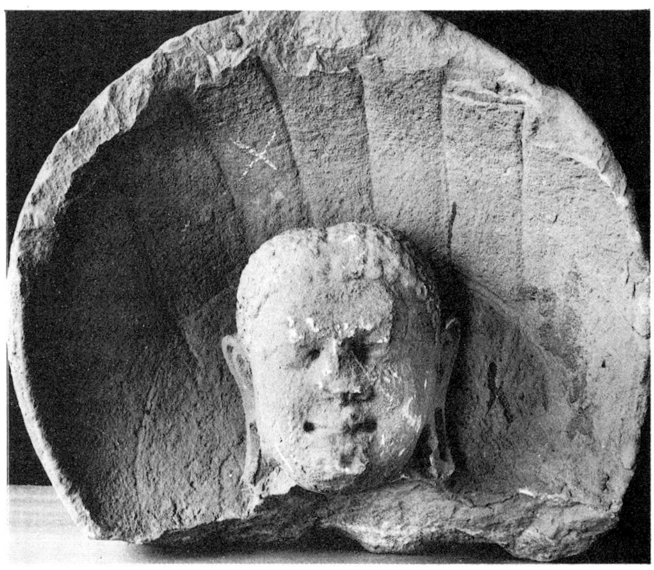

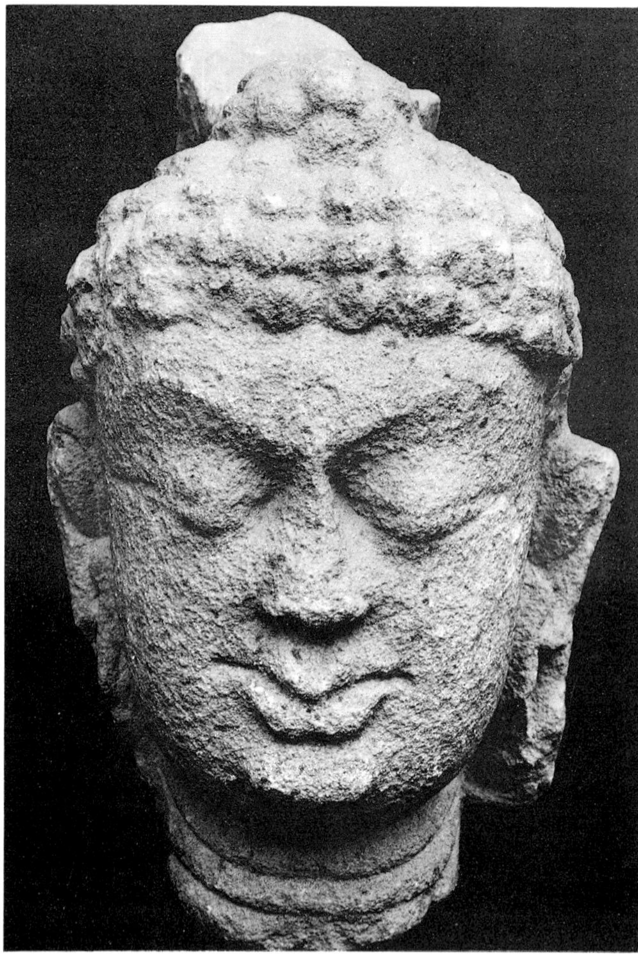

▲ 198

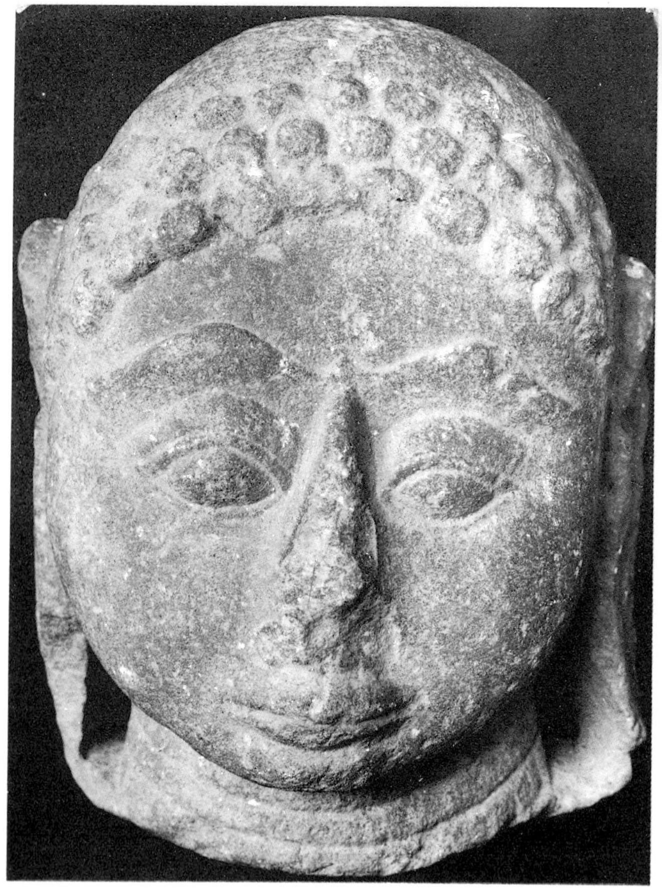

▲ 199

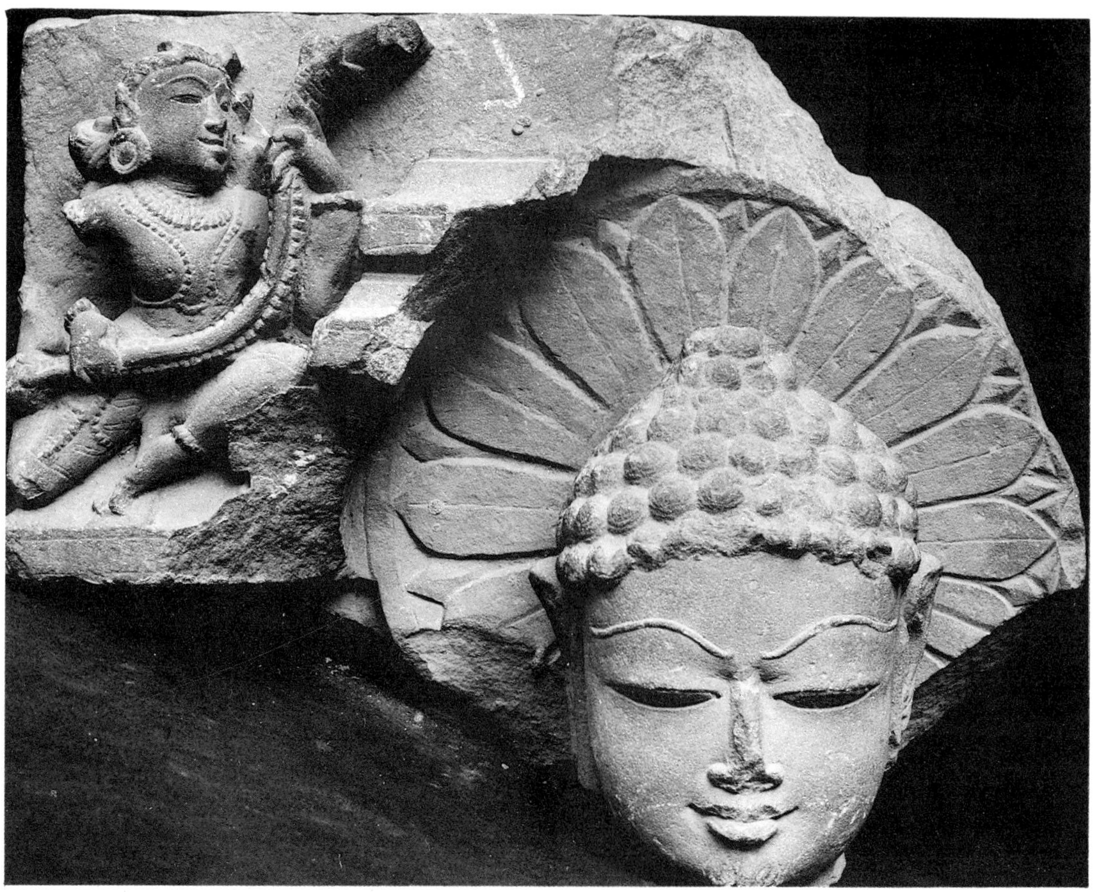

◀ 200

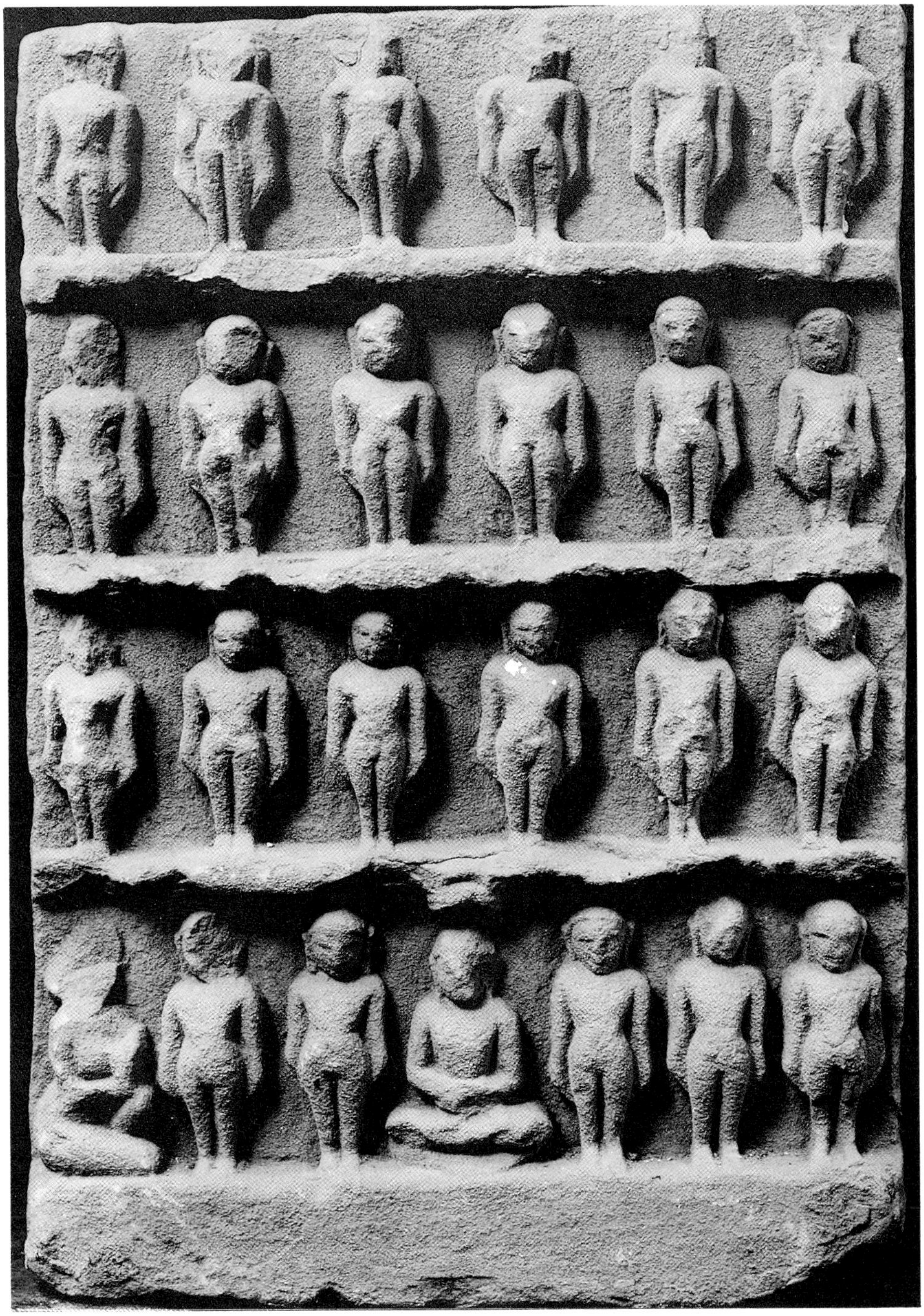

▲ 201

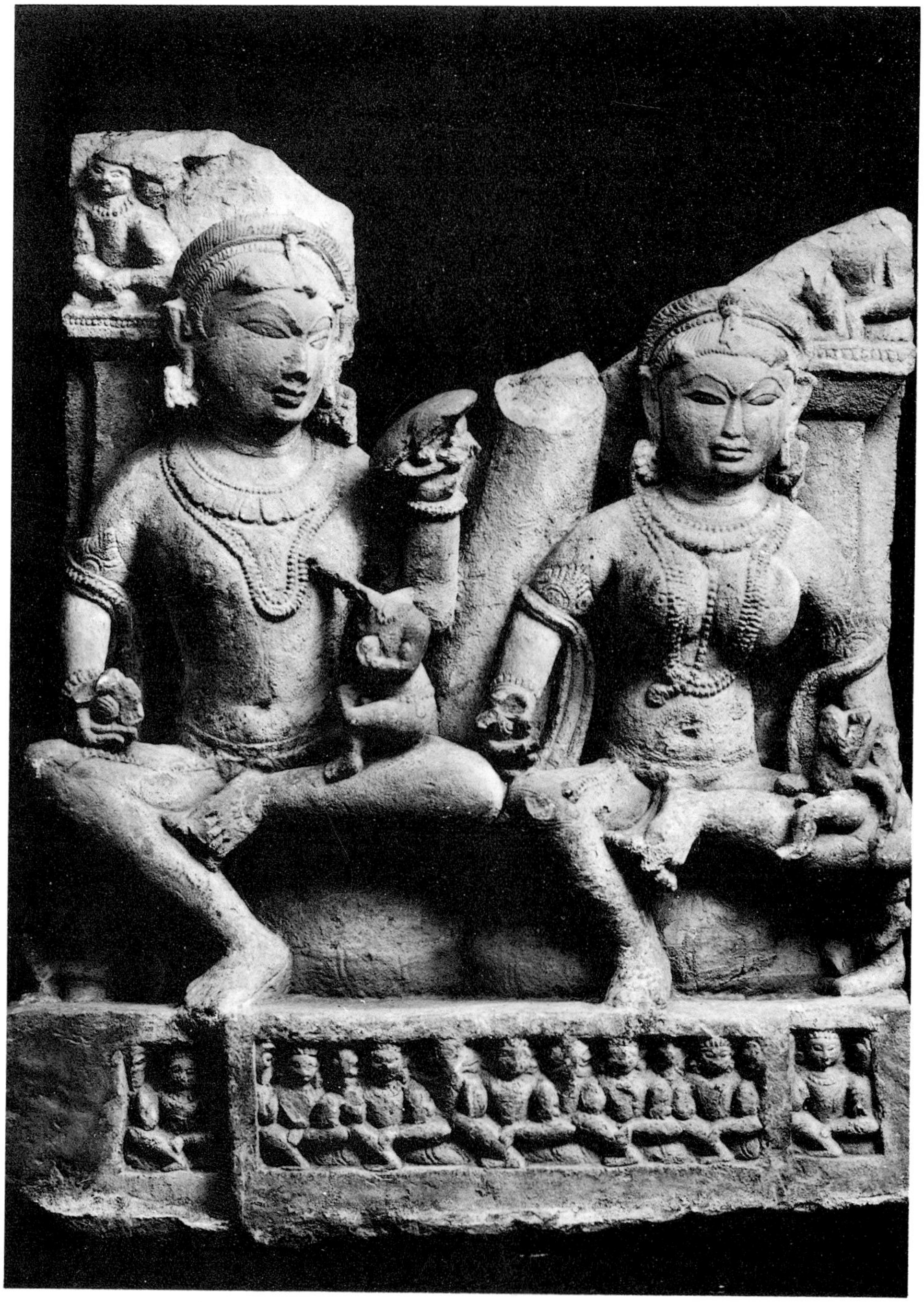

▲ 202

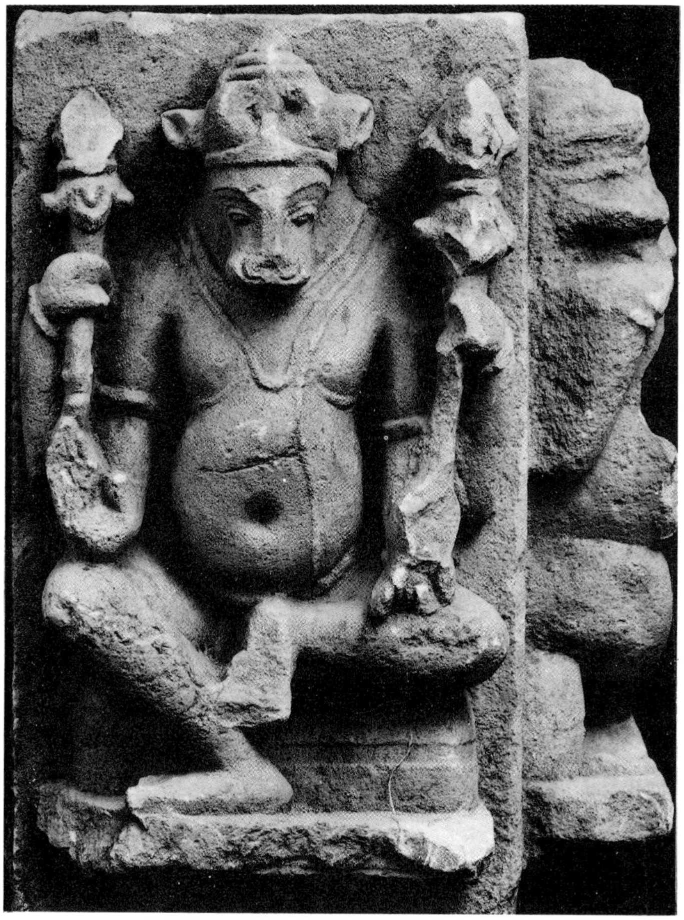

◀
204A

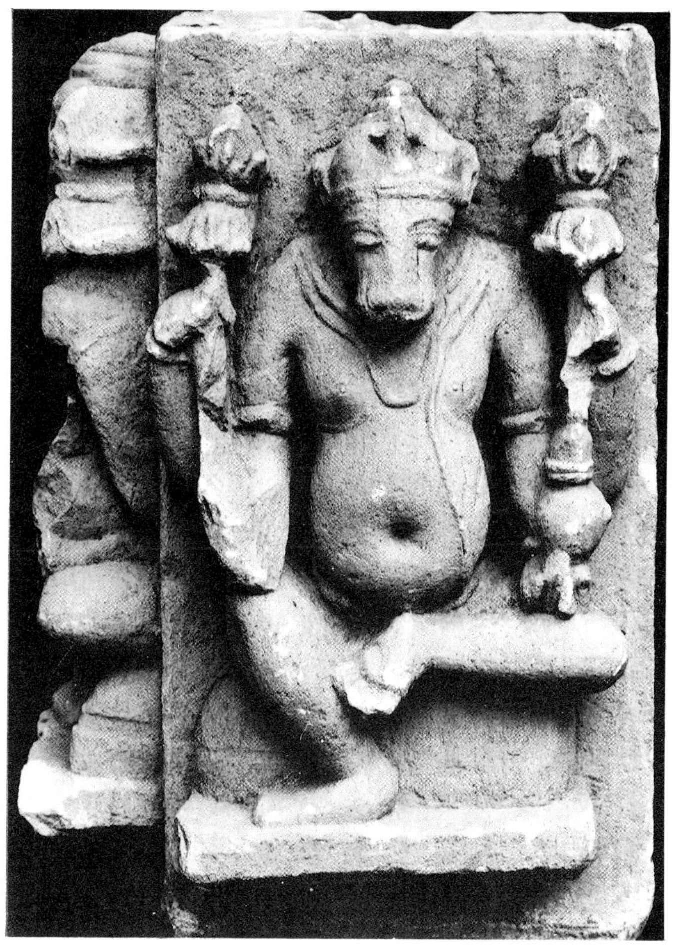

▶
204B

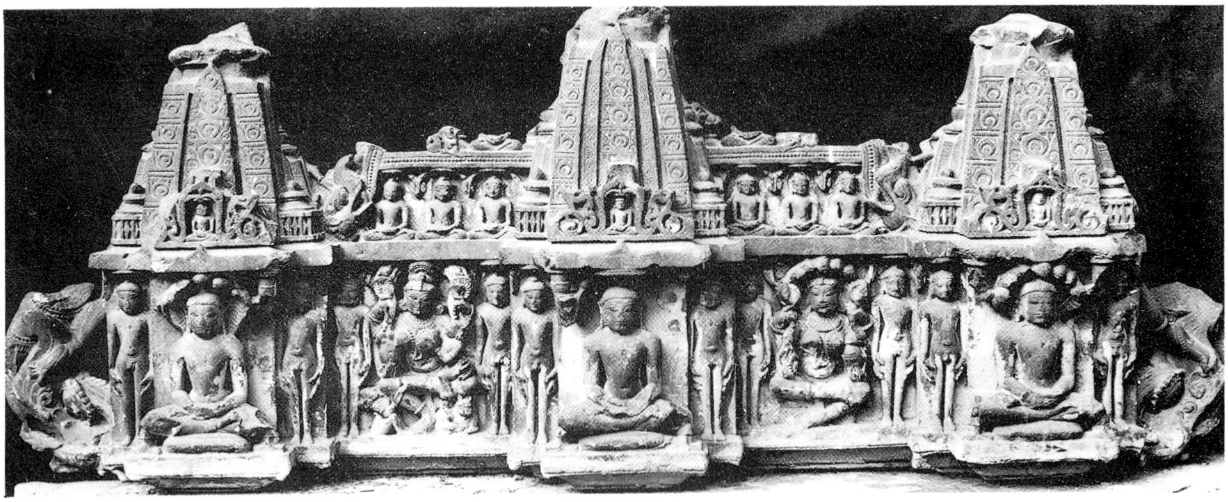

▲ 205

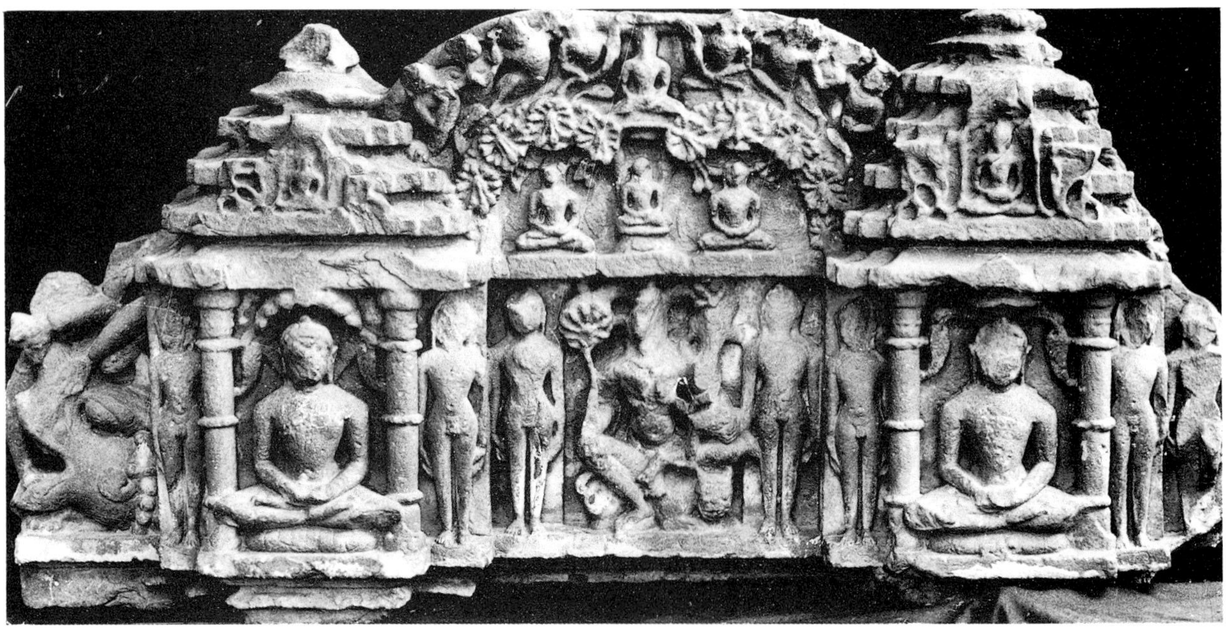

▲ 206

▼ 207

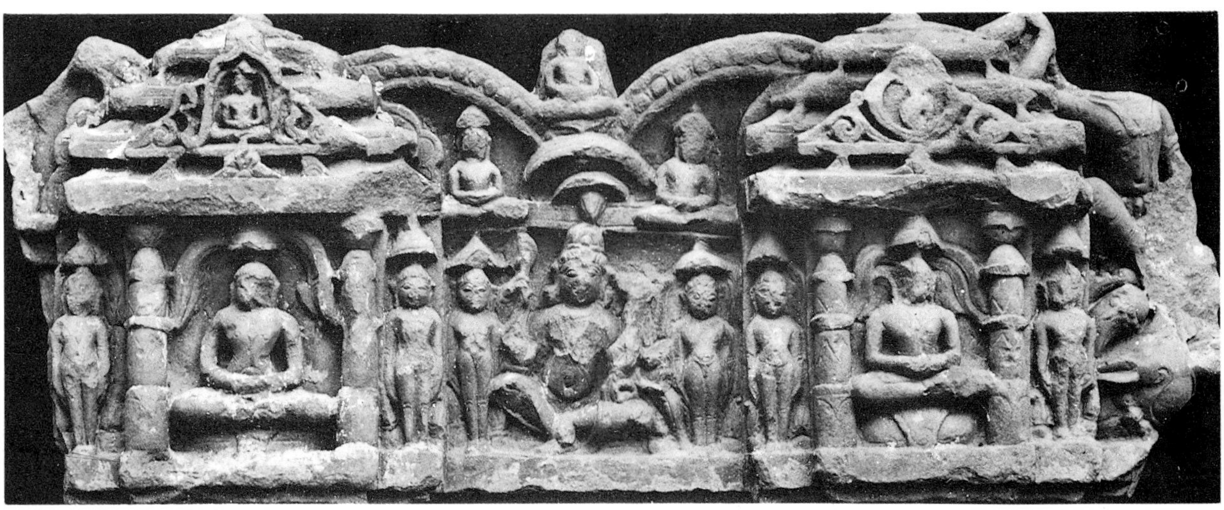

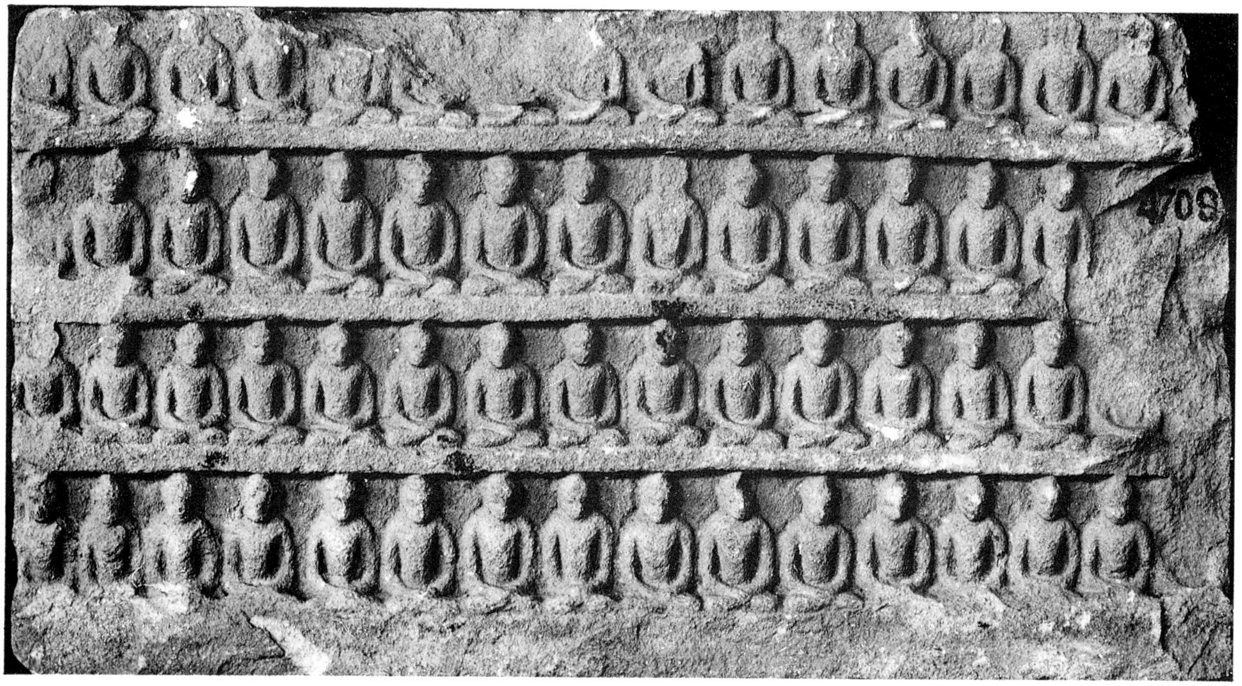

▲ 208

▼ 209

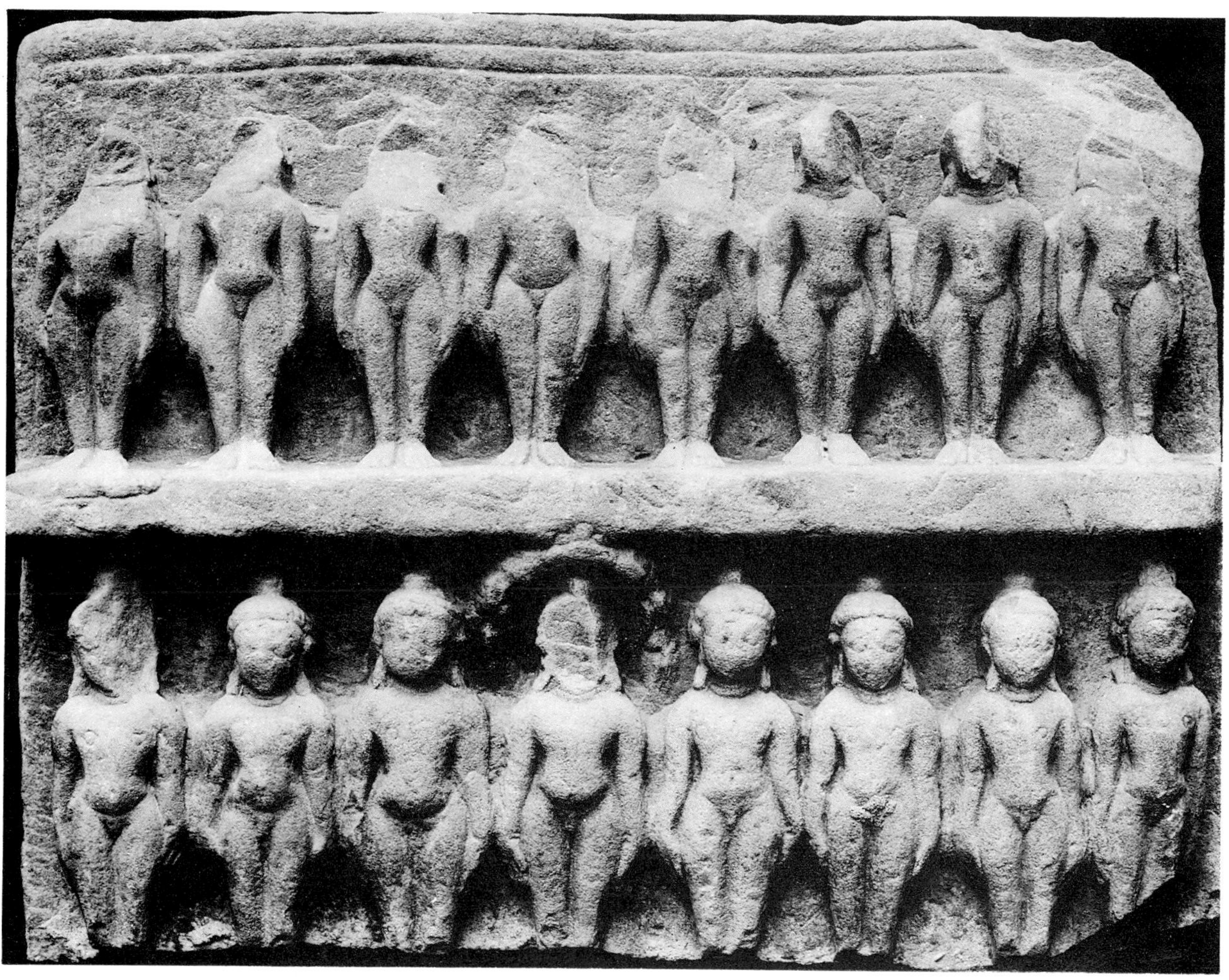

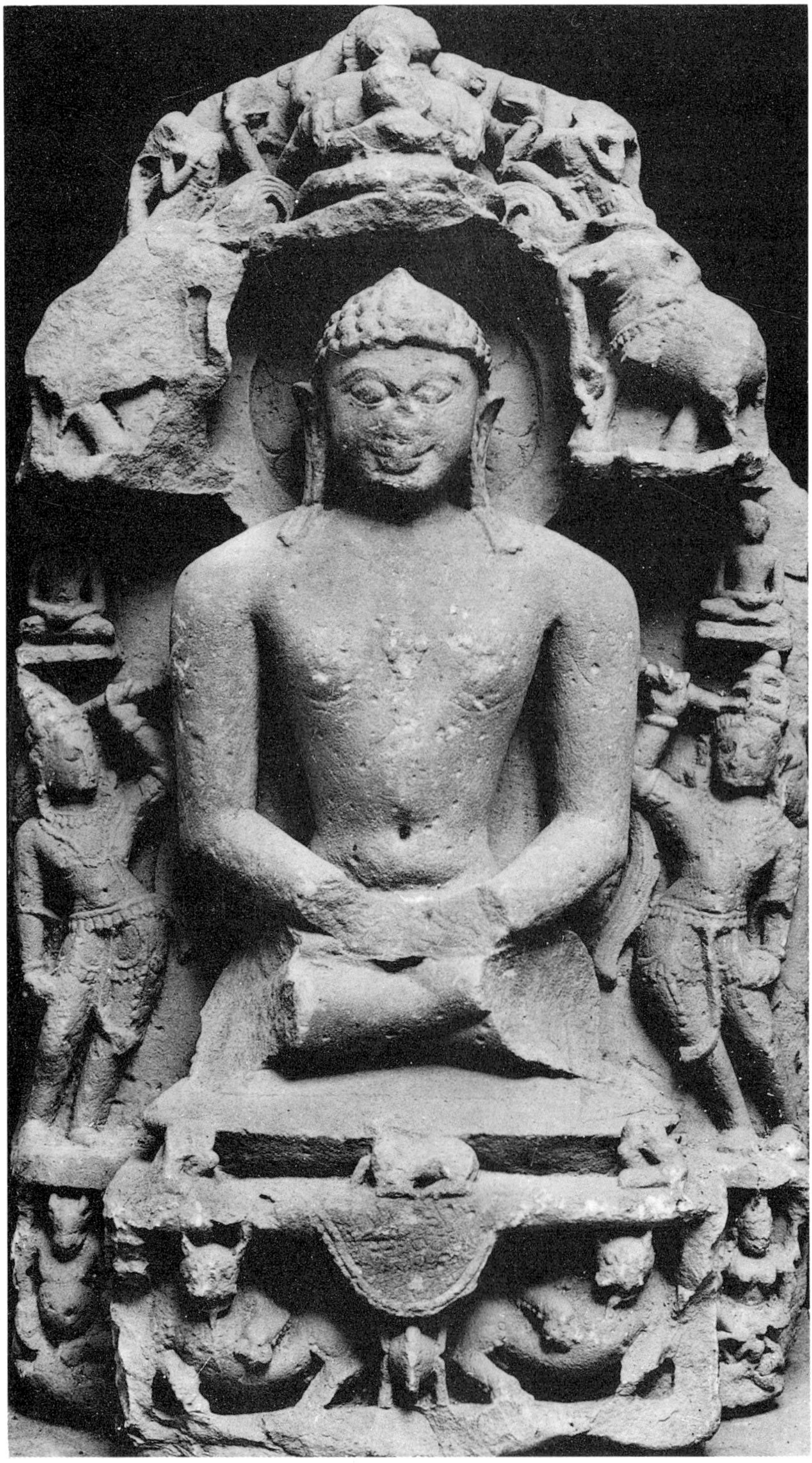

▲ 210

▶ 203

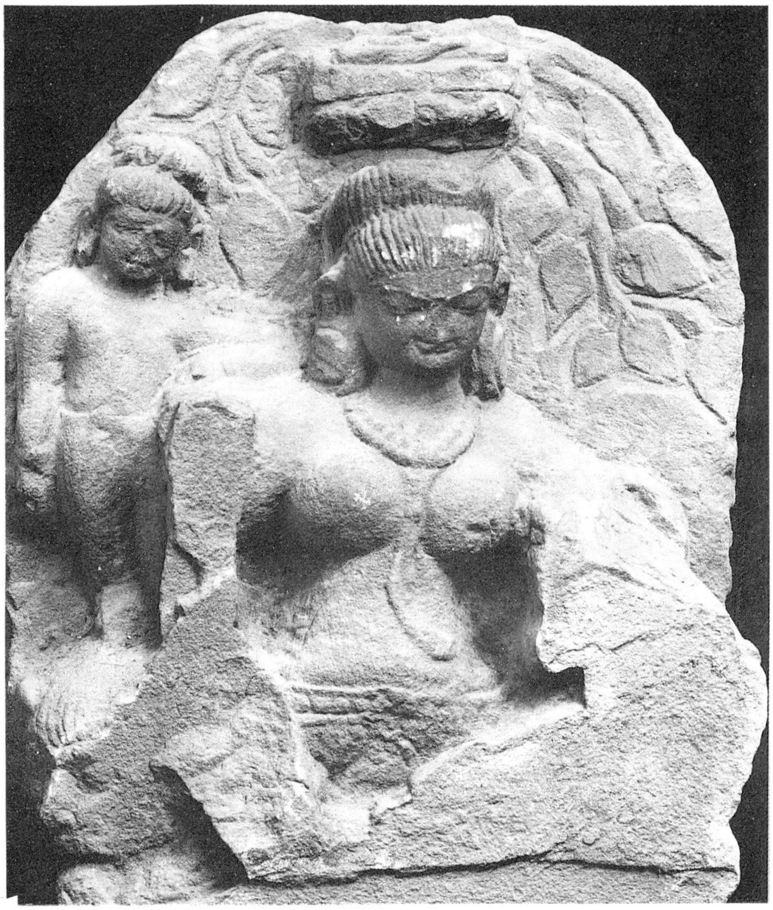

▼ 211

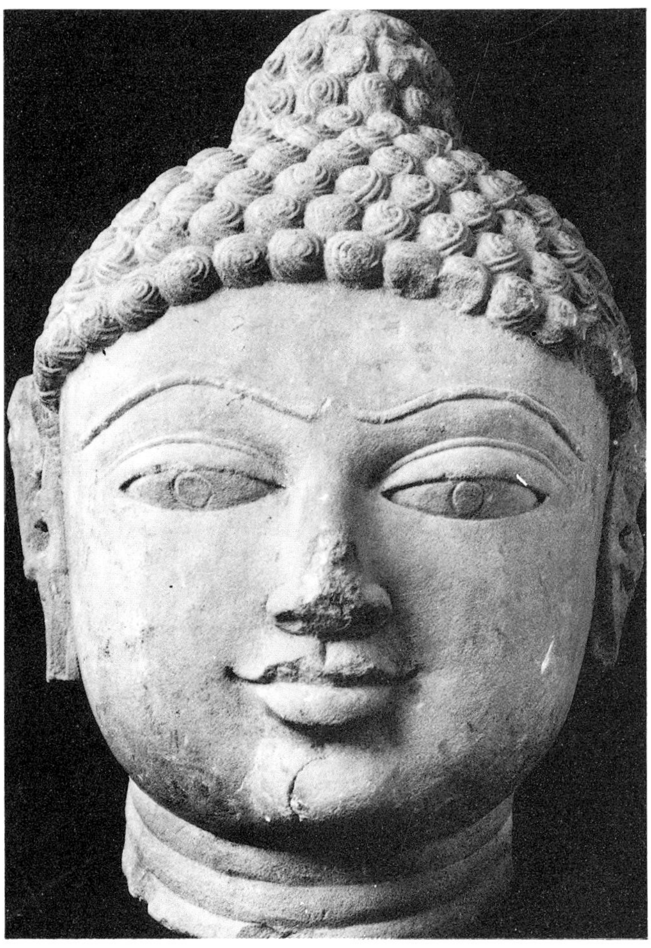

▼ 212

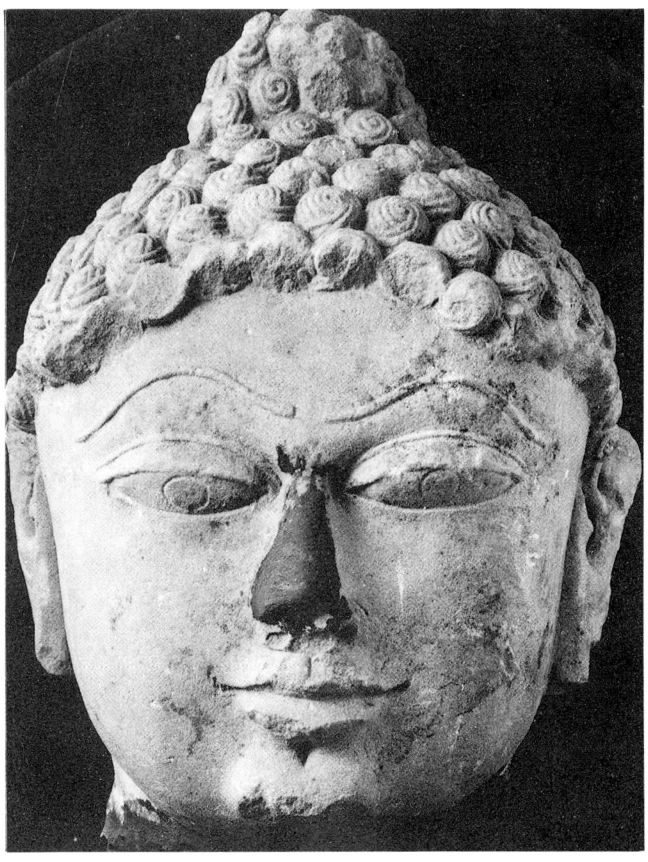

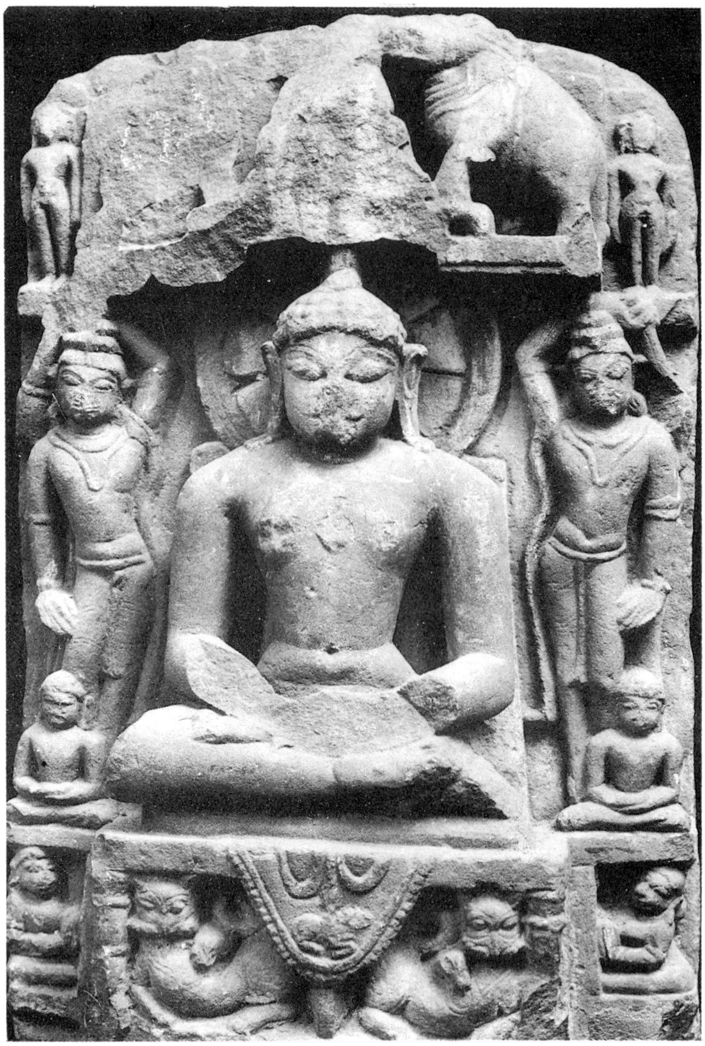

214

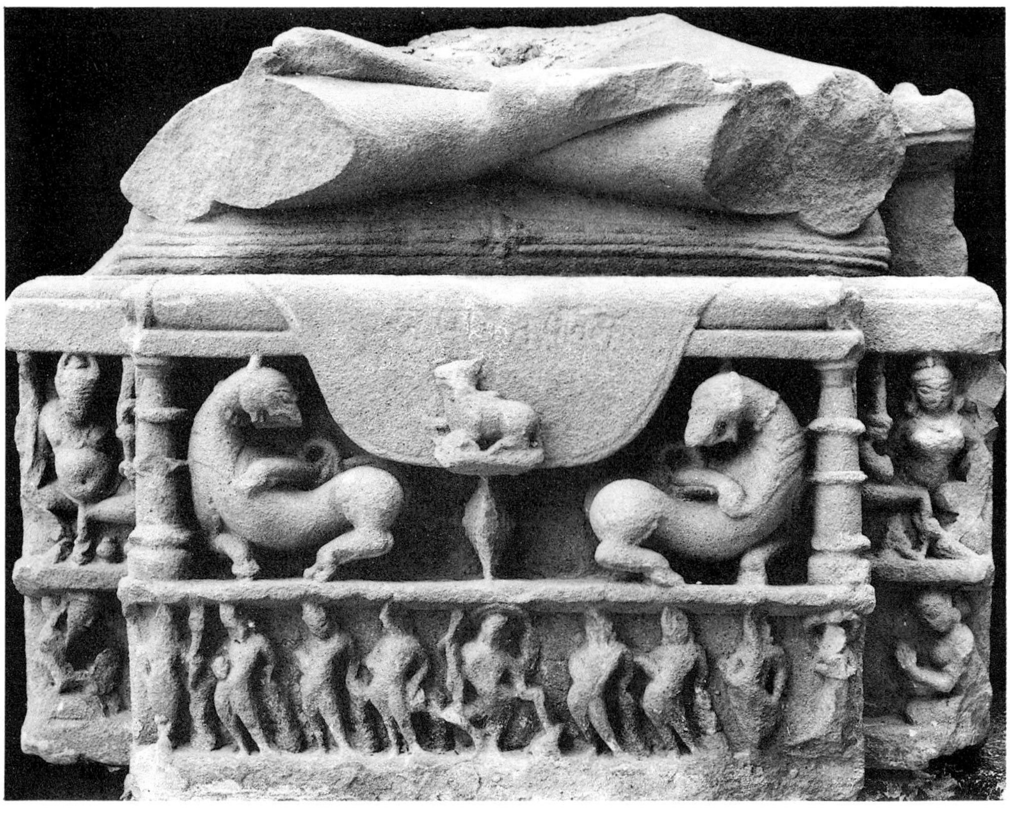

213

▶ 218

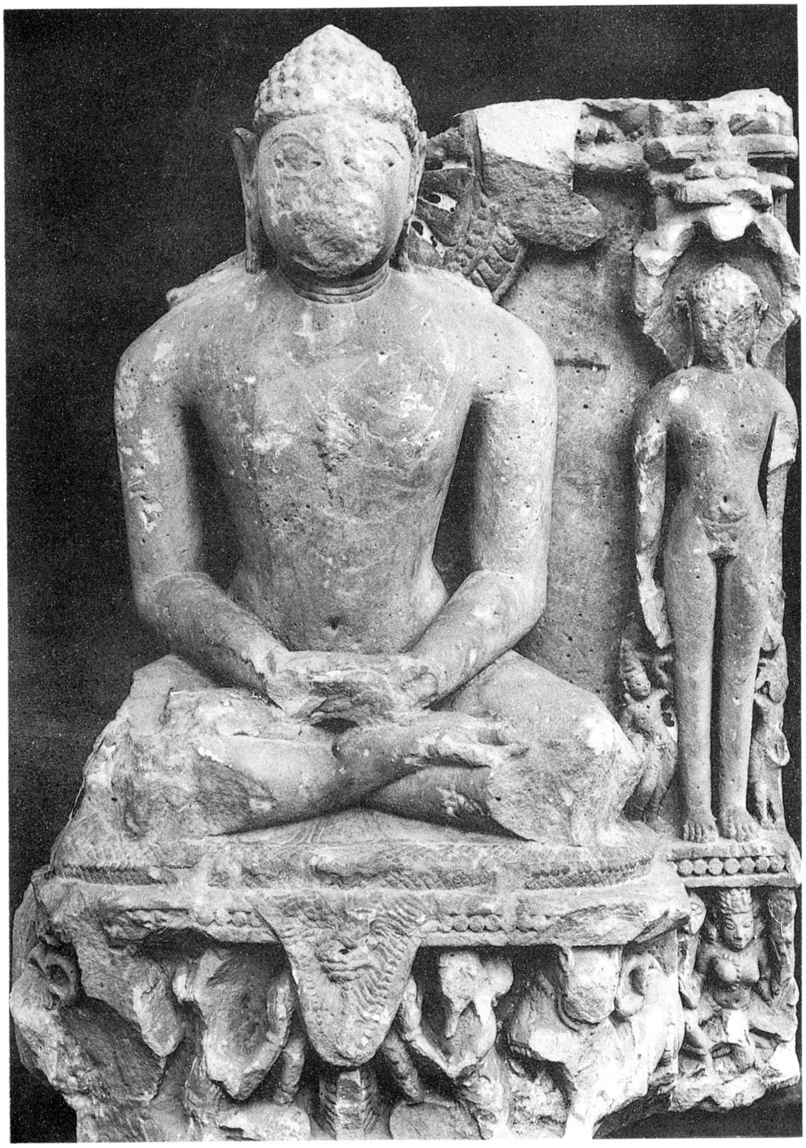

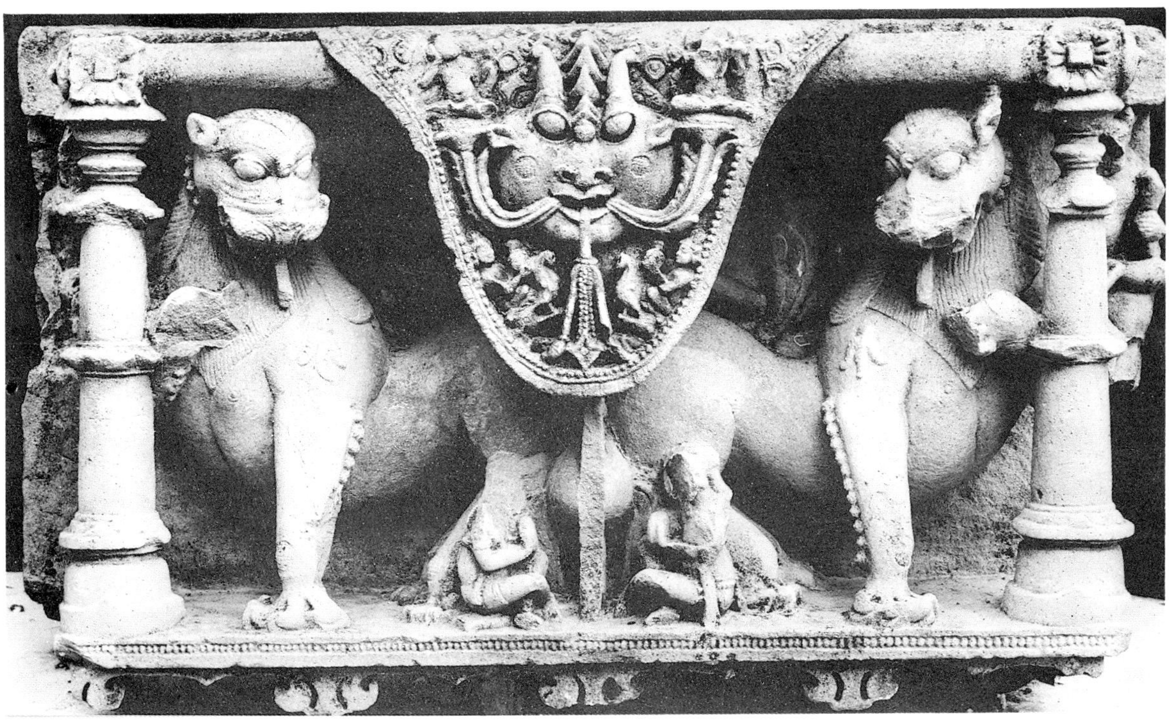

◀ 217

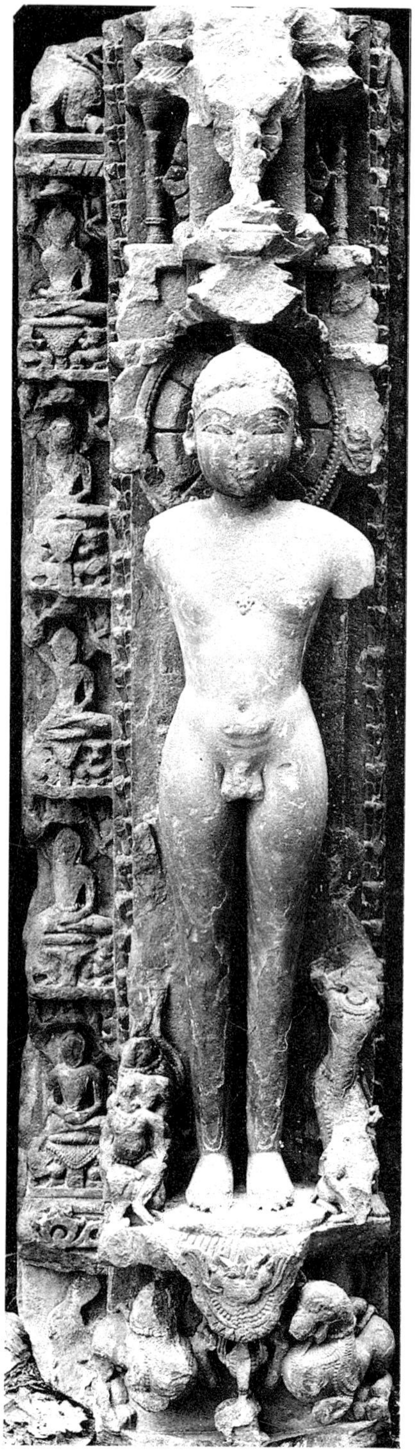

◀ 220

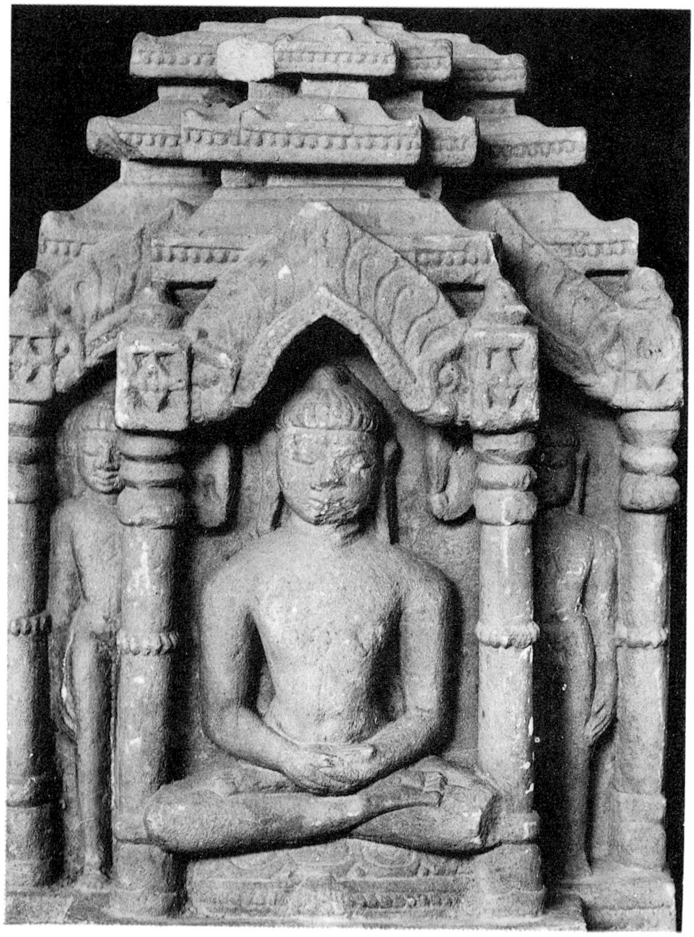

▶ 219

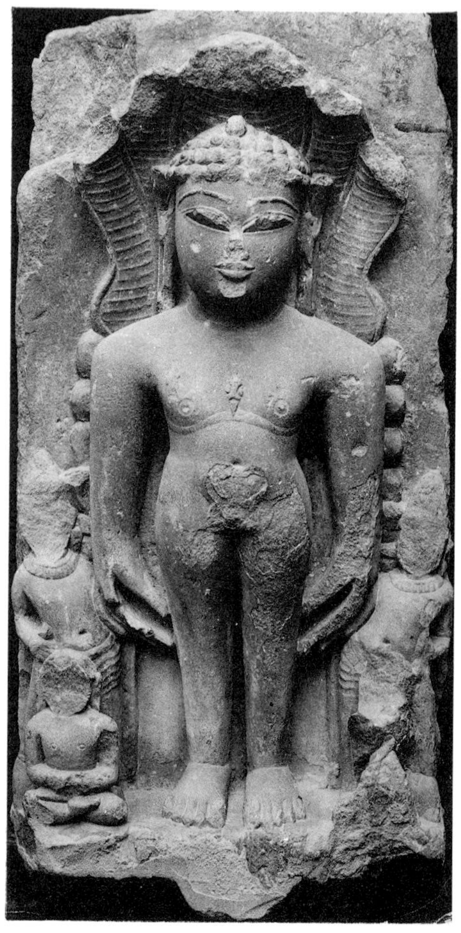

▶ 221

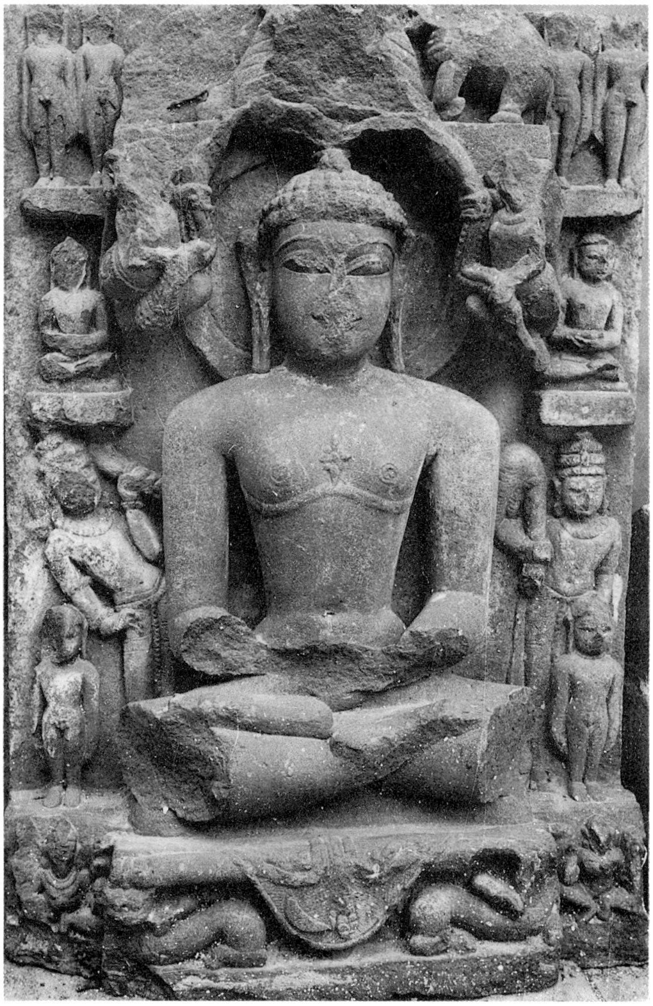

◀
215

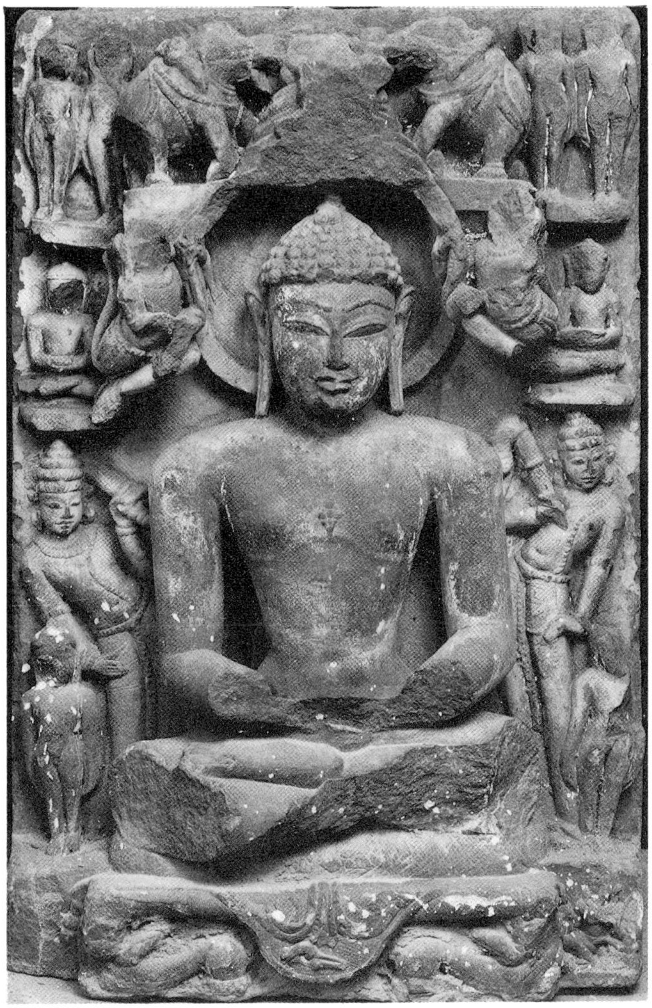

▶
216

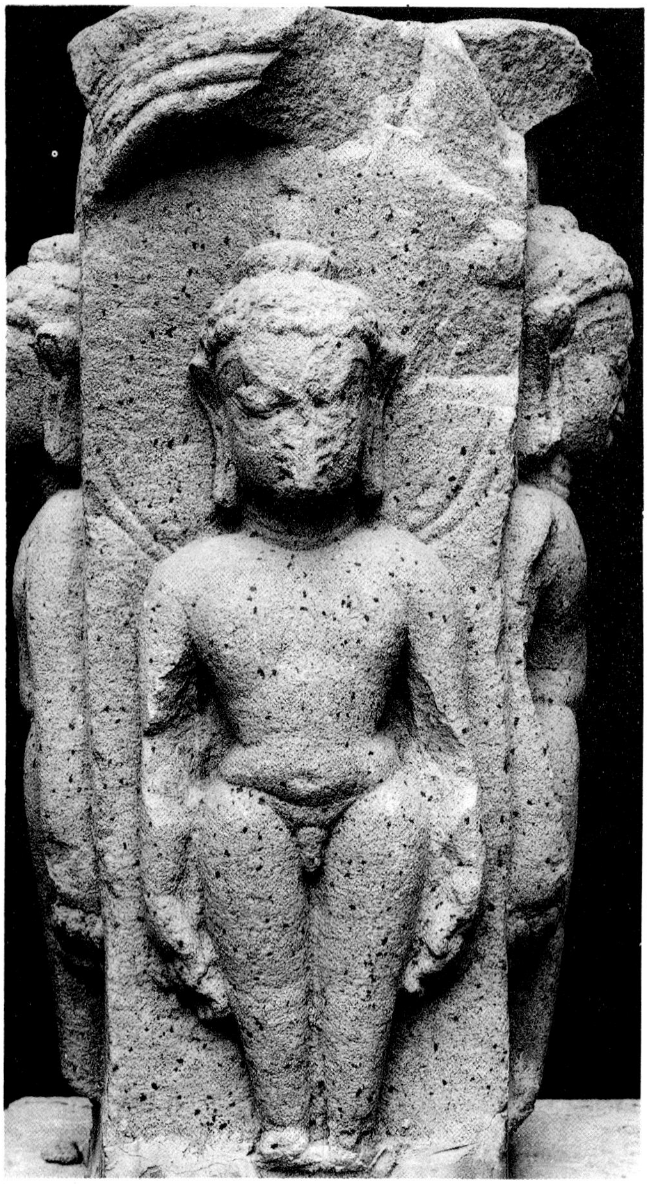

◀ 222A

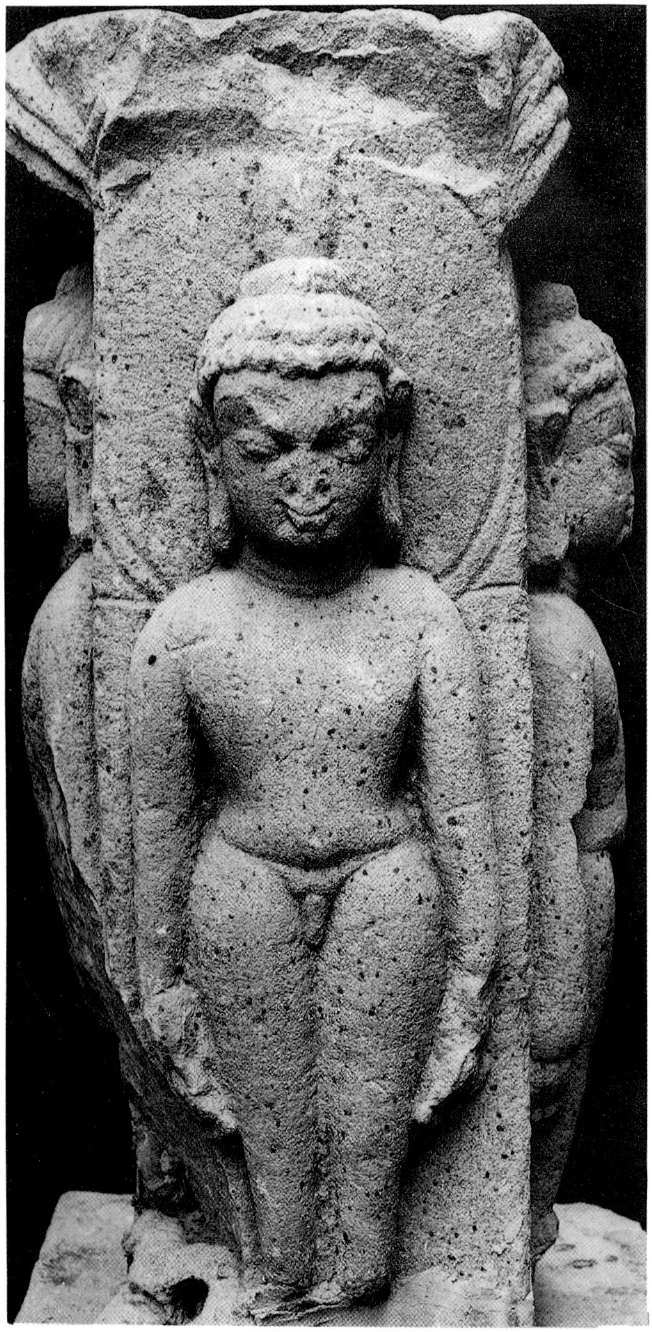

▶ 222B

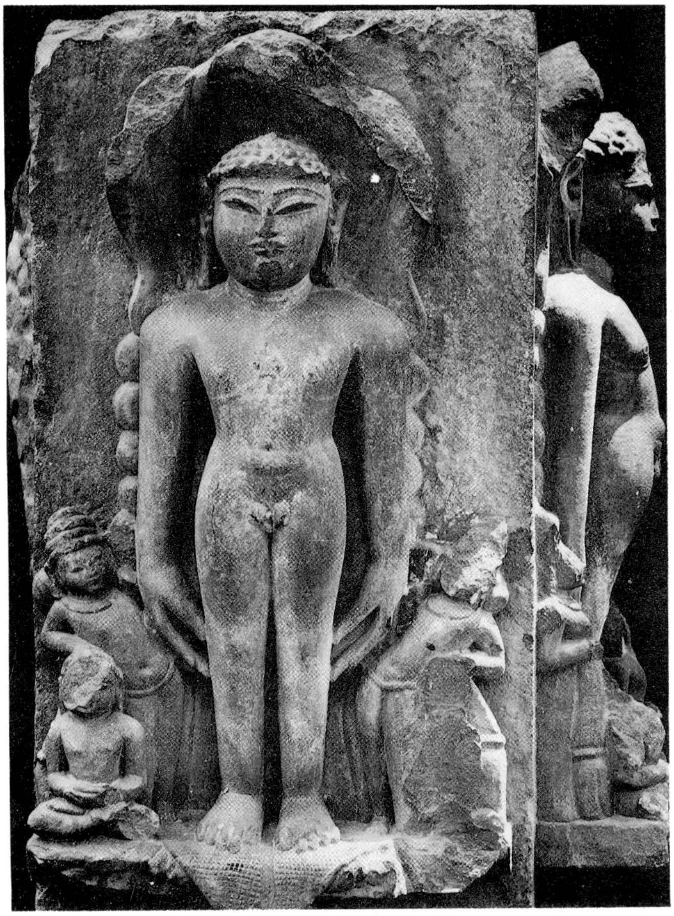

◀
223A

▶
223B

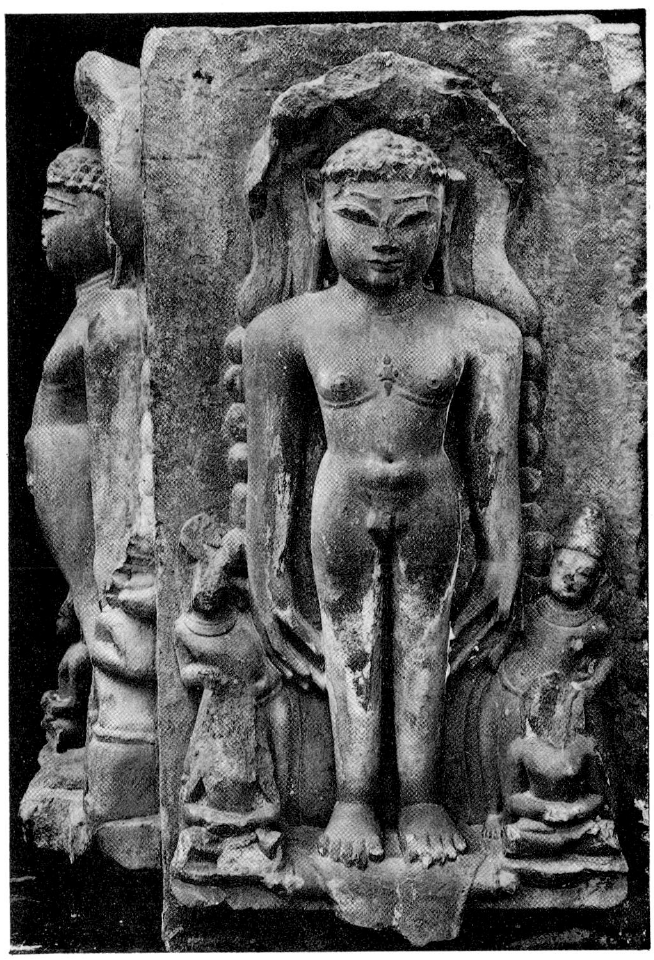

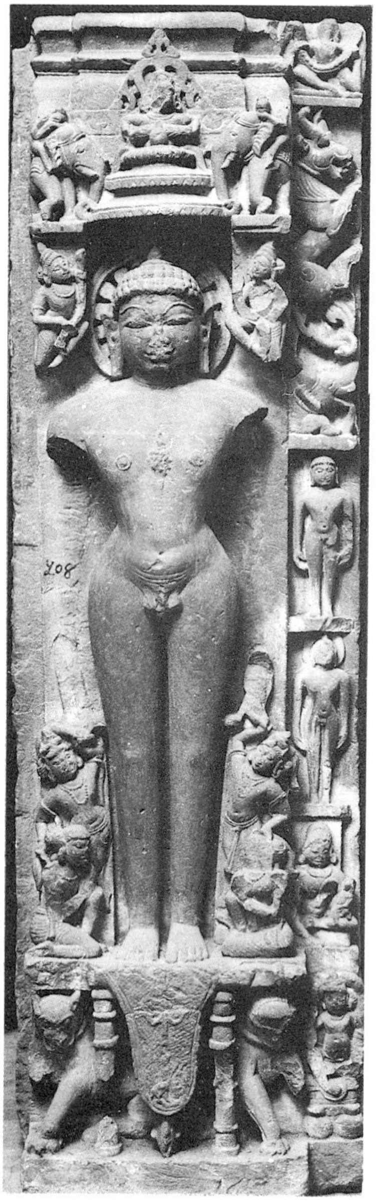

◀ 224

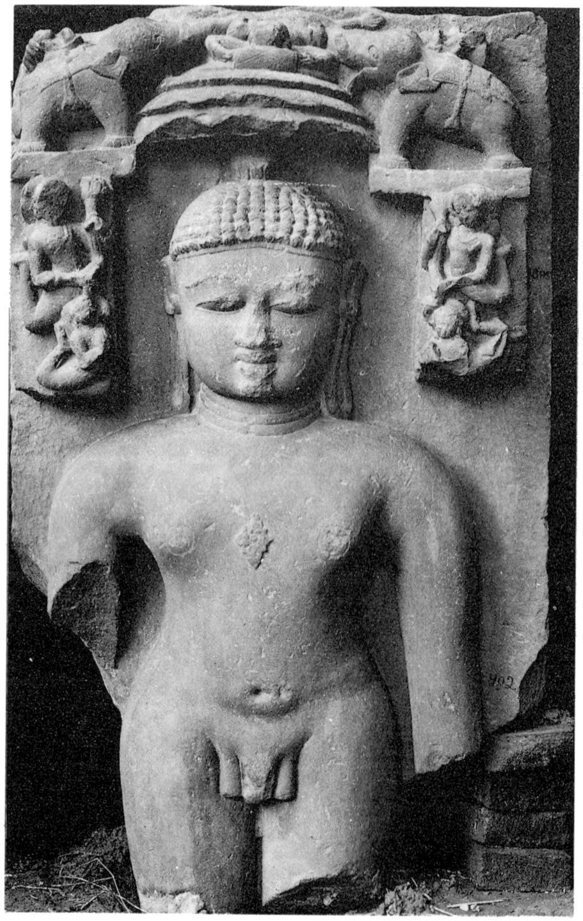

▲ 225

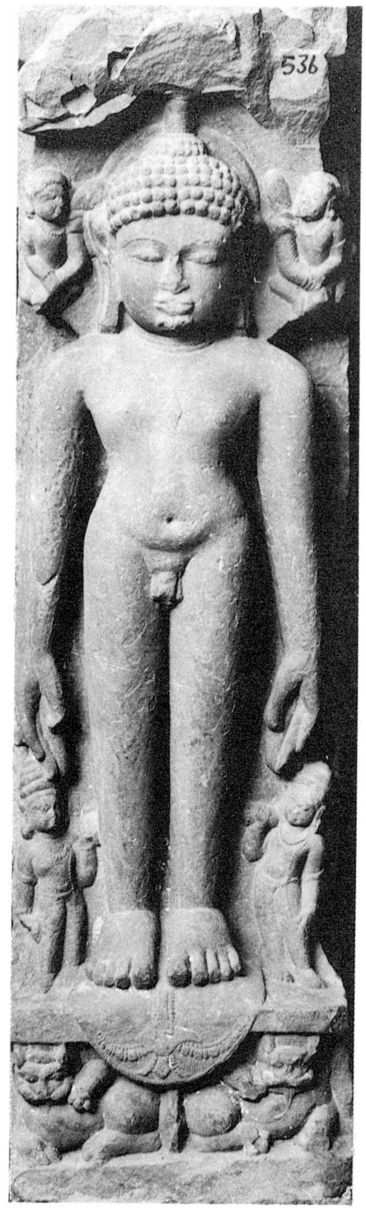

▶ 226

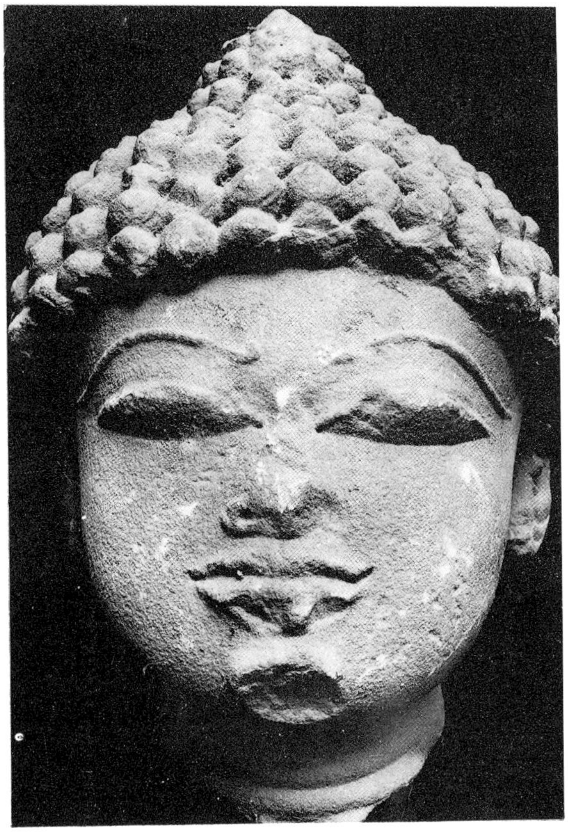

▲ 227

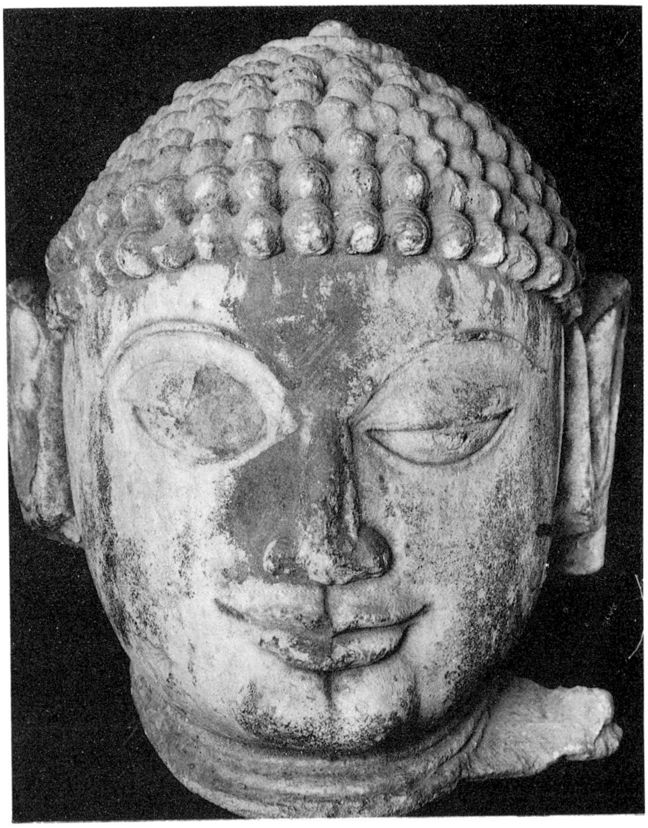

▲ 228

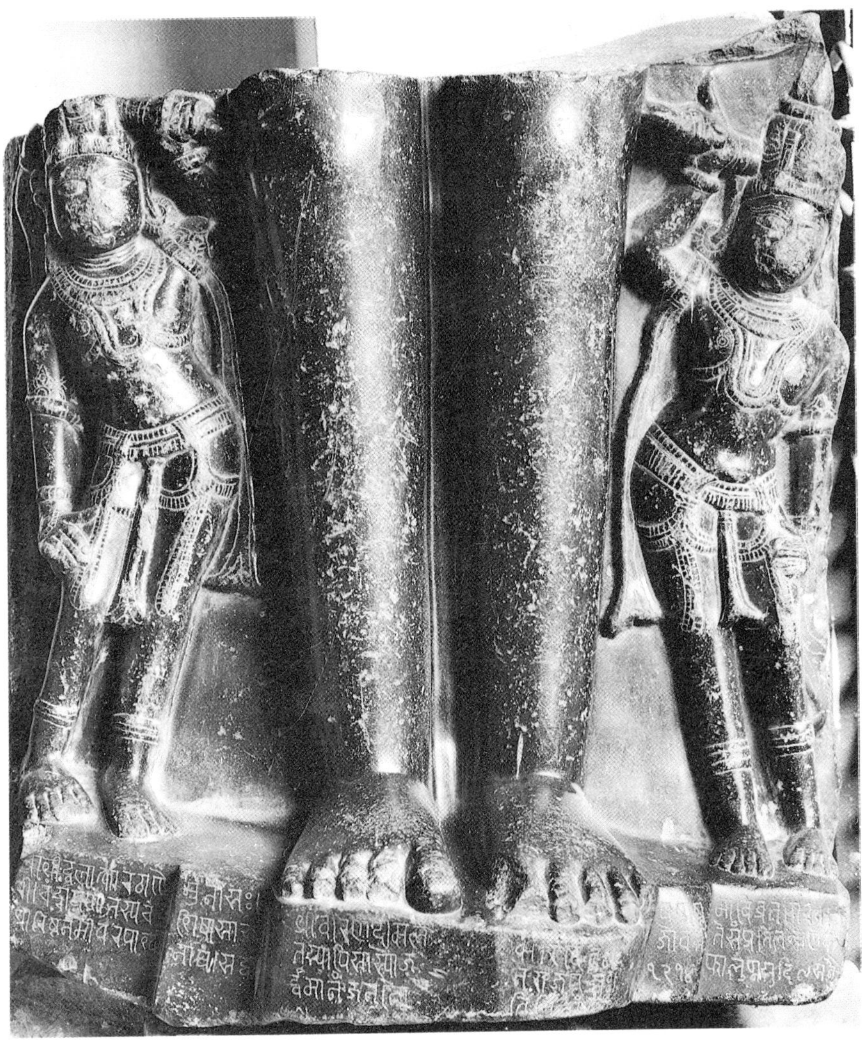

◀ 229

▼ 230A

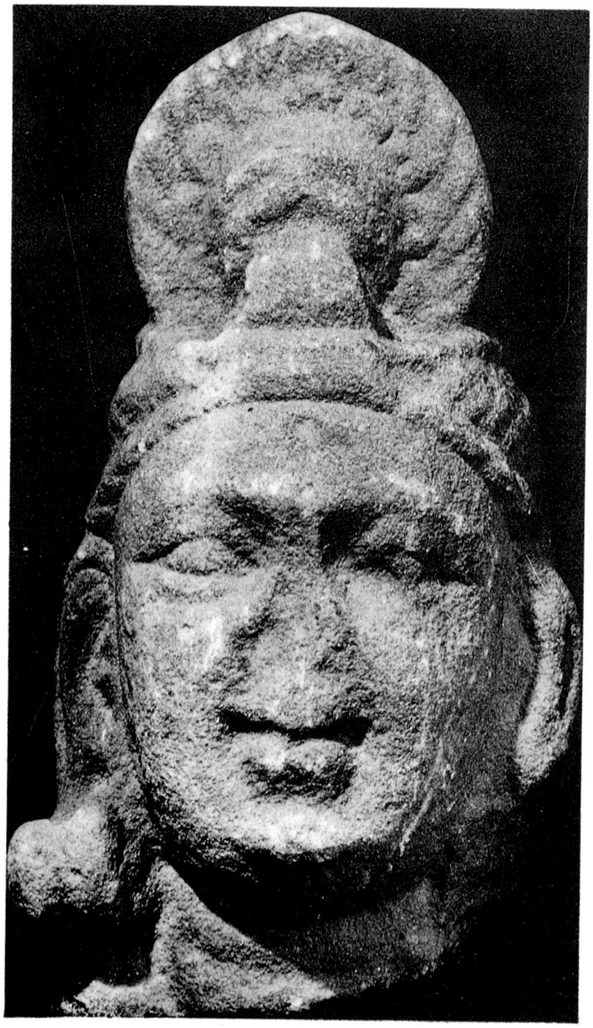

▼ 230B

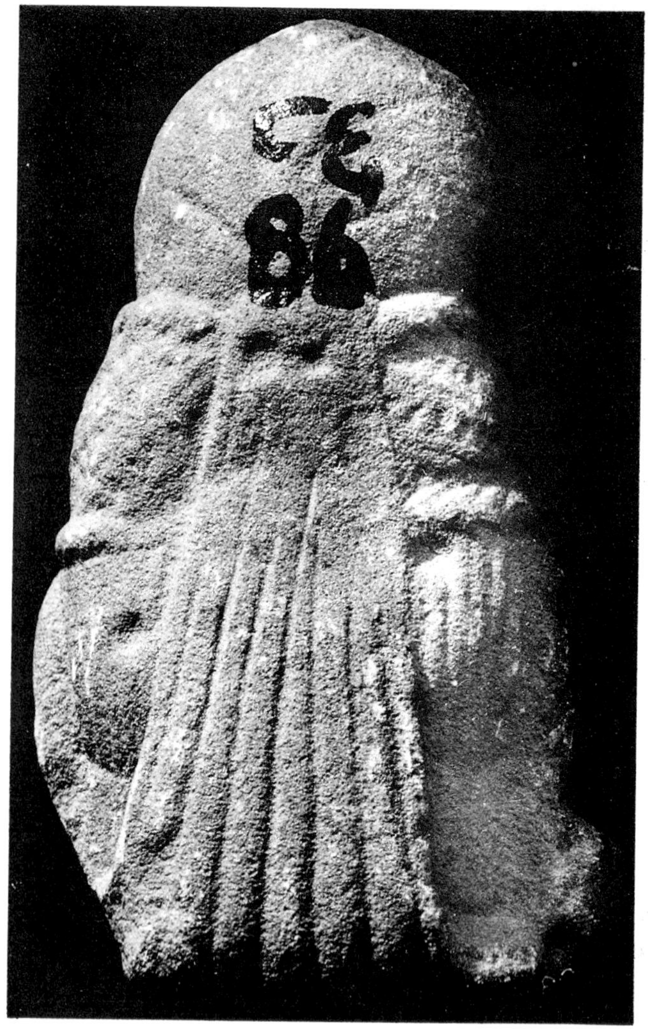

▼ 231

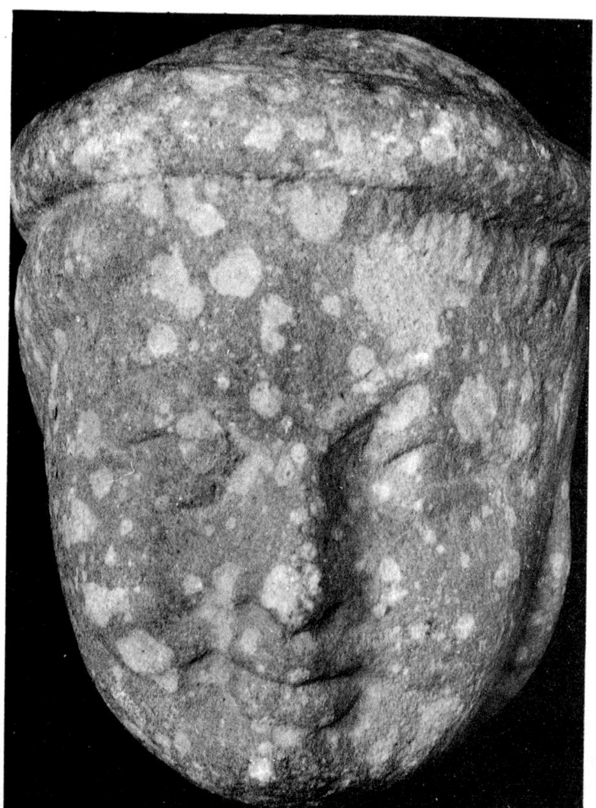

▼ 232

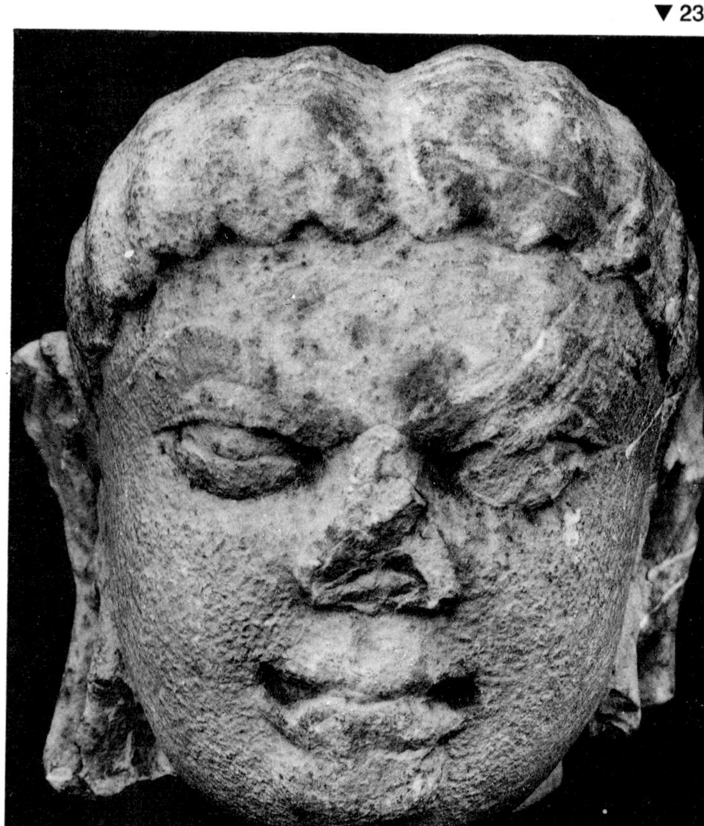

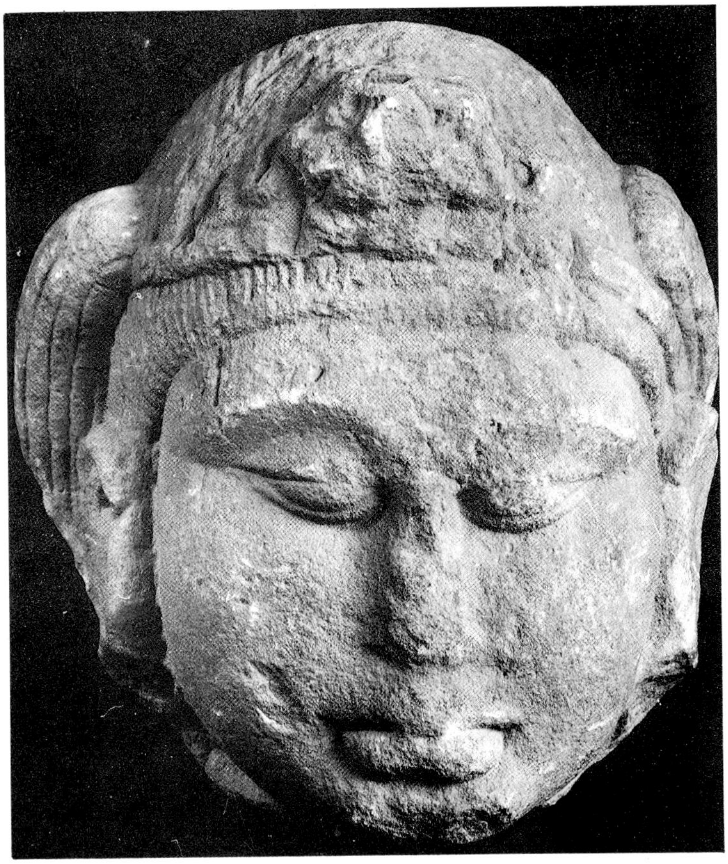

◀
233

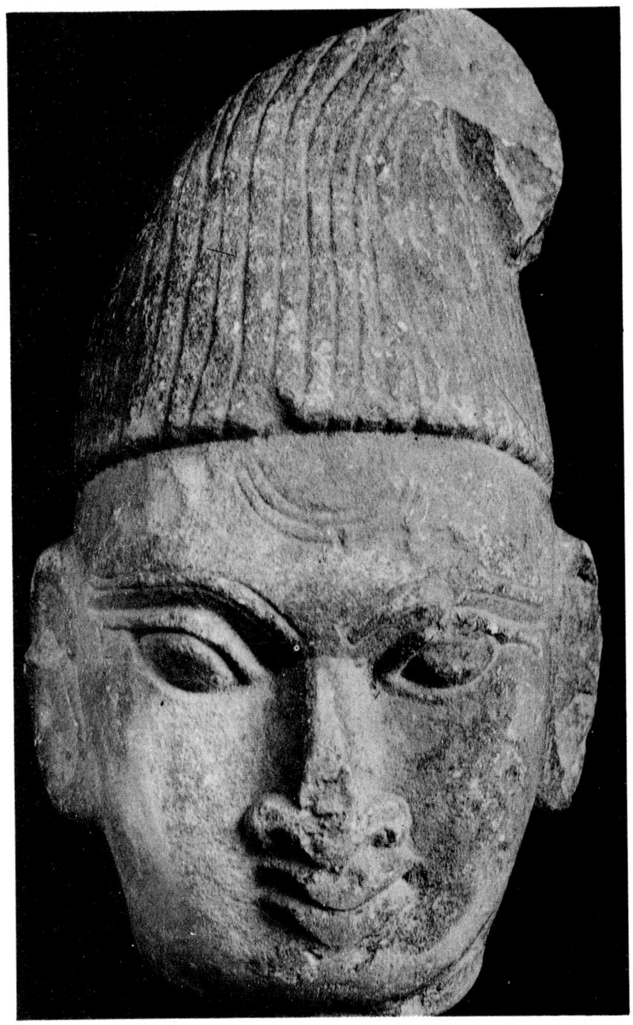

▶
234

▼ 235

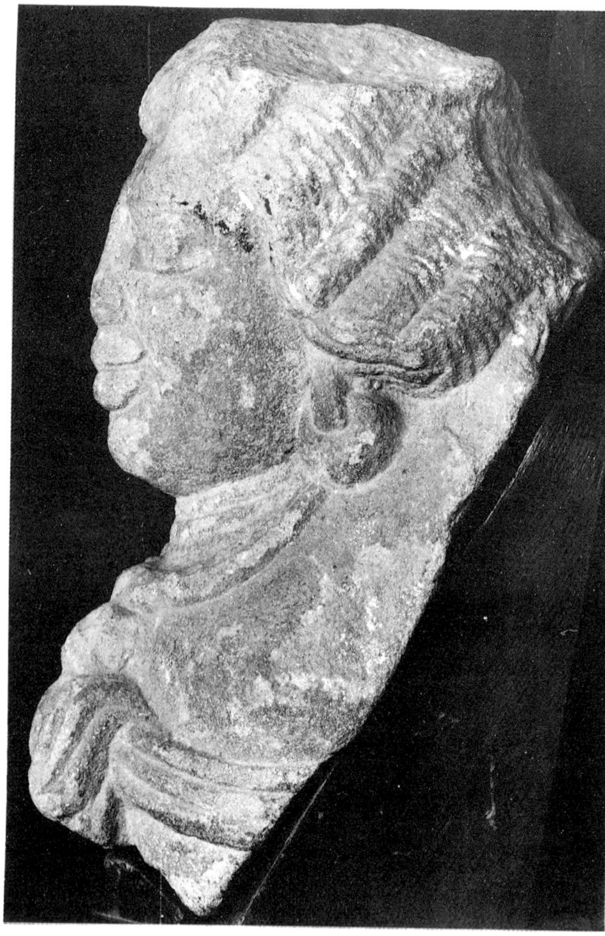

▼ 236

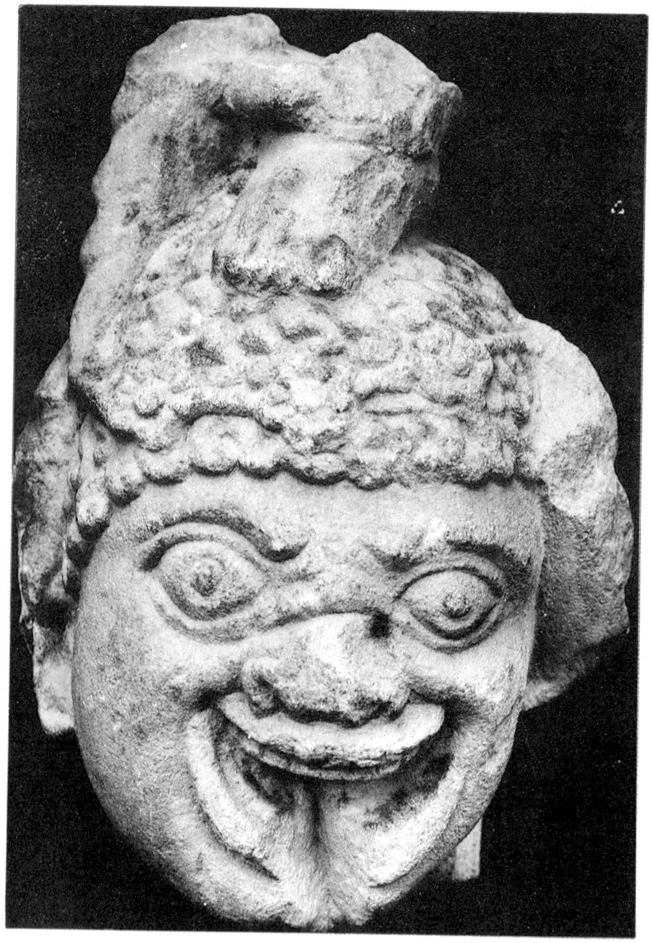

▼ 237

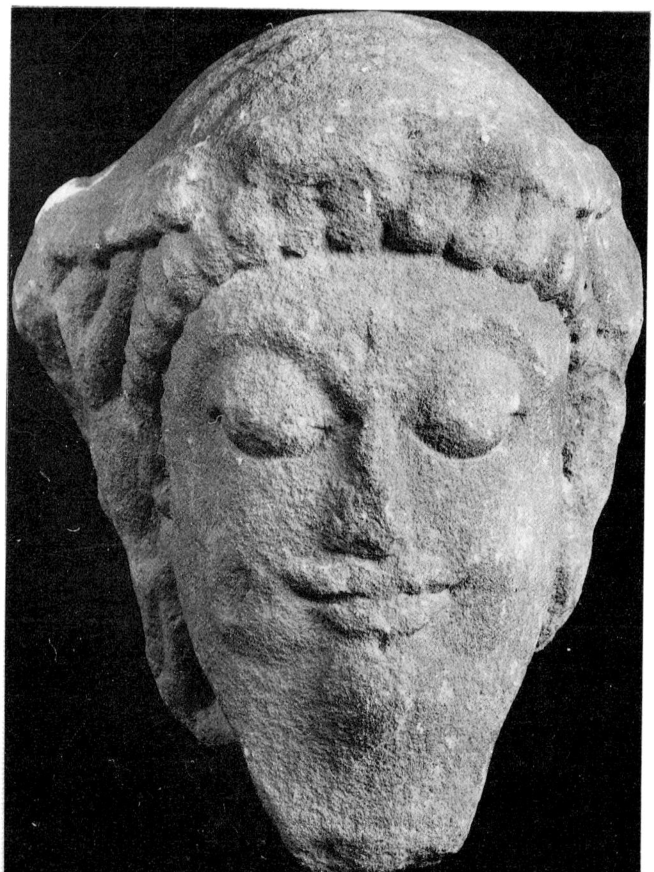

▼ 238

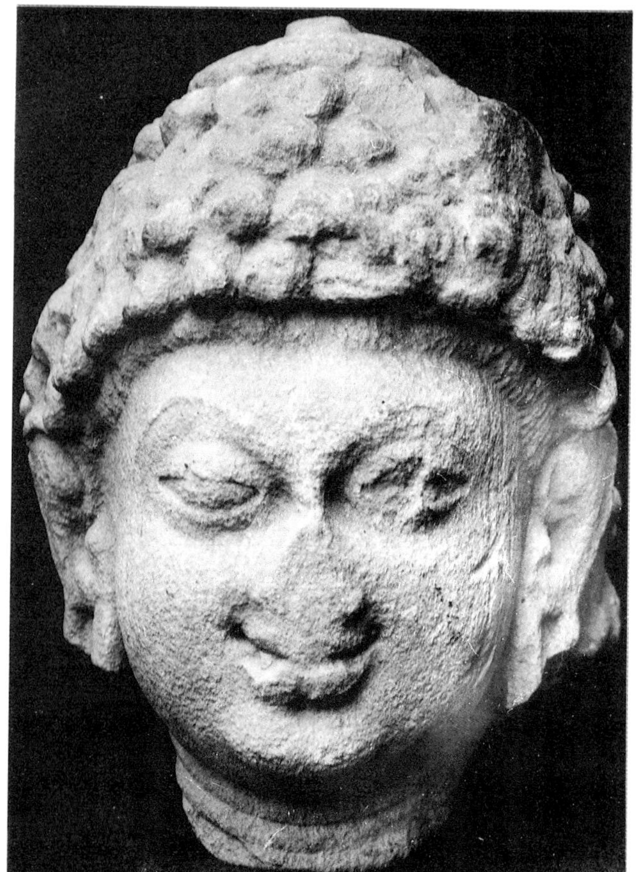

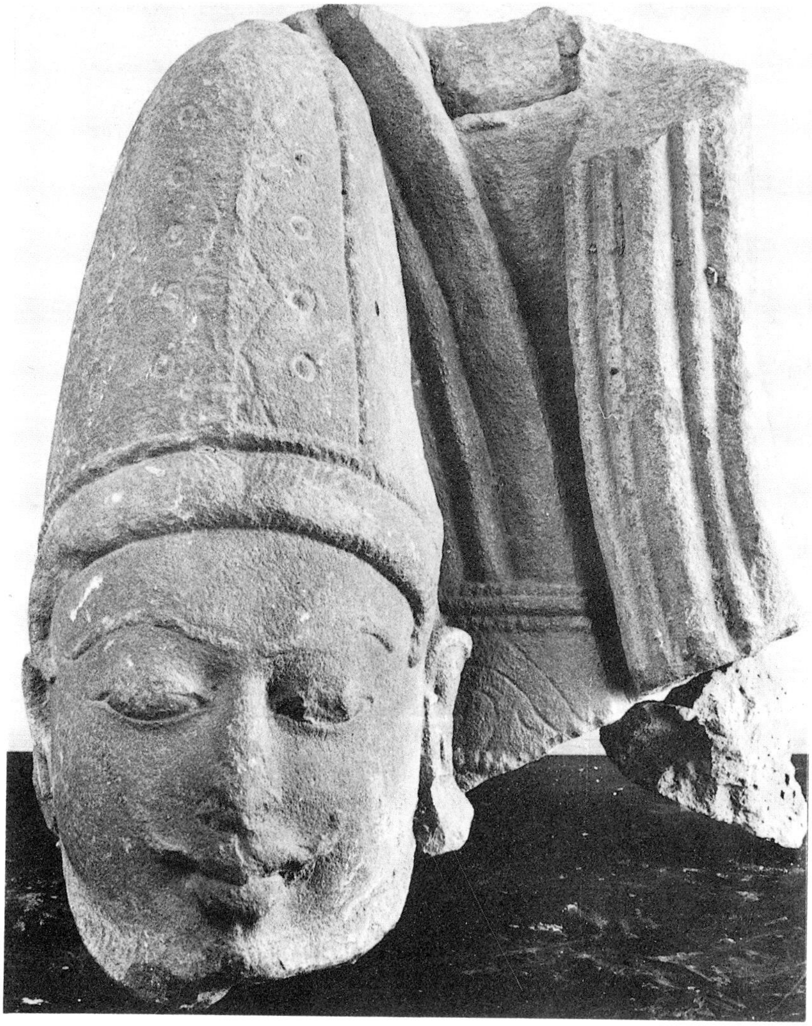

▲ 241

▼ 239

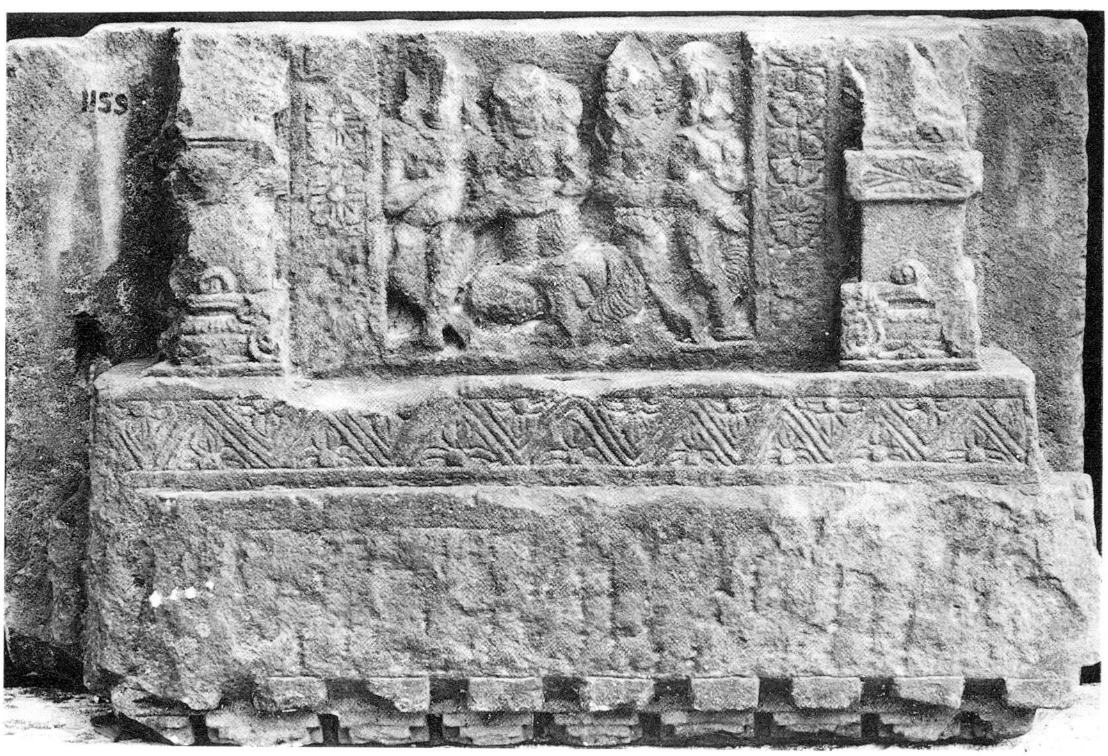

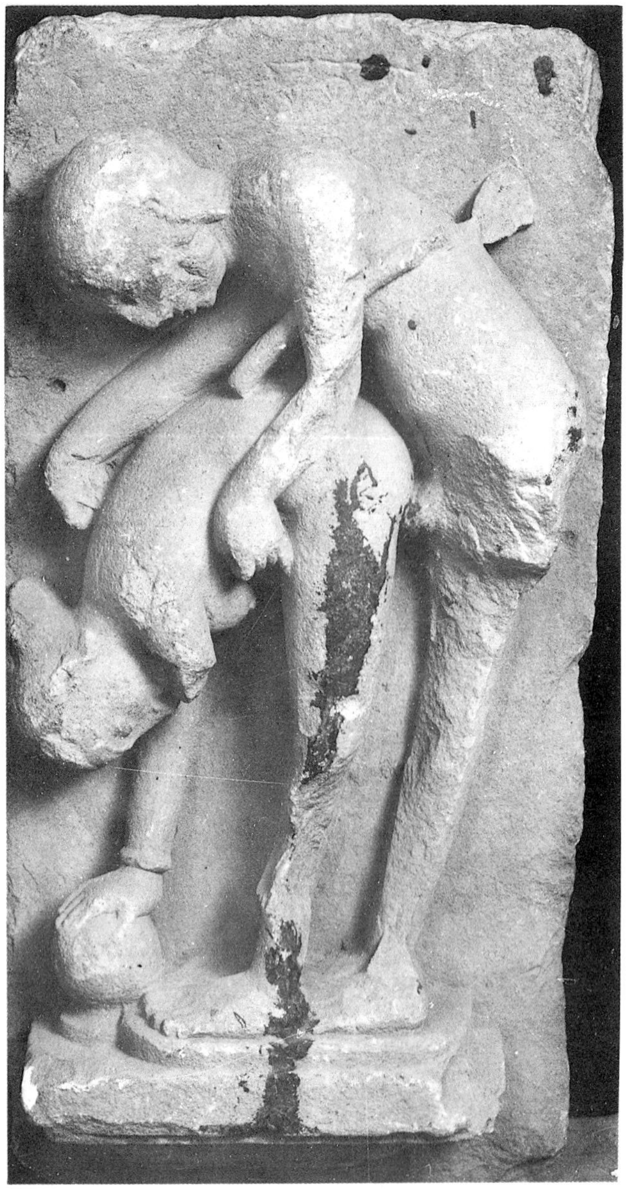

◀ 242

▼ 245

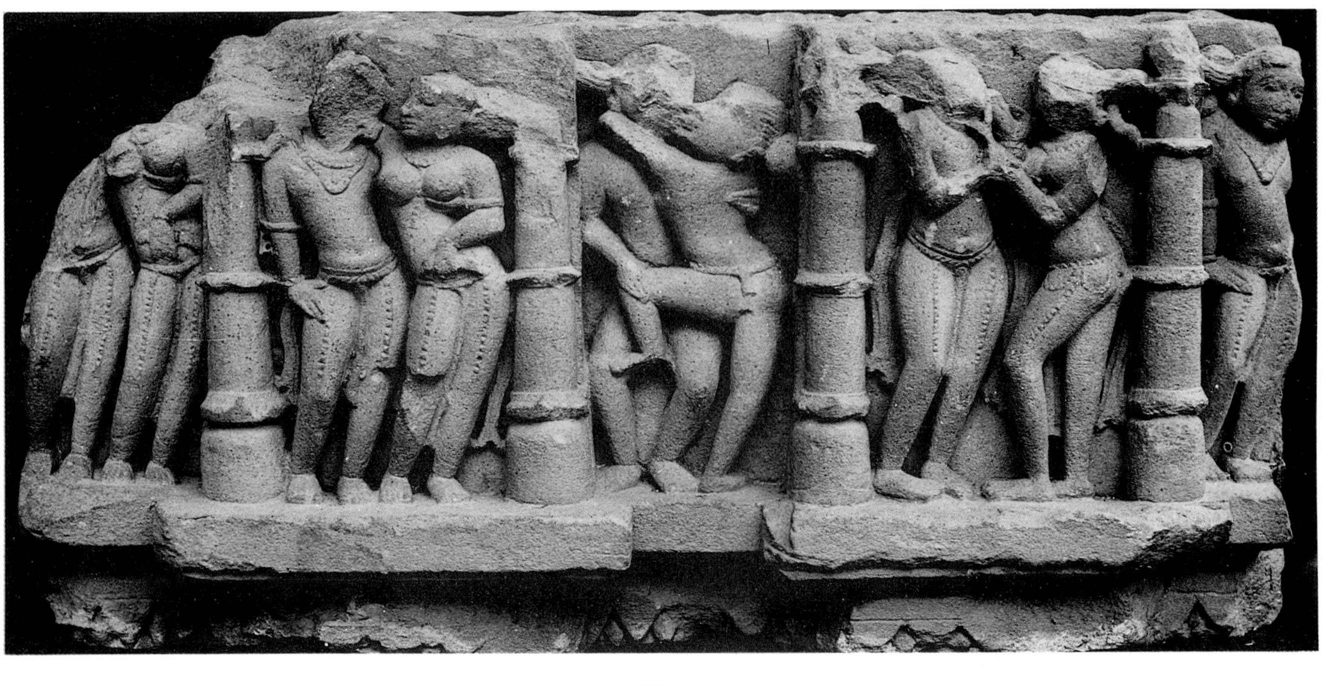

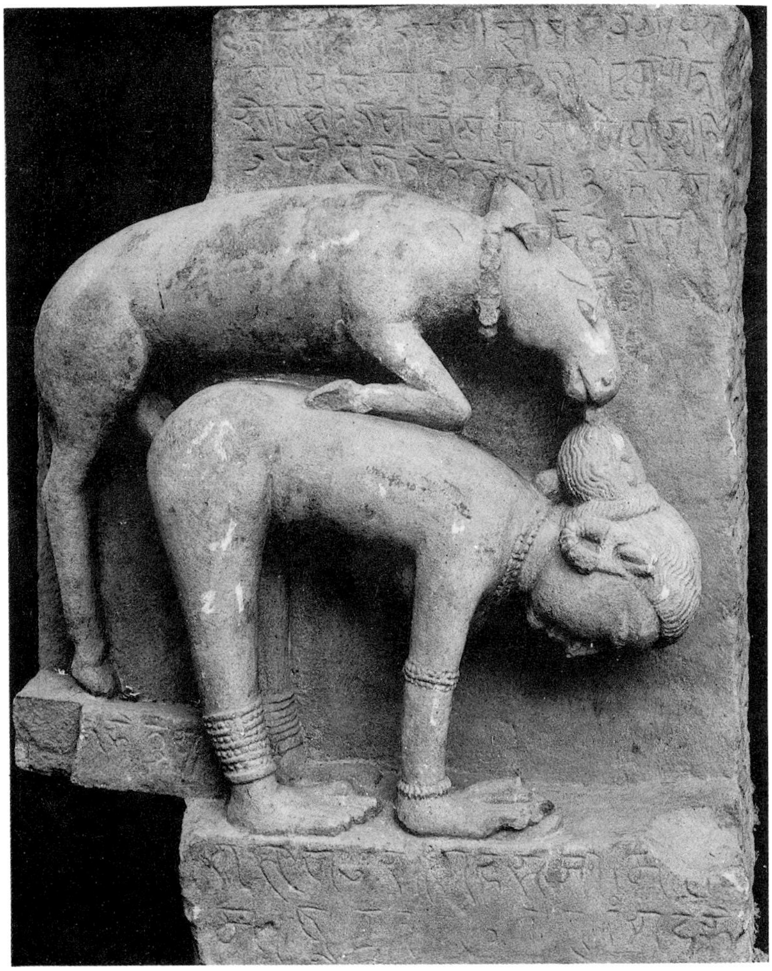

◄ 243A

▼ 243B

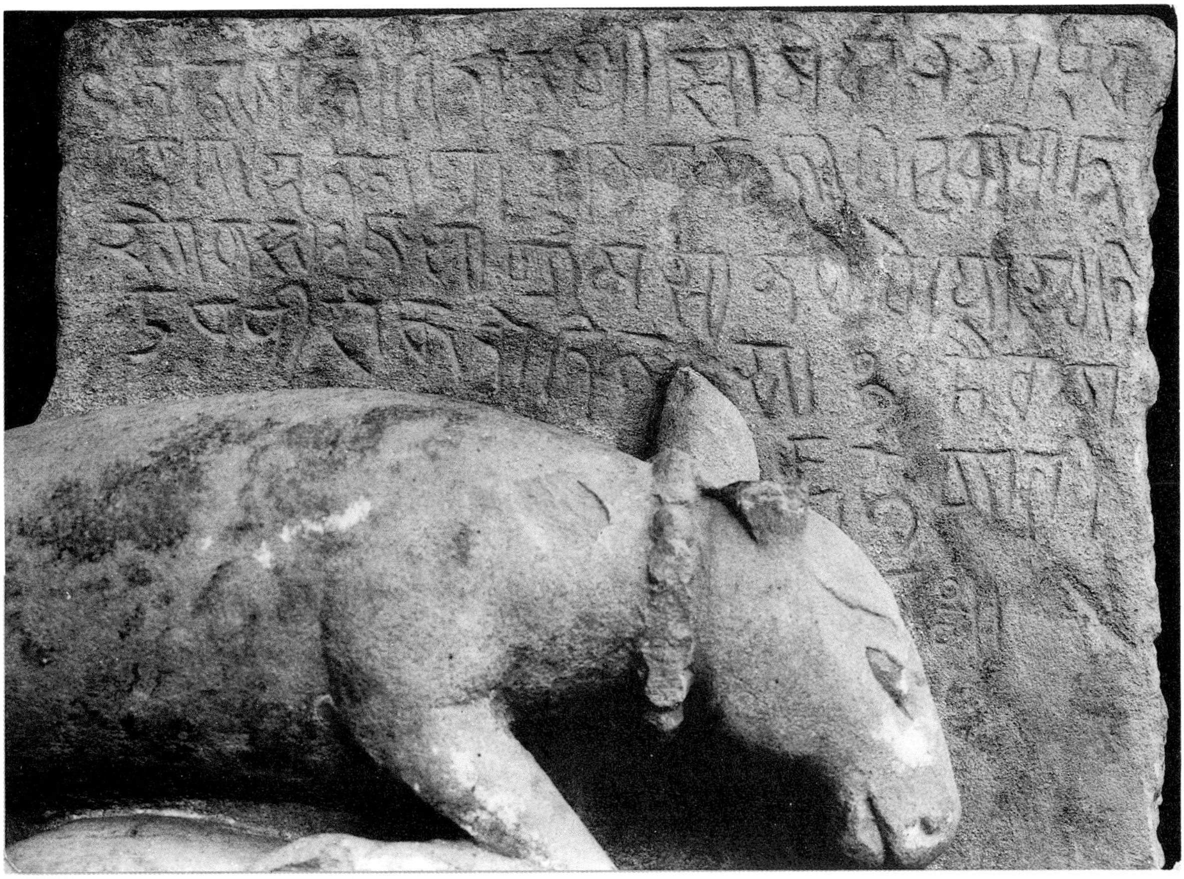

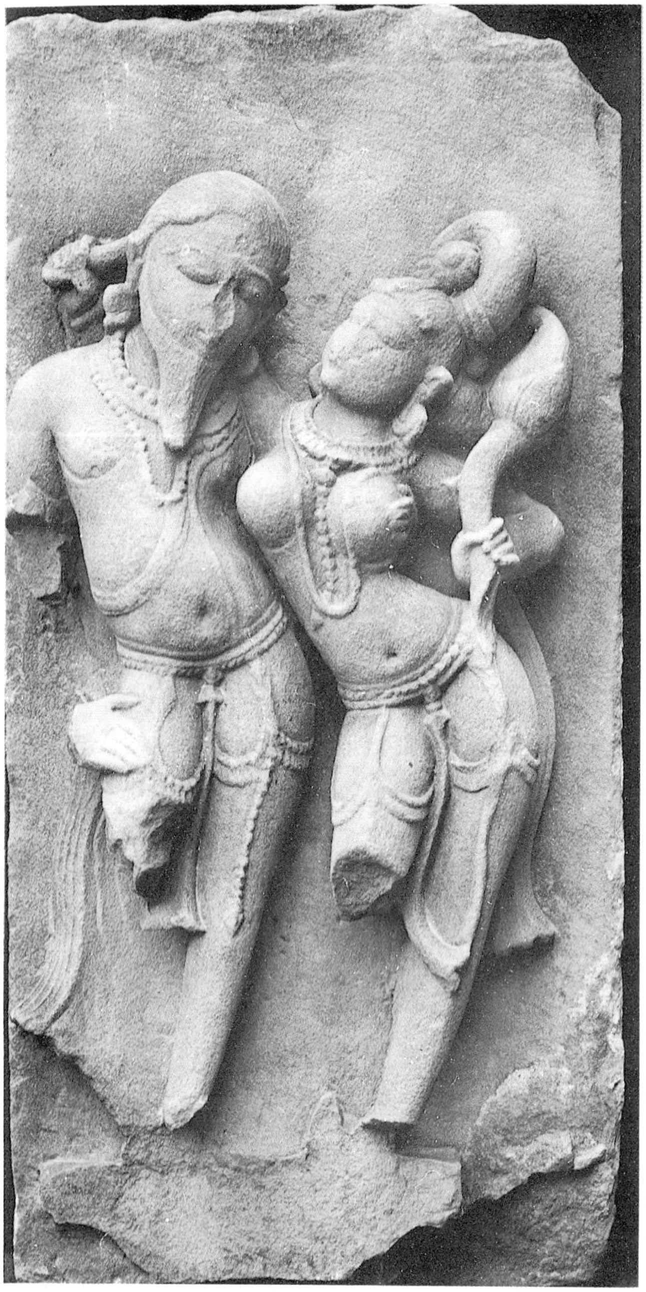

◀ 240

◀ 244

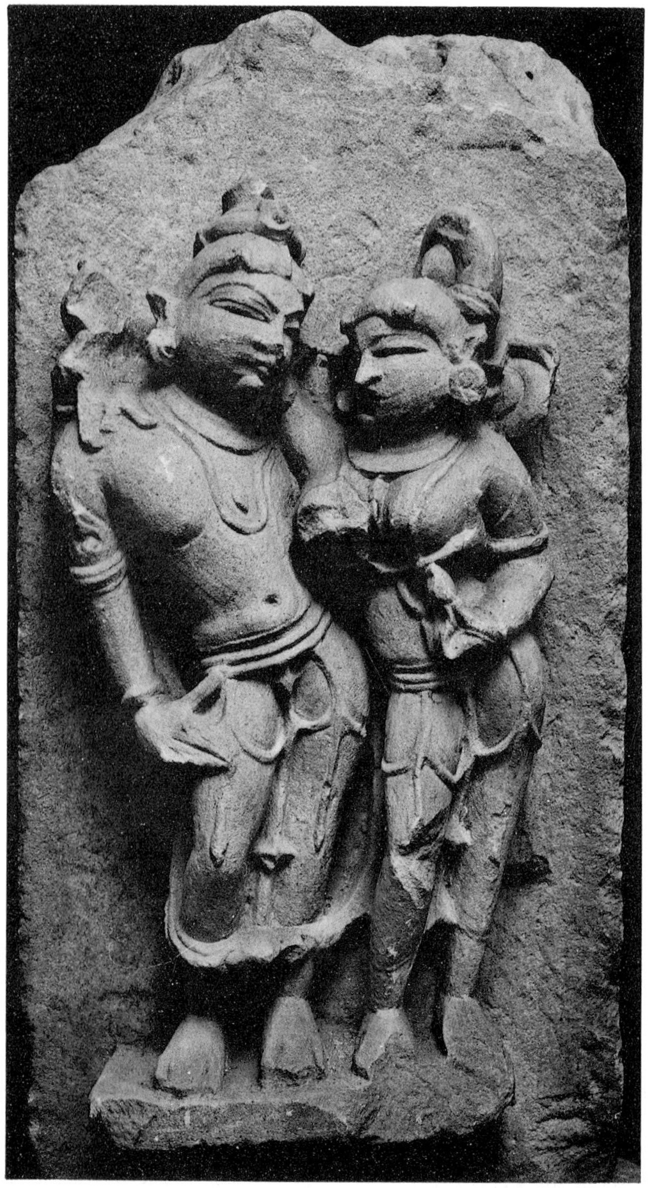

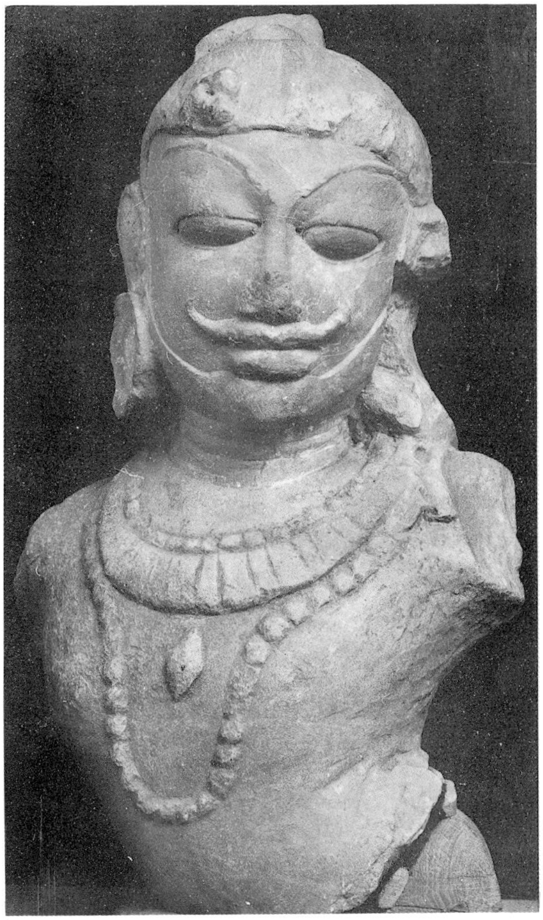

▲ 246A

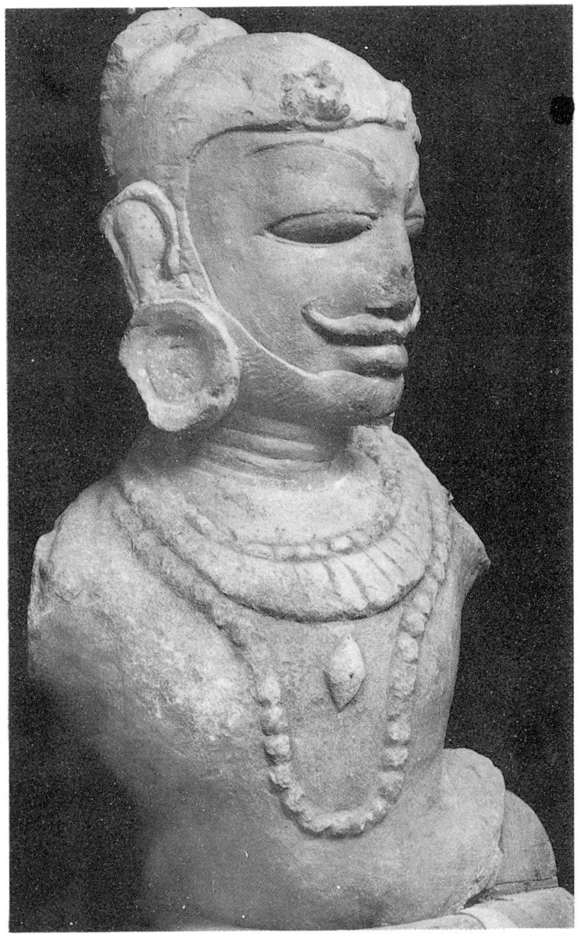

▲ 246B

▼ 247

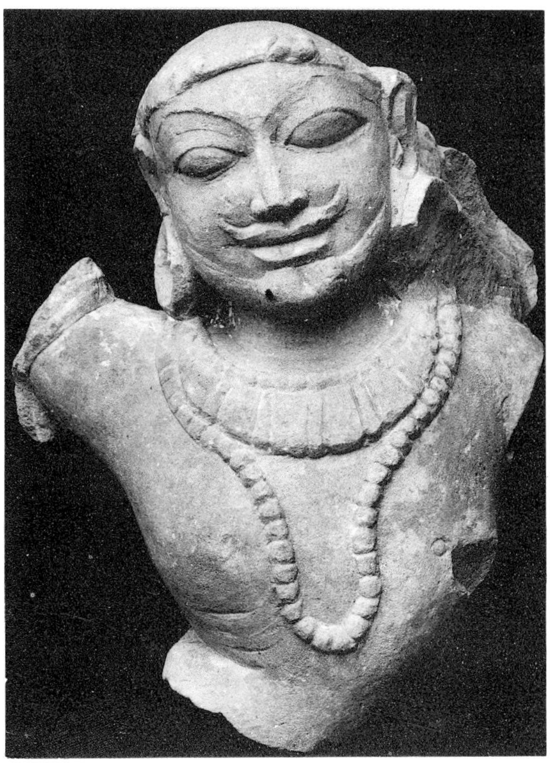

▼ 248

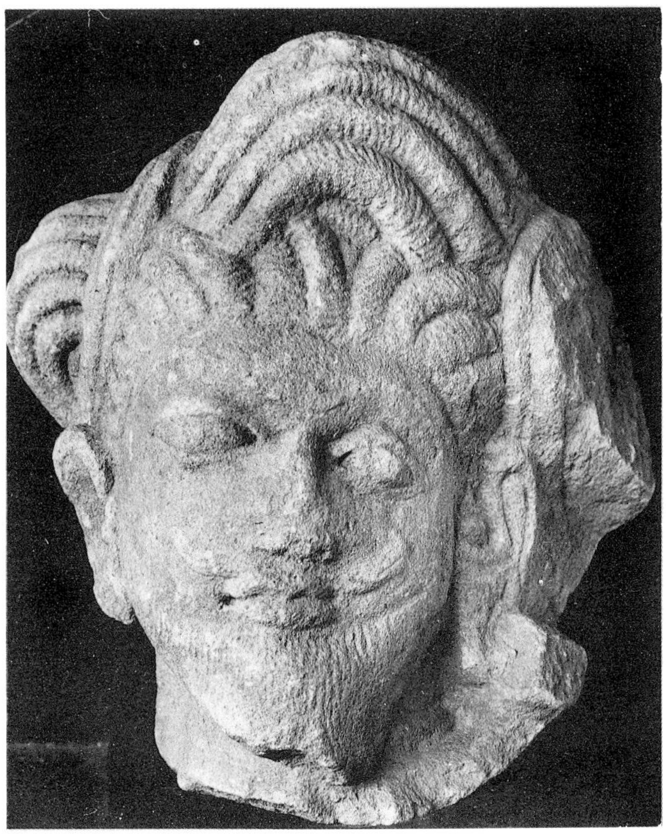

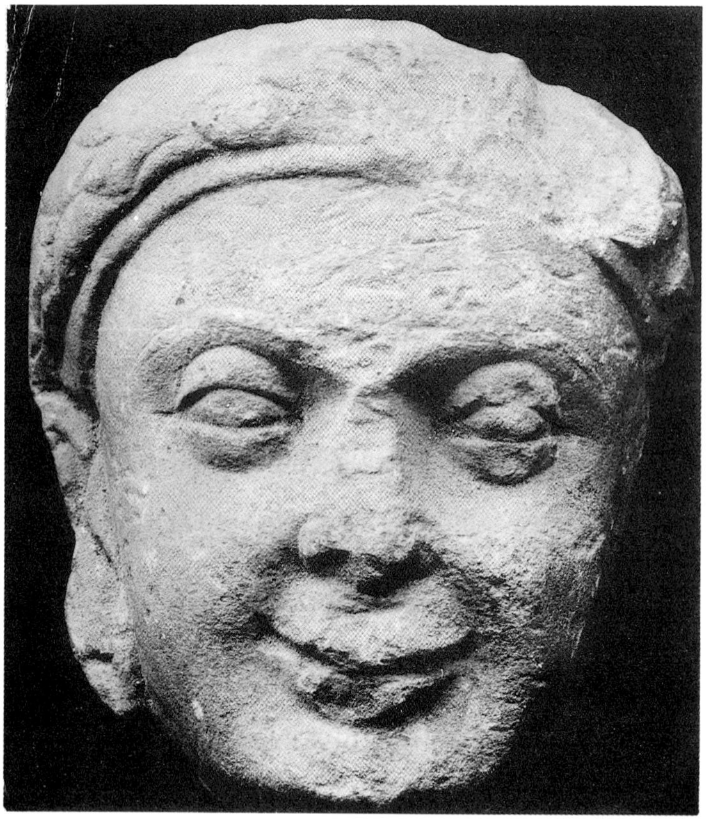

▲ 249

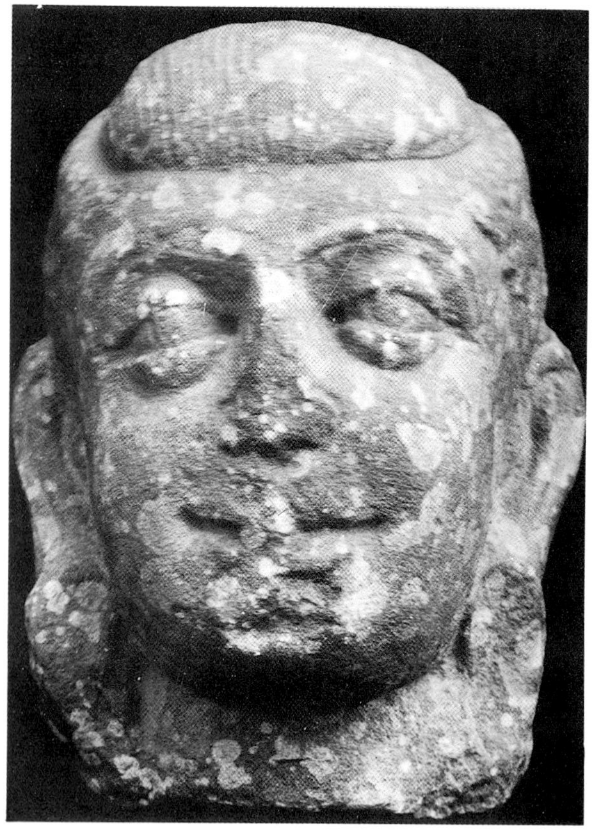

▲ 250

▼ 252

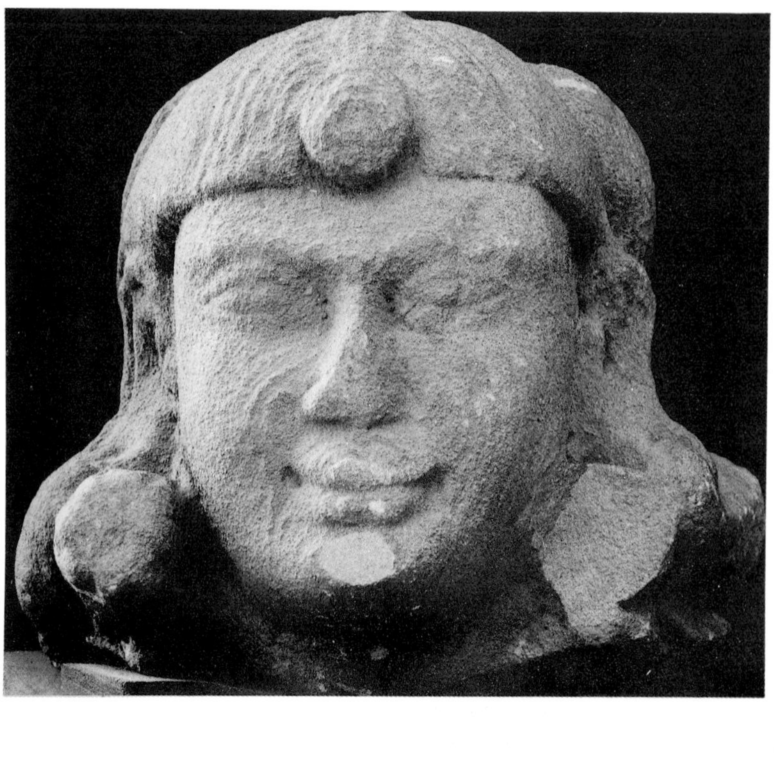

▼ 253

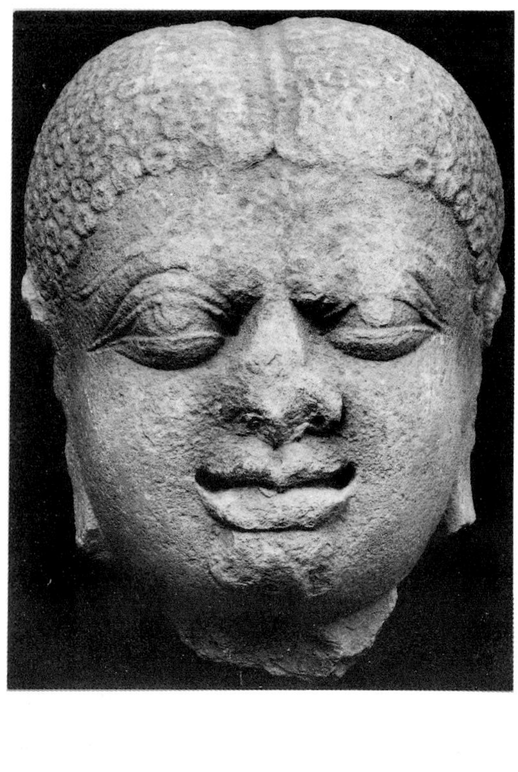

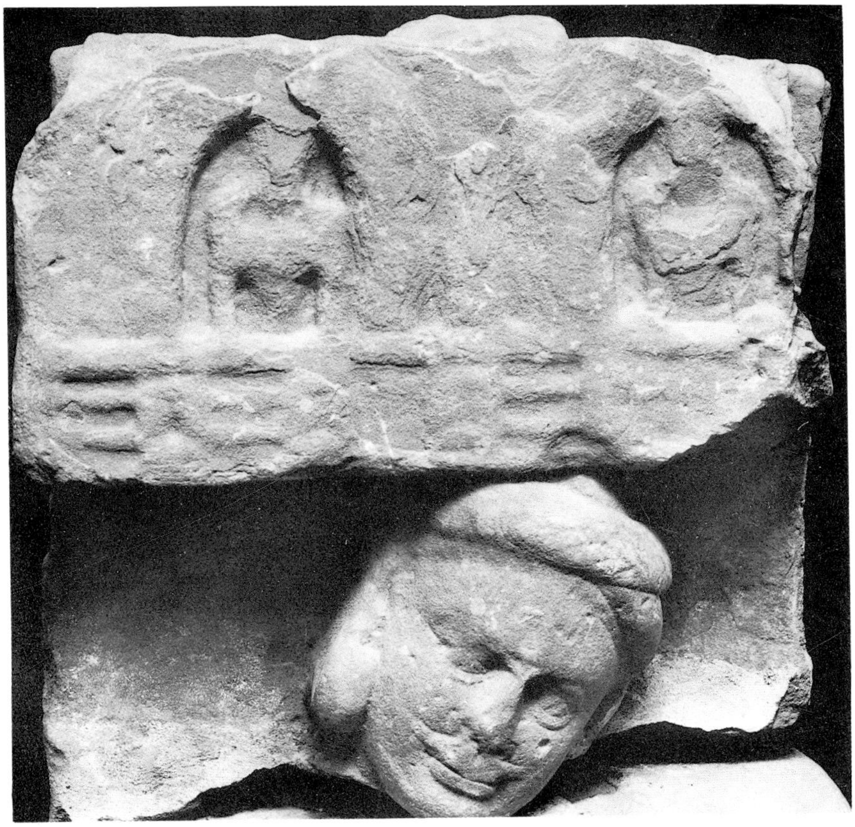

◀
251

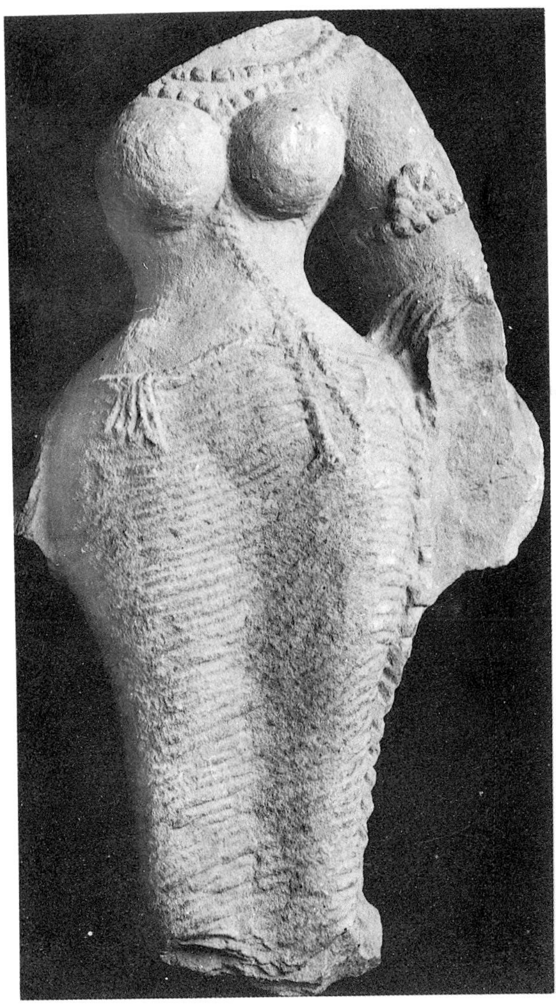

◀
254

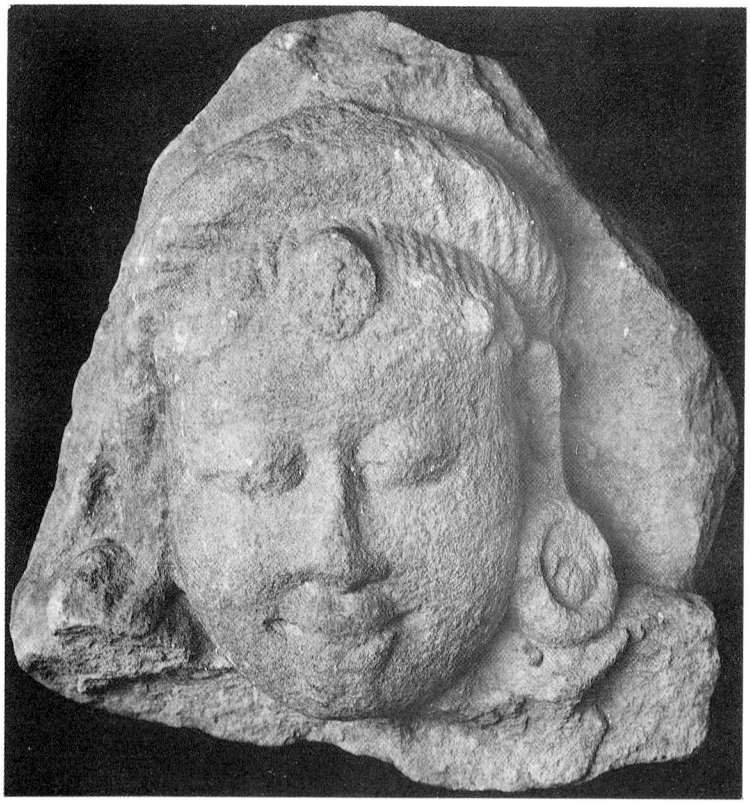

▲ 255

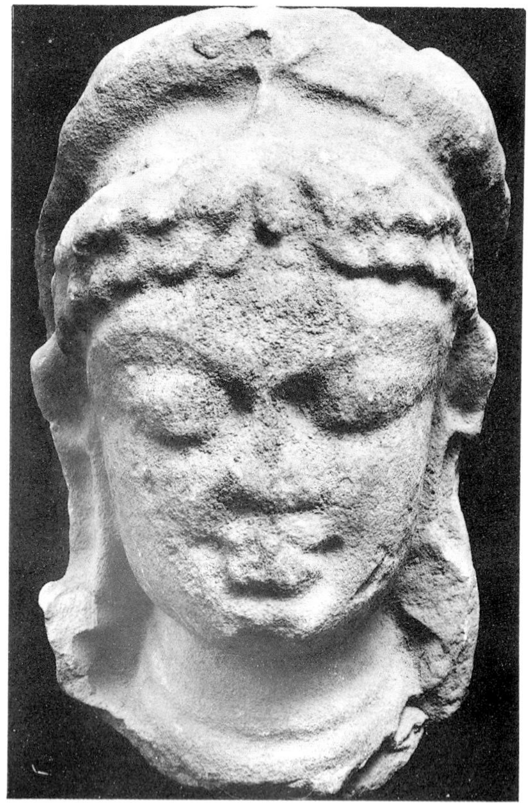

▲ 258

▼ 257B

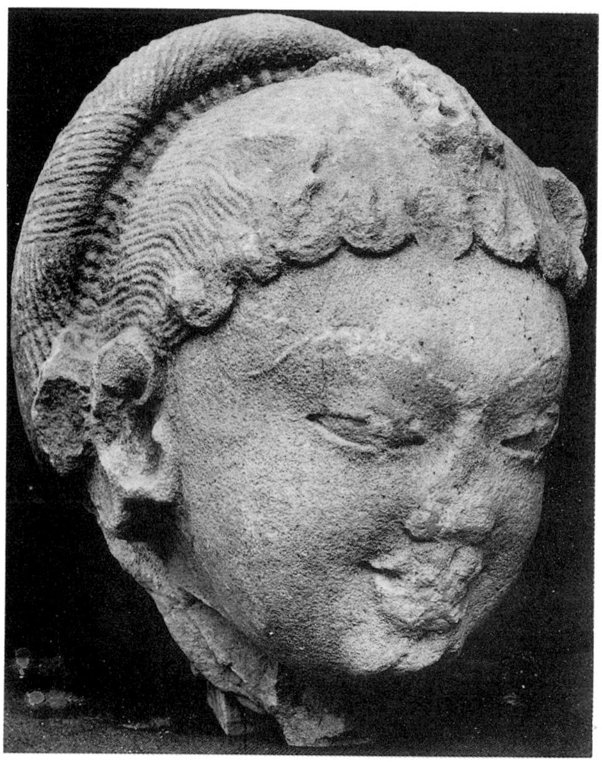

▼ 257A

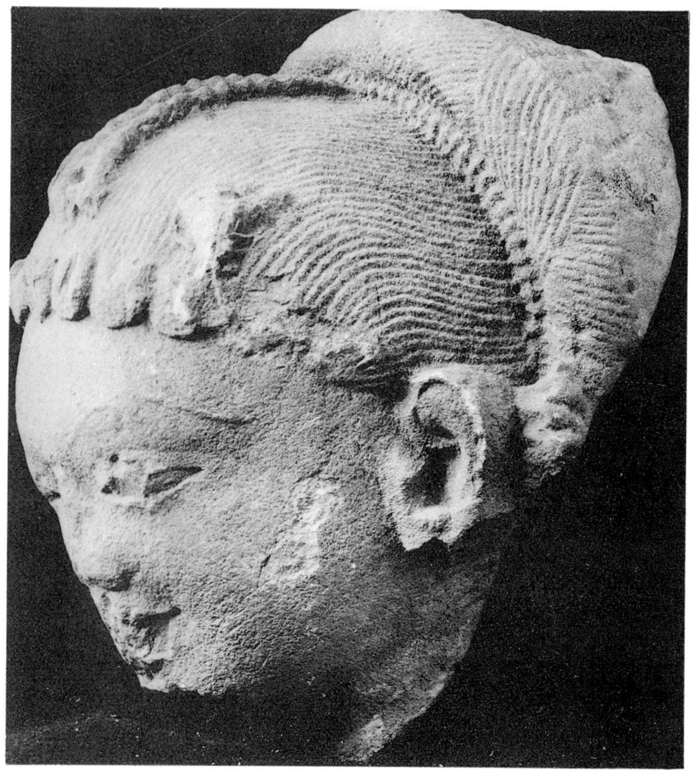

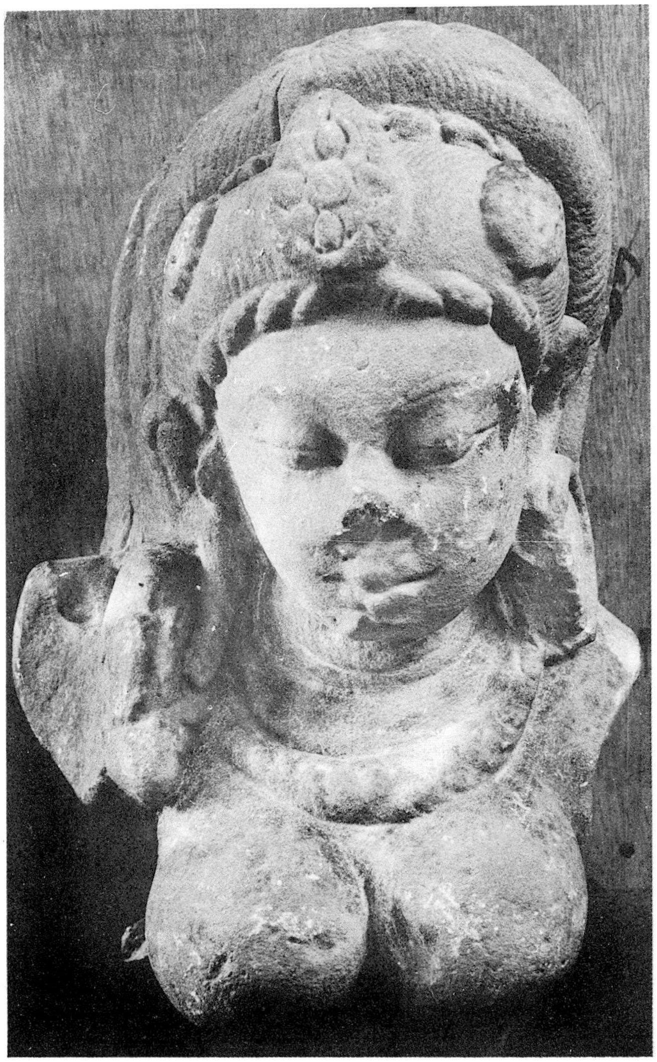

◀
261

▶
259

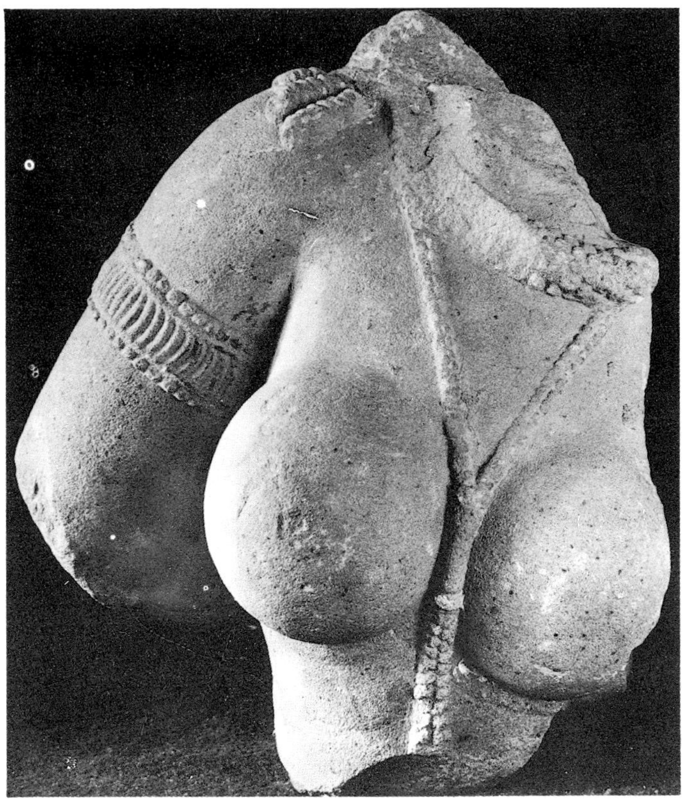

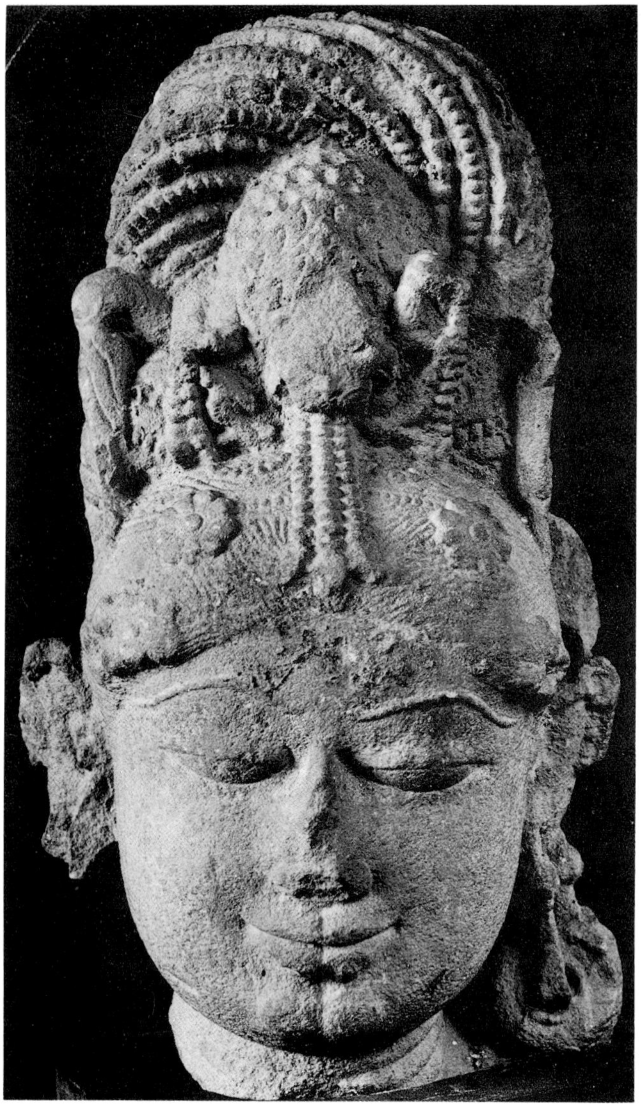

◀
262

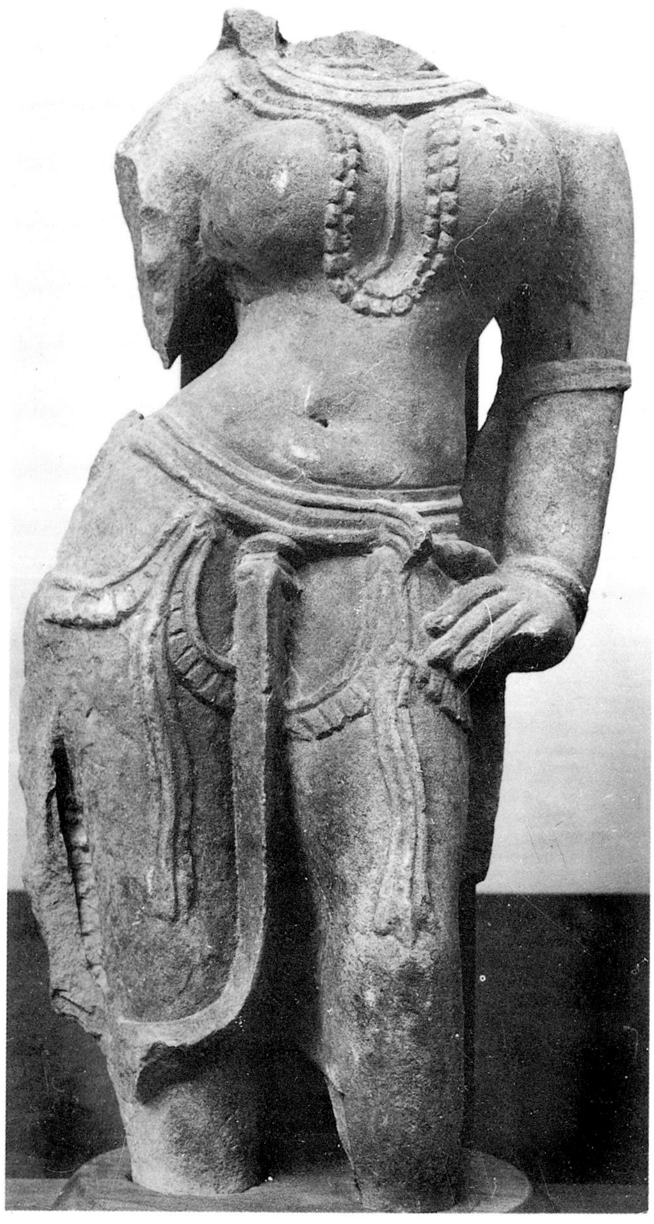

▶
265

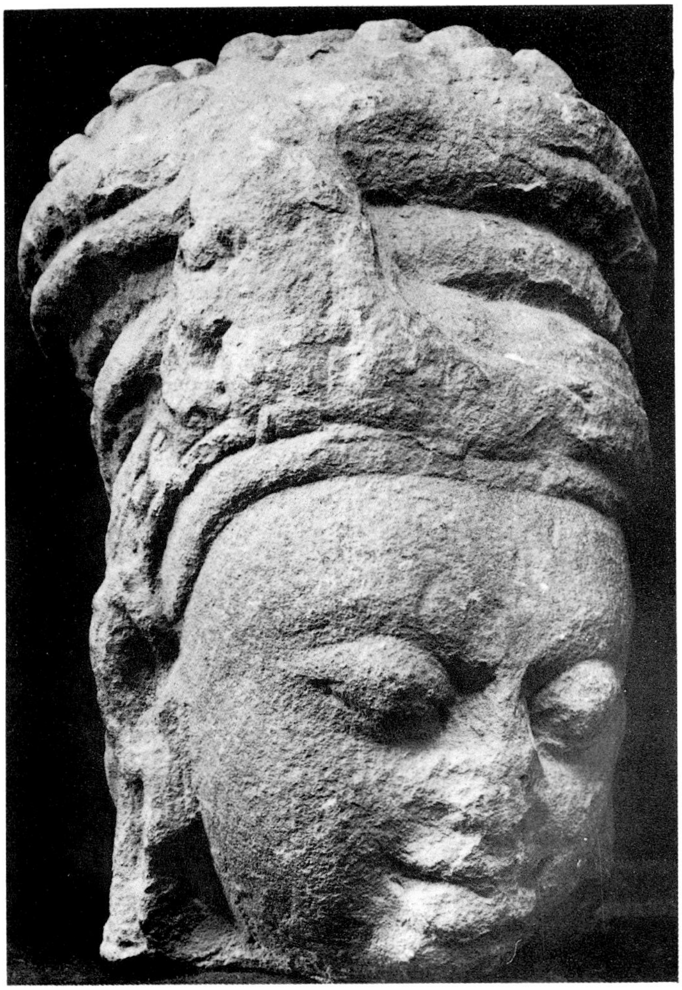

◀ 260

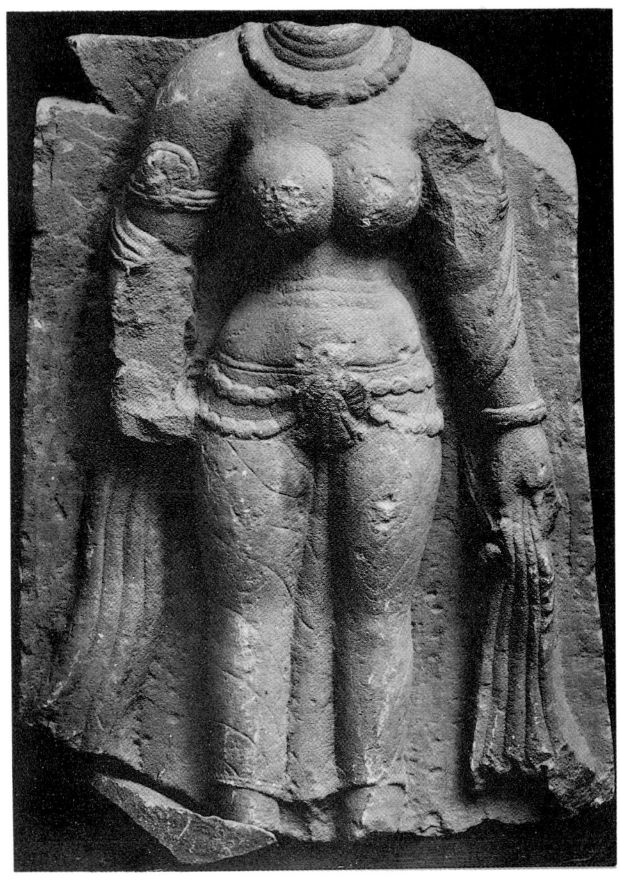

▶ 256

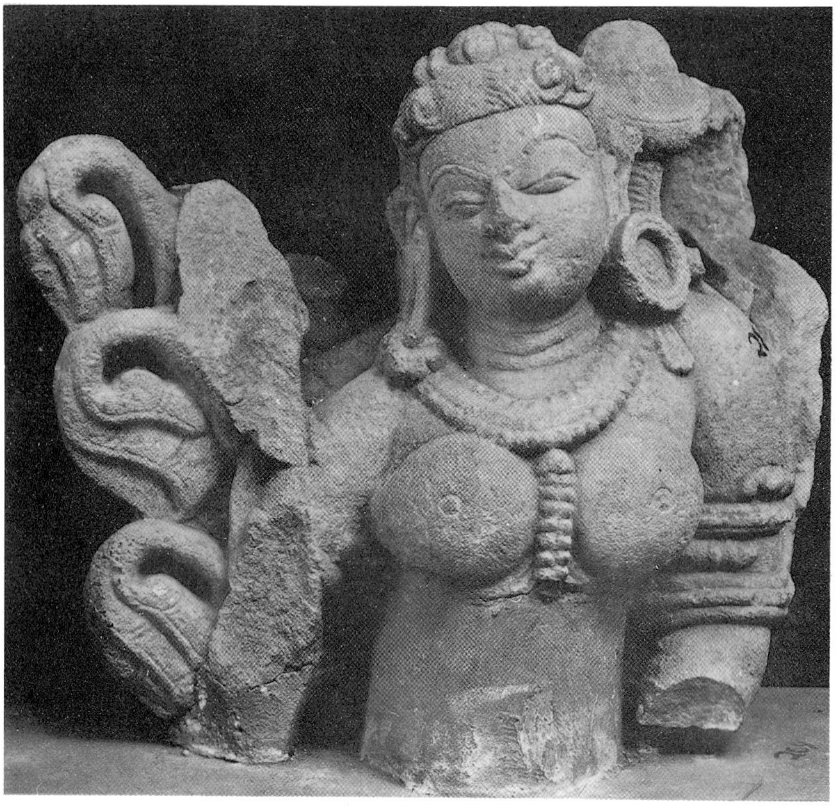

◀ 264

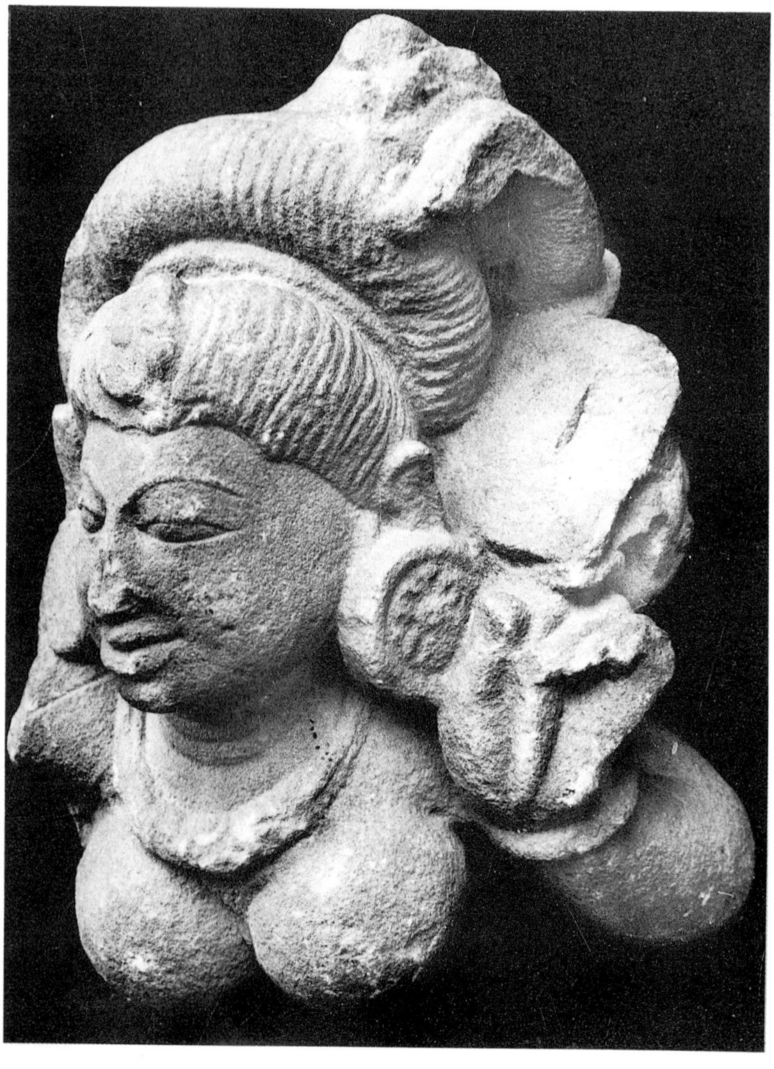

▶ 263

◄ 266

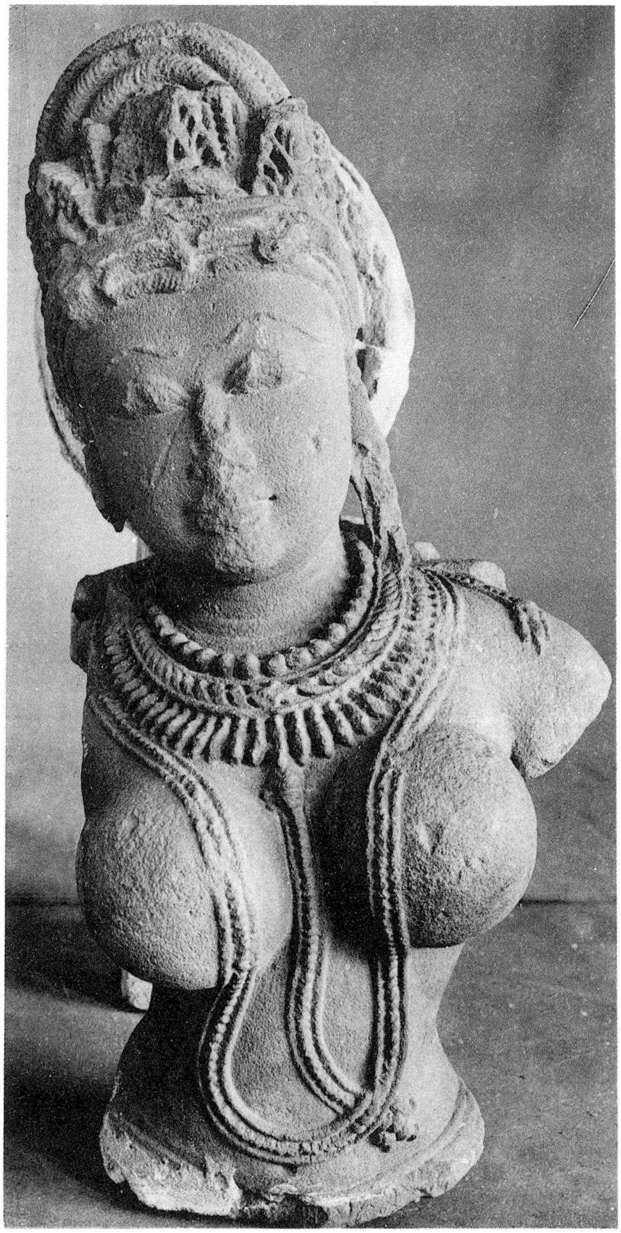

► 269

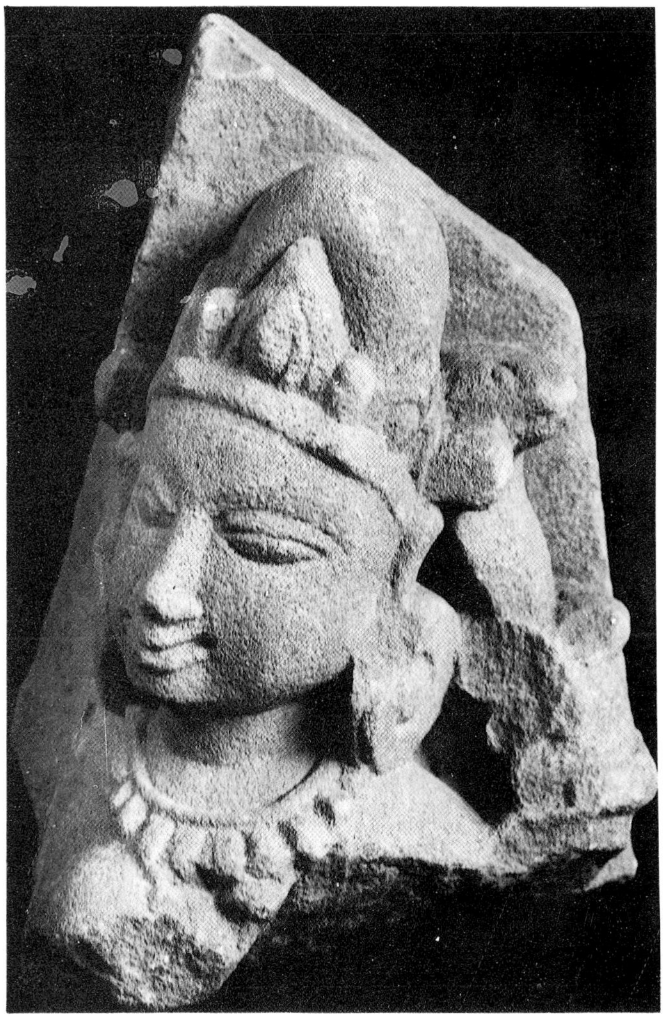

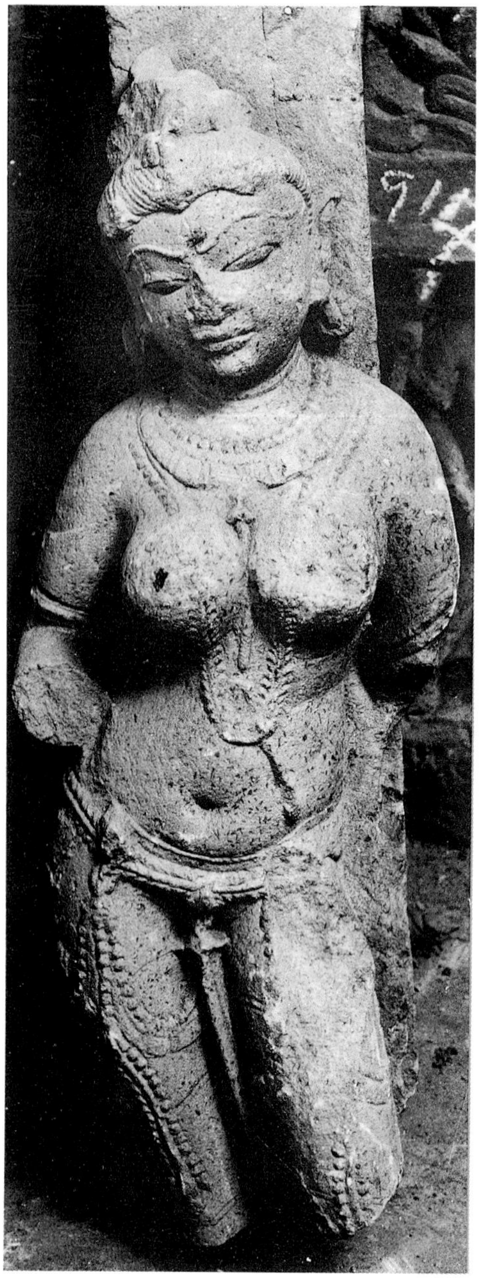

◀ 267

▼ 268

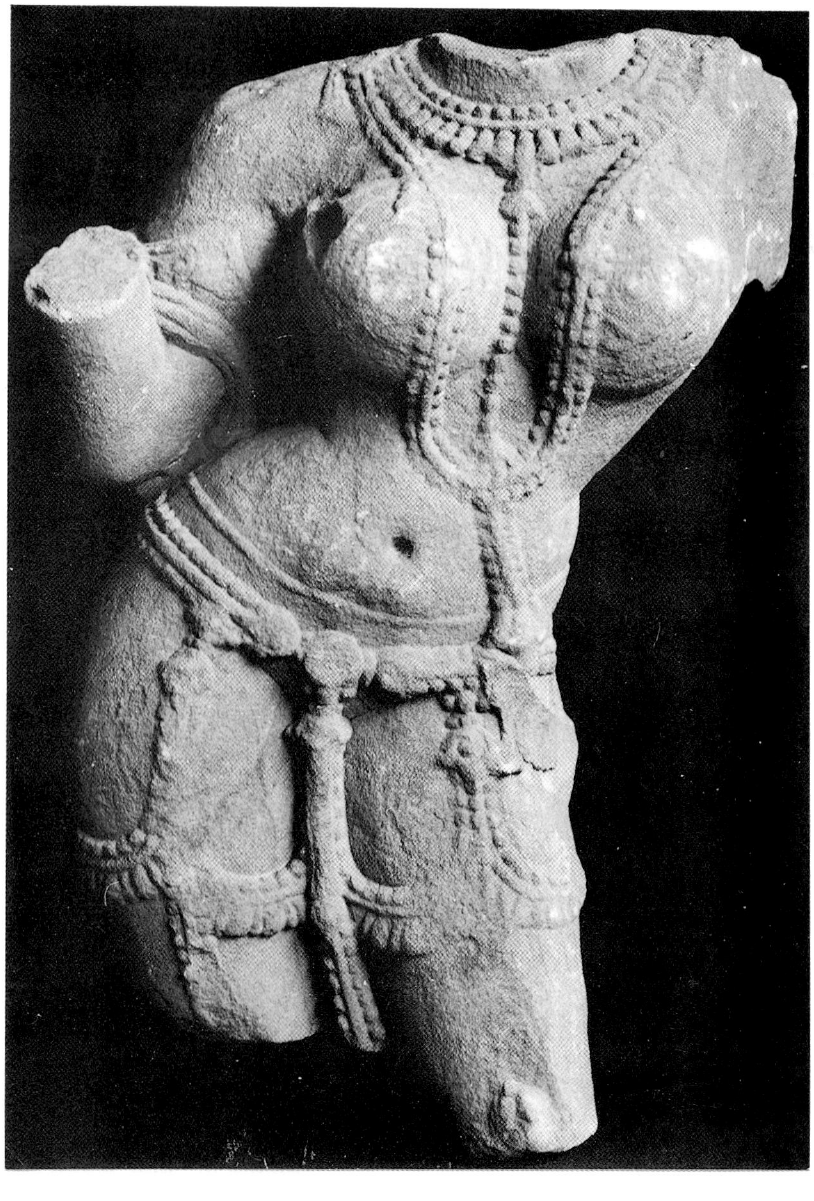

◀ 270

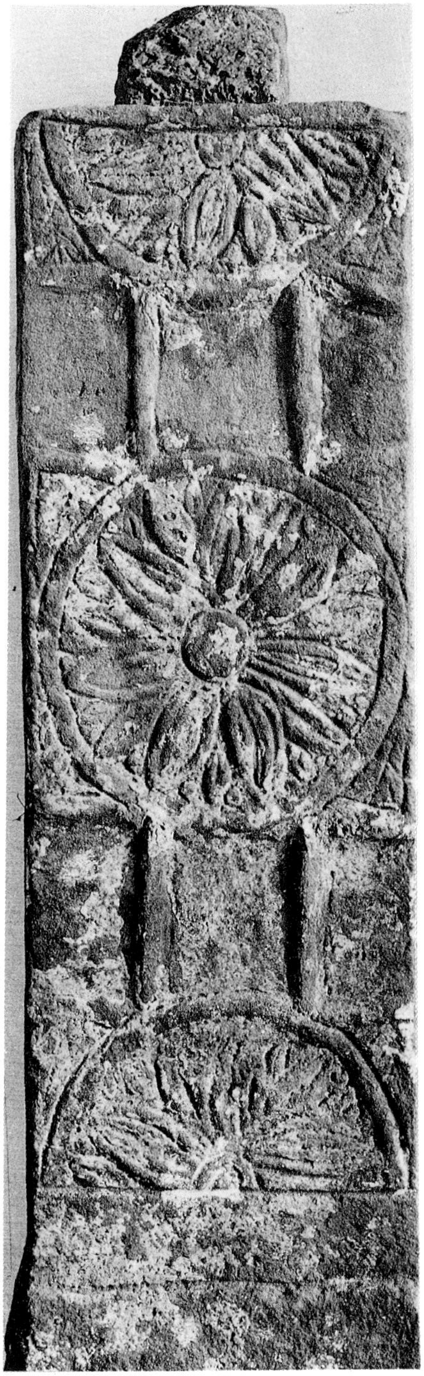

▼ 271

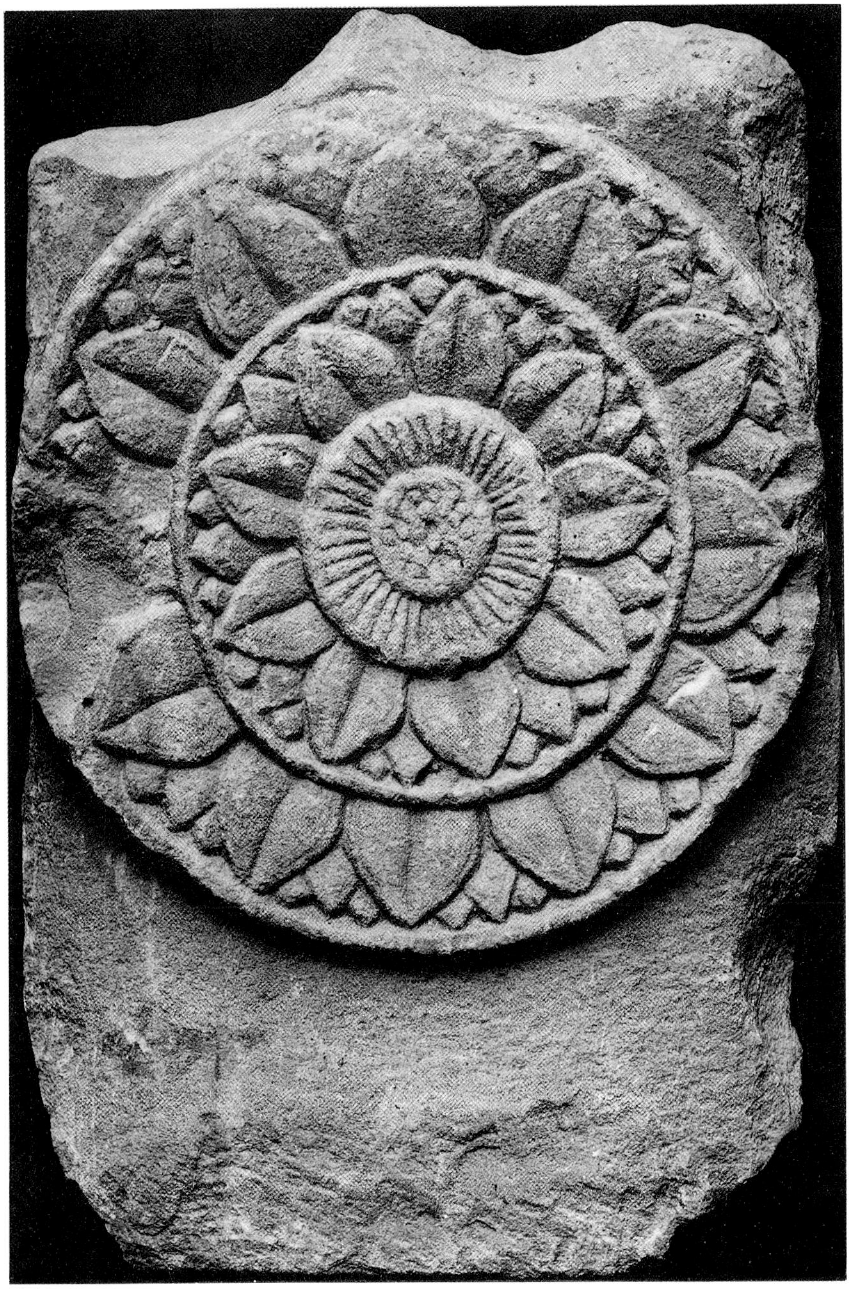

◀
272

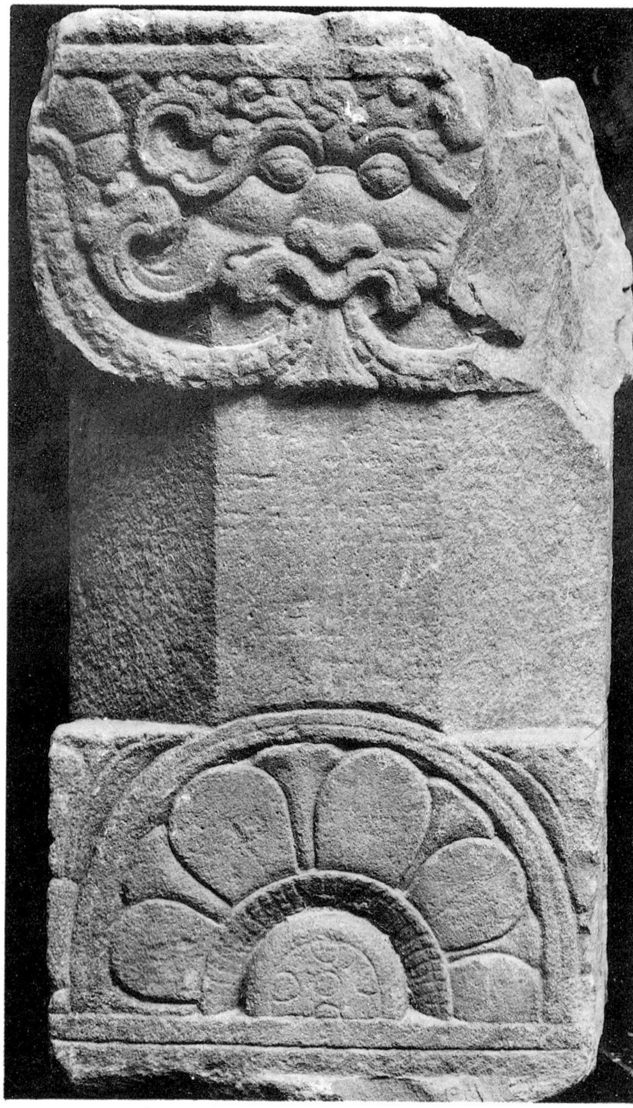

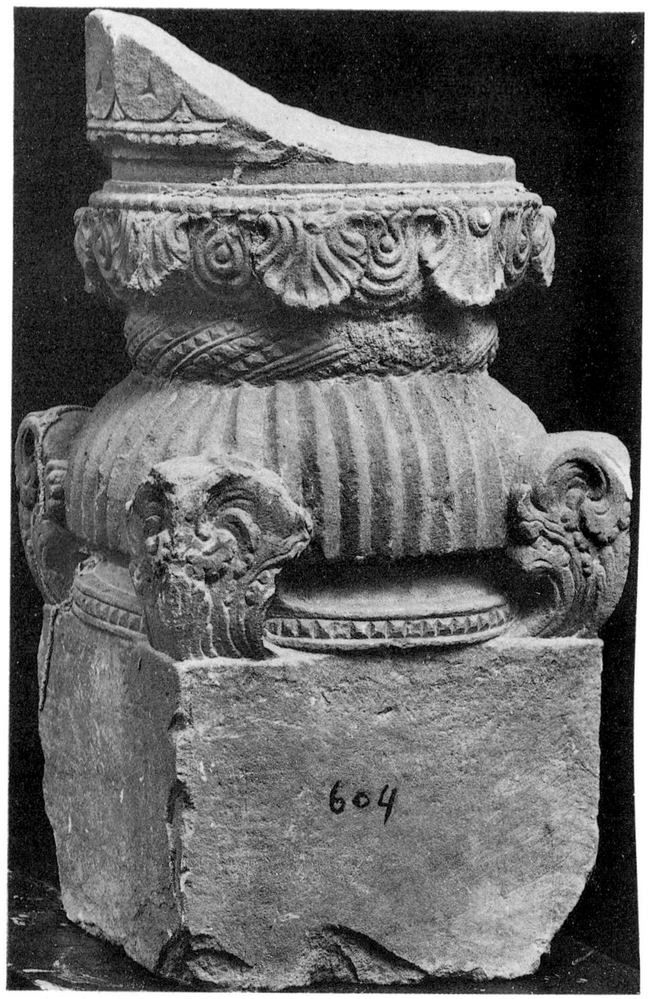

▶
273

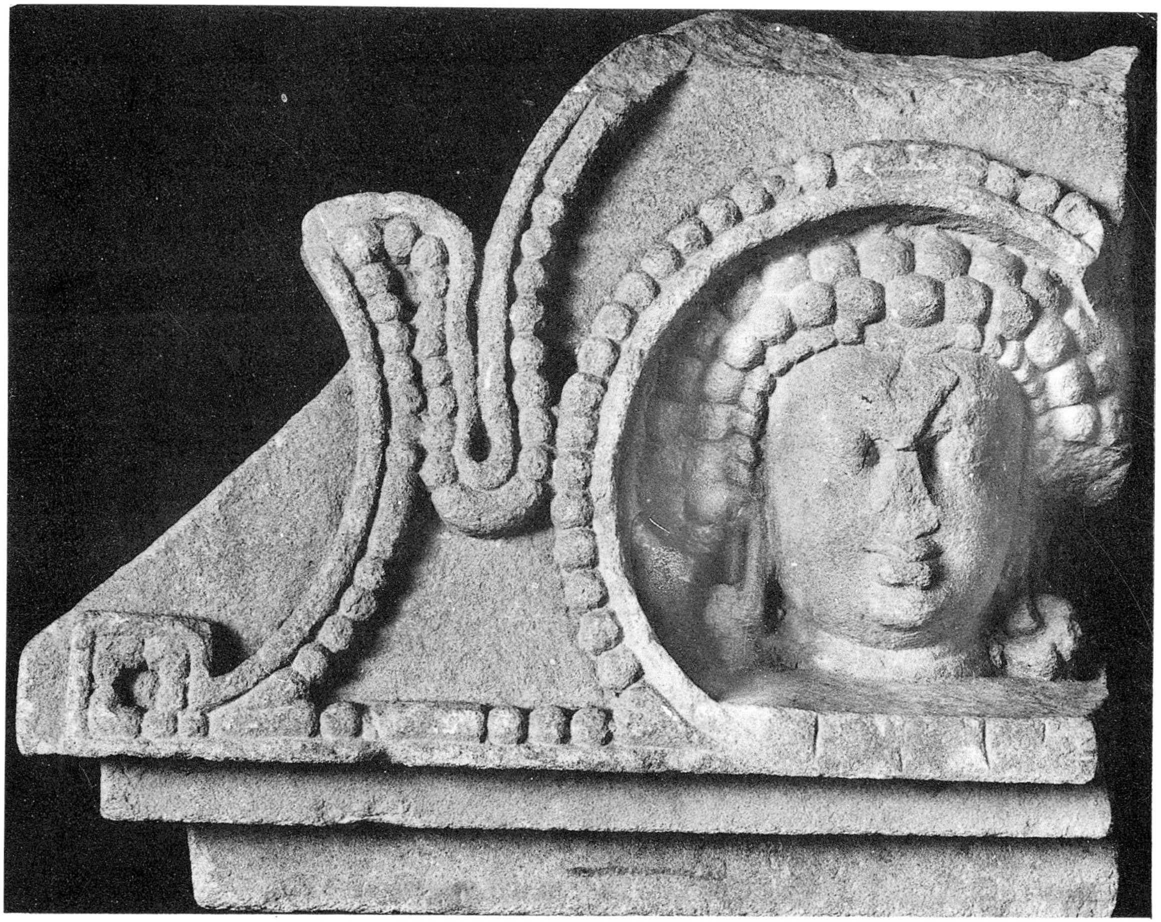

▲ 275

▼ 280

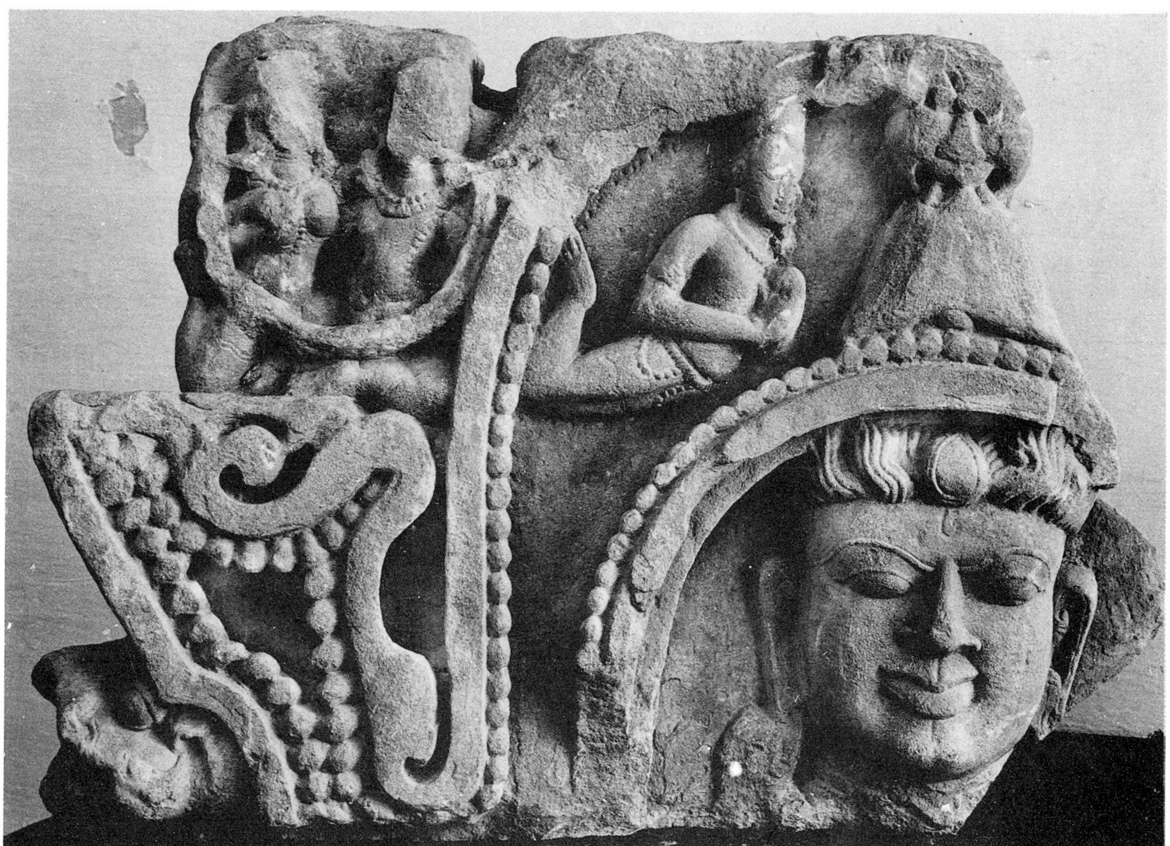

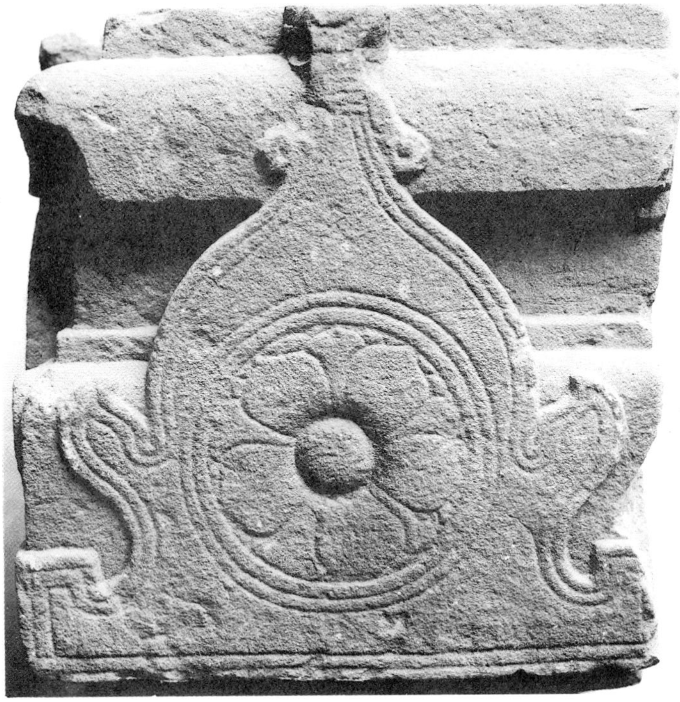

▲ 274

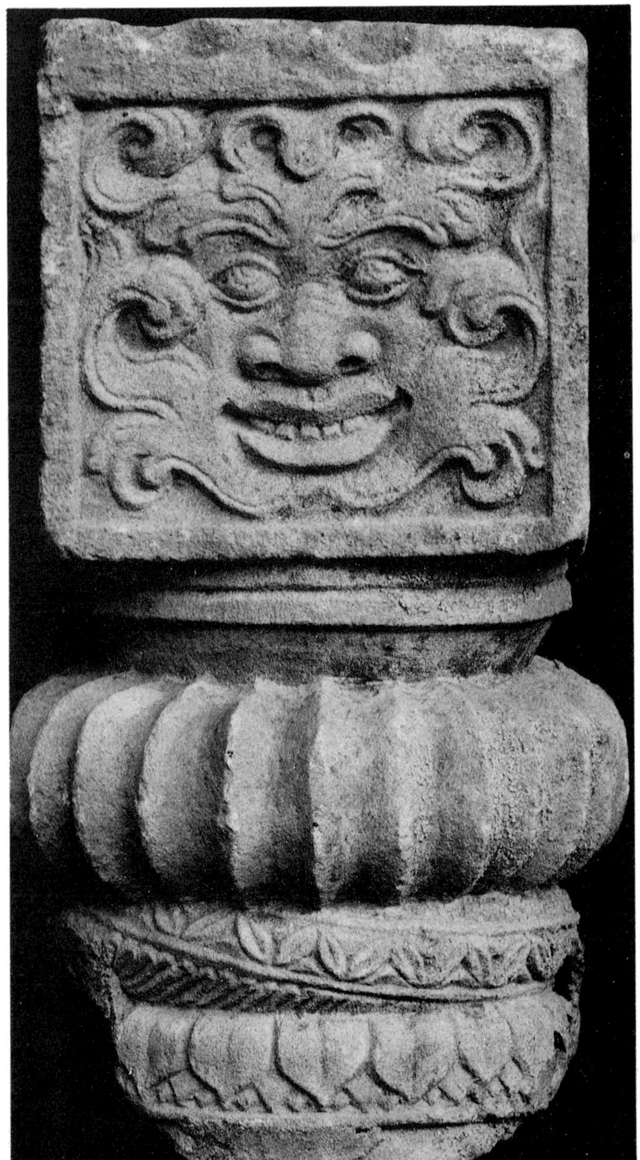

▶
279

▶ 276

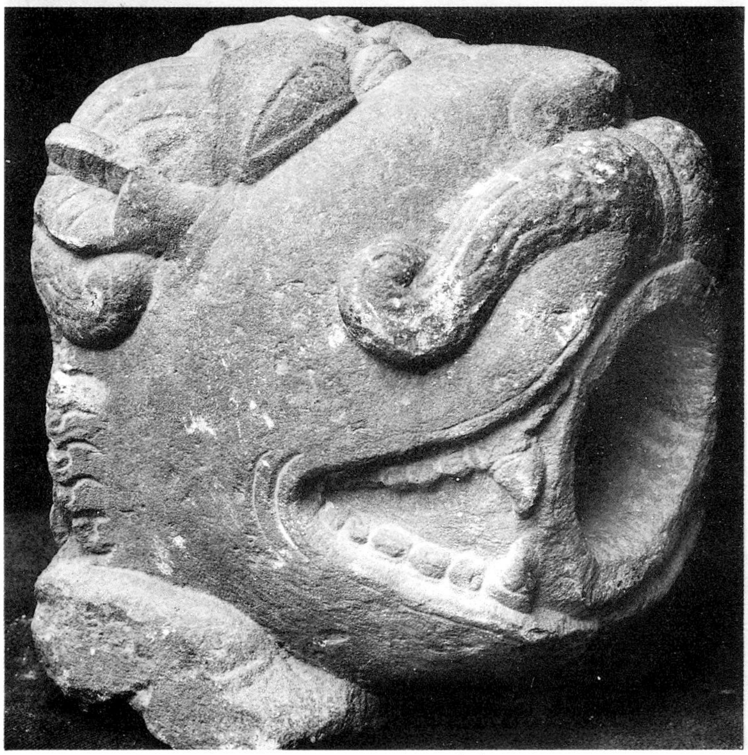

▼ 277

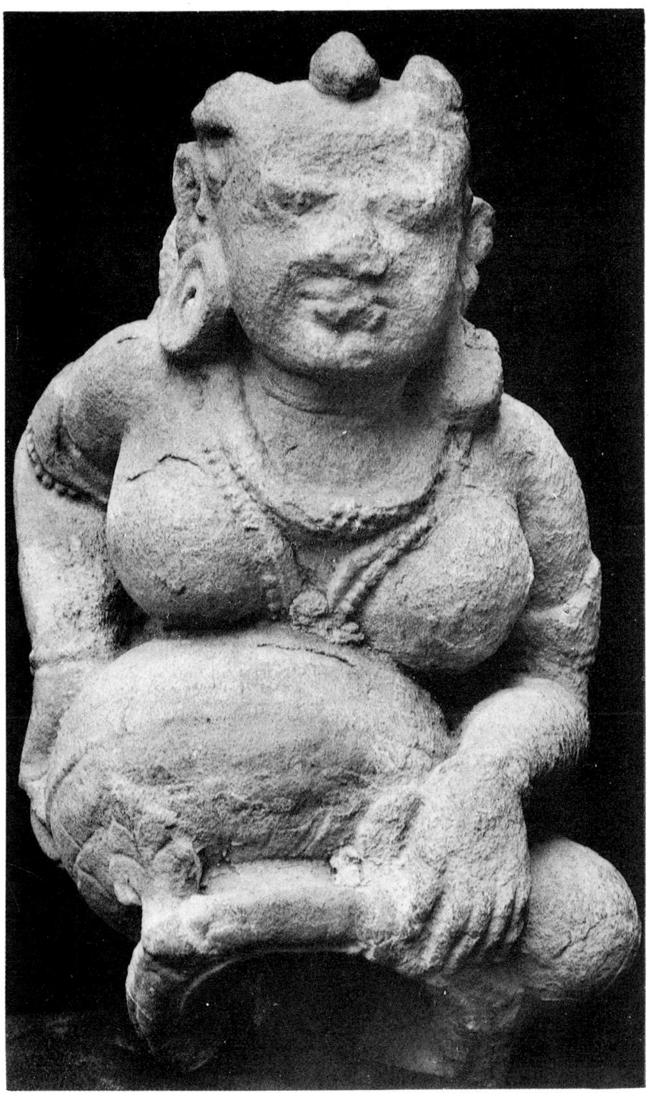

▼ 278

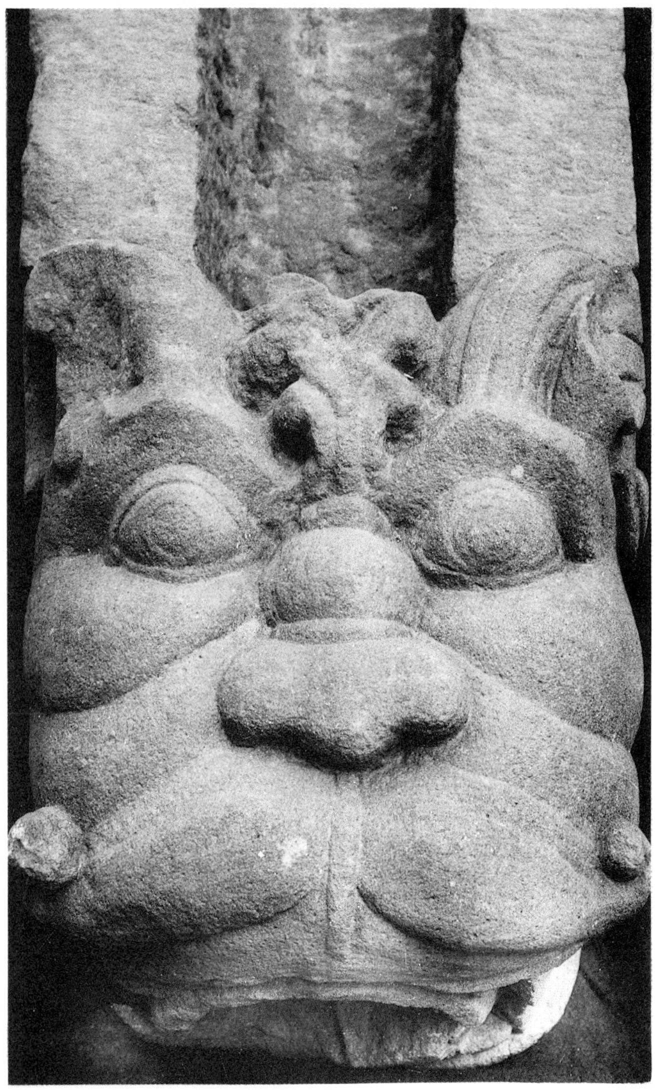

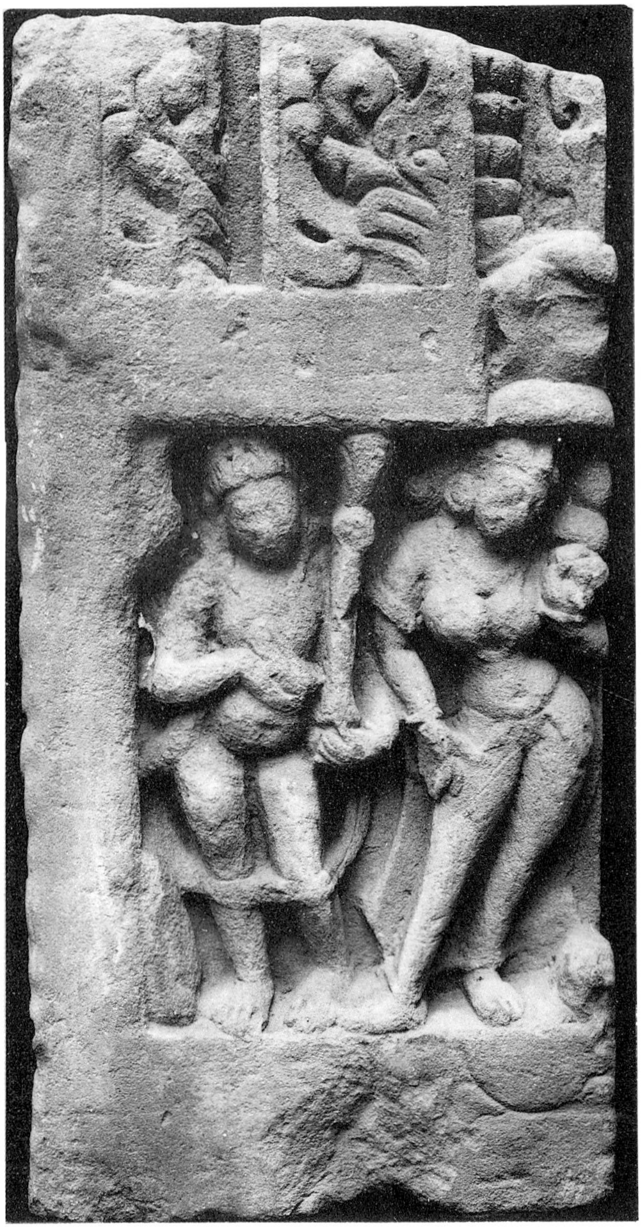

▲ 283

▼ 282

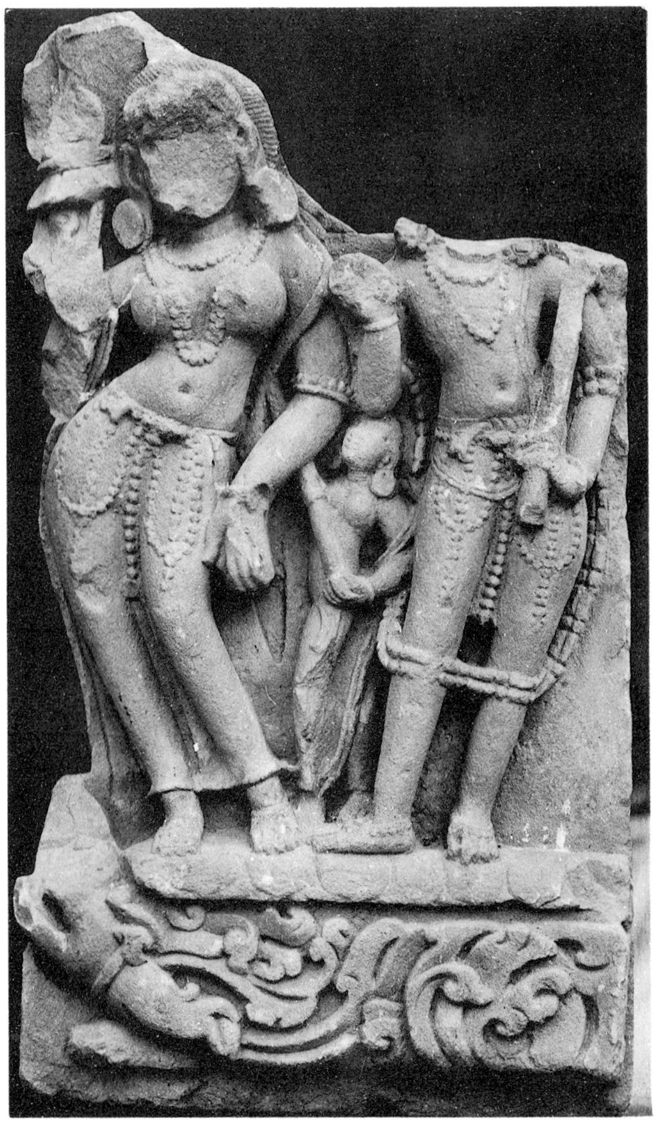

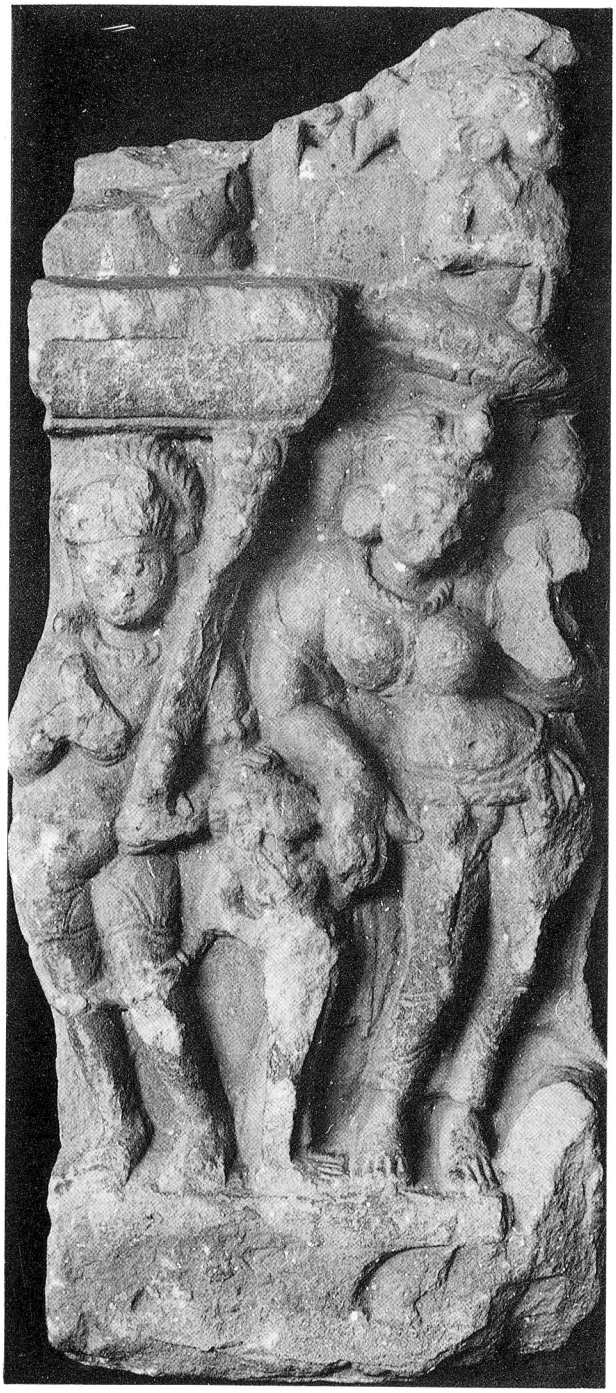

◀
281

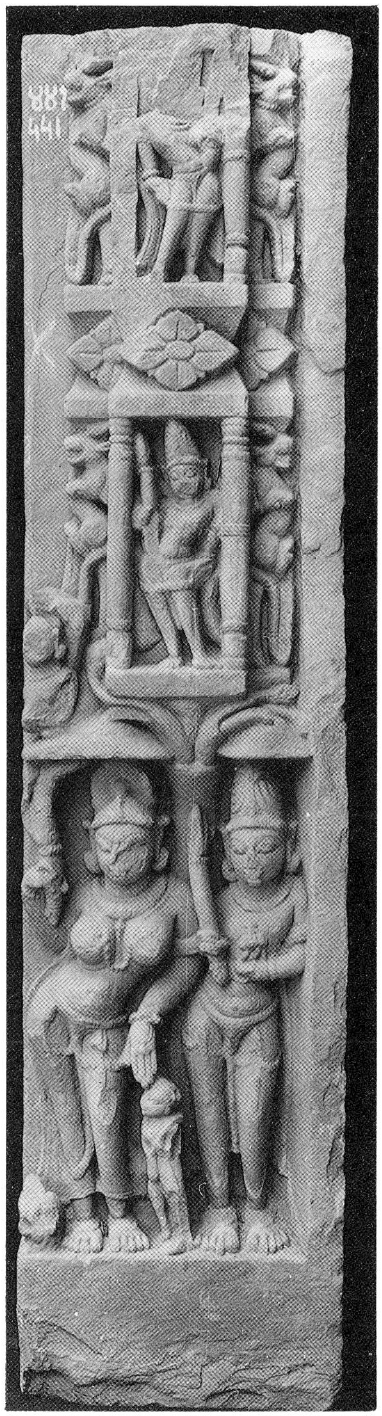

▶
284

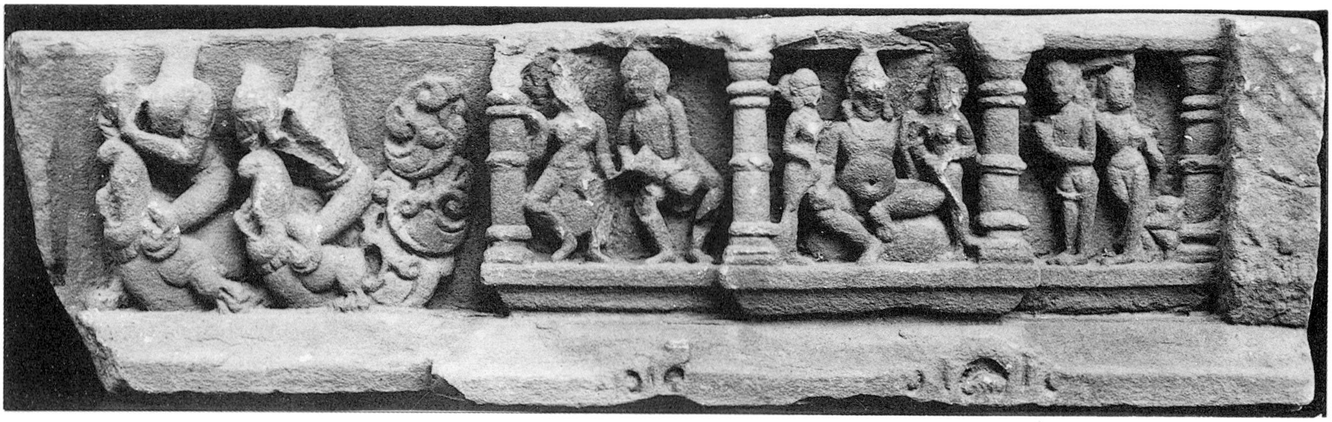

▲ 285

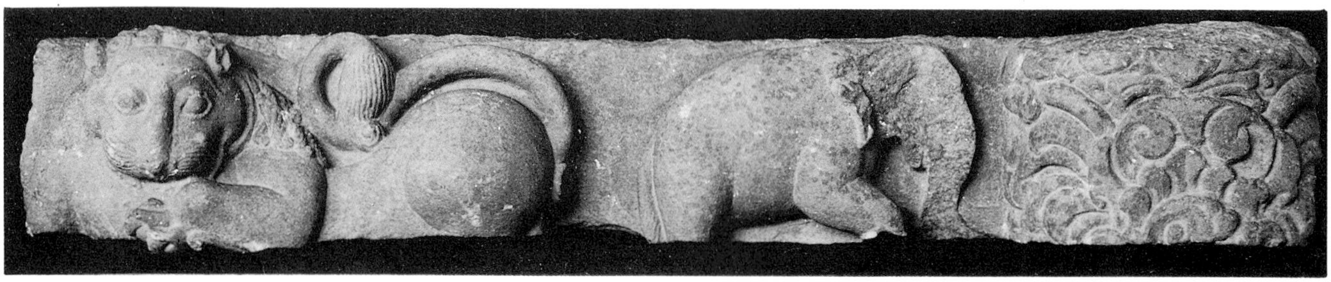

▲ 286

▼ 287

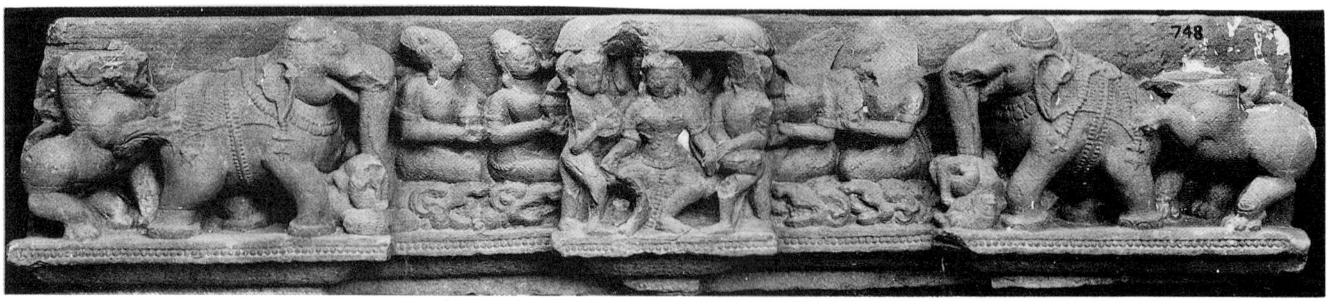

▼ 288

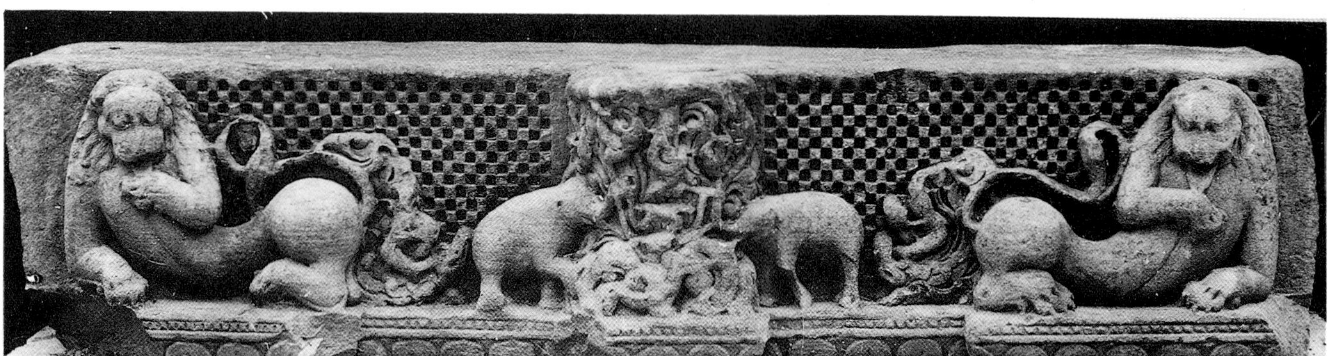

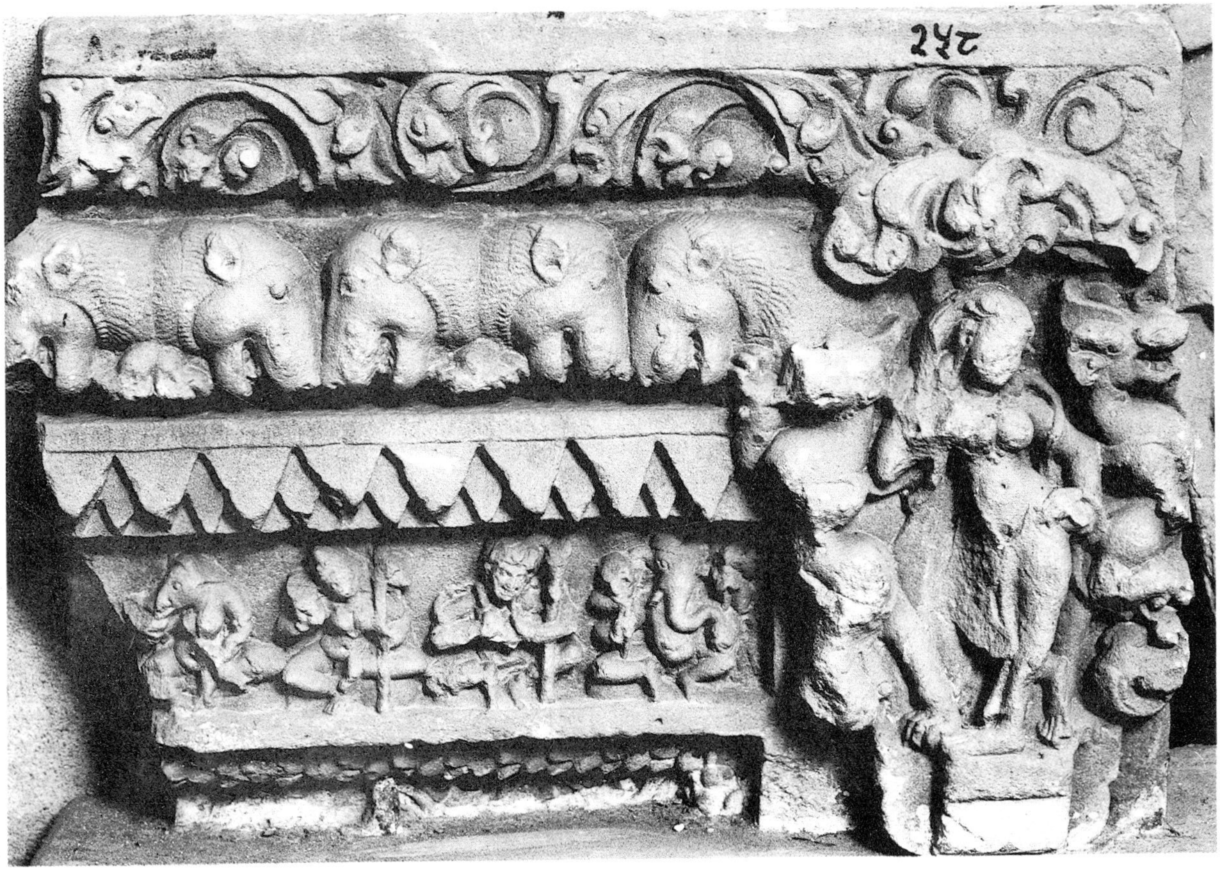

▲ 289

▼ 291

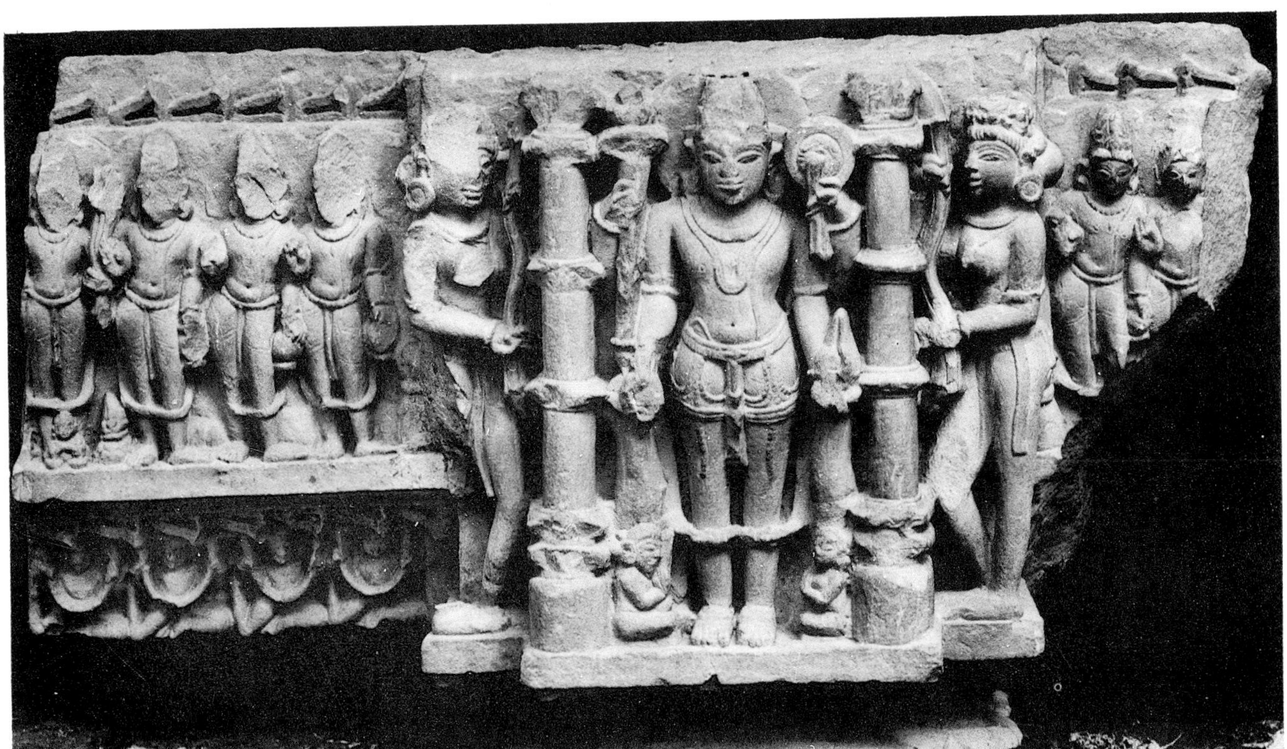

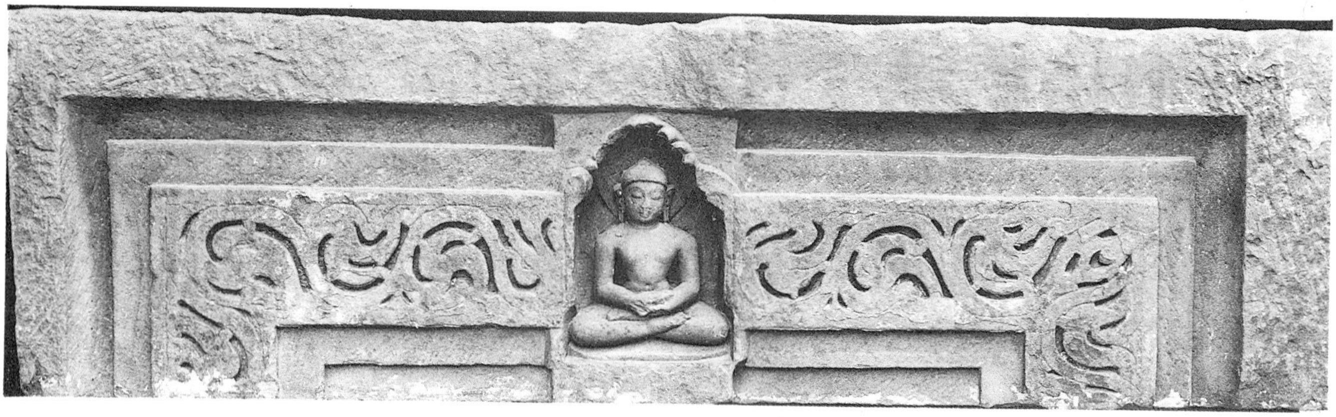

▲ 293

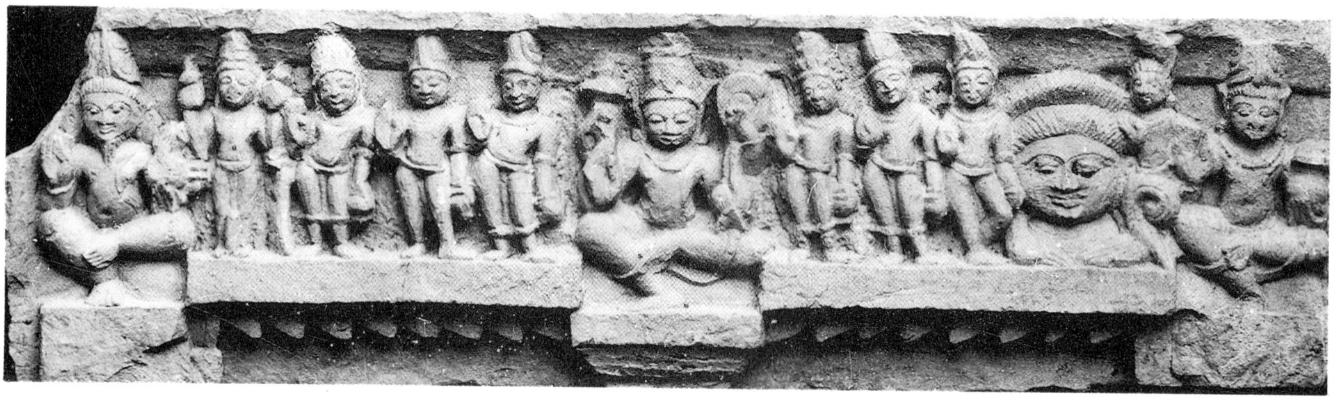

▲ 292

▼ 290

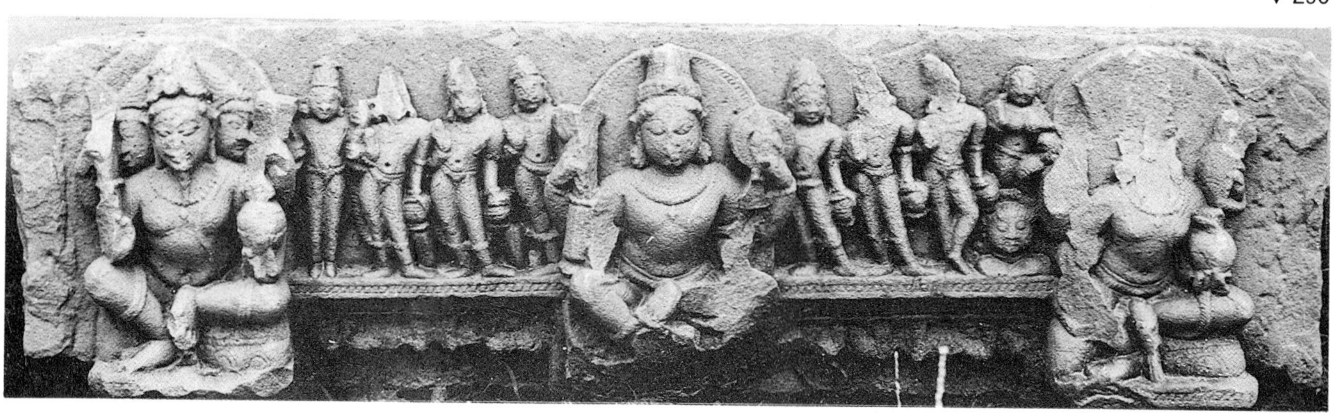

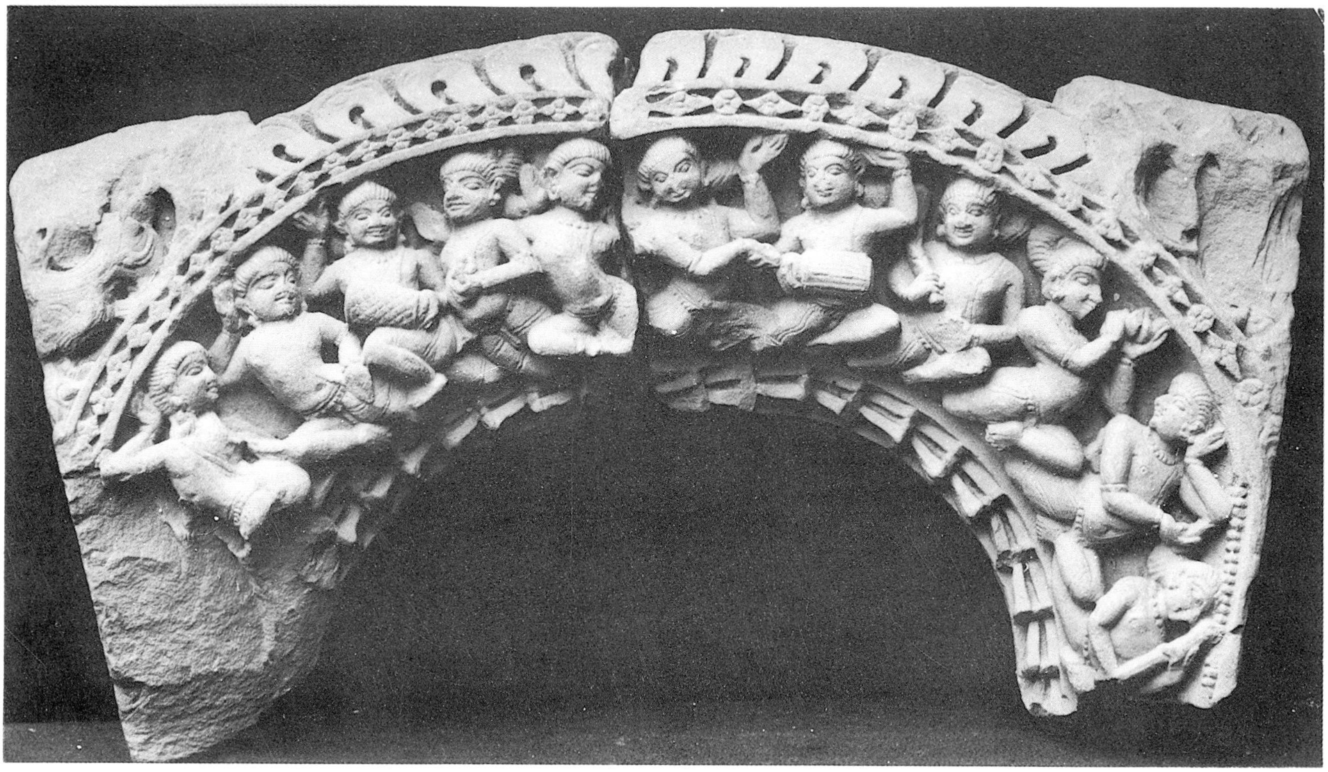

▲ 295

▼ 294

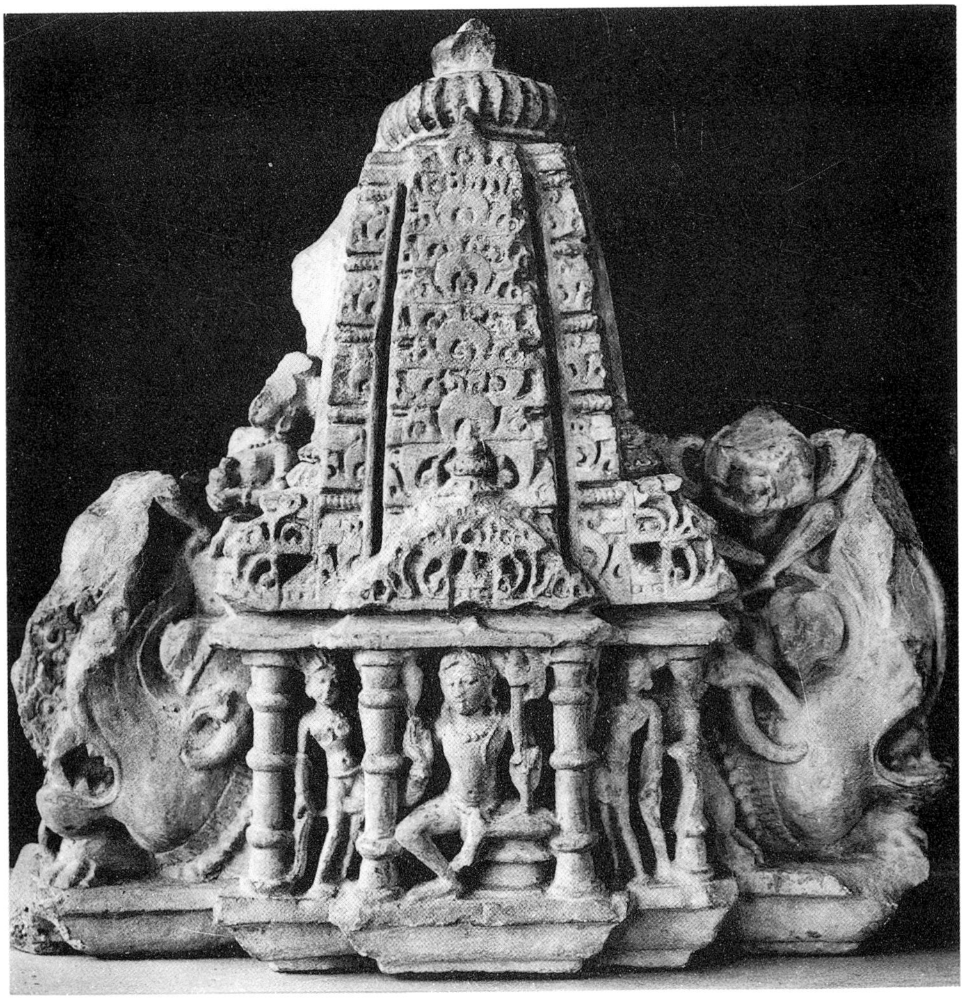

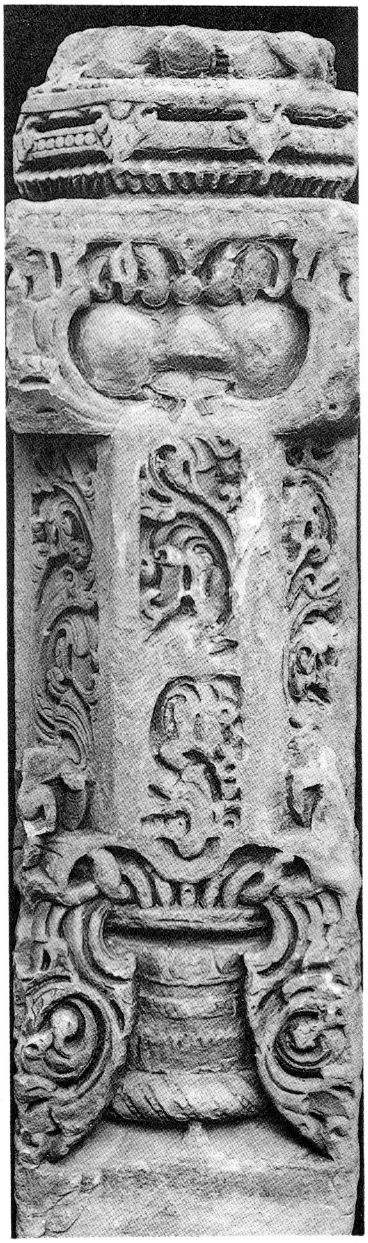

◀ 296

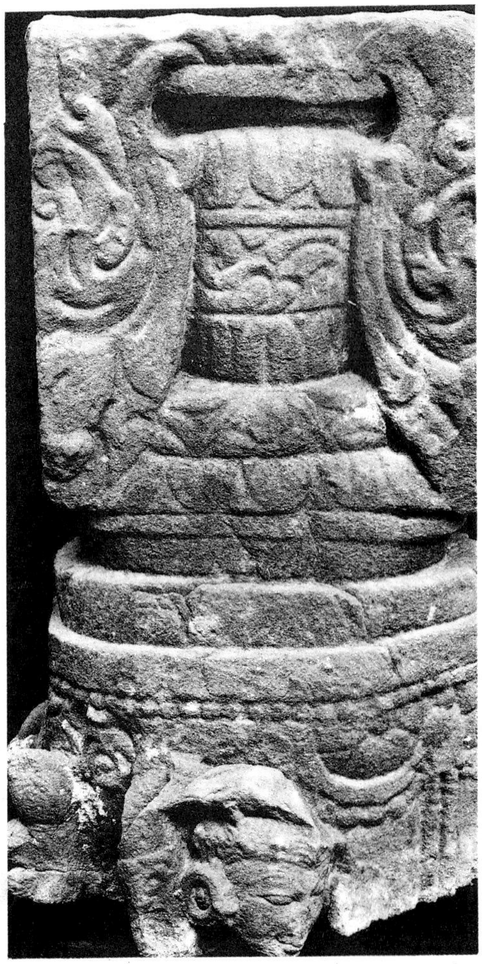

◀ 297

▼ 298

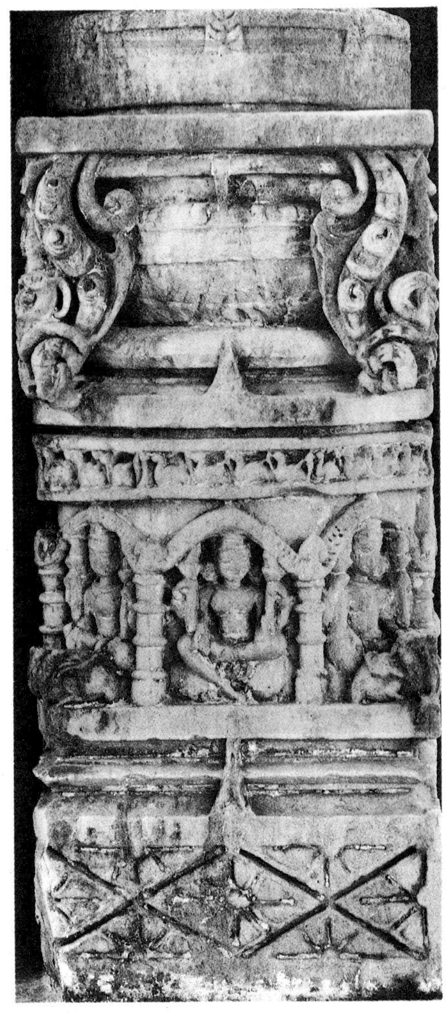

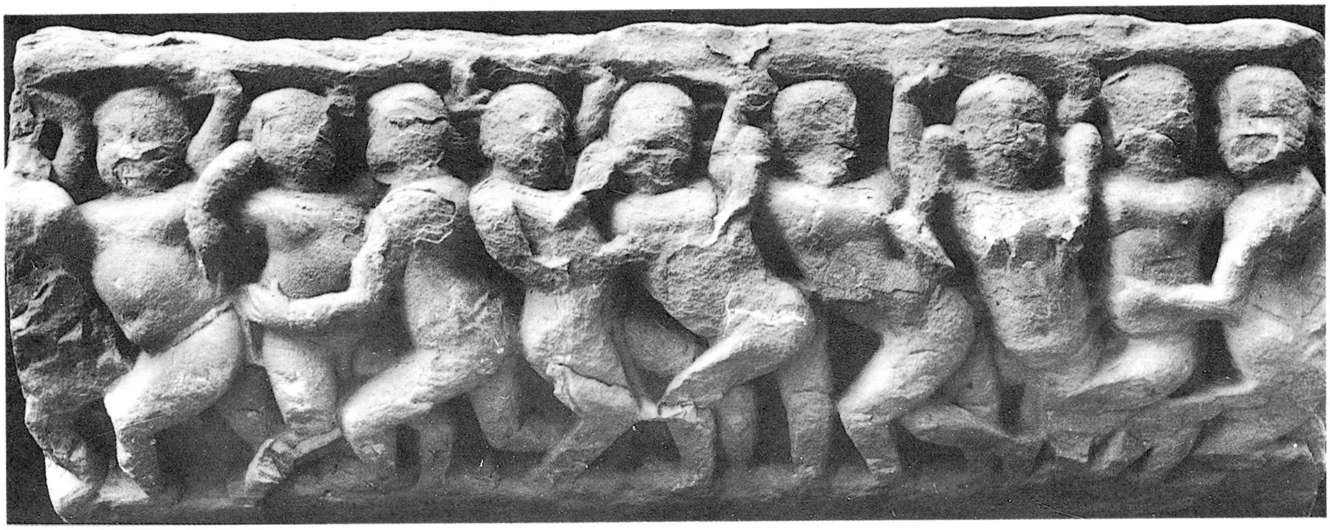

▲ 299

▼ 300

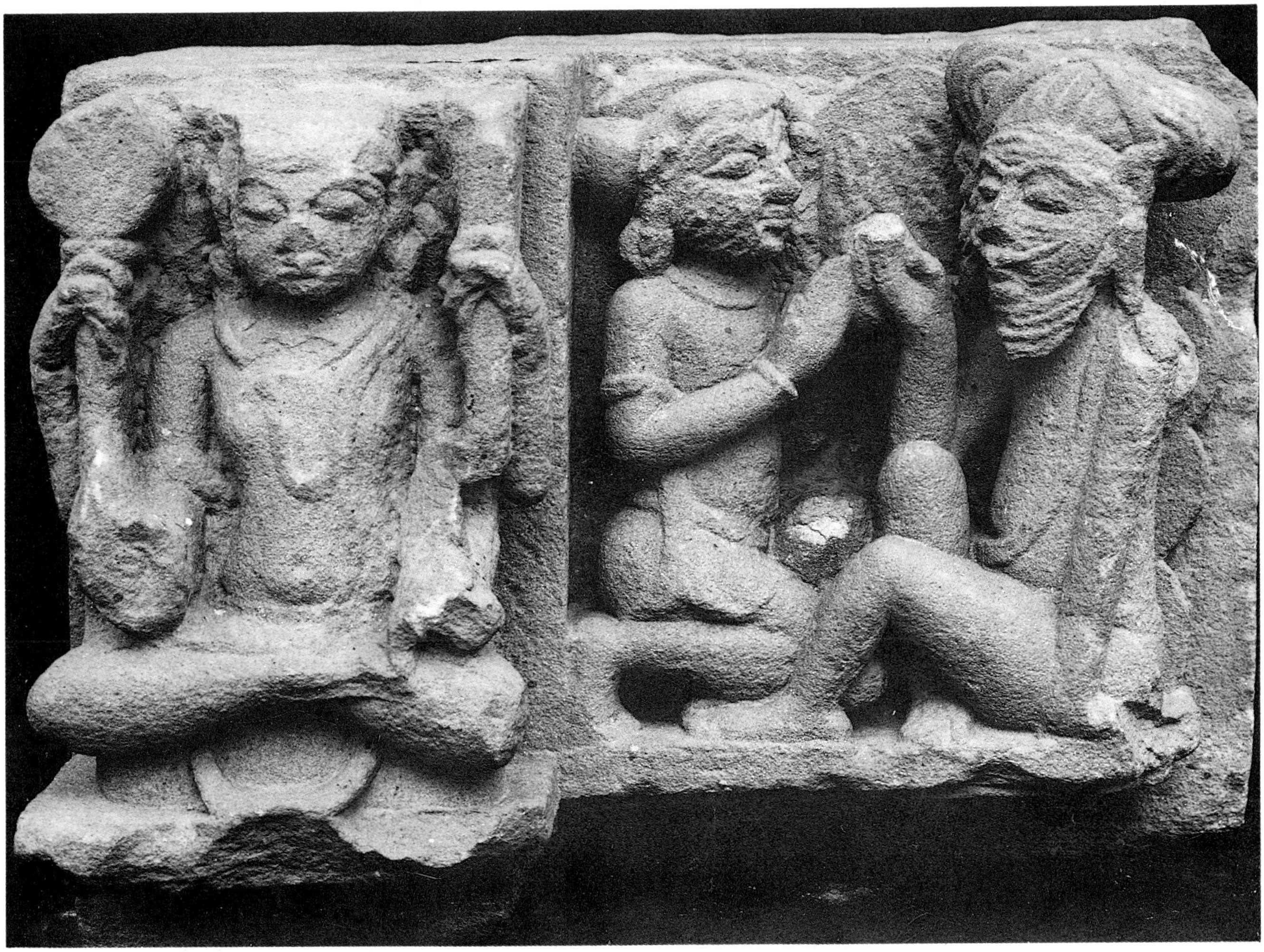

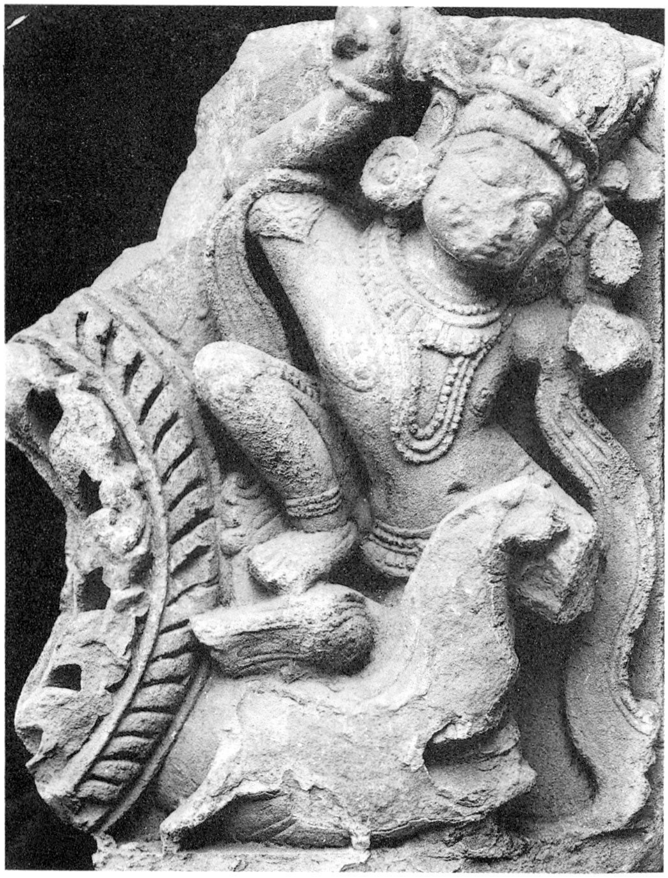

◀ 301

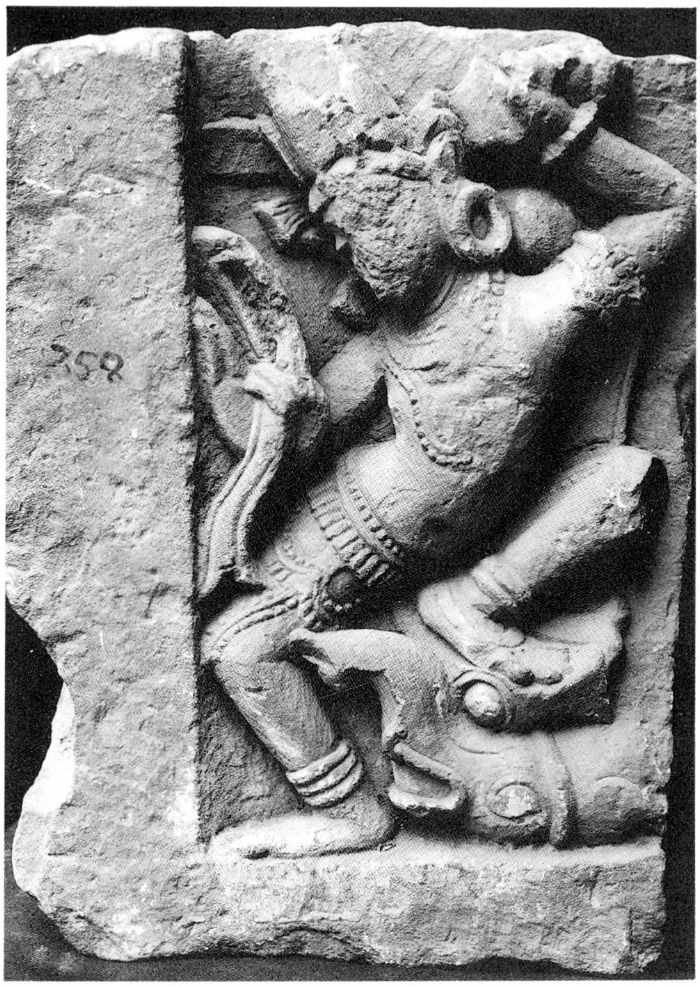

▶ 302

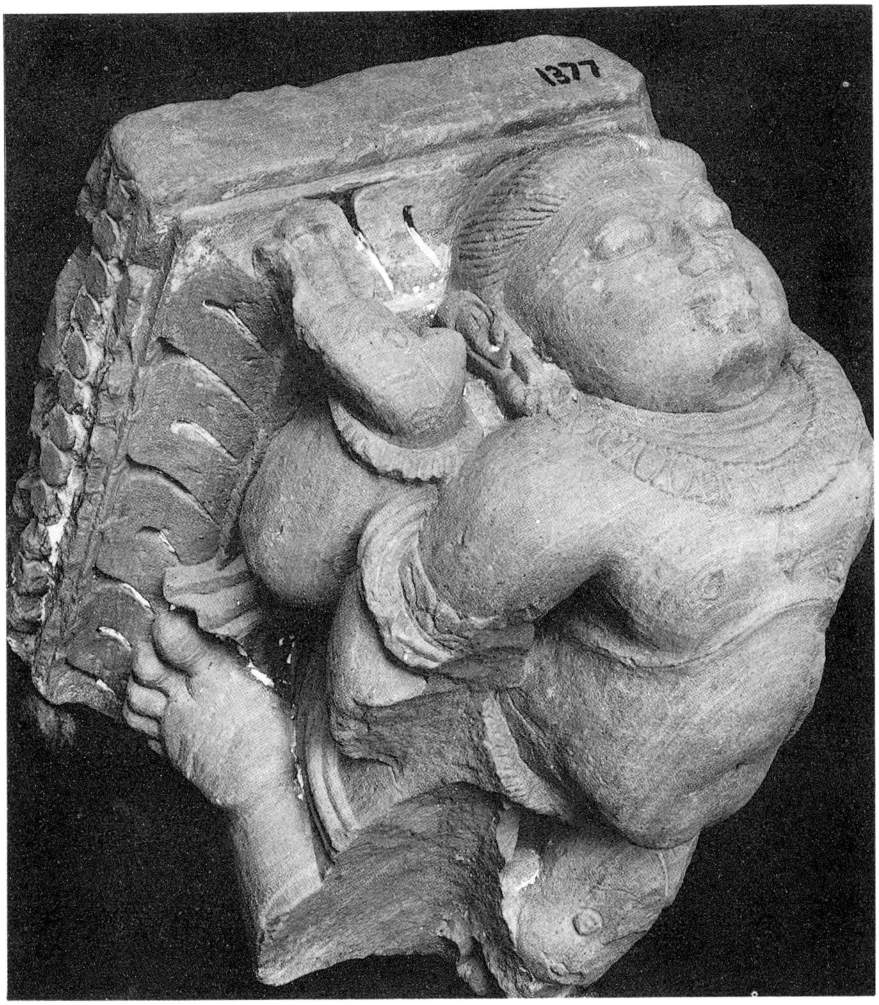

◄ 303

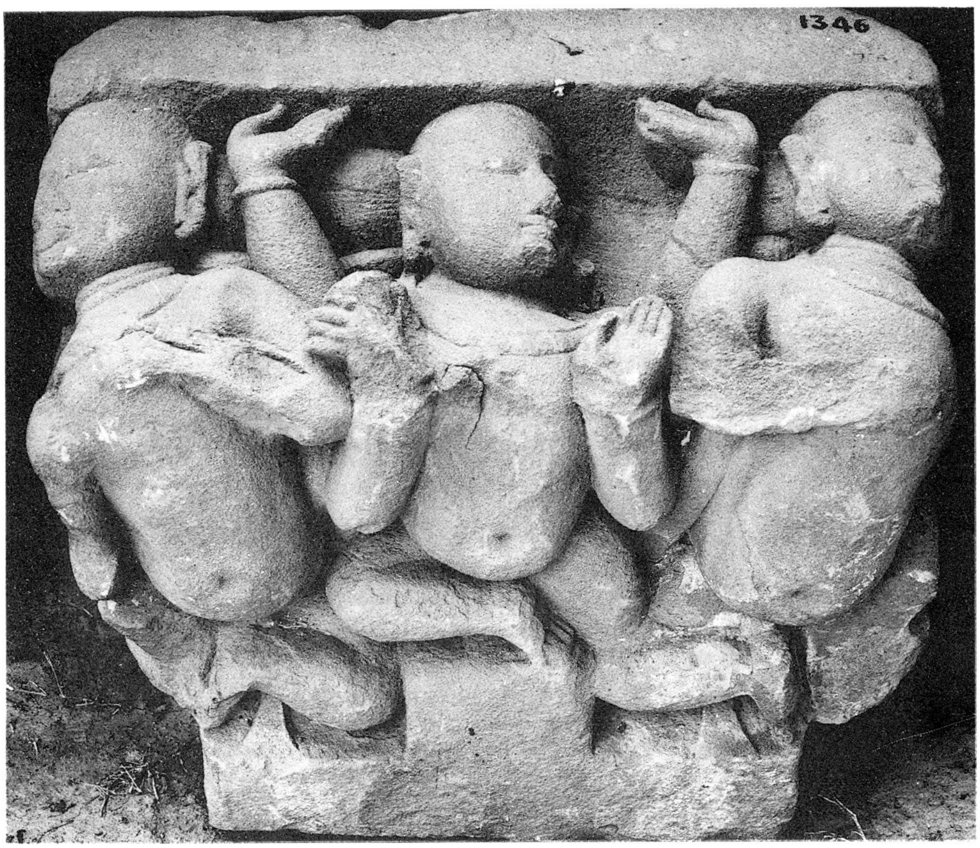

◄ 304

305A

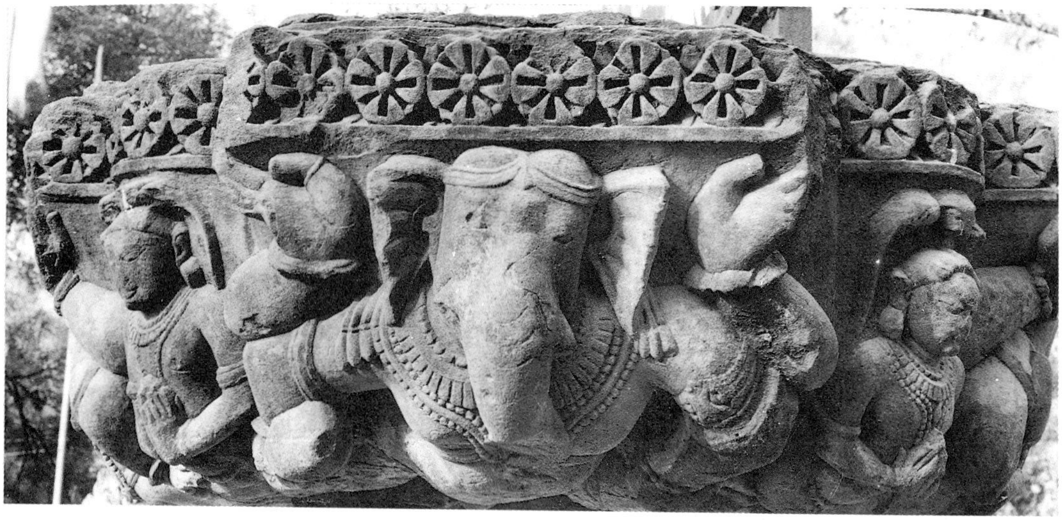

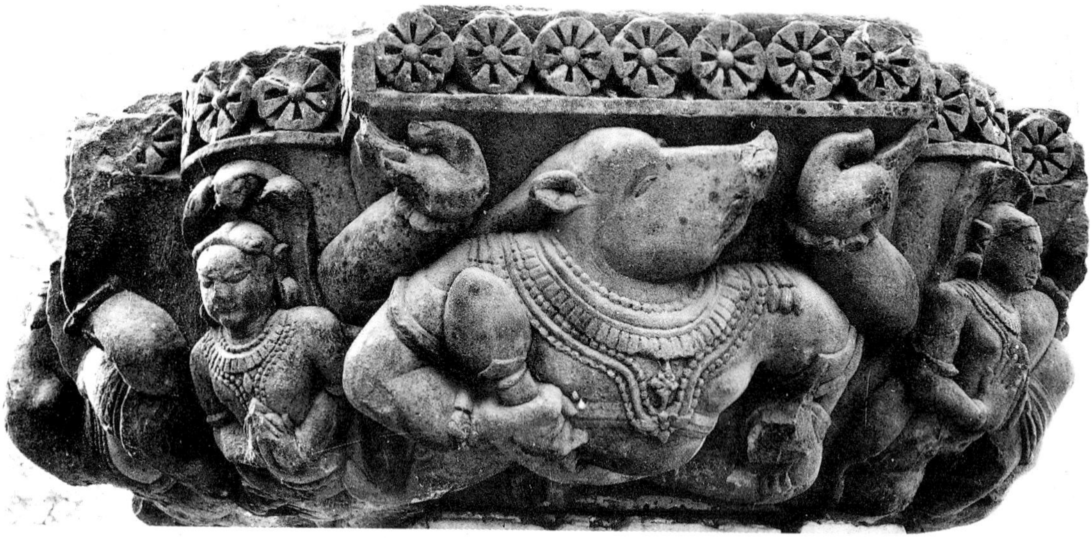

305B

305C

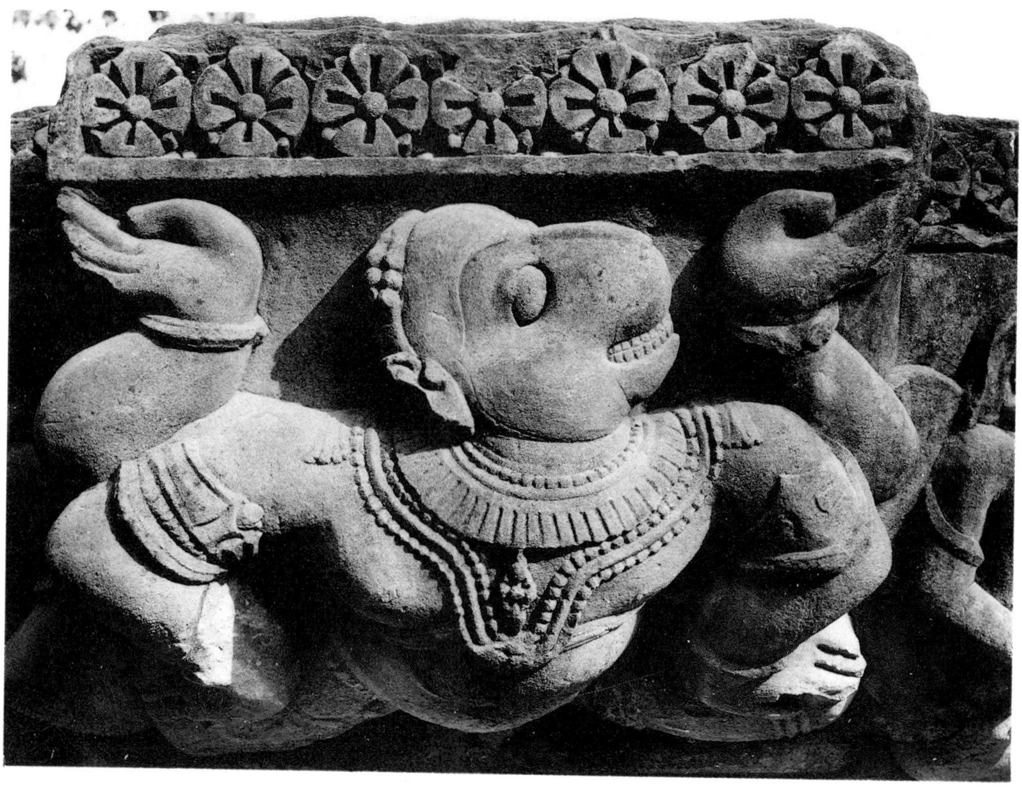

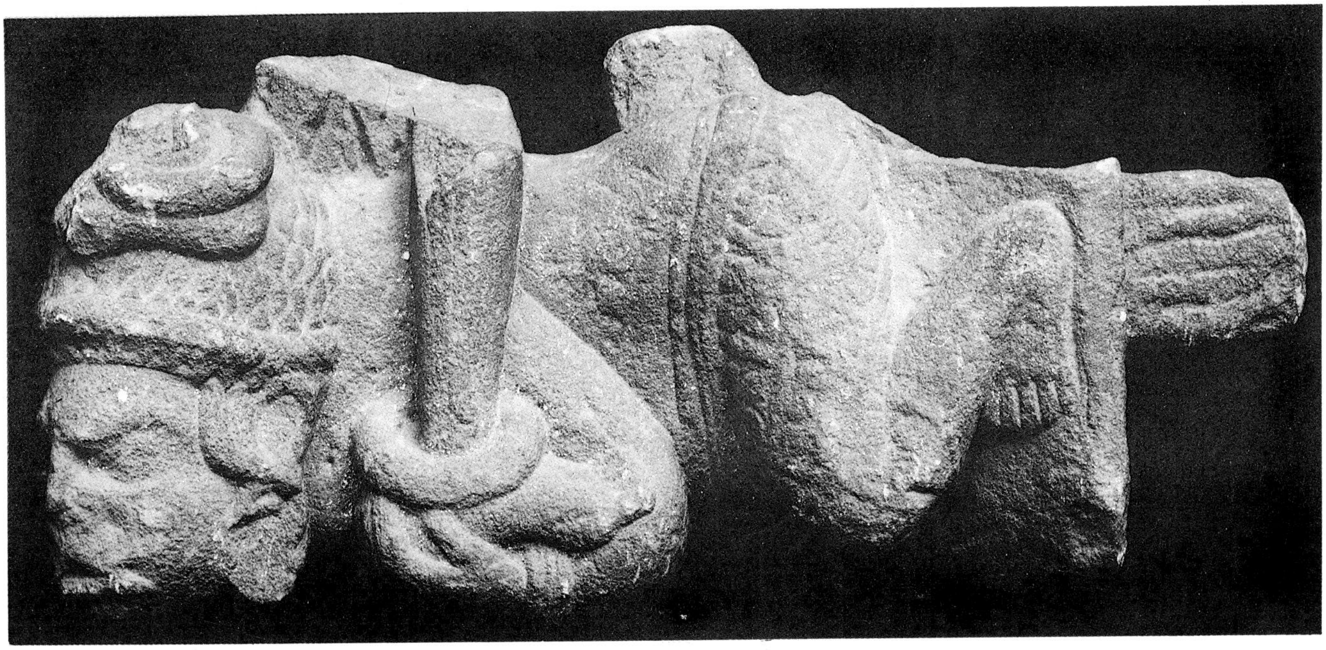

▲ 306

▼ 307

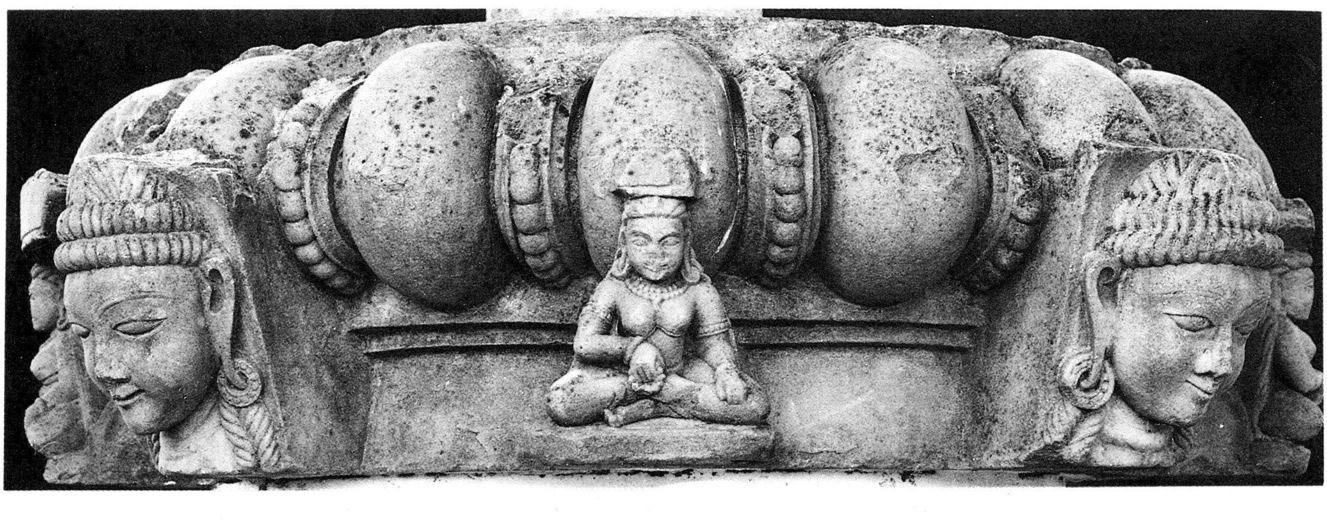

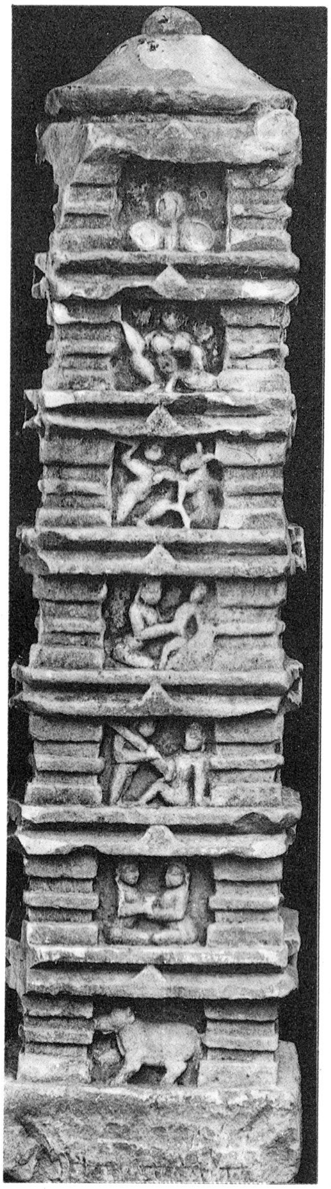

308A

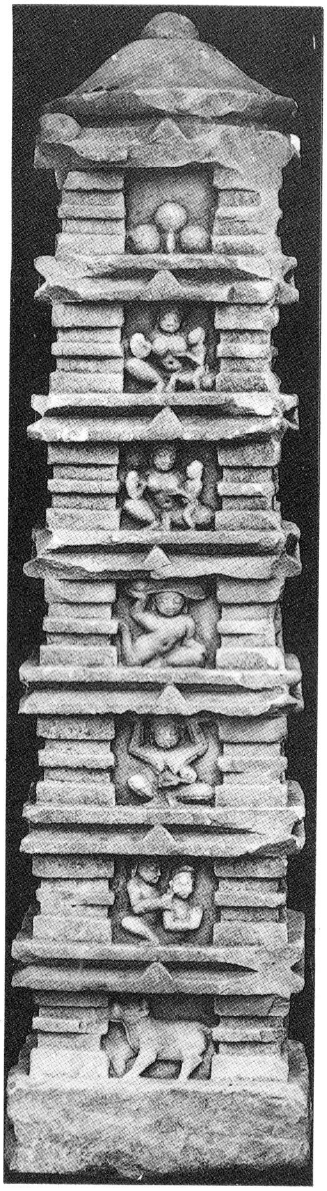

308B

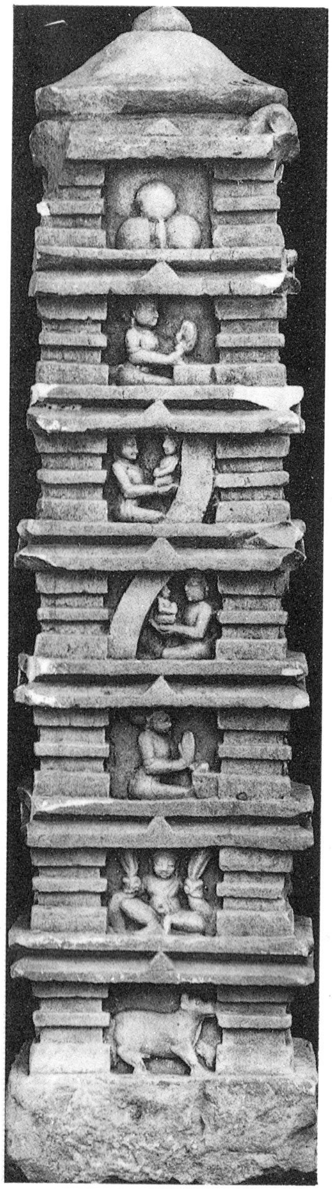

308C

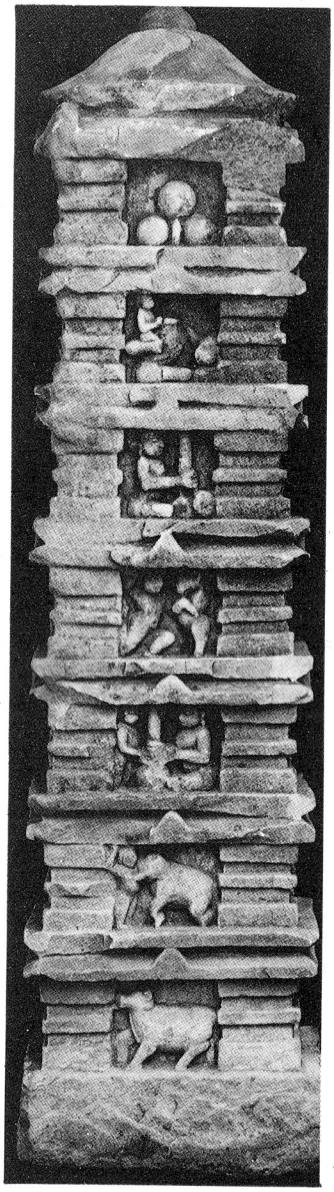

3

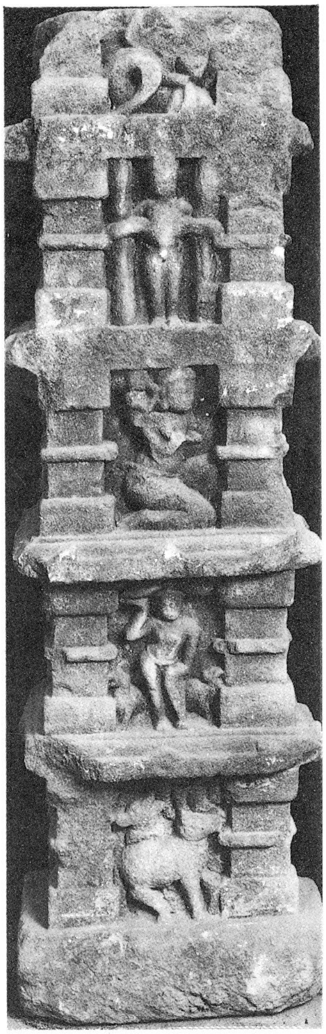

◀ 309A

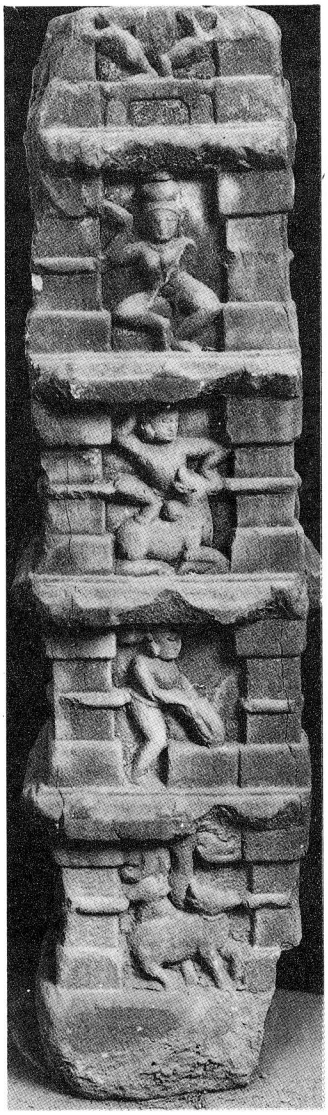

◀ 309B

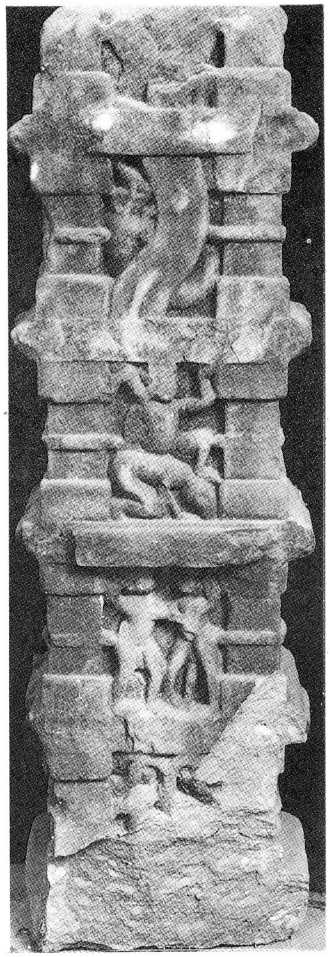

◀ 309C

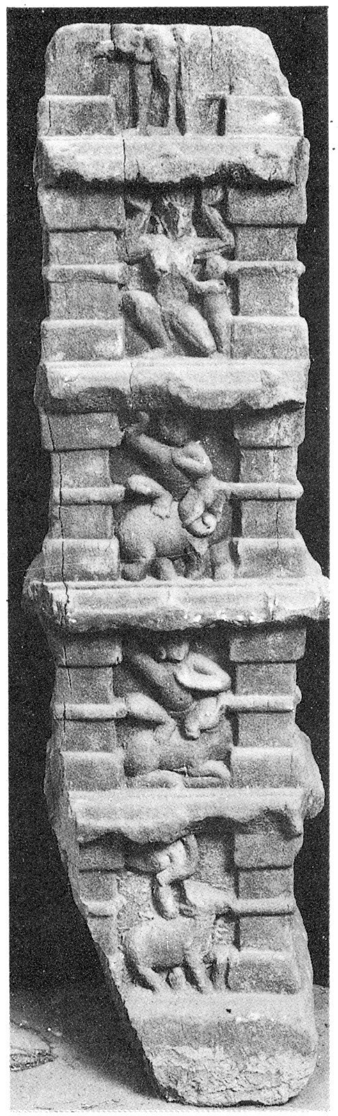

◀ 309D

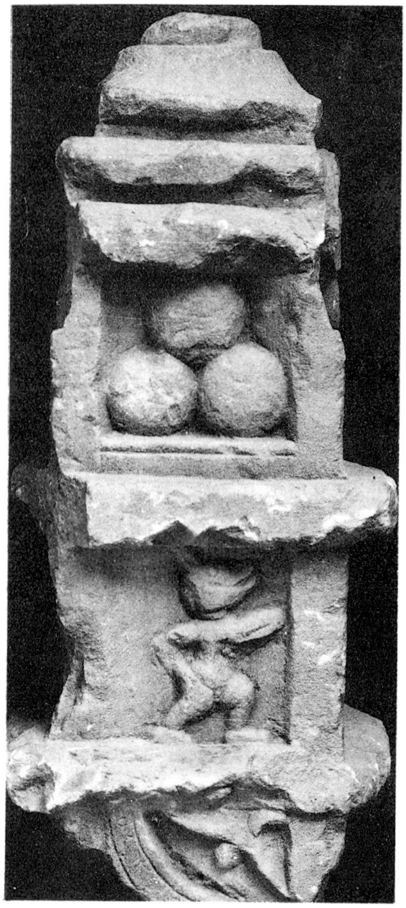

310A

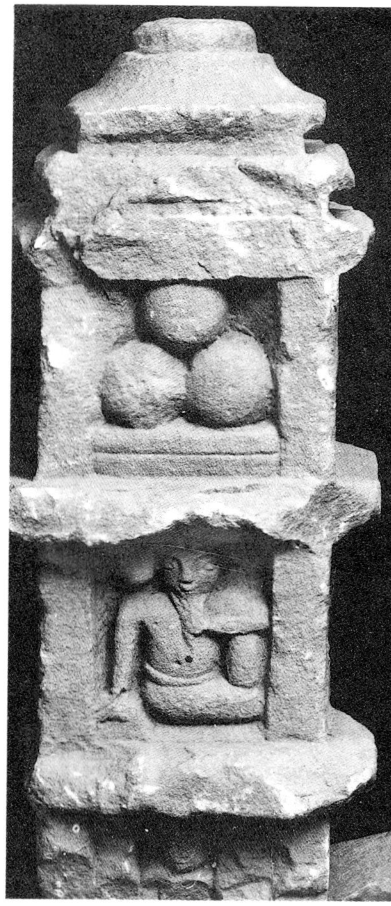

310B

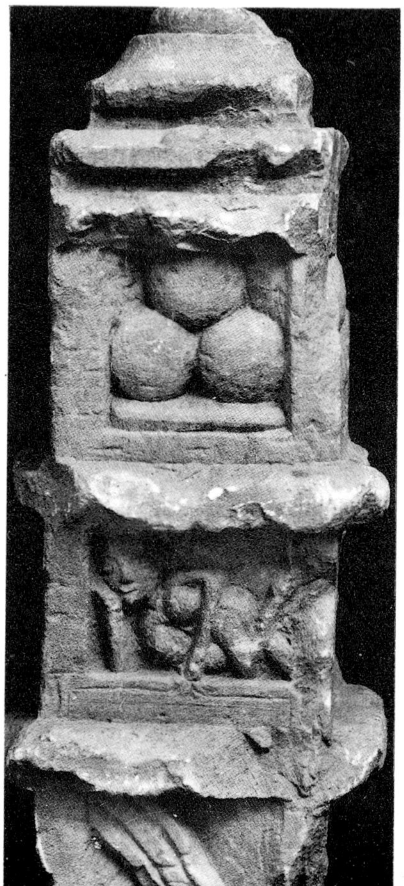

310C

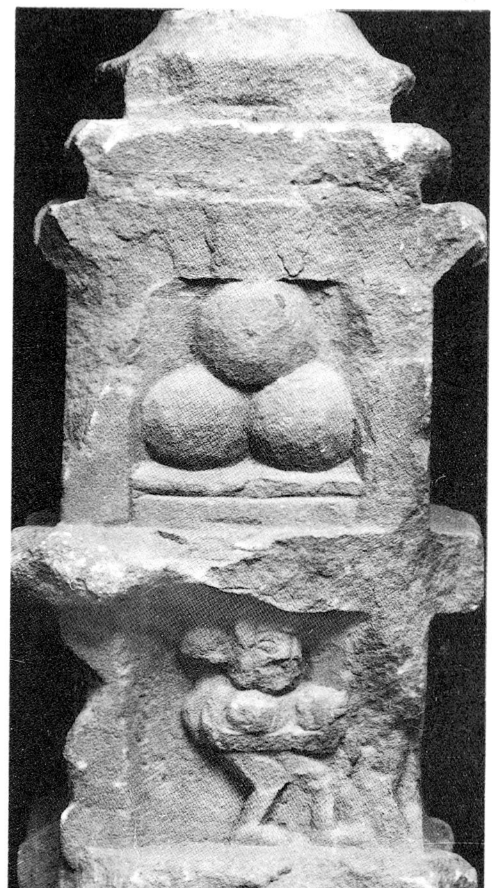

310D

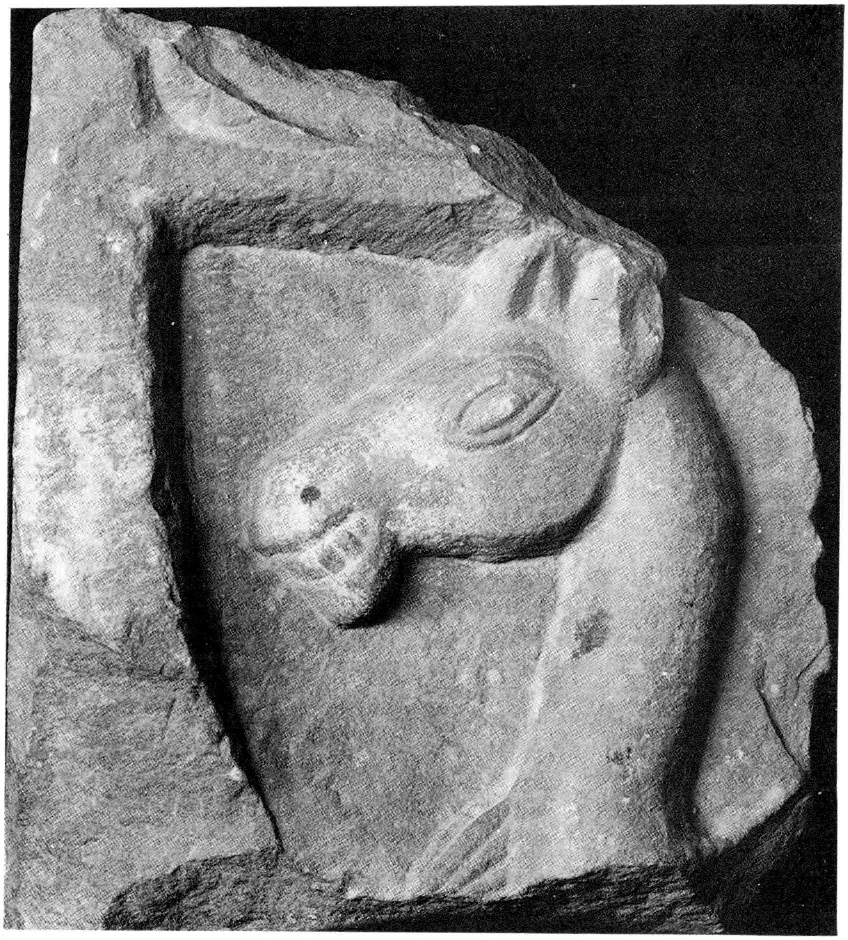

▲ 311

▼ 312

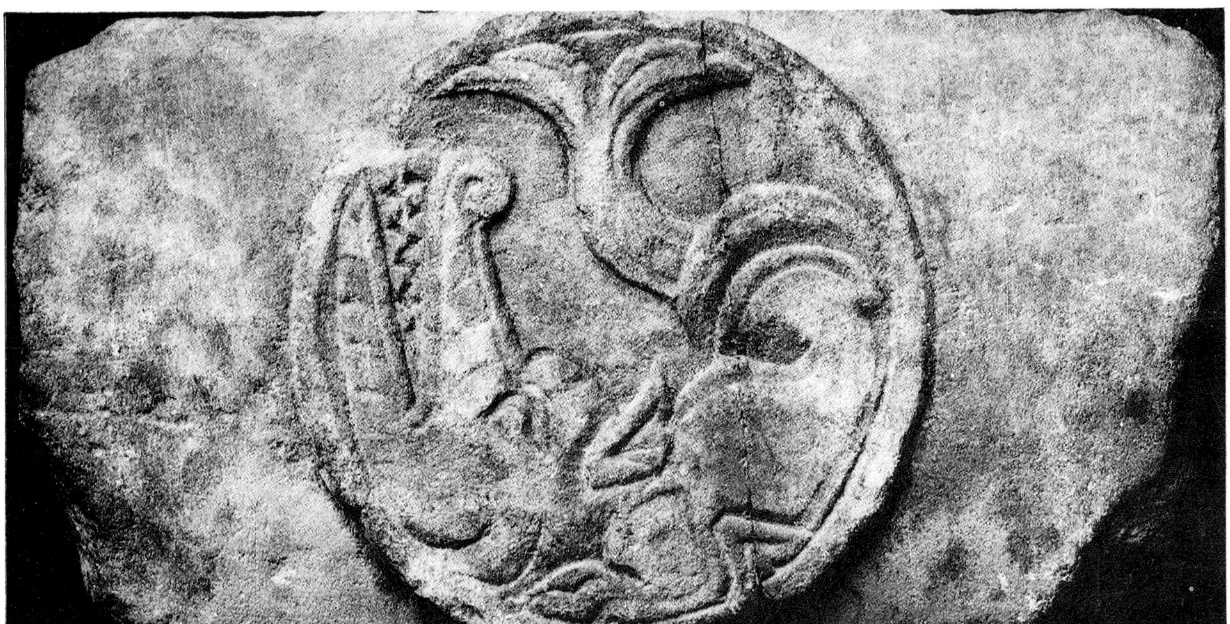

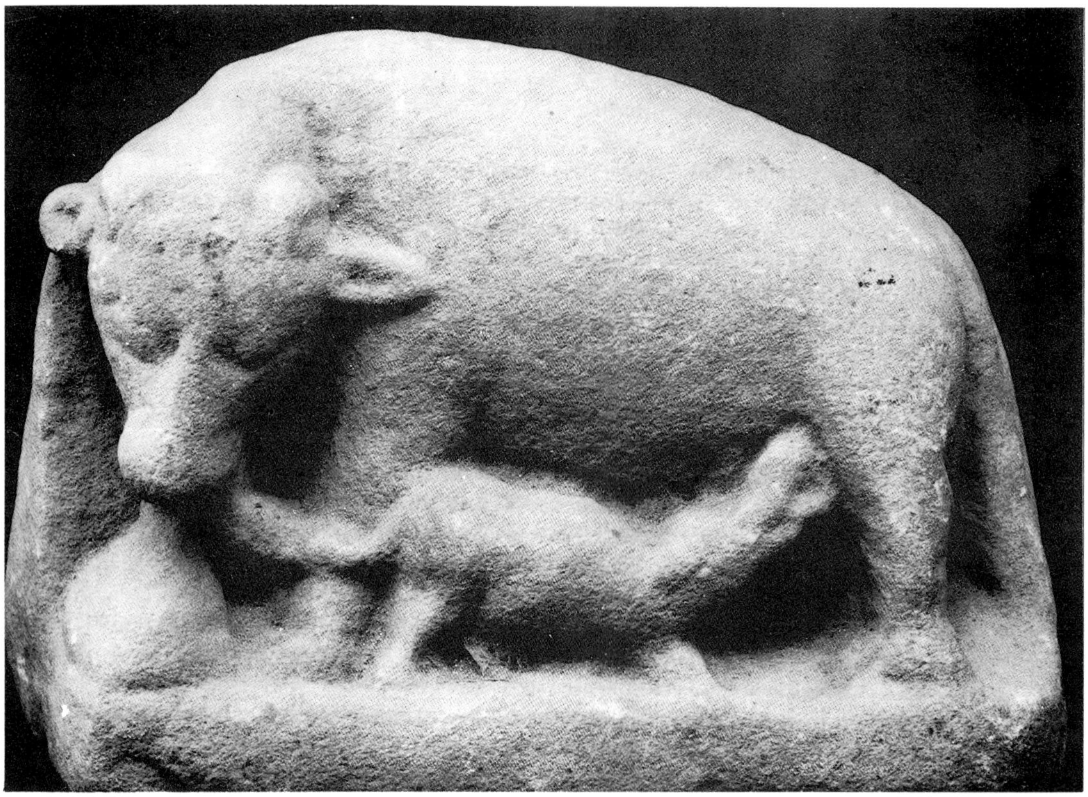

◀ 313

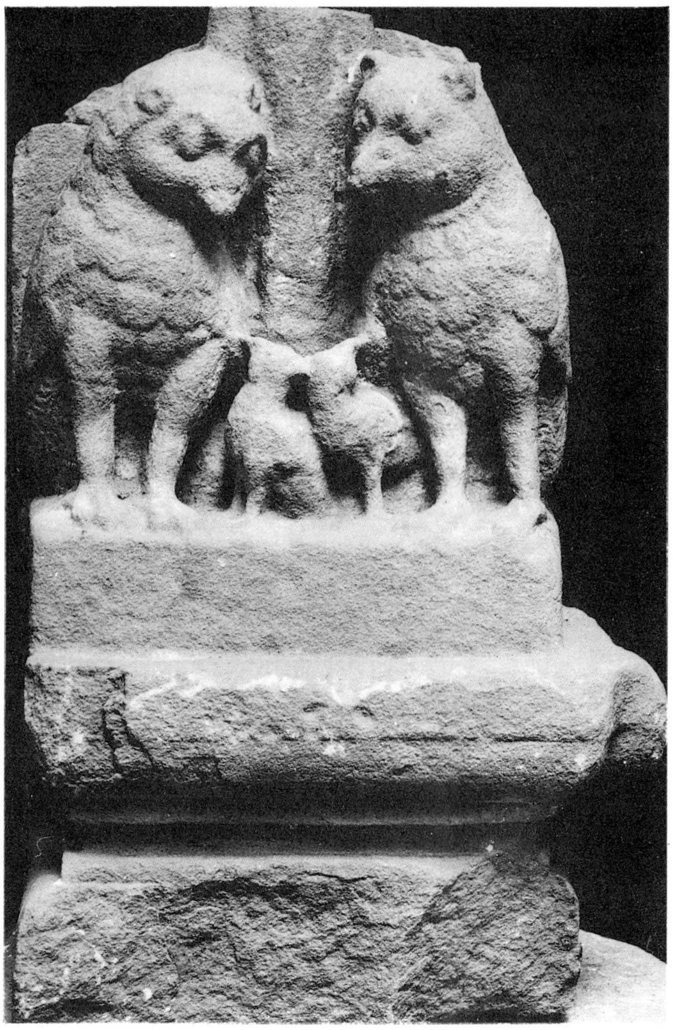

◀ 314

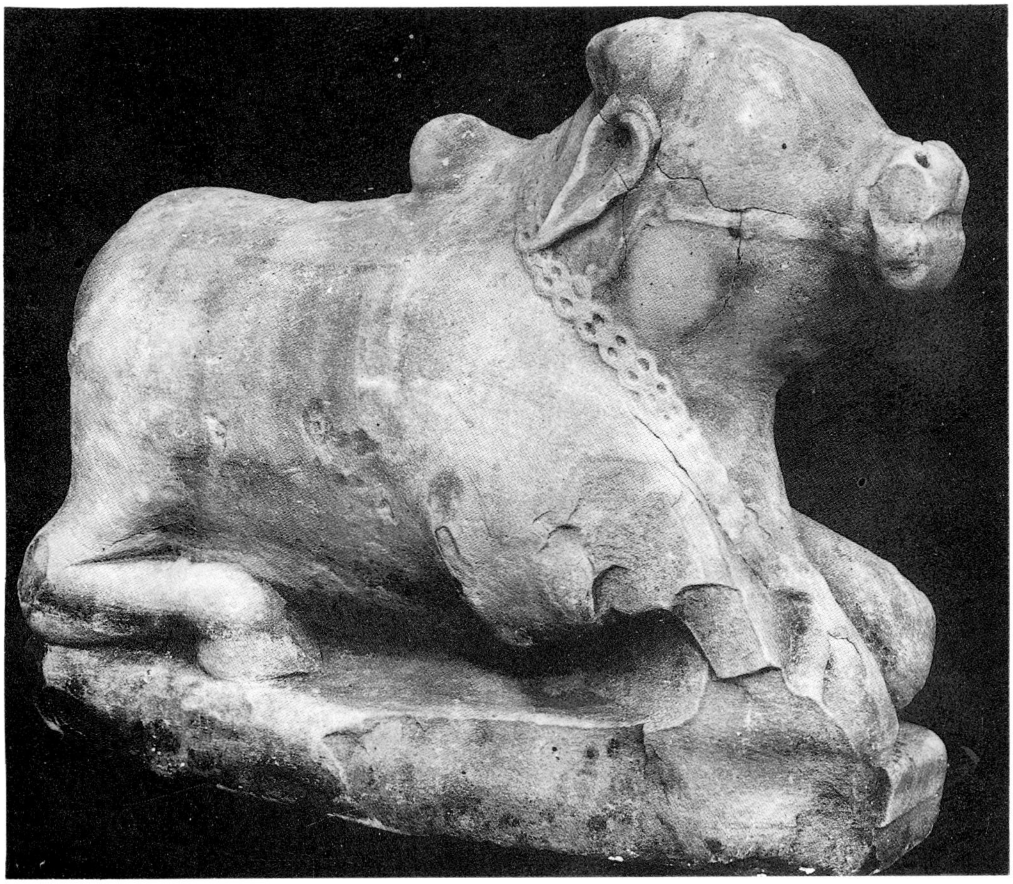

▲ 315

▼ 316

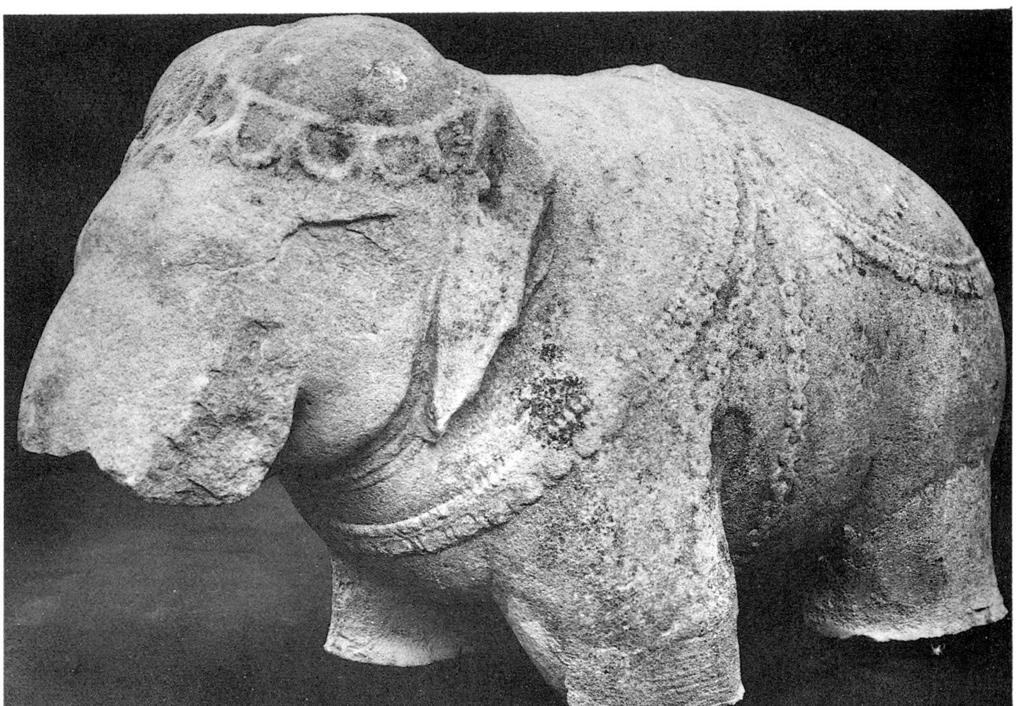

◄ 318

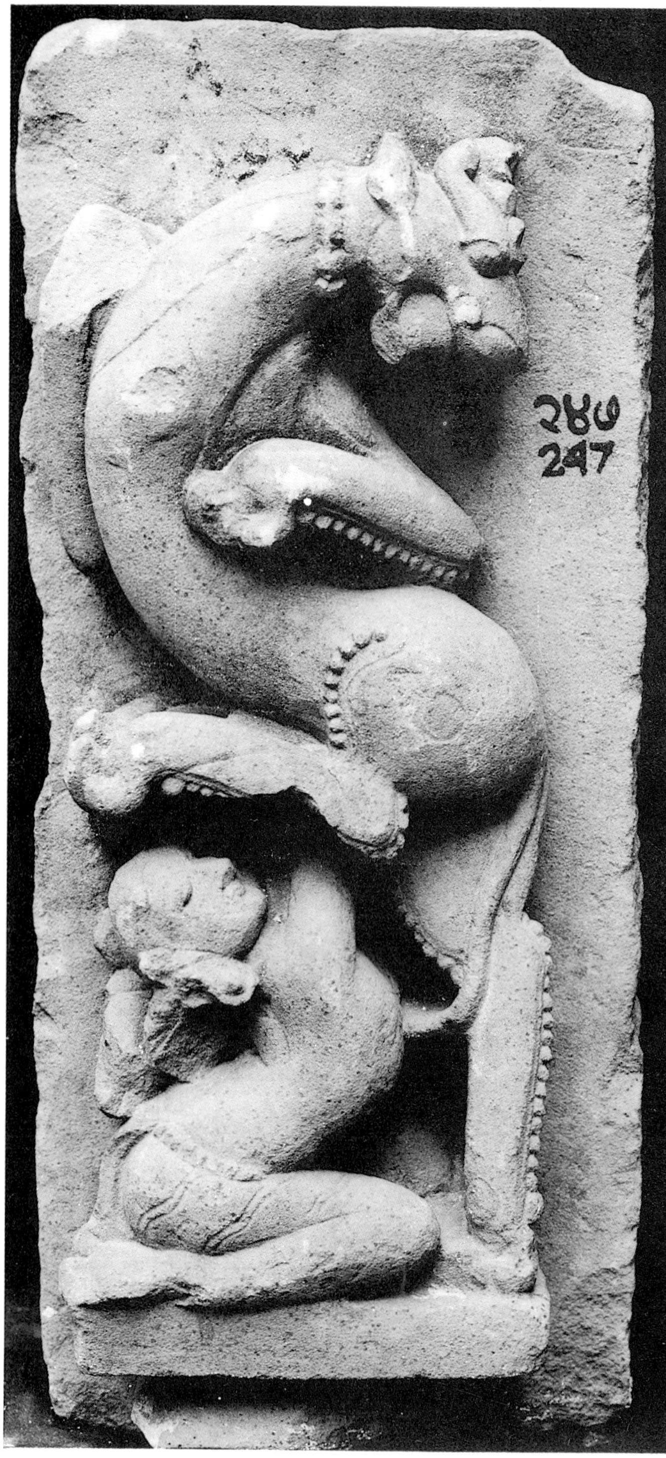

▼ 320

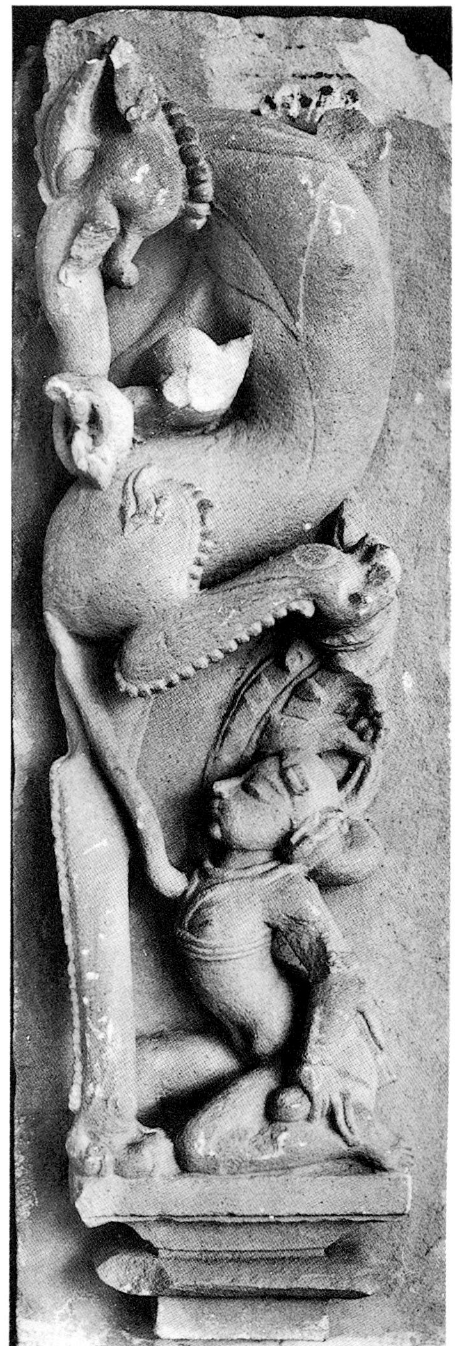

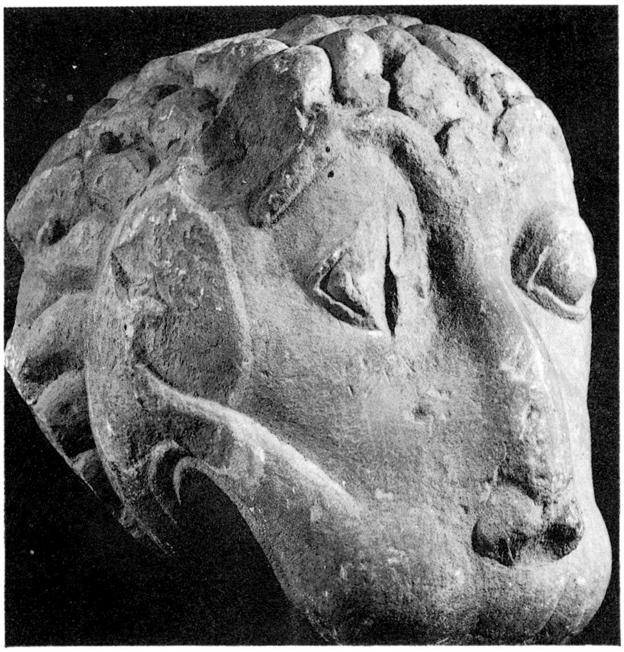

▲ 317

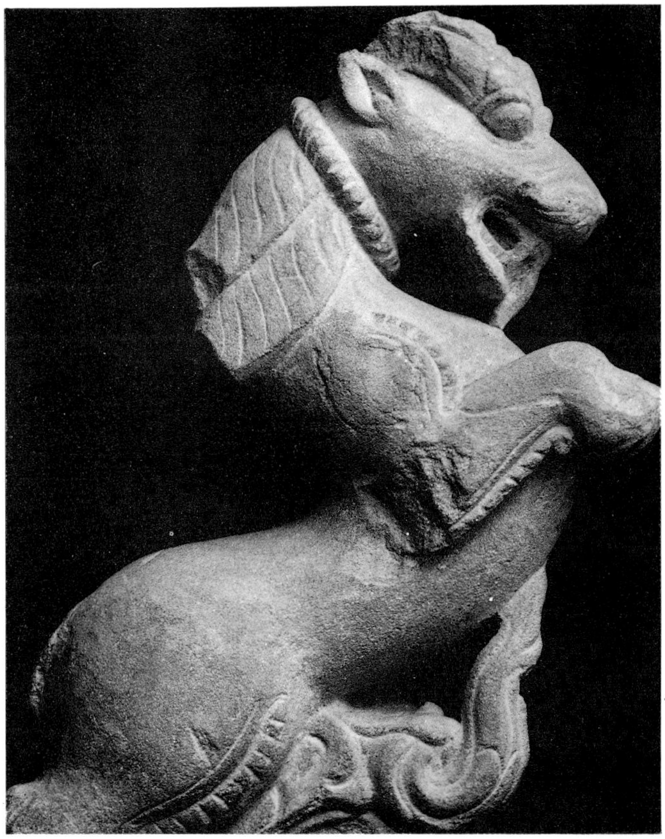

▲ 319

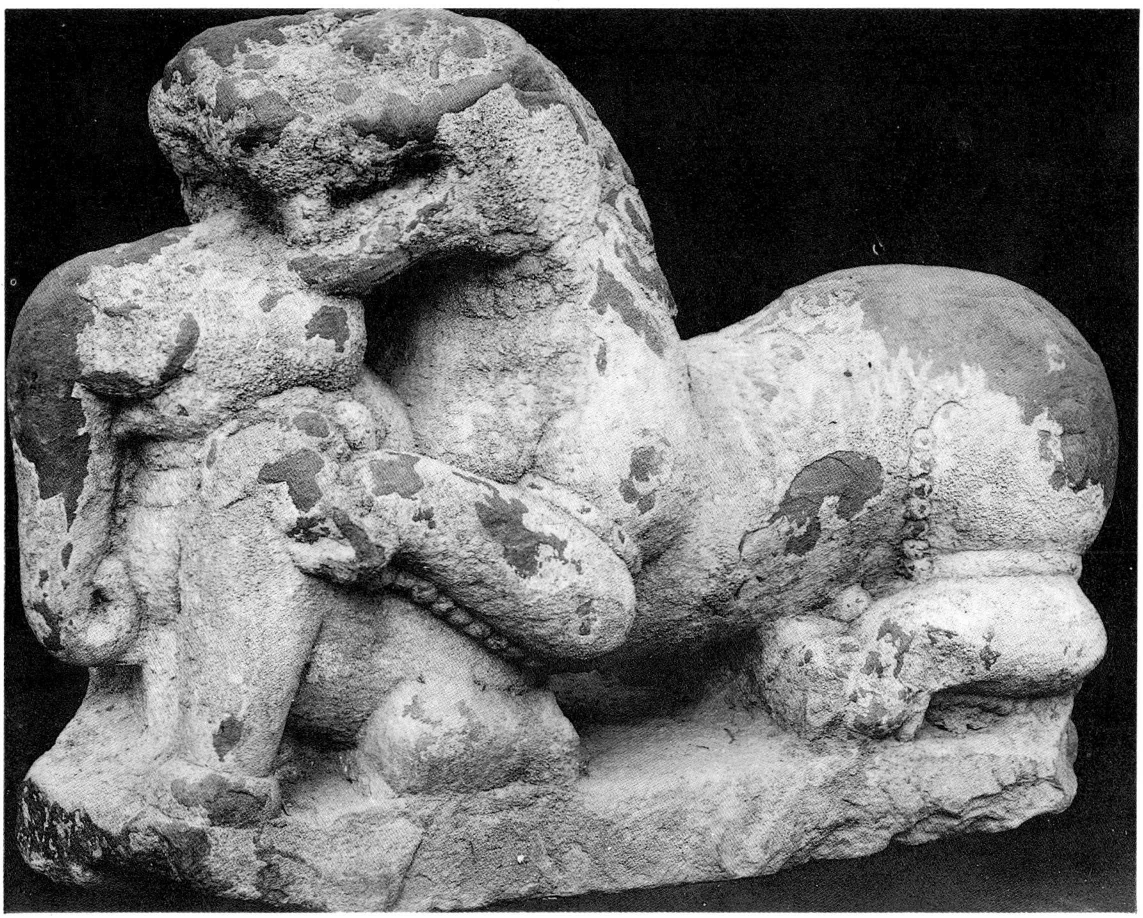

◀ 322

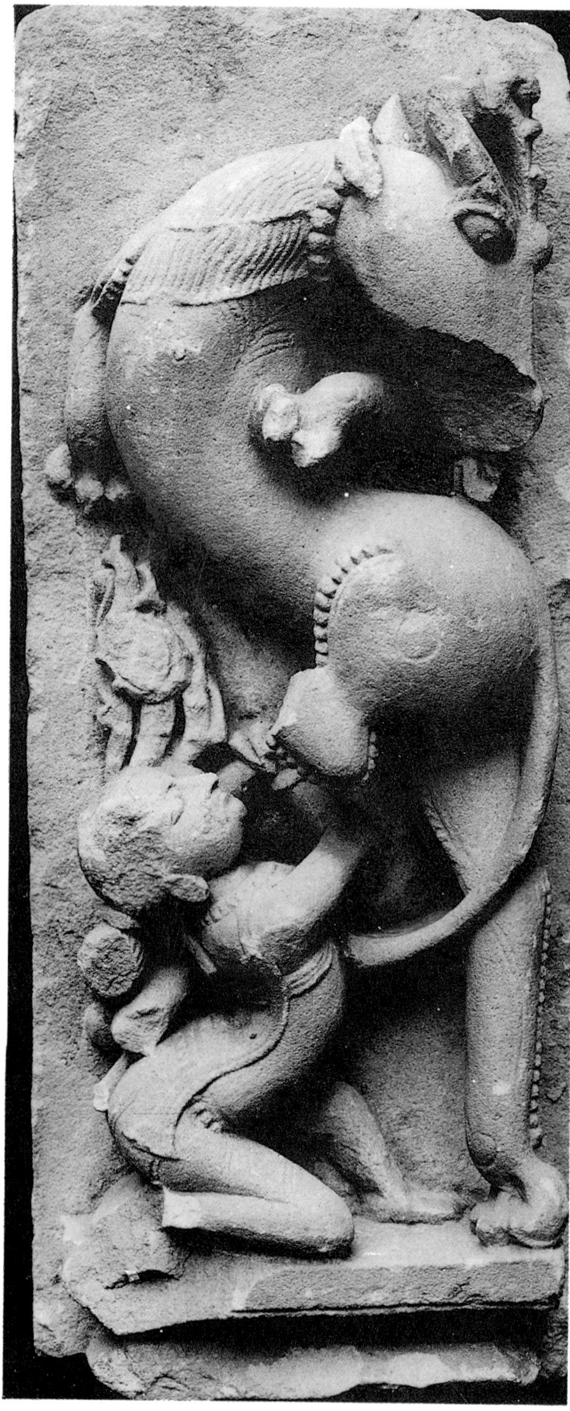

▲ 321

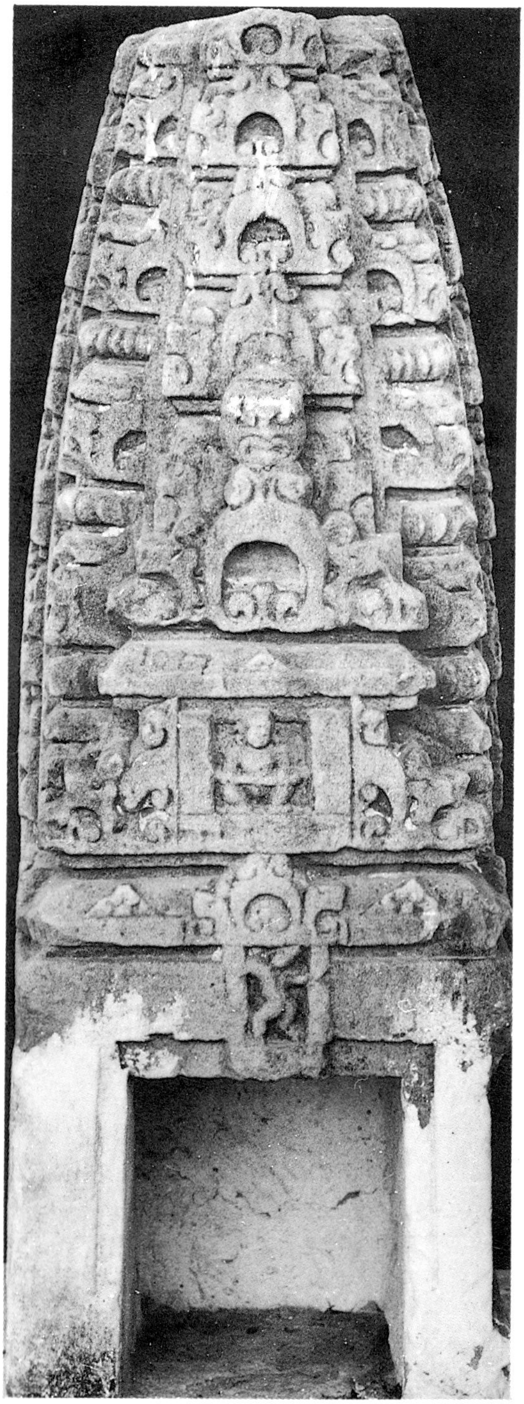

▲ 323

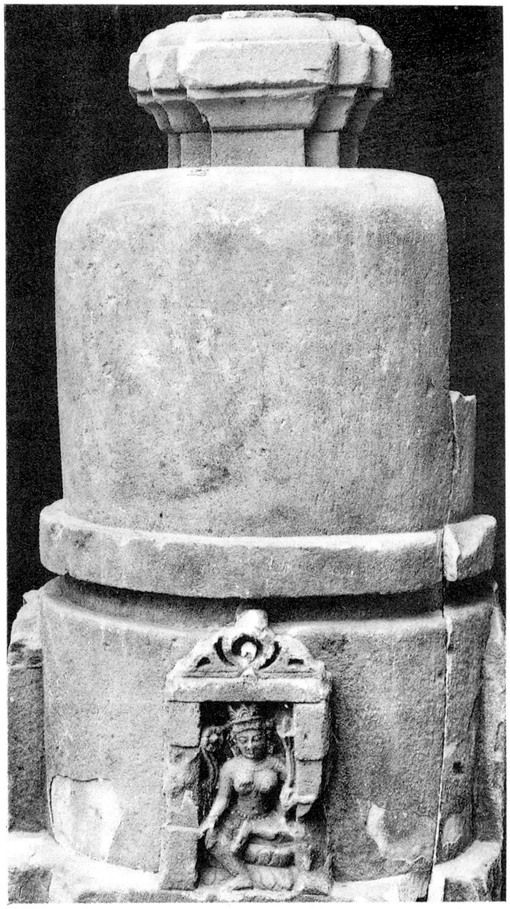

◀ 190A

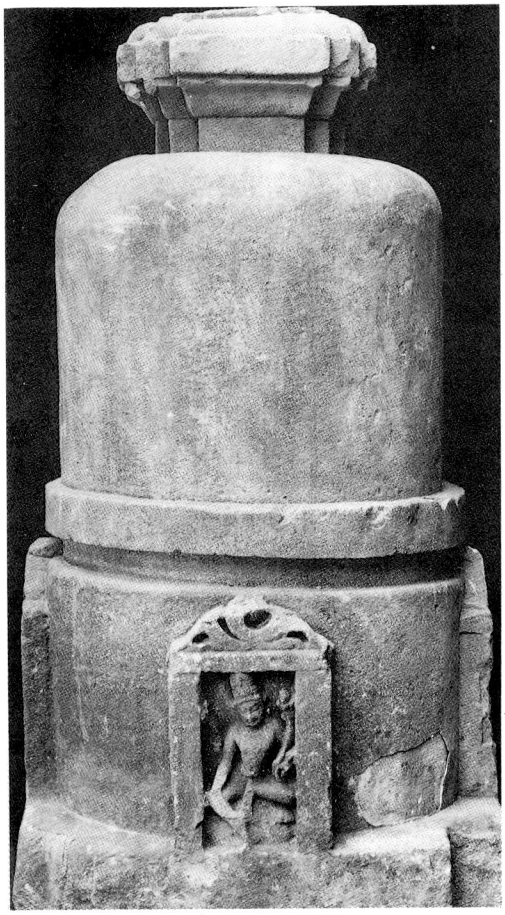

◀ 190B

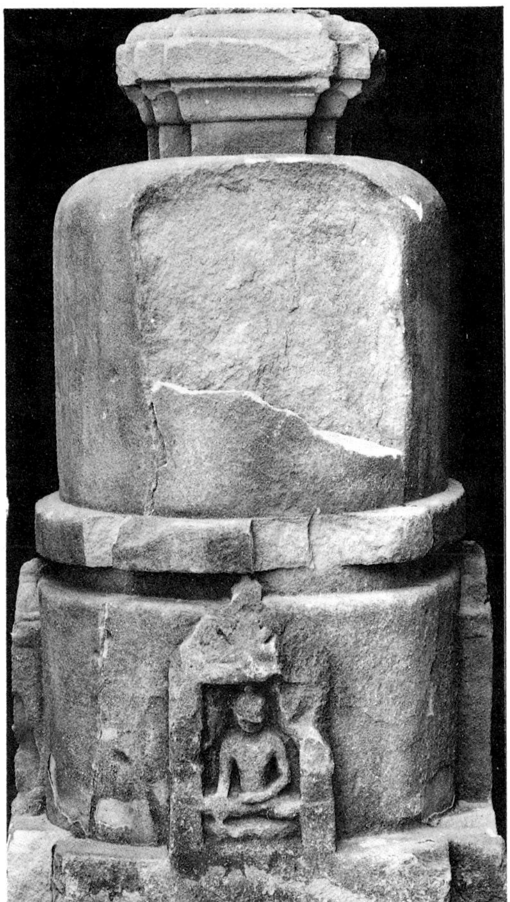

▶ 190C

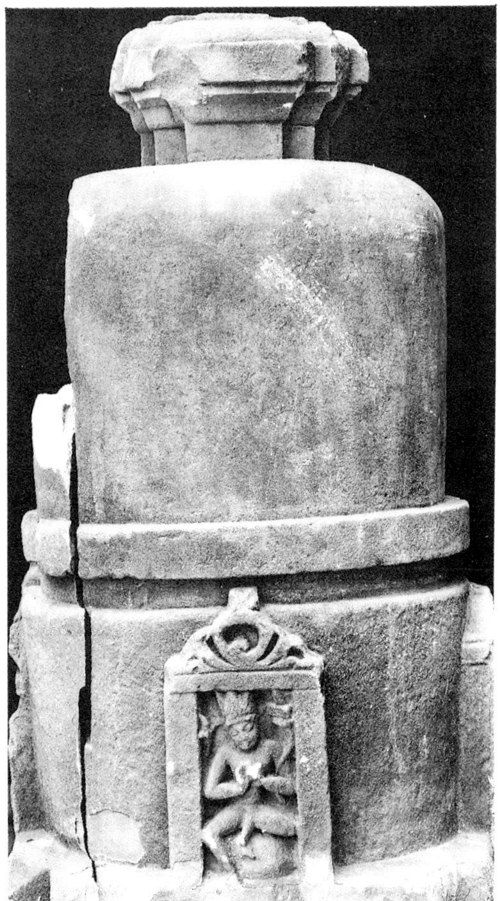

▶ 190D